Computer Networking
Illuminated

Diane Barrett

Remington College
MCSE 2000, MCSE+I NT4, CISSP, CCNA,
A+, Network+, i-Net+, Security+

Todd King

SYS Consulting and Training, Inc.
MCSE 2000, MCSE+I NT4, MCSA, MCT,
CCNP, CCDP, CNX, A+, Network+, i-Net+,
CTT, Security+

JONES AND BARTLETT PUBLISHERS
Sudbury, Massachusetts
BOSTON   TORONTO   LONDON   SINGAPORE

World Headquarters
Jones and Bartlett Publishers
40 Tall Pine Drive
Sudbury, MA 01776
978-443-5000
info@jbpub.com
www.jbpub.com

Jones and Bartlett Publishers
Canada
2406 Nikanna Road
Mississauga, ON L5C 2W6
CANADA

Jones and Bartlett Publishers
International
Barb House, Barb Mews
London W6 7PA
UK

Cover image © Eyewire

Library of Congress Cataloging-in-Publication Data
Barrett, Diane.
  Computer networking illuminated / by Diane Barrett and Todd King.-- 1st ed.
     p. cm.
  Includes index.
  ISBN 0-7637-2676-1
  1. Computer networks. I. King, Todd. II. Title.
  TK5105.5.B365 2005
  004.6--dc22

                                                    2004009047

Acquisitions Editor: Stephen Solomon
Production Manager: Amy Rose
Production Assistant: Kate Hennessy
Marketing Manager: Matthew Payne
Editorial Assistant: Deborah Arrand
Manufacturing Buyer: Therese Bräuer
Cover Design: Kristin E. Ohlin
Text Design: Kristin E. Ohlin
Composition: Northeast Compositors
Technical Artist: George Nichols
Printing and Binding: Malloy, Inc.
Cover Printing: Malloy, Inc.

Printed in the United States of America
08 07 06 05 04   10 9 8 7 6 5 4 3 2 1

Dedications

To the memory of my mother, who taught me more than she'll ever know.
—*Diane Barrett*

To my wife, Lisa, for cheerfully putting up with my late nights while I worked on this book.
—*Todd King*

Preface

Purpose of this book

The study of computer networking concepts and administration is an essential part of the education of computer science and information science students. A basic networking course should provide a strong theoretical background, practice in network design and creation, and the experience of maintaining and managing a network. Having taught computer networking for over ten years, the authors of this book have used many different textbooks and have found that several cover networking using a strictly theoretical or mathematical approach. This text uses an easy-to-understand, practical format, making it not only more interesting to the student but easier for the instructor to explain and hold the attention of the students. With good lab exercises, strong real-world scenarios, and instruction on the use of common, popular tools and utilities, best practices, and recommended strategies and implementations, this book provides coverage of all necessary topics for individuals interested in developing network literacy and competency.

Structure

Chapter 1, "Data Communications," covers data communications, such as multiplexing, signaling, and encoding. Chapter 2, "Communication Networks," introduces the OSI reference model, networking media, hubs, switches, and bridges, and network topologies. Chapter 3, "Network Technologies," defines a local area network, wide area network, and metropolitan area network, and describes the architecture and technologies associated with each. Those foundations and concepts are used throughout the book when discussing practical networking procedures and applications.

Chapter 4, "Managing Multiple Access," focuses on network design issues, such as centralized versus decentralized access. Chapter 5, "Switching," thoroughly explains switching types and the Spanning Tree Algorithm. Chapter 6, "Networking Protocols," describes the higher-level services and protocols used for data communication, including the industry-standard Transmission Control Protocol/Internet Protocol (TCP/IP). Chapter 7, "Naming and Addressing," delves into hierarchical naming, IP addressing, and subnetting.

Chapter 8, "Routing," covers routing tables, protocols (including Address Resolution Protocol [ARP], distance vector and link state protocols, and interior and exterior protocols), and hierarchical routing. Chapter 9, "Network Services and Applications," explains the Domain Name System (DNS), Dynamic Host Configuration Protocol (DHCP), and several e-mail-related protocols; and World Wide Web services. Chapter 10, "Network Security," describes malicious software (viruses, worms, and so on), encryption and decryption, firewalls, IP Security (IPSec), Web and e-mail security, and best practices.

Chapter 11, "Network Operations," steps the reader through installation of a network operating system (that is, Windows Server 2000), and installation of network services. Chapter 12, "Network Administration and Support," discusses management of user access and accounts, network performance, and additional network security measures and practices. Chapter 13, "Network Troubleshooting," covers methods of troubleshooting the operating system and cabling, and includes key resources for additional information. Finally, the appendices offer online networking resources, a list of important networking standards, a tutorial on binary arithmetic and subnetting, and IP tools and software. The last appendix is a glossary of terms used throughout the book.

Learning Features

The writing style is conversational. Each chapter begins with a statement of learning objectives. Step-by-step examples of networking concepts and procedures are presented throughout the text. Illustrations are used both to clarify the material and to vary the presentation. The text is sprinkled with Notes, Tips, and Warnings meant to alert the reader to additional and helpful information related to the subject being discussed. Hands-on lab exercises appear at the end of each chapter, with solutions provided in the Instructor's Guide. The case scenarios at the end of each chapter are an important part of the text, providing real-world application of the materials just presented.

Resources for student laboratory exercises are also available on the website, http://cis.jbpub.com. Chapter summaries are included in the text to provide a rapid review or preview of the material and to help students understand the relative importance of the concepts presented. The Instructor's Guide contains PowerPoint® presentations for each chapter, copies of figures, full statements of objectives for each chapter, alternative student projects, quizzes, chapter tests, comprehensive examinations for multiple chapters, and solutions to exercises.

Audience

The material is suitable for undergraduate computer science majors or information science majors, or students at a two-year technical college or community college, with a basic technical background. The book is intended to be used as a core networking textbook but could also be used for self study.

About the Authors

Diane Barrett has been involved in the IT industry since 1993. She works at Remington College where she taught in the computer networking program for two years before becoming a director. She teaches online classes that include networking, security, and virus protection, and is the president of a security awareness corporation that specializes in training. Diane has co-authored several security and networking books, including *MCSA/MCSE 70-299 Exam Cram 2: Implementing and Administering Security in a Windows Server 2003 Network* (Que, 2004) and *Computer Forensics JumpStart* (Sybex, 2005). Diane currently volunteers for ISSA's Generally Accepted Information Security Principles Project in the ethical practices working group. She currently holds the following certifications: MCSE on Windows 2000, MCSE+I on Windows NT 4.0, CISSP, CCNA, A+, Network+, i-Net+, and Security+.

Todd King currently serves as Chief Executive Officer for SYS Consulting and Training, Inc., a Denver-based computer-consulting firm. He has specialized in several areas of networking, including network design, analysis, and security. Prior to starting SYS, Inc., Todd was in the U.S. Air Force as a survival instructor. He currently holds a B.S. in marketing from Florida State University, and an A.A. Instructor of Technology and A.A. in Survival and Rescue Operations from the Community College of the Air Force. His professional certifications include MCSE on Windows 2000, MCSE +Internet on NT 4, MCSA, MCT, CCNP, CCDP, CNX, A+, Network+, i-Net+, CTT, and Security+.

About the Technical Editors

Bruce Parrish is an accomplished computer instructor and consultant with 20 years' computer experience. Bruce provides networking services and support solutions for small businesses, specializing in Microsoft Small Business Server networks. Additionally, he has authored a Server+ instructor training manual, co-authored a Windows 2000 directory services design lab manual, co-authored *MCSA/MCSE Managing and Maintaining a Windows Server 2003 Environment Exam Cram 2 (Exam Cram 70-292)* (Que, 2003), and is a technical editor and reviewer for LANWrights. Bruce holds the following certifications: MCSE on Windows 2000, MCSE on Windows NT 4.0, MCT, MCSA, MCP, CTT, A+, Server+, and Network+.

Richard Taylor was the envy of his neighborhood when his father brought home an Apple II and quickly learned how to program in BASIC. Since then he has worked as an instructor for numerous CTECs, worked as a consultant for firms such as Honeywell, MicroAge and Pan Energy, and is a former Intel systems engineer where he developed and implemented programs to improve factory automation systems in the United States, Costa Rica, Ireland, Malaysia, and the Philippines. He worked in the Intel Joint Development Program with Microsoft to design and implement a Windows 2000 strategy throughout the company involving over 60,000 workstations and 2000 servers. Rick currently works for Nestlé and is involved in supporting Windows 2000 servers. He is responsible for maintaining the functionality of those servers in four South American countries, the United States, and Canada. Rick also trains for a number of firms in the Phoenix area. Rick holds MCT and MCSE certifications.

Acknowledgments

The authors would like to thank Jones and Bartlett for this opportunity to write a detailed and practical networking textbook. We sincerely appreciate Jones and Bartlett staff, especially Stephen Solomon, our Acquisitions Editor. Hats off to Amy Rose, our production editor, who kept this project on track during author review and page proofs.

The authors would also like to thank Bruce Parrish and Richard Taylor, our technical reviewers, and the LANWrights/iLearning team—Ed Tittel and Kim Lindros. Ed led the book from proposal to project launch, was available throughout the project to offer assistance and guidance, and provided several of the appendices. Thanks to Kim for managing the project on our behalf and wrangling all the pieces that flowed between us and Jones and Bartlett.

Diane Barrett: Thank you to Jones and Bartlett for making this book possible. Thanks to everyone at LANWrights/iLearnings, especially Ed Tittel and Kim Lindros, for keeping everything in perspective. To co-author Todd King, thank you for your fine contributions.

Todd King: I would like to extend my deepest thanks to Ed Tittel and the team at LANWrights/iLearning for their efforts in coordinating this book. Thanks especially to Kim Lindros for helping keep me on track and putting up with me. I would also like to thank Diane Barrett, the lead author on this book, who provided the bulk of the chapters.

Contents

CHAPTER 1

Data Communications

After reading this chapter you will be able to:

- Understand how signaling is used to format data for transmission
- Discuss techniques for encoding and decoding transmissions
- Discuss error detection and recovery
- Understand how flow control works
- Apply methods that control and alleviate congestion

To manage a network, you need to understand how all of the components work together so that you can troubleshoot problems effectively. To be successful in your job as a network administrator, you must be able to discern hardware errors from software errors. If you want to amaze the people you work with by knowing how to fix a computer based on the number of beeps it makes, you have to understand electricity and math. What do electricity and math have to do with networking?

Networking involves much more than managing computers; it means understanding what makes them work. In this chapter, you will start with the basics: how a computer takes what we type on a keyboard, converts it, transmits it, and finally displays it on the computer monitor. A wide variety of techniques exist that can convert and transmit this information over many different types of media. This chapter examines some of these communication techniques to help us better understand what happens to information before it can pass to any type of device or be transmitted over a network.

1.1   Multiplexing

We've come a long way from using two tin cans and a string to communicate. We can now send multiple signals simultaneously over the same cable segment. This is known as multiplexing. **Multiplexing** is about sharing a communications line. It combines several connections into one larger channel. A channel is any distinct conduit for data, such as a TV channel or an Ethernet cable. This technology was originally developed by Bell Labs to allow a single telephone line to carry several phone conversations at the same time. By using multiplexing, Bell Labs was able to establish what is called a T-Carrier network that supports simultaneous links over the same set of cables. Known as a T-1, it combines separate logical data channels and transmits them simultaneously across one physical channel. When it sends these multiple streams or signals of information onto a T-Carrier, the receiving end separates them back into their original sequence.

There are many different types of multiplexing, and the type used depends on what the media, reception equipment, and transmission can handle. Even though there are various types of multiplexing, the device that combines the signals on the sending end of a channel is called a multiplexer, and the device on the receiving end that separates them into their original order is called a demultiplexer. Now that you have learned what all types of multiplexing have in common, let us look at the various types and what makes them differ.

1.1.1   Frequency Division Multiplexing (FDM)

Frequency division multiplexing (FDM) is similar to sending messages through channels using several different colored flashlights. FDM is a method of transmission in which numerous signals are combined on a single communications line or channel. A different frequency is assigned to each signal within the main channel. To explain this, imagine the colored flashlights: You and I are sharing a channel. I transmit data on bits 2, 4, 6, and 8 using a blue flashlight. You transmit data on bits 1, 2, 4, 6, and 7 using a yellow flashlight. If transmitted simultaneously so that they traveled through the fiber together, the combined messages would appear as green. As a result, when our combined message arrives at the other end, it is easy to determine what bits we were each sending on. Each pulse that arrives either will have no light or will be blue, yellow, or green. Thus, frequency division multiplexing makes it possible to send several messages on a single cable simultaneously.

The motivation for using this technology includes using existing physical media more efficiently by maximizing the amount of data that can be transferred. Also, once the data is multiplexed, you can amplify, conduct, or change the frequency of the signal as needed to suit your needs. An attractive feature of FDM is that the transmitting end and the receiving end do not have to be close to each other. This made FDM a popular choice for many of the first telecommunication mediums. In the 1930s, the telephone companies began to combine multiple analog voice signals over one line using FDM. This was later replaced with digital methods. For years, cable TV companies have used FDM to transmit many channels over the same wire. The cable company simultaneously sends you the signals for all the TV channels you want, at the same time, through a single coaxial cable. When FDM is used in a communications network, each input signal is sent and received at maximum speed at all times. However, if many signals must be sent along a single long-distance line and the necessary bandwidth is large, a different method, known as time division multiplexing, is used instead. We will discuss time division multiplexing in the "Time Division Multiplexing" section later in this chapter.

Another method of FDM is orthogonal frequency division multiplexing (OFDM). This technology was first conceived in the 1960s and 1970s during research into minimizing interference among channels that had frequencies near each other. In some respects, OFDM is similar to conventional FDM. The difference lies in the way in which the signals are combined and separated. With OFDM, priority is given to minimizing the interference among the channels rather than focusing on perfecting the individual channels. OFDM is used in European digital audio broadcast services such as digital television, and it is used in wireless local area networks.

1.1.2   Wave Division Multiplexing (WDM)

Now that optical networks have made their way into enterprise networks, they have to be dealt with in ways that are different than copper-based networks. **Wave division multiplexing (WDM)** and dense wave division multiplexing (DWDM, discussed next) are the optical equivalents to early carrier systems. In other words, WDM is a form of frequency division multiplexing specifically for combining many optical carrier signals into a single optical fiber. In fiber-optic transmissions, data is represented as pulses of light traveling through silicon glass. In current optical networks, a single laser signal provides the carrier signal on which the data is multiplexed. The laser is a single color. All the light beams are sent at the same time, with each signal attached to a laser that emits a different color beam. The receiving device splits the colors into the original signals again.

The first WDM systems, which appeared around 1985, combined two signals. Because a single optical fiber has an extremely high capacity, this type of multiplexing offers the greatest potential for future communications. Modern systems can handle up to 128 signals. These systems are sometimes called dense wave division multiplexing (DWDM) systems. DWDM is a technology that puts data from different sources together on an optical fiber, with each signal carried at the same time on its own light wavelength. By combining multiple wavelengths, each representing a separate data channel, the same optic fiber has the bandwidth capacity of multiple cables. Incoming optical signals are assigned to specific frequencies within a designated band. See Figure 1.1. The capacity of the fiber is increased when these signals are multiplexed out onto one fiber. Using this technology, up to 128 separate wavelengths or channels of data can be multiplexed into a light stream transmitted on a single optical fiber. Because each channel is

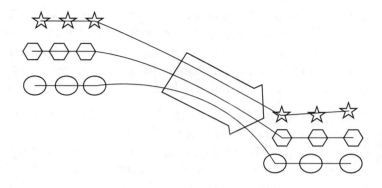

Figure 1.1
Dense wave division multiplexing

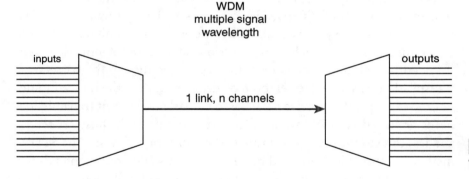

Figure 1.2
Time division multiplexing

demultiplexed back into the original source, different data formats being transmitted at different data rates can be transmitted together.

1.1.3   Time Division Multiplexing (TDM)

In **time division multiplexing (TDM)**, multiple data streams are combined in a single signal and transmitted over the same link by allocating a different time slot for the transmission of each channel. Basically, the data bits take turns traveling across a shared communications line. The single signal accepts the input from each individual user, breaks the input into segments, and assigns the segments to the composite signal in a rotating, repeating sequence. Therefore, the composite signal contains data from multiple senders. At the other end of the long-distance cable, the individual signals are separated out and routed to the proper end users. See Figure 1.2.

TDM is quite popular with today's electrical networks and is straightforward to implement on an optical network. It also enabled telephone companies to migrate from analog to digital on all their long-distance trunks. The technology is used in channel banks, which convert 24 analog voice conversations into one digital T-1 line.

Synchronous time division multiplexing (or slotted time division multiplexing) is a form of TDM in which the time allocated to a device or workstation is fixed. This method is popular for digital voice telephone circuits because each voice call delivers data at exactly the same rate. We should also mention statistical time division multiplexing (STDM). This is a form of TDM that improves sharing efficiency by allowing some of the multiplexed channels to increase their allotted time if other stations are not using theirs to full capacity. This method is based on TDM, and even though TDM works well in many cases, it does not always account for the varying data transmission needs of different devices or users. For example, a busy fax server shared by many users might need to receive or transmit data 70–85% of the time at a much higher transmission rate than a seldom-used laser printer attached to the same line. With TDM, even though the fax server's transmission needs are greater, both devices are allotted the same amount of time to transmit or receive data. Based on past and current transmission needs or statistics, STDM would allocate more time to the busy fax server and less time to the little-used printer. Many data networks use the STDM method because it is considered more efficient. A station only contends for a turn if it has data to transmit; therefore, it does not make sense to waste an allocated time slot with TDM if a station does not have data to send.

1.1.4   Pulse Code Modulation (PCM)

In the 1930s, the necessity to convert analog data to digital format for computer use did not exist because no computers were capable of using it. However, the idea was seen by Alec Reeves as a means of perfect communication because no errors could arise with a system based on 1s and 0s. In 1938, he filed a patent in France that introduced the concept of a digital form of communication that he called pulse code modulation. **Pulse code modulation (PCM)** transmits analog data using a digital scheme. An analog signal is represented as a continuous signal or sine wave as opposed to a digital signal that is represented by an "on" or "off" state denoted as either 0 or 1. Analog signals are real-world signals, such as music, voice, and video.

For them to be stored and manipulated by a computer, these signals must be converted into a digital form that the computer understands. In the process of doing this, the following functions take place: filtering, sampling, quantization, and encoding.

The object of PCM is to convert the human signal into a digital representation. This transformation is similar to how Morse code uses dots and dashes to transmit conversation. PCM is done by sampling the analog signal. A digital signal is obtained by sampling the analog signal at various points in time. These points are generally evenly spaced, with the time between them referred to as the sampling interval. The sampling rate is several times the maximum frequency of the analog waveform in cycles per second. The cycles per second is also called hertz (Hz). The faster the rate at which a signal changes, the higher the frequency of the signal and the higher the sampling rate needed to reproduce it. This critical sampling rate is called the Nyquist sampling rate. The Nyquist sampling rate is a mathematical equation proving that the sampling rate to be used must be greater than twice the highest frequency contained in the analog signal. If the sampling rate is less than this, some of the highest frequency rates in the analog input signal will not be correctly represented in the digitized output so that when the signal is converted back to analog there will be distortion. Before sampling, the signal is filtered to remove any components beyond the Nyquist frequency. If this is not done, these components will appear as noise.

The next step is **quantization**. This stage takes each sample and allocates a level to it. The sampled analog signal can take any value, but the quantized signal can only have a value, from a set of half voltages. Half volts are used because this is the halfway point between two whole numbers. For example, 0–1V is allocated 0.5V. Once this is done, the signal is encoded. Encoding is the process of representing the sampled values with a chosen power of 2 depending on the level of accuracy. The number is always a power of 2, for example, 8, 16, 32, or 64. At this point, the pulse code modulator outputs a series of binary numbers. When this string gets to the receiving end of the communications circuit, a pulse code demodulator converts the binary numbers back into pulses having the same quantum levels as those in the modulator. The pulses then are further processed to restore the original analog waveform. The main parts of this whole conversion system are known as the encoder and decoder. The combined encoder and decoder is called codec. We will next discuss signaling in depth, and then discuss methods of encoding and decoding.

1.2   Signaling

Signaling is a way to communicate when speaking isn't possible. Smoke signals, sports signals, and Morse code are some examples. Signaling is also used to move information around inside of circuits. In this context, signaling is communication of information between network nodes by initiation, transmission, control, and termination of telecommunications signals. Network nodes do not have to be computer network nodes and could easily describe a typical telephone at home. The traditional plain old telephone system (POTS) provides a simple example. When you pick up the telephone receiver to make a call, you take the phone "off hook" and close a circuit connected to a switch at your local phone company. This initiates the call. If your call happens to be local, the phone switch creates a local loop between you and the person you are calling. If you call long distance, your call is sent outside the local switching company onto a different network. The information that is traveling over the network, your voice, is transmitted until you hang up the phone and terminate the call, or open the circuit again.

POTS is called the public switched telephone network (PSTN) today. Signaling can occur "in band" (typically for local phone calls) whereby the call control information shares the same channel as the telephone call. This differs from "out of band" signaling whereby the call control information has a dedicated channel specifically for the control information. This is typical for long-distance telephone carriers today. SS7 is an example of this technology. SS7 stands for Common Channel Signaling System No. 7. In this type of technology, the network elements in the PSTN exchange information over a digital signaling network for wireless or cellular call setup, routing, and control. The SS7 network and protocol are used for wireless services such as personal communications services (PCS), wireless roaming, and mobile subscriber authentication; toll-free (800/888) and toll (900) services; and enhanced call features such as call forwarding, calling party name/number display, and three-way calling. The carrier signal has three major characteristics:

- **Amplitude:** The difference between the crest, or top, of a sine wave and the trough, or bottom (vertical measurement of the sine wave)

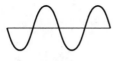 

| Sine waveform | Sawtooth waveform | Square waveform |

Figure 1.3
Analog signal wave forms

- **Frequency:** The number of cycles that occur in a given time period (horizontal measurement of the sine wave from one crest to the next)
- **Phase:** The number of states that a signal can vary

1.2.1 Analog Signaling

Humans are analog, computers are digital. When we speak, we produce analog waves. When we hear a sound, we receive and process analog signals. An **analog signal** has a smooth, continuous signal, which can be represented by a sine wave if you were to view it using an oscilloscope. An oscilloscope is an electronic device that shows variations in voltage for a signal over time and displays the result as a waveform. Analog adds information or encodes information to an alternating current (AC) base signal by modifying the frequency or signal strength. It's possible to represent analog signals using other waveforms as well. Square waveforms are commonly used to represent digital signaling. Figure 1.3 illustrates various analog signals.

1.2.2 Digital Signaling

A **digital signal** uses discrete steps to represent information in binary format as 0s or 1s. The digital signal can be described in more detail according to signal elements such as significant conditions, significant instants, and transitions. Each pulse is considered a signal element. Signal elements can be either unipolar (one state) or bipolar (two states). An oscilloscope can be used to measure the signal variances and display them. Let's say that +3 volts is considered "on" and −3 volts is considered "off." The oscilloscope measures and displays these signal differences and can display them as a rectangular wave form that shows the discrete changes.

1.2.3 Basic Signaling Characteristics

The use of signals is common to many functions in a network operation. We already know that information is represented computers using binary, digital logic. Each binary digit or bit represents one piece of information: a bit being a 1 means one thing, and a 0 means another. Besides transferring

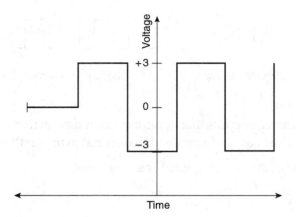

Figure 1.4

Basic signaling characteristics

information digitally, computers are also electronic devices because they deal in electrical terms such as voltage. Within the circuitry of the PC, 1s and 0s are represented by voltage levels. Each component works with a number of different pieces of information, each having a 0 or 1 value at any given time. These values are signals. A signal can be any type of information. The transition from a 0 to a 1 is called the rising edge, and the transition from 1 to 0 the falling edge. Sometimes a response will be triggered on only one or the other of these transitions, while in some cases a response will occur for both. Signals change as time progresses, and this is what enables the flow of data. Figure 1.4 shows the basic signaling characteristics. The following are some common terms used in signaling:

- **Clock:** A clock is a signal that alternates between 0 and 1, back and forth, at a specific speed. It sets the tone for everything that happens within a particular electronic circuit.

- **Cycle:** This is a single pass-through of the signal, from the rising edge, through the falling edge, until the start of the next rising edge.

- **Cycle length:** This is the amount of time required for the signal to complete one full cycle.

- **Rise time and fall time:** This measures how long it takes for the level to change from 0 to 1, or 1 to 0.

Now that we have a basic understanding of signaling, it's time to discuss encoding, which defines the way the signals are represented on the physical communication line.

1.3   Encoding and Decoding Transmissions

Encoding is simply putting electronic data into a standard format. Data is encoded into signals to send them from one place to another. After the data has been encoded and sent along a physical medium, it must be decoded on the other end. The majority of this section focuses on the process of encoding and the methods that are used. Because this process defines the way the signals are represented on the physical communication line, there must be an agreed-upon format. The signal is manipulated so that both the sender and receiver can recognize these changes. Because information can be either digital or analog, and signals can be digital or analog, there are several types of encoding:

- Digital-to-digital
- Analog-to-digital
- Digital-to-analog
- Analog-to-analog

You might also see decoding methods referred to as line coding, but before we go too far into the process, we should review some history.

It is important to understand the history of encoding techniques because as the media types change, you might see an old concept resurface in new technology. This can happen when advances in manufacturing catch up to an old idea that was put on the shelf because it wasn't practical, or even possible, to make something commercially successful at the time. The encoding mechanism chosen will depend on the application needs and technology available at a given point. For instance, radio has been around for more than a century, but widespread use of wireless computer networks using radio frequency (RF) has only taken hold in the past ten years. The changes in encoding mechanisms have increased bandwidth from 1 megabit per second (Mbps) transmissions to 11 Mbps for wireless computer networks using the same transmission medium (air). How is this done? This is discussed in the "Multilevel Signaling" section later in the chapter. Before we delve into multilevel signaling, we'll start with a discussion of the methods of analog-to-analog encoding, such as amplitude modulation and frequency modulation, and then work our way up to digital-to-digital encoding.

Analog data are represented as analog signals at their original frequency, which is called baseband, or at a different frequency in two basic ways.

When we pick up a telephone and speak into it, the telephone network transmits our analog voice signal at face value or baseband signal. Alternatively, the telephone network can combine our signal into another signal (carrier) and then transmit these combined signals at a different frequency. Modifying the strength of a wave is called amplitude modulation, modifying the pitch of a wave is called frequency modulation, and modifying the natural flow of a wave is called phase modulation. We will discuss each of these in the sections that follow.

1.3.1   Amplitude Modulation (AM)

Amplitude modulation (AM) is the encoding of a carrier wave by the changes of its amplitude along with the changes in input signal. The carrier itself does not change in amplitude but the sidebands do. Sidebands are the portion of the signal that are above or below the baseband signal. This means that AM takes a carrier waveform and the bulk of the signal in the baseband. The lower sideband (LSB) is slightly lower than the carrier frequency, and the upper sideband (USB) is slightly higher. These sidebands effectively mirror each other and describe the fluctuations in the signal instead of the carrier.

How does this apply to an AM radio in a car? When you tune your radio into 880 AM, you are receiving a signal being broadcast by a transmitter at 880,000 Hz. Your car antenna picks up all the sine waves broadcasting at different frequencies and your tuner singles out that one particular frequency. The detector in the tuner demodulates the signal and sends it through your car speakers so that you can hear the original signal demodulated.

One of the downsides to AM radio is that it becomes inefficient when you transmit complex information such as music instead of monaural voice. The modulating frequency should ideally be 10% or less of the carrier frequency. When transmitting music, for example, the sidebands can consume 25% of the power, and the carrier frequency consumes 75% of the signal power. If you try to increase the amount of information the sidebands can handle, the bandwidth constraints are exceeded and overmodulation can occur. Overmodulation is consumption of excessive bandwidth that can result in a distorted signal. A more efficient way to transfer music is through frequency modulation.

1.3.2 Frequency Modulation (FM)

Frequency modulation (FM) is the method of encoding data onto an AC wave by changing the instantaneous frequency of the wave. FM can be used to encode digital or analog data. With digital FM, data is represented as 1s and 0s, and the carrier frequency signal changes are also abrupt when compared to the continuous analog waveform. The number of carrier frequencies is typically represented in powers of 2 that correspond with the on/off frequency state. If only two states are used, the mode is called frequency-shift keying (FSK). This is similar to the simplest form of phase-shift keying (PSK), which varies by two states, also known as biphase modulation, represented by 0 degrees and 180 degrees. The state is determined by measuring the previous phase shift bit. If there is no change from low (0) to high (180), then the phase does not shift but remains the same.

Analog FM has a smooth or continuous AC carrier wave, which can be represented as a sine wave. Narrowband FM only varies by 5 KHz (Kilohertz, or 1000 Hz), has less possible variances than standard analog, and is used typically for two-way radio. Wideband FM can vary by several MHz (Megahertz, or 1,000,000 Hz) and is used typically for wireless communications.

NOTE

A hertz is a measurement of frequency in a current that varies, such as AC that is typically found in American households, which is 60 Hz. This means that in 1 second, the current varies in frequency 60 times.

1.3.3 Phase-Shift Modulation (PSM)

When digital signals are conveyed by shifting phases, it is known as **phase-shift modulation (PSM)**. PSM is typically used for digital signaling, or satellite communication. If the number of states used increases beyond the two used for biphase, up to four, then it becomes quarternary, and the shift angles are represented by 0 degree-, 90 degree-, 180 degree-, and 270-degree shifts. The number of phases used to represent the information being transmitted can have significant impact on the amount of information transmitted. The use of more than two phases is also known as multilevel signaling.

1.3.4 Multilevel Signaling

Signaling can be described as the use of light or sound to encode and transmit information. Multilevel signaling encodes a signal using multiple levels or states. Biphase has two states. If you increase the states up to three or four, it is called "ternary" and "quaternary," respectively. Why is this important? It allows you to move more information over the same telecommunications medium to get more bandwidth. The discussion of radio earlier in the chapter mentioned that wireless RF computer networks have increased bandwidth capacity significantly over the past ten years. Now that we know how binary signaling works, it makes sense that if we increase the number of states, the amount of data increases exponentially. For instance, 1-Mbps transmission speeds were accomplished using binary phase-shift keying (BPSK) in which one phase bit is used for each shift bit and only two states are represented. The transmission speed was doubled when quadrature phase-shift keying (QPSK) was introduced and signal encoding could represent four possible states as 0, 90, 180, or 270 degrees instead of just two states. The problem with increasing the amount of information is that it also affects the signal quality, resulting in increasing power levels to compensate for lower signal quality or reducing the distance between transmitting nodes to avoid signal loss or degradation. One of the most recent evolutions in wireless network technology, which has achieved transmission rates of 11 Mbps, is the Institute of Electrical and Electronics Engineers (IEEE) 802.11b standard. This rate is accomplished by using a relatively new multilevel encoding technique called complementary code keying (CCK). Here three computer processors take one of 64 different possible codes and then apply phase QPSK to the code itself. Thus the number of levels that you are able to express increases the amount of information represented in turn to achieve higher bandwidth rates.

NOTE ▣

A bit is a binary digit. A bit represents only two states, on (0) or off (1). Each additional bit increases the amount of information that can be expressed by a factor of 2. So, 2 bits represents four states ($2^2 = 4$) and 3 bits represents eight states ($2^3 = 8$) states. A byte is 8 bits, which can represent $2^8 = 256$ possible values. If you can encode information using four states instead of two, you can express more information during the same time. This results in increased bandwidth.

Bandwidth

Bandwidth is a measurement of how much information can be transmitted over a medium over a prescribed period of time. The bandwidth of an analog signal is the difference between highest to lowest frequency of the signal. A baseband (also called narrowband) connection, for example, is one in which the signal is not multiplexed and has not been shifted from its original frequency to increase the amount of information. Ethernet and Token Ring computer networks are examples of baseband technology. Broadband has a much wider range of frequencies available by comparison, because it does multiplex or combine signals over the transmission media. Coaxial cable used for cable television is an example of broadband.

Before we look into the encoding techniques further, it makes sense to define **synchronous communication** and **asynchronous communication**:

- **Synchronous communication:** Communication whereby a clocking mechanism keeps events in sync to manage flow of information.

- **Asynchronous communication:** Communication that is not synchronized or kept in check with a clocking mechanism between communication devices.

Synchronous communication can be controlled with either character-oriented or bit-oriented clocking. The major difference is that one synchronizes by frame and byte, and one does not. Character-oriented synchronous communications are used to transmit blocks of characters (i.e., American Standard Code for Information Interchange [ASCII] files).

In bit synchronization, each frame is transmitted contiguously. The receiving device maintains bit synchronization in one of two ways:

- **Clock encoding:** The timing information is actually transmitted in the signal instead of relying on the receiving device's local clock.

- **Digital Phase Locked Loop (DPLL):** The receiving device is responsible for synchronization and uses its local clock to synchronize bit transitions.

Now that we've established that clocking and synchronization are factors when trying to communicate over a network, what are some of the other factors that come to mind and who decides how it all works? There are many factors to consider when proposing new communication networks and technologies. The organization responsible for many of the encoding schemes

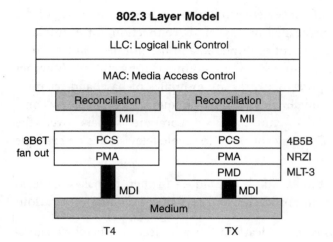

Figure 1.5

Encoding methods in relation to the OSI model

discussed in this chapter is the IEEE. Large groups of people send Requests for Proposals (RFPs) on networking and other technical design specifications to the IEEE. Once an RFP is adopted by the IEEE, it can become a standard, such as IEEE 802.3 (Fast Ethernet). Chapter 2 discusses the Open Systems Interconnection (OSI) reference model, which helps explain system details. Everything needed to connect data networks—from the physical media or wiring used up to the network applications—is broken down in the OSI model. Figure 1.5 provides perspective on how the encoding mechanisms fit into the OSI model. You will learn about the OSI model in Chapter 2.

For now, let's just say that the IEEE 802.3 specification for Ethernet, as an example, has details including and just above the physical media that will be used (copper wire, fiber optics, air, etc.). The layer just above the first Physical layer contains Data Link layer (Layer 2) details. These encoding mechanisms specify how the electrical impulses on the wire get transitioned from polarity changes into binary data or bits. As we describe NRZ, NRZ-L, NRZ-I, and other encoding techniques, keep in mind the way electrical signals are converted at Layer 2 into data. When converting digital data to digital signals and transmitting it across an Ethernet LAN, the data must be it represented as a digital signal. The three common techniques are used for this task are:

1   Non-Return to Zero (NRZ) encoding

2   Manchester encoding

3   Differential Manchester encoding

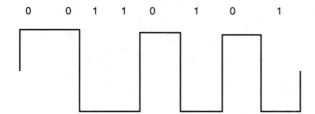

```
0    0   1   1   0   1   0    1
```

Figure 1.6
NRZ

We will now discuss each of these starting with Non-Return to Zero.

1.3.5   Non-Return to Zero (NRZ) Encoding

Non-Return to Zero (NRZ) encoding uses two levels of signaling, known as bipolar. The two levels or states can be expressed as either on or off, or high or low. This is the most basic and simplistic method of encoding. The bit interval does not change, so the encoded data may contain long strings of logic 1s or 0s, which do not result in any bit transitions. See Figure 1.6. If NRZ encoding is used with a DPLL-recovered clock signal, the receiver DPLL could not reliably regenerate the clock, thereby making it impossible to detect the boundaries of the received bits at the receiver. Although it has limitations, NRZ encoding is commonly used in slow-speed communications interfaces for both synchronous and asynchronous transmissions because it is the easiest way to transmit digital signals.

Non-Return to Zero Level (NRZ-L) Encoding

Non-Return to Zero Level (NRZ-L) also uses two different states whereby low voltage is represented as binary 1 and high voltage is represented as binary 0. The level of signal depends on the type of bit. In NRZ-L encoding, the polarity of the signal changes only when the incoming signal changes from a 1 to a 0 or from a 0 to a 1. Figure 1.7 also shows how the digital data word 01001100011 is converted using the NRZ-L encoding method. The

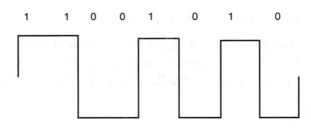

```
1    1   0   0   1   0   1   0
```

Figure 1.7
NRZ-L

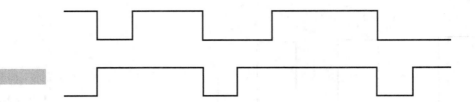

Figure 1.8
NRZ-I

NRZ-L method looks just like the NRZ method, except for the first input 1 data bit. This is because NRZ does not consider the first data bit to be a polarity change, whereby NRZ-L does. Again, as with NRZ, long strings of 1s and 0s would appear as constant voltage pulses, thereby resulting in lack of synchronization and incorrect bit values being transmitted. NRZ-L is used mostly for serial lines.

Non-Return to Zero Inverted (NRZ-I) Encoding

Non-Return to Zero Inverted (NRZ-I) is a variation of NRZ-L. When comparing bits in sequence, a binary 0 does not cause a transition, but a binary 1 does. Binary 1 represents a transition from low to high or high to low at the beginning of a bit interval. NRZ-I is an inverted signal level, so if the bit is a 1, the signal transitions; if the bit is a 0, the level stays current (no transition). See Figure 1.8. NRZ-I differs from NRZ-L by the change in the signal bit. This is considered differential encoding because the difference in the signals is used to determine changes in state, not the value (amplitude). We will cover differential encoding in the next section.

NRZ-I is used on Fast Ethernet and Fiber Distributed Data Interface (FDDI). The 4B/5B (four-bits to five-bits) method is another application of NRZ-I. We will discuss this method later in the chapter.

NOTE
In the exercises at the end of the chapter, you will learn to convert decimal numbers to binary, so don't worry if you can't figure out how some of the numbers are arrived at in the next few sections.

1.3.6   Manchester Encoding

Manchester encoding is a synchronous clock encoding technique used to encode the clock and data of a synchronous bit stream. It uses the rising or falling edge in the middle of each bit time to indicate a 0 or 1. Manchester

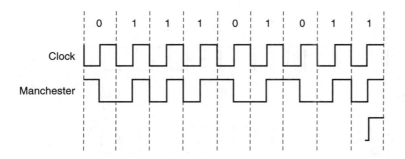

Figure 1.9
Manchester encoding

encoding requires two frequencies: the base carrier and 2 times the carrier frequency, because it changes in the middle of the bit time. The actual binary data to be transmitted are not sent as a sequence of logic 1s and 0s as in NRZ; instead, the bits are translated into a slightly different format. The data bit 1 from the level-encoded signal is represented by a full cycle of the inverted signal from the master clock, which matches with the 0 to 1 rise of the phase-encoded signal, resulting in −V in the first half of the signal and +V in the second half. To clarify, in Manchester encoding, if the original data is a 0, the Manchester code is 0 to 1, and it shifts to an upward transition at bit center. If the original data is a 1, the Manchester code is 1 to 0, and it shifts downward at bit center. There are two bits of Manchester-encoded data for each bit of original data. See Figure 1.9.

The following is a binary example of Manchester encoding:

The pattern of bits " 0 1 1 1 1 0 0 1 " encodes to " 01 10 10 10 10 01 01 10 " (the least significant bit [first] is left-most).

In the previous example, the waveform for a bit stream is carrying a sequence of bits. In Manchester encoding, a logic 0 is indicated by a 0 to 1 transition at the center of the bit, and a logic 1 is indicated by a 1 to 0 transition at the center of the bit. The signal transitions do not always occur at the division between one bit and another because the transition is at the center of each bit.

TIP

In a DPLL, the receiving device is responsible for synchronization and uses its local clock to synchronize bit transitions. Manchester encoding ensures this, allowing the receiving DPLL to correctly extract the clock signal. This happens because a Manchester-encoded signal contains frequent level transitions so that the value and timing of each bit can be correctly decoded.

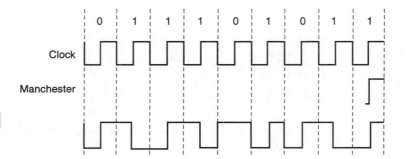

Figure 1.10
**Differential Manchester
encoding**

Frequent transitions in the Manchester-encoded signal cause it to consume more bandwidth than the original signal, as in NRZ. Manchester encoding is used as the physical layer of an Ethernet 802.3 LAN, where the additional bandwidth is not a significant issue. Its main benefit is the ability for error recovery.

1.3.7   Differential Manchester Encoding

Differential Manchester encoding is similar to Manchester encoding in that each bit period is broken into two intervals, and a transition between high and low occurs during each period. The difference is the interpretation of this transition. A 1 bit is indicated by making the first half of the signal equal to the last half of the previous bit's signal so that there is no transition at the start of the bit time. A 0 bit is indicated by making the first half of the signal opposite to the last half of the previous bit's signal. In simpler terms, the interpretation of the transition is a function of the previous bit period so that the presence of a transition at the beginning is coded 0, and no transition at the beginning is coded 1. As in Manchester encoding, there is always a transition in the middle of the bit time. See Figure 1.10 for an example.

As each bit is transmitted, a voltage change always occurs in the middle of the bit time to ensure clock synchronization. Differential Manchester encoding is used in Token Ring networks. You will learn about Token Ring in Chapter 3.

Differential encoding compares the preceding bit to determine change or difference. For example, let's say we have two friends named Ken and Stan

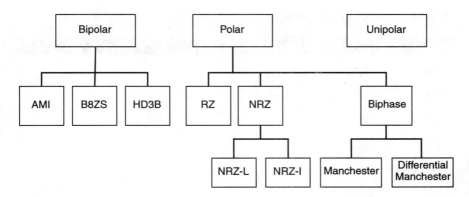

Figure 1.11
Encoding scheme hierarchy

who communicate to each other in binary, or 1s and 0s. If Ken sends Stan sixty 0s in a row and then four 1s in a row, the communication could be expressed counting 64 total bits. A more efficient way to communicate and store that information is for Ken to only let Stan know when he is changing state from 1 to 0.

Instead of Ken saying

"0000000000000000000000000000000000000000000000000000000001111"

He can say

"0x60" and "4x1"

or he can say

"0x60" and "I'm sending 1s until you hear otherwise."

By expressing the stream of 1s and 0s only when there is a change in state, the same information can be expressed using less space. This increased efficiency makes it possible to compress information because you are replacing redundant predictable elements (in this case, bits) with a flag that says, "Only let me know if the preceding bit happens to be different, otherwise I'll assume it's the same."

Figure 1.11 illustrates the hierarchy and relationship of these encoding techniques.

1.3.8   4B/5B Encoding

In this scheme, the data is first encoded to ensure transitions. This is done by what is called the **4B/5B-encoding** scheme. It takes data in 4-bit codes

TABLE 1.1   4B/5B-Encoding Scheme

4B	5B	Hexadecimal Assignment
0000	11110	0
0001	01001	1
0010	10100	2
0011	10101	3
0100	01010	4
0101	01011	5
0110	01110	6
0111	01111	7
1000	10010	8
1001	10011	9
1010	1011	A
1011	10111	B
1100	11010	C
1101	11011	D
1110	11100	E
1111	11101	F

and maps it to corresponding 5-bit codes. This is done to guarantee no more than three 0s in a row so that synchronization is adequate. See Table 1.1 for the encoding scheme. So, the 4B/5B encoding for the bit sequence 1110 0101 0000 0011 is 11100 01011 11110 10101.

4B/5B encoding starts with a "nibble." Remember: A byte is 8 bits, and someone thought it would be humorous to call half a byte a nibble. Each 4-bit block of data has an extra fifth bit added. If input data is dealt with in 4-bit blocks, there are 16 different bit patterns. With 5-bit blocks, there are 32 different bit patterns. Due to the 4B/5B encoding, the clock frequency is now 125 MHz. A 100-MHz signal is not enough to give us 100 Mbps—we need a 125-MHz clock. The use of one extra bit for every five means that there is 20% overhead for every clock encoding. 4B/5B also uses NRZ-I to generate the signal to improve reliability of the differential signal.

The 4B/5B encoding is used with the 100-Mbps Ethernet standard and Fiber Distributed Data Interface (FDDI). You will learn more about Ethernet and FDDI in Chapter 3.

1.3.9 Multi-Level Transition-3 (MLT-3) Encoding

Multi-Level Transition-3 (MLT-3) encoding works much in the same in way that NRZ-I works. Both encode based on presence of a transition or lack of a transition. This is a three-level form of data encoding used to concentrate the signal power below 30 MHz. The difference between the two are the three phases through which MLT-3 moves. Rather than alternating between 0 and 1, MLT-3 alternates between -1, 0, and 1, repeating indefinitely. To reiterate, the states are:

1. -1 to 0
2. 0 to 1
3. 1 to 0
4. 0 to -1

This type of encoding uses the pattern 1, 0, -1, 0. If the next data signal is a 1, the output transitions to the next bit in the pattern. For example, if the output bit was a -1 and the input bit is a 1, the next output bit is a 0. If the next data bit is a 0, the output remains constant because a change occurs only when the input bit is a 1. In this method of data encoding, the highest frequency in the signal occurs when transmitting a long sequence of data bit 1s, in which case the encoded signal repeats the whole pattern. This creates a cycle length of one-fourth of the basic clock rate. In this worst-case scenario, the frequency rate would be at 32.5 MHz when using a 125-MHz clock. For other data bit patterns, the frequency rate would be lower. This type of encoding is used by FDDI to obtain 100MB/s out of a 31.25MHz signal.

1.3.10 8B/6T Encoding

To send information using **8B/6T encoding**, the value of the data byte is compared to the values in the 8B/6T table. The remapping table has nine symbols used for starting and ending delimiters and control characters. The full table is listed in IEEE 802.3 section 23.2.4.1. (For more information

TABLE 1.2   8B/6T Encoding Scheme

Data (Hexadecimal)	8 Binary	6 Ternary
00	0000.0000	+−00+−
01	0000.0001	0+−+−0
02	0000.0010	+−0+−0
03	000.0011	−0++−0
0E	0000.1110	−+0−0+
FE	1111 1110	−+0+00
FF	1111.1111	+0−+00

about IEEE, see Appendix B, "Networking Standards.") The incoming data stream is split into 8-bit values. Each 8-bit value is conveyed in binary numbers. This 8-bit binary number is then converted into a 6-bit pattern using three voltage levels: −V, 0, and V volts, so each 8-bit value has a unique 6T code. For example, 0 x 00 uses the bit pattern 0000 0000 and the code +−00+−. There are 729 possible 6T patterns. Because there are so many possibilities, only a small portion of them is shown in Table 1.2.

Because eight data bits are sent as six voltage-level signals, the carrier needs to be running at only three fourths of the speed of the data rate. Unlike 4B/5B, 8B/6T completely prepares the data for transmission; no further encoding is required.

1.3.11   8B/10B Encoding

8B/10B encoding is an encoding scheme in which 8-bit binary data values are represented by 10-bit symbols. The data octet is split up into the three most-significant bits and the five least-significant bits. This is then represented as two decimal numbers with the least-significant bits first. Each data code group is named /D$x.y$/, where the value of x represents the decimal value of the five least-significant bits and y represents the value of the three most-significant bits. For example:

/D0.0/ = 000 00000

/D6.2/ = 010 00110

/D28.6/ = 110 11100

There are also 12 special code groups that follow the naming convention /Kx.y/. Each octet of data is examined and assigned a 10-bit code group. The 10-bit code groups must contain a minimum of four 0s and 1s to ensure that not too many consecutive 1s and 0s occur between code groups to maintain clock synchronization.

In the actual encoding process, 8 data bits are presented to the encoder. The first five bits are fed into a block that produces functions based on the values of those bits. The last three bits are likewise fed into a similar block. The actual encoding is done in the blocks labeled 5B/6B encoding and 3B/4B encoding. 8B/10B encoding increases transmission time, because 8 bits can only be transmitted in a 10-bit time, but the encoding also enables the creation of additional symbols that can be used for the flow control and error detection of the data being transmitted. We will discuss flow control and error detection later in the chapter.

1.3.12   4D-PAM5 Encoding

4D-PAM5 encoding is a four-dimensional, five-level pulse amplitude modulation. This is a way of encoding bits on copper wires to get a 1 GB per second transfer rate when the maximum rate of a single wire is 125 MHz. This is done by employing a multilevel amplitude signal. A five-level signal, called pulse amplitude modulation 5, is used. This works in a similar manner to MLT-3 except the levels are $-2v$, $-1v$, $0v$, $1v$, and $2v$. The transmitted signal on each wire is a five-level pulse modulation symbol. Four symbols transmitted simultaneously on the four pairs of wire forms the 4D-PAM5 code group that represents an 8-bit frame octet. The symbols to be transmitted are selected from a four-dimensional (4D) code group of five-level symbols.

NOTE

Because there are four separate pairs being used for transmission and reception of data, there are 625 possible codes to choose from when using all four pairs. Therefore, all 8 bits can be transferred using only one 4D-PAM5 symbol.

The data signals have distinct and measurable amplitude and phases, allowing more data bits per cycle. This type of encoding is used by Gigabit Ethernet, whereby 1000 Mbps is squeezed into 125-MHz signals. The electronics are more complex, and the technology is more susceptible to noise. Actually, only four levels are used for data; the 0v level is used to recover the transmitted signal from high noise. This fifth level of coding is used for error detection and correction, which we will discuss next.

1.4   Error Detection and Recovery

Reliable operation of a computer network depends on both error detection and error recovery. As we have seen from the section on encoding, a wide variety of signals are transmitted in a variety of ways over different media types. Some of the encoding methods we previously discussed are more reliable than others. Data communications addresses the reliability shortfalls of media transports by providing error detection and recovery methods and techniques.

WARNING !

The nature of data communications is inherently different from something like high-resolution video or, in some cases, voice. Sometimes a slight delay is acceptable, and other times it is frustrating or simply not acceptable. The delay in propagation when you call someone overseas on the phone can result from a signal being relayed by satellite. Networked computers, on the other hand, may be affected less by delays in communication because data can be queued and sent in batches.

The difference in the needs of the people and communicating devices determines the acceptable amount of errors or the amount of recovery needed. Error detection and recovery is accomplished using parity checking, checksums, cyclic redundancy checks, and error correction, as described in the following sections.

1.4.1   Parity Check

When data is encoded, the method used defines the way the signals are represented on the physical communication line. This information is transformed into bits for transmission over the physical medium. Coded transmissions are essential for reliable digital communications; block and convolutional codes are the most commonly used codes. Some error-correction techniques are called block coding, because a block of data bits is examined to compute the required error control bits. For other applications, a method is required that is suitable for a continuous data stream. In parity checking, the bit stream is packaged into blocks. A block consists of the information bits together with additional bits, called parity check bits. The information bits contain the message, and the parity check bits are

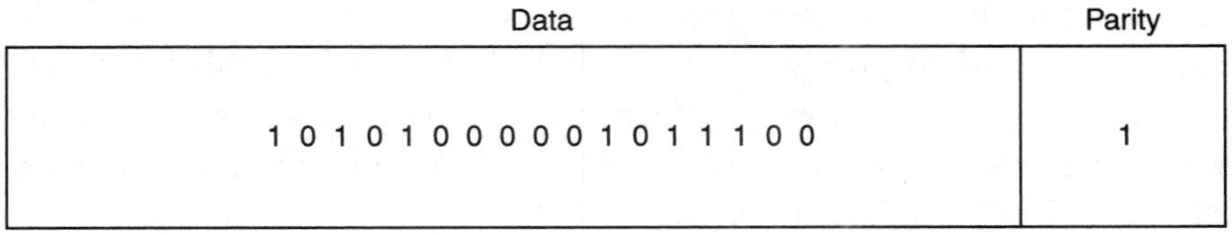

Data	Parity
1 0 1 0 1 0 0 0 0 0 1 0 1 1 1 0 0	1

Figure 1.12
Parity check

determined by the information bits. See Figure 1.12 for an example. If a block has more than one bit in error there is the possibility of wrong correction; however, when bit errors occur infrequently, the probability of multiple bit errors in a block is small. The selection of the parity check bits makes error control and correction possible. There are methods for detecting and correcting single bit errors, which we will discuss later.

A **parity check** ensures that when data is transmitted from one device to another or stored locally, there is a means to recover lost transactions. Parity checks are used during data transmission to detect errors caused by interference or noise. From our previous discussion, you learned that data is transmitted as a sequence of 1s and 0s. Due to electrical interference that occurs during data transmission, a bit may be changed from a 0 to a 1 or a 1 to a 0, thereby causing an error. Parity checks detect this type of error. When data is transmitted, each character is encoded as a 7-bit binary number. Then an eighth bit is added to make a byte. This bit is called a parity bit. Technically this is described as an (8, 7) error-checking code. A system can use either even or odd parity. In even parity, the value of the parity bit is set such that the total number of 1s in the data is even. For example:

- 11110, which has an even number of 1s, becomes 111100.
- 11001, which has an odd number of 1s, becomes 110011.

In odd parity, the value of the parity bit is set such that the total number of 1s in the data is odd. For example:

- 11001, which has an odd number of 1s, becomes 110010.
- 11110, which has an even number of 1s, becomes 111101.

The receiver counts the number of 1s in the byte and checks to be sure this agrees with the parity bit. This is done to detect any errors before stripping the parity off the original data. The method of parity acts as an error flag, indicating an error has occurred somewhere. Often the data has to be retransmitted when a parity error is detected. This method only safeguards against single parity bit errors. To detect complex errors or to pinpoint where the errors have occurred, more sophisticated and complex error-checking algorithms have to be used.

Parity checks are still widely used for error checking in computer memory modules, where errors are likely to occur at random points. Another example of the use of parity checking is in modem communications. The presence or absence of a parity bit in modem communication allows each communicating device to establish a connection and synchronize communication.

WARNING !

The problem with parity checks is that errors do not occur independently; rather, they are often clustered together in bursts. Under burst-error conditions, the probability of undetected errors in a frame protected by single bit parity can approach 50%.

1.4.2   Checksums

A **checksum** is a simple error-detection scheme whereby each message is accompanied by a value based on the number of bits in the message. The receiving device then applies the same formula to the message and checks to make sure the value is the same. If the value matches, it is assumed that the complete transmission was received. If not, the receiver can assume that the message has somehow become corrupt. This type of error detection checks for single-bit errors in a block. To locate a single-bit error using checksum error detection, selected subsets of the block are checked to determine its position. A checksum has no ability to correct errors, but only detect them. For example, if we chose a checksum function, which was simply the sum of the bytes in the message, modulo 256, then it would look like this:

Message	4 22 8
Message with checksum	4 22 8 34
Message after transmission	4 27 8 34

Here the second byte of the message was corrupt from 22 to 27 by the communications channel. However, the receiver can detect this by comparing the transmitted checksum (34) with the computed checksum of 39 (4 + 27 + 8). If the checksum itself is corrupt, a correctly transmitted message might be incorrectly identified as corrupt. An incorrect message occurs where the message and/or checksum is corrupted in a manner that results in a transmission that is consistent. Unfortunately, this possibility is completely unavoidable. To minimize this probability, the checksum can be changed from 1 byte to 2 bytes.

In the previous checksum example, we demonstrated how a corrupt message was detected using a checksum algorithm that sums the bytes in the message, modulo 256. This algorithm is quite simple, and there is a 1 in 256 chance that random corruptions will not be detected. For example:

Message	4 22 8
Message with checksum	4 22 8 34
Message after transmission	4 21 9 34

Replacing the simple summing formula with a more sophisticated formula that causes each incoming byte to have an effect on the entire checksum register can solve this problem. Checksums take on various forms depending upon the nature of the transmission and the needed reliability. For example, the simplest checksum, as we just saw, is to sum up all the bytes of a transmission, computing the sum in an 8-bit counter. This value is appended as the last byte of the transmission. The idea is that upon receipt of 8 bytes, you sum up the first seven 1 bytes, and then see if the answer is the same as the last byte. A variant on this method is, upon transmission, to sum up all the bytes; then, treating the byte as a signed, 8-bit value, negate the checksum byte before transmitting it. This means that the sum of all seven bytes should be 0. The last byte is the checksum number. When you add all the numbers in the package, the sum should be 0. (If the sum reaches 256, it turns to 0.) If for some reason it doesn't sum to 0, we know that an error occurred. The following example demonstrates this:

        12 00 2E 22 12 00 26 75 00 00 FA 12 00 26 25 00 3A

In the example, we see an octet represented in hexadecimal. The last number in the row is a number that, if you sum the whole row and there is no error, should equal 0.

The checksum is usually 8, 16, or 32 bits. The Internet checksum is based on bytes of data being treated as 16-bit integers. A receiver calculates the checksum over the received data and checks whether it matches the checksum carried in the received packet. RFC1071 discusses the Internet checksum algorithm and its implementation in detail. The simplest form of checksum is a parity bit appended on to a 7-bit number so that the total number of 1s is always even or odd, as we have previously learned. A significantly more sophisticated checksum is the cyclic redundancy check (CRC) that is based on algebra, which we will discuss now.

1.4.3   Cyclic Redundancy Checks

Cyclic redundancy checking (CRC) is a technique for checking errors in data transmitted on a communications link. It is substantially reliable in detecting transmission errors and is commonly used in modems. The CRC is a sophisticated form of error checking that is based on algebra. It is calculated by performing a division of the data by a generator polynomial and recording the remainder after division. The CRC is a form of hash function. It compares large chunks of data by precalculating the CRCs for each block. The two blocks are then compared by seeing whether their CRCs are equal, saving a great deal of calculation time in most cases. Because the previous sentences contain many math terms, let's look at how the process works.

> **TIP**
> The basic idea of CRC algorithms is to treat the message as an enormous binary number, divide it by another fixed binary number, and then make the remainder from this division the checksum. When the message is received, the same division can be performed on the other end, and the remainder compared with the checksum.

Although the addition that is used in the simplest form of check summing is clearly not strong enough to form an effective checksum, division is, as long as the divisor is as wide as the checksum register.

Consider the bit pieces of data to be sent, D. The sender and receiver then agree on a r+1 bit pattern, known as a generator, G. The most significant bit, which is the left-most bit of G, is assumed to be a 1. So for a given piece of data, (D), the sender will choose additional bits, R, and append them to D such that the resulting D+R bit pattern is exactly divisible by G using modulo 2 arithmetic. The process of error checking with CRCs is this: The receiver divides the D+R received bits by G; if the remainder is not 0, the receiver knows that an error has occurred; otherwise, the data is accepted as being correct.

All CRC calculations are done in base 2 arithmetic without any carrying in addition or borrowing in subtraction. This means that addition and subtraction are both equivalent to the bitwise exclusive or (XOR) of the operands. For example:

10011011

+11001010

01010001

To understand the above math, realize there are only four cases for each bit position:

0+0=0

0+1=1

1+0=1

1+1=0 (no carry)

Based on these facts, we now can go to multiplication and division. The multiplication is calculated in a regular fashion, whereas the division looks for the numbers to divide into each other without a remainder. Suppose the message consisted of the two bytes (4, 22) as in the previous example. These can be considered the hexadecimal number 0416, which in turn when converted to binary makes the number 0000-0100-0001-0110. If we use, for example, a checksum register 1-byte wide and a constant divisor of 1001, the checksum is the remainder after 0000-0100-0001-0110 is divided by 1001. To calculate this, we do the division using good old-fashioned long division. When was the last time you did long division? Although the effect of each bit of the input message on the quotient is not that significant, the 4-bit remainder moves around a lot during the calculation, and if more bytes were added to the message the value could change very quickly. This is why division works where addition doesn't.

Standards have been defined for 8-, 12-, 16-, and 32-bit generators. The CRC is the only field, by convention, that sends the most-significant bit first. Thus, the first bit of a CRC-16 to be sent is the bit corresponding to X16, and the last is the bit corresponding to X1. The CRC-16 is able to detect all single, double, and odd numbers of errors, as well as errors with burst less than 16 bits in length. In addition, 99.9984% of other error patterns will be detected.

The Ethernet and Token Ring local area network protocols both used a 32-bit CRC.

1.4.4 Error Correction

Error checking and correcting (ECC), also known as error-correction code, is a more sophisticated form of checking than parity because errors are corrected when they are detected. An error-correcting code is an algorithm for expressing a sequence of numbers such that any occurring errors can be detected and corrected based on the remaining numbers. The study of error-correcting codes and the associated mathematics is known as coding theory.

NOTE

Error-correction algorithms are used in a wide variety of applications throughout the electronics industry, from CD-ROMs to spacecraft communications systems. Early space probes used a type of error-correcting code called a block code, and more recent space probes use convolution codes. Error-correcting codes are also used in high-speed modems, cellular phones, network server memory modules, and the ISBN used to identify books and data storage.

Here is how ECC works for data storage:

1. When a unit of data is stored, a code that describes the bit sequence is calculated and stored along with it. For each 64-bit unit, an extra seven bits for ECC are needed in order to store this code.

2. When the unit of data is requested for reading, a code for about-to-be-read data is again calculated using the original algorithm. The newly generated code is compared with the first code generated when the data was stored.

3. If the codes match, it means the data is error free and can be sent.

4. Should the codes not match, the two are compared, and the missing or erroneous bits are sent or corrected.

5. If the error was in the original data and not in the transmission, no attempt is made to correct this data; instead, the error will be logged as a permanent error.

In general, ECC increases the reliability of any computing or telecommunications system without adding too much overhead. As mentioned previously, ECC can be done using different types of algorithms. These algorithms all have one thing in common: Additional bits are appended to the data at its origin. The bits are later removed from the data and then used to check and correct the data at its destination. The location of any single-bit error can be determined when there is a difference in the codes. The defective bit can then be corrected. Once error correction has been incorporated into a system, the probability of errors occurring is greatly reduced.

One particular block algorithm, called a Hamming code, is especially suited to the checking and correction of single-bit errors that originate in large memory arrays. This is actually a method of linear block coding. This particular code is commonly used in computer RAM and is a good choice for randomly occurring errors. The Hamming code is binary code that can also detect two-bit errors but cannot correct them. The code uses additional redundant bits to check for errors and then performs the checks with special equations. A parity check equation adds the bits and makes sure that the sum is even for even parity or odd for odd parity. The extra parity check is checked for errors, along with the other bits. Any odd number of errors shows up as if there were just one error, and any even number of errors looks the same as no error. Even parity is forced by adding an extra parity bit and setting it either to 1 or 0 to make the overall parity come out even. What is important to realize about the Hamming code is that the extra parity check bit actually is included in the check and is checked for errors, along with the other bits. This method for coding actually detects all odd number of bit errors and can be used without correction to detect all single- and double-bit errors. The binary Hamming code is particularly useful because it provides a good balance between error correction and error detection with low overhead. It can correct one error, detect two, and only needs to devote one out of each eight bytes, or 12.5%, to error correction and detection.

Reed-Solomon codes are block-based, error-correcting codes with a wide range of applications in digital communications and storage. These are linear block codes that are used to correct errors in many systems, including storage devices, mobile communications, satellite communications, and digital television. The Reed-Solomon encoder takes a block of digital data and appends redundant bits. The decoder processes each block and attempts to correct errors and recover the original data. The number and type of errors that can be corrected depends on the characteristics of the code. Reed-Solomon codes are particularly well suited to correcting burst errors and can also correct erasures.

Forward error-correction coding or channel coding is a type of digital signal processing that improves data reliability by introducing a known factor into a data sequence prior to transmission. This structure enables a receiving system to detect and possibly correct errors caused by channel or receiver corruption. This coding technique enables the decoder to correct errors without requesting retransmission of the original information. One forward error-correcting technique, known as convolutional coding, has parity check bits depending not only on the current block but on past blocks as well. The technique of convolutional coding is well suited for long bit streams in noisy channels and is readily implemented in hardware. This type of coding transforms a binary message into a sequence of symbols to be transmitted. Upon reception, the received information must be related back to the original message bits. Single-bit errors can be corrected by simple inspection of the received symbols. If there are no errors, the process of decoding is done. Convolutional decoding can be performed using what is called a Viterbi algorithm.

Andrew Viterbi developed a decoding technique that has become the standard for decoding convolutional codes. At each bit interval, the Viterbi decoding algorithm compares the actual received code bits with the code bits that could have been generated for each possible memory-state transition. Based on metrics of similarity, it chooses the most likely sequence within a specific time frame. The Viterbi decoding algorithm requires less memory than sequential decoding because unlikely sequences are eliminated early, leaving a relatively small number of sequences that need to be stored.

Codes that introduce a large measure of redundancy convey relatively little information per each individual code bit. This is advantageous because it reduces the likelihood that all of the original data will be wiped out during a single transmission.

Now that we have covered how errors in transmissions are detected and corrected, it is time to move on and look at how sending too much information at one time is handled. We will cover flow control, windowing and sliding windows, and congestion management in the next few sections.

1.5 Flow Control

We have learned about signals, encoding, and error correction, but how does data flow without flooding the receiving end? How does it know when the receiver has too much data to process? There are methods to control how much data is being sent. **Flow control** is a method by which the data flow between devices is managed so that the data can be handled at an efficient pace. When too much data arrives before a device can handle it, the data is either lost or must be retransmitted. This often happens to us when we give our brains too much to process. What happened when you were reading the math part of the error-correcting section previously? At some point, your brain probably either stopped paying attention, or you had to process the information over again. Well, data works in much the same manner.

Flow control makes it possible for a receiver running on a lower speed to accept data from a sender using a higher speed, without being overloaded. This is because a higher-speed connection generates data faster than the destination device can receive and process it. Because data is transmitted constantly, it requires organization for every device to get what has been requested error-free and at an acceptable speed.

NOTE

Flow control is used to control the flow of a message from the sender to the receiver by transmission as necessary based on the size of the receiver's buffer. It is a way for the receiver to control the rate at which the sender transmits data.

Flow control occurs when the receiving system tells the sending system to stop sending data because it has nowhere to put the data currently being transmitted. This slows the flow of data so that no loss occurs. However, flow control can cause a chain reaction. For example, Computer B is receiving data from Computer A via a modem. Computer B tells its modem to stop. The modem may have space to save the data still coming from the modem from Computer A, but when that space is full, it will have to tell that modem to stop as well. In return, Computer A's modem may have to tell Computer A to stop sending data. This is called end-to-end flow control. If end-to-end flow control isn't working properly, a loss of data will result because any data sent after the stop request is discarded.

Flow control can take place at various levels, such as user process to user process, host to host, and router to router. Two types of flow control are generally supported: hardware and software. Hardware flow control uses two of the wires that are connected between your machine and the modem to tell the other side to stop. Software flow control uses control bytes to tell the other side to stop.

The Ready to Send/Clear to Send (RTS/CTS) protocol uses two additional wires in the cable connecting communicating devices. The RTS wire is an output signal indicating that the device generating the signal has buffer space available to receive. The CTS wire is an input signal indicating that the other device has buffer space available to receive. Xon/Xoff is a protocol for controlling the flow of data between computers and other devices on an asynchronous serial connection. The Xon/Xoff protocol inserts characters directly into the data stream. The X stands for transmitter, so Xon and Xoff are signals used to turn the transmitter on or off. Xon, which is used to enable the flow of data, is hexadecimal 11. Xoff, which is used to stop the flow of data, is hexadecimal 13. The Xon/Xoff protocol is often not a reliable method of flow control because many host systems do not shut off the flow of characters immediately upon receiving an Xoff. Transmission may continue for an additional 20 or 30 bytes before finally stopping. These characters will not be processed because the device is busy processing the previous line.

Besides these protocols, there are several other methods of controlling the flow of data. The first of these is buffering. Buffering is used by devices to temporarily store excess data in memory until they can be processed. Occasional data bursts can easily be handled by buffering, but if the data continues at high speeds, an overflow will occur. The next method is source squelch messages. Source squelch messages are used by receiving devices to keep their buffers from overflowing. The receiving device sends a message to the source, requesting that it reduce the rate of data transmission. The last method for handling flow control is windowing. In windowing, the source requires an acknowledgment from the destination after a certain amount of data has been transmitted. After discussing windowing, we will move on to the concept of sliding window.

1.6   Windowing and Sliding Window

As mentioned previously, windowing is a flow-control method whereby the source requires an acknowledgment from the destination after a certain amount of data has been transmitted. Windowing is reliable because it requires the receiving device to communicate with the sending device by sending back an acknowledgment when it receives data. This happens in a number of steps. First, the source device sends a small amount of data to the destination device. When the data is received, the destination device sends an acknowledgment to the source device. Then the same amount of data is transmitted as was the first time. Should the destination not receive some of the data, the acknowledgment is not sent, and the source then retransmits the data at a lower transmission rate. If the receiving device sends a data packet with a zero window size, it means the buffers are full and it cannot receive any more data. Transmission is restarted when the receiving device sends a data packet with a window size larger than 0. Two mechanisms are used with windowing to ensure the delivery of segments without duplication or data loss. These are:

1.   Acknowledgments (ACKs) and Negative Acknowledgments (NAKs)

2.   Sequencing and Retransmission

All these technologies work together to provide data reliability and optimal performance. These technologies form the characteristics of sliding windows used at the sender and receiver that involve error correction and flow control. Message ordering by the sender can also be incorporated.

Sliding window algorithms are a method of flow control for data transfers. The window is the maximum amount of data can be sent without having to wait for ACKs. The algorithm operates as follows:

1.   Send the data segment in the window that has an assigned sequence number.

2.   Wait for an acknowledgement.

3.   Slide the window to the indicated position and set the window size to the sequence number advertised in the acknowledgment.

4.   If the acknowledgment is not received in some specified time, retransmit the data.

5.   When the acknowledgment arrives, reposition the window.

6.   The transmission continues from the packet following the last one transmitted.

Sliding window protocols use two different methods: data acknowledgment, and stop and wait. The basis of the data acknowledgment sliding window protocol is that both sender and receiver keep a window of acknowledgment. The sender keeps the value of expected acknowledgment, while the receiver keeps the value of expected receiving data. The sender advances the window when it receives an acknowledgment, and the receiver advances the window when it receives the expected data. The Stop-and-Wait is also called the One-Bit Sliding Window Protocol. In this protocol, the sender transmits one data unit and then waits for an acknowledgment before sending the next data unit. The Stop-and-Wait Protocol is very inefficient because at any given moment only one data unit is in transition. The sender has to wait at least one round-trip time before sending the next data unit. Go Back N is the simplest sliding window policy. This strategy corresponds to the receiver having a window of size 1. In other words, the receiver discards all packets except the one requested. Therefore, in the event of a transmission error, the sender's window will fill up and then will empty as the receiver is discarding all the rest of the data packets. The selective repeat protocol works by using both windows and sequence numbers. When a transmission error occurs, the receiver will discard only the data that needs to be retransmitted. The receiver then buffers all subsequent data. In the meantime, the sender continues to transmit data until it notices that there is a timeout. At this point, it retransmits the first unacknowledged piece of data. After a successful retransmission, the sender then acknowledges and passes on all buffered data.

TIP If two devices use a sliding window protocol and the window is large, the link will quickly become congested. If the window size is small, the link won't become congested because the window size limits the total number of data packets that can be in transmission at one time.

It is time now to move from flow control to congestion management. In the next section we will discuss management methods such as traffic shaping, load shedding, and jitter control.

1.7 Congestion Management

Flow control is aimed at preventing a fast sender from overwhelming a slow receiver, and although it can be helpful at reducing congestion, it can't really solve the congestion problem. When one device becomes overloaded, congestion results. Because a device is receiving data faster than it can be processed, one of two things must happen. Either the device must prevent additional data from entering the congested region until the data already present can be processed, or the congested device can discard queued data to make room for new data that is arriving. How do we alleviate the problem of congestion, and what are some possible solutions?

Preallocation is one way to help prevent congestion. Preallocation schemes try to prevent congestion from happening by requiring that resources be preallocated before any data can be sent, guaranteeing that the resources will be available to process the data when it is received. At the other end of the spectrum, we could choose not to preallocate resources in advance and hope that resources will be available when we need them. If insufficient resources are present to process existing data, the queued data is simply discarded. This can lead to potential deadlock and unfairness. If all of a device's buffers hold data, the device has no free buffers. Because it cannot accept additional data, it ignores data packets containing ACKs that would free up some of those buffers. Suppose further that two devices, A and B, are sending data to each other. Because both are waiting for the other to accept the data, neither can proceed. This condition is known as deadlock. The advantage of discarding data when devices become congested is that it is easy to implement; the disadvantage is that it wastes resources. The network may have expended considerable resources processing a data packet that is eventually discarded. In addition, there is less guarantee that data will ever reach its destination, so the sending hosts must pay attention to congestion. If the network cannot prevent a device from sending data, that device can cause the network to become overly congested. In extreme cases, congestion collapse can occur when the network becomes so overloaded that very few data packets reach their destination, and in the meantime the sending hosts continue to generate more and more data in the form of retransmissions and new data.

Isarithmic congestion control is another approach to congestion avoidance. The object is to reduce congestion by setting an upper limit on the number of data packets allowed to be present on the network at any time. When a device accepts data from a host, it must obtain a permit before sending the data onto the network. After a device obtains a permit, it destroys it. The destination device regenerates the permit when it passes the data to the destination host. The level of congestion can be monitored, and when it is present, a choke packet can be sent to the sender that tells it to slow down. The level of congestion can be estimated by measuring such factors as the percentage of buffers in use and line utilization. A choke packet asks the sender to cut back traffic voluntarily. Although the idea of a choke packet is to inform the source to slow down, if one source cuts back while other sources increase traffic, the result could be worse.

1.7.1   Traffic Shaping

Often the network reserves resources that are needed to meet performance guarantees. Several methods are available to be sure that this happens. Among them are traffic policing and traffic shaping. Traffic policing is a device management function on an Asynchronous Transfer Mode (ATM) network. ATM is a dedicated-connection switching technology that will be discussed in the next chapter. **Traffic shaping** is a term given to a range of techniques designed to prioritize the transmission of data over a network link. Traffic shaping involves regulating the flow of data across the network. The main idea behind shaping is to change bursts of traffic to uniform, regular traffic. For communication to occur, the sender and carrier negotiate a traffic pattern or shape allowing specific policies to be set that alter the way in which data is queued for transmission. Upon confirmation of the agreement, data transmission can begin. Sliding windows is the complete opposite of this, because it deals with maximizing the flow of data across the link. Traffic shaping affects only data to be transmitted across a link in a forward direction. The shaper is primarily designed to limit the amount of bandwidth that data paths can consume. The total traffic routed through the shaper is limited to meet the bandwidth cap by discarding any data that would cause the cap to be exceeded.

To police traffic, devices use a buffering technique referred to as a leaky bucket. The leaky bucket algorithm is used to control the data transfer rate in a datagram network by using a single-server queue with constant service time. A queue accepts packets at a variable rate. The output from the leaky bucket is constant. If the bucket overflows, packets are discarded. This technique allows traffic to flow out of the buffer at a constant rate regardless of how fast the traffic inflow is. If the traffic flows in too fast, the data will only be allowed onto the network if there is enough bandwidth. If there is not enough bandwidth, the data is discarded and must be retransmitted by the sending device. Therefore, the algorithm regulates the flow of data across the network, reducing congestion and bursts. This is suitable for multimedia such as TV and audio. A variation of this method uses a counter. The counter is set to a predefined level. Every packet is then compared to the counter. The token bucket algorithm is very similar to the leaky bucket algorithm. Large burst inputs are catered to by allowing the output to speed up. A set number of tokens are generated. For a packet to pass through the queue, it must destroy one of the tokens. The tokens go into the bucket at a constant rate, and each packet must consume one token. If there is no token in the bucket, the packet cannot be sent. This method is less restrictive than the leaky bucket algorithm.

1.7.2   Load Shedding

Load shedding is the process of systematically reducing the system demand by temporarily decreasing the load in response to transmission or capacity shortages. Sometimes there simply may be too much traffic to be able to get it all through. When this happens, some packets must be lost. The packets are lost forever if the stream was unacknowledged; however, if the stream has some form of control, a retransmission can be tried at a later time. A router (discussed in Chapter 2) needs to decide how to choose which packets to drop. If the router knows something about the traffic, it might be possible to make intelligent choices; otherwise, packets are picked at random. For example, suppose a particular stream was a real-time video feed. If a packet was dropped, it might be irritating to the viewer, but because this does not make the transmission unusable, older packets may be discarded. In an instance where the arrival of each packet is critical, such as a file transfer, the decision might be made to drop the newer packets so that a large number of packets won't have to be retransmitted.

1.7.3   Jitter Control

Jitter is deviation in the pulses in a high-frequency digital signal. The deviation can be in terms of amplitude, timing, or the width of the signal pulse. It is the variation in the time between packets arriving due to network congestion, timing drift, or route changes. Jitter can be thought of as shaky pulses. Among the causes of jitter are electromagnetic interference (EMI) and crosstalk with other signals. It can cause monitor flickering, improper processor performance, and loss of data between network devices. In synchronous traffic such as video and audio, having a slightly longer delay is acceptable as long as it's in a constant range. The task of **jitter control** is to make sure that traffic gets through the network smoothly. One mechanism of doing this is to compute the expected transit time for each hop (router) along the path. This information is carried in packets. If at a hop the packet is behind schedule, the router can increase the priority and send it faster; if a packet is ahead of schedule, it can decrease the priority and send it later. The amount of allowable jitter depends greatly on the application.

1.8   Chapter Summary

- Multiplexing is about sharing a communications line. It combines several connections into one larger channel. There are many different types of multiplexing; the type used depends on what the media, reception equipment, and transmission can handle. The different types of multiplexing are frequency division multiplexing (FDM), wave division multiplexing (WDM), and time division multiplexing (TDM).

- The object of pulse code modulation (PCM) is to convert a human signal into a digital representation. This transformation is similar to how Morse code uses dots and dashes to transmit conversation. A digital signal is obtained by sampling the analog signal at various points in time.

- Signaling is communication of information between network nodes by initiation, transmission, control, and termination of telecommunications signals. The carrier signal has three major characteristics: amplitude, frequency, and phase. Analog signaling adds information or encodes information to an alternating current (AC) base signal by modifying the frequency or signal strength. Digital signaling uses discrete steps to represent information in binary format as zeros (0s) or ones (1s).

- Encoding is putting electronic data into a standard format. Data is encoded into signals to send them from one place to another. After the data has been encoded and sent along a physical medium, it must be decoded on the other end. The various types of encoding include amplitude modulation (AM), frequency modulation (FM), Non-Return to Zero (NRZ), Non-Return to Zero Inverted (NRZ-I), Non-Return to Zero Level (NRZ-L) Manchester, Differential Manchester, 4B/5B, MLT-3, 8B/6T, 8B/10B, and 4D-PAM5 encoding.

- Reliable operation of a computing system depends on both error detection and error recovery. Error detection and recovery is accomplished using parity checking, checksums, cyclic redundancy checks, and error correction.

- Flow control is a method by which the data flow between devices is managed so that the data can be handled at an efficient pace. Flow control can take place at various levels, such as user process to user process, host to host, and router to router. Two types of flow control are generally supported: hardware and software. Besides these protocols, there are several other methods of controlling the flow of data—buffering, source squelch messages, and windowing.

- Sliding window protocols use two different methods: data acknowledgment, and stop and wait. The basis of the data acknowledgment sliding window protocol is that both sender and receiver keep a window of acknowledgment. The Stop-and-Wait Protocol is also called the One-Bit Sliding Window Protocol. In this protocol, the sender transmits one data unit and then waits for an acknowledgment before sending the next data unit.

- Congestion can be managed in several ways. Preallocation schemes try to prevent congestion from happening by requiring that resources be preallocated before any data can be sent, guaranteeing that the resources will be available to process the data when it is received. Data discard is a simple but inefficient method of handling congestion. If insufficient resources are present to process existing data, the queued data is simply discarded. Isarithmic congestion control is another approach to congestion avoidance by setting an upper limit on the number of data packets allowed to be present on the network at any one time. Additional methods include choke packets, traffic shaping, load shedding, and jitter control.

1.9   Key Terms

4B/5B encoding: This scheme takes data in 4-bit codes and maps it to corresponding 5-bit codes.

4D-PAM5 encoding: Stands for 4-dimensional, 5-level pulse amplitude modulation. This is a way of encoding bits on copper wires to get a 1 GB per second transfer rate by employing a five-level signal called pulse amplitude modulation 5.

8B/6T encoding: In this type of encoding, the value of the data byte is compared to the values in the 8B/6T table. The remapping table has nine symbols used for starting and ending delimiters and control characters.

8B/10B encoding: An encoding scheme in which 8-bit binary data values are represented by 10-bit symbols The data octet is split up into the three most significant bits and the five least significant bits.

amplitude modulation (AM): The encoding of a carrier wave by the changes of its amplitude along with the changes in input signal.

analog signal: Adds information or encodes information to an AC base signal by modifying the frequency or signal strength.

asynchronous communication: Communication that is not synchronized or kept in check with a clocking mechanism between communication devices.

bandwidth: A measurement of how much information can be transmitted over a medium over a prescribed period of time.

checksum: A simple error-detection scheme whereby each message is accompanied by a value based on the number of bits in the message.

cyclic redundancy checking (CRC): A sophisticated method of error-checking that is based on algebra. It is substantially reliable in detecting transmission errors and is commonly used in modems.

digital signal: Uses steps to represent information in binary format as zeros (0s) or ones (1s).

error checking and correcting (ECC): A more sophisticated form of checking where errors are corrected when they are detected. Also known as error-correction code.

encoding: The process of putting electronic data into a standard format.

flow control: A method by which the data flow between devices is managed so that the data can be handled at an efficient pace.

frequency division multiplexing (FDM): A method of transmission in which numerous signals are combined on a single communications line or channel.

frequency modulation (FM): The method of encoding data onto an AC wave by changing the instantaneous frequency of the wave.

jitter control: A process to make sure traffic gets through the network smoothly.

load shedding: The process of systematically reducing the system demand by temporarily decreasing the load in response to transmission or capacity shortages.

Manchester encoding: A synchronous clock encoding technique used to encode the clock and data of a synchronous bit stream. It uses the rising or falling edge in the middle of each bit time to indicate a 0 or 1.

Multi-Level Transition-3 (MLT-3) encoding: A three-level form of data encoding used to concentrate the signal power below 30 MHz.

multiplexing: Refers to sharing a communications line. It combines several connections into one larger channel.

Non-Return to Zero (NRZ) encoding: Uses two levels of signaling or is bipolar. The two levels or states can be expressed as either on or off, or high or low.

parity check: Ensures that when data is transmitted from one device to another or stored locally, there is a means to recover lost transactions.

phase-shift modulation (PSM): Conveys digital signals by shifting phases.

pulse code modulation (PCM): Transmits analog data using a digital scheme.

quantization: Stage that takes each sample and allocates a level to it. The sampled analog signal can take any value, but the quantized signal can only have a value from a set of half voltages.

signaling: Communication of information between network nodes by initiation, transmission, control, and termination of telecommunications signals.

sliding window: A method of flow control for data transfers. The window is the maximum amount of data that can be sent without having to wait for acknowledgments.

synchronous communication: Communication whereby a clocking mechanism keeps events in sync to manage flow of information.

time division multiplexing (TDM): The process by which multiple data streams are combined in a single signal and transmitted over the same link by allocating a different time slot for the transmission of each channel.

traffic shaping: Regulates the flow of data across the network by changing bursts of traffic to uniform, regular traffic.

wave division multiplexing (WDM): A form of frequency division multiplexing specifically for combining many optical carrier signals into a single optical fiber.

1.10   Challenge Questions

1.1 A sine wave can be used to represent which type of signal?

a. Analog

b. Digital

1.2 Why is broadband able to communicate more information than baseband?

1.3 What are the two major types of bit synchronization, and how do they handle timing differently?

1.4 Explain the leaky bucket algorithm and how it is used.

1.5 When converting digital data to digital signals and transmitting it across an Ethernet LAN, the data must be represented as a digital signal. Name the three common techniques that are used for this task.

1.6 Which method of encoding is the most basic and simplistic method of encoding?

a. 4B-PAM5

b. NRZ

c. Manchester

d. 8B/10B

1.7 For communication to occur, the sender and carrier negotiate a pattern allowing specific policies to be set that alter the way in which data is queued for transmission. This describes which of the following?

a. Checksum

b. ECC

c. Traffic shaping

d. Jitter control

1.8 In which of the following methods does the sender transmit one data unit and then wait for an acknowledgment before sending the next data unit?

a. Preallocation

b. Stop-and-Wait Protocol

c. Leaky bucket algorithm

d. Isarithmic congestion control

1.9 Which of the following is a binary code that can also detect two-bit errors but cannot correct them?

a. Hamming code

b. Reed-Solomon codes

c. Viterbi decoding algorithm

d. Internet checksum

1.10 Which of the following is not a carrier signal characteristic?

a. Amplitude

b. Cycle

c. Phase

d. Frequency

1.11 _____ is a simple error-detection scheme whereby each message is accompanied by a value based on the number of bits in the message. The receiving device then applies the same formula to the message and checks to make sure the value is the same.

1.12 Congestion management methods include _____, _____, and _____.

1.13 Error detection and recovery is accomplished using _____, _____, _____, and _____.

1.14 Four common terms used in signaling are: _____,
_____, _____, and
_____.

1.15 The _____ protocol uses two additional wires in
the cable connecting communicating devices. _____
is a protocol for controlling the flow of data between computers
and other devices on an asynchronous serial connection that
inserts characters directly into the data stream.

1.11 Challenge Exercises

Challenge Exercise 1.1

Being able to convert decimal numbers to binary numbers is an important
part of networking. In the exercise, you do just that in Table 1.3. Do not use
a calculator for this exercise. If you need additional help, refer to Appendix
C, "Binary Arithmetic and IP Address Calculation."

TABLE 1.3   Decimal to Binary Conversion

Decimal Number	Binary Equivalent
6	
24	
32	
48	
64	
72	
96	
108	
128	
192	
255	

Challenge Exercise 1.2

Being able to convert binary numbers to hexadecimal numbers is an important part of networking. In the exercise, take the binary numbers you calculated in Exercise 1.1 and convert them to hexadecimal in Table 1.4. Do not use a calculator for this exercise.

TABLE 1.4   Decimal to Binary to Hexadecimal Conversion

Decimal Number	Binary Equivalent	Hexadecimal Equivalent
6		
24		
32		
48		
64		
72		
96		
108		
128		
192		
255		

Challenge Exercise 1.3

Being able to convert binary numbers to octal numbers is an important aspect of networking. In the exercise, take the binary numbers you calculated in Table 1.3 and convert them to octal in Table 1.5. Do not use a calculator for this exercise.

TABLE 1.5   Decimal to Binary to Octal Conversion

Decimal Number	Binary Equivalent	Octal Equivalent
6		
24		
32		
48		
64		
72		
96		
108		
128		
192		
255		

Challenge Exercise 1.4

Understanding methods of encoding is an important part of networking. In this exercise, take the 4B equivalent and use Table 1.1 to look up the 5B equivalent and the hexadecimal assignment. Record your results in Table 1.6.

TABLE 1.6   4B to 5B with Hexadecimal Assignment

4B	5B	Hexadecimal Assignment
0001		
0010		
1100		
0110		
0101		
1001		
1110		

Challenge Exercise 1.5

In this exercise, you will do research. In 1993, Claude Berrou and his associates developed the turbo code. Research what the turbo code is and how it would apply to networking. For this exercise, you need a pencil and paper, and a desktop or laptop computer with Internet access.

1. Log on to your computer.

2. Open a Web browser and search for **Claude Berrou** and **turbo code**.

3. Write a two-paragraph paper on the research that you found.

Challenge Exercise 1.6

In this exercise, you download an error-checking utility and run it on your computer. For this exercise, you need a desktop or laptop computer with Internet access.

1. Log on to your computer.

2. Go to **http://www.irnis.net/soft/acsv**.

3. Click **Advanced Checksum finder** on the left side of the page.

4. When the file download dialog box opens, click **Save**.

5. When the Save File As dialog box opens, save the file to a directory or to the desktop.

6. When the download is complete, click **Open**.

7. Agree to the user license agreement.

8. Leave the defaults selected on the installation options, and click **Next**.

9. Select the directory you want the program to install in, and click **Install**.

10. When the installation file is complete, click **Close**.

11. Read the tutorial on typical scenarios.

12. Make two sample directories and run the utility.

1.12   Challenge Scenarios

Challenge Scenario 1.1

NetoTech is a newly formed company that has asked for your help. Management recently hired a team of engineers to help them set up a network. In the initial meeting, the engineers asked questions about what type of applications would be run, and several questions came up about encoding. The IT person you are working with has a list of questions and wants you to answer them. They include:

1. What is modulation?
2. Why would you encode digital data into a digital signal?
3. Why would you encode digital data into an analog signal?
4. Why would you encode analog data into a digital signal?
5. Why would you encode analog data into an analog signal?
6. What is the purpose of pulse code modulation?

Challenge Scenario 1.2

NetoTech was extremely happy that you were able to answer their questions in such a timely and professional manner. In their next meeting with the engineers, they discussed different methods of encoding, such as NRZ, Manchester, 4B/5B, 8B/10B, and 4D-PAM5. The IT person you are working with wants you to explain each of these, complete with drawings, if possible.

Challenge Scenario 1.3

In a follow-up meeting with NetoTech, the engineers discussed error detection and correction methods, such as parity, checksum, and CRC. Again, the company wants you to explain each of these, and give examples so it easy for everyone to understand.

Challenge Scenario 1.4

In yet another follow-up meeting with NetoTech, the engineers discussed different methods of flow control, such as sliding windows. NetoTech has asked you to answer the following questions in regard to flow control:

1. What is flow control?
2. How are the sliding window protocols used for error correction?
3. How are the sliding window protocols used for flow control?

Challenge Scenario 1.5

By now, NetoTech is almost ready to start working on the network. In the last meeting, the engineers discussed different methods of congestion control. You are asked to create a document describing congestion control and methods used. What will you submit?

CHAPTER 2

Communications Networks

After reading this chapter you will be able to:

- Understand the benefits of networking
- Understand what telephony networking is
- Identify the layers of the OSI reference model and know what part each one plays in networking
- Discuss how the Internet communicates
- Understand the basics of ATM networks
- Apply knowledge of different networking components
- Explain how network topologies influence planning decisions

In today's complex world, most companies have networks. In fact, most companies have a Web presence as well. A network can range from simply two computers that are linked together to the complexity of computers that can access data across continents. Networks are used to improve communication between departments, foster customer relationships, and share data throughout the world.

As a network administrator, it is your job to manage the network. To do this, you must understand the fundamental networking principles. Having this knowledge will help develop your planning and troubleshooting skills. This chapter provides you with those fundamental principles on which you will build knowledge and experience. It also focuses on the concept of a network, what makes it possible for devices to communicate, and what types of media are used for communication.

2.1   Introducing Networking

A **network** is a group of computers that can communicate with each other to share information. This can range, in its simplest form, from two computers in a home that are connected by one cable to the most complex network that includes many computers, cables, and devices spanning across continents. Before we can explore larger complex networks, we must look at what allows computers to talk to each other.

When computers can communicate with each other, they can share **resources**. These resources can be data (such as documents or spreadsheets), applications (such as Microsoft Word or Microsoft Excel), or hardware (such as modems or printers). What if you want to share a file with a friend who lives down the street? Each of you has your own computer, and neither computer is hooked up to any other computer or the Internet. Each of the computers is considered a **stand-alone computer**. See Figure 2.1.

The two of you can share files by transferring them onto a floppy disk and loading them onto each computer. This is also known as a **sneakernet**. It stems from the fact that you have to physically walk the files on disk back and forth to transfer them. This was the primary method of file transfer before networks became popular. An example of a sneakernet is shown in Figure 2.2.

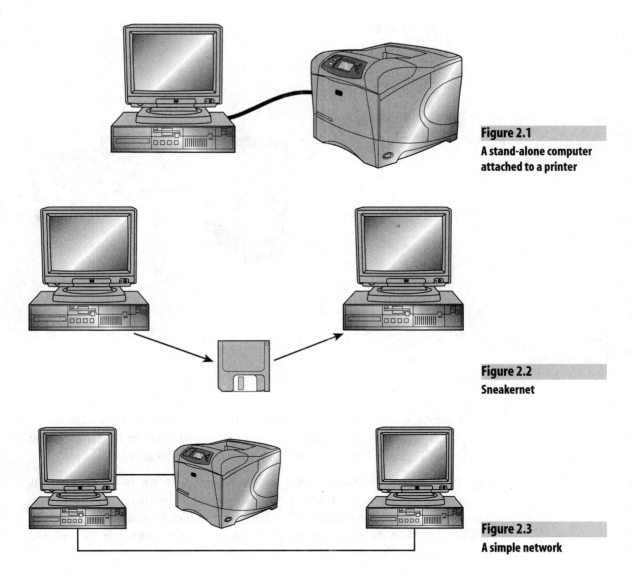

Figure 2.1
A stand-alone computer attached to a printer

Figure 2.2
Sneakernet

Figure 2.3
A simple network

You can connect two computers together with a cable, which results in a simple network. Figure 2.3 illustrates a simple network. In this example, two computers can share information and the same printer.

Before we discuss how computers can talk to each other, we will explore the different types of computers that make up a network. Many times you may hear administrators talk about servers and clients. What exactly are these?

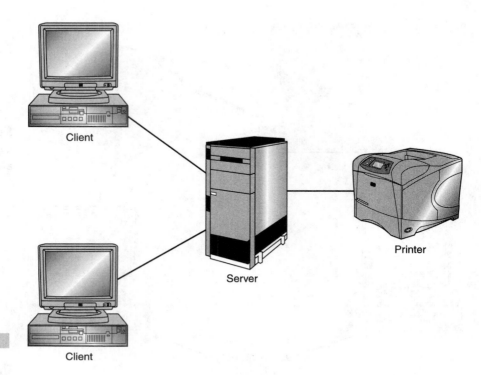

Figure 2.4

A server network

A **server** is a computer that allows its resources to be used by other computers on a network. A **client** is a computer that uses the resources of the server. Figure 2.4 depicts a network with a server and clients.

As we discussed earlier in this section, resources come in many different forms. Resources are the files, applications, and hardware shared by the server for a client to access. When a server provides a resource for a client to access, this is referred to as a *shared resource*. Shared resources are accessed across the network.

NOTE An important concept to remember is that of shared resources. Sharing allows for access across the network. If I share with you, you can use my resources by traversing the network. Shared resources will come into play further in Chapter 12 when the management of access and accounts is discussed.

Technology is advancing rapidly, and most networks tie into some type of telephone system, whether it is a single analog line used to connect a home computer to the Internet or a high-speed digital connection used in most businesses. In Chapter 1 we explained analog and digital signaling. Now that we've introduced what a network is, it's time to look at how analog and digital signaling are used in the communication of a network.

2.2 Telephony Networks

The telecommunications (Telecom), or Private Branch Exchange (PBX), system is a vital part of an organization's infrastructure. A PBX is a telephone system within an organization that switches calls between users on local lines yet allows all users to share a certain number of external phone lines. The main purpose of a PBX is to save the cost of requiring a line for each user to the telephone company's central office. The PBX is owned and operated by the organization rather than the telephone company. Originally, private branch exchanges used analog technology, but most now use digital technology. Digital signals are converted to analog for outside calls on the local loop using plain old traditional telephone service. A PBX includes telephone trunk lines, a computer with memory that manages the calls, a network of lines within the PBX, and a console or switchboard. In essence, users of the PBX share a certain number of outside lines for making telephone calls. Most medium-size or large companies use a PBX because it's much less expensive than connecting an external telephone line to every telephone in the organization. In addition, it's easier to call someone within a PBX because you simply dial a 3- or 4-digit extension. An example of this is a company with one published phone number yet the employees can answer up to five lines at a time. When a call comes in, the receptionist answers the phone and then transfers it to the requested party by dialing their extension.

Not long ago the Internet ran on phone systems, but now many phone systems are running on the Internet. For years, companies carried data traffic on voice networks. During the mid-1990s, advances in technology made it possible to use existing network resources to reduce or eliminate telephony costs. Many companies have moved to **Voice over IP (VoIP)** to integrate computer telephony, videoconferencing, and document sharing. See Figure 2.5.

In analog connectivity, a **plain old telephone system (POTS)** is used. This is also referred to as a **public switched telephone network (PSTN)**. A modem converts the signals from digital to analog to be used over the phone lines and then back to digital for the computer to understand. For example, you and a friend install modems in your computers so that you

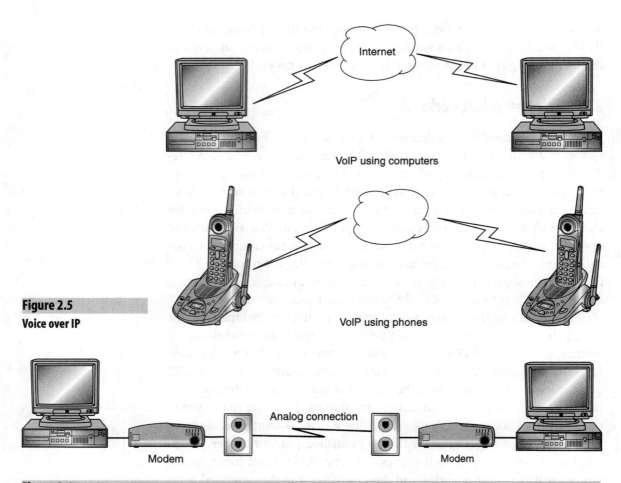

VoIP using computers

VoIP using phones

Figure 2.5
Voice over IP

Analog connection

Modem   Modem

Figure 2.6

A PSTN connection between two computers

can share files without having to use the sneakernet method. You plug a phone line into each modem and use the PSTN to communicate between the computers. Each computer communicates in digital signals. The modem connected to your computer converts the digital signal to analog to travel from your house to your friend's house. Your friend's modem then converts the analog signal to digital for his computer to understand. Figure 2.6 shows an example of communication between modems.

Data networks are based on a technology called packet switching, whereas telephony networks use circuit switching. Because packet switching and circuit switching are discussed in further detail in Chapter 5, we'll just go over some basics.

Here's how circuit switching works: When a call is made, a dedicated connection is opened and maintained between the parties for the duration of the call. No other calls can use those resources until the call is terminated. In contrast, packet switching does not require a dedicated circuit. Data packets are routed over any circuit that is available at any given point, and they don't travel over a fixed path. In other words, numerous users share the same circuit simultaneously because the circuits are available to all users.

A good example of packet switching is sending an e-mail message. You compose an e-mail message and send it to your friend. The message you send is broken down into small pieces called **packets** or frames. This is done because large packets take up a lot of bandwidth, preventing other computers from communicating. After the packets reach the network, they are forwarded from computer to computer until they reach their final destination. All the packets can travel the same route, or each can take a different route depending on how busy the network is. When the packets reach their final destination, they are assembled back into the original message and your friend reads it.

Integrating voice and data communications can be very cost effective. Let's look at an example of this. If you install a modem and use POTS to connect to a computer in New York, you are charged for a long-distance phone call. If you use the Internet to make the connection, you connect via a local number and then use that connection to make contact with the computer in New York, saving the cost of a long-distance phone number.

Because IP telephony networks make better use of available bandwidth, a VoIP network carries voice traffic for less cost than a switched circuit telephone network does. In a PSTN, a dedicated end-to-end circuit is allocated for each call. In a VoIP network, data is much more compressed and carried in packets. Using the same bandwidth, a VoIP network can carry many times the number of voice calls as a switched circuit network and with better voice quality. Now that we have learned how analog and digital communications affect networking, we will go one step further and look at what allows devices to communicate over the network.

2.3   The OSI Reference Model

As networking became the norm for businesses, the need arose for businesses to be able to connect with each other even though their equipment and systems were different. In 1978, the **International Organization for Standardization (ISO)** developed an architecture that would allow the devices of different manufacturers to work together to communicate with different operating systems. In 1984, the ISO architecture became an international standard known as the **Open Systems Interconnection (OSI) reference model**. This architecture determines how hardware, software, topologies, and protocols exist and operate on a network. The OSI model is based on seven layers, as shown in Figure 2.7. Each layer adds functionality to the previous layer and communicates with the layers directly above and below it. Because each layer of the OSI model handles a different part of the

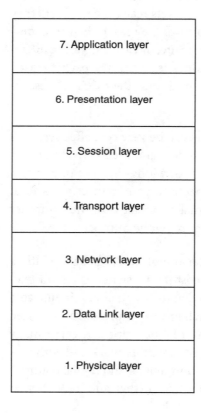

Figure 2.7
The OSI reference model

communications process, it makes the troubleshooting process a little easier because it provides specifications on how components should function.

The main idea behind the OSI model is that exchanging of data between two end points in a network can be divided into layers, with each layer adding its own set of special functions. Each communicating application is at a computer equipped with these layers. In an exchange between users, there will be a flow of data through each layer at one end down through the layers in that computer; and when the message arrives at its destination, there will be another flow of data up through the layers in the receiving computer that ultimately ends up at the application. The actual programming and hardware that furnishes these layers is usually a combination of applications, the computer operating system, transport and network protocols, and the software and hardware that enable you to put a signal on one of the lines attached to your computer.

We will go through each layer and discuss what each does as well as what devices function at that layer. The devices mentioned will be discussed in further detail later in this chapter or Chapter 3. Remember that the OSI model is a communications model. It is used in the telecommunications industry as well as in networking industry.

 NOTE

It is imperative that you grasp the information about the OSI model. Network architecture and devices all operate within the layers of the OSI model.

Before we get into the layers of the OSI model, some background information will help you better understand how it works. We'll just cover the basics because much of this is explained in greater detail in later chapters, and some of it has already been explained in Chapter 1. We will go over protocols, control information, error correction, and flow control.

The OSI model provides a conceptual framework for communication between computers but in itself is not a method of communication. Actual communication is made possible by using communication **protocols.** A protocol is a set of rules and conventions that governs how computers exchange information over a **network medium.** Network medium refers to the cable (metallic or fiber-optic) that links computers on a network. Because wireless

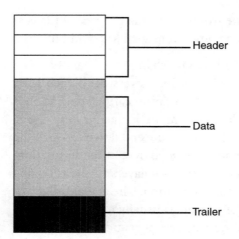

Header

Data

Trailer

Figure 2.8
The structure of a packet

networking is possible, network medium can also describe the type of wireless communications used to permit computers to exchange data via some wireless transmission frequency. A protocol implements the functions of one or more of the OSI layers. A wide variety of communication protocols exist, and many of them rely on others for operation. This concept of building upon the layers already in existence is the foundation of the OSI model.

The OSI layers use various forms of control information to communicate with their equal layers in other computer systems. This information consists of specific requests and instructions that are exchanged between equal OSI layers. The data to be exchanged is broken down into packets. We briefly mentioned packets earlier in this chapter; let's now look at the parts of a packet. All packets consist of a header, data, and a trailer. (See Figure 2.8.) The header contains the source and destination addresses, clocking information, and an alert signal. The data section contains the actual data or payload. The trailer contains information to verify that the contents of the packet are valid.

Control information is then added to the packets. Control information typically takes one of two forms: headers and trailers. Header and trailer information is added or removed as the data passes from layer to layer. An OSI layer may or may not attach a header or a trailer to data from upper layers.

Error checking determines whether transmitted data has become corrupt or damaged while traveling from the source to the destination. Error checking is implemented at several of the OSI layers. A common error-checking method is the cyclic redundancy check (CRC) that detects and discards corrupted data. A CRC value is generated by a calculation that is performed at the source device. The destination device compares this value to its own calculation to determine whether errors occurred during transmission. If the values are equal, the packet is considered valid. If the values are unequal, the packet contains errors and is discarded.

Flow control prevents network congestion by ensuring that transmitting devices do not flood receiving devices with data. A high-speed modem may generate traffic faster than the phone lines can transfer it, or faster than the destination modem can receive and process it. The three commonly used methods for handling network congestion are windowing, buffering, and transmitting source-quench messages.

Windowing is a flow-control scheme in which the source device requires an acknowledgment from the destination after a certain number of packets have been transmitted. If the destination does not receive one or more of the packets for some reason, it does not receive enough packets to send an acknowledgment. The source then retransmits the packets at a reduced transmission rate. Buffering is used to temporarily store bursts of excess data in memory by network devices until they can be processed. Receiving devices use source-quench messages to help prevent their buffers from overflowing.

The seven layers of the OSI reference model can be divided into two categories: upper layers and lower layers. The upper layers of the OSI model deal with application issues and generally are implemented only in software. The lower layers of the OSI model handle data transport issues. The physical layer and the data link layer are implemented in hardware and software. Now we are ready to delve into the different layers and the devices that operate at those layers.

2.3.1   Physical Layer

The **Physical layer** (Layer 1) handles the mechanical and electrical communications. In other words, it translates bits (0s and 1s) into data that can be transmitted. Layer 1 specifications determine the shape, size, and pin-out of connectors; what voltages and currents are used; and how the physical media and electrical components work together.

Devices that operate at the Physical layer include network interface cards, hubs, repeaters, multistation access units, media filters, and transceivers.

2.3.2   Data Link Layer

The **Data Link layer** (Layer 2) provides flow, error control, and synchronization for the Physical layer. It takes information from the Network layer and sends it to the intended device through the Physical layer on the same network. The specifications defined at this layer are network and protocol characteristics. This includes physical addressing, network topology, error notification, sequencing of frames, and flow control. Physical addressing defines how devices are addressed. Network topology determines the specifications that define how devices are to be physically connected. Error notification alerts upper-layer protocols that a transmission error has occurred, and sequencing reorders frames that are transmitted out of order. Flow control monitors the transmission of data so that the receiving device is not overwhelmed with more traffic than it can handle at one time.

The **Institute of Electrical and Electronics Engineers (IEEE)**, a professional organization that defines networking and other standards, further defined the lower layers of the OSI model. The IEEE began this project in February of 1980 and named the project according to the year and the month it came into being. Hence, it became known as the 802 project. The results of this are 12 different specifications that define network connections, topologies, and interface cards. These versions and standards will be discussed in further detail in later chapters, but the standards, along with a brief description, will be listed at the end of the discussion on the OSI model because they work hand in hand. The IEEE 802.2 specification has divided the Data Link layer into two sublayers: the Logical Link Control (LLC) layer and the Media Access Control (MAC) layer. Both layers are shown in Figure 2.9.

The **Logical Link Control (LLC) layer** manages communications between devices over a single link. This includes checking for errors and flow control. The LLC supports both connectionless and connection-oriented services used by higher-layer protocols. Connection-oriented and connectionless communications are discussed later in the "Transport Layer" section. The **Media Access Control (MAC) sublayer** of the Data Link layer manages protocol access to the physical network medium. In other words, the MAC layer controls access and network adapter card drivers. **MAC**

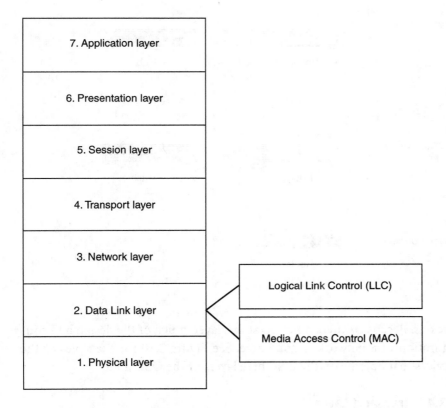

Figure 2.9
The sublayers of the Data Link layer

addresses enable multiple devices to uniquely identify one another. These unique addresses are assigned by the manufacturer. Because it only understands the MAC address, this layer cannot route to other networks—it can only pass on packets in its own segment. Devices that operate at this layer are bridges, switches, and routers.

2.3.3   Network Layer

The **Network layer** (Layer 3) manages the routing of packets that are to be forwarded on to different networks. The Network layer relies on the use of routable protocols to deliver packets to distant networks. The Network layer defines the network address, which is different from the MAC address. The MAC address is considered the physical address, and the network address is considered the logical address. Because this layer defines the logical network layout, routers can use it to determine how to forward

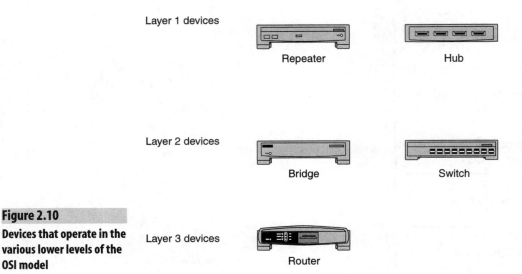

Layer 1 devices — Repeater — Hub

Layer 2 devices — Bridge — Switch

Figure 2.10

Devices that operate in the various lower levels of the OSI model

Layer 3 devices — Router

packets. Because routers function at this layer, much of the design and configuration of a network is done here. See Figure 2.10 for examples of the devices that operate on the first three layers of the OSI model.

2.3.4 Transport Layer

The **Transport layer** (Layer 4) manages the connection between the source and the destination to ensure that the data has reliable delivery. The Transport layer accepts data and segments it for transport across the network. Generally, the Transport layer is responsible for making sure that the data is delivered error free and in the proper sequence. Flow control generally occurs at the Transport layer. Flow control manages data transmission between devices so that the transmitting device does not send more data than the receiving device can process. Reliable delivery involves error checking and recovery. Error checking involves detecting transmission errors, while error recovery involves acting to resolve any errors that occur.

Transport protocols can be characterized as being either connection-oriented or connectionless. Connection-oriented services must first establish a connection with the desired service before passing any data. A connectionless service can send the data without any need to establish a connection first. In general, connection-oriented services provide some level of delivery guarantee, whereas connectionless services do not.

Connection-oriented service involves three phases: establishing the connection, transferring the data, and terminating the connection. The protocol is also responsible for putting the packets in the correct sequence before passing on the data. Connection-oriented network services have more overhead than connectionless ones. Connection-oriented services must negotiate a connection, transfer data, and tear down the connection, whereas a connectionless transfer can simply send the data without the added overhead of creating and tearing down a connection. An example of this is similar to the difference between regular mail and certified mail. Using regular mail delivery, you mail a letter and assume it will get there. Using certified mail delivery, the Post Office contacts the recipient, gives them the mail, and makes them sign for it.

2.3.5 Session Layer

The **Session layer** (Layer 5) manages the communication between the applications after a connection is made. It sets up the session, manages the information exchanges, and then breaks it down when the session ends. The Session layer establishes, manages, and terminates communication sessions. These sessions consist of service requests and responses that occur between applications located in different network devices. The sessions are coordinated by protocols implemented at this layer. It also monitors the identification of the session participants to be sure that only nodes that are authorized can participate in the session. An example of this is a conference call. To connect, you need a participant number. The call is usually run by a moderator who decides who can talk and for how long. The call ends when the moderator disconnects.

2.3.6 Presentation Layer

The **Presentation layer** (Layer 6) formats the data for exchange between the Application layer and the Session layer. Data compression and encryption also occur at this layer. This layer converts incoming and outgoing data from one presentation format to another through the use of standard image, sound, and video formats; standard data compression schemes; and standard data encryption schemes. Presentation layer implementations are not typically associated with a particular protocol stack. Some well-known standards include Motion Picture Experts Group (MPEG), Graphics Interchange Format (GIF), Joint Photographic Experts Group (JPEG), and Tagged Image File Format (TIFF).

2.3.7   Application Layer

The **Application layer** (Layer 7) provides the user interface for communication. The Application layer is the OSI layer closest to the end user, which means that both the OSI Application layer and the user interact directly with the software application. Application layer functions typically include file transfer, file management, message handling, and database query functions. The Application layer also determines the availability of an application with data to transmit, and decides whether sufficient network resources for the communication exist. The Application layer is not itself an application that is communicating; rather it is a layer that provides application services. Some examples of Application layer implementations include Telnet, File Transfer Protocol (FTP), and Simple Mail Transfer Protocol (SMTP).

Let's summarize what we have learned. Each layer of the OSI model performs a particular function. This type of organization allows each layer to communicate only with its surrounding layers within a given host. Applications use layers 5 through 7 to communicate with another computer using the same protocol. Layers 3 and 4 define how data delivery is set up and defined on computers that use the same protocol. Layers 1 and 2 define the physical and electrical signal characteristics. Between hosts, each layer communicates with its corresponding layer on the other computer, but only through the lower layers on both computers. Information being transferred from a software application in one computer system to a software application in another must pass through all of the OSI layers. For example, if a software application in your system has information to pass to a software application in a coworker's system, the application program in your system will pass its information to the Application layer. The Application layer then passes the information to the Presentation layer, which relays the data to the Session layer, and so on, until it reaches the Physical layer. At the Physical layer, the information is placed on the physical network medium and is sent across the medium to the coworker's system. The Physical layer of that system removes the information from the physical medium, and then its physical information is passed up to the Data Link layer, which passes it to the Network layer, and so on, until it reaches the Application layer. The Application layer of the system then passes the information to the application program to complete the communication process. See Figure 2.11 for an overview of data flowing through the OSI model layers.

The OSI reference model is only a guideline. An actual protocol or device may or may not assume all responsibilities of one particular OSI layer. It may also take on functions that span several layers. However, we use the OSI model to help us understand and classify the functions that make up a particular implementation.

TIP

There are several ways to remember the layers of the OSI model. You can make up a sentence of your own but two common ones are, "Please Do Not Throw Sausage Pizza Away" and from the top down, "All People Seem To Need Data Processing."

The ISO created the OSI model and the IEEE further defined the lower layers of the OSI model. Table 2.1 lists those specifications.

2.4   The Internet

The Internet can be considered the largest network in the world. This network is made up of computers used by many different types of businesses, educational institutions, governments, and individuals located around the world. Each network operates independently but can connect to other networks through routers, which are covered in the "Routers" section later in this chapter. Before we discuss how the Internet works, we will go over some of the history behind the Internet.

The name "Internet" refers to the global interconnection of networks made possible by the protocols devised in the 1970s that are still in use today. The Internet was originally called ARPANET (short for Advanced Research Project Agency Network). It was developed by the Department of Defense to provide a way to connect networks. ARPANET grew from four nodes in 1969 to about a hundred by 1975. By mid-1975, it was determined that ARPANET was stable enough to be turned over to a separate agency for

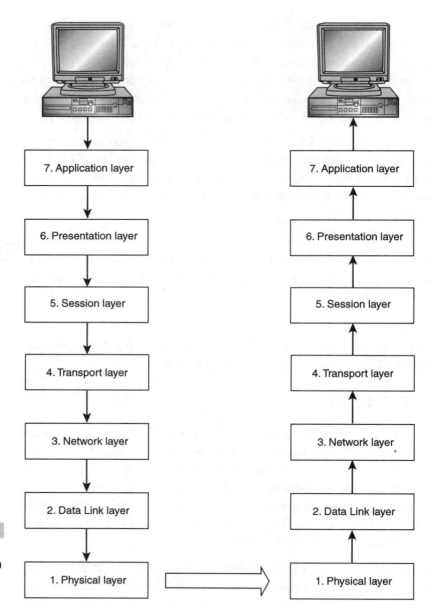

Figure 2.11

Path of an application transmitting data through the layers of the OSI reference model

TABLE 2.1   IEEE 802 Standards

Standard	Name	Description
802.1	Internetworking	Defines internetworking communications, routing, bridging, and switching
802.2	Logical Link Control	Provides addressing, error checking, and flow control for data frames
802.3	Ethernet LAN	Defines all forms of Ethernet interfaces and media
802.4	Token Bus LAN	Defines all forms of Token Bus interfaces and media
802.5	Token Ring LAN	Defines all forms of Token Ring interfaces and media
802.6	Metropolitan Area Network (MAN)	Defines MAN services, technologies, and addressing
802.7	Broadband Technical Advisory Group	Specifies physical, electrical, and mechanical features of broadband cable
802.8	Fiber-Optic Technical Advisory Group	Provides technical direction for the use of fiber-optic technology and media
802.9	Integrated Voice/Data Networks	Defines integration of voice, video, and data on IEEE LANs
802.10	Network Security Technology Advisory Group	Develops a security model for diverse networks that covers authentication and encryption
802.11	Wireless Networks	Defines standards for wireless networks that cover a wide range of frequencies
802.12	Demand Priority	Defines the demand priority access method for 100VG-AnyLAN
802.14	Cable Modems	Creates standards for transmission of data over cable television networks

operation management, so responsibility was transferred to the Defense Communications Agency.

In 1973, the Defense Advanced Research Projects Agency (DARPA) began a series of research programs to extend packet switching to ground mobile units and ships at sea through the use of ground mobile packet radio and synchronous satellites. This process became known as *Internetting*. It was intended to solve the problem of linking different kinds of packet networks together without requiring the users or their computers to know much about how packets traveled. About the same time, DARPA provided additional funding for a research project that began in the late 1960s to explore the use of radio for a packet-switched network. This effort, at the University of Hawaii, led to new mobile packet radio ideas and to the design of what is now Ethernet. The Ethernet concept arose when a researcher realized that the random-access radio system could be operated on a coaxial (coax) cable at data rates thousands of times faster than could then be supported over the air. These efforts came together in 1977 when a four-network demonstration was conducted.

Also in the early 1970s, researchers at Stanford began to design a new set of computer communication protocols that would allow multiple packet networks to be interconnected in a flexible and dynamic way. The first phase of this work was successfully completed in July 1977. This success led to an effort to implement robust versions of the two main Internet protocols— **Transmission Control Protocol (TCP)** and **Internet Protocol (IP)**. By 1980, a serious effort was mounted to require all computers on the ARPANET to adopt the **Transmission Control Protocol /Internet Protocol (TCP/IP)** suite. This was accomplished in January 1983.

As DARPA was preparing to convert the organizations it supported to TCP/IP, the National Science Foundation (NSF) started an effort to interconnect the nation's computer science departments through the use of dial-up connections. The result was "phone-mail," the capability for electronic mail exchange among computers that were not on ARPANET, which pioneered the use of TCP/IP over the X.25 protocol standard. NSF's interest in high bandwidth was heightened in 1986 through its sponsorship of NSFNET, which eventually replaced ARPANET when it was retired in 1990. Among the most monumental decisions that the NSF made was to support the creation of regional networks that would take the demand from the nation's universities and funnel it to the NSFNET backbone. The backbone was initially implemented using gateways and links operating at the speed of 56 Kbps. Because of rapidly increasing demand, a cooperative agreement was made with MCI and IBM to develop a 1.5 Mbps backbone. IBM developed the routers and MCI supplied 1.5 Mbps circuits. The result was a backbone with about 30 times the bandwidth of its predecessor.

Regional networks became the primary means by which universities and other research institutions linked to the backbone. By the mid-1980s, there was sufficient interest in the use of the Internet in the research, educational, and defense communities, so businesses started making equipment for Internet implementation. In 1988, in an effort to test federal policy on commercial use of the Internet, the Corporation for National Research Initiatives approached the Federal Networking Council for permission to experiment with the interconnection of MCI Mail with the Internet. An experimental electronic mail relay was built and put into operation in 1989.

NSFNET backbone traffic more than doubled annually, from a terabyte per month in March 1991 to eighteen terabytes a month in November 1994. The number of host computers increased from 200 to 5 million in the 12 years between 1983 and 1995. One of the major forces behind the exponential growth of the Internet was the variety of new capabilities, especially directory, indexing, and searching services, that helped users find information more readily. Enhancing these services was the arrival of a "killer ap" for the Internet, the World Wide Web.

The World Wide Web was first used in experimental form in 1989. Around 1992, it came to the attention of a programming team at the National Center for Supercomputing Applications (NCSA). This team developed a graphical browser for the Web, called Mosaic. This software was made widely available on the Internet for free. Between 1992 and 1995 a number of commercial versions of Web browsers and servers emerged.

! WARNING

The Internet and the World Wide Web should not be used interchangeably. The World Wide Web is a method to navigate the Internet. They operate at different layers of the OSI model.

The Internet's different services have evolved as technology has. Today some of the more popular Internet services are chat and instant messaging, e-mail, File Transfer Protocol (FTP), newsgroups, telnet, and the World Wide Web. Now that we know how the Internet and browsers were developed, let's explore how the Internet communicates.

As stated earlier, the Internet is a network of interconnected, yet independent networks. Each host is directly connected to some particular network. Two hosts on the same network communicate with each other using the

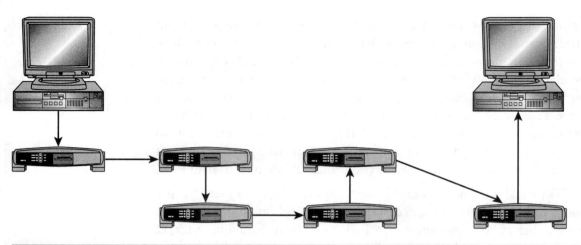

Figure 2.12

Path of a packet traveling through the Internet

same set of protocols that then would be used to communicate with hosts on distant networks. The language of the Internet is TCP/IP. This protocol calls for data to be broken into packets. These packets are designed to have a header for IP as well as TCP, followed by the data. The headers enable packets to be routed across many networks to arrive at their destination. (TCP/IP is described in detail in Chapter 6.) Packets are passed across the networks by devices called routers, which read the headers to determine whether the packet belongs to its network or should be passed on. (See Figure 2.12.) This is like sending a letter through the US mail. The zip code is the ultimate destination for the letter. For example, when you send a letter from California to New York, it may be transported to various other post offices before it actually arrives in New York. If the zip code on the letter does not match the zip code for the post office at which it arrives, the letter will be forwarded on until it reaches its final destination.

For the packets to reach the Internet, there must be some type of connection between the PC and the Internet. The connection is supplied by a company called an **Internet service provider (ISP)**. An ISP provides a gateway to the Internet, along with other online services, primarily as a paid service. The two most common ways to connect to an ISP are dial-up lines using modems and cable modem or digital subscriber lines. ISPs own blocks of addresses that they assign to their customers to give them identity on the network. These addresses are called Internet protocol addresses, or IP addresses. Each address is unique. IP addressing will be covered in Chapter 7. Because IP addresses are numbers and are difficult to remember, hosts are usually found by their domain name. This allows easier navigation on the Internet. All domain names are mapped to IP addresses. This structure behind domain naming and other Internet services is covered in Chapter 9.

The advent of backbones and network infrastructure created the need for high-speed technology. Now it's time to look a high-speed technology that allows networks like the Internet to function.

2.5   Asynchronous Transfer Mode (ATM) Networks

Before there was a need to share resources and communicate, telephone companies built an international network to carry multiple telephone calls using copper cable. Soon the bandwidth limitations of copper cable became apparent, and carriers began looking into upgrading their copper cable to fiber cable. To address these concerns, the **International Telecommunication Union-Telecommunication Standardization Sector (ITU-T)**, formerly called the Consultive Committee for International Telegraph and Telephone (CCITT), and other standards groups started work to establish a series of recommendations to implement a fiber-based network that could solve current limitations and allow networks to efficiently manage future services.

To deliver new services such as video conferencing and video on demand, as well as provide more bandwidth for the increasing volume of traditional data, the communications industry introduced a technology that provided a common format for services with different bandwidth requirements. This technology is **Asynchronous Transfer Mode (ATM)**. As ATM developed, it became instrumental in how companies deliver, manage, and maintain their goods and services. It was first developed at Bell Labs in 1983, but it took several years for standards organizations to agree upon specifications. ATM emerged commercially in the early 1990s. However, at that time few applications could utilize its features. The ATM Forum, established in October, 1991 to accelerate the use of ATM products and services issued its first specifications eight months later.

ATM uses connection-oriented switches to permit senders and receivers to communicate by establishing a dedicated circuit. In this environment, data travels in fixed 53-byte cells. Five bytes are used for header information and 48 bytes are used for data. The data transfer rate can reach up to 9953 Mbps.

NOTE

The cells in ATM are a fixed length of 53 bytes. If the data takes up less space than that, the cells are padded with empty payload.

The use of fixed-length cells enables ATM to work at extremely high speeds. ATM relies on circuit switching, which is done at the Data Link layer of the OSI model. Switches determine the most efficient route between the sender and the receiver, and then establish this path before any data is transmitted. ATM was designed to guarantee a specific **quality of service (QoS)**. QoS is a standard specifying that data will be delivered within a particular time frame after transmission. It is best suited for long-distance, high-bandwidth applications. ATM bandwidths are rated in terms of an optical carrier level. Table 2.2 lists the various rates for optical carrier signaling.

TABLE 2.2   Signaling Rates for Optical Carrier Levels

Optical Carrier Level	Signaling Rate
OC-1	51.84 Mbps
OC-3	155.52 Mbps
OC-9	466.56 Mbps
OC-12	622.08 Mbps
OC-24	1.244 Gbps
OC-36	1.866 Gbps
OC-48	2.488 Gbps
OC-96	4.976 Gbps
OC-192	9.953 Gbps
OC-255	13.271 Gbps
OC-768	39.813 Gbps

Now it's time to look at the devices that make it possible to transmit data via telephony networks, the Internet, and ATM networks. We will next discuss the different types of components that a network comprises, what layer of the OSI model they operate at, and their limitations.

2.6   Networking Components

Computers must share media to communicate successfully. Network media can be a physical cable or it can be wireless. Regardless of the media type, its main function is to carry data from one device to the next. To access the network or communicate with other computers, a network interface card (NIC) is needed. These come in a variety of specifications and, depending on the network setup, may not be interchangeable in all machines. See Figure 2.13 for an example of a NIC.

TIP

You will often hear the term NIC; remember that the C stands for card. Many times the acronym is misused and you will hear "NIC card." This is redundant.

After the network card is installed, it is connected to the media. In the next section, we will describe the various methods of connecting to a network.

2.6.1   Media: Cables and Wireless

Media can be divided into two categories, wired and wireless. We will first look at wired or cabled medium and then look at wireless technology.

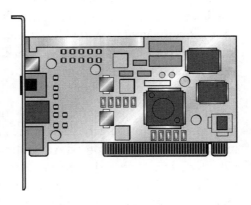

Figure 2.13

A network interface card

Cabling is an important component of any network, because unless the network is wireless, this is how the data will travel from machine to machine. Before we discuss the different types of cable, let's look at the methods of sending signals across these cables. There are two primary methods to do this, baseband and broadband.

Baseband uses a digital transmission pulse at a single fixed frequency. This means that the entire bandwidth of the cable is used to transmit one data signal. It also limits any cable strand to either half duplex or full duplex. **Half-duplex** transmission means that data can be transmitted in both directions on a cable but not at the same time. **Full-duplex** transmission means that data can be transmitted in both directions on the cable at the same time. Because baseband uses a single fixed frequency, as the signal travels farther down the cable, its strength decreases and can distort. For this reason, special devices called **repeaters** are used. A repeater refreshes the signal so that it is restored to its original strength and quality.

Broadband uses analog transmission over a continuous range of values. It travels one way only in optical waves. It is necessary to have two channels, one for receiving and one for sending data. If the cabling supports enough bandwidth, more than one transmission can operate on a single cable. In this situation, you need a tuner to pick up the correct signal. As with baseband, if the signal travels too far, it needs to be strengthened. The device used to do this is called an amplifier. An amplifier detects weak signals, strengthens them, and then rebroadcasts them.

Cabling Media

Several types of network cabling are available. The three main types are coaxial, twisted pair, and fiber optic. They all share certain characteristics, which include grade, bandwidth rating, maximum segment length, maximum number of segments per network, maximum number of devices per segment, and interference susceptibility. Besides these factors, you should also take into consideration the cost of the cable and the installation costs.

Coaxial cable was the first type of cable used to network computers and was instrumental in forming the basis of the Ethernet standard. Coaxial cables are made of a thick copper core with an outer metallic shield used to reduce external interference. External interference can be in the form of electromagnetic interference (EMI), which comes from devices in the surrounding environment, or radio frequency interference (RFI), which comes from other broad-

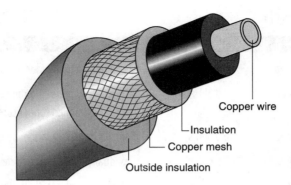

Figure 2.14
Coaxial cable

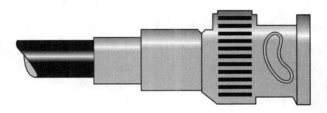

Figure 2.15
A BNC connector

cast signals. Often, the shield is made of woven cooper mesh or aluminum. The cable is then surrounded by a plastic covering, called a sheath. See Figure 2.14.

Although coaxial cables are no longer deployed, they still may be found in legacy environments. The two main types of coaxial cables used are 10Base2 and 10Base5.

10Base2, also known as Thinnet, has a communication speed of 10 Mbps, uses baseband signaling, and is limited in length to 185 meters per segment. 10Base2 uses BNC connectors to attach segments to each other. See Figure 2.15. Terminators are required at both ends of each segment to prevent signal echo.

10Base5, also known as Thicknet, has a communication speed of 10 Mbps, uses baseband signaling, and is limited in length to 500 meters per segment. 10Base5 uses **attachment unit interface (AUI)** external transceivers connected to each NIC by a vampire tap that allows access to the network by piercing the cable.

TABLE 2.3   Types of RG Cable

Specification	Type	Impedance	Description
RG-58/U	Thinnet	50 ohms	U stands for utility grade; solid copper core
RG-58 A/U	Thinnet	50 ohms	A/U indicates braided copper center with foam dielectric insulator; stranded copper core
RG-58 C/U	Thinnet	50 ohms	Solid dielectric insulation; military version of RG-58 A/U
RG-59	CATV	75 ohms	Broadband cable used for television
RG-6	Broadband	75 ohms	A CATV drop cable with higher bandwidth and larger diameter than RG-59
RG-62	Baseband	93 ohms	Used for IBM 3270 terminals and ARCnet
RG-8	Thicknet	50 ohms	0.4" in diameter with a solid core
RG-11	Thicknet	75 ohms	A CATV trunk line; 0.4" in diameter with a stranded core

TIP   To remember 10Base2 and 10Base5, look at the makeup of the type: 10 is for the bandwidth, 10 Mbps per second; base is for the signaling, baseband; and the 2 and 5 are the estimated segment lengths—200, which is rounded up from 185, and 500.

Coax belongs to a family of cable specifications called Radio Government (RG) jointly developed by the US military and cable manufacturers, by the US. Table 2.3 lists the types of RG cable.

If using coaxial cable, keep in mind that the electric signal, conducted by a single core wire, can easily be tapped by piercing the sheath. Another concern of coax cable is reliability. Because there is no focal point involved, a faulty cable can bring the entire network down. Missing terminators or improperly functioning transceivers can cause poor network performance and transmission errors. If you are using coax cable, be sure to have proper cable testing equipment available and periodically scan the network.

Twisted-pair cable is used in most of today's network topologies. Twisted-pair cabling is either unshielded (UTP) or shielded (STP). Plenum cable is also available; this is a grade that complies with fire codes and is used for

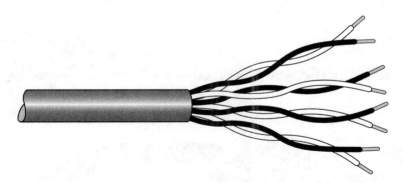

Figure 2.16
UTP cable

running cable either in the area above the ceiling or below the subflooring. The outer casing is more fire resistant than regular twisted-pair cable. UTP is popular because it is inexpensive and easy to install. See Figure 2.16 for an example of UTP.

There are seven types of UTP cable, the most popular being Category 5 (Cat5). Before Cat5, Cat3 type cable was used on Ethernet networks, and some networks may still have it in place. Cat3 is the lowest category that meets standards for a 10BaseT network. The following are the speeds and cable lengths for the seven categories of unshielded pair cable:

- **Category 1 (Cat1):** Traditional telephone cable used prior to 1982 for voice only.

- **Category 2 (Cat2):** Cabling for bandwidth up to 4 Mpbs, consisting of four pairs of wire.

- **Category 3 (Cat3):** Speed capability of 10 Mbps, with cable segments up to 100 meters. Consists of four pairs of wire.

- **Category 4 (Cat4):** The first data-grade cable. Certified for bandwidth up to 16 Mpbs. Consists of four pairs of wire.

- **Category 5 (Cat5):** Speed capability of 1 Gbps, with cable segments up to 100 meters. Consists of four pairs of wire.

- **Category 6 (Cat6):** Consists of four pairs of wire wrapped in foil insulation. The insulation provides shielding against crosstalk and allows for support up to at least six times the throughput of Cat5.

Figure 2.17
STP cable

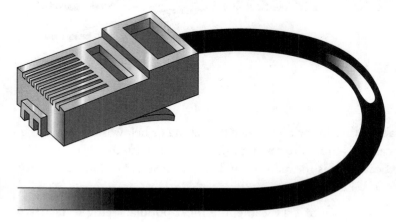

Figure 2.18
RJ-45 connector

- **Category 7 (Cat7):** Speed capability of 1 Gbps, with two layers of shielding. Due to the additional shielding, special connectors are needed.

UTP is eight wires twisted into four pairs. The design cancels much of the overflow and interference from one wire to the next, but UTP is subject to interference from outside electromagnetic sources and is prone to RFI and EMI as well as crosstalk.

STP is different from UTP in that the cable's wires are surrounded by shielding. Some STP has shielding around the individual wires, which helps prevent crosstalk. STP is more resistant to EMI and is considered a bit more secure because the shielding makes wiretapping more difficult. See Figure 2.17.

Both UTP and STP use an RJ-45 connector to plug into network devices such as NICs, hubs, and switches. See Figure 2.18.

Equipment that is associated with STP and UTP cables includes punch-down blocks, patch panels, and wall plates. Punchdown blocks help organize cables and can be used for both network and telephone management. Patch panels allow the cables to be connected in an arrangement beneficial

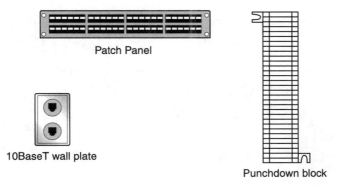

Patch Panel

10BaseT wall plate

Punchdown block

Figure 2.19
Punchdown block, patch panel, and wall plate

to the network design. Wall plates are used to make office wiring easier. Usually, cables are connected on one end to the wall plate and on the other end to the patch panel. Then the RJ-45 connectors attach a patch cable from the wall plate to the computer and from the patch panel to a hub or switch. See Figure 2.19.

10BaseT is an Ethernet standard that replaces 10Base2 and 10Base5. Ethernet will be discussed in detail in Chapter 3. The "10" represents 10-Mpbs throughput, "base" means that it uses baseband transmission, and "T" tells you that it uses twisted-pair wire. On this type of network, two pairs of wires are used for transmission—one for sending and one for receiving. It also requires Cat3 or higher-grade wire, and each segment can be up to 100 meters.

100BaseT is also known as Fast Ethernet. Based on what you have learned so far, it could be determined that this type of media has a throughput of 100 Mpbs, and uses baseband transmission and twisted-pair wire. This type of standard usually requires Cat5 or higher grade wire. There are two 100BaseT specifications, 100BaseTX and 100BaseT4. The difference between the two lies in how they achieve their transmission rates. 100BaseTX uses two pairs of wires within a Cat5 cable, one pair for sending and one for receiving. 100BaseT4 uses all four pairs of wires and can use Cat3 cabling. It achieves its speed by breaking down the data into three 33-Mbps streams, and then using three pairs of wire to send it.

! WARNING

100BaseT4 and 100BaseTX are not interchangeable. You cannot mix devices on the same segment; in other words, you must pick one or the other.

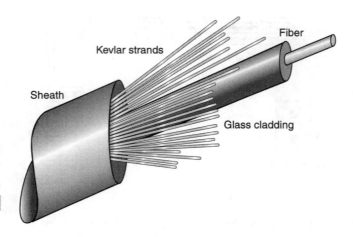

Figure 2.20
Fiber-optic cable

100BaseVG is an alternative to Ethernet technology. "VG" stands for voice grade. This is also known as 100VG-AnyLan. 100BaseVG is more efficient at processing and carrying audio and video, but it requires special NICs and connecting devices. It uses all four wire pairs, so it is slower than 100BaseT.

Fiber was designed for transmissions at higher speeds over longer distances. It uses light pulses for signal transmission, making it immune to RFI, EMI, and eavesdropping. Fiber optic has a plastic or glass center surrounded by another layer of plastic or glass, called cladding. To keep the cable from stretching, another layer of strands of polymer fiber, called Kevlar, is added. Finally, all layers are surrounded with a protective outer coating called a sheath, as shown in Figure 2.20. Data transmission speed ranges from 100 Mbps to 10 Gbps and can be sent a distance of 100 kilometers.

Fiber-optic cable comes in two different types, single-mode fiber (SMF) and multimode fiber (MMF). Single-mode fiber uses a laser for transmission and is used mainly by industries that provide communications over large areas, such as telephone companies. Multimode fiber uses diode transmitters and is used mainly for network and college campuses for distances of up to 2 kilometers. Laser transmissions travel much farther than diode transmitters. There are a variety of connectors that can be used with fiber-optic cable. The two most popular are the ST- and SC-type connectors. Figure 2.21 shows an example of

Figure 2.21
Fiber-optic cable
connectors

TABLE 2.4   Types of Network Cable

Standard	Type of Cable	Bandwidth	Maximum Length per Segment
10Base2	Coaxial	10 Mbps	185 meters
10Base5	Coaxial	10 Mbps	500 meters
10BaseT	UTP	10 Mbps	100 meters
100BaseT	UTP	100 Mbps	100 meters
100BaseT4	Four pairs, Cat3, Cat4, Cat5 UTP	100 Mbps	100 meters
100BaseTX	Two pairs, Cat5 UTP or Cat1 STP	100 Mbps, Fast Ethernet	100 meters
100BaseVG	UTP	100 Mbps, Fast Ethernet	100 meters
10BaseF	Fiber-optic	10 Mbps	2 kilometers
10BaseFX	Fiber-optic	100 Mbps, Fast Ethernet	2 kilometers

the ST-type connector. If you are using a patch cable to run from a router to a patch panel, you should purchase the cable with connectors already installed.

A suffix of "F" or "FX" means that the cable is suitable for an Ethernet environment. 10BaseF requires two strands of multimode cable and uses an ST-type connector. 100BaseFX also requires two strands of multimode cable but can use either the SC- or ST-type connector. The throughput for 10BaseF is only 10 Mbps; due to its low output and high cost, it is seldom found in networks today.

On the down side, fiber is still quite expensive compared to more traditional cabling. It is also more difficult to install, and fixing breaks can be costly. Fiber can transmit data in only one direction at a time; therefore, each cable must have two strands, one for receiving and one for transmitting.

Table 2.4 summarizes types of network cable. Now that we have gone over all the cabling types, it's time to look at wireless technology.

Wireless Technology

Wireless devices have become extremely popular because of the mobility they provide. The term *wireless network* refers to technology that allows two or more computers to communicate using standard network protocols, without network cabling. They are most often referred to as wireless local area networks (WLANs). LANs and wireless technology will be explained in detail in the next chapter. This technology has produced a number of affordable wireless solutions that are growing in popularity with businesses and schools, or when network wiring is impossible, such as in warehousing or point-of-sale handheld equipment.

Wireless networking hardware requires the use of technology that handles data transmission over radio frequencies. The most widely used standard is the IEEE 802.11 standard that defines all aspects of Radio Frequency Wireless networking. Currently, the IEEE standards for wireless are 802.11a, 802.11b, and 802.11g. There are plans to implement 802.11e and i in 2004. Because standards operate on radio frequencies, one of the issues with the current wireless technology is that it is a broadcast signal, so basically it advertises that it is out there, making it easy to pick up.

To connect a wireless network to a wired network, you need some sort of bridge between the wireless and wired network. This can be done either with a hardware access point or a software access point. Hardware access points are available with various types of network interfaces, but typically require extra hardware to be purchased if your networking requirements change. A software access point does not limit the type or number of network interfaces you use; it is only limited by the number of slots or interfaces available in the computer. It may also allow considerable flexibility in providing access to different network types. A software access point may include additional features such as shared Internet access, Web caching, and content filtering.

The 802.11b standard specifies a transfer rate of 11 Mbps, which is sufficient for most broadband connections. As the signal deteriorates, the transfer rate drops dramatically, to 5.5 Mbps, 2 Mbps, and then 1 Mbps, although actual throughput is about half these rates. Optical wireless transmission via a light beam is capable of transmitting data at speeds up to 622 Mbps.

There are two kinds of wireless networks, ad-hoc and access points. An ad-hoc, or peer-to-peer wireless network, consists of computers that are equipped with a wireless NIC. Each computer can communicate directly with all of the other wireless enabled computers. They can share files and printers this way, but may not be able to access wired LAN resources.

A wireless network can also use an access point, or base station. In this type of network, the access point acts like a hub, providing connectivity for the wireless computers. It connects the wireless LAN to a wired LAN, allowing wireless computer access to LAN resources. There are two subcategories of access points: hardware and software access points. Hardware access points offer comprehensive support of most wireless features, but not all devices may be compatible. Software access points run on a computer equipped with a wireless network interface card as used in an ad-hoc or peer-to-peer wireless network.

Each access point has a specific range in which a wireless connection can be maintained between the client computer and the access point. The actual distance varies depending upon the environment. When pushed to the limits of the range, the performance may drop because the quality of connection deteriorates and the system tries to compensate. Indoor ranges for wireless devices are 150 to 300 feet but may be shorter if the construction of the building interferes with radio transmissions. Although longer ranges are possible, performance will degrade with distance. Outdoor ranges are quoted up to 1000 feet, depending on the environment.

2.6.2   Hubs

A **hub** is a multiport repeater that retransmits a signal on all ports. When a packet arrives at one port, it is sent to the other ports so that all segments of the LAN can see it. Because it operates at Layer 1 of the OSI model, it can connect segments or a network but cannot segment a network. Most hubs come with a minimum of 4 ports but can have as many as 48. There are two basic types of hubs: active and passive. Active hubs are the type described previously in this paragraph. A passive hub simply allows the signal to pass through without any amplification or regeneration. Intelligent or manageable hubs add features to active hubs that enable each port to be configured and the traffic passing through the hub to be monitored. A switching hub is a type of active hub that can read the destination address of packets and forward it to the correct port.

Most hubs require no configuration, and passive hubs do not even require power. And remember that the devices connected to hubs all share the same bandwidth. In other words, if you have a 10-Mbps hub and three devices are transmitting at the same time, each device gets one third of the bandwidth (see Figure 2.22).

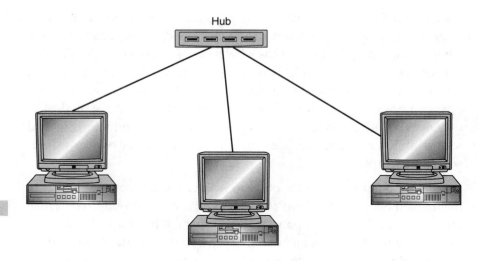

Figure 2.22

A hub connected to three devices

WARNING **!** To connect two hubs you must use a crossover cable, or use the hub's uplink port.

A stackable hub is designed to be connected and stacked on top of another hub, forming an expanding stack. This stackable approach allows equipment to be easily expanded as it grows in size and also reduces clutter.

2.6.3   Bridges

A **bridge** is a device that connects two or more segments of a network to make them one. It could be described as a device that determines whether a message from you to someone else is going to the local area network or to someone on the LAN in the next building. A bridge examines each message, passing on those known to be within the same LAN, and forwarding those known to be on the other connected LANs. It looks similar to a hub but functions at the next layer of the OSI model, the Data Link layer. Bridges have a single input and a single output port. It stores the MAC address for each device and then analyzes the incoming packets to determine what to do with them as they come through. Basically, it learns all the MAC addresses of the network to construct a database used for forwarding or filtering packets. A bridge can connect two different types of topologies because it does not understand anything above the Data Link layer. It doesn't matter whether one machine is using TCP/IP and another is using International Packet Exchange (IPX) Sequenced Packet Exhange (SPX) because they are only concerned with the

MAC addresses and not the protocols. This allows them to move data more rapidly, but it takes longer to transmit because a bridge analyzes each packet.

2.6.4   Switches

Switches are rapidly becoming more popular than hubs when it comes to connecting desktops to the wiring closet. Switches operate at the Data Link layer of the OSI model. Their packet-forwarding decisions are based on MAC addresses. That is, a switch simply looks at each packet and determines from a physical address (the MAC address) which device a packet is intended for and then switches it out toward that device.

Switches allow LANs to be segmented, thereby increasing the amount of bandwidth that goes to each device. This means that, unlike a hub, each port on the switch is like a network segment itself. If you have a 10-Mpbs switch with three devices connected to it, all three devices can use 10-Mbps of bandwidth. A switch repeats data only to the specified port, whereas a hub sends the data to all ports. In this context, it is said that each segment is a separate collision domain but all segments are in the same broadcast domain. Collision and broadcast domains are explained in Chapter 5. The basic functions of a switch include filtering and forwarding frames, learning media access control (MAC) addresses, and preventing loops.

In wide area networks such as the Internet, the destination address requires them to be looked up in a routing table by a device known as a router. Some newer switches also perform routing functions. These switches are sometimes called IP switches or layer 3 switches. Bridges and switches are covered in more detail in Chapter 5.

2.6.5   Routers

Routers operate at the Network layer of the OSI model. They forward information to its destination on the network or the Internet. Routers maintain tables that are checked each time a packet needs to be redirected from one interface to another. The routes may be added manually to the routing table or may be updated automatically using various protocols. Although primarily used to segment traffic, routers have additional useful features. One of the best is its ability to filter packets either by source

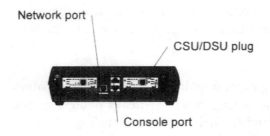

Network port

CSU/DSU plug

Console port

Figure 2.23
Router

address, destination address, protocol, or port. A router may create or maintain a table of the available routes and their conditions, and then use this information along with distance and cost algorithms to determine the best route for a given packet. Typically, a packet may travel through a number of network points with routers before arriving at its destination. Routers can also be configured to use strong protocol authentication.

On the Internet, a router is a device that determines the next network point to which a packet should be forwarded toward its destination. The router is connected to at least two networks and decides which way to send each information packet based on its current understanding of the state of the networks to which it is connected. A router is located at any gateway, including each Internet point of presence. Many times the connection from a router to the Internet is through a device called a Channel Service Unit/Data Service Unit (CSU/DSU). The router is then internal, connected to a LAN port on a switch. See Figure 2.23 for an example of a router. Routing will be discussed further in Chapter 8.

Now that we have defined cabling and the devices that hook everything together, it's time to look at how to lay out the network. The actual geometric layout of the workstations is important because it will determine the type of cable, access, and protocols used.

2.7   Network Topologies

In this section you will get a good grasp of the ways that a network can be designed. The physical layout of a network is called the **topology**, which includes the method of communication. When designing a network, you

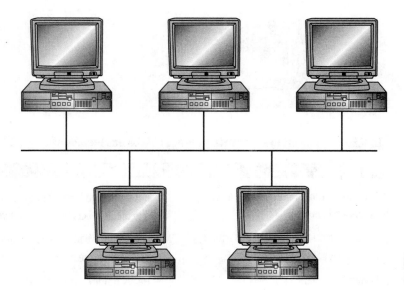

Figure 2.24
Bus topology network

should build in room for expansion. It is much easier to adapt a current network than to have to replace it because it was poorly designed.

2.7.1   Shared Medium

All machines "share" the network. This design as a shared media topology means that all devices on the network compete for access on a single shared piece of media. Only one device can transmit (talk) on the media at a time while all others must listen. When several devices try to talk simultaneously, the competition for access to the media results in a collision of information. Because the devices share the same media, limitations on total throughput and distance limitations of the cabling must be considered. Now we look at the two most common topologies where all devices share media—bus and star.

Bus

The **bus** topology consists of computers connected by a single cable called a **backbone**, as shown in Figure 2.24. All the computers on the bus share in its capacity. This is the simplest method for connecting computers. In a bus environment, 10Base2 or 10Base5 cable is used, and

Figure 2.25
Terminator

TABLE 2.5   Advantages and Disadvantages of the Bus Topology

Advantages	Disadvantages
Cable use is economical because all computers are in one line.	It is difficult to isolate problems because one break affects the entire network.
Cabling is easy to work with and extend, along with being cost-effective.	One break or bad termination brings down the entire network.
Layout is simple.	Heavy traffic can slow it down because all machines share the same bandwidth.

because all devices share the same bandwidth, the more devices the slower the network. In fact, it is probably not feasible for use with more than 10 workstations.

In a bus topology, the computers only listen for data being sent to them—they do not forward data. This is called a passive topology. A generated signal moves from one end of the bus to the other end. If it is not stopped, it will continue bouncing back and forth, preventing the computers from sending data. To prevent this, a terminator is located at each end of the cable. (See Figure 2.25.)

Because the computers are all connected by the same cable, if one segment has a problem the whole network is down. Table 2.5 lists the advantages and disadvantages of the bus topology.

TIP

A bus topology can be likened to a transportation bus—if the bus breaks down, no one gets to where they're going.

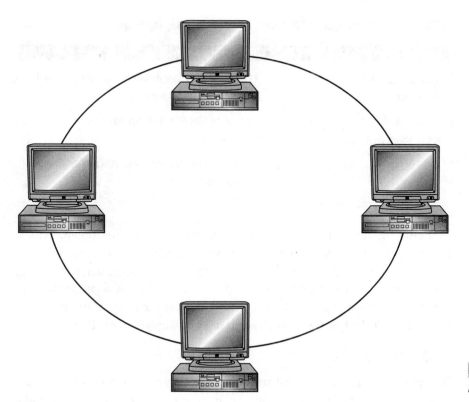

Figure 2.26
A ring topology

Ring

In a **ring** topology, each computer connects directly to the next one in line, forming a circle, as shown in Figure 2.26. Data travels in a clockwise direction, and each computer accepts the information intended for it and passes on the information for other computers. It uses a **token**, which is actually a small packet, to send information. Every computer in the ring is responsible for either passing the token or creating a new one. **Token passing** uses the token, or series of bits, to grant a device permission to transmit over the network. The computer with the token can pass data on the network. When a computer has information to send, it modifies the token and passes it on. After the token reaches its final destination, it lets the sender know it has arrived safely, the sender then makes a new token, and the process starts over. Most ring networks use fiber or twisted pair as the medium.

TABLE 2.6   Advantages and Disadvantages of the Ring Topology

Advantages	Disadvantages
Equal access is granted to all computers.	It is difficult to isolate problems because one break affects the entire network.
Network performance is consistent due to token passing.	If one computer fails, it brings down the entire network.
	The entire network is disrupted when adding or removing computers.

In a ring topology, if one computer fails, the network goes down. This is known as an active topology because each workstation is responsible for sending on the token. Currently, many ring networks implement a dual-ring network or use smart hubs to address this problem. In a dual ring, two rings are used for redundancy while smart hubs remove the failed computer from the ring. Table 2.6 lists the advantages and disadvantages of the ring topology.

2.7.2   Peer-to-Peer

In a **peer-to-peer** network, all machines are equal. They each can act as a server and a client. There is no central control over shared resources; the individual users decide what to share and with whom. There is little control over who has access to what resources and who has what version of each file, so it is less secure than a server-based network. However, it is acceptable for small offices that do not require administration and is much cheaper to implement than a server-based solution. The two most common peer-to-peer networks are the star and mesh topologies.

Star

In a **star** topology, the computers are connected to a centralized hub by a cable segment. (See Figure 2.27.) They require more cabling than ring or bus topologies, but each computer is connected to the hub by its own cable. Therefore, if one computer connection goes down, it does not affect the rest of the network. Because each workstation has its own connection, it is much easier to move them around or connect them to other networks. 10BaseT–100BaseFX can be used with a star topology. A star topology can

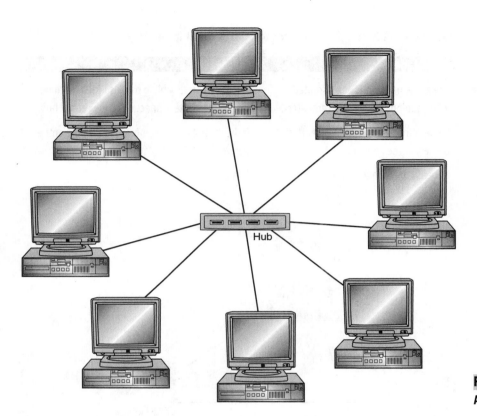

Figure 2.27
A star topology

support up to 1024 workstations, but it may not be feasible to connect them all to the same logical network. Table 2.7 lists the advantages and disadvantages of the star topology.

 TIP

A star topology can be likened to a star in the night sky: If one star falls, the sky still stays lit.

Mesh

In a **mesh** topology, all devices are connected to each other more than once to create fault tolerance. (See Figure 2.28.) A single device or cable failure will not affect the performance because the devices are connected by more than one means. This is more expensive as it requires more hardware and cabling. This type of topology can also be found in enterprise-wide networks with routers connected to other routers for fault tolerance.

TABLE 2.7   Advantages and Disadvantages of the Star Topology

Advantages	Disadvantages
The entire network is not disrupted when adding or removing computers.	It requires more cabling because each machine needs a separate connection to the central hub.
If one computer fails, it doesn't affect the rest of the network.	If the central hub fails, it brings down the entire network.
It is easy to manage and monitor.	N/A

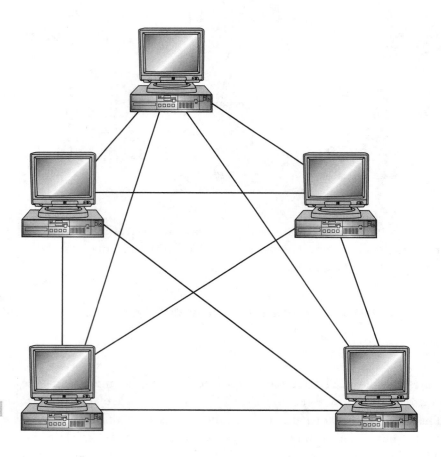

Figure 2.28

A mesh topology

2.7.3   Hybrid Networks

In a **star bus** topology, computers are connected to hubs in a star forma-tion, and then the hubs are connected via bus topology. (See Figure 2.29.) Although it is more expensive to implement, longer distances can be cov-ered, and networks can be isolated more easily.

In a **star ring** topology, data is sent in a circular motion around the star. (See Figure 2.30.) This eliminates the single point of failure that can occur in a ring topology. It uses **token passing** data transmission with the physi-cal layout of a star.

Large networks typically are organized as hierarchies. A hierarchical organ-ization provides advantages such as ease of management, flexibility, and a reduction in unnecessary traffic. In a hierarchical network structure, a high-speed backbone usually connects the servers. Fiber or ATM are the usual choices for these high-speed backbones. The types of large networks and their technologies will be discussed in the next chapter.

2.8   Chapter Summary

- A network is a group of computers that can communicate with each other to share information, and when they can communicate with each other they can also share resources. When a server pro-vides a resource for a client to access, this is referred to as a shared resource. Shared resources are accessed across the network.

- Because IP telephony networks make better use of available band-width, a VoIP network carries voice traffic more cost-effectively than a switched circuit telephone network. In a PSTN, a dedicated end-to-end circuit is allocated for each call. In a VoIP network, data is much more compressed and is carried in packets.

- The ISO developed an architecture that allowed the devices of dif-ferent manufacturers to work together to communicate with dif-ferent operating systems. In 1984, it became an international standard known as the OSI reference model. This architecture determines how hardware, software, topologies, and protocols exist on the network and how they operate. The OSI model is based on seven layers: Physical, Data Link, Network, Transport, Session, Pre-sentation, and Application.

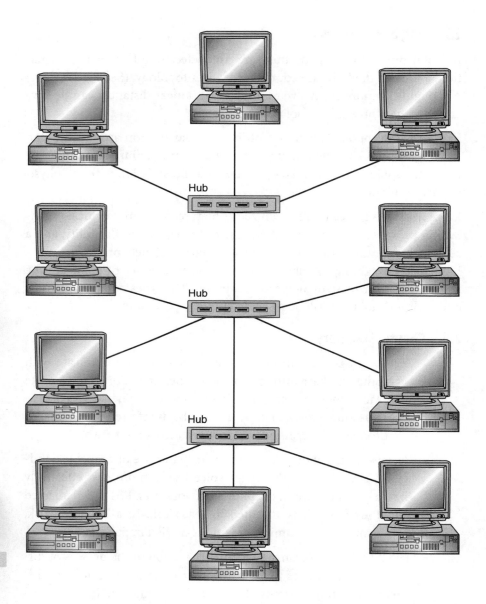

Figure 2.29
A star bus topology

- The Internet was originally called ARPANET. It was developed by the Department of Defense to provide a way to connect networks. The Internet is a network of interconnected, yet independent networks. Each host is directly connected to some particular network. Two hosts on the same network communicate with each other using the same set of protocols that are then used to communicate with hosts on distant networks. The language of the Internet is TCP/IP.

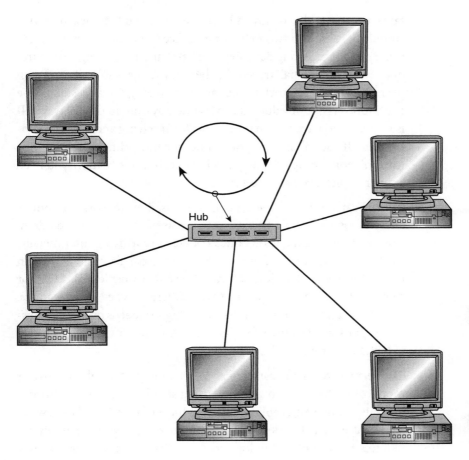

Figure 2.30
A star ring topology

- To deliver new services such as video conferencing and video on demand, as well as to provide more bandwidth for the increasing volume of traditional data, the communications industry introduced ATM technology to provide a common format for services with different bandwidth requirements. ATM uses connection-oriented switches to permit senders and receivers to communicate by establishing a dedicated circuit. In this environment, data travels in fixed 53-byte cells. Five bytes are used for header information, and 48 bytes are used for data. The data transfer rate can reach up to 9953 Mbps.

- Baseband uses a digital transmission pulse at a single fixed frequency. This means that the entire bandwidth of the cable is used to transmit one data signal. It also limits any cable strand to either half duplex or full duplex. Half duplex means that one transmission takes up the entire bandwidth of the cable. Full duplex uses two strands of cable and two network interfaces: one for sending and the other one for receiving data. Because baseband uses a single fixed frequency, as the signal travels further down the cable, its strength decreases and can distort. Broadband uses analog transmission over a continuous range of values. It travels one way only, in optical waves. It is necessary to have two channels, one for receiving and one for sending data. If the cabling supports enough bandwidth, more than one transmission can operate on a single cable. In this situation, you need a tuner to pick up the correct signal.

- Coaxial cable was the first type of cable used to network computers and was instrumental in forming the basis of the Ethernet standard. Coaxial cables are made of a thick copper core with an outer metallic shield to reduce external interference. Twisted-pair cable is used in most of today's network topologies. It is either unshielded (UTP) or shielded (STP), and comes in seven different types, or categories. Fiber was designed for transmissions at higher speeds over longer distances. It uses light pulses for signal transmission, making it immune to RFI, EMI, and eavesdropping.

- The term *wireless network* refers to technology that allows two or more computers to communicate using standard network protocols, but without network cabling. They are most often referred to as wireless local area networks (WLANs). Wireless networking hardware requires the use of technology that handles data transmission over radio frequencies. The most widely used standard is the IEEE 802.11 standard that defines all aspects of Radio Frequency Wireless networking. Currently, the IEEE standards for wireless are 802.11a, 802.11b, and 802.11g.

- A hub is a multiport repeater that retransmits a signal on all ports. When a packet arrives at one port, it is sent to the other ports so that all segments of the LAN can see it. Because it operates at Layer 1 of the OSI model, it can connect segments or a network, but cannot segment a network. A bridge can connect two different types of topologies because it does not understand anything above the Data Link layer. This allows them to move data more rapidly, but it takes longer to transmit because a bridge analyzes each packet. Switches operate at the Data Link layer of the OSI model. Their packet-forwarding decisions are based on MAC addresses. It looks at each packet and determines from a physical address (MAC address) which device a packet is intended for and switches it out toward that device. Routers operate at the Network layer of the OSI model. They forward information to its destination on the network or the Internet. Routers maintain tables that are checked each time a packet needs to be redirected from one interface to another.

- The physical layout of a network is called the topology, which includes the method of communication. Some of the most common topologies are star, ring, bus, and mesh.

2.9 Key Terms

Application layer: Layer 7 of the OSI reference model. This layer provides services to application processes to ensure that effective communication with other application programs is possible.

Asynchronous Transfer Mode (ATM): A communications services technology that provides a common format for services with high bandwidth requirements, such as video conferencing and video on demand. ATM supports transmission rates up to 9953 Mbps.

attachment unit interface (AUI): A transceiver cable between the medium access unit (MAU) and the data terminal equipment.

backbone: A single cable segment used in a bus topology to connect computers in a straight line.

bus: A major network topology in which the computers connect to a backbone cable segment to form a straight line.

bridge: A device that connects two or more segments of a network to make them one.

client: A computer on a network that requests resources or services from some other computer.

Data Link layer: Layer 2 of the OSI reference model. This layer packages raw bits from the Physical layer into logical, structured data packets.

full-duplex: A transmission method whereby data can be transmitted in both directions on a cable at the same time.

half-duplex: A transmission method whereby data can be transmitted in both directions on a cable, but not at the same time.

hub: A multiport repeater that retransmits a signal on all ports.

International Organization for Standardization (ISO): An international standards organization responsible for developing a wide range of standards, including many that are relevant to networking, such as the OSI reference model and the OSI protocol suite.

International Telecommunication Union-Telecommunication Standardization Sector (ITU-T): An international organization that develops communication standards. The ITU-T developed X.25 and other communications standards.

Internet Protocol (IP): The Network layer protocol that is part of the TCP/IP suite.

Internet service provider (ISP): An organization that provides Internet access to customers, primarily as a paid service.

Institute of Electrical and Electronics Engineers (IEEE): A professional engineering organization that defines standards for networking devices, which include network interfaces, cabling, and connectors.

Logical Link Control (LLC) layer: A sublayer of the Data Link layer that manages communications between devices over a single link. This layer includes error checking and flow control.

Media Access Control (MAC) layer: A sublayer of the Data Link layer that manages protocol access to the physical network medium.

MAC address: The unique hardware or physical address of a hardware device. Manufacturers assign MAC addresses to hardware devices.

mesh: A hybrid network topology used for fault tolerance in which all computers connect to each other.

network: A group of computers that can communicate with each other so that they can share information.

Network layer: Layer 3 of the OSI reference model. This layer provides connectivity and path selection between two systems. This is the layer at which routing occurs.

network medium: Refers to the cable (metallic or fiber-optic) that links computers on a network. Because wireless networking is possible, it can also describe the type of wireless communications used to permit computers to exchange data via some wireless transmission frequency.

Open Systems Interconnection (OSI) reference model: A hierarchical, seven-layer abstract structure of communications between application processes running in computer systems.

peer-to-peer: A type of networking in which each computer can be a client to other computers and act as a server as well.

Physical layer: Layer 1 of the OSI reference model. It defines mechanical, functional, procedural, and electrical aspects of networking. It includes connectors, circuits, voltage levels, and grounding.

plain old telephone system (POTS): The public telephone system, also known as PSTN.

Presentation layer: Layer 6 of the OSI reference model. It translates data from the Application layer into an intermediary format provides services such as data encryption, and compresses data.

protocol: A set of rules and conventions that specifically governs how computers exchange information over a network medium. A protocol implements the functions of one or more of the OSI layers.

public switched telephone network (PSTN): *See* plain old telephone system (POTS).

quality of service (QoS): A standard that specifies the time frame in which data will be delivered after transmission. QoS helps control jitter, latency, and loss for long-distance, high-bandwidth applications.

repeater: A device that regenerates electronic signals so that they can travel a greater distance or accommodate additional computers on a network segment.

resources: The files, applications, and hardware that are shared by the server for the client to access.

ring: Topology consisting of computers connected in a circle, forming a closed ring.

router: A device that passes data on from one network to another.

server: A computer whose job is to respond to requests for services or resources from clients elsewhere on a network.

Session layer: Layer 5 of the OSI reference model. It allows two applications on different computers to establish dialog control, regulates which side transmits, and determines the time and length of the transmission.

star: A topology in which the computers connect via a central connecting point, usually a hub.

star bus: A network topology that combines the star and bus topologies.

star ring: A network topology wired like a star that handles traffic like a ring.

switch: A special networking device that manages networked connections between any pair of star-wired devices on a network.

terminator: A device used to absorb signals as they reach the end of a bus, thus freeing the network for new communications.

token: A packet used in some ring topology networks to ensure fair communications between all computers.

token passing: A method of passing data around a ring network.

topology: The basic physical layout of a network.

Transmission Control Protocol (TCP): The Transport layer protocol that's part of the TCP/IP suite.

Transmission Control Protocol/Internet Protocol (TCP/IP): The language of the Internet. This is a suite of protocols that enables packets to be routed across many networks to arrive at their destination.

Transport layer: Layer 4 of the OSI reference model. It helps provide a virtual error-free, point-to-point connection so that communication between two hosts will arrive uncorrupted and in the correct order.

wireless network: A type of LAN that uses high-frequency radio waves rather than physical connections, such as cables or wires, to communicate between devices.

2.10   Challenge Questions

2.1 Match the layers of the OSI reference model with their appropriate function.

a. Physical   ____ Provides error-free packet delivery

b. Data Link   ____ Establishes responses between applications

c Networking   ____ Deals with mechanical and electrical communications

d. Transport   ____ Formats, encrypts, and compresses data

e. Session ____ Determines routes and addressing

f. Presentation ____ Provides user access to the environment

g. Application ____ Packages bits into data

2.2 A _____ accesses shared resources on a network.

   a. router

   b. dumb terminal

   c. client

   d. server

2.3 ATM is based on _____.

   a. dynamic 64-byte packets

   b. fixed 53-byte cells

   c. fixed 64-bit cells

   d. none of the above

2.4 Which of the following are considered an advantage of peer-to-peer networking? (Choose all that apply.)

   a. A network administrator is needed to install and configure a peer-to-peer network.

   b. Peer-to-peer networking is inexpensive to purchase and operate.

   c. Individual users control their own shared resources.

   d. Individual machines depend on the presence of a dictated server.

2.5 Telephony networks are based on _____.

   a. packet switching

   b. circuit switching

   c. data switching

   d. packet filtering

2.6 Which type of network topology is depicted in the following figure?

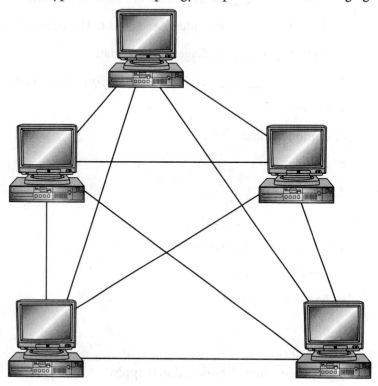

    a. Star bus

    b. Star ring

    c. Hybrid

    d. Mesh

2.7 Which of the following is not an advantage of the ring topology?

    a. All computers have equal access to the rest of the network.

    b. Even with many users, network performance is consistent.

    c. A single computer failure can affect the entire network.

    d. None of the above.

2.8 Which of the following is not an advantage of the bus topology?

    a. It is simple and reliable.

    b. Its cabling is inexpensive and easy to work with.

    c. Any cable can bring the network down.

d. All computers are arranged in a line and use cables economically.

2.9 Which type of cable is depicted in the following figure?

a. Coax

b. Fiber

c. UTP

d. STP

2.10 The layout of a computer network is known as its

_____.

2.11 A(n) _____ absorbs all signals that reach it, clearing the network for new communications.

2.12 A small packet, called a(n) _____, passes around the ring to each computer in turn.

2.13 Describe the purpose of a switch.

2.14 Describe the purpose of data sharing.

2.15 Describe the components that are necessary for two computers to communicate with one another.

2.11   Challenge Exercises

Challenge Exercise 2.1

In this exercise, you make a patch cable. You should know how to do this for several important reasons. You will better understand how cabling works, you will learn how to test cabling, and you will be able to make your own cables if you are ever in a bind. You need UTP cable, RJ-45 connectors, a crimper, scissors, and a cable tester.

To make a patch cable:

1. Cut the UTP cable to a desired length.

2. On one end of the cable, using the stripper on the crimper or a pair of scissors, strip about 1 inch of the outside plastic coating from the cable. Only strip the outside plastic coating from the

wire; do not strip the plastic coating off the inside wires and be careful not to cut through the copper wires. Sometimes it is better to use scissors than the stripper on the crimper because you have better control over the process.

3. Arrange the wires based on the color of the coating on the wires. Start at one end of the cable and arrange them in this sequence: orange/white, orange, green/white, blue, blue/white, green, brown/white, brown. Carefully trim the ends so they are even.

4. Insert an RJ-45 connector over the wires, pushing them to the end of the connector. Hold the connector such that you can see whether the ends of the wire are touching the top of the connector. It is important that the wires touch the top of the connector, otherwise the cable might not work.

5. Crimp the connector.

6. Repeat steps 1 through 5 on the opposite end of the UTP cable.

To test a patch cable:

Each cable tester has different settings to test a cable. Your instructor will help you make sure that the tester is set to the right specification. After this is completed, insert one end of the cable into the larger part of the tester and the other end of the cable into the smaller end of the tester. Check to be sure that all wires go straight through and that the cable is good.

Challenge Exercise 2.2

In this exercise, you make a crossover cable. You need UTP cable, RJ-45 connectors, a crimper, scissors, and a cable tester.

To make a crossover cable:

1. Follow steps 1 through 3 in Challenge Exercise 2.1.

2. Arrange the wires based on the color of the coating of the wires. Start at one end of the cable in this sequence: orange/white, orange, green/white, blue, blue/white, green, brown/white, brown. Carefully trim the ends so they are even.

3. Arrange the wires on the other end of the cable in this sequence: green/white, green, orange/white, blue, blue/white, orange, brown/white, brown. Carefully trim the ends so they are even.

4. Insert an RJ-45 connector over the wires, pushing them to the end of the connector. Hold the connector such that you can see whether the ends of the wire are touching the top of the connector. It is important that the wires touch the top of the connector, otherwise the cable might not work.

5. Crimp the connectors.

To test a crossover cable:

Each cable tester has different settings to test a cable. Your instructor will help you make sure that the tester is set to the right specification. After this is completed, insert one end of the cable into the larger part of the tester and the other end of the cable into the smaller end of the tester. Check to be sure that all wires go straight through and that the cable is good.

Challenge Exercise 2.3

In this exercise, you learn to punch down cable to a patch panel and an RJ-45 jack. You need Cat5 cable, a patch panel, a punchdown tool, and an RJ-45 jack.

1. Cut the UTP cable to a desired length.

2. On one end of the cable, using the stripper on the crimper or a pair of scissors, strip about 1 inch of the outside plastic coating from the cable. Only strip the outside plastic coating from the wire; do not strip the plastic coating off the inside wires.

3. Arrange the wires on one end of the cable in the sequence indicated in the specifications located on the back of the patch panel or in the documentation that accompanied the patch panel. Using the punchdown tool, carefully punch the ends into the panel.

4. Arrange the wires on the other end of the cable according to the specifications that accompany the jack. Using the punchdown tool, carefully punch the ends into the panel.

Challenge Exercise 2.4

In this exercise, you connect a computer to a patch panel with cables. You need two patch cables, a hub or switch, and a desktop PC or laptop with a NIC installed.

1. Attach one end of a patch cable to the NIC in the computer.

2. Attach the other end of the patch cable to the RJ-45 jack.

3. Attach the second patch cable and attach it to the patch panel.

4. Attach the second end of the patch cable to the patch panel.

Challenge Exercise 2.5

In this exercise, you tour an existing network and examine the components, such as topology, media, and hardware. Your instructor has arranged a tour of the school network or the network of a nearby business. During the tour, determine the following:

- What type of topology is used?
- What type of cabling is used?
- How many routers, switches, and hubs are used?
- How many computers are attached to the network?
- Is it a client/server or peer-to-peer network?
- How do users access the Internet?

2.12   Challenge Scenarios

Challenge Scenario 2.1

Acorn Music company occupies four buildings in your city for administrative offices, a warehouse, a record shop, and a multimedia studio. Currently, Acorn has some stand-alone computers but no network. Over the next two months, Acorn plans to implement a network linking all the offices and has asked you to help design it. There are plans for a total of 50 computers at all four sites. Security is not an issue, and the users are fairly computer savvy. What type of network should be installed and why?

Challenge Scenario 2.2

Evergrow, a large, multinational company, is currently running a peer-to-peer network at each of its 60 sites. The sites are not currently connected, but Evergrow is planning to do so. To keep costs low, management would like to continue to use the peer-to-peer network. However, as the sites are linked together, data will be shared between the users, making security a high priority. Should the company continue to use peer-to-peer networking? Why or why not?

Challenge Scenario 2.3

There are 17 computers in Mr. Green's office. They are spread out over three floors of a single building. Each floor has a central telephone room with access to the other floors. You have been asked to connect the computers in a peer-to-peer network. What type of network topology should you implement?

Challenge Scenario 2.4

You are setting up a workgroup for your department, which has seven computers, two printers, and one scanner that need to be connected. All equipment is located on one floor in a relatively small area. Costs must be kept at a minimum, and the network doesn't need to be especially fast. What type of cable would you recommend and why?

CHAPTER 3

Network Technologies

After reading this chapter you will be able to:

- Discuss the differences between local area network (LAN), wide area network (WAN), and metropolitan area network (MAN) configurations

- Describe the architecture, versions, and framing of Ethernet

- Describe the architecture, versions, and framing of Token Ring and Fiber Distributed Data Interface (FDDI)

- Describe the architecture and framing of Fibre Channel

- Describe WAN technologies, including Frame Relay, Integrated Services Digital Network (ISDN), and Synchronous Optical Network (SONET)

- Discuss infrastructure protocols, including Point-to-Point Protocol (PPP), High-level Data Link Control (HDLC), and Logical Link Control (LLC)

- Understand wireless networking technologies, including radio, microwave, and infrared

Chapter 1 introduced the concepts of signaling and electronic transmission methodologies. Chapter 2 covered the concepts of communication networking starting with telephony and finishing with a discussion on network topologies. In this chapter, we focus on the technologies used in data networking. We identify networking terms and the architecture of Data Link (OSI Layer 2) protocols for both wired and wireless communication.

3.1   Defining Network Terms

Understanding networking technologies begins by understanding the terminology used. Modern computer networks can be classified into one of three broad categories centering on the connection and geographic configuration strategy used with the physical devices:

- Local area network (LAN)
- Wide area network (WAN)
- Metropolitan area network (MAN)

Each of these network configurations has similarities but also has its own unique characteristics and deployment strategies.

3.1.1   Local Area Networks (LANs)

A **local area network (LAN)** is best identified using the following characteristics:

- Equipment is located geographically close together.
- Equipment is wholly owned and managed by the company (no leased services).
- Equipment is connected at high speed.

Each characteristic provides a wide range of possibilities, so it's necessary to look at each one more closely.

What does it mean to have all equipment located geographically close together? Is it all in a single wiring closet? Is it located on a single floor of a building, in the entire building, or can it be in two buildings next to each other? The answer is that all of those descriptions could describe equipment that is part of the same LAN.

The second characteristic—that equipment is wholly owned and managed by the company—means that all of the switches, routers, hubs, physical wiring, punchdown blocks, servers, and workstations belong to the company and are under common administrative control. The same people implement, manage, and maintain all of the equipment in a LAN. This would not be true in a WAN in which equipment may be leased and people outside the company help maintain connectivity. (We cover WANs in the following section, "Wide Area Networks.")

The third characteristic is that equipment is connected at high speed. What is high speed? ARCnet was a LAN technology that connected computers at 2.5 megabits per second (Mbps). Early Token Ring connected systems at 4 Mbps. Ethernet systems today can be connected at 1 Gigabit per second (1000 Mbps). Clearly, the definition of fast may change with time or even with the people you talk to. In fact, any one of these characteristics viewed without the others is not enough to qualify a system as being a LAN—you need to consider all three. Exceptions to the rules will always exist, and individual characteristics will be subject to interpretation, but all three characteristics can be found in all LANs.

Let's look at this from the perspective of a fictitious company named Widgets, Inc. Widgets is a manufacturing company currently located on a single floor of a building in Minneapolis, Minnesota. Widgets has all of its computers, printers, and servers connected using 10-Mbps switches and twisted-pair copper cabling. This configuration meets our three criteria for a LAN. Even if Widgets grew to occupy every floor in the building, it would still be considered a LAN as long as all of the networking devices were connected at high speed, with equipment owned and managed by the company. LANs can even span buildings as long as the three basic characteristics are met. So when is a network not a LAN? We answer that question in the following sections, which cover WANs and MANs.

3.1.2   Wide Area Networks (WANs)

A network is considered a **wide area network (WAN)** based on characteristics that are opposite those for a LAN:

- Equipment is geographically dispersed.

- Connection services, and possibly equipment, are leased from telecommunications providers such as phone companies or Internet service providers (ISPs).

- Equipment runs at much slower speeds compared to LANs.

A WAN is the opposite of a LAN in many ways. Our manufacturing company, Widgets, continues to grow and opens a manufacturing plant in Atlanta, Georgia. Both the Minneapolis and Atlanta locations have deployed LANs, and we need to connect these two separated networks so that data can be shared between all networking devices companywide. At this point, we meet the first characteristic: The equipment is geographically dispersed. We have a few choices available to us to connect our two networks—we could run our own wires from Minneapolis to Atlanta. Without going into financial detail and the technology required, running our own wires would be a very expensive and time-consuming proposition. Instead, we investigate the option of borrowing or leasing equipment and wires that are already in place. This would meet the second characteristic of a WAN: connection services, and possibly equipment, are leased. Telecommunications companies that have equipment and wires in place to provide telephone service generally provide the option of leased lines. Widgets can pay a fee and lease time on the wires for data communications. These links are typically much slower than LAN networking (128 kilobits per second [Kbps], up to 1.544 Mbps are typical). This too can be a trap, so don't just consider the speed of a link to qualify a network as a WAN. Some WAN infrastructures run over links that provide speeds in excess of 155 Mbps. This is certainly not a slow link, but because we don't own the equipment, the connection between the two offices is considered a WAN connection. If Widgets continues to grow into a multinational firm with hundreds of offices worldwide, we could inter-connect them all using the same basic techniques and technology. The best known WAN in the world is the Internet.

NOTE The term *wire* as used in this chapter represents any physical medium used to provide connectivity. It can be copper wire or fiber-optic cabling. Its actual composition is irrelevant to the discussion.

3.1.3 Metropolitan Area Networks (MANs)

A **metropolitan area network (MAN)** combines characteristics of both LANs and WANs. A MAN is limited by geography to a single metropolitan area. **Local Access and Transport Areas (LATAs)** are often used to define the boundaries for MANs.

TABLE 3.1 **Network Definitions**

Network	Characteristics	Boundary
LAN	High-speed connectivity between all clients. Company owns all equipment.	Usually limited to a single building, unless the buildings are very close together.
WAN	Lower connectivity speeds than a LAN segment. Company leases lines and possibly equipment from a Telecomm provider.	Connections extend beyond city boundaries.
MAN	A mixture of both LAN and WAN connectivity. Used to connect numerous LANs within a metropolitan area.	Connections are confined to a single metropolitan area.

NOTE

The basic definition of LATA is a defined area where a single company provides phone service. Moving outside a LATA is considered long-distance in phone company terms. When moving between LATAs, Telecomm companies charge additional fees and taxes.

Because of the growth of cities, a metropolitan area may now cross over multiple LATAs, so that alone is not enough to define a MAN. Let's return to our example company. Widgets is now a multinational firm with locations worldwide, and all of the company's LANs are connected with a large WAN. We have expanded in Minneapolis to encompass buildings in the downtown area, but these buildings are too far apart to be connected with only LAN equipment. At this point we can use WAN technologies to interconnect our buildings, creating a MAN architecture for all of the LANs in the Minneapolis area. Multiple companies in a city may get together to connect their respective LANs together for redundancy and higher-speed access to the Internet or other common WANs. This configuration would also be considered a MAN. Colleges and universities also use MANs to interconnect all of their buildings and classrooms.

NOTE

Another possible description for a university or college is a campus area network (CAN), although the distinction is purely one of distance and not well standardized.

Table 3.1 offers a brief review of each technology and shows us the key differences between each.

3.2   Local Area Network Technologies

With a clear understanding of the concepts of LANs, WANs, and MANs, we can now go into more detail about each of the technologies. LANs can use different types of hardware and software to connect equipment. As you learned in Chapter 2, the OSI reference model was developed to provide a standard method of communication between different vendor's equipment. The OSI protocol, as developed, was too complex for wide acceptance. Over the years, it has been used as a guideline or model for building a communications process between network devices. Because the OSI model tells us what to do but does not tell us how to do it, numerous methods have been developed that allow us to establish communications between network devices. These methods are called protocols.

A protocol is most easily thought of as a set of rules for doing something. Many kinds of protocols exist—diplomatic protocols, classroom protocols, and protocols for driving a car. Each protocol defines a set of behaviors that are both acceptable and unacceptable. The most common protocols used (in OSI Data Link layer communications) on a LAN are:

- Ethernet
- Token Ring
- Fibre Channel

Each of these protocols has different rules and standards. Some even support a wide variety of speeds for communications. They all have similarities and differences, but all define a strict set of rules for networked devices to send and receive data communications. Ethernet is arguably the most popular of the three, so we'll look at that protocol first.

3.2.1   Ethernet

Digital, Intel, and Xerox (the DIX consortium) are credited with developing the first version of the Ethernet protocol at the Palo Alto Research Center (PARC) in California. The term is now loosely applied to many different forms and speeds of that original standard. To make it easier to understand this data-link technology, we will first examine the features common to all of the different versions of Ethernet, and then we will look at the different versions and speeds along with their unique characteristics.

Ethernet Architecture

The architecture of Ethernet defines how network clients gain access to the, medium, or network wire, at the beginning of the communications process. The procedure used to gain media access is referred to as **carrier sense multiple access with collision detection (CSMA/CD)**. It sets up the basic rules for:

- Sending data
- Receiving data
- Error identification

Carrier sense requires that a network device wishing to communicate must first listen for a carrier signal. The presence of a carrier signal means that another device on the network is already communicating. The process of listening first ensures that one station does not attempt communications before another station is done. Ethernet defines the listening time as 9.6 microseconds (MS or millionths of a second [ms]). If the wire is free from signals for 9.6 ms, then a network station wishing to communicate can begin the next step in the process. Why 9.6 ms? This time is referred to as the **inter-frame gap** (IFG). In the original specifications of Ethernet, network devices shared the network wire (not so in today's switched networks). When one station was done transmitting, it took a small amount of time for the network interface card (NIC) to transition from transmit mode to receive mode. To allow for the transition time, all stations must wait a minimum of 9.6 ms from the last received signal before attempting to send data on the wire.

NOTE

If network devices were not forced to wait, a station that had just finished transmitting might miss the start of a new data stream because it would still be transitioning between transmit and receive. On the networks of today, systems often run on full-duplex switched Ethernet. In this configuration, the network interface can send and receive data at the same time, so no inter-frame gap is necessary.

Multiple access can have two meanings. For one, it refers to the fact that any station can attempt wire access at any time—it's basically a free-for-all. The other meaning derives from the fact that even if a client machine has just finished sending data, it can attempt to access the wire again as long as it waits the correct amount of time.

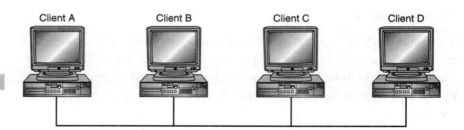

Figure 3.1

Clients on a shared Ethernet segment

Collision detection is used by the network interface to determine whether two stations have attempted to communicate at the same time. Note that this behavior is not only probable, but also expected, as part of the original design. Given at least two network devices on a common network wire, the stations are likely to listen and find the wire free of traffic. Both will then attempt to communicate, and the resulting signals will interfere with each other to cause a **collision**. This probability increases as the number of network devices increases. All devices with the potential to send signals that will collide are said to be in the same **collision domain**.

From this understanding of how Ethernet operates, a number of other rules can be explored. We know that the network interface needs to be able to detect collisions, but how fast does this process have to occur? We know how to gain access to the wire, but after the network interface begins, how long is it allowed to transmit? If a collision occurs, how is the network interface supposed to react? To answer these and other questions about the Ethernet protocol, let's analyze a network communication process between two Ethernet clients on the same shared network. Figure 3.1 illustrates several clients.

Client A wishes to send data to client D, so it listens for 9.6 ms and then begins the transmission process. The first 64 bits of data transmitted are the preamble. The preamble allows the other stations time to lock on to the transmission and identify the length of a bit's electronic signal. As Client A transmits, it is also listening for changes in the signal indicating that a collision has occurred. The preamble is an alternating pattern of 1s and 0s ending in 11. Ending the preamble with 11 will signal the other NICs that the preamble is over and the actual data is about to be sent.

Client A now sends the data. The electronic signal from start to finish (not including the preamble) is called a frame. Client A continues to listen for signal changes for the first 64 bytes of data that is transmitted. If the first 64 bytes are transmitted and no collision is detected, it is assumed that no collision will occur and the rest of the frame is transmitted. Clients B, C, and D receive the frame and must determine whether the data is intended for its interface. This is done with **addressing**.

NOTE

All NICs have a unique hardware address. The address on a NIC is burned into the read-only memory to uniquely distinguish it from all other network interfaces. It is composed of 12 hexadecimal digits (48 bits). The first six hexadecimal digits are a manufacturing code assigned to the company that produced the NIC. The last six hexadecimal digits are a production code used by the company for uniqueness. This address is called the Media Access Control (MAC) address or the burned-in address (BIA).

As clients B, C, and D receive the frame, the first series of 1s and 0s correspond to the destination MAC address of the intended recipient. This allows clients B and C to discard the packet without further processing. However, Client D continues to process the packet after recognizing its own MAC address in the electronic signal and continues to move the frame into memory.

By looking at this process, we discover additional information about collisions. We now know that a collision must occur within the first 64 bytes of transmission. By identifying collisions early in the transmission process, the NIC can retransmit the frame until it is successful. This fact gives us insight as to cable length limitations of cable length on Ethernet segments. We know that collisions must occur in the first 64 bytes (or 512 bits) of transmission. A physical fact is that electricity on a copper wire travels roughly two thirds the speed of light, or 200 million meters per second. If we combine this with the speed of the network, we can determine the maximum distance between two client computers that can operate within the collision limitation. Let's assume we are on a 10-Mbps network. The math works out as follows:

- (200 million meters per second) / (10 million bits per second) = 20 meters per bit
- 512 bits (smallest packet allowed) × 20 meters = 10,240 meters

Divide this number in half to yield about 5000 meters between two clients on a shared Ethernet segment. Why do we divide in half? Assume Clients A and D in Figure 3.2 are 5000 meters apart. Client A begins to transmit. Client D begins to transmit the instant before Client A's frame reaches it, resulting in a collision at the last moment. The reflection of the collision must travel a full

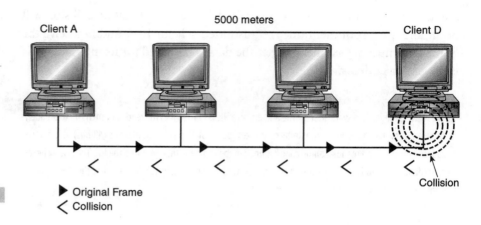

Figure 3.2
Collision

▶ Original Frame
< Collision

5000 meters back to Client A before the network interface on Client A has transmitted the 512th bit. The round trip is 10,000 meters. This behavior is called **propagation delay** and will be discussed in the "Ethernet Media Limitations" section.

When you exceed the maximum cable length between hosts, a **late collision** occurs after the designated 64-byte limitation. In our previous example, when Client A transmitted to Client D, as soon as the first 64 bytes were transmitted without incident the rest of the data frame was transmitted. The NIC on Client A emptied its transmit buffer and cannot retransmit the packet without the help of a higher-level process. This can cause a large delay and unexpected problems for the transmitting client.

NOTE

While working on a mixed Novell and Microsoft network, the authors noticed that systems periodically disappeared from the network list. Different systems were affected at different times throughout the day. We eventually learned the problem was caused by several of the computers being outside the maximum cable length.

How should a system react when a collision does occur? The Ethernet protocol tells us that as soon as a NIC recognizes a collision it should transmit a jamming signal. The most common jamming signal is a series of 32 binary 1s. The two NICs that caused the collision will both send the jamming signal the instant they recognize the collision. Each NIC then uses a mathematical algorithm known as the **Truncated Binary Exponential Backoff algorithm** to generate a random wait-time before trying to transmit again. This randomization effect prevents the stations from attempting to communicate at the same time again.

The last rules that we will look at concern packet size. We have discussed how the minimum allowable frame size on the network is 64 bytes. The maximum frame size, often referred to as the maximum transmission unit (MTU), is 1518 bytes. The MTU limits the amount of time a station is allowed to transmit and allows other stations equal access attempts at using the network. If a collision occurs, the resulting signals on the network are often seen as runts and giants. A **runt** is any packet below the minimum, and a **giant** is any packet above the maximum.

This discussion introduced many facts about the Ethernet protocol, so let's do a quick review:

- Ethernet controls transmissions through CSMA/CD.

- Any NIC can attempt access at any time (multiple access).

- However, before a NIC can transmit, the network wire must be free of signals for 9.6 ms (carrier sense). While transmitting, a NIC must listen for changes in the electronic signal indicating a collision (collision detection).

- The minimum packet size is 64 bytes. The maximum packet size (or MTU) is 1518 bytes.

- A runt is any packet below the minimum size. A giant is any packet above the maximum size.

- A collision occurs when two stations transmit at the same time. A late collision occurs after the first 64 bytes of data are transmitted. If a collision does occur, the responsible systems transmit a jamming signal and use an algorithm to determine a wait time before attempting to communicate again.

Ethernet Media Limitations

The speed of electronic signaling has changed dramatically over the years. As covered in Chapter 2, Ethernet has evolved from a signaling rate of 10

TABLE 3.2   Types of Network Cable

Standard	Type of Cable	Bandwidth	Maximum Length per Segment
10Base2	Coaxial	10 Mbps	185 meters
10Base5	Coaxial	10 Mbps	500 meters
10BaseT	UTP	10 Mbps	100 meters
100BaseT	UTP	100 Mbps	100 meters
100BaseT4	Four pairs, Cat3, Cat4, Cat5 unshielded twisted pair (UTP)	100 Mbps	100 meters
100BaseTX	Two pairs, Cat5 UTP or Cat1 shielded twisted pair (STP)	100 Mbps, Fast Ethernet	100 meters
100BaseVG	UTP	100 Mbps, Fast Ethernet	100 meters
10BaseF	Fiber-optic	10 Mbps	2 kilometers
10BaseFX	Fiber-optic	100 Mbps, Fast Ethernet	2 kilometers

Mbps to a current speed of 1 Gbps. There are current implementations utilizing 10 Gbps, although this specification is not yet formally standardized. Each change in speed has brought with it a change in the physical media over which the signals are transmitted. Chapter 2 discussed these media types:

- Thick coaxial cabling
- Thin coaxial cabling
- Unshielded twisted pair
- Shielded twisted pair
- Multimode fiber
- Single-mode fiber

Use Table 3.2 for a quick review of the media cable type, supported speed and allowed distance.

In addition to the rules and information covered in Chapter 2, you should consider other details when dealing with media and Ethernet.

Recall that Thicknet is used in the 10Base5 specification of Ethernet. The cable is about ½ inch thick and can be run 500 meters in a single bus configuration. Network nodes attach to the bus directly through an attachment unit interface (AUI) connector. The bus can be extended using a total of four repeaters for a total of five segments and a network length of 2500 meters. Implementations of Ethernet on coax only allowed three of these segments to be populated. This is known as the 5-4-3 rule (5 segments, 4 repeaters, 3 populated segments) and applies to both Thicknet and Thinnet network topologies.

From our earlier mathematical formula we determined that an Ethernet network could be a total of 5000 meters long. The actual implementation of 10Base5 allowed a total network length of 2500 meters and required two of the connecting segments to be free of network nodes. Each time a frame passes through a repeater, a small amount of time is added to the total round trip a signal takes on the network. This added time is called **latency** or **delay**. When moving frames (also called propagating frames) across multiple repeaters, the delay is called propagation delay. If a signal passing through four repeaters is involved in a collision, the collision result needs to pass back through all four repeaters to the original sender within the specified time limit (before the 64th byte is transmitted). So, by factoring in propagation delay and the conservative attitude of the Ethernet designers, lower distances ensured that early specifications of the Ethernet protocol were well within the mathematical limits.

Running Ethernet over twisted-pair-wire has similar limitations. Overcoming the distance limitation of 100 meters for UTP and STP is a simple matter of deploying repeaters or hubs. Like coax, however, there is a limitation on how many repeaters are used in a UTP network. If you are currently running at 10 Mbps, you are limited to four total repeaters, although all segments can be populated. If your network is running at 100 Mbps, you are limited to one Class I repeater or two Class II repeaters. The difference between the two types of repeaters is how much latency (delay) is added to the delivery of frames. A Class I repeater can add as much as 1.4 microseconds of latency while a Class II typically adds only .7 microseconds.

These limitations apply only to the use of hubs and repeaters when configuring or designing a network. A switch or bridge can buffer traffic flow, which prevents collisions. This behavior exempts them from adding latency (with respect to the collision rule) and should not be a factor when designing or implementing these devices in your network.

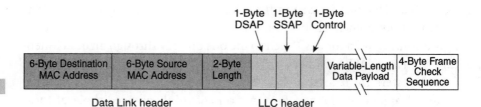

Figure 3.3

802.3 Ethernet frame

Ethernet Versions and Frame Formats

In the previous section, we covered common attributes of the Ethernet protocol, including media limitations. Here we look at specific differences in the Data Link layer framing of Ethernet and the evolution of the protocol into its current standards. There are four different frame types or versions of Ethernet:

1. Ethernet (version I)

2. Ethernet II

3. Ethernet SNAP

4. Novell Proprietary Ethernet (Ethernet raw)

Ethernet (version I) is the original Ethernet developed at PARC by the DIX consortium. Development of the protocol began in the early 1970s, and the protocol was released as a standard in 1980. Most references and updates to the protocol are managed through the Institute of Electrical and Electronic Engineers (IEEE). The managing project number specifically for Ethernet is 802.3. An 802.3 Ethernet frame is illustrated in Figure 3.3.

NOTE

Each of the four Ethernet frame formats begin with an 8-byte (64-bit) preamble. References often subdivide the preamble into 7 bytes of alternating 1s and 0s with a 1-byte start-of-frame (SOF) field that ends with the last two bits as 11b.

Numeric annotations ending with a *b* (as in 11b) identify the characters as base 2, or binary, format. Numeric values ending in an *h* (as in 11h) identify the characters as represented in base 16, or hexadecimal, format.

The Ethernet version I frame fields are:

-   **Destination MAC Address:** A 6-byte field that identifies the MAC address of the destination network interface.

- **Source MAC Address:** A 6-byte field that identifies the MAC address of the source network interface.

- **Length:** A 2-byte field that identifies the length of the data payload.

- **Destination Service Access Point (DSAP):** A 1-byte field that tells the destination NIC where to place the packet in buffer memory. This is necessary for controlling multiple frames from the same computer but is generated from different applications or processes.

- **Source Service Access Point (SSAP):** A 1-byte field that contains the corresponding buffer memory location on the source computer's NIC.

- **Control:** A 1-byte field that identifies the type of LLC communications in use (connection-oriented or connectionless).

- **Data payload:** A variable-length field, ranging from 43 to 1497 bytes of data. The data itself consists of upper-layer protocol headers, checksums (such as TCP/IP, IPX, AppleTalk), and working data.

- **Frame Check Sequence (FCS):** A 4-byte field that contains a mathematical result of the binary information in the packet. This is known as a checksum. The FCS sent is compared to a calculated FCS at the destination. If the two values don't match, the frame was corrupted during transport and is discarded.

NOTE

Remember that a packet cannot be shorter that 64 bytes. The Data Link layer information is 21 bytes total, so the payload must be a minimum of 43 bytes. If it is less, the packet is padded with bits, as needed, to bring it up to an appropriate length. The maximum length of an Ethernet frame is 1518 bytes. If the data payload exceeds this number with the Data Link layer information included, additional frames must be created and transmitted.

Ethernet II was developed quickly after the original 802.3 specification and published in 1982. Its frame format is almost identical to that of Ethernet version I. (See Figure 3.4.)

The Ethernet II frame fields are:

- **Destination MAC Address:** A 6-byte field that contains the MAC address of the destination network interface.

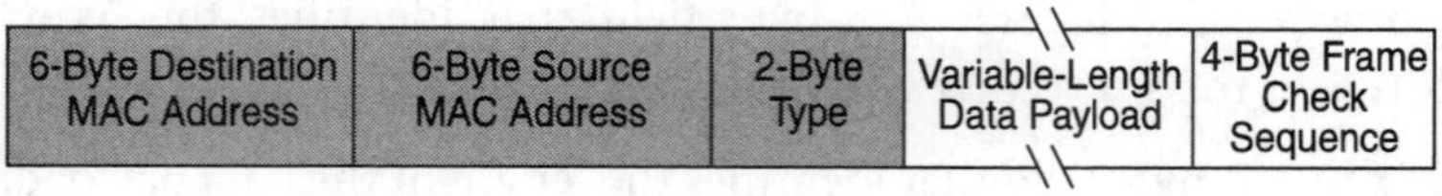

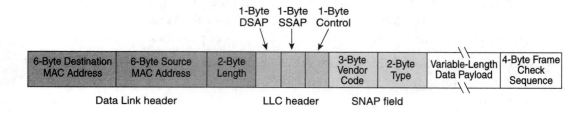

Figure 3.4

Ethernet II frame

Figure 3.5

Ethernet SNAP frame

- **Source MAC Address:** A 6-byte field that contains the MAC address of the source network interface.

- **Type:** A 2-byte field that serves the same purposes as the SAP fields in Ethernet version I.

- **Data payload:** A variable-length field that contains data. This field is slightly larger than the corresponding Ethernet version I field because it includes the LLC information.

- **Frame Check Sequence (FCS):** A 4-byte field that contains checksum information.

NOTE The key differences between Ethernet II and Ethernet version I are that Ethernet II includes a Type field instead of the LLC and does not have a Length field.

Not long after the 802.3 Ethernet standard was published, concerns were raised about using a 1-byte field for service access points. This allowed for only 256 logical addresses or port identities. A new frame format was developed to expand this capability and is referred to as the Sub-Network Access Protocol (SNAP). An additional function of SNAP was to include the Type field found in Ethernet II. The **Ethernet SNAP** frame format is illustrated in Figure 3.5.

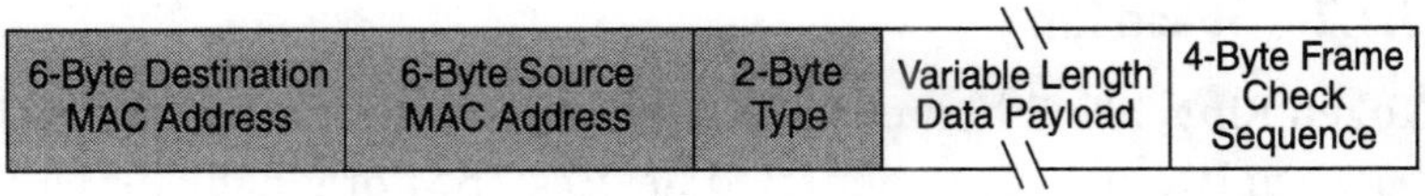

6-Byte Destination MAC Address	6-Byte Source MAC Address	2-Byte Type	Variable Length Data Payload	4-Byte Frame Check Sequence

Figure 3.6
Ethernet raw frame

The SNAP frame is essentially an 802.3 Ethernet frame with the addition of a 5-byte SNAP field following the Control field at the end of the LLC header. The significant changes in the 802.3 Ethernet SNAP frame are:

- The SSAP field is set to AAh to indicate the frame is a SNAP frame.

- The first three bytes of the SNAP field are vendor code that usually map to the vendor code of the source MAC address.

- The last two bytes of the SNAP field contain an Ethertype that matches the Type field found in Ethernet II.

The last frame format we'll look at is the proprietary frame of Novell. Early in the lifecycle of Ethernet, numerous papers were released with proposed frame configurations of 802.3. Novell developed its Ethernet implementations based on one of these early release papers. After Novell released its adaptation with its own IPX/SPX network protocol, the LLC header information was added to 802.3, making Novell's configuration incompatible. The proprietary format is often referred as **Ethernet raw**, which is illustrated in Figure 3.6.

The Ethernet raw frame fields are:

- **Destination MAC Address:** A 6-byte field that contains the MAC address of the destination network interface.

- **Source MAC Address:** A 6-byte field that contains the MAC address of the source network interface.

- **Type:** A 2-byte field that identifies the length of the data payload.

- **Data payload:** The data payload works the same as in Ethernet I but is slightly larger because no LLC information is included. The first two bytes of the payload are set to FFFFh to differentiate Novell raw frames from other Ethernet frames.

- **Frame Check Sequence (FCS):** A 4-byte field that contains checksum information.

3.2.2   Token Ring

Token Ring, like Ethernet, defines a method for sending and receiving data between two network-connected devices. IBM originally developed Token Ring in the 1970s. The IEEE published it as a standard (IEEE 802.5) in 1985. Although some minor differences exist between the two standards, they are essentially the same. The differences are covered later in this section.

NOTE

IBM's Token Ring standard was the first to be published, and any changes made to it are generally reflected in updates to the 802.5 standard. For the purposes of this discussion, any reference to Token Ring is meant to refer collectively to IBM and 802.5.

Token Ring Architecture

Token-passing technology was developed to interconnect external devices to mainframe and manufacturing computer architectures. A method of prioritizing important data and delivering data reliably had to be developed for these environments. Because mainframes are intolerant of unreliable sessions and traffic, it was necessary to avoid a collision-based topology, such as Ethernet, because of the potential loss of frames and required time for retransmission. ARCnet and Manufacturing Automation Protocol (MAP) were two early implementations of token-passing architectures.

As we learned in the "Ethernet" section, Data Link protocols set up basic procedures for:

- Sending data
- Receiving data
- Identifying errors

Sending data in a token-passing environment is far different than the chaos of Ethernet. Remember that in Ethernet a client need only listen to ensure that the wire is free from signals and can then transmit. To communicate in a token-passing environment, any client must wait until it receives an electronic token. The token is a special frame transmitted from one device to the next. When one device needs to communicate with another, it converts the token frame into a data frame and transmits it on to the wire.

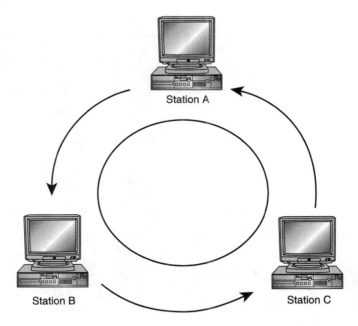

Station A

Station B

Station C

Figure 3.7

Token Bus logical ring structure

There are two types of token-passing architectures:

- Token Bus
- Token Ring

Token Bus is similar to Ethernet because all clients are on a common bus and can pick up transmissions from all other stations. The destination MAC address of the frame allows each network client to accept or discard frames as necessary. To work properly, each client has to establish *neighbors* so that the token is passed in a logical ring from one neighbor to the next. (See Figure 3.7.) Examples of Token Bus architecture are 802.4 and ARCnet.

Token Ring is different from Token Bus in that the clients are set up in a true physical ring structure. Each client plugs into a device called a **Multistation Access Unit (MAU)**, which is similar to an Ethernet hub or switch. Each network interface has both transmit and receive ports. The transmit port of one station is wired to the receive port of the next station. In this way, a Token Ring client can communicate with only two systems—its neighbors. The physical ring structure is illustrated in Figure 3.8.

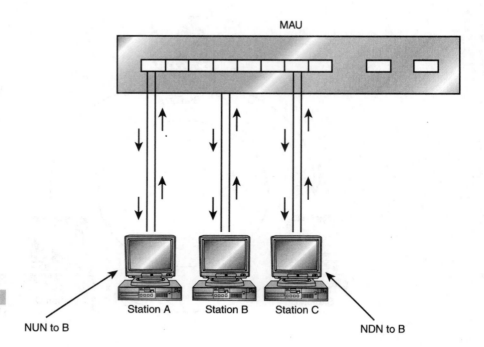

MAU

Figure 3.8
Token Ring physical ring structure

Station A   Station B   Station C

NUN to B   NDN to B

From the perspective of Station B, Station A is the Nearest Upstream Neighbor (NUN) and Station C is the Nearest Downstream Neighbor (NDN). Station B can only receive traffic from A and can only transmit traffic to C.

Before exploring the Token Ring communications process in detail, it is important to introduce some of the key components and activities of this Data Link technology. These components are implemented as software and include:

- Active Monitor
- Standby Monitor
- Monitor contention
- Ring polling
- Ring purge

The Active Monitor (AM) role is a process that can be enabled on any Token Ring station. On a correctly functioning ring, there will only be one AM. The election process is called monitor contention, which is covered later in this section. The responsibilities of the AM include:

- **Setting master clocking:** This is a signal that all stations on the ring use to synchronize their internal clocks. It is used to identify proper bit times and is similar in function to Ethernet's preamble.

- **Managing the latency buffer:** This is a 24-bit latency buffer used by the AM on small ring configurations to ensure that a station completely finishes sending a frame before pulling the next frame off of the wire.

- **Ring polling:** The AM will send an Active Monitor Present (AMP) frame every 7 seconds so that all stations know of its presence.

- **Monitoring of ring polling process:** If the AM does not receive an AMP frame from its upstream neighbor, it issues a ring poll error.

- **Monitoring of token frame:** The AM is responsible for maintaining the token frame to ensure that it is regenerated if lost. It also manages the reset of token priority if a station raises the priority and does not lower it back down. The AM needs to see a good token every 10 milliseconds.

- **Adjusting jitter:** All stations on a Token Ring network are repeaters. Each in turn resends data that was received from its NUN. Each repetition of the frame produces a small shift in the signal, referred to as jitter. The AM adjusts the signal by using its own master internal clocking signal rather than the clock signal received from its NUN.

The Standby Monitor (SM) is any station that is not the AM. The SM stations periodically check:

- **Token passing:** An SM must see a valid token or data frame every 2.6 seconds or it begins monitor contention.

- **Ring polling:** An SM must see an AMP frame every 15 seconds or it begins monitor contention.

- **Ring frequency:** If an SM detects that its own clock signal differs significantly from the AM, it begins monitor contention.

Monitor contention is the election process used to determine the AM. If the current AM is not performing properly or is no longer transmitting AMP frames, then a standby station will force an election. The station with the highest MAC address usually wins the role as the AM. If an AM currently exists when an election is called, it will not participate in the process.

Ring polling, in addition to the AM function previously listed, allows a station to learn its nearest active upstream neighbor (NAUN). Ring polling occurs every 7 seconds and allows a ring fault to be isolated to a particular domain.

Ring purge is used to reset the ring after monitor contention and other errors. This is accomplished by the AM by sending a ring purge frame. When Token Ring stations receive a ring purge frame, all current activity is stopped and the stations transition to Bit Repeat Mode. When the AM receives its own ring purge frame, a new token can be placed on the wire.

All of the functions described are built into the Token Ring interface card. There is a processor on board along with the imbedded software functions discussed so far. This functionality offloaded the work from the PC or server and relieved it of network interrupts for ring functions. Although this intelligence and complexity was more expensive than its Ethernet counterpart, there were significant benefits to running Token Ring in its heyday.

Token Ring functions at two speeds, 4 Mbps and 16 Mbps. There are no collisions (remember that 10-Mbps shared Ethernet was the competing technology) and the MTU on Token Ring is 4464 bytes for 4 Mbps and 17,914 for 16 Mbps. Therefore, a Token Ring network could deliver a minimum of 2.5 times as much data with far better reliability than Ethernet. Also, keep in mind that on shared Ethernet, 40% utilization was considered the maximum due to collision problems. Token Ring networks were commonly run at 75 to 85% utilization with few problems.

Token Ring Media and Topologies

Token Ring topologies are physically wired in a star configuration using STP or UTP (Cat4 or higher for 16 Mbps) cabling. IBM classified its cabling by using type instead of category. Networks were further classified as:

- Small movable
- Large non-movable

Small movable networks support up to 96 connected nodes and up to 12 MAUs. The clients are connected using thinner (26 AWG [American Wire Gauge]), more flexible Type 6 cabling. Type 6 is STP and supports limited distances but is easy to work with.

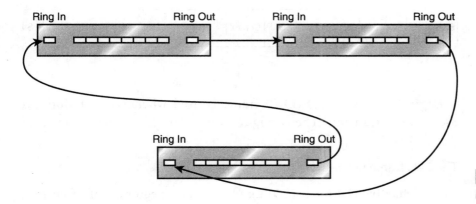

Large non-movable networks support up to 260 nodes and up to 33 MAUs. Clients are connected using Type 1 or Type 2 cabling, which is thicker (22 AWG) than Type 6, and supports longer cable runs.

Type 1 cable contains two twisted pairs for data while Type 2 contains two twisted pairs for data and four twisted pairs for voice.

■ **NOTE**

MAUs have regular client ports as well as Ring In and Ring Out ports. You can connect multiple MAUs together to form larger rings, as shown in Figure 3.9.

Token Ring Framing Protocols

There are three types of frames on a Token Ring network:

1. Token
2. Logical Link Control (LLC)
3. Media Access Control (MAC)

The token is a 3-byte packet consisting of a 1-byte Starting Delimiter (SDEL) field, a 1-byte Access Control (AC) field, and a 1-byte Ending Delimiter (EDEL) field. The SDEL serves the same function as the Ethernet preamble. The AC is in all frames and identifies the incoming signal as a frame or token. It also identifies priority and contains bits used by the AM.

Figure 3.10
LLC frame

SDEL	AC	FC	DA	SA	DSAP	SSAP	Control	Data	EDEL	FS

A **Logical Link Control (LLC)** frame is used whenever a station has user data to transmit. The configuration of an LLC frame is shown in Figure 3.10.

The LLC frame fields are:

- **Starting Delimiter (SDEL):** Identifies the beginning of a frame.

- **Access Control (AC):** Identifies the signal as a frame or token.

- **Frame Control (FC):** Identifies a frame as either LLC or MAC.

- **Destination Address (DA):** A 6-byte hexadecimal address that is set to the destination station, null address for ring-clearing purposes, or broadcast.

- **Source Address (SA):** The 6-byte MAC address of the source station.

- **Destination Service Access Point (DSAP):** Tells the destination NIC where to place the packet in buffer memory. This is necessary for controlling multiple frames from the same computer but generated from different applications or processes.

- **Source Service Access Point (SSAP):** The corresponding buffer memory location on the source computer's NIC.

- **Control:** Holds commands, responses, sequence numbers, and other data.

- **Data payload:** A variable-length field that contains actual user data.

- **Ending Delimiter (EDEL):** Identifies the end of the frame.

- **Frame Status (FS):** A 1-byte field used to notify the source of the data traffic as to what happened with the frame. The status can be Frame copied, Host nonexistent, or Frame received but not copied.

A **Media Access Control (MAC)** frame type is used for Token Ring functions such as Active Monitor Present frames, ring purge, and ring polling

SDEL	AC	FC	DA	SA	MAC Data	EDEL	FS

Figure 3.11
MAC frame

frames. These frames normally never pass through a bridge or router, limiting their impact to the local ring segment. The MAC frame is similar to the layout of an LLC frame but does not contain the SAP or Control fields, and the data payload is replaced with Token Ring maintenance information. The format is shown in Figure 3.11.

One of the final points to evaluate with Token Ring is the difference between IBM's Token Ring and the IEEE 802.5 specification.

IBM's Token Ring and 802.5

The differences between the two versions of Token Ring are minimal, as summarized in Table 3.3. As you can see, the real difference is that IBM specifies information concerning wiring and equipment, whereas the 802.5 specification does not.

Fiber Distributed Data Interface (FDDI)

Fiber Distributed Data Interface (FDDI) is another token-passing environment that relies on a dual-ring configuration for fault tolerance. In addition to its ability to recover from a primary ring failure, FDDI also functions at 100 Mbps. Although this might not sound impressive today, it

TABLE 3.3   Differences between IBM and 802.5

	IBM Token Ring	IEEE 802.5
Stations/Segment	260 on Type1/Type 2 96 on Type 6	250
Topology	Star	Not specified
Media	Twisted-pair cable with MAUs	Not specified

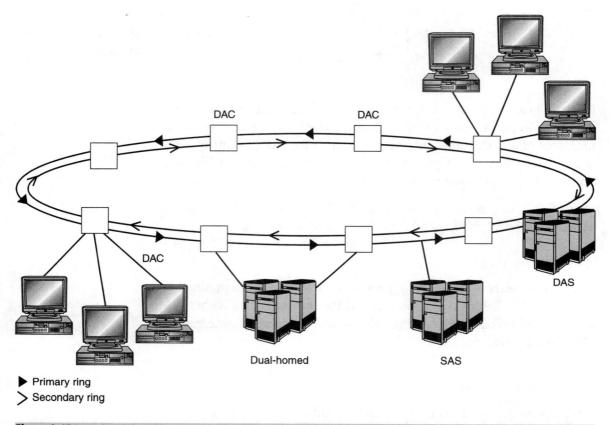

Figure 3.12
Dual-ring topology

was remarkably faster and more reliable than any other technology available when it was released in the mid-1980s.

Figure 3.12 shows the dual-ring topology with the following equipment identified:

- **Dual-attached station (DAS):** This system is attached to both the primary and secondary ring and is capable of wrapping the ring in case of a primary ring failure (explained later).

- **Dual-attached concentrator (DAC):** This system is attached to both the primary and secondary ring and is capable of wrapping the ring in case of a primary ring failure. Additionally, it has one or more ports that allow workstations and other devices access to both rings.

- **Single attached station (SAS):** This system is attached to the primary ring only. In the event of a local primary ring failure, this device will be off the network.

- **Dual-homed:** This system is attached to two individual DACs using two separate interface cards. One card is transmitting, and one card is on standby in case of failure.

FDDI is commonly used as a backbone network architecture because of its failover capability. If the primary ring fails for any reason, the nearest DAC/DAS will wrap the signal on the wire, as shown in Figure 3.13. This failover takes less than one second.

NOTE

The single attached station shown in the failover would not be able to communicate because it was only attached to the primary ring and the failure occurred on its local segment.

3.2.3   Fibre Channel

Most LAN protocols function in a chaotic environment. On Ethernet, Token Ring, and FDDI, any client can talk to any other client at any time. No preconfigured communication path or routing must be in place for this communication to take place. **Fibre Channel** is an emerging technology that moves away from this behavior.

Fibre Channel Architecture

Three different layouts are possible for Fibre Channel technology:

1. Point-to-point
2. Arbitrated loop
3. Fabric

Point-to-point is one of the most common configurations in Fibre Channel and is used to connect external drive arrays, printers, and other hardware component resources to servers. This configuration allows the components to be managed independently of the server hardware (secured in a vault, for example). Point-to-point sets up a single channel between two hosts such that the send circuit of one is wired to the receive circuit of the other.

An **arbitrated loop (AL)** has become the preferred configuration for Fibre Channel, although it is considerably more complex to set up. It is a mixture

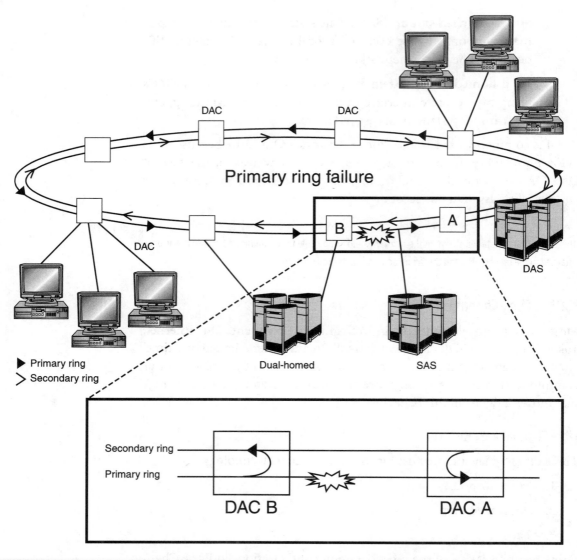

Figure 3.13

FDDI primary ring failure

of both Ethernet and Token Ring topologies, and can support as many as 127 devices. When a device has data to send, rather than using a token it sends a frame notifying the other stations that it wishes to communicate. This frame is known as an arbitrate frame and is sent to each station through a logical loop configuration. If a station receives its own arbitration frame back, it can now communicate with other devices. If multiple devices are arbitrating at the same time, the client with the lowest physical address will win. (This is discussed later in this section.)

Another difference in the Fibre Channel technology is that there is no time limit on how long a station can transmit. Once finished, however, a station may not send out an arbitrate frame again until all other stations have had a chance to communicate.

Addressing in a Fibre Channel AL configuration is done when the loop is initialized. A loop master is selected first, based on a lowest configured numeric port ID. The Fibre Channel client selects an address from an available 127 addresses and sends a frame to the loop master. If the address is available, the loop master then repeats the frame back to the requesting client.

Fibre Channel configured in a **fabric** is used to connect as many as 2^{24} (16,777,216) devices in a switched configuration. Unlike an AL configuration, the devices in a fabric can communicate at the same time. Fabric is a more expensive solution because it requires the purchase of a switch, but may well be worth the price for the performance gained.

Fibre Channel Media and Topologies

Fibre Channel can run on fiber-optic cable and copper (usually STP). Table 3.4 shows the possible configurations. Note that speeds are given in both megabytes (MBps) and megabits (Mbps) measurements.

3.3 Wide Area Network Technologies

WAN technologies can be traced back to the early days of mainframe computer systems. There was a need to move operator terminals out of the room where the mainframe was located (due to noise and cold). A link-control mechanism was created to manage data between the mainframe and the terminal. The Data Link Control (DLC) protocol was one of the eventual standards that came out of this process and is the basis for many of the modern WAN protocols in use today. The concept continued to evolve to include terminals that were physically remote. Although LANs serve most communications and resource needs, WANs give companies the ability to leverage information technology across wide geographic areas.

TABLE 3.4   Differences between IBM and 802.5

Media	Speed	Name
Copper or fiber	12.5 MBps or 133 Mbps	Eighth speed
Fiber	25 MBps or 266 Mbps	Quarter speed
Fiber	50 MBps or 531 Mbps	Half speed
Fiber	100 MBps or 1063 Mbps	Full speed
Fiber	200 MBps or 2126 Mbps	Double speed
Fiber	400 MBps or 4252 Mbps	Quadruple speed

WANs are classified in one of three ways:

1. **Circuit switching:** This involves creating a circuit between two points when needed. The communications path is created only when data is present, and the circuit is torn down when the data delivery is complete.

2. **Packet switching:** This allows multiple companies to share the cost of WANs by sharing the network transmission path. Packet switching uses virtual circuits for data delivery. **Permanent virtual circuits (PVCs)** are predefined paths for data flow between two end points. The virtual circuit is up even when no data is present. **Switched virtual circuits (SVCs)** function the same as circuit switching. The path is built when data needs to be transferred and torn down when data transfer is complete.

3. **Cell switching:** PVCs and SVCs are also used in cell switching technology for data delivery. The key difference is that cells do not vary in size. Asynchronous Transfer Mode (ATM), as an example, has a 53-byte cell length. This fixed size allows equipment to function much more quickly because the incoming cell will always be the same length.

3.3.1   Integrated Services Digital Network (ISDN)

Integrated Services Digital Network (ISDN) is a circuit-switching technology similar in function to public switched telephone network (PSTN).

When using ISDN, you dial a number just as with PSTN, but the signal is digital instead of analog. The two types of ISDN service are:

- **Basic Rate Interface (BRI):** Composed of two 64-Kbps B channels and one 16-Kpbs D channel. Because of the channel configuration, you may see ISDN BRI annotated as 2B+D. The total bit width of ISDN is 192 Kbps. It is composed of the B channels (128 Kbps) for transmitting data, the 16-Kbps D channel for signaling and link control, and the final 48 Kbps for framing and protocol overhead.

- **Primary Rate Interface (PRI):** Composed of twenty-three 64-Kbps channels and one 64-Kbps D channel. This is a T1 specification in North America and has a total bit rate of 1.544 Mbps. In Europe, Japan, Australia, and New Zealand, a PRI has thirty 64-Kbps B channels and one 64-Kbps D channel. This is an E1 specification and has a total data rate of 2.048 Mbps.

A company connects into an ISDN network using standard ISDN equipment such as routers, phones, or even PCs. This equipment is owned by the company and referred to as customer premise equipment (CPE). The copper wire used to connect into the service provider's network is called the last mile, or local loop. The provider is responsible for any errors or maintenance required from the local loop back to the provider network. (See Figure 3.14 for more detail.)

ISDN is widely available and still popular for small WAN configurations. The price varies based on the market and other available alternatives. As an

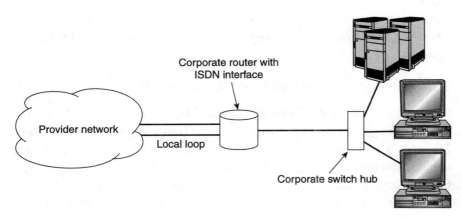

Figure 3.14
ISDN configuration

example, digital subscriber line (DSL) and cable data-networking technologies are quickly surpassing ISDN in many markets as low-cost, high-speed alternatives.

3.3.2   Frame Relay

Frame Relay is a very popular high-speed, packet-switching WAN protocol. Much of the error-checking and retransmission capabilities offered in earlier protocols (such as X.25) have been stripped out of Frame Relay because the underlying WAN switches and wiring have been greatly improved since the 1970s. This streamlined WAN protocol offers higher speed and greater efficiency than its X.25 predecessor using a simple FCS for error correction. The Frame Relay standard is controlled by the International Telecommunication Union (ITU) and the American National Standards Institute (ANSI), and updates to this protocol continue today.

Frame Relay utilizes PVC and SVC technology for data transfer and is a subscriber-based WAN service. A service provider connects a company into the provider's network by using Data Terminating Equipment (DTE). This DTE device (often a router) connects into the service provider's Data Communications Equipment (DCE) within the Frame Relay switching network. Each possible network destination is given a circuit ID called a **Data Link Connection Identifier (DLCI)**. The DLCI is assigned to each Frame Relay packet sent, allowing it to be correctly delivered to its destination through the switching fabric, as shown in Figure 3.15.

In addition to the DLCI, the Local Management Interface (LMI) controls signaling and provides services such as multicasting, Virtual Circuit (VC) status messages, and other extensions for managing the Frame Relay configuration between the company and the local interface at the service provider.

3.3.3   Switched Multimegabit Data Service (SMDS)

Switched Multimegabit Data Service (SMDS) is high-speed, cell-switching technology that supports data rates from Digital Signal 1 (DS1, at 1.544 Mbps) to Digital Signal 3 (DS3, at 44.736 Mbps). Similar to Frame Relay, companies connect their networks to a service provider's network through CPE devices (usually a router). SMDS utilizes connectionless datagrams that are large enough to encapsulate entire LAN protocols such as Ethernet

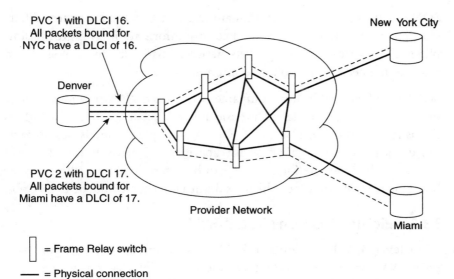

PVC 1 with DLCI 16.
All packets bound for
NYC have a DLCI of 16.

New York City

Denver

PVC 2 with DLCI 17.
All packets bound for
Miami have a DLCI of 17.

Provider Network

Miami

⬚ = Frame Relay switch

—— = Physical connection

Figure 3.15
Frame Relay cloud

and Token Ring without altering them. SMDS supports different access rates or classes of service on DS3 configurations, allowing customers to subscribe to lower and less-expensive data rates ranging from 4 Mbps to 34 Mbps. SMDS is a common MAN protocol but can be used for long-haul WAN configurations.

SMDS interface protocol (SIP) uses a 10-digit addressing system (similar to phones) and works at Layers 1 and 2 of the OSI model. Three distinct SIP levels exist. SIP Level 3 works at the MAC layer and encapsulates user data into frames called **protocol data units (PDUs)**. SIP Level 2 segments the PDUs into uniform 53-octet cells. SIP Level 1 transmits the cells as 1s and 0s onto the physical medium.

3.3.4   Synchronous Optical Network (SONET)

Synchronous Optical Network (SONET) is a WAN technology that allows different data stream formats to be combined into a single synchronous high-speed signal over fiber. DS1 and DS3 technologies use different line code and signaling rates such as AMI, B8ZS, HDB3, and B3ZS. These different signaling technologies often require complex multiplexing (muxing) and demultiplexing (demuxing) in order to send data between them.

SONET offers a common denominator signaling method for these different signals by adding overhead and control information. This greatly simplifies the transmission of packets between dissimilar technologies and removes the need for complicated multiplexing operations.

SONET is often used in large companies with varied WAN solutions in place or between service providers. The basic unit, or signaling rate, is 51.84 Mbps and is known as Optical Carrier 1 (OC-1). Multiple OC levels can be combined to achieve very large bandwidth capacities. OC-256 is the fastest current standard. The total rate for OC-256 can be determined by multiplying the base rate of 51.84 times 256, which results in a total bandwidth of 13.28 Gpbs.

3.3.5   High-level Data Link Control (HDLC)

High-level Data Link Control (HDLC) is commonly used on **point-to-point** WAN interfaces and between local serial interfaces as needed. It is a derivative of IBM's Synchronous Data Link Control (SDLC) protocol used in Systems Network Architecture (SNA). SDLC was modified by the ISO and the resulting protocol was HDLC. The IEEE further modified HDLC to generate Link Access Procedure (LAP) and Link Access Procedure Balanced (LAPB), which can be found in many of the modern WAN protocols including X.25, X.21, ISDN, and Frame Relay, to name a few.

HDLC functions using two primary configurations:

- **Point-to-point:** This configuration comprises only two nodes, one on each end of the link.
- **Multipoint:** Configurations using multipoint allow multiple nodes on the same link configuration.

The benefit of this protocol is that it is simple, well understood, and easy to configure when using equipment from the same vendor. Unfortunately, many of the vendors have added their own proprietary fields to HDLC, making it incompatible with other vendors.

3.3.6   Logic Link Control (LLC)

IEEE 802.2 defines LLC as a protocol. It is used in Ethernet, Token Ring, and other environments such as mainframe communications. LLC offers three types of service: Type 1, Type 2, and Type 3.

Type 1 service is unacknowledged and connectionless. It relies on upper-layer protocols such as Transmission Control Protocol (TCP) and Sequenced Packet Exchange (SPX) for retransmission in the case of lost packets.

Type 2 service is connection-oriented and provides acknowledgments for positive receipt of data during communications. Type 2 is commonly used in IBM mainframe environments.

Type 3 service is connectionless but does provide acknowledgment of receipt of data. In essence, frames are sent before establishing any communications path or far-end availability, but when Type 3 frames are received, they are acknowledged by the receiving system.

Table 3.5 summarizes the covered WAN technologies.

3.4   Metropolitan Area Network Technologies

MANs can use a combination of the WAN/LAN technologies discussed so far for interconnecting networks. As stated earlier in the "Metropolitan Area Networks" section, MANs are limited in scope to a single metropolitan area or LATA. IEEE 802.6 and IEEE 802-2001 define a wide range of characteristics of a MAN relating to technologies used, affordability, and supported transmission speeds and transport capability (for video, voice, and data).

3.5   Infrastructure Protocols

Infrastructure protocols differ from LAN and WAN protocols, because they tend to focus on extending network functionality to a small subset of users or even to a single client. Numerous protocols exist that might fall into this category, but we are going to focus on three of the most popular:

- Point-to-Point Protocol (PPP)
- Point-to-Point Tunneling Protocol (PPTP)
- Layer 2 Tunneling Protocol (L2TP)

3.5.1   Point-to-Point Protocol (PPP)

Point-to-Point Protocol (PPP) is used to connect client systems into an existing WAN infrastructure and can be used over dial-up or dedicated links. It

TABLE 3.5   WAN Protocols

Protocol	Technology	Characteristics
ISDN	Circuit switched	Uses traditional copper media
		Similar to phone service
		128 Kbps for BRI
		1.544 Mbps for PRI T1
		2.048 Mbps for PRI E1
Frame Relay	Packet switched	Uses traditional copper media
		Uses DLCIs to identify different VCs
		Can use PVC or SVC configuration
		1.544-Mbps data rate
SMDS	Cell switched	Uses copper or fiber media
		Frames are fixed 53-octet cells
		Has three distinct levels
		Supports data rates from DS1 to DS3
SONET	Packet switched	Uses fiber-optic media
		Primarily used to aggregate bandwidth from multiple sources and signaling types
		Base rate is 51.84 Mbps measured as OC-1
		Current fastest rate defined is OC-256 (13.28 Gbps)
HDLC	Packet switched	Simple serial protocol
		Basis for numerous WAN protocols
		Uses point-to-point and multipoint configurations
		May not interoperate between different vendors' equipment
		Supports data rates through E1
LLC	Packet Switched	Defined by IEEE 802.2
		Used in Ethernet and Token Ring
		Supports three levels of service:
		• Type 1 is connectionless and unacknowledged
		• Type 2 is connection-oriented and acknowledged
		• Type 3 is connectionless and acknowledged
		Data rate based on other technologies in use

replaces the older Serial Line Internet Protocol (SLIP) and has significant improvements. PPP uses two sublayers to offer these improvements:

- Link Control Protocol (LCP)
- Network Control Protocol (NCP)

LCP is the workhorse of the protocol and is responsible for link negotiation, link establishment, and link termination. In addition, LCP provides the following support:

- **Encrypted logons:** Allows passwords to be encrypted before being sent across the link.

- **Encrypted data transfers:** Different encryption algorithms may be employed to protect data sent between two connected devices.

- **Compression:** Allows more efficient use of the link through data compression if both end points support it.

- **Multilink:** Multiple physical links can be combined to form one logical link. For example, you can link the two individual channels of ISDN to form one 128-Kbps link. This technology can even be used with analog phones, combining, for example, four 56-Kbps dial-up links into one logical 224-Kbps connection.

NCP is the negotiator of the Layer 3 (OSI) protocol stacks including dynamic assignment of Network layer addresses. It supports TCP/IP, IPX/SPX, AppleTalk, Pathworks, and any other protocols for which an NCP module is written.

3.5.2 Point-to-Point Tunneling Protocol (PPTP)

Point-to-Point Tunneling Protocol (PPTP) is most often used when connecting users using virtual private networks (VPNs). The concept behind VPNs is that a user can dial in to a local service provider for Internet access and then connect to the corporate LAN through the Internet connection (the tunnel). This configuration is an enormous cost savings to companies because they avoid costly direct-dial, long-distance charges. Packet encryption (using a 40- or 56-bit algorithm) provided by PPP ensures that only users on the corporate network can read the data. This protocol is well standardized and has gained wide acceptance in recent years.

3.5.3   Layer 2 Tunneling Protocol (L2TP)

Layer 2 Tunneling Protocol (L2TP) is the next generation of tunneling and is similar in function to PPTP. The tunneling mechanism is provided by Cisco's layer-2 forwarding technology, which is more streamlined and stable compared to PPTP. The encryption mechanism has been separated from the tunneling protocol so that it can be upgraded later without having to overhaul the entire protocol mechanism. The encryption is currently provided by IP Security (IPSec) protocol and supports a higher-bit (currently 128-bit) encryption algorithm than its PPTP counterpart.

3.6   Wireless Network Technologies

Wireless networking capabilities have been available for many years. The recent drop in price and advancement in the speeds offered by wireless technology has contributed to the rapid rise in its popularity. One-time set-up fees, speeds ranging from DS1 to OC3, and freedom from ongoing monthly WAN provider fees make wireless a viable and attractive solution for companies in a MAN situation. In addition to these benefits, wireless offers redundancy for hard-wired links that may be dug up by utility workers or knocked out by storms.

Before deploying wireless, you should consider several things. Wireless generally requires line of sight (LOS) between the two connection points. Buildings and natural formations, such as hills or depressions, can cause connection and transmission problems. Wireless offers freedom from monthly WAN fees, but the up-front cost of purchasing and installing wireless may be prohibitive. Microwave configurations, for example, cost $20,000 to $25,000 just for two sites. Monthly fees may still be incurred for rental charges if the company does not own the building or property where the wireless equipment needs to be deployed. Additional training for maintenance and troubleshooting of the wireless network may be advisable as well. Overall, however, wireless does offer attractive alternatives to traditional wired LAN and MAN solutions. Wireless can be configured using several different signaling technologies such as radio, microwave, and infrared.

3.6.1   Radio Frequency (RF)

Radio frequency (RF) wireless technologies have evolved to include multiple frequencies and speeds. Setting up RF wireless communications involves configuring two or more transceivers (devices capable of transmitting and receiving) for delivering data through point-to-point or multipoint configuration over a range of 1 to 10 miles.

3.6.2 Microwave Frequency

Microwave wireless technology is similar in function to RF technology but uses microwave signaling, has the ability to be transmitted distances of 30 miles (or more), and can achieve significantly higher speeds (OC3 is possible). A significant drawback to this technology is that the frequencies are regulated by the Federal Communications Commission (FCC) and must be licensed before being deployed.

3.6.3 Infrared Frequency

Infrared frequency is a low-power wireless technology that is good for short distances, typically on an office floor. It is often used when other wireless signals would interfere with existing electronic equipment (in a hospital, for example). You can set it up as a directed or diffused technology. Directed infrared requires that the wireless devices be pointed at a concentrator in order to make a connection. With diffused infrared, the signal bounces off of walls and other materials, allowing the equipment to be easily placed in an area without specific direction needed.

Infrared is currently used to connect laptops, printers, and personal data devices easily with little or no extra equipment needed.

3.6.4 Important Standards and Capabilities

This section briefly covers some of the current standards and capabilities associated with wireless technologies.

802.11

Wireless technologies are currently defined in the following IEEE standards:

- **802.11a:** Operates at 5.0 GHz and has a data rate of 54 Mbps.
- **802.11b:** Operates at 2.4 GHz and has a data rate of 11 Mbps.
- **802.11g:** Operates at 2.4 Ghz and has a data rate of 54 Mbps.

A benefit of the 802.11a standard is that it is out of the frequency range normally used by telephones, microwave ovens, and other appliances. Other frequencies are under consideration that support faster transmission speeds, but these three are the most current and widely supported standards.

802.1x

802.1x defines a common authentication mechanism for both wired and wireless LANs. It uses standard Ethernet frames to encapsulate Extensible Authentication Protocol (EAP) requests. When used on wireless LANs, EAP requests are sent to an authentication server through **wireless access points (WAPs)**, which are devices used to connect wireless devices into a managed network. After authentication is deployed, users are required to log on successfully before using available wireless access points.

Bluetooth

Bluetooth is an open standard that allows interoperation between equipment from different vendors, and is aimed primarily at LAN devices and components. The technology is highly resistant to interference and allows connectivity between devices without the use of wireless concentrators (WCs) or WAPs. This type of connectivity mode is referred to as ad hoc mode and gives users of Bluetooth technology freedom from proprietary cabling and the need to purchase intermediate connectivity devices such as hubs or switches. Bluetooth-enabled cell phones can download phone lists from a Bluetooth-compliant laptop. Both devices can use headsets, microphones, or other equipment manufactured under the Bluetooth standard. Printers, scanners, handheld devices, and even home entertainment systems are all being built with Bluetooth technologies. (Maybe we really can get down to one remote!)

Home RF

Home RF is one of the newest standards in RF wireless technology and is being standardized to help meet demands in the home networking arena. A working group was formed in 1997 to help define a more complete wireless solution that could meet the following four demands:

- Networking with no new wires
- Simple and easy to install and use
- Integration with other wireless technologies such as phones, home entertainment systems, and home automation equipment
- Low cost and secure

Home RF can be configured in ad hoc mode as in the Bluetooth technology or as a managed network with WAPs. One of the drawbacks to current 802.11 wireless technologies is that it uses a common 2.4 GHz frequency that is also used by phones, microwaves, and other home appliances. Home RF overcomes this issue by using Shared Wireless Access Protocol (SWAP), allowing current and future appliances to share the 2.4 GHz range.

3.7   Chapter Summary

- A local area network (LAN) is a collection of networking equipment located geographically close together, owned by a single company, and capable of high-speed data transfer.

- A wide area network (WAN) is a collection of networking equipment that's geographically separated and connected by leased equipment and services that typically run at slower speeds than a LAN.

- A metropolitan area network (MAN) combines the characteristics of both LANs and WANs within a metropolitan area.

- A protocol is a set of rules governing a given activity. Network protocols create standard methods of communications for networked devices. Standard LAN protocols include Ethernet, Token Ring, and Fibre Channel.

- Ethernet clients rely on Carrier Sense Multiple Access with Collision Detection (CSMA/CD), whereas Token Ring clients rely on token passing.

- Ethernet has four frame types: Ethernet, Ethernet II, Ethernet SNAP, and Novell Proprietary Ethernet (Ethernet raw).

- Fiber Distributed Digital Interface (FDDI) and Fibre Channel both use fiber-optic cabling technologies. FDDI uses a token-passing method whereas Fibre Channel uses preconfigured connection points.

- WAN protocols use either packet-switching or circuit-switching technologies. WAN connections include Integrated Services Digital Network (ISDN), Frame Relay, Switched Multimegabit Data Service (SMDS), Synchronous Optical Network (SONET), High-level Data Link Control (HDLC), and Logical Link Control (LLC).

- Infrastructure protocols include Point-to-Point Protocol (PPP), Point-to-Point Tunneling Protocol (PPTP), and Layer 2 Tunneling Protocol (L2TP).

- Wireless protocols include 802.11a, 802.11b, and 802.11g.

- Wireless technologies now exist for both business and home. Wireless uses radio, microwave, and infrared frequencies to connect devices together. Wireless standards currently include Bluetooth and home RF.

3.8   Key Terms

802.1x: A standard that governs internetworking and link security. 802.1x governs authentication mechanisms for both wired and wireless technologies.

addressing: A method of identifying network-connected equipment with a unique value.

ad hoc: A wireless network setup between clients without using a WAP.

arbitrated loop (AL): A Fibre Channel configuration that creates a multipoint configuration between a maximum of 127 nodes.

Bluetooth: An open standard of wireless communication that allows communications between devices from different vendors.

carrier sense multiple access with collision detection (CSMA/CD): A method used in Ethernet that allows clients access to the medium. Clients must listen for a carrier signal before transmitting and must then listen for collisions.

collision: Refers to when two network stations attempt to communicate at the same time and the signals cross over each other on the wire.

collision domain: All networking clients with the potential to send signals and have them collide are said to be in the same collision domain.

Data Link Connection Identifier (DLCI): A method of identifying multiple virtual circuits in a Frame Relay network.

delay: *See* latency.

dual-attached concentrator (DAC): A network node in FDDI that is attached to both rings and can wrap the ring in case of a primary ring failure. It is also responsible for connecting end-nodes to the FDDI ring.

dual-attached station (DAS): A network node in FDDI that is attached to both rings and can wrap the ring in case of a primary ring failure.

dual-homed: A network node in a FDDI network that is attached to two DACs.

Ethernet : A Layer 2 network protocol used for delivering frames between two network interface cards. Network access is achieved through CSMA/CD.

Ethernet II: A modification of the original Ethernet standard. Ethernet II uses a Type field instead of an LLC field.

Ethernet raw: A Novell proprietary implementation of the original Ethernet I standard. It does not use an LLC field.

Ethernet SNAP: An extension of the Ethernet I specification that allows for more service access points.

fabric: A Fibre Channel configuration that creates a multipoint configuration between an infinite number of nodes. It requires a special switch.

Fiber Distributed Data Interface (FDDI): A Layer 2 protocol similar to Token Ring. It uses token passing for media access and a dual-ring topology for redundancy.

Fibre Channel: A Layer 2 networking protocol used to create a channel between communicating nodes.

Frame Relay: A packet-switched WAN technology whereby bandwidth is shared among subscribers.

giant: A frame that is larger than the defined current protocol and media.

High-level Data Link Control (HDLC): A Layer 2 WAN protocol used on point-to-point serial links.

home RF: A wireless technology being developed for use with home appliances.

Integrated Services Digital Network (ISDN): A packet-switched digital connection method similar to phone service.

inter-frame gap: The 9.6-microsecond required wait time between the receipt of the last signal and the start of a new signal on an Ethernet network.

late collision: A collision that occurs after the first 64 bytes of data have been transmitted.

latency: Delay associated with the transmission, retransmission, or processing of network frames.

Local Access and Transport Area (LATA): A geographic zone supported by a single telephone service provider.

local area network (LAN): A group of devices under common administrative control, connected at high speed, and located close together.

Logical Link Control (LLC): A Layer 2 protocol defined by IEEE 802.2 and used in other protocols such as Ethernet and Token Ring.

metropolitan area network (MAN): A group of LANs connected using WAN and LAN technologies but limited in distance to a metropolitan area or LATA.

multipoint: A network configuration that involves multiple network nodes or end points.

multistation access unit (MAU): A device used to attach clients to a Token Ring network.

permanent virtual circuit (PVC): A circuit path defined in software for the delivery of packets between two end points. The circuit is up even when no data is being sent.

point-to-point: A network configuration involving only two nodes.

propagation delay: The delay an electronic signal experiences when transmitted between two end points.

protocol data unit (PDU): A defined amount of data that can be transmitted using the current protocol and media.

runt: A frame that is smaller than the defined minimum size for the protocol and media.

single-attached station (SAS): A network node in FDDI attached only to the primary ring.

Switched Multimegabit Data Service (SMDS): A subscriber WAN service for connecting networks together over high-speed links.

switched virtual circuit (SVC): A circuit path defined in software for the delivery of packets between two end points. The circuit is only up when there is data to send.

Synchronous Optical Network (SONET): A subscriber WAN service that aggregates multiple signaling types into a single large pipe.

Token Bus: An early definition of a token-passing environment in which systems were wired in a physical bus.

Token Ring: A Layer 2 networking protocol used for delivering frames between two network interfaces. Network access is achieved by possessing an electronic token.

Truncated Binary Exponential Backoff Algorithm: A mathematical formula used by Ethernet clients after a collision has occurred. It insures that the clients do not attempt to communicate at the same time again.

wide area network (WAN): A group of LANs connected over a wide geographic area, at slower speeds than LAN, and under shared administrative control.

wireless: The ability to transmit data without using wires.

wireless access point (WAP): A device used to connect wireless cards into a managed network.

3.9   Challenge Questions

3.1   Which of the following best describes how an Ethernet client accesses the physical medium when transporting data?

   a. It waits for a special frame on the wire. It reconfigures the frame with data and transmits it to its downstream neighbor.

   b. It listens to ensure that no signal is present on the wire and then begins to transmit.

   c. It sends a signal notifying other stations of its intent to send data. If no collision occurs, then the station transmits.

   d. It sends out a special packet attempting to gain control of the network. If the client receives its own packet back, it has successfully won the right to communicate.

3.2   What is the inter-frame gap?

   a. The amount of time that a Token Ring client must wait before releasing a data frame

   b. The amount of time that a Token Ring client must wait before releasing a token frame

   c. The amount of time that an Ethernet client must wait from the end of the last transmission before beginning a new transmission on the wire

    d. The amount of time that an Ethernet client must wait at the beginning of a transmission before copying data into the NIC buffer

3.3 A client must wait for a special frame before communicating. After the special frame is received, it is converted to a data frame and transmitted to its nearest downstream neighbor. What type of network is this client on?

    a. Token Ring

    b. Fibre Channel

    c. Frame Relay

    d. Ethernet

3.4 Which of the following does the Active Monitor perform? (Choose all that apply.)

    a. Removes lost or unclaimed tokens

    b. Resets the ring after each successful transmission

    c. Sets the master clock signal for the ring

    d. Identifies all neighbors through a negotiation process

3.5 Ethernet uses _____ as its access methodology.

    a. token passing

    b. packet passing

    c. CSMA/CA

    d. CSMA/CD

3.6 Which three topologies are valid in a Fibre Channel configuration? (Choose all that apply.)

    a. Arbitrated loop

    b. Full mesh

    c. Fabric

    d. Point-to-point

    e. Arbitrated point

3.7 Data Link Connection Identifiers are used with which of the following technologies?

    a. SMDS

    b. SONET

    c. Frame Relay

    d. HDLC

    e. LLC

3.8 IEEE 802.2 defines which of the following?

    a. LLC Type 1 connection-oriented acknowledged data

    b. LLC Type 1 connectionless unacknowledged data

    c. LLC Type 2 connectionless acknowledged data

    d. LLC Type 2 connection-oriented unacknowledged data

    e. LLC Type 3 connection-oriented acknowledged data

3.9 Which WAN technology is circuit switched?

    a. Frame Relay

    b. ISDN

    c. SMDS

    d. HDLC

3.10 _____ is a three-layer protocol that functions at the Physical and Data Link layers of the OSI model and produces a uniform 53-octet cell when transmitting data.

    a. SMDS

    b. Frame Relay

    c. LLC

    d. SONET

    e. HDLC

    f. SDLC

3.11 When deploying ISDN BRI, it is often annotated as 2B+D. What does the annotation represent?

    a. Two data channels at 64 Kbps with one control channel at 16 Kbps

    b. Two data channels at 128 Kbps with one control channel at 16 Kbps

c. Two control channels at 64 Kbps with one data channel at 16 Kbps

d. Two control channels at 64 Kbps with one data channel at 64 Kbps

3.12 What is the total data rate of an E1?

a. 64 Kbps

b. 1.5.44 Mbps

c. 2.048 Mbps

d. 51.84 Mbps

3.13 LCP as a subfunction of the Point-to-Point protocol manages which of the following? (Choose all that apply.)

a. Link compression

b. Link encryption

c. Authentication encryption

d. Network layer addressing

e. Network layer protocol configuration

f. Link termination

3.14 Dual-attached stations and dual-attached concentrators are found on which of the following networks?

a. Fiber-optic

b. Ethernet

c. Token Ring

d. Frame Relay

e. SONET

f. FDDI

3.15 Which of the following frame types are 802.3 standard? (Choose all that apply.)

a. Ethernet II

b. 802.3 with an 802.2 LLC header

c. 802.3 with SNAP

d. 802.3 raw

3.16 IEEE 802.11 specifies the connectivity standard for which type of network?

    a. Ethernet

    b. Wireless

    c. Token Ring

    d. MAN

3.17 Wireless technologies offer which of the following?

    a. Low-cost, low-speed solutions for WAN connectivity over long distances

    b. High-cost, high-speed solutions for WAN connectivity over long distances

    c. One-time cost, high-speed solutions for LAN/MAN connectivity with distances under 30 miles

    d. One-time cost, low-speed solutions for LAN/MAN connectivity with distances under 30 miles

3.18 Which of the following is primarily a built-in wireless networking technology?

    a. Microwave

    b. RF

    c. Bluetooth

    d. Laser

3.19 What frequency range is associated with 802.11b?

    a. 2.4 GHz

    b. 2.4 MHz

    c. 5.0 GHz

    d. 5.0 Mhz

3.20 Wireless MANs often require _____ between transmission points.

    a. ad hoc

    b. infrared

     c. SWAP

     d. line of sight (LOS)

3.21 SWAP is a new protocol that allows _____.

     a. MAN wireless networks to properly connect

     b. home RF networks to share the 2.4 GHz frequency range with other devices

     c. home RF networks to share the 5.0 MHz frequency range with other devices

     d. home RF networks to share the 2.4 MHz frequency range with other devices

     e. MAN wireless networks the ability to share the 2.4 GHz frequency range

3.22 You have been asked to purchase a WAN technology that will allow your company to aggregate multiple DS1 and DS3 lines together back to the corporate offices. The DS1 and DS3 configurations vary widely among your regional offices. Which of the following WAN technologies would best serve your current requirements?

     a. SMDS

     b. HDLC

     c. Frame Relay

     d. PPP

     e. SONET

3.23 Which of the following infrastructure protocols has the highest encryption strength when used as a VPN solution?

     a. PPP

     b. L2TP

     c. PPTP

     d. LLC

3.24 How long is a Data Link layer destination address?

     a. 36 bits

     b. 40 bits

c. 6 bytes

d. 12 bytes

3.25 What IEEE specification created the LLC protocol layer?

a. 802.2

b. 802.3

c. 802.4

d. 802.5

e. 802.6

f. 802.11

3.10 Challenge Exercises

Challenge Exercise 3.1

In this exercise, you research ISDN on the World Wide Web. You need a computer with a Web browser and Internet access. The Web site that you will visit is the Cisco Web site.

1. In your Web browser, enter the following address:
   http://www.cisco.com/univercd/cc/td/doc/cisintwk/ito_doc/isdn.htm

2. Read the description of ISDN.

3. Write a two- or three-paragraph summary of the functional components of ISDN and its framing characteristics.

Challenge Exercise 3.2

In this exercise, you research wireless LAN technologies and associated security issues on the World Wide Web. You need a computer with a Web browser and Internet access. The Web site that you will visit is the WLAN Web site.

1. In your Web browser, enter the following address:
   http://www.wlana.org/learn/security.htm

2. Read the white papers on wireless LAN security, such as those listed under "Introduction to Wireless LAN Security" and "Basic Wireless LAN Security."

3. Write a two- or three-paragraph summary outlining the major security issues associated with implementing wireless LANs.

Challenge Exercise 3.3

In this exercise, you research the characteristics of metropolitan area networks. You need a computer with a Web browser and Internet access. You will visit the Institute of Electrical and Electronic Engineers Web site.

1. In your Web browser, visit the following Web sites:

   http://grouper.ieee.org/groups/802/16/sysreq/contributions/80216sc -99_02.pdf

   http://standards.ieee.org/getieee802/download/802-2001.pdf

2. Read the IEEE standards.

3. Write a two- or three-paragraph summary outlining the characteristics of MAN technologies.

3.11   Challenge Scenarios

Challenge Scenario 3.1

Top Peak is a small, specialty mountain bike company. The company specializes in custom-built mountain bikes for racing. Top Peak has a small plant in Colorado Springs, Colorado, with four buildings. In addition, it has seven retail stores in Denver, Boulder, Los Angeles, Seattle, Portland, San Francisco, and Phoenix.

Top Peak has a total of 200 computers located throughout the company. None of the computers is currently networked. Top Peak management has asked you to plan the deployment of LAN and WAN technologies so that all of their stores and buildings are connected and capable of network communications. They would like a solution that uses current technologies, is inexpensive, and is easy to maintain. What would you recommend for Top Peak?

Challenge Scenario 3.2

The Gray Seagull is a bed-and-breakfast located in a coastal resort town in the United States. The owners would like to offer Internet access for their guests, as well as to deploy a LAN for their own use. The building is in the National Register of Historic Places and cannot be altered in appearance or structure. You have been asked to present a fast and easy solution that will not require altering the building in any way. What LAN/WAN solution would be most appropriate for the Gray Seagull?

Challenge Scenario 3.3

An executive at a local marketing firm has called and asked you to deploy a network for his corporate office. He has done a small amount of research on LAN technologies but would like you to explain the pros and cons of Ethernet and Token Ring, and then make a recommendation on which technology to deploy. He wants to use current technology, and the network has to be upgradeable in the future. How would you present the differences between Ethernet and Token Ring, and which technology would you recommend?

Challenge Scenario 3.4

You are the CIO of a large office building management firm. Your company manages office buildings worldwide. You have been asked by the board of directors to research the possibility of combining the current data network with the voice and video conferencing networks. You have five sites that need to be consolidated, and the timeline for a return on investment is five years. The following table outlines the current cost of the networks:

Current Technology in Use	Current Costs for All Five Sites
Video conferencing	$250,000/year
Telephone	$150,000/year
WAN connectivity	$150,000/year

In addition to the current annual costs for the technology, an additional $1.5 million per year is spent on support staff.

To support the combination of the networks, an additional $20,000 per month must be spent on the WAN connections. A one-time charge of $900,000 for the purchase of new equipment will be amortized over a 5-year period. After the migration to a single network structure, the video and telephone networks will be dismantled, and the firm will save $6,000 per month in support staff salaries.

Given the current and proposed costs, would you recommend a combined network? Besides money, what other benefits might there be to having a single network configuration for video, voice, and data?

CHAPTER 4

Managing Multiple Access

After reading this chapter you will be able to:

- Understand network design types
- Recognize what to consider to avoid implementation issues
- Describe types of centralized access
- Describe different methods of distributed access
- Comprehend how hardware addressing works

In previous chapters, we have looked at how data gets from one place to the next and the different network technologies that are available. Communication originally was set up for human-to-human contact, not computer-to-computer. In Chapter 1, we discussed time division multiplexing (TDM) and frequency division multiplexing (FDM), which is good for voice communication, but neither is appropriate for data traffic.

In real life, when someone is speaking, you can usually hear that person clearly. What happens when you walk into a room in which many people are speaking? It can be difficult to understand any one person because all of the voices mix. A network operates the same way. It consists of many devices, each sending data simultaneously. There has to be some way for data traffic to flow efficiently, without crashing into one another, thus being destroyed or lost. In this chapter, we will explore those avenues by discussing design and implementation issues. We will find ways to maximize the number of messages exchanged per second while minimizing the time spent waiting to communicate. We will then move on to learn about centralized and distributed methods of access, how they work, and what their advantages and disadvantages are. Finally, we will cover how and why hardware uses addresses.

4.1   Design Issues

With many devices running on a network, they must be managed properly to communicate at the same time. **Multiple access** allows more than one device to communicate simultaneously. As technology advances, this is a consistent issue. Several types of multiple access links are available, such as point-to-point, broadcast, and switched. In Chapter 3, you learned about these different types of networks. None of these is immune to this type of issue; in fact, there are multiple access problems in wired local area networks (LANs), wireless local area networks (WLANs), packet radios, cellular telephones, and satellite communications.

A LAN is composed of devices that are linked together by means of some type of cabling, as discussed in Chapters 2 and 3. A wireless network is made of devices with wireless adapters communicating with each other using radio waves. These wireless devices are called nodes. The signal transmitted can be received only within a certain distance from the sender. A

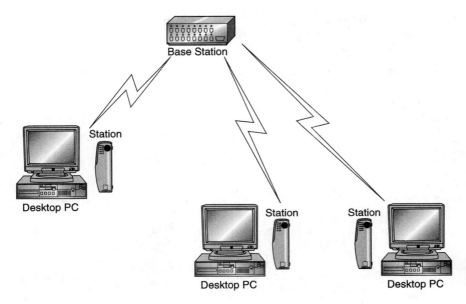

Figure 4.1
Wireless LAN

base station (BS), or wireless access point (WAP), is a special fixed node on the network located in a central location. See Figure 4.1 for an example.

 TIP

Wireless networks differ from wired networks in the **duplexing** mechanism and the network architecture used.

Satellite technology is based on an overhead wireless repeater station that provides a microwave communication link between two geographically remote sites. Each satellite is equipped with various transponders consisting of a transceiver and an antenna tuned to a certain part of the allocated spectrum. The incoming signal is amplified and then rebroadcast on a different frequency. In the last few decades, the use of satellites in packet data transmission has been on the rise. They are typically used on WAN networks where they provide backbone links to geographically dispersed LANs and metropolitan area networks (MANs). Satellite communication channels typically have long transmission delays. Figure 4.2 demonstrates how satellites communicate. Satellite links can operate in different frequency bands and use separate carrier frequencies for the uplink and downlink.

When designing a way for network devices to communicate, you must first choose a base technology. This will isolate traffic from different stations.

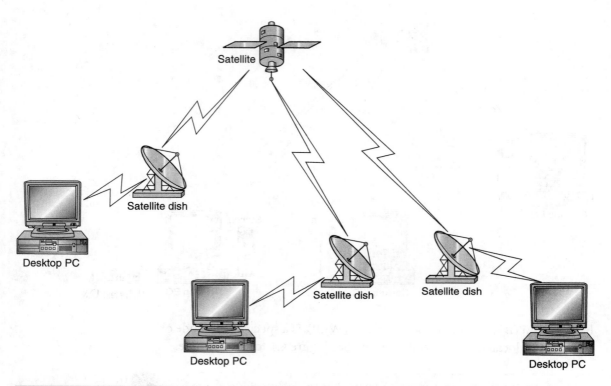

Figure 4.2
Satellite communications

Then you can decide whether to use a time domain or a frequency domain. Next, plan and choose how to allocate a limited number of transmission resources to many contending users. To do this, several fundamental questions must be answered, including:

- Should one device manage the communications?
- Should the management responsibilities be shared among the devices?
- Do we want to send steady streams of data?
- Do we want to limit the amount of data sent at one time?

Because of these choices, several basic schemes have been designed to handle communication media to facilitate multiple access. What if a traffic cop is used to direct traffic? There needs to be something directing the traffic so that network data flows in an orderly fashion. This describes a centralized design. Sounds good, but what if something happens to the traffic cop? In a distributed design, a device can communicate only if no other device is communicating. However, if two devices are waiting for one to finish communicating and then both begin sending data packets at the same time, a collision will occur. You see the dilemma: We cannot have collisions, a central point of failure, or a system that is dependent on one device to control the communication. Besides centralized and distributed designs, design methods exist for how data flows and is sent, such as in streams or bursts of packets. We will discuss all these design methods in the following two sections.

4.1.1 Distributed versus Centralized

In Chapter 1, we explained multiplexing. Multiplexing is about sharing a communications line. It combines several connections into one larger channel. The duplexing method of communication refers to how the data transmission and reception channels are multiplexed. They can be multiplexed in either different time slots or different frequency channels. **Time division duplex (TDD)** refers to multiplexing of the transmission in different time periods but in the same frequency band. **Frequency division duplex (FDD)** uses different frequency bands for uplink and downlink. With FDD, it is possible for the node to transmit and receive data at the same time because different frequency bands are used.

NOTE

These methods of duplexing are usually combined with other technology types. For example, TDD is combined with frequency division multiple access (FDMA) for use in second-generation cordless phones, and FDD is combined with either time division multiple access (TDMA) or frequency division multiple access (FDMA) in digital cellular phones. We discuss TDMA and FDMA in the "Implementation Issues" section that follows.

Based on the network architecture, networks can be divided logically into two classes: distributed and centralized. In a centralized design, there is a central node or a manager, which keeps the important information and makes all decisions. Because this node is the central point, if it fails, all communication stops. Usually the controlling device is called the master and the others are slaves. Master to slave is considered downlink communication. Slave to master is considered uplink communication. An example of this slave is the use of a hub to network several machines. On the hub is a button or port called Uplink. This is used to send communication from the devices connected to the hub to the main server or router.

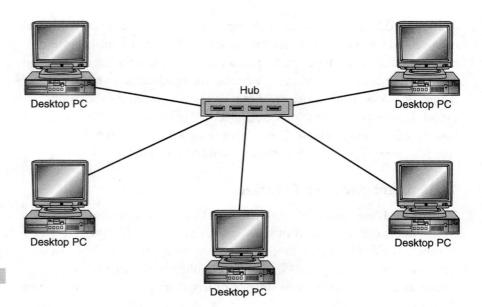

Figure 4.3
Centralized network

Centralized wireless networks are extensions to wired networks, with wireless in the last section of the network. These networks have a BS that interfaces between the wireless and wired networks. The transmissions from the BS to wireless nodes (downlink) are broadcast and can be heard by all the devices on the network. The uplink from the wireless devices to the BS is shared by all the nodes, making it a multiple access channel. The system architecture of a centralized network is shown in Figure 4.3. A centralized network can operate both in TDD mode and FDD mode.

Centralized solutions often include recovery mechanisms. In these cases, although there is still a central decision maker, if it fails, procedures are in place for a new master to be elected. If no recovery method exists, the failure of the master causes the entire network to fail.

In a distributed design, there is no central node or manager. All nodes have approximately the same kinds and amounts of information. They are peers and all nodes are equal. Decisions are made using the information that is local to them, they all spend about the same amount of resources in arriving at a decision, and they all share responsibility for the final decision. If one node fails, it does not cause the whole system to fail.

Distributed wireless networks are wireless devices communicating with one another without any predefined infrastructure in place. These types of

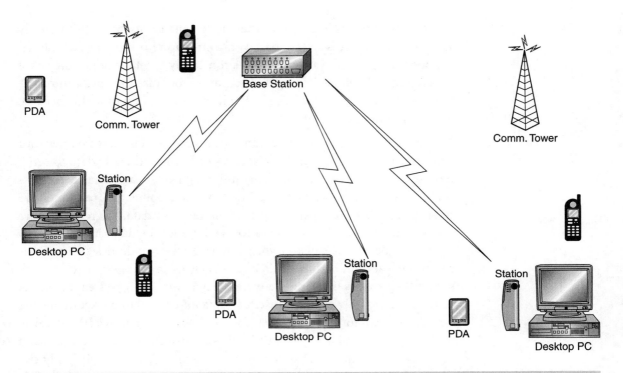

Figure 4.4

Distributed network

networks can also be referred to as ad hoc networks. A typical distributed network is illustrated in Figure 4.4.

Wireless terminals have a wireless interface, whether it be radio frequency (RF) or infrared (IR), and exchange information between one another in a distributed manner. As mentioned previously, this type of network has no central administration. The network will not be affected when one of the nodes goes down or is relocated. In a distributed network, all data transmission and reception has to be in the same frequency band because there are no special nodes to translate the transmission from one frequency band to another. Therefore, all wireless ad hoc networks operate in TDD mode.

4.1.2 Circuit Mode and Packet Mode

Circuit mode is used to send steady streams of data at a continuous bit rate. It provides a physical, dedicated path called a time slot for the data. Because this time slot is dedicated, no other node can use its path. With steady streams, the resources are not based on contention for every packet; rather, the nodes hold on to system resources constantly, whether or not they have data to send. Circuit switching is synchronous because the node's information is transmitted in a specific time slot, and only in that time slot, because it is a continuous bit rate.

A variable bit-rate method of communication provides increased network efficiency by allocating system resources only when there is data to send. Resources are shared because they are assigned on an as-needed, first-come, first-serve basis. When a burst of data comes in, resources are assigned for that burst. At the end of the burst of data, the resources are released for the next burst of data to use. Because the data can arrive anytime, this method is called asynchronous. Packet mode design—such as common packet channel (CPCH), which is a wireless packet data method—provides increased network efficiency by giving system resources to system users only when the user has data to send. With packet mode, the nodes contend for every packet to avoid wasting bandwidth. Because packet mode is a shared system, it allows network media to serve many more users with the same system resources than they could with only circuit mode.

4.2   Implementation Issues

After the design considerations are in place, implementation issues must be addressed. The first is spectrum scarcity. Radio spectrum is hard to come by because only a few frequencies are available for long-distance communication. When designing and implementing communications, it is imperative that multiple access schemes do not waste bandwidth. The next issue is the properties of radio links. In wireless systems, it is difficult to receive data when the transmitter is sending data because when a node is transmitting data, a large fraction of the signal energy leaks into the receive path. This is known as **self-interference**. The leaked signal typically has much more power than the received signal, making it impossible to detect a received signal while transmitting data. Therefore, collision detection is not possible while sending data, so Ethernet-like protocols cannot be used. We discuss collision detection in the "Distributed Access" section later in this chapter.

Radio links are error prone, and are susceptible to fading and multipath interference. Radio signals propagate according to reflection, diffraction, and scattering. The signal received by a node is a time-shifted and attenuated version of the transmitted signal.

As a consequence of the time-varying channel and varying signal strength, errors are more likely in wireless transmissions. Upon data collision, the station with more power overpowers the others, so lower-powered stations may never get a chance to be heard. With this in mind, due to spectrum scarcity, performance needs to be taken into consideration. Because radio spectrum is a limited resource shared by all users, a method must be devised to divide up the bandwidth among as many users as possible. There also has to be a method devised for communication that can help control errors, fading, and interference.

4.2.1   Performance Considerations

Before we talk about performance, let's look at a parameter that we will use throughout this chapter. The parameter is a, where $a = D/T$, D is the propagation delay, and T is the time taken to transmit. This formula gives us the number of packets sent before the farthest station receives the first bit. See Figure 4.5 for an illustration. In communications, any delay between the time a signal enters the transmission channel and the time it is received can be critical. The propagation delay is relatively small across a LAN, but can become considerable in satellite communications, in which the signal must travel from one earth station to the satellite and back to earth again. Unusually long propagation delays may require the use of specialized hardware to ensure that the link is not broken prematurely.

We will look at four factors:

- **Normalized throughput:** In normalized throughput, a fraction of the link capacity is used to carry nonretransmitted packets. For example, if we send 5000 packets/second with no collisions, our throughput would be 5000 packets/second. This is unrealistic. With a specific design and workload, 1250 packets/second equals an output of .25. This is called the goodput. In actuality, most protocols have goodputs between 0.1 and 0.95.

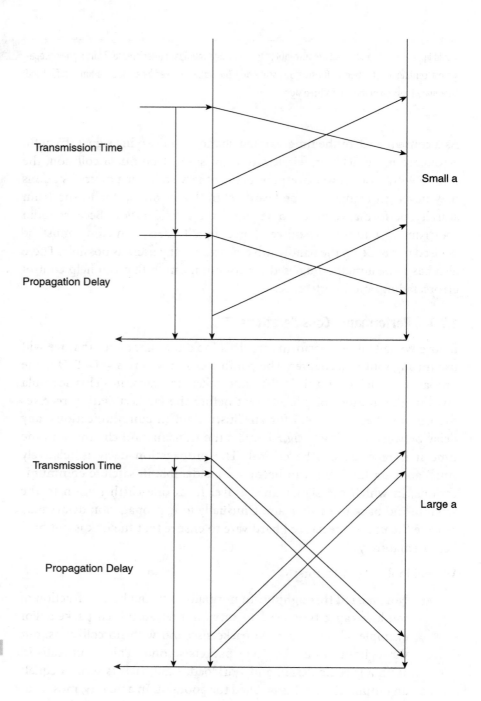

Figure 4.5
The parameter a

- **Mean delay:** Mean delay is the amount of time a node has to wait before it successfully transmits a packet. This depends on the type of medium as well as the size of the packet.

- **Stability:** When a load becomes heavy and the majority of time is spent on resolving contentions, the process becomes unstable. With a stable algorithm, throughput stays the same and is not affected by the load. Stability is also a factor when an infinite number of nodes share a link. When overload is detected, stability can be achieved by reducing load.

- **Fairness:** Each contending node should receive an equal share of the bandwidth and an equal chance to send data.

4.2.2 Base Technologies

As early analog cellular systems started to become overcrowded, new methods of communication had to be developed. Because cellular systems are fixed in channel capacity with a limited number of frequencies available, a digital solution could increase the capacity of the channel. Base technologies isolate data from different sources. A base technology uses a line driver to introduce voltage shifts in digital signals onto a channel. The channel acts as a transport mechanism for the digital voltage pulses as they travel through the channel. In general, only one communication channel is available at any given time.

The wireless industry began to explore converting the existing analog network to digital as a means of improving capacity back in the late 1980s. In 1982, the Conference of European Posts and Telegraphs (CEPT) formed a study group called the Groupe Spécial Mobile (GSM) to study and develop a European public land mobile system. Although standardized in Europe, GSM is not specifically a European standard. GSM systems exist worldwide, and the acronym GSM now stands for Global System for Mobile Communications. Because development was taking place in the United States as well, the Cellular Telecommunications Industry Association (CTIA) decided to let carriers make their own technology selection.

Since then, several technologies have emerged. Currently there are three basic choices: frequency division multiple access, time division multiple access, and code division multiple access.

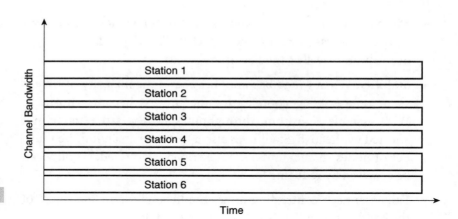

Figure 4.6

FDMA

4.2.3   Frequency Division Multiple Access (FDMA)

Frequency division multiple access (FDMA) is the oldest of the three main methods for multiple radio transmissions to share the radio spectrum. FDMA works by dividing the frequency spectrum allocated for wireless cellular telephone communication into channels of equal bandwidth. Each of these channels can carry voice or digital data. FDMA is a basic technology used by analog systems such as advanced mobile phone service (AMPS), total access communication system (TACS), and the narrowband analog mobile phone service (NAMPS). With FDMA, each channel can be assigned to only one user at a time, and other users cannot access that channel until the call is finished or transferred to another channel. Figure 4.6 demonstrates this concept.

NOTE

TDMA and CDMA can be used in combination with FDMA; in other words, a given frequency channel may be used for either TDMA or FDMA regardless of signals being transmitted on other frequency channels.

For example, digital-advanced mobile phone service (D-AMPS) uses FDMA but adds TDMA to get three channels for each FDMA channel, tripling the number of calls that can be handled on a channel. Ultra-wideband (UWB) is an exception, as it uses essentially all of the usable radio spectrum in one location. We will talk about UWB after we discuss TDMA and CDMA.

The following is a recap of FDMA:

- Simplest and best suited for analog links

- Channel spectrum is divided into frequency bands
- Each station has its own assigned, fixed-frequency band
- Number of frequencies is limited
- Unused transmission time in frequency bands stays idle
- Can be combined with other methods

Although technically FDMA is simple to implement, it wastes bandwidth because the channel is assigned to a single station whether or not that station has data to send, and it cannot handle any alternate forms of data, only voice.

FDMA is the method of choice for allowing in-home networking systems and last-mile access systems to coexist because it divides the frequency spectrum between isolated systems to eliminate contention. FDMA is used in the TACS. D-AMPS also uses FDMA but adds TDMA to get three channels for each FDMA channel, tripling the number of calls that can be handled on a channel. Speaking of TDMA, it's time to learn more about it.

4.2.4   Time Division Multiple Access (TDMA)

Time division multiple access (TDMA) is a digital transmission technology that allows users to access a single RF channel without interference by dividing the channel into time slots for each user. Basically, TDMA is analog's FDMA with a built-in, timesharing component. The access method used in TDMA is multiplexing. This allows three users to share one 30 KHz carrier frequency. The current TDMA standard for cellular divides a single channel into six time slots, with each signal using two slots, providing a 3-to-1 gain in capacity over AMPS. Figure 4.7 shows us the concept behind TDMA.

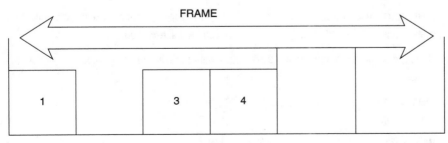

1, 3, and 4 have data
packets to send. Slots 2,
5, and 6 are idle.

Figure 4.7

TDMA

TDMA relies upon a digitized audio signal. (We discussed digitization in Chapter 1.) When the signal has been digitized, it is divided into a number of milliseconds-long packets. TDMA allocates a single-frequency channel for a short time and then moves to another channel. The digital samples from a single transmitter occupy different time slots in several bands at the same time. The basic unit of time in the TDMA scheme is called a burst period, which lasts 15/26 ms. Eight burst periods are grouped into a TDMA frame, which in turn forms the base unit for a logical channels. One physical channel is one burst period per TDMA frame.

The number and position of the corresponding burst periods define channels. Channels can be divided into dedicated channels, which are allocated to a mobile station and common channels. A traffic channel (TCH) is used to carry speech and data traffic. Traffic channels are defined using a group of 26 TDMA frames. The length of this multiframe is 120 ms, which is how the length of a burst period is defined. Out of the 26 frames, 24 are used for traffic, 1 is used for the Slow Associated Control Channel (SACCH), and 1 is currently unused. Uplink and downlink traffic channels are separated in time by three burst periods. This simplifies the process so that the mobile station does not have to transmit and receive simultaneously.

NOTE The TDMA system is designed for use in a wide range of environments and situations, and supports a variety of services for the end user, such as voice, data, fax, short message services, and broadcast messages. Table 4.1 lists the pros and cons of using TDMA.

TABLE 4.1   TDMA Pros and Cons

Pros	Cons
All users transmit data on the same frequency, but at different times.	Time synchronization is needed, causing additional overhead.
Users can be given different amounts of bandwidth.	Multipath interference is greater.
Idle time can be used to determine best base station.	N/A
When not transmitting, can be powered off.	N/A

TDMA is a well-proven method used in commercial operation in many of today's systems. TDMA is also the access technique used both in the European digital standard, GSM, and in the Japanese digital standard, personal digital cellular (PDC).

4.2.5   Code Division Multiple Access (CDMA)

The last of the three wireless telephone transmission technologies, **code division multiple access (CDMA)**, is a military technology first used during World War II to outwit German attempts at jamming transmissions. The English allies decided to transmit over several frequencies, instead of just one, making it difficult for the Germans to pick up the complete signal. Originally known as IS-95, this type of transmission takes an entirely different approach than TDMA. After the data is digitized, it is spread out over the entire bandwidth available. Called spread-spectrum technology, it allows multiple frequencies to be used simultaneously. CDMA combines spread-spectrum technology with analog-to-digital conversion. Audio input is first digitized into binary elements. The frequency of the transmitted signal is then made to vary so that every packet it sends is sent with a unique frequency code. This is known as pseudo-random code sequencing. The data is then scattered across the frequency band in a random pattern. A CDMA receiver responds only to that code, and can pick out and demodulate the associated signal. There are well over a trillion possible frequency-sequencing codes, enhancing privacy and making cloning difficult. Spreading the data across the frequency spectrum makes the signal resistant to noise, interference, and snooping. Table 4.2 lists the pros and cons of CDMA.

TABLE 4.2   CDMA Pros and Cons

Pros	Cons
Difficult to eavesdrop on	Complex implementation
Immune from narrowband noise	Needs a large contiguous frequency band
Stations don't need to be synchronized	Problems installing in the field
No limit on capacity of a cell	N/A
All frequencies can be used by all cells	N/A

TABLE 4.3   Wireless Telecommunications Characteristics

Standard	Technology Type	Multiple Access Method	Duplex Method
AMPS	Analog cellular	FDMA	FDD
TACS	Analog cellular	FDMA	FDD
NMT (Nordic Mobile Telephone)	Analog cellular	FDMA	FDD
IS-54/I36 (North American Digital Cellular)	Digital cellular	TDMA/FDMA	FDD
IS-95 (North American Digital Cellular)	Digital cellular	CDMA/FDMA	FDD
GSM (Global System for Mobile) Communications	Digital cellular	TDMA/FDMA	FDD
IEEE 802.11 Wireless LAN	WAN/LAN	CSMA	TDD

The CDMA channel is 1.23 MHz wide. CDMA networks use a technique called soft handoff, which reduces signal breakup as a handset passes from one cell to another. The combination of digital and spread-spectrum modes supports many more signals per unit bandwidth than analog modes. CDMA is also compatible with other cellular technologies, thus allowing for cellular roaming. CDMA is characterized by high capacity and small cell radius. This technology is used in ultra-high-frequency cellular telephone systems in the 800 MHz and 1.9 GHz bands, WLANs, and cable modems.

Table 4.3 shows some of the characteristics of the various wireless telecommunication standards.

TIP There are now different variations, but the original CDMA is known as cdmaOne. Still common in cellular telephones, cdmaOne offers a transmission speed of up to 14.4 Kbps in its single channel form and up to 115 Kbps in an eight-channel form.

Newer technologies such as cdma2000 and wideband CDMA deliver data many times faster then cdmaOne. Also enhancing today's data capabilities is the 1XRTT CDMA standard. 1XRTT enables 144-Kbps packet data in a mobile environment while supporting all channel sizes. It also provides circuit and packet data rates up to 2 Mbps, incorporates advanced multimedia capabilities, and includes a framework for advanced 3G voice services such as voice-over packet and circuit data. It works on both the forward and reverse links and helps extend battery life for handsets. CDMA is constantly evolving; third-generation CDMA technology, including Multi-Carrier (cdma2000, 1×MC, and HDR in 1.25 MHz bandwidth and 3×MC in 5 MHz bandwidth) along with Direct Spread (WCDMA in 5 MHz bandwidth) are now in use. Another developing technology is ultra-wideband (UWB). If this technology is successful, eventually we may see tiny routers embedded in all electronic devices. Before we get too far into UWB, let's back up and discuss how CDMA works. We already know that it combines spread-spectrum technology with analog-to-digital conversion whereby audio input is first digitized into binary elements. The frequency of the transmitted signal is then made to vary so that every packet it sends is sent with a unique frequency code. How does this happen? All users share the same frequency but each has its own code or chipping sequence to encode data. It is this chipping sequence that we will explore more closely.

The encoded signal is the original data times the chipping sequence. For example, in Figure 4.8 we can see the data bits converted to binary in slot 1 = 1; therefore, when it is multiplied by the code or chipping sequence, it produces the output shown.

In newer technologies such as cdma2000 and WCDMA, there is often debate about the system chip rate used. WCDMA uses a chip rate value of 4.096 Mbps, while cdma2000 uses 3.6864 Mbps. Proponents of WCDMA tend to believe the higher rate has more power, but how the technology will be deployed and all factors affecting system performance should be considered. The usable spectrum along with chip rate affects capacity. Greater overall capacity is achieved with 10, 15, and 20 MHz bands, respectively. One of the main factors in determining the capacity of a CDMA system is the ratio of energy per information bit to noise power spectrum density (Eb/No). The required Eb/No value depends on such factors as frame structure, coding and modulation characteristics, and diversity techniques. The small difference in chip rate between 3.6864 Mbps and 4.096 Mbps has very little impact on the Eb/No requirement. System design factors such as channel structure, power control mechanisms, handoff efficiency, and base station synchronization have a much greater impact on system capacity than chip rate. Lastly, there are negative effects on spectrum use and power emissions when using higher value chip rates.

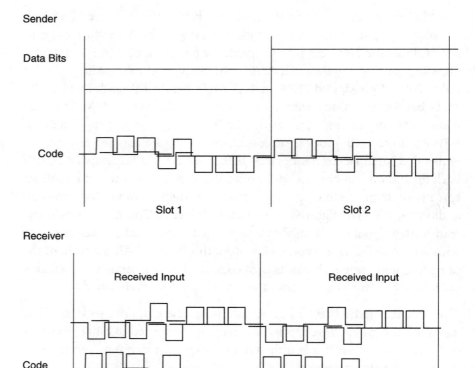

Figure 4.8
CDMA chipping

All major wireless technologies use guard bands to separate their signal spectrum from those of services in adjacent bands. Sometimes, due to the higher power emissions, the system cannot meet the FCC out-of-band requirements, so the capacity gain will not be realizable in markets that need to consider adjacent channel interference or FCC power emission requirements.

Returning to UWB, the target speed is 100-Mbps real throughput. In addition to speed, it could extend battery life to years instead of hours. UWB abandons the concept of carrier waves. Instead, it broadcasts on many frequencies simultaneously, sending its signal across a vast bandwidth. It is similar to CDMA, but UWB spreads the signal over a wider band and potentially over the entire radio spectrum. This, of course, would be of concern because unrestricted UWB transmissions could interfere with cur-

TABLE 4.4   Bandwidth Spectrum of Wireless Technologies

Type	Bandwidth Used	Regulations
AMPS or D-AMPS	.03 MHz	Licensed spectrum
GSM	.2 MHz	Licensed spectrum
IS-54 CDMA	1.25 MHz	Licensed spectrum
Wideband CDMA	5 MHz	Licensed spectrum
IEEE 802.11a or 802.11b	25 MHz	Confined to ISM band
UWB	75 MHz	Power restricted

rent radio spectrum users, affecting the bandwidth of existing networks. The FCC has initially restricted UWB to a bandwidth of 75 GHz, which is much broader than the spectrum allowed to all other systems combined. See Table 4.4 for a list of the allocated bandwidths of wireless technologies.

UWB offers higher data rates and lower energy consumption because of the way it generates the signal. Instead of using modulation schemes and antennas, it emits staccato pulses of white noise directly from a chip. The pulses are much shorter that the gap between them, so the system is idle most of the time. This could enable a device to run for months between battery charges. Research is being done into eliminating the battery altogether and using energy scavenging, as in self-winding watches.

There is another cellular architecture for radio access called **capture-division packetized access (CDPA)**. This is an alternative to systems based on bandwidth subdivision methods such as TDMA, FDMA, and CDMA. In CDPA there is no subdivision of bandwidth. All cells and terminals use a single-frequency channel while transmitting packets on a slotted channel. Parallel transmission in the different cells is achieved through a capture capability, which is the ability of a receiver to detect a signal even in the presence of other signals, called interferers. Capture is achieved if the ratio between the power of the signal and the power of interference is greater than a certain threshold, called capture ratio.

A dynamic polling mechanism called centralized PRMA (C-PRMA) is managed by the base station and guarantees almost immediate retransmission of packets that are not captured. The base station acts as a central scheduler so that collisions among terminals in the same cells are avoided. In C-PRMA, the base station marks the time slots as available or reserved. A terminal is allowed to transmit only when polled. Reserved slots are scheduled by the base station according to a Scheduling Algorithm (SA).

Now that we have looked at implementation methods of technologies, it's time to discuss how devices access this technology. In the "Distributed versus Centralized" section earlier in this chapter, we discussed centralized design; we will next explore centralized access.

4.3   Centralized Access

Recall that in a centralized design, a central node or a manager keeps the important information and makes all decisions. Usually the controlling device is called the master and the other devices are referred to as slaves. Centralized access works pretty much the same way; one station is master and all the others are slaves. The slaves can transmit only when the master allows them to. This is a good fit in some situations such as a wireless LAN where only the base station can communicate with the wireless clients, or in cellular telephony where the base station is the only one capable of high transmit power. Centralized access is simple, and the master provides a single point of coordination. But the master is the single point of failure, and it needs a reelection protocol. Because all communication goes through the master, it is involved in every data transfer, which causes an added delay and thus slows the network.

Now we will explore several different methods of centralized control, including circuit-mode, polling or packet mode, and reservation based.

4.3.1   Circuit Mode

The way circuit-mode data transfer works is:

1. When a station wants to transmit data, it sends a message to the master.

2. The master allocates transmission resources to the slave.

3. The slave uses the allocated resources until it has completed the transmission.

Because this is an assigned resource allocation, there is no contention during the data transmission. Both TDMA and CDMA make provisions for

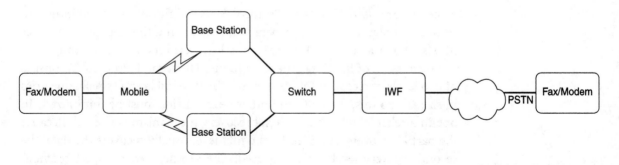

Figure 4.9
Pattern for cellular circuit-mode data

circuit-mode data transfers driven by a need to provide good support for fax transmissions on a cellular network. Figure 4.9 shows a pattern for cellular circuit-mode data transmission. This standard reflects an **interworking function (IWF)** to terminate the cellular circuit data, and to connect to a modem or fax over a wired network.

IWFs provide the necessary protocol conversions so that wireless data users can continue to access existing wired applications without requiring modifications to the applications. The conversion between the air interface and wired applications takes place in the radio system or wired network, as demonstrated in Figure 4.9. For example, for wireless data users to access modems on the PSTN, conversion has to occur between the digital data on the air interface and the voiceband data on the remote applications.

NOTE

The Interworking Control Protocol (ICP) provides reliable transfer of data between a radio system and the interworking function. By making this protocol generic, multiple radio systems can interface with the network using a common set of protocols over different transmission facilities.

All of the digital cellular systems, such as GSM communications and IS-95, support direct access to digital channels using circuit-switched data connections. This allows them the capability of offering a messaging service similar to those provided by today's paging services.

Radio link protocols for circuit-mode data transmissions on cellular systems are based on the premise that the error-prone link must be reliable. For circuit-mode data recovery to work over CDMA and TDMA, two radio link protocols are used. The first, Protocol S, uses a flexible segmentation and recovery sublayer to package data frames into multiplexed physical layer bursts. When a radio link bursts or is lost, recovery is done through the retransmission of the Data Link layer frame. The second, Protocol T, consists of two levels of recovery. In this method, the Physical layer is small and varies in size. To do this, the CRC and other header fields must be minimized. To obtain a reliable link, an additional recovery mechanism is needed. Because the partial recovery provided by the first level usually recovers the data, the second recovery level is seldom used. The second recovery level provides additional CRC and header fields that are missing from the first level of recovery. Protocol T has been standardized for CDMA circuit-mode data as IS-99. When the two protocols are compared, the complexity of the two-level recovery system can obtain higher throughput because of the reduced retransmission data unit size. This type of centralized access is used primarily in cellular home systems that utilize EAMPS: (Extended Advanced Mobile Phone System) FDMA, GSM/IS-54:TDMA, and IS-95:CDMA.

4.3.2   Polling or Packet Mode

In polling- or packet-mode access, a user's data stream is broken down into smaller segments, called **packets**. Each packet then has network control information added before it is transmitted through the network. The size of the packet varies. When a user has data to send, the packet is placed on the network. Once the packet transmission is complete, that resource becomes available for use by other nodes to transmit packets.

Polling is the process in which the master broadcasts a query to every node on the network asking each node in turn whether it has anything to communicate. The master then waits to receive a unique response from each node.

TIP

Polling continuously checks the nodes to find out what state they are in, usually to determine whether they are still connected or want to communicate. Polling can be thought of as a combination of broadcasting and gathering information from the nodes.

To ensure that only one message is transmitted at any time, the master either polls or selects each terminal connected to the line in a specific sequence. Each node is allocated a unique identifier with which the central computer communicates. The messages exchanged are either control or data. This type of polling, also known as roll-call polling, consists of the master simply sending a message to each terminal in turn, inquiring whether or not the terminal has anything to say. The poll control message is used to request that a specific terminal send any waiting data message it may have. If the polled node doesn't have data to send, it sends back a special poll reject message. The master then continues by polling the next node. It may take a long time to complete a cycle on a line with many nodes, even if most are idle most of the time, because each node in the network must be polled before it can send or receive a message. Usually the master polls all the nodes in round-robin fashion, but in certain circumstances some nodes may get more than one poll per cycle. On half-duplex lines, each poll requires two line turnarounds, one for the master to send and one for the node to send.

The poll protocol operation begins with the master sending an ENQ poll control message with the address of a polled node preceding the ENQ character. If the polled node has a message awaiting transmission, it responds by sending it. Upon receipt of the data, the master recalculates the parity check sequence. If there are no transmissions errors, it acknowledges the receipt by sending an acknowledgment (ACK) if the data is correct or a negative acknowledgment (NAK) if it has errors. This exchange may occur several times until the node is finished sending data. The node must then send an indication that it has completed its transmission and the connection is clear. It does this with an end-of-transmission (EOT) control message.

With recent advancements in Ethernet passive optical networks (EPON), a proposed protocol called Bandwidth Guarantee Polling is used to control the sharing of upstream channels. This protocol is based on roll-call polling in which the optical line terminal (OLT) polls the optical network units (ONUs). The ONUs are divided into two groups, one with bandwidth guarantees and one with non-bandwidth guarantees. The OLT maintains an Entry Table that keeps track of the sequence of polls. The OLT polls ONUs one by one in order of entry sequence in the Entry Table. If the entry is not allocated to a bandwidth-guaranteed ONU, it can be used to poll the non-bandwidth guarantee group. This type of design is intended to provide efficient network service to various kinds of ONUs that have diverse bandwidth requirements.

Multipoint communication uses cluster controllers. Each cluster controller is connected to its nearest neighbor rather than to the master. The master manages all transfers to and from the cluster controllers. The master selects and sends a data message to any of the controllers at any time using special select lines. This is called hub polling. With hub polling, the master first polls the controller farthest from it. If the controller has data, it sends it back to the master; otherwise it sends a nothing-to-send control message on another poll line to its nearest neighbor on the master side. When the next controller receives this message, if it has data it responds by adding its own data to the tail of the received message. The appended message is then forwarded to its downstream neighbor. The procedure continues with each controller adding its own response message as it passes the message toward the master. When the process is complete, the message is disassembled and the data is passed on for further processing. Unlike roll-call polling on half-duplex lines, it is not necessary to keep returning the transmission line just to discover that the terminal has nothing to say.

Polling is considered an inefficient method, especially if only a few stations are active. Because it is centrally controlled, a network will slow if the system has many terminals. The overhead for polling messages is high because all nodes have to be polled. This causes performance to suffer when the controllers on the link become overloaded.

Another process used is probing. With probing, the stations are numbered with consecutive logical addresses. This type of communication assumes that the node can listen both to its own address and to a set of multicast addresses. Instead of individually polling each node, the master does a binary search to locate the next active node.

4.3.3 Reservation Based

In the "Performance Considerations" section earlier in this chapter, we calculated a, which is equal to D/T, where D is the propagation delay and T is the time taken to transmit. This gives us the number of packets sent before the farthest station receives the first bit. When a is large, a distributed scheme for packet mode cannot be used because there are too many collisions. (We will discuss distributed access and data collisions in the next section.) Also, if it takes a long time for the data the reach the farthest station, polling would not be an option. So instead, the master coordinates access to links using reservations. The master assigns slots that are devoted to sending just these reservation messages. Sometimes for the sake of efficiency, these are smaller-than-regular data slots. When this occurs, the slots are known as minislots. The nodes either

contend for a minislot or they own one. When the nodes contend for the minislots, the master decides who will get access and then grants access to the link.
In this type of environment, packet collisions are limited only to minislots, so
the overhead on contention is reduced. This type of access is used mainly for
satellite links.

Although all these methods of access have good points, sometimes it just
isn't feasible to have one central control for all data communication. It is
important in communication media to have methods for multiple access.
In order to do this, distributed access was developed. We will now take a
look at the methods that compose this type of access.

4.4   Distributed Access

The premise behind distributed access is similar to that of a distributed
design: There is no central node or manager. All nodes have equal access.
Decisions are made using the information that is local to nodes. If one
node fails, it does not cause the network to fail. Compared to centralized
access, a distributed scheme is more reliable, or has lower message or propagation delays, and often allows higher network utilization but is more
complicated. Almost all distributed access methods are packet mode. Most
companies use the distributed access method.

With a distributed access scheme, a station starts transmission after it satisfies a set of network requirements by using a random access Media Access
Control (MAC) protocol that uniquely identifies each network node. These
protocols specify how to detect collisions and how to recover from them,
especially because during heavy transmission times, collisions may occur in
some systems. This is the preferred method of access for LANs, and many
WANs also use it.

There are several methods of distributed access, which we will cover next.
These include decentralized polling, carrier sense multiple access, busy
tone multiple access, multiple access collision avoidance, token passing,
and ALOHA.

4.4.1   Decentralized Polling

The principle behind decentralized polling is similar to centralized
polling except that there is no master to control the transmission and collection of packets. All stations must share a time base. The access time is

divided into slots, and then each station is assigned a slot that it uses for transmissions. This type of access is a reservation-based protocol, so mini-slots are used for reservations that all nodes see. After reservation slots are transmitted, the message transmissions are ordered by known priority. Because the time slots are assigned, if a node has nothing to send, the slot is wasted.

Decentralized probing, also called tree-based multiple access, is another method used and is similar to decentralized polling. In this method, the stations are all placed in subtrees of the root station. All stations in a sub-tree place their packets on the transmission medium, and when there is a collision, the root repeats the process until it is successful. This method works poorly in a network design where there is a large number of active stations or when all active stations are in the same subtree. This is because if two nodes with successive logical addresses have a packet to send, it may take many collisions before one of them is granted access.

4.4.2   Carrier Sense Multiple Access (CSMA)

Ethernet networks use **carrier sense multiple access (CSMA)** to improve performance and reduce traffic. When a node has data to transmit, it first listens on the cable by using a transceiver to check whether a signal is being transmitted by another node. This is done by monitoring the current flowing in the cable. Individual bits of data are sent using Manchester encoding by encoding them with a 10- or 100-Hz clock. Data is transmitted when there is no current present and the physical medium is idle. CSMA is a fundamental advance in access and performance because it checks whether the medium is active before sending a packet. In other words, it listens before it transmits. If the channel is sensed as idle, it transmits. If the channel is sensed as busy, it holds off the transmission until it can sense that the medium is idle. Unlike polling or probing a node, CSMA doesn't have to wait for a master or for its turn in a schedule. There are two types of CSMA:

1. **Persistent:** The transmission is immediately retried based on a probability (p) of when the transmission medium will become available.

2. **Nonpersistent:** The transmission is retried after random intervals.

An issue with persistent CSMA is that if two stations are waiting to transmit, they will send, as soon as each sense the medium is idle, causing a collision. So how do you solve the collision problem?

Before we discuss how the collision issue can be resolved, let's talk about how collisions occur. Earlier in this chapter, we discussed a—this gives us the number of packets sent before the farthest station receives the first bit. Due to the propagation delay, two nodes may not hear each other's transmissions. So, the role that distance and propagation delay play in collisions is important because these factors determine the probability of a collision. Based on this, it is safe to say that CSMA works best when a is small.

⚠ WARNING

When a collision occurs, the entire packet transmission time is wasted. The collision will corrupt the data being sent, which will subsequently be discarded by the receiver because a corrupted frame will not have a valid 32-bit CRC at the end.

Now that we know a little about collisions, let's go over what can be done to resolve this issue. Obviously, if a collision happens, we want to detect and resolve it. Earlier we mentioned persistent CSMA. In this model, the transmission is retried immediately based on a probability (p) of when the transmission medium will become available. This works to a certain extent, but remember that this is based on probability. It is hard to actually calculate the probability of when the medium will be available. If the probability is small but a large probability is calculated, then time is wasted. In the opposite case, if the probability is large but a small one is calculated, then more collisions occur. The other method that can be used to solve collision issues is exponential backoff. In this method, when a collision occurs, a timeout is randomly chosen from a doubled range and the backoff range adapts to the number of contending stations. There is no need to calculate probability. CSMA/CD uses exponential backoff, the topic of the next section.

Carrier Sense Multiple Access with Collision Detection (CSMA/CD)

In Chapter 3 you learned about Ethernet networks and how they work. Ethernet provides shared access to network resources to a group of nodes. These nodes are said to form a collision domain, which will be covered in detail in the next chapter. All nodes receive all frames of data sent on the medium. Even though the packet is received by all nodes, the MAC header of the packet contains a destination address that verifies that only the specified destination actually forwards the received frame. The other computers all discard the frames not addressed to them. For example, let's look at an Ethernet network consisting of five computers:

1. Computer 1 sends a packet that has a destination address corresponding to the address of Computer 3.

2. The cable signal sends the frame in both directions so that the signal reaches all five computers.

3. All five computers receive the frame, and each examines it, checking its length and checksum. The header destination address is examined next to determine whether the computer should accept the packet.

4. Only Computer 3 recognizes the destination address as valid, and therefore this computer alone forwards the contents of the frame to the Network layer.

5. The shared cable allows any networked computer to send whenever it wishes, but if two computers happen to transmit at the same time, a collision will occur, resulting in corrupted data.

Because this is a decentralized access method, when data is waiting to be sent, each transmitting node monitors its own transmission. In CSMA/CD, if a node observes a collision, it stops transmission immediately and instead will send a random 32-bit pattern for a short period of time, referred to as jam sequence or a jam signal. The purpose of this sequence is to ensure that any nodes currently receiving this frame will receive the jam signal in place of the correct 32-bit MAC CRC. This causes the other nodes to discard the frame and ensure that all stations are aware of a collision so that they can increment a timeout range.

When two or more transmitting nodes detect a collision, each responds in the same way by transmitting the jam sequence. The following sequence explains a collision based on the five computers we used in the last example:

1. Computer 2 sends a frame on the idle medium.

2. A short time later, Computer 4 also transmits because the medium, as observed by the computer, is idle.

3. After a period 'a' (equal to the propagation delay of the network), Computer 4 detects the transmission from Computer 2 and is aware of a collision, but Computer 2 has not yet observed that Computer 4 is also transmitting. Computer 4 continues to transmit, sending the 32-bit jam sequence instead of the intended data.

4. After one complete round trip of propagation time, both computers are aware of the collision. Computer 4 stops transmission of the jam sequence while Computer 2 continues to transmit a complete jam sequence. As Computer 2 finishes sending the jam sequence, the cable becomes idle.

Ethernet requires a minimum packet size, so that a collision is detected before packet transmission completes ('a' <= 1). The minimum frame size is related to the distance that the network spans, the type of media being used, and the number of repeaters that the signal may have to pass through to reach the farthest part of the LAN. The minimum frame size is 512 bits, or 64 bytes, and is called the Ethernet Slot Time. The packet should be at least 64 bytes long for the longest allowed segment while the maximum packet size is 1500 bytes. The upper limit is set to prevent a single station from monopolizing the bandwidth.

CSMA/CD uses exponential backoff. In this method, when a collision occurs, a timeout is randomly chosen from a doubled range, and then the backoff range adapts to the number of contending stations. Let's start with the transmission process and then move on to the retransmit procedure:

1. The sending node initializes the number of transmissions of the current frame (n) to zero and starts listening to the cable using the carrier sense logic.

2. If the cable is not idle, it waits until the cable is idle.

3. It then waits for a small inter-frame gap (IFG) to allow time for all receiving nodes to prepare themselves for the next transmission.

4. Transmission then starts with the preamble, followed by the frame data and the CRC-32.

5. When transmission is complete, the sending node returns to passively monitoring the cable for other transmissions.

During this process, the node must continuously monitor the collision detection logic to detect whether a collision occurs. If it does, it stops sending bits within a few bit periods, starts the collision procedure by sending a jam signal, and then calculates a retransmission time.

What would happen if all nodes immediately attempt to retransmit following a collision? Certainly more collisions would result. On a busy network, it is possible that a retransmission may still collide with new data being sent or with another retransmission. Therefore, a procedure to assure that there is only a small possibility of simultaneous retransmissions has been developed. The scheme is called exponential backoff. Because exponential backoff is actually multiplication scaling for a large number of nodes, we will explore the theory behind the process. To calculate the retransmission time, nodes use a random backoff period. Each node selects a random number, multiplies this by the slot time, adds the IFG, and then waits for this period before attempting retransmission. The protocol allows for up to 15 retransmission attempts of the same frame.

- For each retransmission, the node constructs a set of numbers.

- A random value R is picked from this set, and the node waits for a period that is calculated as: $R \times$ slot time; for example, $R \times 51.2$ microseconds.

In exponential backoff, the backoff waiting time for the node having collisions is scaled to a larger value. The reason for this is that the more attempts required, the greater the number of computers that are trying to send at the same time; therefore, the transmission needs a longer period of time to be deferred.

WARNING !

Each transmitting node also limits the maximum number of retransmission attempts of a single frame to 16. After this number of attempts, the node gives up transmission and discards the frame, logging an error. This is more than a sufficient number of attempts to complete the transmission, so a network that is not overloaded should never discard frames in this way.

Ethernet nodes monitor the CD (collision detection) signal during the first slot time after it starts transmission because it is common for a node to have a collision within this time. If the CD circuit is faulty or the network interface card (NIC) is noisy, either can cause a late collision. A late collision happens when there is a collision after the slot time. Most nodes continue to monitor the CD signal during the entire transmission. If they observe a late collision, they will inform the sender of the error.

Now that we understand CSMA/CD, what about performance issues? Earlier in this chapter, we discussed four performance issues:

- **Normalized throughput:** A fraction of the link capacity used to carry non-retransmitted packets.

- **Mean delay:** The amount of time a node has to wait before it successfully transmits a packet.

- **Stability:** The network status achieved by reducing the load.

- **Fairness:** The ability of each contending node to receive an equal share of the bandwidth and an equal chance to send data.

If there was only one node attempting to transmit at any time, performance would not be an issue because we would have almost 100% utilization of the network, providing close to 10 Mbps of throughput on a 10-Mbps LAN. However, the performance of Ethernet is less predictable when two or more nodes attempt to transmit at the same time. Throughput is reduced because some bandwidth is wasted by collisions and backoff delays. In real life, a busy shared 10-Mbps Ethernet network will typically supply 30 to 40 Mbps of throughput to the connected nodes. As network traffic increases and many nodes are competing to share the bandwidth, an overload condition or network bottleneck may occur. In this case, the throughput is reduced considerably because much of the capacity is wasted by the CSMA/CD algorithm, and very little is available for sending data. A LAN with higher traffic will observe a high collision rate and a variable transmission time due to backoff. This is why a shared Ethernet LAN should not connect more than 1024 computers. There are resolutions to this overload problem:

- The LAN can be separated into two or more collision domains using bridges or switches.

- Use Gigabyte Ethernet, which operates at 1000 Mbps. (Because Gigabyte Ethernet uses fiber-optic or twisted-pair cable, a hub or switch is required.)

Another issue with using CSMA/CD is that the sharing is not necessarily fair. If each node connected to the LAN has only a small amount of data to send, the network exhibits almost equal access time for each node. This, however, is not the case on most networks. When one node starts sending an excessive number of packets, it can dominate the network. For example, if one node is sending text files and another node is sending video files, which will have more packets to send? The one sending the video files. This effect is known as Ethernet capture. Ethernet capture occurs when many nodes compete with one node that has much more data to send than the other nodes. Under these situations, some nodes may be locked out from transmitting data for a period of time. Let's look at how this happens based on the example we have been using:

1. Both Computer 3 and Computer 5 have data to transmit. Computer 3 transmits first.

2. Both Computer 3 and Computer 5 try to transmit simultaneously.

3. A collision occurs, and Computer 5 chooses a larger retransmission interval than Computer 3.

4. In the meantime, Computer 3 sends, and then re-sends packets.

5. After a short pause, both computers attempt to resume transmission, causing another collision.

6. Both back off, but Computer 5 was already in backoff because it failed to retransmit, so it chooses from a larger range of backoff times, allowing Computer 3 a better chance of transmitting.

7. At the next pause in transmission, both computers attempt to send, causing a collision.

8. Computer 5 further increases its backoff and is now unable to fairly compete with Computer 3.

The use of higher-speed network transmission such as 100 Mbps significantly reduces the probability of capture, and using full-duplex cabling will eliminate it.

CSMA/CD supports two or more nodes on a shared, common bus. As we have learned, with CSMA/CD a transmitting node postpones transmitting of data packets until the network is free of traffic. Of course, this is all based on the Ethernet standard. CSMA/CD is difficult to implement in wireless LANs because of the transmission design. Another method of CSMA used for wireless and Appletalk networks is called carrier sense multiple access with collision avoidance. (We discuss Appletalk in Chapter 6.)

Carrier Sense Multiple Access with Collision Avoidance (CSMA/CA)

The most important difference between the wireless LAN and the MAC protocol of most wired networking designs is the ability to detect collisions. Because both the receiving and sending antennas in a wireless network are next to each other, a wireless station is unable to see any signal but its own. As a result, the entire data packet is sent before the checksum discloses that a collision has occurred. So in a wireless environment, it is very important that the number of collisions be limited to the absolute minimum. This can be achieved by a protocol called **carrier sense multiple access with collision avoidance (CSMA/CA)**, which is actually a variation of CSMA/CD. The idea behind CSMA/CA is to prevent collisions at the moment they are most likely to occur. All nodes are forced to wait for a random number of timeslots and then check the network medium again, before starting a transmission. If the medium is busy, the node freezes its timer until it becomes free again. Thus, the chance of two nodes starting to send data packets simultaneously is reduced.

! WARNING

Because collision detection can't be used, the sending node needs some type of acknowledgment from the receiving node that the transmission was received.

In collision avoidance, when a node wants to send a data packet, it sends a message called a Request to Send (RTS) to the destination device. If the node receives a Clear to Send (CTS) message back from the device, it sends its data. When the data packet has been received, the receiving device sends an acknowledgment (ACK) packet.

The CSMA algorithm is based on avoiding collisions rather than detecting them. Here is how the process works:

1. The node checks to see if the medium is busy. The node, wishing to transmit, sends a jamming signal. It stops if another jamming signal is detected and waits for the medium to become idle.

2. The node waits for a small IFG to allow time for all receiving nodes to prepare themselves for the next transmission.

3. The protocol sets the contention timer to a randomly chosen interval.

4. The sending node sends the packet and waits for an ACK from the receiving node.

5. If no ACK is received, the sending node assumes that the packet is lost.

6. The transmission is tried again, after doubling the contention timer.

    7.   If another transmission occurs during the timer countdown, the node holds the current timer, and when the channel is clear, it restarts the current timer.

The performance issues of CSMA/CA start with the delays introduced by the collision avoidance. The delays should be as small as possible. The protocol should also keep the number of collisions to a minimum, even under the highest possible network traffic. The range of the contention timer is set to vary with the load. When a collision occurs, the delay is doubled progressively until a successful transmission occurs and the delay is reset to the minimal value.

Remember that in CSMA/CD we used the formula $a = D/T$ to calculate the probability of collisions. In normal configurations, all stations apply a standard mechanism to avoid collision of wireless messages. In CSMA/CA, the carrier cannot detect whether a collision has occurred, so it attempts to avoid collisions by waiting for the wireless medium to clear the amount of time it takes a packet to be sent from the station farthest away. This protocol works fine when every station can receive transmissions from every station, and in many cases the user of a wireless device may hardly notice the delay time. However, there are two issues with this type of design: hidden and exposed terminals.

Hidden terminal describes a situation in which the stations farthest away from each other or other stations in the area cannot hear each other's packets quickly enough, because the time it takes for a packet sent from one station to reach the second station is greater than the second station's wait time, even though the base can hear both transmissions. With an exposed terminal, some but not all stations can hear transmissions from stations that are not in the local area. With a hidden terminal, collisions occur because a station is not detected, and with an exposed terminal the station sits idle because it incorrectly detects a node that isn't in its local area. See Figure 4.10 for an illustration of hidden and exposed terminals.

To deal with hidden and exposed terminals, two solutions have been developed: busy tone multiple access (BTMA) and multiple access collision avoidance (MACA).

4.4.3   Busy-Tone Multiple Access (BTMA) and Multiple Access Collision Avoidance (MACA)

Packet-radios or stations use the MAC protocol for sharing a common broadcast channel. As we just learned, even though CSMA tries to prevent

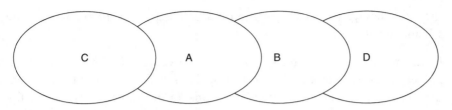

A is the sender
B is the receiver
C is the exposed station
D is the hidden station

Figure 4.10

**Hidden and exposed
terminals**

a station from transmitting at the same time as other stations, hidden and exposed terminals degrade the performance because the carrier either isn't sensed or isn't in the local area. Hidden terminals are the nodes in the range of the receiver but out of the range of the transmitter. Collisions occur at the receiver, so when the channel is sensed for activity, the transmitter doesn't sense that the receiver is already receiving transmissions. On the other hand, exposed terminals occur when the nodes are in the range of the transmitter and not the range of the receiver. Again, remember that the major issue with this is that collisions occur at the receiver and channel sensing is done from the transmitter. Several protocols have been developed to help resolve this issue.

Busy-tone multiple access (BTMA) is designed for station-based networks and divides the channel into two categories: message channel and busy-tone channel.

The base station will transmit a busy-tone signal on the busy-tone channel when transmission is occurring. The station is in line of sight of all terminals, so each terminal can sense the busy-tone channel to be able to determine whether it can send data. When the station is receiving a message, it places a tone on this channel. Everyone who wants to send data packets to a station knows that it is busy even if they cannot hear transmissions that the station hears. BTMA relies on a centralized network composed of base stations. When a base station senses a terminal transmission, it broadcasts a busy-tone signal to all the terminals. This broadcast keeps them from accessing the channel. Although technically it could be used in ad hoc networks with distributed control, it is mainly implemented in a centralized environment. In the implementation area, BTMA requires a split frequency band, meaning more complex receivers and two tuners. Because there are two separate bands, they may have different propagation characteristics, which could cause the scheme to fail.

In the receiver-initiated busy-tone multiple access (RI-BTMA) scheme, a packet preamble is sent to the receiver by the transmitter. After it is received, the receiver sets up an out-of-band busy tone for the transmitter to see, so the data packet can be sent. This type of design allows acknowledgment along with preventing other nodes from sending. The principle behind this is similar to the CSMA/CA principle. The transmitter sends an RTS. Once received, the receiver sends a busy tone, and then the transmitting node sends the data packet.

Several different protocols have been developed to overcome the hidden and exposed terminal issues in packet radio. One possible solution, which we already discussed, is through the use of BTMA; there are several disadvantages to this approach however. In a full-duplex mode, the hardware expense will normally be much higher, and the system will occupy two frequencies but may only realize the maximum throughput of one. A better solution might be to increase the throughput by reducing the collisions on a single-channel system rather than spreading the load onto two channels. One of the methods used that attempts to solve the hidden station problem while still using a single frequency is called demand assigned multiple access (DAMA). Here is how it works:

1.   The node attempts to connect to the master by means of a channel access without any coordination. Collisions might occur during this phase but they are acceptable because they are relatively rare.

2.   Once the master recognizes a connection request, the connecting station's identification is added to the polling list, and now the master controls the connected station.

3.   Permission to send data is granted by means of polls, which might be included in ACK packets or transferred data frames.

4.   Once permission is granted, several frames might be transmitted in a block. However, if the user does not respond within a given time frame, the master assumes that the node never received it.

5.   The master passes permission to transmit to all other active stations and, when completed, comes back to the first node and gives it another chance to transmit.

On the other hand, if the node actually receives the poll and replies, the master will not acknowledge it until after it has served all the other active stations. If the node has no data to send, when polled by the master, the node responds with an empty frame. The master reduces the node in polling priority and skips the node the next time. The polling priority of inactive nodes might be further decreased, but when they respond with a data frame they will again regain their original priority.

Multiple access collision avoidance (MACA) attempts to detect collisions at the receiver by establishing a request-response channel of communication between the sender and receiver. Instead of using two channels like BMTA, it uses a single frequency band, but uses explicit messages to tell others that the receiver is busy. Here's how MACA works:

1. Before sending data, the transmitter sends an RTS to the intended receiver station.

2. If the station is idle, it sends a CTS to the transmitter.

3. The transmitter sends data.

4. If another station overhears the RTS, it waits for the transmission to end.

Even though this protocol was designed to solve the hidden and exposed terminal issues, it doesn't completely eliminate them.

Another protocol that can be used is the MACAW protocol. MACAW uses a message exchange that consists of five steps:

1. Before sending data, the transmitter sends an RTS to the intended receiver station.

2. If the station is idle, it sends a CTS to the transmitter.

3. The transmitter sends a data sending (DS) packet to notify all the nodes in the transmitter's range that the channel is in use.

4. The transmitter sends data.

5. The receiver sends an ACK to the transmitter letting it know the data has been received.

Included in this protocol is a backoff algorithm called multiple increase and linear decrease (MILD). The algorithm is meant to address the issue of unfairness that happens in normal backoff. Even though the algorithm has accommodations for calculating multiple backoff intervals for different destinations, it still doesn't solve the hidden and exposed terminal dilemma.

Next is the floor acquisition multiple access (FAMA) protocol. The objective of FAMA is for a station with data to send to acquire control of a channel, also called a floor, before it sends a data packet while ensuring that no data packet collides with any other packet at the receiver. This amounts to a single channel BTMA using either packet sensing or carrier sensing and a three-way RTS-CTS handshake. There are two versions of FAMA:

- **FAMA Non-Persistent Packet Sensing (FAMA-NPS):** The stations do not sense the channel before sending data. It is comparable to MACA.

- **FAMA Non-Persistent Carrier Sensing (FAMA-NCS):** This method uses a carrier-sensing scheme and longer CTS packets to ensure correct floor acquisition and collision-free data packet reception.

Multiple access-based collision avoidance MAC protocols have made a case for the sender–receiver pair to first acquire a floor, as in FAMA. Acquiring a floor allows the sender–receiver pair to avoid collisions due to hidden and exposed stations. The fundamental difference in power-controlled multiple access (PCMA) is that instead of using the reception of the RTS/CTS as an on–off trigger, it uses signal strength of the RTS/CTS to bound the transmission power of the stations. The goal of PMCA is to achieve power-controlled multiple access within the framework of CSMA/CA. The power control component of PCMA has two main mechanisms:

- A request-power-to-send (RPTS)/acceptable-power-to-send (APTS) handshake between the data sender and the receiver that is used to determine the minimum transmission power that will result in a successful transmission. This is done before the data is sent, and once the transmission is complete, the receiver sends back an ACK.

- The noise-tolerance advertisement is used to advertise the additional noise power it can tolerate given its current status. The noise-tolerance advertisement or the busy tone is periodically pulsed by each receiver in the busy-tone channel.

The last major component in PCMA is collision resolution, which is backoff-based. Because PCMA uses power control, more sophisticated collision resolution algorithms can be used.

The last method is dual busy-tone multiple access (DBTMA). Using the DBTMA protocol, two narrow-bandwidth tones are implemented in a single channel. The two tones are the transmit busy tone and the receive busy tone.

These tones indicate whether a node is sending or receiving data. The transmit busy tone is used to increase the probability of successful RTS receipt at the receiver, and the receive busy tone is used to acknowledge the RTS packet. Any node sensing any busy tones is not allowed to send RTS requests. A node implementing DBTMA can be in one of seven states:

1. **IDLE:** A node with no packets to send

2. **CONTEND:** A node that has data to send but is not allowed to send yet

3. **S_RTS:** A node sending an RTS

4. **S_DATA:** A node sending data

5. **WF_BTR:** The RTS sender state while waiting for an acknowledgment from the receiver

6. **WF_DATA:** The receiver state while waiting for a data packet

7. **WAIT:** The state a node is in after WF-BTR and before the S_DATA. This is a mandatory waiting time to allow all RTS transmissions in the vicinity of the receiver to be aborted.

The channel throughput using DBTMA is greater than that of FAMA-NCS and MACAW. DBTMA resolves the hidden and exposed terminal issues, but extra hardware is required because two busy-tone transmitters and sensing circuits have to be incorporated into each communication node.

4.4.4 Token Passing

In the Distributed Access section earlier in this chapter, we discussed distributed polling. In distributed polling, every station has to wait for its turn. The access time is divided into slots, and then each station is assigned a slot that it uses for transmissions. Because the slots are assigned, if there is nothing to send, the slot is wasted. How can we skip past idle stations? Skipping the idle stations is the main idea of a token-passing network. Token passing is an alternative to CSMA/CD Ethernet networks. Tokens are special data packets that circulate from node to node when there's no data traffic. This small packet gives a station the right to transmit data. Possession of the token allows exclusive access to the network for transmission of

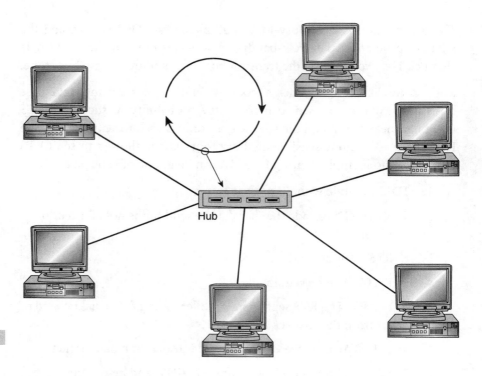

Figure 4.11
Logical ring

a message. When the transmission is finished, the node passes the token to the next station. Every computer in the network is responsible for either passing the token or creating a new one. Once a computer has information to send, it modifies the token and passes it on. When the token reaches its final destination, it lets the sender know it has arrived safely. The sender then makes a new token and the process starts over. A node waits for an empty token in order to transmit a message. A destination address and message are appended to the token. Tokens are reviewed by each node to establish a destination. Upon receipt, the status of the token is reset to empty and transmitted to the next node. A token is guaranteed to rotate once every Target Token Rotation Time (TTRT) so that each station is guaranteed a synchronous allocation within every TTRT.

The stations form a logical ring. Logical rings can be on a nonphysical topology as demonstrated in a hub or star ring, and as shown in Figure 4.11.

Here's how token passing works:

1. During normal operation, on a token-passing network, nodes copy packets from input buffer to output.

2. If the packet is a token, it checks that the packet is ready to send. If not, it forwards the token on. If the packet is ready to send, the node deletes the token and sends the packet.

3. The receiving node copies the packet and sends an ACK flag to the sender.

4. The sender removes the packet and deletes it.

5. When it is finished, the node reinserts the token.

6. If the ring is idle and no token has passed for a long time, the node regenerates the token.

NOTE

Token-passing networks, also called Token Ring networks, can be either single or double rings. With a single ring, the failure of a single link or station breaks the network, so this type of access can be susceptible to a single point of failure. With a double ring, if there is a failure on one ring, the second ring can be used to avoid the issues with just a single ring.

This is the method used in Fiber Distributed Data Interface (FDDI). FDDI was explained in detail in the previous chapter, so we will just recap this access method for purposes of demonstrating token passing. A FDDI network contains two token rings, one for possible backup in case the primary ring fails. FDDI uses dual-ring architecture with traffic on each ring flowing in opposite directions. The dual rings consist of a primary and a secondary ring. During normal operation, the primary ring is used for data transmission, and the secondary ring remains idle. The primary purpose of the dual rings is to provide superior reliability and robustness.

FDDI is frequently used as high-speed backbone technology because of its support for high bandwidth and greater distances than copper. Table 4.5 show the pros and cons of using token passing for network access.

It is time to move on to one more method of distributed access before we discuss hardware addressing.

4.4.5   ALOHA

In the 1970s, Norman Abramson and his colleagues at the University of Hawaii devised a new method to solve the channel allocation problem. Although Abramson's work, originally called the Aloha System, was used for

TABLE 4.5   Pros and Cons of Using Token-Passing Access

Pro	Con
Medium access protocol is simple and explicit.	Token is single point of failure.
No need for carrier sensing, time synchronization, or complex protocols to resolve contention.	Lost or corrupted token disrupts the network and, if necessary, must regenerate token.
Guarantees zero collisions.	All stations must cooperate. The network must detect unresponsive stations.
Can give some stations priority over others.	Stations must actively monitor network.
Supports both single-attached and dual-attached stations.	Stations must actively monitor network.

satellite communication systems in the Pacific, the fundamental design is applicable to any system in which random users are competing for the use of a single shared channel. **ALOHA** is one of the earliest multiple access schemes.

Random access protocols address situations in which traffic is bursty. With this type of traffic, a station can be busy for short amounts of time and idle for long stretches. When the channel assignment is fixed in implementations such as FDMA and TDMA, those idle periods amount to wasted bandwidth even though other stations may have data to transmit. One solution would be to allow stations to transmit anytime they have data to send. Of course, when this type of access is allowed, collisions result. Because there is no guarantee of successful transmission in advance, the individual stations account for and recover from corrupted data packets.

A protocol controls which computers are allowed to transmit at any given time. So far we have discussed many distributed access protocols. The simplest one of these is known as ALOHA. It is a simple communications scheme in which each transmitter in a network sends data whenever there is a frame to send. If the frame successfully reaches the receiver, the next frame is sent. If the frame is not received, it is sent again.

There are several variants of ALOHA:

- Pure ALOHA
- Slotted ALOHA
- Reservation ALOHA

Pure ALOHA allows the stations access to the channel whenever they have data to transmit, but each station must add a checksum at the end of its transmission to allow the receiver to recognize whether the frame was properly received. ALOHA is a best-effort service that does not guarantee that the frame of data will actually reach the remote recipient without corruption. Because the threat of data collision exists, each station must either monitor its transmission on the rebroadcast or await an acknowledgment from the destination station. If it does not receive an ACK, the node tries after a random waiting time to reduce the probability of re-collision. There is no backoff calculated like in CSMA/CA or MACAW.

In a wireless broadcast system or a half-duplex two-way link, pure ALOHA works great, but as networks become more complex, such as where data travels many paths at once, issues occur because data frames collide. A pure ALOHA network can also work well when the medium has a low bandwidth utilization, because this leads to a low probability of the transmission colliding with that of another computer, therefore allowing a good chance that the data is not corrupted. The heavier the communications traffic, the worse the collision problems become.

To minimize the number of collisions, thereby optimizing network bandwidth efficiency and increasing the number of subscribers that can use a given network, a scheme called slotted ALOHA was developed. We will discuss slotted ALOHA right after we look at the advantages and disadvantages of pure ALOHA, as shown in Table 4.6.

TIP

Ethernet uses a refinement of ALOHA, known as CSMA, which improves performance when there is a higher medium network utilization. Figure 4.12 demonstrates the theory of pure ALOHA.

By making a small restriction in the transmission of the individual stations, the throughput of the ALOHA protocol can be doubled. Assuming that the

TABLE 4.6   Advantages and Disadvantages of Pure ALOHA

Advantages	Disadvantages
Superior to fixed assignment when there is a large number of bursty stations.	Theoretically proven throughput maximum of 18.4%.
Useful when 'a' is large and carrier sensing doesn't help; often used for satellite links.	Requires queuing buffers for retransmission of packets.
Adapts to varying number of stations.	At high loads, collisions are very frequent.
Simple; there is no carrier sensing, no token, and no time-based synchronization.	Sudden burst of traffic can lead to instability unless backoff is exponential.

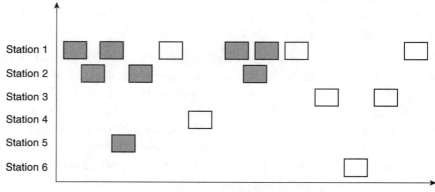

Figure 4.12
Pure ALOHA scheme summarized

packet lengths are constant, transmission time is broken into slots equivalent to the transmission time of a single packet. All transmissions must start at slot boundaries. When packets collide, they will overlap completely instead of partially, and the packet is retransmitted in a future slot until the transmission is successful. This has the effect of doubling the efficiency of the ALOHA protocol and has come to be known as **slotted ALOHA**. Slotted ALOHA is commonly used in cellular phone uplinks. Table 4.7 lists the advantages and disadvantages of slotted ALOHA, and Figure 4.13 demonstrates the theory of slotted ALOHA.

The previous two variations of ALOHA demonstrated the designs of restrictive to unrestrictive access to the channel. On the one hand, slotted ALOHA restricts access to the channel and limits a station's capability to

TABLE 4.7   Advantages and Disadvantages of Slotted ALOHA

Advantages	Disadvantages
Doubles the efficiency of ALOHA.	Theoretically proven throughput maximum of 36.8%.
Adaptable to a changing station population.	Requires queuing buffers for retransmission of packets.
	Synchronization required.

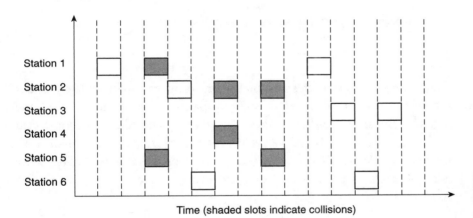

Time (shaded slots indicate collisions)

Figure 4.13
Slotted ALOHA scheme summarized

handle bursty data. On the other hand, pure ALOHA gives stations the freedom to transmit whenever required, and therefore the channel efficiency is limited due to collisions. Protocols in which a station's intentions are announced in the form of some kind of explicit or implicit reservation are called Demand Assignment protocols. The last variation of ALOHA, reservation ALOHA, is a Demand Assignment protocol. **Reservation ALOHA** is a combination of a slot reservation design with slotted ALOHA. This channel allocation scheme divides the channel bandwidth into slot sizes equal to the transmission time of a single packet, assuming that the packet sizes are of constant length. The slots are then organized into frames

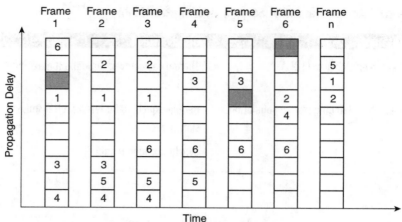

Figure 4.14

Reservation ALOHA

Time
(numbers indicate statioin ownership, shaded slots indicate collisions)

of equal size whose length spans that of one propagation delay. (Remember our formula, a = D/T, where D is the propagation delay and T is the time taken to transmit.) Earlier in the chapter we discussed reservation-based access. In reservation-based access, the reserved slots are smaller than regular data slots. When this occurs, the slots are known as minislots. The nodes either contend for a minislot or they own one. Here's how reservation ALOHA works:

1.   A station makes an implicit reservation by successfully transmitting in an available slot.

2.   After a successful transmission, the station is guaranteed that slot in all succeeding frames until it is no longer needed.

3.   The slot becomes available by going empty or by a collision in the previous frame.

4.   The remaining stations then contend for the reservation minislots in the next frame by using slotted ALOHA.

If the frame size did not span the propagation delay, a slot could go unused several times before the stations sense its availability. Reservation ALOHA is most commonly found in cable modem uplinks. Figure 4.14 demonstrates this protocol using several frames. In Frame 1, two stations (stations 2 and 5) collide in an attempt to acquire the same slot. They succeed in

TABLE 4.8 Advantages and Disadvantages of Reservation ALOHA

Advantages	Disadvantages
Handles bursty data traffic efficiently.	Inefficient for single-packet messages.
Supports both circuit- and packet-mode transfers.	Arriving packet has to wait for entire frame before it has a chance to send.
Works with large a.	If propagation delay is large, frame size can be excessive.
Simple.	Cannot preempt stations that hog bandwidth.

Frame 2. The same scenario occurs in frames 5 and 6, except the collisions occur between stations 2 and 4, and 5 and 1, respectively.

Table 4.8 lists the advantages and disadvantages of reservation ALOHA.

4.5 Hardware Addressing

Now that we have addressed how we can manage many devices on the network when they all want to communicate at the same time through different multiple access methods, how is data transmitted from a single computer to a single computer on a LAN? Do all computers get a copy of the data? Moreover, how does a computer know that it is the destination of a data frame?

Most network technologies have a unique physical address scheme that identifies computers on the network. Each LAN technology uses an addressing scheme where each node is assigned a unique physical address. As signals are sent across a shared network, two computers can communicate directly across a shared LAN using this physical addressing scheme. This unique physical address is also called a hardware address, or **Media Access Control (MAC) address**. This address is the MAC hexadecimal address of the system's NIC and is 48 bits long. A MAC address looks like 00-10-A4-A8-DA-D0.

The data information is sent across the network in a frame format usually consisting of a frame header followed by a larger payload area that contains the data being sent. Each computer is assigned a numeric hardware address

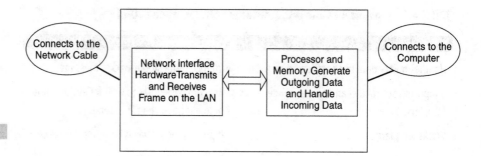

Figure 4.15

The face of a NIC

(MAC). The sender includes the destination hardware address in each transmitted frame so that only the computer identified in the frame receives a copy of the frame. Most LAN technologies also include the sender's hardware address in the frame.

These addresses are located in fields inside the packet header. The NIC handles all the details of sending and receiving frames. The network interface hardware can detect the delivery of a frame and extract that frame from the media. It checks the destination address for all incoming frames to determine whether it matches the node's address and, if so, a copy of the frame is passed to the attached computer. Frames not addressed to the attached computer are ignored or passed down the transmission media. It handles the details of transmission and receipt of frames by adding frames, headers and footers, hardware addresses, data, and error-detection codes (CRCs) to outgoing frames. See Figure 4.15 for an illustration of the workings of a NIC.

The NIC operates separately from the CPU, transmitting outgoing data in frames and accepting incoming data if the destination address matches its own physical address. The two main functions of a NIC are to establish and handle the computer's network connection and to translate the digital data into signals that the outgoing media can understand. In essence, the NIC is link between a computer and a network. This link, or exchange of information, is handled at the Data Link level of the OSI model and must include a device called a transceiver that is designed for the specific network media. These days, many NICs can be configured for more than one type of media. The exchange obeys access rules when transmitting and receiving, such as CSMA/CD.

As mentioned earlier, each NIC has a unique address. But where does this address come from? IEEE designates an addressing scheme and assigns unique blocks of addresses to NIC manufacturers. Each time a NIC is manufactured, the MAC address is burned onto or built into a chip on the NIC. This is composed of six 2-digit hexadecimal numbers separated by colons. The first three 2-digit hexadecimal numbers (24 bits) are used to identify the vendor, the second three 2-digit hexadecimal numbers are assigned by the vendor. For example, let's look at the MAC address 00-10-A4-A8-5F-5B. The portion 00-10-A4 indicates that it is an IBM NIC address. For a list of manufacturer NIC assignments, go to *http://standards.ieee.org/regauth/oui/index.shtml* or *http://www.coffer.com/mac_find/*. The second site is easier to use provided that you have the MAC address. You can identify your MAC address by going to a command prompt and typing ipconfig /all. The results display your TCP/IP configuration and your NIC's physical address.

4.6 Chapter Summary

- Multiple access allows more than one device to communicate. This is necessary in a networked environment. Based on the network architecture, networks logically can be divided into two classes: distributed and centralized. In a centralized design, there is a central node or a manager, which keeps the important information and manages all communication decisions. In a distributed design, there is no central node or manager. All nodes have approximately the same kinds and amounts of information.

- Circuit mode is used to send steady streams of data at a continuous bit rate. Circuit mode provides a physical, dedicated path, called a time slot, for the data. Packet-mode design provides increased network efficiency by providing system resources to the system users only when the user has data to send. With packet mode, the nodes contend for every packet to avoid wasting bandwidth. Because packet mode is the shared type, it allows network media to serve many more users with the same system resources than they could with only circuit mode.

- With multiple access, implementation issues need to be addressed. The first issue is spectrum scarcity. The next is the properties that radio links possess. In wireless systems it is very difficult to receive data when the transmitter is sending data. This is because when a node is transmitting data, a large fraction of the signal energy leaks into the receive path. There also has to be a method devised for communication that can help control errors, fading, and interference. The four factors that affect performance are normalized throughput, mean delay, stability, and fairness.

- In the late 1980s the wireless industry began to explore converting the existing analog network to digital as a means of improving capacity. Currently there are three basic choices: frequency division multiple access (FDMA), time division multiple access (TDMA), and code division multiple access (CDMA). FDMA works by dividing the frequency spectrum allocated for wireless cellular telephone communication into channels of equal bandwidth. TDMA is analog's FDMA with a built-in, time-sharing component. CDMA combines spread-spectrum technology with analog-to-digital conversion. Audio input is first digitized into binary elements. The data are then scattered across the frequency band in a random pattern.

- There are several methods of distributed access, including decentralized polling, carrier sense multiple access (CSMA), busy-tone multiple access (BTMA), multiple access collision avoidance (MACA), token passing, and ALOHA. BTMA is designed for station-based networks, and divides the channel into a message channel and busy-tone channel. ALOHA allows the stations access to the channel whenever they have data to transmit, but each station must add a checksum at the end of its transmission to allow the receiver to recognize whether the frame was properly received. MACA is a multiple-access method that attempts to detect collisions at the receiver by establishing a request-response channel of communication between the sender and the receiver.

- Ethernet uses CSMA to improve performance on larger networks with medium to heavy traffic. When a node has data to transmit, it first listens to the cable by using a transceiver to check whether a signal is being transmitted by another node. There are two kinds of CSMA, CSMA/CD (collision detection) and CSMA/CA (collision avoidance). The idea behind CSMA/CA is to prevent collisions at the moment they are most likely to occur. All nodes are forced to wait for a random number of timeslots and then check the medium again before starting a transmission. In carrier sense multiple access with collision detection (CSMA/CD), if a node observes a collision, it stops transmission immediately and instead will send a random 32-bit pattern for a short period of time, referred to as jam sequence or a jam signal.

- Token passing is an alternative to CSMA/CD Ethernet networks. Tokens are special data packets that circulate from node to node. This small packet gives a station the right to transmit data. Possession of the token allows exclusive access to the network for transmission of a message. When the transmission is finished, the node passes the token to the next station. Every computer in the network is responsible for either passing the token or creating a new one.

- Most network technologies have a unique physical address scheme that identifies computers on the network. This unique physical address is also called a hardware address or Media Access Control (MAC) address. The MAC address is located on the system's network interface card (NIC) and is 48 bits long.

4.7 Key Terms

ALOHA: One of the earliest multiple access schemes. It allows network stations access to the channel whenever they have data to transmit, but each station must add a checksum at the end of its transmission to allow the receiver to recognize whether the frame was properly received.

base station (BS): A special fixed node on a network. It is located in a central location for use in a wireless or cellular network.

busy-tone multiple access (BTMA): An access method designed for station-based networks, it divides the channel into a message channel and a busy-tone channel.

capture-division packetized access (CDPA): An alternative to systems based on bandwidth subdivision methods such as TDMA, FDMA, and CDMA. In CDPA there is no subdivision of bandwidth.

carrier sense multiple access (CSMA): A fundamental advance in network access because it checks whether the medium is active before sending a packet; that is, it listens before it transmits.

carrier sense multiple access with collision avoidance (CSMA/CA): Designed to prevent collisions at the moment they are most likely to occur. All nodes are forced to wait for a random number of timeslots and then check the medium again before starting a transmission.

code division multiple access (CDMA): An access method that combines spread-spectrum technology with analog-to-digital conversion. After the data is digitized, it is spread out over the entire bandwidth available.

duplexing: Refers to the transmission of packets. Half-duplexing transmits packets in one direction only. Full-duplexing transmit packets in two directions simultaneously.

frequency division duplex (FDD): Uses different frequency bands for uplink and downlink.

frequency division multiple access (FDMA): Provides multiple and simultaneous transmissions to a single transponder.

interworking function (IWF): Provides the necessary protocol conversions so that wireless data users can continue to access existing network-wired applications without requiring modifications to the applications.

Media Access Control (MAC) address: A unique physical address, also called a hardware address, that all NICs have.

multiple access: Allows more than one device to communicate.

multiple access collision avoidance (MACA): A multiple access method that attempts to detect collisions at the receiver by establishing a request-response channel of communication between the sender and receiver.

packet: A small segment of a data stream message transmitted over a packet-switched network. A packet contains a destination address in addition to data.

polling: A process in which the master broadcasts a query to every node on the network, asking each node in turn whether it has anything to communicate.

pure ALOHA: A multiple-access scheme that allows stations to access a communications channel whenever the stations have data to transmit, but each station must add a checksum to the end of its transmission to allow the receiver to determine whether the frame was properly received.

reservation ALOHA: Combination of a slot reservation design with slotted ALOHA. This channel allocation scheme divides the channel bandwidth into slot sizes equal to the transmission time of a single packet, assuming that the packet sizes are of constant length.

self-interference: A process by which a large fraction of the signal energy leaks into the receive path when a node is transmitting data.

slotted ALOHA: Doubles the efficiency of the ALOHA protocol by completely overlapping packets when they collide so that the packet is retransmitted in a future slot until the transmission is successful.

time division duplex (TDD): Multiplexing of the transmission in different time periods but in the same frequency band.

time division multiple access (TDMA): A digital transmission technology that allows users to access a single radio-frequency (RF) channel without interference by dividing the channel into time slots for each user.

4.8 Challenge Questions

4.1 Which of the following is a multiple access method that attempts to detect collisions at the receiver by establishing a request-response channel of communication between the sender and receiver?

a. TDMA

b. MACA

c. CSMA

d. FDMA

4.2 Which of the following is one of the earliest multiple access schemes?

a. MACAW

b. CSMA

c. ALOHA

d. DBTMA

4.3 Several different methods of centralized control include which of the following?

a. Circuit mode

b. Polling or packet mode

c. Reservation based

d. All of the above

4.4 Which of the following is not a method of distributed access?

a. CSMA

b. Circuit-mode

c. BTMA

d. Token passing

4.5 When a collision occurs, which of the following is true?

a. The packet will subsequently be discarded.

b. The entire packet transmission time is wasted.

c. The collision will result in the corruption of the data being sent.

d. All of the above

4.6 Back in the late 1980s, the wireless industry began to explore converting the existing analog network to digital as a means of improving capacity. Since then, several technologies have emerged. Which of the following is *not* a wireless access method?

a. FDMA

b. TDMA

c. CSMA/CD

d. CDMA

4.7 BTMA is designed for station-based networks and divides the channel into what categories?

a. Message channel and busy-tone channel

b. Message channel, idle channel, and busy-tone channel

c. BTMA is only one channel.

d. Receiving channel, idle channel, sending channel, and busy-tone channel

4.8 Explain the difference between circuit-mode and polling or packet-mode.

4.9 Explain the difference between a distributed and a centralized network design.

4.10 What is an IWF, and how is it used?

4.11 Describe and compare pure ALOHA and slotted ALOHA.

4.12 The following four factors affect performance: _____,
_____, _____, and
_____.

4.13 A node's unique physical address is also called a _____,
or a _____. This address is the address of the system's _____ and is _____ bits long.

4.14 Ethernet uses a refinement of ALOHA, known as
_____, which improves performance when there is
a higher-medium network utilization.

4.15 _____ networks can be either single or double
rings. With a single ring, the failure of a single link or station
breaks the network, making this type of access susceptible to
_____. With a double ring, a failure on one ring
results in _____.

4.9   Challenge Exercises

Challenge Exercise 4.1

In this exercise, you research CDMA. You will then draw the encoding
scheme or chipping sequence used in this type of access. You need a computer with Internet access and either a drawing program such as Visio or a
pencil and paper.

4.1 Log on to your computer and open an Internet connection.

4.2 Go to your favorite search engine, such as Google.com, and
search for CDMA.

4.3 Spend about 20 minutes reading about CDMA.

4.4 When you are finished, draw the encoding and decoding scheme
that CDMA uses.

Challenge Exercise 4.2

In this exercise, you research common packet channel (CPCH), which is a
wireless packet data access method. You will then write a short description
of this type of access. You need a computer with Internet access, and either
a word processing program such as Microsoft Word or a pencil and paper.

4.1 Log on to your computer and open an Internet connection.

4.2 Go to your favorite search engine and search for CPCH.

4.3 Spend about 20 minutes reading about CPCH.

4.4 When you are finished, write one to two paragraphs about this type of access.

Challenge Exercise 4.3

In this exercise, you determine the MAC address of your computer. You will then access the Internet and verify the NIC manufacturer. You will need a computer with network connectivity and Internet access, and a pencil and paper. This exercise assumes you are using Windows 2000 or Windows XP Professional.

4.1 Log on to your computer.

4.2 To open a command prompt window, click **Start**, click **Run**, type **cmd** in the Open text box, and press **Enter**.

4.3 At the command prompt, type **ipconfig /all**. Your screen should look similar to Figure 4.16.

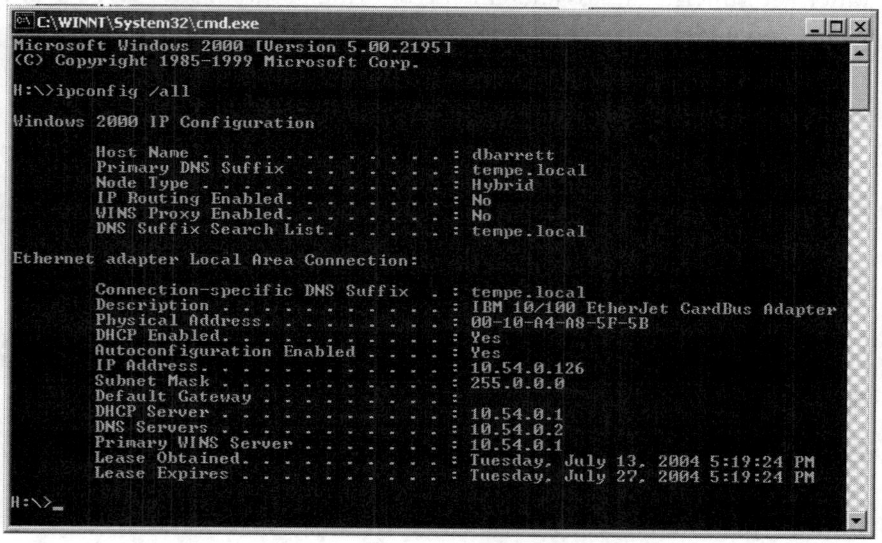

Figure 4.16
Ipconfig

4.4 Look for the line labeled Physical Address. This is the MAC address of your NIC. Write down the address. The line above it should have a description of the NIC manufacturer.

4.5 To verify the manufacturer, open an Internet connection.

4.6 Go to *http://www.coffer.com/mac_find/*.

4.7 Enter the first six characters of your MAC address, separating each pair of characters with a colon, in the String to Search For text box. For example, type **00:10:A4**.

4.8 Does the manufacturer match?

Challenge Exercise 4.4

In this exercise, you research satellite systems. You will then write a short description about this type of access and draw a satellite system. You need a computer with Internet access, and either a word processing program (such as Microsoft Word) and a drawing program (such as Visio) or a pencil and paper.

4.1 Log on to your computer and open an Internet connection.

4.2 Go to your favorite search engine and search for satellites.

4.3 Spend about 20 minutes reading about satellite communications.

4.4 When you are finished, write one to two paragraphs about this type of communication and draw a satellite system.

Challenge Exercise 4.5

In this exercise, you design a network and determine the methods of access of each type of device. You need a computer with either a word processing program (such as Microsoft Word) and a drawing program (such as Visio) or a pencil and paper.

4.1 You are going to design a network that includes:

   a. 12 wireless laptop computers

   b. 12 workstations

   c. 25 PDAs

   d. 20 cell phones

4.2   Decide whether you will use a centralized or decentralized design.

4.3   Decide which methods of access you will use for the laptops, workstations, PDAs, and cell phones.

4.4   Draw your plan and explain why you chose the methods you did.

Challenge Exercise 4.6

In this exercise, you research ALOHA and its variants (pure, slotted, and reservation). Then you will write a short description of each type of ALOHA access and draw a picture to compare how all three variants access media. You need a computer with Internet access and either a word processing program (such as Microsoft Word) and a drawing program (such as Visio) or a pencil and paper.

4.1   Log on to your computer and open an Internet connection.

4.2   Go to your favorite search engine and search for pure ALOHA, slotted ALOHA, and reservation ALOHA.

4.3   Spend about an hour reading about the various ALOHA variants.

4.4   When you are finished, write one to two paragraphs about each ALOHA variant and draw a picture of how each ALOHA variant accesses media.

4.10   Challenge Scenarios

Challenge Scenario 4.1

NetoTech is a newly formed company that has asked for your help. Management recently hired a team of engineers to help set up a network. In the initial meeting, the engineers asked questions about what type of applications would be run, and several questions came up about centralized and decentralized designs. The IT manager needs explanations of these types of designs. What will you tell him?

Challenge Scenario 4.2

NetoTech is now considering wireless phones and how they will affect the network. The IT manager has a list of questions, which include the following:

4.1   What methods are used for wireless access?

4.2   Why is one method better than another?

4.3   What is the purpose of a satellite?

How would you answer these questions? He wants you to explain each of these, complete with drawings, if possible.

Challenge Scenario 4.3

In a follow-up meeting with NetoTech, the engineers discussed network access and brought up CSMA. They asked about which devices would access the network and whether they should use CDMA/CD for the LAN and CDMA/CA for the wireless laptops. The IT manager again asked for your help. He wants you to explain each of these and offer examples.

Challenge Scenario 4.4

The engineers continued their discussion of CSMA with NetoTech IT staff and brought up performance issues. They specifically asked about normalized throughput, mean delay, stability, and fairness. Explain each of these to the company IT staff.

Challenge Scenario 4.5

In a final meeting with NetoTech, the engineers want to discuss hardware addressing. They have asked you to put together a document describing this type of addressing and how it works. What will you submit?

CHAPTER 5

Switching

After reading this chapter you will be able to:

- Understand bridges and bridging behavior
- Understand switches and switching behavior
- Discuss circuit switching and packet switching
- Understand the usefulness of virtual local area networks
- Understand how switches can be integrated with hubs and routers

The primary focus of this chapter is on moving electronic signals from one interface to another. *Switching* is the term used to describe this basic behavior. We start with a discussion of bridges and LAN technology. Then we move on to circuit switching and the original behaviors of phone systems, as well as packet switching and current digital WAN connectivity. Finally, we examine VLAN technology and the integration of switches with hubs and routers on data networks. Although some of the information in this chapter might seem dated, it is worthy of discussion because it sets a framework for where the technology has come from and where it is going.

5.1   Bridges and Bridging

Understanding bridges and bridging technology requires a brief review of networking history. Keep in mind that, as we discuss bridges, many of the same principles apply to the modern evolution of bridging: the concept of switches and switching technology. It will be easier to understand switching technology if we first uncover where and why bridging was invented and explore its evolution. Our discussion will look at both Ethernet and Token Ring LAN topologies. We'll start by looking at the most popular of the two, Ethernet.

Recall that Ethernet networks started as a single-segment bus topology with all clients able to receive the electronic signals of all other clients on their network. In the early days of networking, this was considered a good thing, as clients could easily use broadcast and unicast traffic. Many of the simpler network software solutions, such as Windows for Workgroups, AppleTalk, and those provided by Novell, used broadcasts extensively as a simple way to find network resources such as logon servers, shared folders, and printers. Because there were few network clients in those days, having all systems receive and process traffic was not a big issue. In addition, using a single segment, broadcast architecture greatly simplified the installation and maintenance of networks.

As networks increased in popularity, they grew to support more clients that were further apart. One way of extending a network was to implement a repeater or hub. This allowed network designers to span larger areas. On a network that uses a repeater, the signal is cleaned and repeated at its original strength. This process occurred at Layer 1 of the OSI model, so all clients were still in the same collision domain. As networks continued to

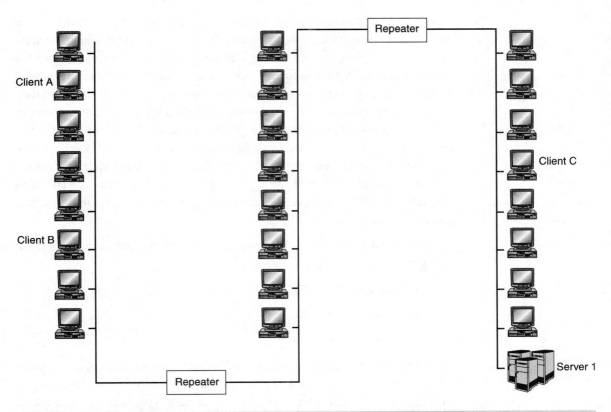

Figure 5.1
Clients on a shared Ethernet network

grow, problems with this architecture became evident. One of the concerns was the number of physical devices connected to a single network bus. As large populations of clients were connected on single or multiple repeated segments, access to the wire and signal collisions became an issue. A common early network layout is shown in Figure 5.1.

Because early Ethernet networks operated at 10-Mbps half-duplex, only one system could have access to the wire at a time. Figure 5.1 helps to explain this. If Client C transfers a large file to Server 1, clients A and B will have more difficulty communicating because all clients on this network can potentially collide with each other. As clients are added, collisions increase. Any devices involved in a collision use the Truncated Binary Exponential

Backoff Algorithm (covered in Chapter 3) to generate a random amount of wait time before attempting to resend the data. Too many collisions cause the devices to have to wait longer and longer to gain proper access to the network media. With collisions come retransmissions of data, and this adds to the overall problem. In addition to the post-collision wait time and data retransmission, network devices would have to listen longer for the wire to be free simply because there was a greater demand. These two issues made growing (or scaling) a network difficult. The solution was to isolate groups of network devices, segmenting the wire signals of one group from another group by bridging. Each of the separate groups is referred to as a **collision domain**. With fewer devices competing per network segment, normal communications could resume.

As with most technologies there are several different implementations of bridging. The most common are:

- Transparent bridging
- Source route bridging
- Translational bridging

Each has a specific purpose in controlling traffic flows and collisions. Each form of bridging also has a newer configuration called switching, and we will examine the differences as we introduce each type. Let's first take a look at the most popular type, transparent bridging.

5.1.1   Transparent Bridging

The word *transparent*, as it is used here, means that the network devices are unaware of the presence of the bridge. Much like a repeater or a hub, a bridge operates by simply plugging it into the wall and connecting network devices to it. So what does a transparent bridge do, and how does it accomplish its goal of segmenting network signals? Let's take a look at how the basic process works using Figure 5.2.

We start the example by assuming that the two bridges were just turned on and have no configuration yet. Each bridge contains memory and is able to learn and store Media Access Control (MAC) addresses. To properly build a Layer 2 header in a network communications packet, MAC addresses are required. The steps are as follows:

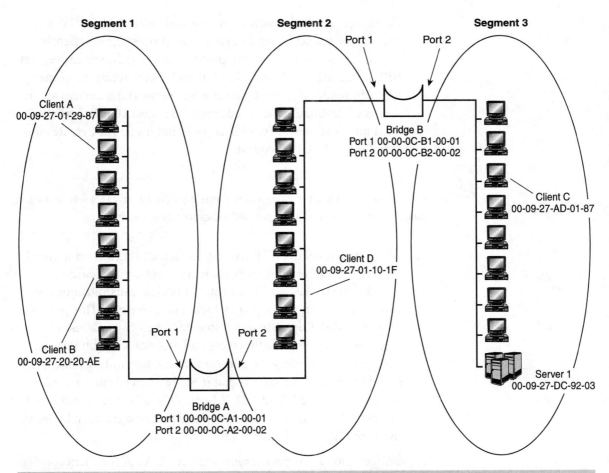

Figure 5.2

Clients on a bridged Ethernet network

1. Client A wishes to communicate with Client B and sends out a
    broadcast request looking for the MAC address of Client B.
    Remember from previous chapters that both source and destina-
    tion MAC addresses are required for the Layer 2 header informa-
    tion. The source is easy: It's Client A's address of
    00-09-27-01-29-87. The destination MAC address is currently
    unknown (we're looking for Client B's address), so a destination
    MAC address of FF-FF-FF-FF-FF-FF-FF is used to reach all

clients. This is the broadcast address and requires that all clients process the packet beyond Layer 2. The process differs slightly depending on which network protocol is in use (for example, Net-BEUI, TCP/IP, and AppleTalk), but each client sends out some type of broadcast request packet when networking devices are in search of destination MAC addresses. Because TCP/IP is the standard for most networks, we'll assume that it's an Address Resolution Protocol (ARP) request.

> **NOTE**
>
> ARP is a Data Link layer protocol that converts an IP address into a MAC address on Ethernet networks. In our example, Client A broadcasts an ARP request. ARP is discussed fully in Chapter 6.

2. Client B receives the ARP request. In fact, all stations on network Segment 1 receive the broadcast, including Port 1 of Bridge A. Because the packet is a broadcast, the bridge transmits it out of every port except the port on which it was received. This process is known as **flooding**. Bridge A also enters the MAC address of Client A into its forwarding table and associates it with Port 1. The process of adding the address into the forwarding table is called **learning**. The logic is that if Bridge A needs to forward a packet to 00-09-27-01-29-87 (Client A's MAC), it forwards it out of Port 1. It is important to remember that bridges learn by using the *source* MAC address.

3. Bridge A floods the packet onto Segment 2. All of the clients on Segment 2 receive the packet, including Bridge B. Because it is a broadcast, Bridge B floods the packet out of all ports except the port on which it was received. Bridge B also builds a forwarding table, entering Client A's MAC address and associating it with Port 1.

4. Bridge B finishes the initial process for Client A's search for Client B by flooding the packet out of Port 2 to Segment 3.

5. Client B answers the broadcast request for its MAC address. This is a unicast packet with a source address of Client B (00-09-27-20-20-AE) and a destination address of Client A (00-09-27-01-29-87). Client A's MAC address was in the header of the first packet, so Client B now has it in memory. All clients on Segment 1 receive the signal. Each device (except Client B) processes the packet up

TABLE 5.1   Bridge A Forwarding Table

Port	MAC Address
1	00-09-27-01-29-87 (Client A)
1	00-09-27-20-20-AE (Client B)
2	00-09-27-01-10-1F (Client D)
2	00-09-27-AD-01-87 (Client C)
2	00-09-27-DC-92-03 (Server 1)

to Layer 2 and then discards it because it is addressed to Client A. Client A processes the packet fully. Bridge A also receives the packet from Client B. It looks up the destination MAC address of the packet (Client A), determines that the destination address is local, and does not forward the packet out of Port 2. This process is known as **filtering**, and the result is that segments 2 and 3 do not hear the conversation between clients A and B. The filtering behavior prevents Bridge B from learning about the MAC address of Client B during this particular communication. The learning process would occur the first time that Client B sourced a broadcast packet.

The described process would continue for each network device, with each bridge building a forwarding table identifying a MAC addresses with an appropriate exit port. As its name suggests, a forwarding table is used by a bridge to decide which port will receive a particular frame. **Forwarding** describes the process of transmitting (or copying) a frame to a particular port based on the learned MAC address. See Tables 5.1 and 5.2 for the forwarding tables for each of the bridges and their clients.

Notice that the only difference between the tables is the location of Client D. Bridge A uses Port 2 to reach this client, while Bridge B uses Port 1. An important feature of bridges with respect to the forwarding table is the use of an aging timer. When an entry is made to the forwarding table, a countdown starts (the timer) and, if it reaches 0, the entry is flushed from memory. This action is known as **aging**. The timer is reset each time the bridge uses an entry in the table. Aging allows the bridge to conserve memory and ensures that the most-often-used entries (such as busy servers) stay in the

TABLE 5.2   Bridge B Forwarding Table

Port	MAC Address
1	00-09-27-01-29-87 (Client A)
1	00-09-27-20-20-AE (Client B)
1	00-09-27-01-10-1F (Client D)
2	00-09-27-AD-01-87 (Client C)
2	00-09-27-DC-92-03 (Server 1)

forwarding table. The timer is also useful when network devices are moved from one segment to another. If the entries did not periodically timeout, the bridge would never realize that a MAC address had moved, and it would continue to forward traffic out of an incorrect port. We have learned that bridges flood broadcast packets and filter packets when the destination is on the local segment. The last behavior to examine is the process of forwarding. Using Figure 5.2 and the two bridge forwarding tables, let's follow the communication process between Client A and Client D:

1. Client A sends out a broadcast to find the MAC address of Client D. As with our previous example, this broadcast is flooded throughout the network. Bridges always flood broadcasts, multicasts, and packets with an unknown destination MAC address.

2. Client D responds to Client A with a unicast packet that has 00-09-27-01-29-87 (Client A) as the destination and 00-09-27-01-10-1F (Client D) as the source. Both Bridge A and Bridge B will receive the unicast on their respective ports. Bridge A looks up the destination MAC address in its table (Table 5.1) and discovers that the packet should be sent out of Port 1 to reach that client. Bridge A forwards the frame from Port 2 to Port 1. The decision process to copy a frame from one port to another based on a known destination address is known as forwarding.

3. At the same time, Bridge B receives the packet and, using its forwarding table (Table 5.2), identifies Port 1 as the correct destination port for Client A. Because this is the same port that the packet was originally received on, Bridge B filters (or drops) the

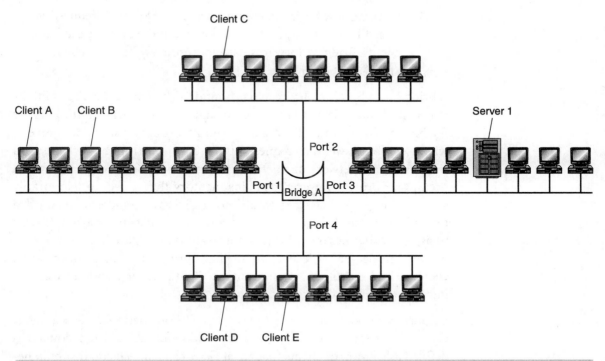

Figure 5.3

Buffering on a bridged Ethernet network

packet. This behavior isolates Segment 3 from the conversation, allowing Segment 3 clients to access the wire.

In addition to providing filtering, flooding, and forwarding capabilities, bridges also offer the ability to **buffer** traffic flows. Buffering occurs when the bridge receives frames of data and holds them in memory before forwarding or filtering. Both Figure 5.3 and the following scenario illustrate the benefit of buffering.

1.   Clients A and C both need to communicate with Server 1. Each client sends out a broadcast and receives the correct information back from the server. Bridge A learns the location of clients A and C and Server 1.

2.   Client C begins a large file transfer from Server 1. Bridge A begins forwarding the packets between Client C and Server 1.

3. Client A now begins to communicate with Server 1, requesting a large file transfer as well. Packets arrive at the bridge from both clients. Bridge A forwards data appropriately between clients A and C and Server 1.

A bridge is an Ethernet device and is bound by the same rules as any Ethernet client. It must listen to the wire for signals prior to transmitting. There is a high probability that during these simultaneous transmissions Server 1 will receive or answer data requests at the same time from both clients. In a single-segment network or a network using only repeaters, collisions would occur. Our bridge, however, contains memory that it uses to temporarily store or buffer packets that would normally have collided if forwarded immediately. The bridge forwards traffic on a first-in, first-out (FIFO) basis, so it combines the transmissions to allow multiple clients to communicate with Server 1. Keep in mind that during this entire conversation clients D and E could have communicated with Server 1 without interfering with any of the other transmissions.

Because each port on a bridge prevents collisions between the segments, each port is said to be its own collision domain. A collision domain is defined as a group of clients that are at risk of signal collision if simultaneous transmission occurs. Figure 5.3 shows four collision domains, one for each port.

NOTE ◼

It is also common to refer to each of the ports as an "Ethernet segment," or simply a "segment," because traffic is segmented at OSI Layer 2 through the use of the bridge.

Clients on the same wire segment will still contend for access to the media and can still produce collisions locally. But we have shown that by using a bridge to create smaller segments, this is less likely to occur. We have also shown that through the use of a bridge, clients have better access to bandwidth. By isolating transmissions, more network devices can communicate at the same time.

NOTE ◼

The placement of the clients, servers, and other resources is critical to realizing the benefits of using a bridge. Clients that access the same resources should be placed on the same segment together, along with the resources they use. If too many network segments separate the clients from their resources, it will greatly diminish the benefit of using a bridge because traffic will be forwarded across multiple segments, reducing the possible number of transmissions that can take place between clients.

It is also important to understand that network transmissions take a small amount of time, and the bridge must be fast enough to keep up. It is possible to overwhelm a bridge with too many clients communicating with a single device, such as the server in our most recent example. The bridge has a limited amount of memory for buffering, and can run out of available memory for data storage. This condition is called **oversubscription** and can occur even on modern network switches (discussed in detail later in this chapter).

WARNING

Whenever you introduce a network device that uses memory to buffer traffic flow and make forwarding decisions, you can run into oversubscription. This includes bridges, switches, routers, firewalls, and so forth. Make sure that you calculate the expected traffic load on each of the ports and buy a device that is capable of handling the expected load.

Source Route Bridging (SRB)

Source route bridging (SRB) is designed for use with Token Ring networks. As its name implies, the source of traffic (the client) determines the best path through the Layer 2 network. This differs from transparent bridging in which a Spanning Tree Algorithm is used on the bridges to determine the best path. (This will be discussed in the "Spanning Tree Algorithm" section later in this chapter.)

NOTE

SRB has been updated to source route switching (SRS) and offers benefits similar to those discussed in the section on transparent bridging. We will use the terms *bridging* and *switching* interchangeably unless otherwise noted.

We discussed Token Ring architecture in Chapter 3. You should recall that a group of clients interconnected and passing the same token are part of the same ring. In much the same way that broadcast traffic and collisions can bog down an Ethernet network, too many clients configured in a single Token Ring can cause unacceptable delays waiting for access to the wire.

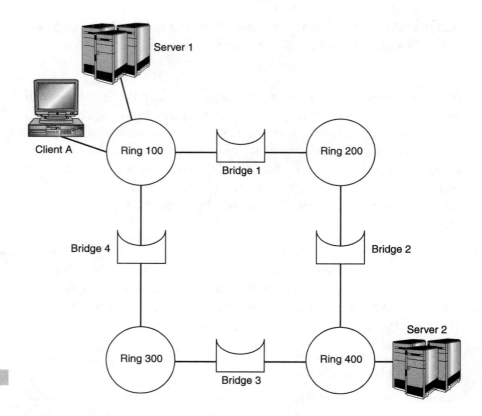

Figure 5.4

Multi-ring environment

NOTE

Remember that in Token Ring networks collisions are not a concern because two clients cannot communicate at the same time, so we are primarily concerned with media access. Figure 5.4 shows the process of SRB in a Token Ring environment.

On Token Ring networks, rings and bridges have an assigned numeric value. Bridges interconnect each of the rings and, in the case of our example network, we have a loop created for redundancy. Let's assume that Client A needs to communicate with Server 1. The following steps outline how Client A would determine the best path to Server 1:

1. Client A sends out a local explorer frame to determine whether Server 1 is on the same ring as itself. A special bit in the frame called the **routing information indicator (RII)** is set to 0, indicating to all bridges that the frame should be ignored.

2. Server 1 sees a frame with its address and responds to the local explorer frame. At this point all communications take place locally without involving any of the bridges or other rings.

Now let's look at a more complex example. Client A wishes to communicate with Server 2. The process begins in the same manner as in the previous example:

1. Client A sends out a local explorer frame to determine whether Server 2 is on the same ring as itself.

2. No response is received to the local explorer frame, so Client A sends out an **all routes explorer (ARE)** frame. When an ARE is sent, the RII field is set to 1, indicating that bridges should pass the frame and fill in the **routing information field (RIF)**.

3. Bridge 1 receives the ARE from Client A and fills in the RIF. The first entry indicates the source ring and the local bridge ID. The RIF entry on Bridge 1 would look like this:

    `ring100-bridge1`

4. Bridge 1 retransmits the frame as a local explorer frame attempting to find Server 2 on ring 200.

5. No response to the local explorer frame is received, so Bridge 1 retransmits the frame with the RII set to 1 and the discovery process continues at Bridge 2.

6. Bridge 2 receives the frame and notes that the RII is set to 1. It fills in the RIF field with the next set of entries, as follows:

    `ring100-bridge1-ring200-bridge2`

7. Bridge 2 sends the frame out as a local explorer frame attempting to find Server 2 on ring 400.

8. Server 2 responds to the local explorer frame and retransmits the RIF field, sending the frame back to Client A along the same path.

Bridge 4 and Bridge 3 also participate in the same process at the same time, with the final RIF entries for both paths looking like this:

```
ring100-bridge1-ring200-bridge2-ring400
ring100-bridge4-ring300-bridge3-ring400
```

Server 2 responds to both of the explorer frames, reversing the fields in its reply to Client A. So, which path does Client A use when continuing the communication process with Server 2? The answer depends on how the SRB is configured. The default behavior is to use the path identified in the first response received. Additional criteria can be used, such as least number of bridges (smallest number of hops), largest **maximum transmission unit (MTU)**, or a combination of any of these criteria. Using the default behavior of quickest response allows Client A to find the fastest path through the network at the time the ARE was sent out.

5.1.2   Translational Bridging

Some networks contain a mixture of Ethernet and Token Ring clients. To bridge these networks we can use **translational bridging**. Several key differences need to be overcome when attempting to connect Ethernet and Token Ring clients, including:

- Media access
- MAC address format
- Framing format
- RIF
- MTU size

There are other differences, but the preceding list represents the most significant. A bridge that communicates both Ethernet and Token Ring can translate mismatched fields and allow networks to communicate properly. Unfortunately, few standards exist for translational bridging and implementations vary between vendors.

WARNING

Some translational bridging implementations may not work between vendors, so it's important to research compatibility if you plan to implement translational bridging or switching.

Because of the nonstandard behaviors of translational bridging, most network design engineers (us included) strongly recommend that when communicating between Token Ring and Ethernet networks, a more intelligent router or other Layer 3 device should be used instead of a Layer 2 bridge or switch.

NOTE

When communicating through a router, the Layer 2 header is completely rebuilt, eliminating the need for translation of Layer 2 data fields.

With a firm grasp of the concept of bridging, we can now move on to the current area of switching.

5.2   Switches and Switching

The concept of switching is identical to bridging: They both forward, flood, and filter traffic using the same rules. Both bridges and switches create multiple collision domains as well (one collision domain per port). However, switching offers the following improvements over bridging:

- Higher port density
- Faster packet-processing capabilities
- Quality-of-service (QoS) capabilities
- Use of virtual LAN (VLAN) technology

Regarding port density, early bridges typically had two ports, and some had as many as four. It was rare and very expensive to find a bridge with a total of six or more ports. Most early switches came with a minimum of eight ports, with some having as many as 16 or 24 ports. Some of the switches used in today's network environment are expandable to more than 350 full-duplex 100-Mbps ports. Each port is, in essence, a single bridging device that creates its own collision domain and uses port-based memory for buffering incoming and outgoing data.

Switches achieve faster packet-processing capabilities than bridges in a number of different ways:

- **Application-specific integrated circuits (ASICs):** Bridges accomplish their decision-making process almost exclusively via software. Although it was adequate for its time, today's networking applications and services require much faster processing capabilities. This is achieved by imbedding the decision routines into hardware ASICs installed on each port on a switch. Deciding how to manage a packet is handled at the lowest level possible, allowing switches to achieve packet throughput in excess of 150 million packets per second, which was inconceivable 10 years ago.

- **Better central processing units (CPUs):** In addition to the ASICs, switches use the latest and most powerful CPUs on the market that help process all of the port-based ASIC decisions as well as other switching functions such as QoS and VLAN configuration (discussed in the "VLANs" section later in this chapter).

- **Cut-through switching:** This process enables switches to forward packets immediately after receiving the destination MAC address. Bridges manage frames by using **store-and-forward** processing, whereby the bridge receives the entire frame in memory before forwarding it to a different interface. **Cut-through processing** allows the switch to forward frames much more quickly because the destination MAC address is received in the first six bytes of a frame. The major drawback to cut-through switching is that malformed frames from collisions or a misbehaving network interface card (NIC) are also forwarded.

- **Fragment-free switching:** This technique is similar to cut-through except that it eliminates the forwarding of collision packets and still achieves a faster processing capability than store-and-forward bridge behavior. In the **fragment-free switching** technique, the frame is forwarded after receipt of the 64th byte frame. Because Ethernet requires that collisions are detected prior to this byte being transmitted, a successful transmission to the 64th byte ensures a high probability that the frame is good (not a collision).

Another switching benefit is the ability to implement QoS. Bridges process packets based on a FIFO scheme. Switches, by default, do the same type of processing but also have the ability to process packets based on rules set up by administrators. QoS allows a switch to process higher priority frames first so that data is not lost on busy networks. Common uses of QoS are found in implementations of Voice-over IP (VoIP), video conferencing, mainframe connectivity, and manufacturing, to name a few. Many of today's network services are sensitive to delay and packet loss, and QoS guarantees that higher-priority frames are properly processed.

NOTE   VoIP is a technology that allows you to run your phone system over a data network. This is becoming a more popular method of deploying phone service as the technology stabilizes.

Our final switching benefit is **virtual local area network (VLAN)** capability. VLAN technology gives a switch the ability to control broadcast, multicast, and unknown frame propagation by creating virtual LAN segments that simulate a Layer 3 network. Both bridges and switches will, by default, flood all broadcast, multicast, and unknown traffic out of all ports except the port of entry. We will learn about problems that can occur on large complex networks with these specific traffic types in the "Broadcast Storms" section later in this chapter. VLANs are covered in detail later in the chapter as well. First, let's examine the building blocks of a switch and the switching environment, and then discuss the two main types of switching: circuit switching and packet switching.

5.2.1   Switching Fabric

Switching fabric is the combination of switching elements, which are the basic building blocks of switches. Switching fabric includes the switches in a node, the hardware that they contain, and the software programs that control switching paths. Switching fabric is independent of the bus technology. The term is sometimes used to mean all switching hardware and software in a network.

The term is also used (rather confusingly) to refer to the highway that data takes as it passes from one port to the next inside a switch. In this case, it is sometimes referred to as the data plane. The size (capacity, or bandwidth) of a switching fabric is defined by its data width in bits and the speed at which it can transmit these bits. The calculation also depends on whether data frames move across the fabric in only one direction at a time (half duplex) or whether the fabric can support the transmission and receipt of a frame simultaneously (full duplex). For example, a Cisco Catalyst 6000 series switch provides a switching fabric that is 256 bits wide and operates at 62.5 MHz/sec. This switch provides a switching fabric bandwidth of 16 Gbps half duplex and 32 Gbps full duplex. Switching fabric typically includes data buffers and the use of shared memory.

Crossbar

A **crossbar switch** is a device that directly switches data between any input port and any output port, without sharing a bus with any other data. The paths set up between devices can be (and usually are) fixed for a predefined duration or changed when desired.

Crossbar topology can be contrasted with bus topology, in which there is only one path that all devices share. A major advantage of crossbar switching is that the traffic between any two devices does not affect traffic between other devices. In addition to offering more flexibility, a crossbar switch environment offers greater scalability than a bus environment. We will look at crossbar switches based on a matrix topology when we consider space-division circuit switching later in this chapter.

Broadcast

An increasing number of communication and computing environments require the ability to simultaneously transfer text, voice, graphics, or video information from a transmitting device to a set of receiving devices. Also, parallel processing systems transfer data between processing and memory units. When a transmitting device simultaneously sends information to more than one receiving device, a one-to-many connection is required. This is called a *broadcast connection*. A set of broadcast connections is called a *broadcast assignment*. Networks that satisfy this requirement are called *broadcast networks*.

Using a broadcast connection in a nonblocking, multistage network, an input port is connected simultaneously to several unused output ports. (We discuss blocking in the "Packet Switching" section later in this chapter.) However, an output port cannot be connected to more than one input port. The network must be capable of satisfying a request from an idle input port for a connection to a set of idle output ports without causing any disturbance or rearrangement of other existing broadcasting connections. The network must be nonblocking for broadcast assignments.

Sometimes these two requirements are contradictory, and some network structures can require the rearrangement of existing connections in order to alleviate a blocking condition. Such networks are known as rearrangeable networks, but should be used with caution because of the possible disruption of ongoing communication and the time delay in setting up the path.

In standard nonblocking broadcast networks, it is always possible to provide a connection path through the network for any legitimate broadcast connection request from an input port to a set of output ports without disturbing existing connections. If more than one such path is available, then any path can be selected without concern for future requests.

5.2.2   Circuit Switching

Circuit switching is the oldest form of switching (originally used on traditional telephone networks). Its basic behavior is to create a path between two endpoints (phones) for the duration of a call. While the call is in progress, a point-to-point connection exists between the devices, and no other device can use the resources along that path. After the call is over, the circuit path goes through a process referred to as "teardown" that makes the resources available again.

Circuit switching establishes calls over the most efficient route available at the time. This means that a call from Los Angeles to El Paso could go through a switching center in Detroit, because a more direct route was not available when the connection was made. That path or circuit remains the same throughout the call, even if a less expensive route becomes available during the connection.

Circuit-switched networks are used for delivering information that must be received in the order in which it was sent—for example, real-time audio and video. Circuit switching ensures that data is delivered as quickly as possible over a dedicated connection. It can, however, be wasteful compared to other types of communication, because the circuit remains active even if the end stations are not currently transmitting.

Examples of circuit-switched networks include:

- Asynchronous Transfer Mode (ATM)
- Integrated Services Digital Network (ISDN)
- Leased digital line
- T1
- Analog dial-up line

NOTE

Leased analog lines do exist but are seldom used today. Historically, they were used to connect mainframe computers to dumb terminals.

Types of switching include time-division, space-division, time-space, and time-space-time, as discussed in the following sections.

Time-Division Switching

Federal Standard 1073C defines **time-division switching** as the switching of **time-division multiplexed (TDM)** channels by shifting bits between time slots in a TDM frame. The same standard defines time-division multiplexing as digital multiplexing in which two or more apparently simultaneous channels are derived from a given frequency spectrum (i.e., bit stream) by interleaving pulses representing bits from different channels.

In time-division switching, slow data streams are partitioned into pieces, or data segments, that share time on a higher-speed stream. The segments are switched one at a time. This switching method is based on synchronous TDM, and the source and destination of data in each time slot are known. As a result, address bits are not required in the slot.

A time slot has fixed endpoints and a fixed circuit, but different slots occupying the same high-speed link can have different endpoints and circuits (and typically do). When data is being transmitted on one channel, the data for the next channel is prepared for transmission and may be buffered at the gate. The time allocated to a slot must equal the transmission time for the slot data plus any propagation delay across the bus.

For time-division switching to be successful, the transmitting station must connect in the same time slot as the appropriate receiving station. The process of coordinating time slots is called the **time-slot interchange (TSI)**. It involves holding received samples in a buffer memory for only the time necessary to shift their positions in the cycle—that is, to move them from one time slot to another. This process can cause delays in time-division networks.

Time-division switching can be implemented only on digital links. However, voice and video traffic are frequently digitized (sampled) for transmission over wide-area, high-speed links. The technique can handle devices of differing speeds by allocating more time slots to fast devices.

Space-Division Switching

In **space-division switching**, single transmission-path routing is accomplished using a switch to physically separate a set of matrix contacts or cross-points. Space-division is, therefore, closely linked to the concept of the crossbar switch. A cross-point connects an incoming and an outgoing circuit to create a path element or link. A dedicated physical path is created for each traffic stream, and several signals are switched in parallel. Although the technique was originally developed for analog environments, space-division circuits can carry either analog or digital traffic.

Number (N) input paths form a crossbar matrix with number (M) output paths, often forming a square N-by-M matrix. The number of cross-points in an N-by-M matrix grows as the square of the number of stations increases. Space-division switching is fast, because each path is assigned to one call, and exclusively to that call, throughout its duration. Once a continuous path has been established, signals are transferred between the two channels (input and output) at the full transmission speed of the circuit, without the need for time-division. At any time, a large number of completed paths can exist through a network between different pairs of communication channels.

The process of identifying the cross-points that must be closed to set up a continuous path between two given channels, without disturbing other existing connections, is known as path-finding. This requires that the system identify the links to and from the cross-points. The system must, therefore, be able to determine at any time which links are free and which are busy. There is a requirement for central control that can check the status of the links at the network itself or can consult a map of the network's dynamic status in memory.

Space-division switching has a number of disadvantages. If the matrix becomes too large (typically if N is greater than 64), set-up times can be a problem. In addition, the loss of a single cross-point can prevent a connection.

To minimize these problems, multistage switching is implemented in all but the smallest switching configurations. For each path through the switching network, several matrices (typically four to eight) are interconnected by links. Each matrix belongs to a different switching stage, and the middle stages usually have fewer cross-points than the first and last stages. This arrangement results in fewer cross-points for the same number of input and output circuits. In a well-designed network, a large number of possible paths exists between any input channel and any output channel, even if many cross-points are already busy. Reliability is therefore greatly improved.

NOTE

The original, space-division telephone exchanges always switched continuous analog speech signals. For this reason, the term *analog switching* is often used as a synonym for space-division switching while *digital switching* is a commonly used synonym for time-division switching. However, you should remember that space-division circuits can carry both analog and digital signals (although not on the same circuit at the same time), and that time-division systems can carry voice and video data, albeit in digital form.

Time-Space Switching

Space-division switching has the advantage of having no delays due to TSI processing, but has the disadvantage of having too many cross-points. Time-division switching, on the other hand, requires no cross-points, but TSI processing causes propagation delays. You can create a switching fabric that combines both types of switching to get the best of both techniques. **Time-space switching** precedes each input trunk in a crossbar with a TSI and delays samples so that they arrive at the right time for the space-division switch's schedule.

The time stages have buffer memories for temporary storage of samples. The space stages employ electronic cross-points (gates). Buffer memory read/write operations and gate opening/closing are executed at times defined by the connections established through the switching network, using information held in control memory. The related operations of entering and clearing data in control memory to establish and release connections are generally known as marking operations, and are performed in accordance with instructions from central control.

Space switches that work in conjunction with time switches should be able to change their connection patterns on every time slot. Such switches are known as time-multiplexed state switches (TMSS). Thus in time-space switching, each transmission has a separate path, but these paths are not fixed.

Time-Space-Time Switching

You implement time-space-time (TST) switching using a switching fabric that includes a number of TDM inlets. The data pass through a space switch (or multiplexed space switches) to create circuits for TDM outlets. This arrangement gives more flexibility and lowers the probability of call blocking (see the "Blocking" section later in this chapter).

In practice, networks use switching fabrics that are combinations of both space and time stages.

5.2.3   Packet Switching

Packet switching is implemented by protocols that divide messages into packets before sending them. Each packet is then transmitted individually. Packets can follow different routes to the message destination and may not arrive in the order that they were sent. After all of the packets forming a message arrive at the destination, they are recompiled into the original message. Most modern wide-area network (WAN) protocols, including TCP/IP, X.25, and Frame Relay, are based on packet-switching technologies.

One of the key features of a packet is that it contains the destination address in addition to the data. On IP networks, packets are often called datagrams.

In contrast, normal telephone service is based on circuit switching, in which a dedicated line is allocated for transmission between two parties. Circuit switching is used when data must be transmitted quickly and must arrive in the order in which it is sent (for example, live audio and video). Packet switching is used to transmit data that can withstand some delays in transmission (for example, e-mail messages and Web pages).

NOTE

Technologies such as Cellular Digital Packet Data (CDPD) and VoIP using code division multiple access (CDMA) are currently implementing voice communication using packet switching, with little or no perceptible decline in quality.

Port Mapping

To the home computer user, a port is a hardware device to which a peripheral such as a printer may be connected. However, to packet-switching protocols, such as TCP, a port is represented by a number (the allowed range is 1 through 65535) within a packet that indicates the type of packet. For example, a value of 80 normally indicates a Hypertext Transfer Protocol (HTTP) packet that contains Web information. Ports are essential to packet switching. In TCP/IP, for example, communication between a source and a destination is implemented by a socket, which is defined by three pieces of information: the IP address (either of the source or destination), the port number, and the transport protocol (either TCP or User Datagram Protocol [UDP]). Because IP datagrams contain source and destination information, a channel of communication is set up between the transmitting and receiving socket for each packet.

In packet switching, the route that the packet takes is (in theory) unimportant. It is even possible that a packet that is too large to be transmitted over part of a network is split up, and the resulting smaller packets take different routes. A packet that contains its source and destination address and its port number is identified by its destination socket, which is **listening** on the appropriate port number, and processed accordingly. When a reliable protocol such as TCP is used, any packets that do not reach their destination are retransmitted.

Ports are used to address applications and services that run on a computer. Several applications can run simultaneously on a particular computer, each running on a different port. Thus, a port number may be seen as an address of an application within the computer.

Port mapping, or **port address translation (PAT)**, is a process in which packets arriving for a particular socket can be translated and thus redirected to a different socket. This technique is used, for example, to create a persistent passage using **network address translation (NAT)**. Port mapping is necessary only for incoming transmissions, not for returning traffic.

A network uses port mapping if, for example, a Web or e-mail server is running on a station with a private IP address and needs to gain access to, and be accessed from, the Internet using a fixed public IP address. Port mapping is also used if a network is running an applications, such as an instant messenger, that needs incoming connections on a client computer with a private IP internal address.

Some port mappers, such as the IP Masquerade feature provided by IPNetRouter, combine NAT with port mapping to allow multiple hosts to connect to the Internet using a single user ISP account and single public IP address. Others, such as the port mapping services provided by MultiNet, mirror services provided by other computers on the Internet or LAN. A port on the MultiNet server is mapped to a port on another device. Traffic from client software connected to the MultiNet port is tunneled through MultiNet and passed to the mapped device. The mapped device sees MultiNet as the client. The client software sees MultiNet as the server.

A key use of port mapping is to enable client software that is not capable or configured to use a proxy server (such as a news client) to securely access Internet servers without introducing a security risk. A software proxy server is similar in function to a hardware firewall. When a firewall protects an intranet (which is normally the case), port mapping can be used to establish a tunnel through the firewall, allowing a trusted server on the local network to provide Internet services. Firewalls are discussed in Chapter 10.

Port mapping on a switch is relatively straightforward and normally requires only a look-up table. Configuring port mapping on a router is more complex, because the router selects the end station using the longest match algorithm. This means that the router needs to route the incoming packets to the most specific subnet for which the target station's IP address is valid—that is, the subnet with the longest network mask. (Subnetting is covered in Chapter 7.)

Blocking

Blocking occurs when a network is unable to connect stations and complete a circuit. In circuit switching, this occurs when all paths are in use. Some voice-switching networks accept blocking, particularly if they are used for short-duration calls. On many networks, however, the goal is to reduce the incidence of blocking to an acceptable level. This is done by using multiplexed space-division switching and by implementing combined space-time systems.

In packet switching, blocking is caused by congestion. This occurs when several items are trying to access the same port simultaneously, or when the switching fabric is receiving more data than it can handle. The latter condition is due to oversubscription. A nonblocking switching implementation is one in which the switch fabric has a greater capacity than the sum of the bandwidth of all the ports.

If blocking occurs within a packet-switched network, congestion management is used to help ensure that the blocked packet is not lost and that the condition is invisible to the user. Remember that in a packet-switching network, packets do not have to arrive in the order that they were transmitted and any packet that arrives before its **time-to-live (TTL)** expires will be placed in its correct place in the data stream. Congestion management also handles ports that have different capacities as well as switching fabrics that have different capacities from the ports. In the absence of congestion management, a 100-Mbps port will soon overwhelm a 10-Mbps port.

Congestion management is implemented using buffers or queues. A queue is memory that is allocated to hold a packet (or frame) until a switch or port can process it. Queues can use fixed-buffer queuing or dynamic-buffer queuing, and are implemented as input queues, output queues, and shared queues.

In fixed-buffer queuing, a fixed amount of memory, which is usually set to the size of the MTU, is allocated for each frame that enters a switch or router. This is an easy system to control but is an inefficient use of memory, because each buffered frame is allocated the maximum amount of memory to hold the largest possible frame, regardless the actual frame size.

Input queue buffers are implemented in small increments (typically 64 bytes). Each frame uses as many buffers as it needs. This is an efficient use of memory but requires more complex (and expensive) control.

Input queues handle blocking due to oversubscription. In effect, they reduce the rate at which data enters the switching fabric and buffer the excess data during busy periods. This adds latency to the overall process of switching the frame, slows throughput, and can lead to head-of-line blocking.

As frames enter an input queue, they are handled on a FIFO basis. A frame cannot be transmitted until the frames before it are transmitted. Also, it cannot be transmitted until an **egress port** is available. If the egress port for a frame at the head of the line is congested, then the frame waits in the queue, blocking all the frames behind it.

Output queues are used to prevent, or minimize, head-of-line blocking by allowing the egress port to buffer a frame until the receiving device is ready to accept it. This removes the frame from the beginning of the input queue and thus allows the frames behind it to be processed.

The use of shared queues is the most efficient queuing technique. All ports on a system share the same queues. When a frame enters a switch, it is placed in the shared buffer space. It is then switched to the output port without moving to another buffer. Shared queues also prevent head-of-line blocking because frames can be switched to their egress port as soon as that port is available. Because there is no buffer transfer, the FIFO restriction no longer applies.

ATM Switching

Asynchronous transfer mode (ATM) is a high-speed packet-switching technique capable of supporting many classes of traffic. It uses short, fixed-length packets called *cells*. This reduces the delay and jitter (variance of delay) for delay-sensitive services such as real-time voice and video. ATM is capable of supporting a wide range of traffic types such as voice, video, image, and data.

ATM switching architecture operates at bandwidths from 150 Mbps through 600 Mbps. ATM is *connection oriented,* and the switching elements have predefined routing tables to minimize the complexity of single-switch routing. The ATM cell has a fixed-length *payload* (48 bytes) and a fixed-length *header* (5 bytes). Header functionality is limited and allows the implementation of different switching architectures, such as queuing functions. Conceptually, an ATM switching network has two parts, transport and control.

The transport network is the physical means by which information is transferred from the incoming logical ATM channel (inlet) to the outgoing logical ATM channel (outlet). The control portion of the switch controls the transport network. It decides, for example, which inlet to connect to which outlet based on incoming signaling information.

All ATM cells belong to a virtual connection preestablished by the transport network. All traffic is segmented into cells for transmission across this network, and the sequence integrity of all the cells in the virtual connection is preserved across each ATM switch. This simplifies the reconstruction of the original traffic at the destination and, hence, reduces the total delay on the network. Each cell header contains a virtual channel identifier (VCI) that identifies the virtual connection to which the cell belongs.

When a connection is established on an ATM network, it defines the virtual path through different switches across the network. The VCI is local to each switch port. As each cell travels across an ATM switch, the switch translates the VCI into a new value and builds a new cell header containing the new VCI, and possibly a new virtual path identifier (VPI). The ATM switch is also responsible for transporting cells from an inlet to an outlet port.

Two identifiers characterize the logical ATM channel:

- **Physical inlet/outlet:** Identified by a physical port number
- **Logical channel on the physical port:** Identified by the VCI and/or the VPI

During the switching process, the physical and logical identifiers of the incoming cell have to be related to physical and logical identifiers of the outgoing cell. ATM switches implement both space-switching and time-switching functions. The space-switching function allows a connection between any input and any output, and implements cell routing within the switch. The time-switching function is necessary because ATM works in asynchronous mode, and cells that arrive in various time slots from different inputs need to be delivered in different time slots to different outputs. Because there is no preassigned time-slot connection, a contention occurs when more than two logical channels are connected to the same output in the same time slot. The ATM switch solves this problem by implementing a queuing function.

The basic unit of the ATM switch fabric is the switching element, which is implemented in a single integrated circuit element. At the inlet, the routing information of the incoming cell is analyzed and the cell is then directed to the correct outlet. The switching element consists of an interconnection network, an input controller (IC) for each incoming line, and an output controller (OC) for each outgoing line. The IC synchronizes arriving cells to the internal clock. The OC transports cells that have been received from the interconnection network toward their destination. The interconnection network couples the IC and OC.

An ATM switch performs statistical multiplexing in the switch inputs and demultiplexing in the switch outputs. If two ATM cells arrive at two inlets simultaneously and are directed toward the same outlet, then blocking can occur. To deal with this, arbitration and queuing mechanisms are required. ATM switches utilize input and output queues. They also implement shared queues, although this last technique is known as *central queuing* in ATM terminology.

NOTE

Space permits only a brief description of ATM switching in this book. More details can be obtained from the Internet or any technical library.

As you can see from our discussion, switches are far superior and have all but replaced the older bridging technology. Switches have added functionality and speed, but the basic process of forwarding frames based on the destination MAC address has remained constant as technology has improved.

For the rest of this chapter the terms *bridge* and *switch* will be used interchangeably because the technologies are so similar that in most discussions the actual hardware in use (switch or bridge) is irrelevant. If you remember that switches are hardware-based, super fast, port-dense bridges, all of the discussions will make sense. Use Table 5.3 as a quick review.

Now that you have a firm grasp of the benefits of bridging and switching, it's time to take a closer look at the potential problems that can be created if these technologies are not deployed correctly.

TABLE 5.3   Bridge and Switch Review

Feature	Bridge	Switch
Decision making	Software based	Hardware based
Ports	2 to 4 ports average High cost/port	16 to 300+ ports Low cost/port
Forwarding process	FIFO	FIFO by default, but can use QoS rules for more advanced processing capabilities.
Switching method	Store and forward	Store and forward by default, but can be configured to use advanced processing techniques such as cut-through and fragment-free.
Broadcast control	Not available	Available through the use of VLAN technology.

5.3   Spanning Tree Algorithm

The **Spanning Tree Algorithm (STA)** was created to overcome a specific weakness inherent in bridges and continues to be deployed today in switching technologies. Implementations of STA are governed by IEEE specification 802.1d. The algorithm is implemented as the Spanning Tree Protocol and is used as a communication and configuration protocol between Layer 2 devices.

5.3.1   Broadcasts

The specific weakness managed by STA is the flooding behavior of broadcast, multicast, and unknown traffic types. Consider the behavior as illustrated in Figure 5.5.

Client A sends a broadcast, which is flooded out of all the local ports of Switch 1. When the broadcast reaches switches 2 and 3, they also flood the broadcast packet out of all ports. This behavior is not only expected, but desired. However, you will run into problems when you configure two or more bridges into a loop.

NOTE

The broadcast is never sent back out of the port on which it was received.

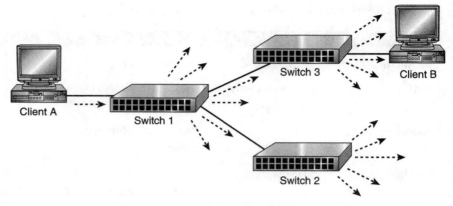

Figure 5.5

Normal broadcast flooding

Broadcast from Client A is flooded out of all ports of all switches.

Broadcast Storms

Why would you configure your network with bridging loops? The most common reason is for connection redundancy. By interconnecting multiple switches with redundant paths, you can overcome problems with faulty cables or port failures. The other, less common reason for loops in a network is accidentally plugging a cable into the wrong port on the wrong switch (but that *never* happens). Figure 5.6 illustrates the effect of a bridging loop.

The following phases, along with Figure 5.6, illustrate the communications process in a looped topology:

- **Phase 1:** Client A broadcasts an ARP request for the MAC address of Client B.

- **Phase 2:** Switch 1 floods the packet as expected out of all ports, including ports 2 and 3 connected to switches 2 and 3, respectively.

- **Phase 3:** Switch 2 receives the broadcast and floods it out of all ports, including Port 2 connected to Switch 3. At the same time, Switch 3 is receiving the broadcast in Port 1 and floods it out of all ports, including Port 2 connected to Switch 2.

- **Phase 4:** The loop begins when switches 2 and 3 receive the broadcast from each other and, following standard bridging rules, flood the broadcast back out of all ports including Port 1 back to Switch 1.

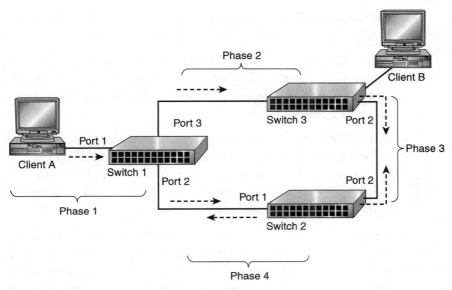

Because the switches are plugged together in a looped
topology, the broadcasts will loop endlessly.

Figure 5.6

**Clients on a bridged
Ethernet network**

This example uses a very simple three-switch network with one client broadcasting a single ARP packet. A moderately complex network might have 20 or 30 switches and 400 to 500 clients connected. If you multiplied our example behavior by the actual number of clients and switches involved on a medium-size network, the network would be brought down by a series of simple broadcast requests! The entire process as illustrated is often referred to as a *broadcast storm*. The endless looping of broadcasts is maintained because Layer 2 of the OSI model does not provide a timeout mechanism for packets, unlike Layer 3 that provides a TTL mechanism for pulling stray frames off of a segment.

Another less well-known side effect of a bridging loop is the corruption of the forwarding tables on all of the switches. Recall that a switch learns based on reading the source MAC addresses of received packets. Looking back at Figure 5.6:

- **Phase 1:** Switch 1 receives a broadcast packet in Port 1 with Client A's MAC address as the source and the all F's broadcast MAC address (all Fs) as the destination. Switch 1 associates Client A's MAC with Port 1 in the forwarding table.

- **Phase 2:** Switches 2 and 3 receive the broadcast packet with Client A's MAC address. The packet enters both switches on Port 1 and the appropriate entry is made in the forwarding table of switches 2 and 3.

- **Phase 3:** We begin to see the corruption take place. Switches 2 and 3 flood the packet out of their respective Port 2. Each switch then receives Client A's broadcast packet from the other in Port 2. Learning from the source MAC address again, the forwarding table is updated to reflect the new port for Client A.

- **Phase 4:** Switch 1 receives packets back from both Switch 2 and Switch 3 and updates its forwarding table associating Client A's MAC address with either Port 2 or Port 3, depending on which port the broadcast packet was last received. This flip-flop behavior will continue on all of the switches until they are unplugged or manually reset.

You can see from our examples that bridging loops are bad. It would take very little time for Layer 2 broadcast loops to completely destroy the functionality of any network. The solution to this problem, as stated at the beginning of this section, is the use of Spanning Tree.

Spanning Tree Protocol (STP)

The Spanning Tree Protocol (STP) prevents bridging loops by identifying a preferred path through a series of looped bridges. Administrators can provide redundancy and fault-tolerance by wiring a loop, and then using STP will turn off ports that would cause loops to occur. If a primary link fails, STP will reactivate the back-up port, allowing normal operation of the network to continue. The STP process is accomplished by:

- Election of a root bridge
- Identification of a root port
- Identification of a designated port

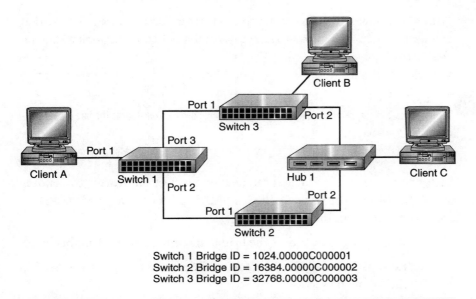

Figure 5.7

Root bridge election

Root Bridge Election

The first task of STP is the election of a root bridge and it is managed by using a **bridge ID**. The bridge ID is 8 bytes long and consists of a bridge priority and a MAC address. The **bridge priority** is a user-configurable 2-byte field offering a range of values from 0 to 65535 (2^{16}). The MAC address portion of the bridge ID is a 6-byte field and varies from vendor to vendor but is typically the lowest configured MAC address on the bridge. It is important to remember that the *lowest* bridge ID wins the root bridge election. An administrator can control the election process by setting the bridge priority of a given bridge to be lower than any other bridge on the network, ensuring that it wins as the root bridge. A bridge ID might look something like this:

32768.00000C12AF01

Looking at Figure 5.7, we can step through the process of electing a root bridge.

TIP
The term "bridge" is used in this chapter section for simplicity and consistency, and represents both bridges and switches. The term *root bridge* persists in most documentation and is used here, although the term *root switch* is becoming more common.

WARNING
The figures used in our examples do not necessarily represent good network layouts. They are used to illustrate points concerning the current topic.

Each bridge, when first turned on, begins the election process by sending out a special type of packet called a bridge protocol data unit (BPDU). Some of the fields in the BPDU are:

- **Root bridge ID:** This is the bridge ID of the current root bridge.

- **Root path cost:** This is the cost of the path to the root (discussed in the following section).

- **Sender bridge ID:** This is the ID of the bridge that sent the BPDU.

Each bridge believes itself to be the root until it receives a BPDU with a lower root bridge ID. In Figure 5.7, let's assume that switches 2 and 3 have been turned on. Switch 3 would begin transmitting BPDUs with the root bridge ID field and sender bridge ID field both set to its own bridge ID of 32768.00000C000003. At the same time, Switch 2 begins sending BPDUs with the root bridge and sender bridge ID fields set to 16384.00000C000002.

The next step in the process begins when Switch 2 receives Switch 3's BPDU. Switch 2 discards it because the local root bridge ID is lower than the one proposed in the BPDU from Switch 3. Switch 3 receives the BPDU from Bridge 2 and recognizes that Switch 2 is the root bridge because it has a lower bridge ID. Switch 3 now begins to advertise a BPDU with the root bridge ID field set to Switch 2 and the sender ID field still set to its own bridge ID. Switch 2 is now the root bridge.

Later, we turn on Switch 1. It begins advertising BPDUs with its root and sender bridge ID fields set to 1024.00000C000001. It discards the BPDUs sent to it from switches 2 and 3 because its own bridge ID is lower. When switches 2 and 3 receive a BPDU from Switch 1, they recognize Switch 1 as the new root and begin advertising BPDUs with the root bridge ID field set to Switch 1. Now that our root bridge has been determined, we can begin the process of identifying the best path to the root.

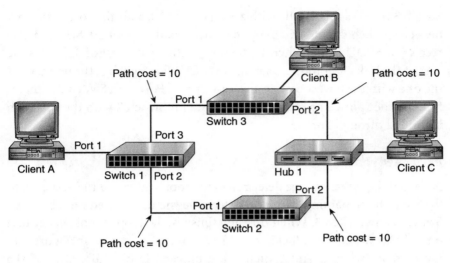

Switch 1 Bridge ID = 1024.00000C000001
Switch 2 Bridge ID = 16384.00000C000002
Switch 3 Bridge ID = 32768.00000C000003

Figure 5.8
Path cost determination

Root Ports and Path Cost

Once the root bridge is determined, each nonroot bridge finds the best path to the root using **path cost**. Path cost is a numeric value that bridges use to determine the preference of a given path and is derived by dividing 1000 MBps by the speed of the link. A 100-MBps link has a path cost of 10 (1000/100). Many vendors are adjusting the base of this formula because of the rise of faster links such as 10 GBps, but for simplicity we will stick with the original formula throughout our examples. Continuing with our previous example, Switches 2 and 3 need to find the best path to the root. In Figure 5.8, we have added the appropriate path cost and can now illustrate how this is done.

Switch 1 sends out BPDUs with the root bridge ID and sender ID set to the same value. The BPDU also has a field for path cost. Because Switch 1 is the root, it advertises a path cost of 0. Switch 2 receives this BPDU and adds the cost of the link on which the packet arrived, in this case 10. It then advertises a BPDU to Switch 3 with the following fields:

Root Bridge ID	1024.00000C000001
Path cost	10
Sender Bridge ID	16384.00000C000002

Switch 3 receives this BPDU with a path cost of 10, adds the cost of the link between Switch 2 and Switch 3 to produce a path cost of 20. Switch 3 also receives a BPDU from Switch 1 (the root) with a path cost of 0. It adds the cost of the link and produces a path cost of 10. For Switch 3, the best path is the one with the lowest cost; in this case Port 1. Port 1 on Switch 3 is therefore the root port. The same would be true for Switch 2 with the best path identified through Port 1.

Designated Port

Now that the switches have determined the root bridge and the best path to the root, the remaining step is to determine the **designated port** between Switch 2 and Switch 3. When this step finishes, the loop is broken, because one of the switches is blocking traffic on one of its ports. In Figure 5.8, notice that Switch 2 and Switch 3 are plugged into a hub. One of the switches has to be allowed to forward traffic for the segment. To determine which switch forwards and which does not, let's return to the bridge ID. The switch with the lowest bridge ID forwards traffic while the other blocks it. In this case, Switch 2 has the lowest bridge ID and continues to forward traffic through Port 2 toward the root bridge. This port is known as the designated port. Switch 3 filters all traffic coming in on its Port 2.

NOTE

The switch continues to receive traffic on the port and evaluates each frame. If the frames are configuration frames such as BPDUs or VLAN configuration frames (discussed next), the switch forwards these frames as required. All user traffic is filtered, including unicasts, broadcasts, and multicast frames. If Switch 3 no longer receives BPDUs from Switch 2, Switch 3 takes over the forwarding duties for the segment.

We now have a loop-free switch environment, and are protected from broadcast storms and forwarding table corruption. A few issues can surprise the uninitiated switch administrator. Anytime a new switch is plugged in, the process of determining the root bridge occurs. If the bridge priority is set as illustrated in our examples, the impact is minimal. Additionally, problems can arise when clients are plugged into an active switch. Client services, such as Dynamic Host Configuration Protocol (DHCP) and Network layer address allocation, may run into timeout issues based on how long a bridge or switch works through the port activation process. Most bridges and switches go through the following phases when activating ports to determine which system is the root bridge (as needed) and which ports are active or disabled. These phases and their purposes are:

- **Blocking:** Most Layer 2 devices will initially block traffic while a port activates. This can be roughly compared to the boot process. The port is monitored for BPDU traffic that may indicate an alternate path to the root bridge. If the port does receive BPDU traffic, then the process of determining the root port is undertaken.

- **Listening:** No user data is being forwarded in this phase, but the switch begins to send BPDU traffic out the port and continues to listen for BPDU traffic inbound.

- **Learning:** At this stage the device will begin reading the source address of all traffic received on the port and update its forwarding table appropriately.

- **Forwarding:** Upon entering the forwarding state, the device begins to send and receive data on the active port.

Depending on the device manufacturer and the default configuration, it may take as long as 50 to 60 seconds before the port will begin to forward data. This can cause timeouts and configuration errors on network clients that receive their TCP/IP configurations from DHCP or Trivial File Transfer Protocol (TFTP) servers. To help overcome this, most vendors have a command that allows the bridge or switch to immediately begin forwarding traffic without the phase transitions listed above.

NOTE

DHCP is a service that runs on many networks and allows clients to automatically receive IP address and network configuration information. TFTP is used on Unix systems and some network devices the same way DHCP is used on PC-based systems.

WARNING

Disabling the phases and allowing a port to go directly to a forwarding state may introduce loops into your bridged or switched network. If you use this command on your devices, ensure that it is properly documented and never plug another Layer 2 device into ports configured for immediate forwarding.

The purpose behind Spanning Tree and the processes just discussed is to protect our networks from issues associated with the way Layer 2 devices handle broadcast, multicast, and unknown traffic frames. Another configuration option exists on newer switching equipment that offers the same protection from these traffic types and also allows network administrators greater flexibility and security. This configuration option is known as a virtual local area network.

5.4   Virtual Local Area Networks (VLANs)

Prior to the concept of VLANs, the only way for administrators to block broadcast traffic was to implement a router. Routers by default will not pass broadcast, multicast, or frames with an unknown destination MAC address. The problem with routers is that they far more expensive on a per-port basis than are switches. **VLANs** represent an interim solution, allowing administrators to group ports on their switches so that broadcast traffic is passed only among ports within the group.

NOTE ▢ For ease of reading, we represent broadcast, multicast, and unknown frames simply as broadcast traffic.

Figure 5.9 shows a switch with 24 ports hosting a total of 23 PCs and one server. Among these clients is a group of four Web programmers. These programmers are constantly testing their applications and generating an enormous amount of traffic. The traffic often interferes with other network clients and their ability to use shared server resources. As network administrators, we decide to separate the Web programmers from the main network into their own smaller network. To do this, we create a VLAN and place the Web programmers' ports into that VLAN. Because different vendors use different commands, we explain the process in a generic fashion. Using the correct commands, we create a VLAN named WebProg and assign it a value of 10. The naming and numbering have been randomly generated for this example and do not represent any defaults or required steps. With the VLAN defined, we can now associate the Web programmer's ports with this new VLAN. After this step is accomplished, the Web programmers' ports will only flood broadcast traffic to their own members. This configuration creates two separate **broadcast domains**. A broadcast domain is a group of network devices capable of receiving each other's broadcast traffic.

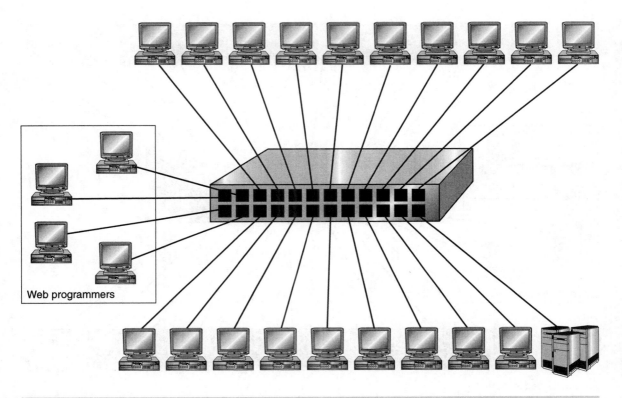

Figure 5.9
24-port switch

The configuration also calls for two separate Layer 3 network segments. If we are using the TCP/IP protocol, for example, our hosts need to have separate network IDs. Another way to visualize a VLAN is to think of coloring the ports that are assigned to a given VLAN, as shown in Figure 5.10.

We now have two VLANs, the default VLAN (usually 1) represented by the black ports and WebProg VLAN 10 represented by the gray ports. If the switch now receives any broadcast traffic on a gray port, it is only flooded out of other gray ports. This action reduces the impact of the Web programmers on the rest of the network clients. After the VLANs are created, it is necessary to have a Layer 3 router, otherwise the clients on separate VLANs will no longer be able to communicate with each other. This is because the network devices can no longer discover each other with Layer 2 broadcast requests (ARP broadcasts, which are discussed in Chapter 6).

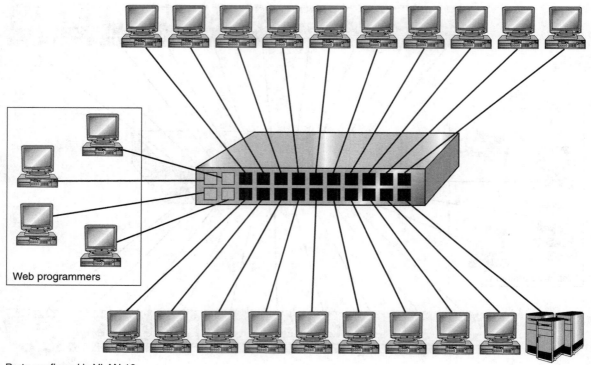

Web programmers

Ports configued in VLAN 10

Figure 5.10

Ports of a different color

5.4.1   VLAN Tags

The basic process of creating a VLAN involves tagging the inbound packet with a VLAN ID. Tagging can be accomplished using one of two methods, frame insertion and frame encapsulation.

Frame insertion involves inserting a small identifier into the frame as it is received at the switch's port. IEEE 802.1q is a VLAN standard that identifies the insertion of a 4-byte identification field inside each received frame. Let's assume that one of our Web programmers sends out a broadcast looking for a shared resource on one of the local Web servers. The frame would be received at the switch and an ID inserted. The switch then checks the status of all of the ports currently associated with that VLAN ID and floods the broadcast only to the outgoing buffers on those ports. As the frame

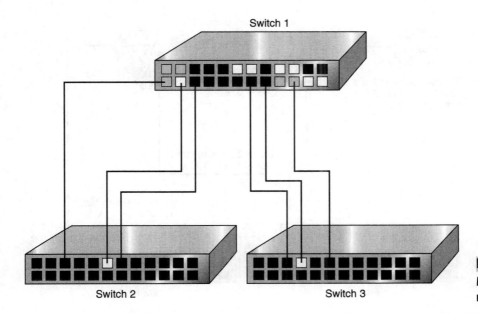

Figure 5.11
Managing VLANs across multiple switches

leaves the port headed to the client, it is necessary for the switch to remove the ID because a standard networking client would be unable to recognize a tagged frame.

Frame encapsulation is a less complicated procedure. The entire frame is simply encapsulated inside a VLAN ID header and checksum. The entire underlying frame is left undisturbed. The process for the switch is the same from this point forward, copying the frame only to those ports with the same VLAN ID. The VLAN encapsulation is removed when the packet is sent to the client. Encapsulation is still a proprietary method of VLAN tagging but is gaining in popularity because it is fast at frame insertion and less prone to damaging the underlying frame.

5.4.2   VLAN Trunking

VLAN trunking uses the VLAN concept and applies it to more than one switch at a time. Figure 5.11 illustrates three switches and three VLANs.

In Figure 5.11, for all white ports to communicate with each other requires that a white port on each switch be used for cross-switch communications. As shown in Figure 5.11, by connecting a white port on Switch 1 to a white port on Switches 2 and 3, we can now forward data traffic and broadcasts between all white ports on all switches. We would then do the same for the

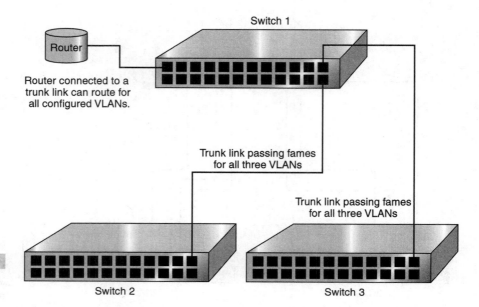

Figure 5.12
Trunking VLANs between switches

other VLANs. The final configuration uses three ports each on Switches 2 and 3 and six ports on Switch 1 just for interswitch VLAN communication. At this point we haven't even started routing frames between our VLANS!

The solution for routing frames is trunking, or making one port forward traffic for all of our VLANs. In effect we are going to make one port communicate with all of the ports at once. Looking at Figure 5.12, notice that doing so cuts our port usage down considerably. On Switches 2 and 3 we use one port for all three VLANs, and on Switch 1 we use two ports, a far more reasonable configuration.

Figure 5.12 also shows one possible configuration of a VLAN router. The router is plugged into a trunked port and can therefore see and route frames for all three VLANs and properly route frames between the three groups of clients. Figure 5.13 depicts the logical configuration of our VLANs.

Although VLANs may seem complex at first, they offer enormous flexibility for administrators. If a particular networking device needs to be moved from one broadcast domain to another, only the port configuration on the switch needs to be changed, not the physical location of the device. We also use fewer ports on our routers, saving money and configuration time.

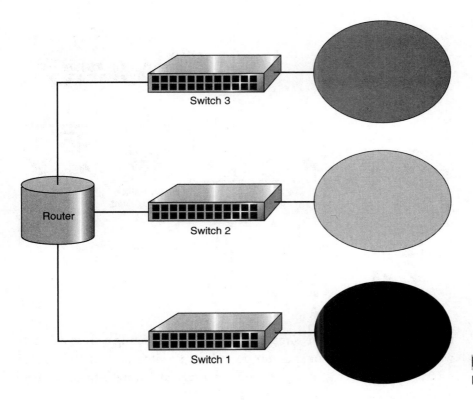

Figure 5.13
Logical VLAN configuration

In this section we examined one of the newest switching technologies in use, VLANs. Our final section explores the integration of switches with hubs and routers.

5.5 Integrating Switches

Companies often continue to use old network equipment while continuously upgrading their networks with newer and better network devices. Network administrators must be able to integrate old equipment with new. This final section looks at integrating switches with older hub technology as well as newer technologies such as multilayer switching.

5.5.1 Integrating Hubs and Switches

Integrating hubs and switches provides a migration path as networks are upgraded from the traditional hub environments to the newer switching

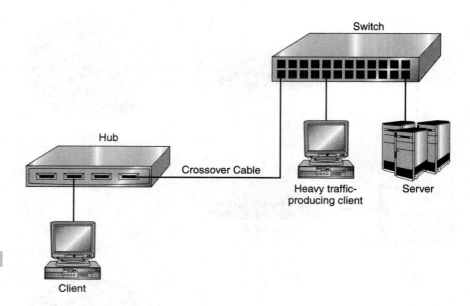

Figure 5.14

Hub and switch environment

topologies. The process is simple and involves connecting a crossover network cable from one of the hub ports into a switch port. If the hub or switch includes a crossover port, you use a regular (straight-through) networking cable.

When designing a network using both hubs and switches, it is essential to remember that all ports on a hub are in the same broadcast and collision domain. All ports on a switch are in the same broadcast domain, but each port is its own collision domain (unless VLANs are used). It is a good practice to connect your servers and other high-traffic workstations directly to a switch so that they are free from collisions. The rest of your clients can remain on the hub until enough switch ports are available for all clients. Networks in the process of migrating from a hub to a switch often look similar to Figure 5.14.

5.5.2   Integrating Routers and Switches

Our final topic of this chapter is the concept of a switch that also routes. This concept has developed rapidly over the past five years, reaching a point where packets are routed at the same speed as the network wire. Most, if not all, of the enterprise-class switching devices sold by various vendors provide this ability. As with a PC, you can add functionality to a switch by adding modules (also called blades) to the chassis. Some of these modules allow you to add functions such as:

- Packet filtering
- Encryption
- Auditing/accounting
- Tunneling
- Routing

The significant benefit of adding these modules directly to the switch is that frames are copied into the memory of the switch once and then forwarded to the next destination without further copying. This allows a switch to route frames at network wire speed. Compare this with a traditional switch and external router combination where the switch has to copy the frame and then forward it to the router. The router then copies the frame and makes additional forwarding decisions, slowing down the entire process. An additional side benefit of integrating switches with routing technology is the simplification of network design. Although the initial cost of these enterprise-class switches is often higher than the simpler and more traditional stand-alone switch, they are, in the long-term, well worth the price.

5.6   Chapter Summary

- Switching fabric consists of an interconnection of switching elements that facilitate a switching mechanism. Switching fabric typically includes data buffers and the use of shared memory.

- Although single stage time- and space-switching elements may be used, many switching fabrics use both space- and time-division elements in multi-stage switches.

- In a crossbar matrix switch (or space-division switch), the conceptual interconnection of a network consists of a rectangular matrix of cross-points. Buffering can be used at the inputs, at the outputs, at the cross-points, or at any of these in combination.

- Circuit-switched networks deliver information that must be received in the order in which it was sent—for example, real-time audio and video.

- Space-division switching has the advantage of having no delays due to TSI processing, but the disadvantage of having too many cross-points. Time-division switching requires no cross-points, but TSI processing causes delays.

- Packet switching is implemented by protocols that divide messages into packets before sending them, with each packet transmitted individually.

- Blocking occurs when a network is unable to connect stations and complete a circuit.

- ATM is a high-speed, connection-oriented packet-switching technique that is capable of supporting many classes of traffic, and uses short, fixed-length packets called cells.

- Bridges are used to segment a network into collision domains; more collision domains mean fewer collisions.

- Bridges learn by reading the source MAC address of a frame and associating it with a particular port; they forward, filter, or flood the frame based on the destination MAC address of a frame.

- VLAN technology provides a switch with the ability to control broadcast, multicast, and unknown frame propagation by creating virtual LAN segments that simulate a Layer 3 network.

- Spanning Tree Protocol prevents bridging loops by identifying a preferred path through a series of looped bridges.

- Most bridges and switches use the blocking, listening, learning, and forwarding phases while activating ports to determine which system is the root bridge (as needed) and which ports are designated or disabled.

- A router or other Layer 3 device should be used instead of a bridge or switch when communicating between Token Ring and Ethernet networks.

5.7   Key Terms

all routes explorer (ARE): A frame used to discover the best path to a client in source route bridging networks.

application-specific integrated circuit (ASIC): A hardware circuit with embedded code used in switching.

blocking: A state on a bridge or a switch in which traffic is not passed to or from the port.

bridge ID: A two-part ID consisting of bridge priority and MAC address.

bridge priority: A 2-byte user-configurable field that provides administrators control over which bridge becomes the root.

broadcast domain: A group of network devices that are capable of receiving each other's broadcast packets.

buffering: The act of temporarily storing data in memory while waiting for access to the media or for further processing.

crossbar switch: A device that directly switches data between any input and any output port, without sharing a bus with other data.

cut-through switching: A type of switching method where the switch forwards packets as soon as the 6-byte destination MAC address is received.

designated port: In a looped bridge or switch environment, the port that is designated to forward traffic for a given segment. All other switches on that segment will filter all client traffic.

egress port: The designated outbound port for a given frame.

filtering: The process of reading information in a packet, such as the destination address, and either forwarding or dropping the packet based on that information.

flooding: When a bridge receives a broadcast, multicast, or a packet with an unknown destination, and copies the packet to all ports except the port of entry.

forwarding: The process that a bridge uses when copying a frame from one port to another using a known destination MAC address.

fragment-free switching: A form of switching used instead of cut-through to eliminate forwarding collision fragments. The packet is forwarded after the 64th byte of data is received.

learning: When a bridge or switch adds an address into its forwarding table.

listening: A phase used on a bridge or switch port that allows it to send BPDU traffic.

maximum transmission unit (MTU): The maximum frame size allowed to travel through a network, using a given protocol and media type.

network address translation (NAT): The process of replacing the source or destination network address in a frame with a valid address.

oversubscription: A condition that exists when a network device is too slow or has too little memory for the current traffic load. The result is dropped packets.

path cost: The cost of a link between two bridges or switches. It is determined by dividing 1,000 Mbps by the speed of the link.

port address translation (PAT): The process of replacing the source or destination network and port address in a frame with a valid address and port number.

proxy aware: Software applications that can be configured to use a proxy server.

root bridge: The bridge with the lowest bridge ID in the Spanning Tree Algorithm. All traffic forwards along the best path toward the root bridge.

root port: The port with the lowest-cost path to the root bridge.

routing information field (RIF): A field used in source route bridging that maintains the correct path that frame used to traverse a series of Token Ring networks. Token Ring bridges or switches populate this field.

routing information indicator (RII): A field used in source route bridging that identifies the packet as a local frame if set to 0, or a source route frame if set to 1.

Source Route Bridging (SRB): A type of bridging used on Token Ring networks where the client sends out a special frame used to determine the best path to a given destination.

space-division switching: Single transmission-path routing accomplished using a switch to physically separate a set of matrix contacts or cross-points. Space-division is closely related to the concept of the crossbar switch.

Spanning Tree Algorithm (STA): An algorithm that prevents bridging and switching loops.

store-and-forward switching: A standard type of bridging and switching process where the entire frame is received before a forwarding decision is made.

switching fabric: The combination of hardware and software that transfers data coming into a network node to the appropriate output port on the next node on the network. Switching fabric includes the switches in a node, the hardware that they contain, and the software programs that control switching paths.

time-division multiplexing (TDM): Digital multiplexing in which two or more apparently simultaneous channels are derived from a given frequency spectrum (i.e., bit stream) by interleaving pulses representing bits from different channels.

time-division switching: Switching of TDM channels by shifting bits between time slots in a TDM frame.

time-slot interchange (TSI): In time-division switching, the process of coordinating time slots between the transmitting station and the receiving station.

time-space switching: A combination of space-division and time-division switching. Time-space switching precedes each input trunk in a crossbar with a TSI, and delays samples so that they arrive at the right time for the space-division switch's schedule.

time-to-live (TTL): A number, assigned to a frame, that is decremented to prevent it from infinitely circulating through the network.

translational bridging: A form of bridging that allows bridging between Ethernet and Token Ring networks.

virtual local area network (VLAN): A configuration on a switch that groups ports into a single broadcast domain.

5.8   Challenge Questions

5.1   Which of the following best describes the process of bridging and switching?

    a. Packets with known destinations are either filtered or flooded. Packets with an unknown destination are forwarded.

    b. Packets with known destinations are filtered. Packets with unknown destinations are either forwarded or flooded.

    c. Packets with known destinations are forwarded or filtered. Packets with unknown destinations are flooded.

    d. Packets with known destinations are forwarded or flooded. Packets with unknown destinations are filtered.

5.2   Bridges and switches learn using the _____ and make decisions based on _____ .

    a. destination MAC address; source MAC address

b. broadcast address; source MAC address

c. destination MAC address; broadcast address

d. source MAC address; destination MAC address

5.3 When a bridge receives a broadcast, what action is taken?

a. The bridge copies the packet to all ports except the port on which the packet was received.

b. The bridge copies the packet to all ports including the port on which it was received.

c. The bridge filters the packet.

d. The bridge forwards the packet to the appropriate network segment based on the source MAC address.

5.4 Examine the following forwarding table:

Port	Client	MAC Address
1	A	00-09-27-01-29-87
1	B	00-09-27-20-20-AE
2	C	00-09-27-01-10-1F
2	D	00-09-27-AD-01-87
1	E	00-09-27-BA-D1-00
2	F	00-09-27-AB-01-10

What will the bridge do with packets sent from Client A to Client E?

a. Flood

b. Filter

c. Forward

d. Buffer

5.5 Using the same table from Question 4, what will the bridge do with packets sent from Client A to Client F?

a. Flood

b. Filter

c. Forward

d. Buffer

5.6 Which of the following are benefits found in switches but not traditional bridges? (Choose all that apply.)

a. Processes frames in hardware

b. Creates separate collision domains

c. Lower cost per port

d. Allows transparent connectivity between clients

5.7 What is the primary purpose of the Spanning Tree Protocol?

a. Elimination of broadcasts

b. Creation of a loop-free switching environment

c. Election of a root bridge

d. Elimination of multicasts

5.8 Which of the following is used to elect a root bridge?

a. Highest bridge ID

b. Lowest path cost

c. Fewest hops from any point in the network (central bridge)

d. Lowest bridge ID

5.9 What is the key factor used in determining the root port?

a. Lowest bridge ID

b. Fewest hops

c. Lowest path cost

d. Highest bridge ID

5.10 The bridge ID is composed of which of the following? (Choose all that apply.)

a. Bridge priority

b. Bridge number

c. Port priority

d. Lowest configured MAC address

e. Highest configured MAC address

5.11 What is the major benefit of implementing VLANs?

a. Creation of additional broadcast domains

b. Creation of additional collision domains

c. Elimination of broadcasts

d. Simplification of switch configuration

5.12 What configuration on a switch port will allow it to carry VLAN frames for more than one VLAN?

a. Buffering

b. Trunking

c. Routing

d. Forwarding

5.13 You have just implemented VLANs on 15 switches in your network. What additional device is now required for complete communications between VLAN clients?

a. Hub

b. Root switch

c. Router

d. Trunk

5.14 When using source route bridging, which system determines the best path through the network?

a. Bridge

b. Router

c. The systems that initiates a communication request

d. The system that responds to a communication request

5.15 What is the purpose of an all routes explorer (ARE) frame?

a. It is a frame with the RII set to 0 and is forwarded by bridges when determining the best path through the network.

b. It is a frame with the RII set to 1 and is filtered by bridges when looking for a client on the local segment.

c. It is a frame with the RII set to 0 and is filtered by bridges when looking for a client on the local segment.

d. It is a frame with the RII set to 1 and is forwarded by bridges when determining the best path through the network.

5.16 What is the purpose of translational bridging?

a. Interconnection of different TCP/IP subnets

b. Interconnection of Ethernet and Token Ring networks

c. Interconnection of different VLANs

d. Interconnection of Ethernet 1 and Ethernet 2 networks

5.17 Which of the following is not a significant benefit of integrating routers and switches?

a. The ability to move frames at wire speed

b. Simplification of frame processing

c. Increased processing overhead because of multiple frame copies

d. Simpler network design

5.18 In TCP/IP, which of the following define a socket? (Choose all that apply.)

a. Port number

b. Routing protocol

c. Transport protocol

d. Source or destination MAC address

e. Source or destination IP address

f. Subnet mask

5.19 An ATM cell has a header size of _____ and a payload size of _____.

a. 5 bytes; 48 bytes

b. 16 bytes; 64 bytes

c. 5 bytes; 53 bytes

d. 16 bytes; 128 bytes

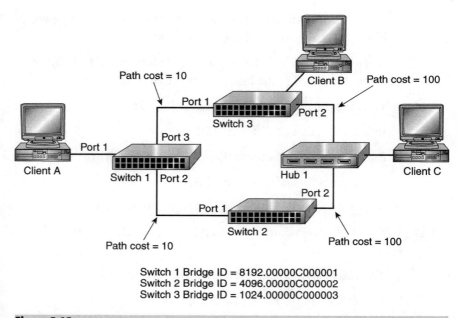

Figure 5.15
Spanning Tree

5.20 An ATM switching element consists of which of the following? (Choose all that apply.)

a. A multiplexer/demultiplexer

b. A central queuing buffer

c. A VCI

d. An interconnection network

e. An OC for each outgoing line

f. An IC for each incoming line

5.9 Challenge Exercises

Challenge Exercise 5.1

This exercise helps you to review your understanding of Spanning Tree Algorithm and Spanning Tree Protocol. Use Figure 5.15 to answer the following questions.

5.1 Which system becomes the root bridge?

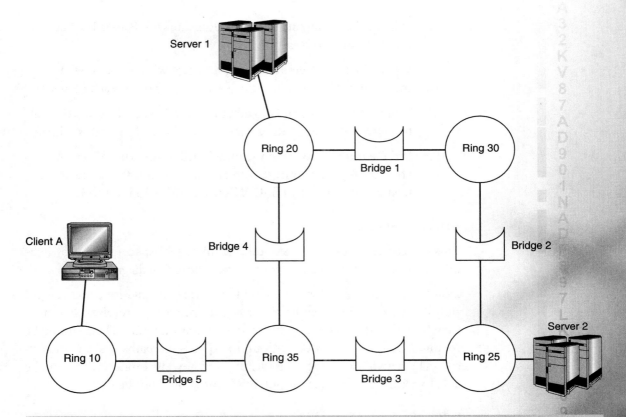

Figure 5.16
Source route bridging

5.2 When Client C transmits data to Client A, which switch forwards the data?

5.3 Which switch and what port will be in a blocking mode based on STA rules?

5.4 What are the two path cost values from Switch 2 to the root bridge?

5.5 When Client A broadcasts, which systems will it reach?

Challenge Exercise 5.2

This exercise tests your understanding of the source route bridging process. Use Figure 5.16 to answer the questions that follow.

5.1 When Client A attempts to communicate with Server 1, what is the first frame to be sent?

5.2 When Client A attempts to communicate with Server 1, what is the pattern of the two RIF fields when the frames reach Server 1?

5.3 When Client A attempts to talk to Server 2, what default path will be taken if the Token Ring network is using SRB default settings?

5.4 If there is no response to the initial SRB frame when Client A attempts to communicate with Server 2, what is the name of the next frame that is sent out? (Hint: The RII field is set to 1.)

Challenge Exercise 5.3

This exercise tests your understanding of multistage space-division switching. It is a design exercise, and your answer should be diagrammatic.

Design a simple space-division switching fabric that can interconnect eight stations. Each station may be either a transmitter or a receiver. No more than four circuits can exist in the network at any one time. There should be redundancy in the network, with up to 16 possible paths for any one circuit. The network must be nonblocking, and any idle input must always be able to connect to any idle output. Buffering should not be used.

5.10   Challenge Scenarios

Challenge Scenario 5.1

You are the network administrator for a company that is migrating from Token Ring to Ethernet. You will be required to run both networks for a period of approximately eight weeks. Your boss has asked you for a proposal on the technologies necessary for the migration and any recommendations on hardware needed or desired both during the transition and after the migration to Ethernet is completed. What would be in your list of requirements and recommendations?

Challenge Scenario 5.2

You are the network administrator for a small manufacturing firm that runs Ethernet. You are currently using hubs and repeaters for connectivity but have decided to upgrade to a switched infrastructure. The CFO has looked over your proposal and would like more information on the benefits of migrating to a switched network. What benefits would you list and why? What additional features of switching might your company deploy as it grows?

Challenge Scenario 5.3

You are the network administrator for a sales and marketing firm that currently uses a single Ethernet subnet as its intranet. A private addressing scheme is used and NAT is implemented. Your firm has three main departments: sales, marketing, and accounts. These departments are not on separate floors but are distributed in groups throughout your premises. Most traffic is interdepartmental. You are currently using hubs and repeaters for connectivity. The network is performing poorly and you want to segment it into collision domains. You decide to implement VLANs. You are asked to justify this strategy, as opposed to using bridges or subnetting the intranet using routers. How do you justify the use of VLANs?

CHAPTER 6

Networking Protocols

After reading this chapter you will be able to:

- Identify the different types of protocols

- Describe how TCP/IP came into being

- Understand how TCP/IP communicates at different layers of the OSI model

- Use ICMP commands to test connectivity

- Understand what common applications communicate using the TCP/IP layer

In previous chapters, we learned how data moves across wires, about different architectures and topologies, and how switches and hubs determine where packets go. Most of this discussion was concentrated on how data moves through media and devices. We haven't actually discussed how the devices communicate with each other. For example, to get to Germany from the United States, you can travel by plane, rail, or boat. Once you arrive in Germany, to communicate you either need to speak German, find someone who speaks English, or use an interpreter. The same holds true for networks.

All networked devices need a set of rules to follow when they communicate with each other. In this chapter, we discuss these rules.

6.1   Protocol Basics

A protocol is a set of rules and conventions that determines how computers exchange information over a network medium. A protocol implements the tasks that are performed at one or more of the OSI layers. The more complex a protocol is, the higher the layer at which it functions. Protocols vary according to their speed, utilization of resources, ease of setup, transmission efficiency, and ability to travel between LAN segments. A layer does not define a single protocol; instead, it defines a data communication function that may be performed by any number of protocols. Because each layer defines a function, it can contain multiple protocols, each of which provides a service suitable to the function of that layer. A wide variety of communication protocols exist, and many of them rely on others for operation. Because the protocols that compose the various layers of the OSI model are stacked on one another, similar to a pile of building blocks, groups of related protocols are often called stacks. Many times, a connection-oriented protocol works in conjunction with a connectionless protocol. Remember from Chapter 2 that connection-oriented services provide some level of delivery guarantee, whereas connectionless services do not.

6.2   A Brief Protocol Prospectus

Many protocols are available in today's networks. A good way to see this is by going to *http://www.decodes.co.uk/content/chart.htm*. Here you find a protocol decode chart. It has all the layers of the OSI model listed on the left side, with all the protocols that exist at each layer along with the layer boundaries. As you can see, there are about 100 protocols. We won't discuss them all, but we will cover the more common ones.

NOTE

To effectively manage, support, and maintain a network, you must have a thorough understanding of network protocols and how they operate.

6.2.1   Proprietary versus Standard Protocols

Because a protocol determines what language is spoken by the computers on a network, an important decision when designing a network is the choice of protocols. What access is needed and to what types of networks, and whether an interpreter can be used for communicating with networks that speak different languages will all help in determining this. Remember that when you decide on a protocol, consideration must be given to speed, overhead, efficiency, and routing.

Data packets can be sent over the medium using any one of a number of protocols. These protocols are either standard or proprietary. With a standard protocol, users can purchase equipment from any manufacturer because it is programmed to communicate universally. A proprietary protocol is usually protected by patents or other legal stipulations, so users are restricted to purchasing equipment from the developing company or authorized vendors. In a proprietary environment, additional equipment or protocols may be needed in order for the network devices to communicate with devices on standard protocol networks. We will first discuss the proprietary protocols and move to the more standard protocols.

6.2.2   Xerox Network Systems (XNS)

Xerox Network Systems (XNS) is a suite of protocols created by Xerox in the late 1970s and early 1980s to be used in Ethernet networks. XNS was adopted by most of the early LAN companies because of its availability and early entry into the market. Because many companies purchase or use other technologies for the basis of their own, XNS became the foundation of Novell's IPX/SPX, which will be discussed shortly. XNS is used in very few new networks today.

Although several XNS protocols resemble the standards developed by the Defense Advanced Research Projects Agency (DARPA), the XNS concept of

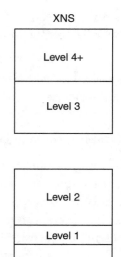

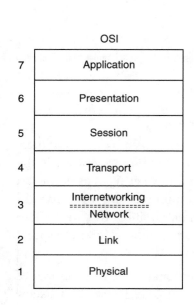

Figure 6.1

XNS layers as they correspond to the OSI layers

a protocol hierarchy is somewhat different. Figure 6.1 compares the OSI model layers to the XNS model layers.

Xerox provides a five-level model for packets to communicate. Level 0 maps to OSI Layers 1 and 2, handling bit-stream manipulation and data link access. Level 1 maps to the part of OSI Layer 3 that deals with network traffic. Level 2 maps to the part of OSI Layer 3 that pertains to network routing, and to OSI Layer 4, which handles error-free data delivery and proper sequencing. Level 3 maps roughly to OSI Layer 6, which formats data exchange, and Level 4 maps roughly to Layer 7 of the OSI model, handling application communications. XNS has no protocol corresponding to OSI Layer 5.

XNS does not really define what a Level 0 protocol is. It leaves media access an open issue, allowing any protocol, such as X.25, Ethernet, or High-level Data Link Control (HDLC), to host the transport of packets over a physical medium.

The following XNS protocols provide routing capability and support for both sequenced and connectionless packet delivery:

- **Internet Datagram Protocol (IDP):** Performs standard OSI Layer 3 (network) functions, including logical addressing and end-to-

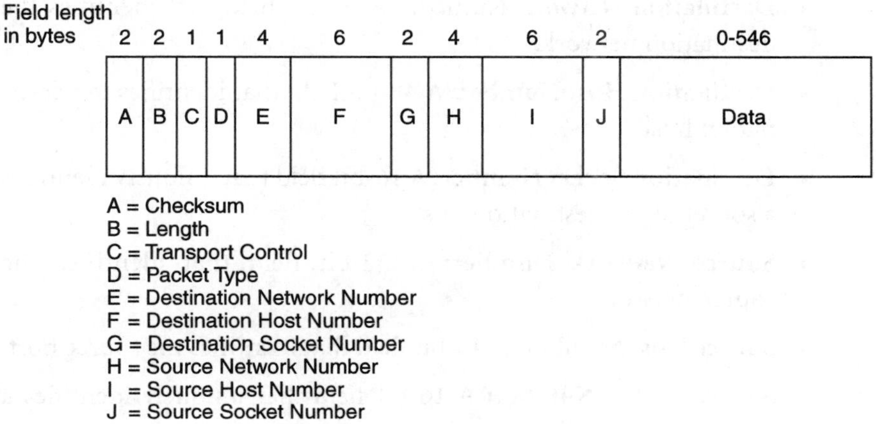

Field length
in bytes

2	2	1	1	4	6	2	4	6	2	0-546
A	B	C	D	E	F	G	H	I	J	Data

A = Checksum
B = Length
C = Transport Control
D = Packet Type
E = Destination Network Number
F = Destination Host Number
G = Destination Socket Number
H = Source Network Number
I = Source Host Number
J = Source Socket Number

Figure 6.2

IDP packet fields

end datagram delivery. XNS generally limits the IDP packets to a maximum size of 576 bytes, excluding the Data Link header.

- **Routing Information Protocol (RIP):** Used by XNS to maintain a database of network hosts and exchange information about the topology of the network. RIP is explained in Chapter 8.

- **Packet Exchange Protocol (PEP):** Provides a semireliable packet delivery service that is single packet-based. It provides retransmissions but no duplicate packet detection.

- **Sequenced Packet Protocol (SPP):** Provides reliable transport delivery with flow control. SPP packets cannot be longer than 576 bytes.

Figure 6.2 illustrates the format of an IDP packet.

The following are IDP packet fields and their descriptions:

- **Checksum:** A 16-bit field that gauges the integrity of the packet.

- **Length:** A 16-bit field that carries the length of the datagram, including the checksum.

- **Transport Control:** An 8-bit field that contains the hop count and Maximum Packet Lifetime (MPL) subfields. The MPL subfield provides the maximum amount of time that a packet can remain on the network.

- **Packet Type:** An 8-bit field that specifies the format of the data field.

- **Destination Network Number:** A 32-bit field that identifies the destination network.

- **Destination Host Number:** A 48-bit field that identifies the destination host.

- **Destination Socket Number:** A 16-bit field that uniquely identifies a socket in the destination host.

- **Source Network Number:** A 32-bit field that identifies the source network.

- **Source Host Number:** A 48-bit field that identifies the source host.

- **Source Socket Number:** A 16-bit field that uniquely identifies a socket in the source host.

XNS uses the Echo protocol to determine the existence and accessibility of another host on the network, and uses the Error protocol to signal routing errors. It also offers several upper-layer protocols. The Courier Protocol provides conventions for data structuring and process interaction. Each of these three protocols runs on top of the Courier Protocol:

- **Printing Protocol:** Provides print services.

- **Filing Protocol:** Provides file access services.

- **Clearinghouse Protocol:** Provides name services.

6.2.3   NetBIOS and NetBEUI

The **Network Basic Input/Output System (NetBIOS)** interface was developed in 1983 for International Business Machines Corporation (IBM) by Sytec Inc. Its intention was to allow applications on different computers to communicate within a local area network. It operated over proprietary protocols on IBM's local PC Network and could accommodate up to 72 devices. NetBIOS was not designed for large networks. The **NetBIOS Extended User Interface (NetBEUI)** was introduced in 1985 to allow Token Ring networks to accommodate up to 260 devices on one ring. Later it was adopted by Microsoft and became an industry standard. NetBIOS is used in Ethernet, Token Ring, and Windows NT networks.

NOTE NetBIOS can operate over IPX/SPX and TCP/IP, so NetBEUI is not required to run NetBIOS. Older Microsoft operating systems require NetBIOS naming to function, but they can use IPX/SPX or TCP/IP. Beginning with

Windows 2000, Microsoft operating systems have migrated from using NetBEUI as a default protocol. In fact, Windows XP and Windows Server 2003 do not use it at all.

NetBIOS was actually designed as an application programming interface (API) as a means to provide networking services to the BIOS. The term *NetBIOS protocol* refers to the set of protocols developed with the NetBIOS API, which is NetBIOS Frames Protocol (NBF) and the protocols that followed—Server Message Block (SMB) and Common Internet File System (CIFS). Many operating systems use SMB including those developed by Microsoft, IBM, Novell, and Linux.

To communicate, all nodes need to be uniquely identified on a network. Names are the method of identification used by each node in a NetBIOS network. These names represent a flat name space. They are 16 bytes long with few restrictions on the byte values that can be used. They are non-hierarchical and, because there is no method to identify networks with the NetBIOS name scheme, protocols using this name scheme cannot be routed. After the NetBIOS name is found, the permanent node name—the physical adapter card's name (MAC address of the card)—is determined. NetBIOS names use from one to 15 characters containing no periods or spaces. Letters, numbers, underscores, and hyphens are commonly used.

An example of a NetBIOS name is STATION_1. NetBEUI does not have the type of addressing that allows packet forwarding on routed networks, but the NetBIOS interface is adaptable to other protocols that are, such as IPX and TCP/IP. Thus it can be encapsulated and many times is used in conjunction with other protocols.

NetBIOS is a Layer 5 (Session) protocol whereas NetBEUI works at both Layer 3 (Network) and Layer 4 (Transport), as illustrated in Figure 6.3. Net-BEUI defines the arrangement of information in a data transmission that was not specified as part of NetBIOS and adds additional functions. It specifies the way that upper-level software sends and receives messages over NBF. When NetBEUI was developed in 1985, it was assumed that LANs would be segmented into workgroups of no more than 200 computers and that gateways would be used to connect those LAN segments to other segments or mainframes. Therefore, NetBEUI is optimized for very high performance when used in small LANs or LAN segments.

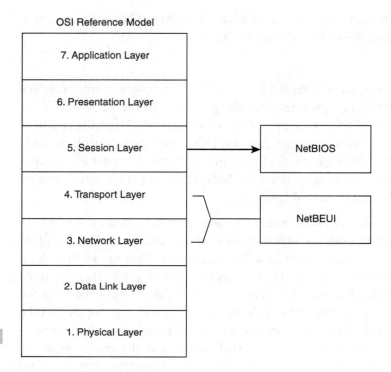

Figure 6.3
NetBIOS/NetBEUI suite

6.2.4 Internetwork Packet Exchange/Sequenced Packet Exchange (IPX/SPX)

Introduced in the early 1980s, NetWare was developed by Novell, Inc. It was derived from XNS. Besides an operating system, Novell has also developed its own network-protocol stack called Internetwork Packet Exchange/ Sequenced Packet Exchange (IPX/SPX), which is based on the XNS network protocol family, where IPX is the Network layer protocol and SPX is the Transport layer protocol.

Figure 6.4 illustrates the NetWare protocol suite, the media-access protocols on which NetWare runs, and the relationship between the OSI reference model and the NetWare protocols. The NetWare suite of protocols supports the following Layer 2 protocols: Ethernet/IEEE 802.3, Token Ring/IEEE 802.5, Fiber Distributed Data Interface (FDDI), and Point-to-Point Protocol (PPP).

Internetwork Packet Exchange (IPX) is a connectionless datagram-based Layer 3 (Network) protocol used to route packets through networks. IPX

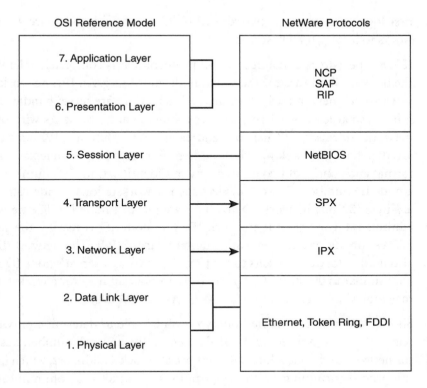

OSI Reference Model	NetWare Protocols
7. Application Layer	NCP SAP RIP
6. Presentation Layer	
5. Session Layer	NetBIOS
4. Transport Layer	SPX
3. Network Layer	IPX
2. Data Link Layer	Ethernet, Token Ring, FDDI
1. Physical Layer	

Figure 6.4
NetWare's protocol suite

uses the services of a distance vector routing protocol such as RIP, or a link-state routing protocol such as NetWare Link-State Protocol (NLSP). Distance vector and link-state protocols are discussed in Chapter 8.

⚠ WARNING

Novell's version of RIP is not identical to the RIP implementation of TCP/IP. Novell added an extra field—Number of Ticks—to the official XNS protocol.

Service Advertisement Protocol (SAP) is an IPX protocol through which network resources such as file servers and print servers advertise their addresses and the services they provide. Advertisements are sent via SAP every 60 seconds. Services are identified by a hexadecimal number called a SAP identifier. SAP is prevalent in networks based on NetWare 3.11 and earlier. It is used less frequently in NetWare 4.0 networks because workstations can locate services through a NetWare Directory Services (NDS) server. However, because clients use SAP to request the *nearest server* when first logging in to the network, SAP is still required in NetWare 4.0 networks to locate an NDS server.

IPX is a peer-to-peer connectionless protocol that is completely reliant on the network hardware for the actual node addressing. An IPX network is a server-based network, which means all interactions are server handled. You must have at least one server to have a functional network. As with other network addresses, IPX network addresses must be unique. IPX addresses are 10 octets (80 bits) long. These addresses are represented in hexadecimal format and consist of two parts: a network identification (ID) number and a node ID number. Network devices such as workstations are identified by a 4-byte (32-bit) network ID and a 6-byte (48-bit) node ID. The network administrator assigns the network ID. The node ID is usually the MAC address of the system's network interface card (NIC). The network ID is also used to forward packets to the proper network. A server's node ID may look similar to 00-00-00-00-00-01. The complete address for a workstation may look similar to 00-00-05-B7:00-10-A4-A8-DA-D0.

Should you have to troubleshoot, you will be able to determine on which segments the computers are located based on the network number. Besides the network and node addresses, there are also socket addresses, which identify processes running on the workstations. A socket is a communication endpoint within a node on the network. Processes request socket numbers, which are then appended to the IPX address. An example of a complete IPX address for a socket is 00-00-05-B7:00-10-A4-A8-DA-D0:456h.

The IPX packet is the basic unit of Novell NetWare internetworking. Figure 6.5 illustrates the format of a NetWare IPX packet.

The IPX packet fields are described as:

- **Checksum:** A 16-bit field that provides integrity checking for the packet.

- **Packet Length:** Specifies the length, in bytes, of a complete IPX datagram.

- **Transport Control:** Indicates the number of routers through which the packet has passed. When this value reaches 16, the packet is discarded.

- **Packet Type:** Specifies which upper-layer service should receive the packet's information.

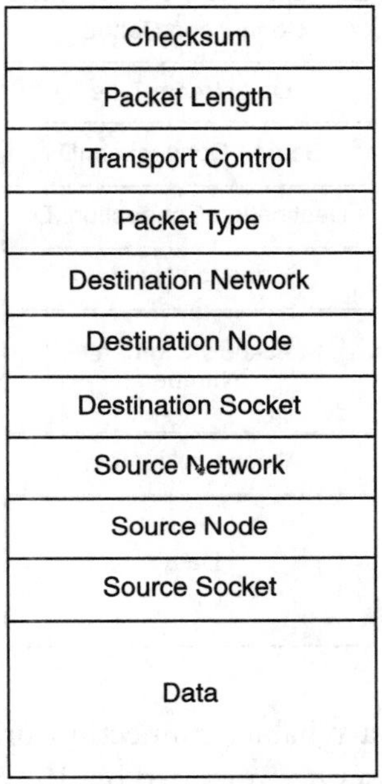

Checksum
Packet Length
Transport Control
Packet Type
Destination Network
Destination Node
Destination Socket
Source Network
Source Node
Source Socket
Data

Figure 6.5
IPX packet

- **Destination Network, Destination Node,** and **Destination Socket:** Specify destination information.

- **Source Network, Source Node,** and **Source Socket:** Specify source information.

- **Data:** Contains information for upper-layer processes.

IPX can support multiple encapsulation schemes. **Encapsulation** is the process of packaging upper-layer protocol information and data into a frame. NetWare supports the following encapsulation schemes:

- **Novell Proprietary:** Also called 802.3 raw or Novell Ethernet_802.3, it serves as the initial encapsulation scheme that Novell uses.

- **802.3:** Also called Novell_802.2, 802.3 is the standard IEEE 802.3 frame format.

- **Ethernet version 2:** Also called Ethernet-II or ARPA.

- **SNAP:** Also called Ethernet_SNAP.

Sequenced Packet Exchange (SPX) is the most common NetWare transport protocol at Layer 4 of the OSI model. SPX resides on top of IPX and is

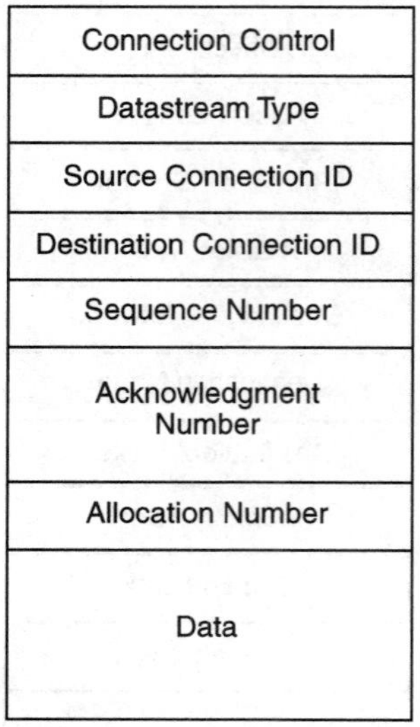

| Connection Control |
| Datastream Type |
| Source Connection ID |
| Destination Connection ID |
| Sequence Number |
| Acknowledgment Number |
| Allocation Number |
| Data |

Figure 6.6

SPX packet header

a reliable, connection-oriented protocol that supplements the datagram service provided by IPX. SPX was derived from the XNS Sequenced Packet Protocol (SPP). The SPX packet header is illustrated in Figure 6.6.

The SPX header fields are described as:

- **Connection Control:** The first octet (eight bits) of the SPX header, which provides four 2-bit flags that determine whether it is a system or application packet.

- **Datastream Type:** The next eight bits of the header, which defines the type of data.

- **Source Connection ID:** A 16-bit field used to identify the source connection.

- **Destination Connection ID:** A 16-bit field used to identify the destination.

- **Sequence Number:** A 16-bit field that provides the destination host's SPX protocol with a count of packets transmitted.

- **Acknowledgment Number:** A 16-bit field that indicates the next expected packet.

- **Allocation Number:** A 16-bit field used to track the number of packets sent, but not yet acknowledged, by the intended recipient.

- **Data:** The last field in the SPX header, which contains the data of up to 534 octets.

NetWare supports a wide variety of upper-layer protocols, including:

- **NetWare Shell:** Runs clients along with intercepting application input/output (I/O) calls to determine whether network access is needed for task completion.

- **NetWare Remote Procedure Call (RPC):** A more general redirection mechanism similar in concept to the NetWare shell.

- **NetWare Core Protocol (NCP):** A series of server routines designed to satisfy application requests, including file access, printer access, name management, accounting, security, and file synchronization.

- **Network Basic Input/Output System (NetBIOS):** A Session layer emulation protocol that allows programs written to the industry-standard NetBIOS interface to run within NetWare.

The Application layer contains protocols and functions required by User applications to perform communication tasks such as checking the availability of software components. The NetWare Application layer services include:

- **NetWare Directory Services (NDS):** A relational database that can be accessed across the network, making it easy to share services and resources.

- **NetWare Message Handling Service (MHS):** Provides electronic mail transport.

- **Btrieve:** Novell's implementation of the binary tree (btree) database-access mechanism.

- **NetWare loadable modules (NLMs):** Add-on modules that can be added to the system.

- **NWLink:** An IPX/SPX-compatible protocol for Windows NT. NWLink, when used with a redirector such as Microsoft's Client Service for NetWare (CSNW) or Novell's NetWare Client for Windows NT, allows a Windows NT computer to access files or printers on a NetWare server, or to act as a file or print server to a NetWare

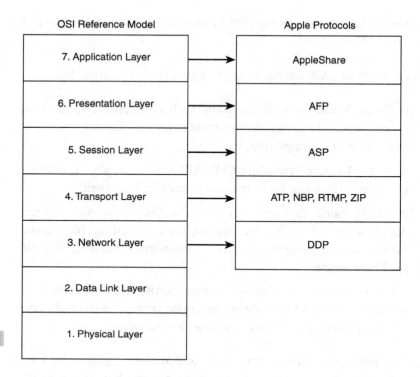

Figure 6.7
Apple's protocol suite

client. The client portion can be run on a Windows NT computer accessing the server portion on a NetWare server or vice versa.

6.2.5   Apple Protocols

AppleTalk is a Macintosh networking protocol. It was designed to be a flexible, simple, and inexpensive network means for connecting computers, peripherals, and servers. AppleTalk consists of a bus topology that uses a trunk cable between connections.

> NOTE Many times AppleTalk is confused with LocalTalk. AppleTalk is a protocol and LocalTalk is a media type.

The term *AppleTalk* was originally used for both the protocol and connecting cables. LocalTalk now describes the simple shielded twisted-pair cable used to connect Macs to other Macs or printers. TokenTalk is AppleTalk via Token Ring networks, while EtherTalk is AppleTalk over Ethernet. Figure 6.7 shows the relationship between the OSI model and Apple protocols.

For the Physical layer, any transmission medium can be used for the network as long as connection modules conform to the signal specifications. This layer is responsible for bit encoding, synchronization, signal transmission, and carrier sensing.

AppleTalk Link Access Protocol (ALAP) is a Layer 2 (Data Link) protocol that determines when the bus is free, and then it encapsulates, sends, and acknowledges data that should be received. It must be common to all systems on a single AppleTalk network bus because it assigns node numbers to each station on the network and handles the node-to-node delivery of data between devices. ALAP uses AppleTalk CSMA/CA for access control, thus all transmitters wait until the bus is idle for a minimum amount of time plus a random amount of added time before transmitting.

The **Datagram Delivery Protocol (DDP)** is a Layer 3 (Network) protocol that extends the concept of ALAP to include an interconnected group of AppleTalk networks. ALAP provides delivery of data over a single AppleTalk network, while DDP is used to connect more than one network. One of the fields in the DDP packet header is a 16-bit checksum. This is used to protect packets against data corruption in intervening routers and noisy networks. AppleTalk's address header consists of a socket number, node number, and network number. Sockets belong to software processes that are implemented in the node.

The DDP header fields are described as:

- **Hop Count:** Contains a counter that is incremented by 1 for each router device it travels across. Hop count is only used in the extended header.

- **Datagram Length:** Contains the length of the datagram and can be used to determine whether it was corrupted in transit.

- **DDP Checksum:** Provides a more robust form of error detection than simply checking the length of a datagram. Checksum verification detects whether the contents were changed even slightly, regardless of whether or not the length of the datagram changed. This is an optional field.

- **Source Socket Number:** Identifies the communicating process on the machine that initiated the connection.

- **Destination Socket Number:** Identifies the communicating process on the machine that responded to the connection request.

- **Source Address:** Contains the network and node numbers of the originating computer. This field is used only in the extended header format and enables routers to forward datagrams across multiple subnetworks.

- **Destination Address:** Contains the network and node numbers of the destination computer. This field is used only in the extended header format and enables routers to forward datagrams across multiple subnetworks.

- **DDP Type:** Identifies the upper-layer protocol that is encapsulated in the datagram. The destination computer's Transport layer uses it to identify the appropriate protocol to which to pass the contents.

- **Data:** This field contains the data that is being transmitted. It can vary in size from 0 to 586.

TIP   AppleTalk and IPX headers both consist of the same three elements: a network address, a node address, and a socket address.

DDP requires that each network be assigned a network number. Node numbers are unique only within a single physical network. Because one Mac may have many connections open at one time, socket numbers are also required. DDP takes care of assigning socket, node, and network numbers so that a unique identifier exists for every process that occurs on the network. A possible network/node/socket AppleTalk address could be written as 54.164/220/129.

The node is an 8-bit or 16-bit randomly chosen number when the computer first connects to the network. The network number is a unique 16-bit number. Node numbers can range from 1 to 253 or from 1 to 254 on LocalTalk. Network numbers can range from 1 to 65535. This can also be written in dotted decimal notation as 0.1 to 255.255. On EtherTalk and TokenTalk extended networks, a network range may be assigned to the cable. In other words, the nodes on the cable are free to choose a network number from any of those within the specified range. LocalTalk networks may be assigned only a single network number. The theoretical upper limit for the number of nodes on a LocalTalk network is 254, although there are physical limitations on the length of each type of cable and the number of possible connections to it.

At Layer 4 (Transport), the following protocols exist to add functionality to the underlying services:

- **Routing Table Maintenance Protocol (RTMP):** Allows bridges and routers to dynamically discover routes to the different AppleTalk networks in zones.

- **AppleTalk Transaction Protocol (ATP):** A transaction-oriented protocol responsible for controlling the flow of data between sockets.

- **Name Binding Protocol (NBP):** Translates common names into the addresses of the corresponding clients.

- **Zone Information Protocol (ZIP):** Used to maintain the mapping of networks to zone names. ZIP is used by NBP to determine which networks belong to a given zone.

- **Echo Protocol (EP):** Used for network maintenance functions. This simple protocol allows a node to send data to any other node on a network and receive an echoed copy of that data back.

NBP also introduces the concept of a zone, which is a subset of networks, where each network is in one, and only one, zone. Zones are provided to assist in establishing departmental or other groupings of entities. AppleTalk names consist of three fields: the object name, the type name, and the zone name. An example is Hibbert:LaserWriter[at]HR2C, in which Hibbert is the object name, LaserWriter is the type name, and HR2C is the zone name. A Macintosh user typically only encounters object and zone names. The Chooser takes care of looking up NBP types and mapping the results to AppleTalk addresses.

In Layer 5 (Session), the AppleTalk Session Protocol (ASP) is an asymmetric protocol designed to interact with ATP for establishing, maintaining, and closing sessions. The workstation initiates the session connection and issues sequences of commands to which the server responds; the server may not send commands to the workstation.

AFP is a Layer 6 (Presentation) protocol designed to control access to remote as well as local file systems. AppleShare file server software, which uses AFP, is a Layer 7 protocol. Besides file sharing, it provides print queue services and user access information.

Newer versions of Macintosh operating systems use TCP/IP and SMB as default protocols rather than AppleTalk. This is because most operating system developers have stopped using proprietary protocols and instead use industry-standard protocols for easy integration with other operating systems.

6.2.6   DECnet

DECnet is a proprietary network protocol designed by Digital Equipment Corporation. The first version of DECnet was released in 1975. Later releases expanded the functionality while remaining backward compatible. Currently, two versions of DECnet are in use: DECnet Phase IV and DECnet/OSI. DECnet Phase IV is the more popular of the two, while DECnet/OSI is the more recent.

DECnet Phase IV is based on Phase IV Digital Network Architecture (DNA). **Digital Network Architecture (DNA)** is a layered network architecture that supports standard and proprietary protocols. Phase IV DNA is similar to the OSI model, except it is composed of eight layers instead of seven. Figure 6.8 shows how the layers of Phase IV DNA map to the OSI reference model.

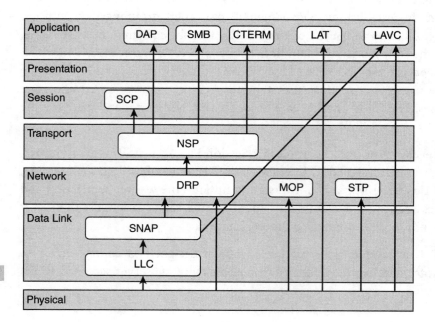

Figure 6.8

Phase IV DNA protocol suite

The Physical layer maps to the OSI Physical layer. It manages hardware interfaces and determines the electrical and mechanical functions of media. It supports Ethernet/IEEE 802.3, Token Ring/IEEE 802.5, and FDDI.

The Data Link layer manages physical network channels and maps to the OSI Data Link layer. DECnet hosts do not use MAC addresses; hosts are located using area/node address pairs instead of the physical networks to which the nodes are connected. Area address values range from 1 to 63, and node address values range between 1 and 1023. Therefore, approximately 65,000 nodes (63 $\times$ 1023) can be addressed in a DECnet network. Areas can span multiple routers, so if a node has several network interfaces, it uses the same area/node address for each interface.

The Routing layer performs routing and other functions, and corresponds to the OSI Network layer. DECnet routing occurs at this layer and is implemented by the DECnet Routing Protocol (DRP). DRP is a relatively simple and efficient protocol whose primary function is to provide the most efficient path through a DECnet Phase IV network.

The end Communications layer handles flow control, segmentation, and reassembly functions, and maps to the OSI Transport layer. **Network Services Protocol (NSP)** is a connection-oriented protocol developed by Digital to manage these functions, which includes two types of flow control: a simple start/stop mechanism and a more complex scheme in which the receiver tells the sender how many messages it can accept.

The DECnet Phase IV DNA specifies four upper layers to provide user interaction services, network-management capabilities, file transfer, and session management. These are:

- **Session Control layer:** Maps to the OSI Session layer; manages logical link connections between end nodes.

- **Network Application layer:** Maps to the OSI Presentation and Application layers; provides various network applications, such as remote file access and virtual terminal access.

- **User layer:** Maps to the OSI Application layer; supports user services and programs.

- **Network Management layer:** Maps to the OSI Application layer; represents the user interface to network-management information by interacting with all the lower layers of the DNA.

DECnet/OSI is sometimes called DECnet Phase V. It is a layered model that implements three protocol suites:

- **OSI:** Conforms to the OSI reference model and supports many of the standard OSI protocols.

- **DECnet:** Provides backward compatibility with DECnet Phase IV and supports multiple proprietary Digital protocols.

- **TCP/IP:** Supports the lower-layer TCP/IP protocols and enables the transmission of DECnet traffic over TCP transport protocols.

Few networks still use DECnet, but you may encounter them in some legacy systems.

6.3   Transmission Control Protocol/Internet Protocol (TCP/IP)

TCP/IP is considered the language of the Internet and probably the most widely used protocol today. Like many of the protocols we have already discussed, it a suite or stack of small, specialized protocols. To this point, we have discussed proprietary protocols. Because of its routing ability, TCP/IP has become the protocol of choice for many LANs as well as the basis for the Internet, making it a standard.

TIP

TCP/IP is an extensive topic, and there are volumes written on the subject. It is imperative to understand how TCP/IP works as it will be used extensively in routing. If you plan to be a network administrator, you will need some good reference sources on this subject.

Before we learn how TCP/IP works, we'll review some history about how it evolved.

6.3.1   A Brief History of TCP/IP

In the early 1970s, the Department of Defense funded the Advanced Research Project Agency (ARPA) at Stanford for research to design a new set of computer communication protocols that would allow multiple packet networks to be interconnected in a flexible and dynamic way. The first phase of this work was successfully completed in July 1977. By 1979, so many researchers were involved in the TCP/IP project that ARPA formed a committee to coordinate and guide the design of the protocols and architecture. This committee was called the Internet Control and Configuration Board (ICCB), and it was active until 1983 when it was reorganized.

The protocol developed was originally called Network Control Protocol (NCP). This success led to the implementation of the two main Internet protocols, Transmission Control Protocol (TCP) and Internet Protocol (IP). By 1980, a serious effort was mounted to require all computers on the ARPANET to adopt TCP/IP. To encourage usage of the new protocols, ARPA made a low-cost implementation available for university researchers. ARPA was able to reach almost all of the university computer science departments in the United States, a feat accomplished in January 1983. Meanwhile, the Internet Architecture Board (IAB) was created from the reorganization of the ICCB. The primary task of the IAB is to set official policies and determine which protocols form the TCP/IP suite.

The success of TCP/IP technology and the Internet among computer science researchers led other groups to adopt it. The National Science Foundation (NSF) realized the importance of computer communication and took an active role in expanding the use of TCP/IP among scientists. In 1985, networks were established around six supercomputer centers. The NSF's interest in high bandwidth was heightened in 1986 through its sponsorship of NSFNET, a new wide-area backbone network. NSFNET gradually reached all the supercomputer centers and tied them to the ARPANET, eventually replacing ARPANET, which was retired in 1990.

In 1992, the U.S. Congress gave the National Science Foundation statutory authority to commercialize the NSFNET. As a result, the Internet Society was created. This is an international organization that encourages participation in the Internet around the world. By 1994, the Internet had reached over 3 million computers in 61 countries. Today, the Internet is growing exponentially, and computers almost everywhere are connected using TCP/IP.

6.3.2 TCP/IP Networking Model

As mentioned previously, a layer does not define a single protocol. Instead, it defines a communication function that may be performed by any number of protocols. Because each layer defines a function, it can contain multiple protocols, each of which provides a service suitable to the function of that layer. TCP/IP's implementation of the OSI model makes functionality simpler by mapping the same seven layers of the OSI model to a four-layer model instead. Unlike the OSI reference model, the TCP/IP model focuses

TABLE 6.1   Comparison of OSI Reference Model and TCP/IP Networking Model

OSI Reference Model	TCP/IP Networking Model
Application	Application
Presentation	
Session	
Transport	Transport
Network	Internet
Data Link	Network Interface
Physical	

more on delivering interconnectivity than on functional layers. It does this by acknowledging the importance of a structured hierarchical sequence of functions, yet leaves protocol designers with the flexibility for implementation. The OSI reference model is much better at explaining the mechanics of intercomputer communications, but because TCP/IP has become the internetworking protocol of choice you may find this model more commonly used.

Table 6.1 compares the OSI and TCP/IP models.

> **TIP**
>
> Just like using the phrases "Please Do Not Throw Sausage Pizza Away" or "All People Seem To Need Data Processing" to remember the layers of the OSI model, similar mnemonics can be applied to the layers of the TCP/IP model: "Not In Time Again" or, from the top down, "Always Think In Numbers."

- **Application layer:** Maps to Layers 5 (Session), 6 (Presentation), and 7 (Application) of the OSI model. This is how applications and certain services access the network.

- **Transport layer:** Maps to Layer 4 (Transport) of the OSI model. It accepts data and segments it for transport across the network, making sure that the data is delivered error-free and in the proper sequence.

- **Internet layer:** Maps to Layer 3 (Network) of the OSI model. It manages the routing of packets that are to be forwarded on to different networks, relying on routable protocols for delivery.

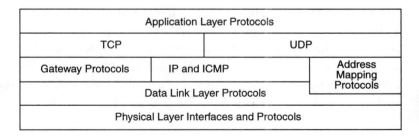

Figure 6.9
TCP/IP protocol stack

- **Network Access layer:** Maps to Layers 1 (Physical) and 2 (Data Link) of the OSI model. It is responsible for the delivery of datagrams by creating a frame for the network type and then sending the data to the wire.

TCP/IP is a suite of protocols and applications that enable a computer to communicate with other computers in a network. It doesn't matter what operating system the computers are using as long as each system supports TCP/IP. The computers can then communicate and share information. Figure 6.9 shows the general layout of how the various protocols are related to each other. The parts comprising the protocol stack are the protocols found on the Transport and Network layers.

6.4   TCP/IP Network Access Layer Protocols

The Network Access layer is the lowest layer in the TCP/IP networking model. It contains the protocols used to deliver data to computers and devices on the network. The design of TCP/IP hides the function of this layer from the user because it is concerned with getting data across a specific type of physical network.

TCP/IP calls for data to be broken into packets. These packets are designed to have a header for both IP and TCP, followed by the data. The headers enable packets to be routed across many networks to arrive at their destination. The protocols at this layer perform the following functions: They define how the network transmits a frame, they exchange data between the computer and the physical network, and they deliver data between two devices on the same network. To deliver data on the local network, the Network Access layer protocols use the physical addresses of the nodes on the network. The Network Access layer relies on the use of routable protocols to deliver the packets to distant networks. The Network Access layer also defines the network address, which is different from the MAC address. The MAC address is considered the physical address, and the network address is considered the logical address. This layer defines the logical network layout so that routers can use it to determine where to forward packets. Logical addressing is addressed in great detail in Chapter 7. We will now discuss the various protocols used at the Network Address layer.

6.4.1 Serial Line Interface Protocol (SLIP) and Point-to-Point Protocol (PPP)

Serial Line Interface Protocol (SLIP) and **Point-to-Point Protocol** (PPP) are communication protocols for serial data transmission between two devices. They are methods by which IP packets can be sent over a modem. Remember from Chapter 2 that a modem is used to convert the signals from digital to analog to be used over the phone lines, and then back to digital for the computer to understand. SLIP and PPP are the protocols used to send the data in analog format.

SLIP is an extremely simple framing scheme for putting IP packets on a serial line. Because SLIP is a simple protocol, it doesn't have many special features. It has no provision for error detection because it assumes that the upper-level services will handle that. SLIP can only transport TCP/IP traffic, supports only asynchronous communication, and does not support compression. If compression is desired, Compressed SLIP (CSLIP) should be used. CSLIP is a version of SLIP that compresses the IP headers. To use CSLIP, the client and host must both support it. Use of CSLIP requires manual configuration, although for the same host it only needs to be done once. With SLIP, you have to know the IP address assigned to you by your service provider. You also need to know the IP address of the system you will be dialing into. If the service provider automatically assigns IP addresses, the SLIP software needs to be able to pick up the IP assignments. You may also need to configure additional settings.

PPP is a newer protocol that does essentially the same thing SLIP does but has extra features such as error detection and IP address negotiation. It is a Data Link layer protocol that encapsulates Network layer protocols. It can operate across a variety of environments. The Point-to-Point Protocol is designed for simple links transporting packets between two peers. The links provide full-duplex, simultaneous bi-directional operation, and are assumed to deliver packets in order. PPP provides a common solution for easy connection of a wide variety of hosts, bridges, and routers. In Chapter 3 we discussed how PPP operates over HDLC and consists of the Link Control Protocol (LCP) and Network Control Protocol (NCP). As a PPP link comes up, first LCP defines the configuration and negotiation options, such as authentication, and then NCP is used to negotiate various IP parameters, such as the IP address. Therefore, all the variables that may make a PPP connection unsuccessful are subject to negotiation.

A PPP implementation can easily report link failures. It supports either bit-oriented synchronous transmission, byte-oriented transmission, or asynchronous transmission. It requires full-duplex capability and can be used over switched or dial-up links. PPP also has some additional benefits. Unlike SLIP, PPP is a multi-protocol transport mechanism. This means that besides TCP/IP traffic, PPP can also transport IPX and AppleTalk traffic, and it allows you to transport all of these protocols at the same time on the same connection. This is generally not a concern because the purpose of using either SLIP or PPP is to connect to the Internet, and the Internet uses only TCP/IP. The most significant advantage PPP can offer is the automatic login and configuration negotiation. With these features, the software only needs to know your login user ID and password, and the telephone number of your service provider. The software can then dial in to your service provider and configure everything else on its own. PPP provides two methods with which logins can be automated: PAP (Password Authentication Protocol) and CHAP (Challenge-Handshake Authentication Protocol). Table 6.2 compares SLIP and PPP features.

6.4.2   Address Resolution Protocol (ARP) and Reverse Address Resolution Protocol (RARP)

As we learned earlier, the Network layer defines the network address, which is different from the MAC address. The MAC address is considered the physical address, and the network address is considered the logical, or IP, address. In IP version 4, an address is 32 bits long, whereas in an Ethernet local area network, addresses for devices are 48 bits long. How does a network know the physical (MAC) address of a machine and map it to a logical (IP) address? And how does a machine with a MAC address find out the network address of another machine? Relating different addresses to each

TABLE 6.2   A Comparison of SLIP and PPP

Feature	SLIP	PPP
Compression	None; CSLIP added later as an option.	Automatically negotiated as part of the connection process.
Connection configuration	Manual effort required for IP settings, or separate programs are needed to configure.	Automatic; IP configuration is part of the connection process and is transparent to the user.
Error detection	None; SLIP is vulnerable to noisy lines, although error-correcting modems can cover for this deficiency.	Built-in error detection.
Industry support	None.	Widespread industry support for PPP.
Protocol handling	IP only.	Multi-protocol handling on a single serial connection.
Reliability	No error-correction capabilities.	Uses LCP to negotiate reliable connections at the highest possible speed.
Speed	Maximum capability is 56 Kbps.	Supports bandwidth on demand via PPP Multilink Protocol or Bandwidth Allocation Control Protocol.

other is done through two protocols, the Address Resolution Protocol and the Reverse Address Resolution Protocol.

The **Address Resolution Protocol (ARP)** is used by the Internet Protocol (IP) Network layer protocol to map IP network addresses to the hardware addresses used by a Data Link protocol. It operates below the Network layer as a part of the OSI Data Link layer, and is used with IP over Ethernet. A table, called the ARP cache, is used to maintain each MAC address and its corresponding IP address. ARP provides the protocol rules for address resolution in both directions and hides the MAC address from upper-layer protocols.

When an incoming packet destined for a host machine arrives, a device such as a gateway asks the ARP program to find the MAC address that corresponds to the IP address. The ARP program looks in the cache. If the cache finds the address, it is sent back to the requester so the packet can be converted to the right format and then forwarded to the proper machine. If

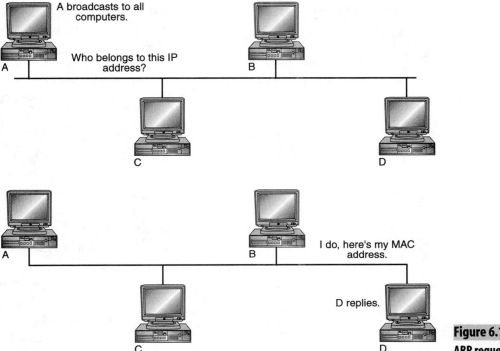

Figure 6.10
ARP request and reply

no entry is found, ARP broadcasts a request to all the machines on the LAN to see if any of them have that IP address associated with it. This broadcast is called the ARP request. It contains the destination IP address. When a machine recognizes the IP address as its own, it returns an ARP reply. The reply contains the MAC address of the host. ARP updates the cache and then sends the packet to the MAC address that replied. For example, Computer A broadcasts a request to all computers. Computer D, which has the address that Computer A seeks, responds by sending its MAC address. Computer A can then add that address to its ARP cache. An example of an ARP request and reply is shown in Figure 6.10.

Network hosts such as diskless workstations frequently do not know their protocol addresses when booted; they often know only their physical addresses. To communicate using higher-level protocols, their network address must be obtained from an external source. **Reverse Address Resolution Protocol (RARP)** is the network protocol belonging to the OSI Data

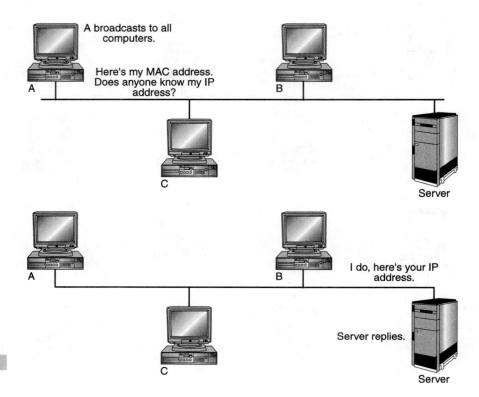

Figure 6.11
RARP request and reply

Link layer that is used to resolve a Data Link layer address to the correspon-ding Network layer address. This is a means by which a physical machine in a local area network can request to learn its IP address from a server's ARP table or cache. When a new diskless system is booted up, it broadcasts a RARP request packet with its MAC address, asking to be sent its IP address. Because the request is a broadcast, the packet reaches all hosts on the net-work, but only a RARP server responds. When the RARP server receives this packet, it looks up this MAC address in the configuration file, assum-ing that an entry has been set up in the router table, and determines the corresponding IP address. It then sends this IP address in the RARP reply packet. The diskless system receives this packet and gets its IP address, which can store it for future use. A RARP request and a reply are illustrated in Figure 6.11.

Because RARP is intended to operate at the hardware level, it has some dis-advantages. It contains limited information and can be difficult to manage from an applications program.

WARNING

ARP and RARP are two different operations. ARP assumes that every host knows the mapping between its own hardware address and network address, and that all hosts are equal in status; thus, there is no distinction between clients and servers. On the other hand, RARP requires one or more server hosts to maintain a database of mappings from hardware address to network address and respond to requests from client hosts. ARP and RARP are discussed in more detail in Chapter 8.

In Windows, Apple, and NetWare operating systems, the protocols in the Network Access layer appear as NDIS and ODI drivers and related programs. The modules that are identified with network devices usually act as an interface between the Data Link layer MAC sublayer and the device driver to encapsulate and deliver the data to the network, while separate programs perform related functions such as address mapping. Device drivers are covered in Chapter 11.

6.5   TCP/IP Internet Layer Protocols

The layer above the Network Access layer is called the Internet layer. It manages the routing of packets that are to be forwarded on to different networks, relying on routable protocols for delivery. The devices responsible for routing messages between networks are routers and gateways. A router is a dedicated hardware device that passes packets from one network to a different network. A gateway is a computer that has two network adapter cards. The computer accepts packets from one network on one card and routes those packets to a different network through the second card.

 NOTE

The terms *router* and *gateway* are often used interchangeably but may have distinct differences in their ability to route packets, particularly if the term is used in a strictly hardware sense.

It is a common practice in Internet language to use the term *gateway* for any machine that performs route discovery or uses routing protocols, thus allowing IP packets to be forwarded. Routing protocols are covered in Chapter 8.

6.5.1   Internet Protocol (IP)

The Internet Protocol (IP) is responsible for making data packets routable. It is a forwarding protocol that uses routing tables that are created by routing protocols. It is a simple, connectionless internetworking protocol. This means that IP does not exchange control information, often called a hand-shake, to establish an end-to-end connection before transmitting data. IP relies on protocols in other layers to establish the connection if connection-oriented services are required, as well as to provide error detection and error recovery. Because it doesn't contain connection, error-detection, or error-recovery code, IP is sometimes called an unreliable protocol. The actual service IP uses is unreliable datagram delivery. IP simply promises to make a reasonable effort to deliver every datagram to its destination. However, IP is free to occasionally deliver datagrams with errors in them, or duplicate or even lose datagrams. IP relies on the Internet Control Message Protocol (ICMP) to report errors in the processing of a datagram and provide for additional administrative and status messages. ICMP is discussed later in the chapter.

The basis of IP is its use of routing tables and how it uses them to make decisions about routing an IP packet. Knowing how addresses and route tables are used is important to understanding internetworking and is necessary for the successful administration and maintenance of a network. A Network Access layer address identifies a network or subnetwork and may also identify a device connected to that network. Every host on the network needs an IP address. TCP/IP uses a 32-bit Layer 3 address in the format xxx.xxx.xxx.xxx to identify the network and the host computer. Each set of xxx is called an octet. IP addresses are classified by their formats. The five classes of IP addresses and their corresponding numbers are:

1. **Class A:** Has a first octet number between 1 and 126 and can support a network with 16,777,216 hosts.

2. **Class B:** Has a first octet number between 128 and 191 and can support 65,536 hosts.

3. **Class C:** Has a first octet number between 192 and 223 and can support 254 hosts per network.

4. **Class D:** Begins at 224 and ends at 239. This address class is reserved for sending multicast messages.

5. **Class E:** Begins with 240 and ends at 255. This address class is reserved for experimental use.

In the preceding list, notice that the number 127 is missing. The IP address 127.0.0.1 is the loopback address, most often used for troubleshooting. Loopback means that a computer sends a message back to itself.

The version of IP we are discussing in this section is IPv4. IPv6 is a newer implementation. Both are covered ▣ **NOTE**
in Chapter 7.

IP Datagrams

Remember from Chapter 2 that TCP/IP protocols were built to transmit data over the ARPANET, which was a packet-switching network. In this type of network, the addressing information in the packets is used to switch packets from one network to another. Each packet travels the network independent of any other packet. A **datagram** is the packet format defined by IP. Datagrams are packets that consist of a header, data, and a trailer. The header contains information that the network needs to route the datagram, such as the destination address, source address, and security labels. Trailers typically contain a checksum value, which is used to ensure that the data is not modified in transit. The incoming data is stored in a queue. Next, the datagram header is checked for modifications with a checksum field. Then the IP address is checked. If it is local, it is passed to an upper-layer protocol. If it is not, it is sent to the routing table to determine whether there is a matching route. If there is, it's forwarded on; if not, it is either dropped or sent to a default route.

Resolving Routes

IP delivers the datagram by checking the destination address in the header. IP itself does not do route discovery; instead, it uses the routing tables that are created by gateway protocols to make the routing decision for each individual packet. Routing protocols find a route for the traffic to travel through the Internet. IP checks the destination address in the header, and if it is the address of a host on the local network, the datagram is delivered directly to the destination. If it is not on the local network, the datagram is passed on for delivery.

Each router that a datagram passes through is considered a *hop*. Establishing a maximum hop count ensures that datagrams do not loop continuously in a routed network. Many gateway protocols route traffic based on the premise that the datagram should travel through the fewest number of networks and hops. IP places no constraints on how fast a system can generate or receive datagrams. A system transmits IP datagrams as fast as it can generate them. However, IP does have two features that can affect throughput: the IP Time to Live (TTL) and IP Fragmentation.

IP Datagram Lifetime

Each node is required to check the TTL parameter. This is used to measure how long a datagram has been in the Internet. The TTL field is actually the number of hops the datagram has made. Each time an IP node processes a datagram it decreases this value, and when the value gets to zero the datagram gets discarded. In certain situations, a datagram may loop through a set of routers. To protect against continuous circulation, IP places a limit on how long a datagram may live in the network. This is the limit imposed by the TTL field in the IP datagram header. Originally, the IP specification required that the TTL be decremented at least once per second. Because the TTL field is 8 bits, a datagram could live for just over four minutes, but specifications for higher-layer protocols usually assume that the maximum time a datagram can live in the network is only two minutes. The significance of the maximum datagram lifetime is that higher-layer protocols must be careful not to send two similar datagrams within a few minutes of each other with the same sequence number so that the second datagram gets delivered first.

Fragmentation and Reassembly

When dissimilar physical networks are interconnected, an IP datagram may travel across networks that use different protocol data unit (PDU) sizes. Each type of network has a **maximum transmission unit (MTU)**, which is the largest packet it can transfer. A datagram received from one network may be too large to be transmitted in a single packet on another network; therefore, it may be necessary to divide the datagram into smaller pieces. This division process is called fragmentation. When an IP gateway receives a datagram that is too large to be transmitted, it divides it into two or more 8-octet pieces. Each piece has a header that contains the identification, addressing, and options that pertain to the original datagram. IP uses three fields to control fragmentation and reassembly: Identifier, Flags, and Fragmentation Offset. The Identifier field is used to identify the fragments from the original datagram; the Flags field is used to determine whether the datagram can be fragmented and then indicates which fragment is the last one; and the Fragment Offset field is used to tell reassembly the order in which to put the datagram. IP handles each fragment independently. The fragments may travel through different gateways and become further fragmented. For reassembly to occur, the receiving host's IP module sets up

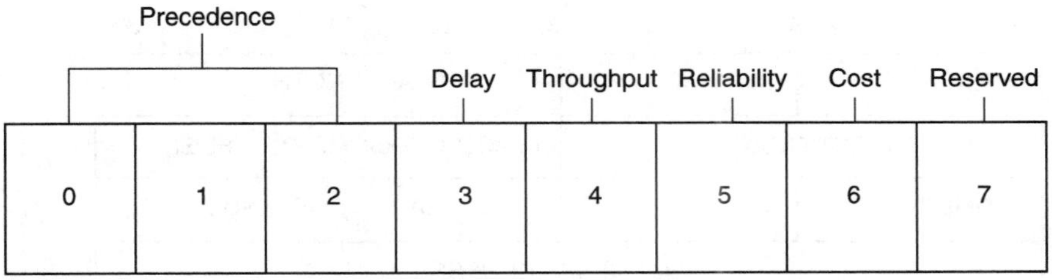

Figure 6.12
TOS field

buffer space when the first fragment arrives. A buffer is reserved for each fragment, and the fragments are placed there in order.

Service Delivery Options

The Type of Service (TOS) component is used to determine the type of service that must be provided, which is determined by the type of application for which the data transfer is occurring. The types of services that can be provided by IP maximize reliability and throughput as well as minimize cost and delay. The TOS field contains six entries consisting of 8 bits. The TOS field is shown in Figure 6.12.

These values are used to transfer data. Only one of the TOS bits can be set at any point in time, and the TOS bits will be meaningful only if the network devices through which a datagram is routed are programmed to support and provide quality service.

IP Header

The IP header contains quite a bit of information. Routers generally only pay attention to the destination address. The IP header is typically 20 bytes long, with the maximum possible header being 60 bytes. An IP header is illustrated in Figure 6.13.

The IP header fields are described as:

- **Version:** This 4-bit field identifies the version of IP.

- **Header Length:** This 4-bit field contains the length of the header, expressed in 32-bit words. A header without options contains 20 octets; therefore, the value is usually 5 (5 × 32-bit words).

- **Type of Service:** This 8-bit field contains 1-bit flags that can be used to request delay, throughput, and reliability parameters.

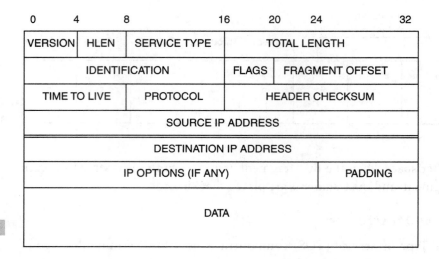

Figure 6.13
IP header

- **Total Length:** This 16-bit field contains the total length the IP datagram takes up including the header. Values can range from 576 to 65,535 octets.

- **Identifier:** This field contains a unique 16-bit number assigned to a datagram fragment to help in the reassembly of fragmented datagrams.

- **Flags:** This field contains three 1-bit flags that indicate whether fragmentation of the packet is permitted.

- **Fragment Offset:** This 8-bit field, measured in units of 8 octets (64 bits), specifies a value for each data fragment in the reassembly process.

- **Time to Live (TTL):** This 8-bit field is the time that the datagram is allowed to exist on the network. Each router that processes the packet decrements this by 1 until it reaches 0 and is discarded.

- **Protocol:** This 8-bit field specifies the Layer 4 protocol sending the datagram.

- **Checksum:** This 16-bit error-checking field checks only the header.

- **Source IP Address:** This field contains a 32-bit address of the computer sending the datagram.

- **Destination IP Address:** This field contains a 32-bit address of the computer to which the datagram is being sent.

- **IP Options:** This field contains optional routing and timing information.

- **Padding:** Extra zeros are added to this field to ensure that the datagram is a multiple of 32 bits.

6.5.2   Internet Control Message Protocol (ICMP)

Internet Control Message Protocol (ICMP) is part of the Internet layer and uses IP datagram delivery to send its messages. Of course, because ICMP uses IP, ICMP packet delivery may be unreliable. The messages typically report errors in the processing of datagrams, control, and informational functions related to network operations. ICMP uses the basic support of IP as if it was a higher-level protocol but is actually an integrated part of IP. Every ICMP packet must have a type value, but only some ICMP types have an associated code value. Message formats for ICMP can be found in RFC 792.

To avoid infinite repetition, no ICMP error messages are sent in response to ICMP error messages; they are only sent for errors on the first fragment of fragmented IP datagrams and are never sent in response to a datagram that is destined to a broadcast or a multicast address. Basically, ICMP is a protocol meant to be used as an aid for other protocols, as well as system administrators, to test for connectivity and search for configuration errors in a network. We now look at some of the functions that can be performed via ICMP.

Understanding and Using PING

PING was created by Mike Muuss of the Army Research Laboratory in December 1983. It is named after the sound that a sonar makes, inspired by the principle of echolocation. When submarine crews wanted to test the distance of an object, they would send a sonar ping and wait to hear the echo from the wave when it bounced off something, such as another submarine or the ocean floor. Like many other terms in networking, you will also find documentation that PING is actually an acronym for the words *Packet InterNet Groper*.

PING uses the ICMP echo function. A small packet containing an ICMP echo message is sent through the network to a particular IP address. The

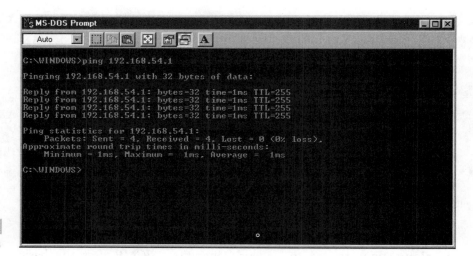

Figure 6.14

PING command and results

computer that sent the packet then waits for a return packet. If the connections are good and the target computer is up, the echo message return packet will be received. It is one of the most useful network tools available because it tests the most basic function of an IP network. It also shows the TTL value and the amount of time it takes for a packet to make the complete trip, also known as round-trip time (RTT), in milliseconds (ms). If the trip takes an extended period of time, it indicates that something may be wrong. When PING works, it tells you that there is a functioning path between the source and the destination, and that the machine with the target IP address is running. See Figure 6.14 for an example of PING results.

Some other advantages of using PING include:

- It places a unique sequence number on each packet it transmits.

- There are checksums each packet.

- It places a timestamp in each packet.

- It reports other ICMP messages.

6.5.3   Understanding and Using Traceroute

Traceroute was originally developed for the Unix operating system but now is used by many operating systems and most routers to track the path a packet takes to get to its destination. In other words, it measures how long it takes to travel through each hop to get to its target. Traceroute uses an

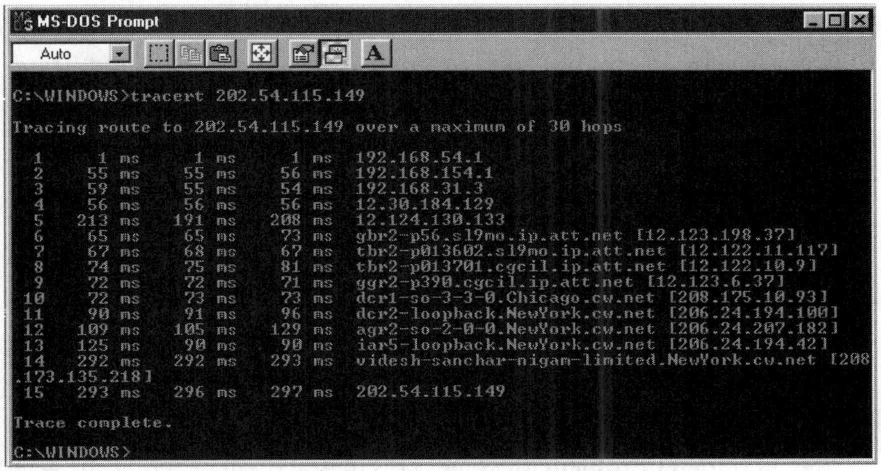

Figure 6.15
Tracert command and results

ICMP echo request packet to find the path. It sends an echo reply with the TTL value set to 1. When the first router sees the packet with TTL 1, it decreases it by 1 to 0, and then discards the packet. As a result, it sends an ICMP time-exceeded message back to the source address. The source address of the ICMP error message is the first router address. Now the source knows the address of the first router. Generally, three packets are sent at each TTL, and the RTT is measured for each one. See Figure 6.15 for an example of a successful Tracert command, which is the Windows equivalent of Traceroute. The source address then sends another packet with TTL 2, which passes the first router. If the destination network is directly attached to the first router, it will reach the destination. If not, it will end at the second router, and the process is repeated. Most implementations of Traceroute keep working until they have gone 30 hops, but this can be extended up to 254 routers (maximum TTL).

Most implementations of Traceroute also add a reverse name lookup to the process for each router IP address, which could make it pause too long between hops, giving the impression that there is a network problem.

! **WARNING**

Many firewalls will not issue ICMP error messages, so the Traceroute client may time out. This doesn't necessarily mean that there is a connectivity problem, just that it stops at a certain point due to firewall restrictions.

Other ICMP Tests and Functions

Besides assisting in troubleshooting functions such as PING and Trace-route, ICMP capabilities include announcing network errors, congestion, and timeout notification. The following is a list and descriptions of the functions that ICMP can perform:

- **Destination Unreachable Message:** If the IP module cannot deliver the datagram because the protocol or port is not active, the destination host sends a destination unreachable message to the source host.

- **Time Exceeded Message:** If the gateway processing a datagram finds the TTL field is 0, it discards the datagram and notifies the source host via the time exceeded message.

- **Parameter Problem Message:** This message will be sent if the gateway or host processing a datagram finds a problem with the header parameters and discards the datagram.

- **Source Quench Message:** A destination host may send a source quench message if datagrams arrive too fast to be processed. This is a request to the host to slow down the rate at which it is sending traffic to the destination host.

- **Redirect Message:** The gateway sends a redirect message to a host when it finds that the source address of a datagram is on the same network as the next gateway. The redirect message advises the host to send its traffic to next gateway, which is a shorter path to the destination.

- **Timestamp or Timestamp Reply Message:** The data received in the message is returned with an additional timestamp.

- **Information Request or Information Reply Message:** This is a way for a host to find out the number of the network it is on. It may be sent with the source network in the IP header source and destination address fields set to 0.

6.6   TCP/IP Transport Layer Protocols

The protocol layer above the Internet layer is the Transport layer. It is responsible for providing end-to-end data integrity. It also provides a reliable communication service so that an extended two-way conversation may take place. This layer accepts and returns information to be transmitted as a stream of characters while using open and close commands to initiate and terminate the connection. It consists of two protocols, TCP and User Datagram Protocol (UDP). An experimental protocol called Transaction Transmission Control Protocol (T/TCP) is an extension of TCP, which is transaction based. T/TCP solves TCP performance problems for transactions. You can find information on this in RFC 1644 (*http://www.faqs. org/rfcs/rfc1644.html*).

TCP provides connection-oriented data transmission, can support multiple data streams, and provides for flow and error control. It uses sequence numbers and acknowledgments to guarantee delivery. UDP does not provide either sequencing or acknowledgments. It is a connectionless protocol that is used a lot in telephony traffic and the Remote Procedure Call (RPC). The major difference between TCP and UDP is reliability. TCP is highly reliable, and UDP is a *best effort* simple delivery method. This difference results in vastly different uses of both protocols. One of the main functions of TCP and UDP is as a port manager for the applications that are in the top layer. The destination port number is placed in the header and is used to pass traffic to the correct application. There are 65,535 ports that can be accessed on a machine. The well-known ports are those from 0 through 1023. Some of the common well-known port numbers will be discussed later in the chapter.

6.6.1   Transmission Control Protocol (TCP)

TCP is the part of the protocol suite that provides functionality for packets and error checking. Applications that require reliable data delivery use TCP because it verifies that data are delivered accurately and in the proper sequence. It also ensures that data are resubmitted when transmission results in an error, and also enables hosts to maintain multiple, simultaneous connections.

Sockets make up a TCP connection. In Chapter 2, we discussed that a socket consists of an IP address and a port number. Connections are determined by the IP addresses and the socket numbers of the two computers trying to communicate. To establish a connection, a machine needs to know the IP address and port number on which the application communicates. When the application first starts using TCP, the receiver's computer sets up a buffer large enough to accommodate traffic for the data from the application. An acknowledgment (ACK) is periodically sent to the sender. If TCP receives ACKs that indicate a missing segment, it resends the missing segment and any segments sent after that to ensure that all the data was sent. The two TCP endpoints hold state information that in essence forms a virtual circuit. The virtual circuit is full duplex, meaning that data can go

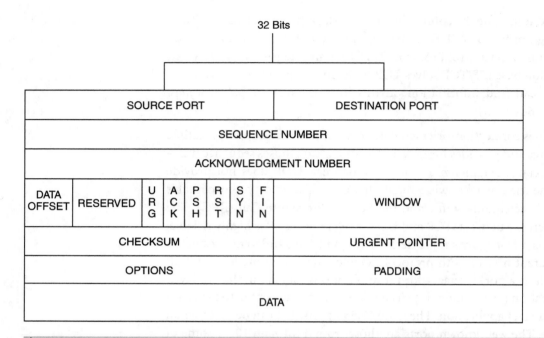

Figure 6.16

TCP protocol header

in both directions simultaneously. This virtual circuit consumes resources in both TCP endpoints; therefore, it requires more CPU and network bandwidth.

The two most typical network applications that use TCP are File Transfer Protocol (FTP) and Telnet. Telnet uses port 23 and FTP uses port 21. Clients can find the desired server simply by connecting to port 23 or 21 of TCP on the specified computer. The TCP protocol header is illustrated in Figure 6.16.

The TCP protocol header is a minimum of 20 octets and contains the following fields:

- **Source Port:** This 16-bit field contains the port number of the application requesting the connection.

- **Destination Port:** This 16-bit field contains the port number of the application called in the connection.

- **Sequence Number:** This field contains a 32-bit number that is used to reconstruct the data back into its original form at the destination computer.

- **Acknowledgment Number:** This field contains a 32-bit number that identifies each sequence number of the packet being acknowledged. It contains the sequence number of the next expected octet.

- **Data Offset:** This field contains the size of the TCP header, measured in 32-bit words. It is used to determine where the data field begins.

- **Reserved:** This 6-bit field is always set to 0. These are reserved for future use.

- **Flags:** This 6-bit field contains six 1-bit control flags that are used to specify services and operations during the session. These are:

  - **URG:** Significant urgent pointer field

  - **ACK:** Significant acknowledgment field

  - **PSH:** Use the push function

  - **RST:** Reset connection

  - **SYN:** Synchronize sequence numbers

  - **FIN:** Data has finished sending

- **Window Size:** This 16-bit field tells the source host how many octets the destination host is willing to accept per segment.

- **Checksum:** This 16-bit field compares calculated mathematical values based upon the segment's contents to determine whether the segment has arrived error free.

- **Padding:** Extra zeros are added to this field to ensure that the TCP header is always an even multiple of 32 bits.

6.6.2 User Datagram Protocol (UDP)

User Datagram Protocol (UDP) is the other main protocol that resides on top of IP. UDP is a connectionless datagram service that does not guarantee delivery and does not maintain an end-to-end connection. It merely pushes the datagrams out and accepts incoming datagrams. UDP adds to what IP

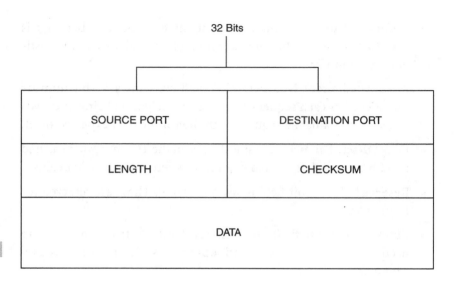

Figure 6.17
UDP protocol header

provides by multiplexing information between applications based on port number. In other words, UDP gives application programs direct access to a datagram via ports. This direct access allows applications to exchange messages over the network with a minimum of protocol overhead.

If UDP is unreliable, why is it used as a data transport service? If the amount of data being transmitted is small, the overhead of creating connections and ensuring reliable delivery may be greater than the work of retransmitting the entire datagram. Other applications provide their own techniques for reliable data delivery and do not require that service from the Transport layer protocol. Imposing another layer of acknowledgment is redundant. Some applications have a *query/response* mechanism. The response can be used as an acknowledgment to the query, thereby verifying the connection. UDP can also be used for exchanges of data, such as broadcasting NetBIOS names and system messages, because they do not require any of the functionality that TCP provides. The UDP protocol header is illustrated in Figure 6.17.

The UDP protocol header has the following fields:

- **Source Port Number:** This 16-bit field contains the port number of the application requesting the connection.

- **Destination Port Number:** This 16-bit field contains the port number of the application called in the connection.

- **Message Length:** This field contains the length of the datagram, which includes the header and the data. The minimum length is 8 octets.

- **Checksum:** This 16-bit field compares calculated mathematical values, based on the segment's contents, to determine whether the segment has arrived error free. It also does a checksum on any padding.

Example network applications that use UDP are Network File System (NFS) and Simple Network Management Protocol (SNMP). Both are discussed in the following section.

6.7   TCP/IP Application Layer Protocols

The top layer in the TCP/IP networking model is the Application layer. This is where applications and certain services access the network. It provides the services that applications use to communicate over the network, and is a service provider for workstations and applications. It also provides protocols for remote access and resource sharing. Familiar applications, such as e-mail, file transfer, terminal services and name server, reside and operate in this layer while depending on the functionality of the underlying layers. The most widely known and implemented TCP/IP Application layer services are:

- **File Transfer Protocol (FTP):** Performs basic interactive file transfers between hosts, allowing files to be uploaded and downloaded. It opens a connection on port 21.

- **Trivial File Transfer Protocol (TFTP):** Performs simple file transfers and is the predecessor of FTP. The TFTP protocol uses UDP for transferring files between server and client, and uses port 69 to transfer.

- **Telnet:** Provides a remote login capability on TCP. It uses terminal emulation for access to remote hosts. Implementations of Telnet usually work between different operating systems. It connects using port 23.

- **Simple Mail Transfer Protocol (SMTP):** Supports basic message delivery services between mail servers. SMTP uses port 25 to transfer data.

- **HyperText Transfer Protocol (HTTP):** Supports the transport of files containing text and graphics. This low-overhead Web browser service protocol uses port 80 to connect the browser and the Web server.

- **Network File System (NFS):** First developed by Sun Microsystems Inc., it uses UDP and enables computers to mount drives on remote hosts and operate them as if they were local drives.

- **Simple Network Management Protocol (SNMP):** Uses UDP port 161 and is designed to collect management information from network devices. A central station is used to collect data from other computers on the network.

- **Network News Transfer Protocol (NNTP):** Handles distribution and posting of news articles. It uses port 119 to communicate.

- **Dynamic Host Configuration Protocol (DHCP):** Allows for automatic IP addressing. Clients can lease an address from the server, making administration easier.

- **Domain Name Service (DNS):** Uses UDP port 53. Its hierarchical structure makes it easier to contact machines by resolving domain names to IP addresses.

Many of these protocols and services will be discussed in Chapter 9.

6.8   Chapter Summary

- A protocol is a set of rules and conventions that determines how computers exchange information over a network medium. A wide variety of communication protocols exist, and many of them rely on others for operation. Groups of related protocols are often called stacks or protocol stacks.

- Protocols can be either standard or proprietary. Proprietary protocols include XNS, NetBIOS, IPX/SPX, AppleTalk, and DECNet. XNS stands for Xerox Network Systems. This is a suite of protocols created by Xerox in the late 1970s and early 1980s for use in Ethernet networks. The NetBIOS interface was developed in 1983 for IBM by Sytec Inc. NetBIOS allows applications on different computers to communicate within a local area network. In the early 1980s, Novell introduced its own network protocol stack called Internetwork Packet Exchange/Sequenced Packet Exchange (IPX/SPX). This stack was based on the XNS network protocol family. IPX is the Network layer protocol, and SPX is the

Transport layer protocol. AppleTalk is Apple's networking protocol. It is designed to be a flexible, simple, and inexpensive network means for connecting computers, peripherals, and servers. DECnet is a proprietary network protocol designed by DEC. The first version of DECnet was released in 1975. Later releases expanded the functionality while remaining backward-compatible. Currently, two versions of DECnet are in use: DECnet Phase IV and DECnet/OSI.

- TCP/IP is considered the language of the Internet and probably the most widely used protocol today. It a suite, or stack, of small, specialized protocols. Because of its routing ability, TCP/IP has become the protocol of choice for many LANs, as well as the basis for the Internet, making it the standard. TCP/IP's implementation of the OSI model makes functionality simpler by mapping the same seven layers of the OSI model to a four-layer TCP/IP model instead. The TCP/IP model focuses more on delivering interconnectivity than on functional layers.

- The Network Access layer is the lowest layer in the TCP/IP networking model. It contains the protocols used to deliver data to computers and devices on the network. The various protocols used at the Network Access layer include Serial Line Interface Protocol (SLIP) and Point-to-Point Protocol (PPP). They are communication protocols for serial data transmission by which IP packets can be sent over a modem. Other protocols used at the Network Access layer include a means to relate different types of addresses to each other. This is done through two protocols: the Address Resolution Protocol (ARP) and the Reverse Address Resolution Protocol (RARP).

- The layer above the Network Access layer is called the Internet layer. It manages the routing of packets that are to be forwarded on to different networks, relying on routable protocols for delivery. The Internet Protocol (IP) is responsible for making data packets routable. It is a forwarding protocol that uses routing tables created by routing protocols. It is a simple, connectionless internetworking protocol. Internet Control Message Protocol (ICMP) is part of the Internet layer and uses IP datagram delivery to send its messages. PING uses the Internet Control Message Protocol (ICMP) echo function. It is one of the most useful network tools available because it tests the most basic function of an IP network. Traceroute was originally developed for the Unix operating system but is used for many operating systems and most routers. It is used to track the path a packet takes to get to its destination. In other words, it measures how long it takes to travel through each hop to get to its target. Traceroute uses an ICMP echo request packet to find the path. The Windows version of Traceroute is Tracert.

- The protocol layer above the Internet layer is the Transport layer. It is responsible for providing end-to-end data integrity. It also provides a reliable communication service so that an extended two-way conversation may take place. It consists of two protocols, Transmission Control Protocol (TCP) and User Datagram Protocol (UDP). TCP provides connection-oriented data transmission, can support multiple datastreams, and provides for flow and error control. It uses sequence numbers and acknowledgments to guarantee delivery. UDP does not provide either sequencing or acknowledgments. It is a connectionless protocol that uses a "best effort" simple delivery method.

- The top layer in the TCP/IP networking model is the Application layer. This is where applications and certain services access the network. It provides the services that applications use to communicate over the network and serves as service provider for workstations and applications. The most widely known and implemented TCP/IP Application layer services are FTP, TFTP, Telnet, SMTP, HTTP, NNTP, SNMP, DNS, and DCHP.

6.9   Key Terms

Address Resolution Protocol (ARP): A protocol used by IP Network layer protocols to map IP network addresses to the hardware addresses used by a Data Link protocol.

AppleTalk: The protocol suite used to interconnect Macintosh computers. It is designed to be a flexible, simple, and inexpensive network means for connecting computers, peripherals, and servers.

datagram: A packet that consists of a header, data, and a trailer.

Datagram Delivery Protocol (DDP): An AppleTalk Network layer protocol used to connect more than one network.

DECnet: A proprietary network protocol designed by Digital Equipment Corporation.

Digital Network Architecture (DNA): A layered network architecture that supports standard and proprietary protocols.

encapsulation: The process of packaging upper-layer protocol information and data into a frame.

Internet Control Message Protocol (ICMP): A part of the Internet layer that uses IP datagram delivery to send messages notifying the sender if something has gone wrong in the transmission process.

Internetwork Packet Exchange (IPX): A connectionless datagram-based Layer 3 (Network) protocol of the IPX/SPX suite that is used to route packets through networks.

maximum transmission unit (MTU): The maximum frame size allowed to travel through a network, using a given protocol and media type.

NetBIOS Extended User Interface (NetBEUI): Specifies the way that upper-level software sends and receives messages over the NetBIOS Frames Protocol (NBF). It has become an industry standard.

NetWare Core Protocol (NCP): One of the core protocols of the IPX/SPX suite. NCP handles requests for services, such as printing and file access, between clients and servers.

Network Basic Input/Output System (NetBIOS): Developed in 1983 for IBM to allow applications on different computers to communicate within a local area network.

Network Services Protocol (NSP): A connection-oriented protocol developed by Digital to manage flow control, segmentation, and reassembly functions.

PING: An ICMP echo function used to test network connectivity.

Point-to-Point Protocol (PPP): A newer protocol that does essentially the same thing as SLIP but has extra features, such as error detection and IP address negotiation.

Reverse Address Resolution Protocol (RARP): A network protocol belonging to the OSI Data Link layer that is used to resolve a Data Link layer address to the corresponding Network layer address.

Sequenced Packet Exchange (SPX): Resides on top of IPX and is a reliable, connection-oriented protocol that supplements the datagram service provided by IPX. SPX works with IPX to make sure that data is received whole, in sequence, and error-free.

Serial Line Interface Protocol (SLIP): An extremely simple framing scheme for putting IP packets on a serial line.

Service Advertising Protocol (SAP): A protocol in the IPX/SPX suite through which network resources, such as file servers and print servers, advertise their addresses and the services they provide.

Traceroute: In Unix, an ICMP function used to track the path a packet takes to get to its destination. Windows uses a similar utility called Tracert.

User Datagram Protocol (UDP): A connectionless datagram service in the TCP/IP suite that does not guarantee delivery and does not maintain an end-to-end connection. It merely pushes the datagrams out and accepts incoming datagrams.

Xerox Network Systems (XNS): A suite of protocols created by Xerox in the late 1970s and early 1980s to be used in Ethernet networks.

6.10   Challenge Questions

6.1 Of the major protocols, _____ is the most commonly used.

a. IPX/SPX

b. TCP/IP

c. NetBEUI

d. AppleTalk

6.2 The component of an IP datagram header that indicates the maximum time in seconds that a datagram can remain on the network before it is discarded is called _____.

a. Time to Destiny

b. Time to Line

c. Time to Activate

d. Time to Live

6.3 The IP component of TCP/IP is an unreliable, connectionless protocol. This means that _____.

    a. it does not need a connection to perform its function

    b. it does not have a way to connect and must rely on other components

    c. it does not guarantee delivery of data

    d. none of the above

6.4 The numbers 128 through 191 in the first octets of an IP address indicate that the address is _____.

    a. Class E

    b. Class B

    c. Class A

    d. Class C

6.5 IPX addresses contain two parts: the _____ address and the _____ address.

    a. network, node

    b. platform, node

    c. protocol, platform

    d. network, protocol

6.6 The length of the IP datagram including its header and data cannot exceed _____ bytes.

    a. 6,535

    b. 65,535

    c. 512

    d. 5,126

6.7 Protocols vary according to _____.

    a. speed

    b. transmission efficiency

    c. utilization of resources

    d. all of the above

6.8 TCP sits on top of the IP protocol and enhances IP reliability by providing _____, _____, and _____.

6.9 NetBIOS is a protocol originally designed by _____ to provide Transport and Session layer services for applications running on small networks.

6.10 A(n) _____ is a logical address assigned to a specific process running on a computer.

6.11 The _____, an Application layer protocol in the TCP/IP suite, can automatically assign IP addresses.

6.12 In the IP datagram, the component that tells IP how to process the incoming datagram by indicating speed, priority, or reliability is the _____.

6.13 What is ICMP, and how is it used?

6.14 What is SAP, and how does it function?

6.15 What is the difference between ARP and RARP?

6.11   Challenge Exercises

Challenge Exercise 6.1

In this exercise, you install and remove NWLink. This will allow you to see the configuration settings needed when installing IPX/SPX. You need a desktop or laptop computer with a Windows-based operating system, such as Windows 2000, and a network card installed.

To add the IPX/SPX protocol to a computer's configuration:

1. Right-click **My Network Places** on the desktop and select **Properties**. The Network and Dial-up Connections window opens.

2. Double-click the **Local Area Connection** icon. The Local Area Connection Status dialog box opens.

3. Click the **Properties** button. The Local Area Connection Properties dialog box opens.

4. Click the **Install** button. The Select Network Component Type dialog box opens.

5. Select **Protocol** and then click the **Add** button. The Select Network Protocol dialog box opens.

6. Select the **NWLink IPX/SPX/NetBIOS Compatible Transport Protocol** entry and click **OK**.

7. Click the **Close** button.

To view the settings of the IPX/SPX protocol:

1. Return to the Local Area Connection Status dialog box and click **Properties**. Click **NWLink IPX/SPX/NetBIOS Compatible Transport Protocol** and click the **Properties** button. The NWLink IPX/SPX/NetBIOS Compatible Transport Protocol Properties dialog box opens.

2. The General tab shows both the network number and the frame type configuration, as shown in Figure 6.18. Click **OK**.

3. Click **OK** twice and then close all open windows associated with this exercise.

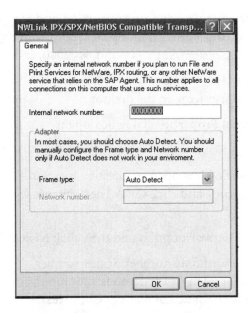

Figure 6.18

Network number and frame type

To uninstall the IPX/SPX protocol:

1. Right-click **My Network Places** on the desktop and select **Properties**. The Network and Dial-up Connections window opens.

2. Double-click **Local Area Connection**. The Local Area Connection Status dialog box opens.

3. Click the **Properties** button. The Local Area Connection Properties dialog box opens.

4. Select the **NWLink IPX/SPX/NetBIOS Compatible Transport Protocol** entry in the Components Checked Are Used by this Connection list box.

5. Click the **Uninstall** button.

6. When prompted to confirm your action, click **Yes**.

7. When prompted to restart your computer, click **Yes**.

Challenge Exercise 6.2

In this exercise, you learn how to create a new dial-up connection and see where PPP and SLIP are configured. You need a desktop or laptop computer with a Windows-based operating system, such as Windows 2000, and an installed modem.

6.1 Right-click the **Internet Explorer** icon on the desktop.

6.2 Select **Properties**. The Internet Properties dialog box opens.

6.3 Click the **Connections** tab.

6.4 Click the **Add** button. (If a dialog box opens requesting location information, enter your area code and click **OK**.) The Network Connection Wizard starts.

6.5 Select the **Dial-up to private network** option and then click **Next**.

6.6 Enter a phone number (use your home number or the number given to you by your instructor). This is for demonstration purposes only and is not being used for actual dial-up. Click **Next**.

6.7 In the Connection Availability screen, confirm that the **For all users** option is selected. Click **Next**.

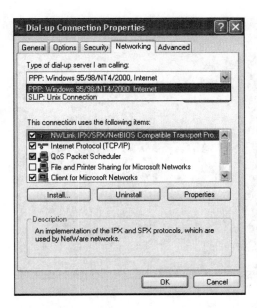

Figure 6.19
PPP configuration

6.8 Enter a connection name or leave the default. Click **Finish**. The Dial-Up Connection Settings dialog box opens.

6.9 Click the **Properties** button.

6.10 Click the **Networking** tab. The first list box shows the type of server you are dialing into (see Figure 6.19). This is where you could change the configuration to SLIP, if needed. For this exercise, leave the default PPP entry selected.

6.11 Click **OK** twice. You are returned to the Connections tab in the Internet Properties dialog box.

6.12 Select the connection you just made and then click **Remove**. When prompted to delete the connection, click **OK**.

6.13 Close all open windows associated with this exercise.

Challenge Exercise 6.3

In this exercise, you explore the purpose of the PING utility. You will see how ICMP messages are displayed using various commands. You need a

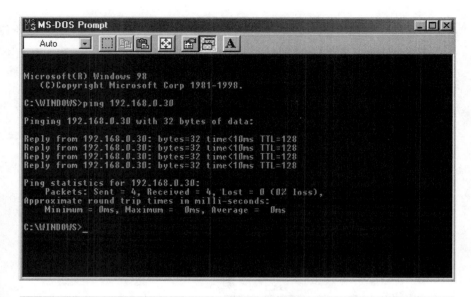

Figure 6.20
Results of ping command

desktop or laptop computer with a Windows-based operating system, TCP/IP installed, network connectivity, and Internet access.

6.1 Log on to your computer.

6.2 Click **Start**, click **Run**, type **cmd** in the Open text box, and then click **OK**.

6.3 At the command prompt, type **ping** and press **Enter**. The commands that can be used with PING are displayed.

6.4 At the command prompt, type **ipconfig** and press **Enter**. The IP address of your computer is displayed.

6.5 Type **ping** with the IP address of someone else in the class, and then press **Enter**. What happens?

6.6 Type **ping 207.46.138.20** and press **Enter**. This is a DNS server IP address associated with *www.microsoft.com*. The results should look similar to Figure 6.20.

6.7 Type **ping 10.10.10.10** and press **Enter**. What happens? What does this mean?

6.8 Type **exit** and press **Enter** to close the command prompt window.

```
MS-DOS Prompt                                          _ □ ×
Auto        ▼   □  🗎🗎  ⊠  🖼🖼  A

C:\WINDOWS>tracert 202.54.115.149

Tracing route to 202.54.115.149 over a maximum of 30 hops

   1    1 ms     1 ms     1 ms  192.168.54.1
   2   55 ms    55 ms    56 ms  192.168.154.1
   3   59 ms    55 ms    54 ms  192.168.31.3
   4   56 ms    56 ms    56 ms  12.30.184.129
   5  213 ms   191 ms   208 ms  12.124.130.133
   6   65 ms    65 ms    73 ms  gbr2-p56.s19mo.ip.att.net [12.123.198.37]
   7   67 ms    68 ms    67 ms  tbr2-p013602.s19mo.ip.att.net [12.122.11.117]
   8   74 ms    75 ms    81 ms  tbr2-p013701.cgcil.ip.att.net [12.122.10.9]
   9   72 ms    72 ms    71 ms  ggr2-p390.cgcil.ip.att.net [12.123.6.37]
  10   72 ms    73 ms    73 ms  dcr1-so-3-3-0.Chicago.cw.net [208.175.10.93]
  11   90 ms    91 ms    96 ms  dcr2-loopback.NewYork.cw.net [206.24.194.100]
  12  109 ms   105 ms   129 ms  agr2-so-2-0-0.NewYork.cw.net [206.24.207.182]
  13  125 ms    90 ms    90 ms  iar5-loopback.NewYork.cw.net [206.24.194.42]
  14  292 ms   292 ms   293 ms  videsh-sanchar-nigam-limited.NewYork.cw.net [208
.173.135.218]
  15  293 ms   296 ms   297 ms  202.54.115.149

Trace complete.

C:\WINDOWS>
```

Figure 6.21

Results of tracert command

Challenge Exercise 6.4

In this exercise, you learn the purpose of the Tracert (aka Traceroute) utility. This exercise shows you how ICMP messages are displayed using various commands. You need a desktop or laptop computer with a Windows-based operating system, TCP/IP installed, network connectivity, and Internet access.

6.1 Log on to your computer.

6.2 Click **Start**, click **Run**, type **cmd** in the Open text box, and then click **OK**.

6.3 At the command prompt, type **tracert** with the IP address of someone else in the class, and then press **Enter**. What happens?

6.4 Type **tracert 207.46.138.20**. The results should look similar to Figure 6.21.

6.5 Type **tracert 10.10.10.10** and press **Enter**. What happens? What does this mean?

6.6 Open Internet Explorer and go to *http://www.whois.com*. Search for some common company names (ask your instructor for assistance, if necessary) and do a traceroute to their DNS servers. Record the number of hops and the milliseconds.

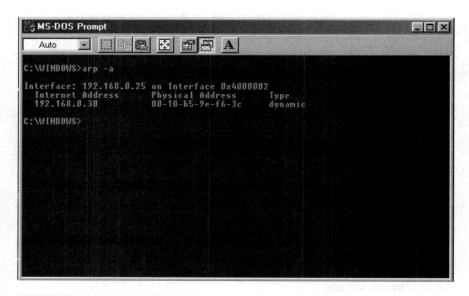

Figure 6.22
Results of arp -a command

6.7   Type **tracert 200.200.200.200** and press **Enter**. What happens? Why?

6.8   Type **exit** and press **Enter** to close the command prompt window.

Challenge Exercise 6.5

In this exercise, you learn the purpose of ARP. The exercise shows the information that can be viewed through the various commands. You need a desktop or laptop computer with a Windows-based operating system, TCP/IP installed, and network connectivity.

6.1   Log on to your computer.

6.2   Click **Start**, click **Run**, type **cmd** in the Open text box, and then click **OK**.

6.3   At the command prompt, type **arp** and press **Enter**. The commands that can be used with ARP are displayed.

6.4   Type **arp -a** and press **Enter**. You should see a mapping of IP addresses to MAC addresses similar to the one shown in Figure 6.22. The ARP cache holds actively changing information for 10 minutes but deletes it if it is not used within 2 minutes. If you took a break between exercises, you may have to ping or traceroute to an IP address to add entries in the cache.

6.5 Type **rarp** and press **Enter**. What happens? Why?

6.6 Type **exit** and press **Enter** to close the command prompt window.

Challenge Exercise 6.6

In this exercise, you learn how to install Network Monitor and then capture and read packets. You need a desktop or laptop computer running Windows 2000 Server, TCP/IP installed, and network connectivity.

To install Network Monitor:

6.1 Log on to your computer.

6.2 Right-click **My Network Places** on the desktop and select **Properties**. The Network and Dial-up Connections window opens.

6.3 Double-click **Local Area Connection**. The Local Area Connection Status dialog box opens.

6.4 Click the **Properties** button. The Local Area Connection Properties dialog box opens.

6.5 Click the **Install** button. The Select Network Component Type dialog box opens.

6.6 Select **Protocol** and then click **Add**. The Select Network Protocol dialog box opens.

6.7 Select the **Network Monitor Driver** entry and click **OK**.

6.8 Click **OK** again and then close any open windows.

To capture and view packets with Network Monitor:

6.1 On the server, click **Start**, click **Programs**, point to **Administrative Tools**, and click **Network Monitor**.

6.2 Click **Capture** in the menu bar and select **Start**.

6.3 Let the monitor run for a few minutes, and then click **Capture** in the menu bar and click **Stop and View**.

6.4 Examine the captured packets. Beginning with the first frame, go through each category and look at the source MAC address, destination MAC address, and the protocol.

6.5 Double-click the first frame to see additional details. Notice the frame, Ethernet, IP, and UDP entries. Expand each category and view the packet information.

6.12   Challenge Scenarios

Challenge Scenario 6.1

You have been asked to design a network for a small law firm. It is currently running 20 Windows 2000 and 15 NetWare computers. The firm is interested in installing a server to connect all the computers. You are told that there is a good possibility that the law firm will be merging with another firm twice its size. Except for the price of the server, management would like to keep costs low. They also want to be sure that they can easily integrate with the merging law firm when the time comes. Choose the server type and protocol you would recommend, and explain why you made that recommendation.

Challenge Scenario 6.2

A movie company that specializes in animation and graphics has asked you to assess their shop. Currently, the employees have individual, stand-alone computers. Management plans to hire additional employees due to a pending contract. They received a large advance for the project and have some money to spend on IT-related purchases. They want the staff to be able to share files and work together. What protocol would you recommend they use? Explain your answer.

Challenge Scenario 6.3

Your friend is a network administrator at a large company. One of the workstations can no longer access the Internet. He checked all the cables and they seem to be fine. All the other computers appear to be operating appropriately and can access the Internet. He suspects that the user has changed some settings, but the user denies doing so. The network administrator asks for your help. How would you help him troubleshoot the problem?

Challenge Scenario 6.4

You have been asked to review the network of a small bank. Management wants some of the employees to be able to telecommute. For security reasons, they do not want to allow the employees to use high-speed Internet connections that could be left on all day. They have had modems installed in the employee's home computers and want you to suggest a protocol to use for the connection between the home users and the bank. What protocol would you recommend and why?

CHAPTER 7

Naming and Addressing

After reading this chapter you will be able to:

- Identify why naming is important

- Create and identify hierarchical naming schemes

- Describe addressing concepts for a variety of technologies and protocols

- Develop addressing for TCP/IP

- Subnet TCP/IP addresses

- Identify the function of variable-length subnet masking (VLSM)

- Identify the characteristics and benefits of classless inter-domain routing (CIDR)

- Discuss the basic concepts of IP version 6

The focus of this chapter is identifying standard methods used in addressing and naming network devices. We first focus on naming, highlighting why naming is important and common methods used to properly name network equipment. We then focus on addressing, looking first at the familiar telephone network method and then identifying addressing used in IPv4 and IPv6 networks.

7.1   Why Naming Is Important

A router by any name will route frames, a switch will forward packets even if it is named Euripides, and a server named Caesar will still serve resources to network clients. So why is naming so important? Generally speaking, networks are created to offer resources to users and proper naming is critical to this purpose. Naming network resources has a direct impact on usability, security, and productivity, and if done properly it has a positive impact in other areas, including:

- Teaching employees (old and new) about the network
- Identifying the network layout and traffic flow
- Documenting the network
- Identifying systems using network-monitoring software and packet captures
- Identifying systems using graphical browse lists and network sutilities

Using names that have meaning or that follow a naming scheme (or naming convention) allows users to better understand the function and placement of computers and networking equipment throughout the network. The benefits of proper naming are not limited to employees in the IT department, but extend to anyone who uses the network for resource access.

In Figure 7.1 we illustrate problems associated with poor naming and then give you guidelines for proper naming of network devices.

NOTE   The names used in Figure 7.1 come from real clients and their actual network naming practices.

As you can see from Figure 7.1, it is difficult to identify what services or resources any of the computers offer. What type of equipment is Riker? Is

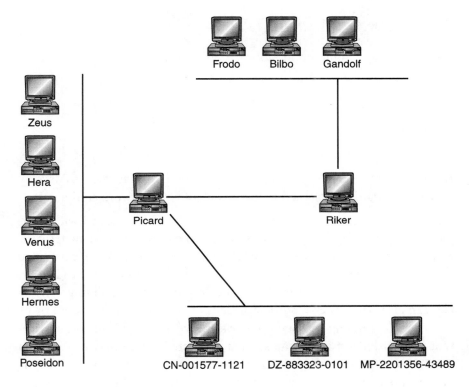

Figure 7.1
Naming network devices

Zeus a server or a client workstation? If you were troubleshooting the network and saw a large number of packets coming from Gandolf, would that be expected? If you are a brand new end user on this network, what server is likely to house your personal folders?

Given the current lack of information supplied by the names of the systems, all of these questions would have to be answered by trial and error, or by calling the help desk or IT department. What happens to you, as a network administrator, when you have to install and configure server number 300 and you are all out of Greek and Roman gods? The better approach to naming your network resources is to use a systematic naming methodology that will serve an infinite (or nearly so) number of devices.

7.2   Hierarchical Naming

Proper naming is built around four key elements:

1. Hierarchy
2. Location
3. Function
4. Unique identifier (ID)

By placing these elements together in a structured format, you can develop a useful standardized method to identify all of your network equipment.

Hierarchy is a characteristic of good naming and is developed within the naming structure by going from less specific to more specific characteristics. As an example, you can start by identifying a network device according to which country it is in, then which state or province, and finally by identifying the city, building, and potentially the floor within the building. Hierarchy can also be built around object identity (servers, workstations) or by function (identifying the operating system, current version, and services that are in use). Admittedly, most hierarchies are built around location, but on a few occasions with our clients we have seen a benefit in creating object-based hierarchical naming instead of or in addition to location-based naming. We will give you some examples of both as we discuss the next two characteristics.

> **NOTE** You can reverse the process and go from more specific to less specific, but it is unusual to do it this way. The important points to remember are to incorporate hierarchy when possible and to make sure that it makes sense and adds value for your internal processes.

7.2.1   Developing a Common Naming Scheme

Location can be identified at several different layers, and it depends on the needs of the users and administrators as well as the size and needs of the company. We'll use a fictitious company called Widgets, Inc. as an example. Widgets is a small firm with all of its computer systems currently located in Miami, Florida. In this situation, you might decide to use any of the following as a location code in the name of all network devices:

- MIAMI (the full name of the location)

- MIA (the airport code for the nearest airport)

- MIFL (the first two characters of the city and the standard two letter postal code for the state)

- FLMI (the reverse of the previous code, with state first and then city)

- FL (the two-letter state postal code)

As shown, there are many possibilities for assigning a location code to your devices. You are probably asking the question, why? The company is small and has only a single location, so why put a location in the name at all? Change is constant, and the possibility of growth or acquisition is a real business factor that should be considered by every network administrator. If Widgets opens a branch office in Los Angeles or is acquired by a larger firm, the location in the name will benefit network users and administrators alike.

In a large company that has multiple locations or an international presence, a regional or country code may also be used. Looking at Widgets again, let's assume it has grown and now has offices in Hong Kong, Sydney, Berlin, London, Paris, Rome, Nairobi, and Rio de Janeiro, as well as in Miami. You might decide that it is best to include a region or country code in the naming scheme. The following list is an example and does not necessarily represent the best naming format for all situations:

- USMIA (United States, Miami)

- AUSY (Australia, Sydney)

- UKLO (United Kingdom, London)

- ITRO (Italy, Rome)

Continuing with our example, Widgets continues to expand its offices to include eight buildings in the downtown Miami area, two office buildings in London, and four buildings in Hong Kong. This situation warrants the use of codes to identify buildings and maybe even floors, so that a server in Miami in Building 1 on the 3rd floor might have a name that starts with MIA0103.

Don't focus too much on the exact examples. The key here is to understand the concept of using a standard method to create names and include a location code so that it will be easier to identify where a network device is located. Another feature that will make life easier for all concerned and

TABLE 7.1   Functional Abbreviations

Function	Abbreviation
Logon server	LS
DNS server	NS
Web server	W
E-mail server	EM
File and print server	FP
Database server	DB
Workstation	WK
Router	RTR
Switch	SW
Firewall	FW

should be included in naming network devices is some type of function code or service ID.

Function, similar to location, allows users, administrators, and even the occasional outside contractor a quicker insight when using, viewing, or troubleshooting the network. It is an integral part of the naming scheme for modern networks. Table 7.1 represents some common functional abbreviations that we have seen used by various companies.

This is by no means a comprehensive code map but should give you some good ideas for naming your equipment. With our new naming convention in place, we can now break down the name of a system and know where it is and what primary function it serves within the network, as follows:

- **MIA0103LS:** This name would be assigned to a system in Miami (MIA) that is located in Building 1 (01) on the 3rd floor (03) and whose primary service is as a logon server (LS).

- **MIA0201NSW:** This name would represent a DNS (NS) server and a Web server (W) located in Miami in Building 2 on the 1st floor.

- **MIA0201RTR:** This name would represent a router located in Miami in Building 2 on the 1st floor.

Many times, on networks both large and small, several of the same device types will be in the same location offering the same service. Logon servers, user workstations, routers, and switches represent groups of devices that are often physically located in the same area. Using our naming scheme, how do we properly name these systems without duplication? The answer is the last of our three characteristics of naming—a unique ID code.

Unique ID codes are sequential numeric values added to the end of a system name to make a situation unique when otherwise the name code would be the same. For instance, in Building 1 of our Widgets Miami office, we have three logon servers on the first floor. The names of the servers are as follows:

- MIA0101LS01
- MIA0101LS02
- MIA0101LS03

Incorporating a systematic naming methodology makes naming new servers an easy task. If we added a fourth logon server in the same location in Miami, the name would be MIA0101LS04. At this time, the names might look strange, but after a few weeks of seeing and using these codes, it would be an easy process to identify where a device is, what it does, and how many other devices of that type are in the same location. This type of naming scheme provides location, functionality, and ID to assist you in the field when you are trying to troubleshoot a network problem.

By utilizing each of the three components of proper naming—location, function, and unique ID—you can eliminate common problems such as trying to identify what device is malfunctioning to the more mundane issue of what to name a new device when it is deployed. Unfortunately, a key argument against logical naming or developing an obvious naming scheme as we have illustrated is lack of security.

7.2.2 Developing a Secure Naming Scheme

Security has become a major concern in the last few years, even on small networks. Looking at the codes for one of our Widgets servers might give a hacker enough information to make a more precise attack. We can adapt our principles of naming to better obscure the location and/or the function of the equipment that we manage and still keep our three characteristics

TABLE 7.2 **Obscured Location Abbreviations**

Location	Abbreviation
Miami, Florida	A
Sydney, Australia	B
Rome, Italy	C
Paris, France	D
Hong Kong, China	E
Berlin, Germany	F
Rio de Janeiro, Brazil	G
London, United Kingdom	H
Nairobi, Kenya	I

and the benefits of standardized naming. As shown in Tables 7.2 and 7.3, we can convert the more obvious code structure to one that is less likely to offer desirable information to unauthorized users.

The names for our Widgets servers using our new more secure code structure are as follows:

- **A0103Z01:** A server in Miami in Building 1 on the 3rd floor that is providing logon services.

- **A0201XY01:** A server in Miami in Building 2 on the 1st floor that is providing naming and Web server services.

- **F0101SQ01:** The first router located in Berlin in Building 1 on the 1st floor that is also providing firewall services.

Comparing the two different naming styles side by side, you can see that the second style makes it considerably harder to glean information. (See Table 7.4.) Although the second style makes it harder to identify the location and function of a server, codes can still be broken. It is important that the necessary security features be implemented to properly protect systems and information from unwanted access and use. Firewalls, packet filtering, auditing, security permissions on files and directories, intrusion detection,

TABLE 7.3 Obscured Functional Abbreviations

Function	Abbreviation
Logon server	Z
DNS server	Y
Web server	X
E-mail server	W
File and print server	V
Database server	U
Workstation	T
Router	S
Switch	R
Firewall	Q

TABLE 7.4 Comparing the Two Naming Styles

Device	Style 1	Style 2 (more secure)
Miami, Building 1, 3rd floor, first logon server	MIA0103LS01	A0103Z01
Miami, Building 2, 1st floor, DNS and Web server	MIA0201NSW	A0201XY
Berlin, Building 1, 1st floor, router and firewall	BER0101RTRFW	F0101SQ

backing up important user and company data, and other security features will ensure that if an attack does occur, your information and systems will be protected.

⚠ WARNING

Do not rely on name codes alone to protect your servers, services, and information. Individuals can randomly attack systems without using system names, or the codes can be inadvertently disclosed or cracked. This is just one component of a security puzzle that should be implemented to make the function and location of network devices less obvious.

We have shown that naming is important and can be both useful and easy if some simple rules are followed. Use the following list to review:

- Naming should be structured and standardized.

- Hierarchy allows names to flow from more generic to more specific references, and it may include location and object or service references.

- When possible and practical, naming should include location, function, and a unique ID.

- Security may require that you create a less obvious naming structure.

With the challenge of naming devices behind us, it's now time to discuss the concept of network device addressing.

7.3   Addressing

Network device addressing can generally be thought of as a user-defined value given to equipment that allows logical grouping by location, function, user base, or a number of other administrative functions. Addressing is composed of at least two parts: a network address portion and an endpoint (also called a host or node) or device portion. As you will see in the next section, an address can be divided into more than two sections, but at a minimum is composed of two parts, network and node.

7.3.1   Telephone Networks

The telephone network is one of the oldest and probably one of the most familiar forms of addressing used with internetworked devices. The telephone addressing system is a structured hierarchical format comprised of four key elements:

1. Country code
2. Area code
3. Switching prefix
4. Endpoint

Let's begin by looking at each portion of the address in the order of its hierarchy. The country codes allow telephone calls to be placed internationally. The telephony network system evaluates how each call is dialed and identifies the proper route based on the numeric values entered. Making a call

TABLE 7.5   International Dialing Codes

Country	Code	Zone
United States	1	1
Kenya	254	2
Portugal	351	3
United Kingdom	44	4
Brazil	55	5
New Zealand	64	6

outside your current country requires a specific beginning sequence that notifies the switching system to route the call to a particular country. In the United States, the international dialing sequence is 011; in many other countries it is 00. The international prefix value is then followed by the country code. The world is divided into nine zones, and each country within a zone has been assigned a code by the International Telecommunications Union (ITU). A short list of country codes is shown in Table 7.5.

For example, if you were to place a call from the United States to a city in the United Kingdom, you would first dial 011-44. The next number dialed would be the area code.

Area codes further divide the telephony switching system within a country into regions. In the United States, area codes are three digits in length and are used to group users by local service, allowing devices with the same area code prefix to connect without long-distance charges being applied.

NOTE

Due to population increases, some large metropolitan areas may use more than one area code within the same local dialing area.

Similar to an international call, a prefix is used for long-distance dialing. In the United States, a 1 is dialed, followed by the area code and then the remainder of the number. For dialing locally, neither the 1 nor the area code is required.

> If your region uses two or more area codes for local dialing, the area code is generally included with the standard number. This is often referred to as 10-digit dialing.

The third division of the telephony addressing system is the exchange number or local prefix. Inside the United States and most of the Caribbean, a 3-digit number identifies a particular switch within an area code. This could be a neighborhood, subdivision, or even an entire town.

The final address division is called the subscriber number and is usually four or more digits in length. This number identifies the actual endpoint or device in a telephone network, and is used to initiate the ringing or connection to the phone in a home or business. A complete number dialed from within the United States would look something like this:

- 1-303-555-1212
- 011-44-01869-000000

In the first example, the 1 specifies a long-distance call (out of the local dialing area) and the 303 is the area code (Denver, Colorado). The 555 prefix identifies an area within Denver, and 1212 specifies a phone line or subscriber. In the second example, we are making an international call (011) to the United Kingdom (44). The 01869 value represents the area code of Oxfordshire, and the last portion is the actual subscriber number.

> We have used fictitious or partial telephone numbers to avoid problems with publishing active phone listings. As shown in our examples, different countries deploy the numeric addressing system for telephony differently. A majority of our examples are based on the US phone system.

The main point here is that we simplify connecting a complex network of devices (telephones, in this case) by using a hierarchical addressing system broken down into smaller segments. This concept will carry forward when you begin to create addresses for your data network as we discuss in the next sections titled "Internet" and "IP Version 4 (IPv4)."

7.3.2 Internet

The Internet as we know it today evolved from an early military project of the 1960s. The original concept included the ability to interconnect (or network) dissimilar computer and communication systems across large geographic boundaries, allowing them to easily exchange data. Also included in this original concept of networking was the idea that if certain parts of the network were destroyed or damaged, network traffic would gracefully route around these trouble areas. One of the critical aspects of the project was the protocol to use and the addressing structure.

As discussed in Chapter 6, the protocols that were first considered for what has become the Internet included the Open Systems Interconnection (OSI) protocol and Transmission Control Protocol/Internet Protocol (TCP/IP). The OSI protocol proved to be too complex and instead evolved as a guideline (or model) for a majority of the networking protocols in use today. TCP/IP became the de facto standard protocol on the public Internet soon after a version of Unix (FreeBSD) shipped to universities with a preconfigured and stable TCP/IP software protocol component.

Time proven and well supported by network administrators and software manufacturers, addressing on the public Internet and on many private networks is now based solely on TCP/IP. Proper network addressing is crucial to ensure reliable network communications. The following sections familiarize you with the addressing format, features, functions, and future development of TCP/IP in the following sections.

NOTE

You will often read and hear TCP/IP referred to as just IP. It saves you from getting tongue-tied when discussing the protocol and saves a few letters when reading. TCP/IP and IP are used interchangeably throughout the rest of the chapter.

7.3.3 IP Version 4 (IPv4)

IP version 4 (IPv4) is the widely deployed version of the protocol and is in use on both private networks and on the Internet. Due to the strong possibility that the Internet will deplete the available IPv4 addresses, a new version—IPv6—is in development. IPv6 is set to debut as the next addressing standard due to the huge supply of unique IP addresses.

NOTE

IP version 6 is annotated as IPv6 or IPng (IP next generation) and represents a version of the protocol undergoing extensive testing and experimental deployment and development. This version is briefly discussed in the "IP Version 6 (IPv6)" section later in this chapter.

The addressing function in IPv4 is built around two key elements:

- Address
- Subnet mask

IP Address

The address space for IP is built on the binary numbering system and is composed of 32 bits. A bit is the most basic form of electronic storage and is either a 1 or a 0 (on or off, respectively). The bits are grouped into a byte (8 contiguous bits), also known as an octet. In an address, each of the octets is separated by a period and might look something like this:

10010011.00001001.10101101.01110110

Each **host** on an IP network must have an address, and it must be unique. The computer processes information in binary form but we humans do not, so to make it easier, the address is converted to decimal format and looks like this:

147.9.173.118

To visualize the conversion from binary to decimal, let's look at a single octet (set of 8 bits) and identify the value of each bit. Starting with the familiar is often easier, so let's look at a base10 number such as 1,426. This number is in decimal format is familiar to your eye. It can be read as four-teen hundred twenty-six, one thousand four hundred twenty-six, or just fourteen twenty-six. When you first learned about numbers, a number such as 1,426 may have been taught to you like this:

$$1426 = 1 \times 1000 + 4 \times 100 + 2 \times 10 + 6 \times 1$$

Each place in base10 has a value that is multiplied by the number in that place as annotated. In our example, the 6 (in 1,426) is in the 1s place, the 2 is in the 10s place, the 4 is in the 100s place, and so on. With that under-standing, we can determine the total value represented by 1,426. Binary numbering uses the same concept and is actually simpler because there are only two possible values, 1 or 0, for any place. Looking at a single octet in binary format, we can map out the place values like this:

10000010 or

Current value	1	0	0	0	0	0	1	0
Place value	128	64	32	16	8	4	2	1

TABLE 7.6   Binary Values to 15

Binary	Decimal	Binary	Decimal
00000000	0	00001000	8
00000001	1	00001001	9
00000010	2	00001010	10
00000011	3	00001011	11
00000100	4	00001100	12
00000101	5	00001101	13
00000110	6	00001110	14
00000111	7	00001111	15

The binary number shown would be represented in decimal as 130 (1 × 128 + 1 × 2 = 130). Table 7.6 shows the first 16 binary values so that you can visualize the pattern clearly.

Remember that we have an address that consists of four binary octets (a total of 32 bits). Each octet can have a binary value from 0000000 to 11111111, or from 0 to 255 in decimal. Putting all of this together, we come up with an address space that can support 4,294,967,296 (2^{32}) individual addresses as seen in the following sample addresses:

00000000.00000000.00000000.00000000 (first four possible addresses)
00000000.00000000.00000000.00000001
00000000.00000000.00000000.00000010
00000000.00000000.00000000.00000011
⋮
(4,294,967,288 other addresses omitted for the sake of brevity)
⋮
11111111.11111111.11111111.11111100 (last four possible addresses)
11111111.11111111.11111111.11111101
11111111.11111111.11111111.11111110
11111111.11111111.11111111.11111111

TABLE 7.7   Address Classes

Class	Beginning Range	End Range	Binary Pattern of First Octet
A	0.x.x.x	127.x.x.x	**0**0000000 to **0**1111111
B	128.x.x.x	191.x.x.x	**10**000000 to **10**111111
C	192.x.x.x	223.x.x.x	**110**00000 to **110**11111
D	224.x.x.x	239.x.x.x	**1110**0000 to **1110**1111
E	240.x.x.x	255.x.x.x	**1111**0000 to **1111**1111

As we can see, the address space for IPv4 is enormous (almost 4.3 billion) and, much like the telephone addressing system, is broken into more manageable blocks. The blocks do not correspond to geography like the telephony address space but instead are broken into blocks based on estimated numbers of hosts. The address blocks were assigned a letter value and can be identified by the numeric or binary pattern of the first octet (see Table 7.7).

TIP

The governing binary pattern has been bolded to make it easier to see. For each class address, the pattern in bold remains constant in the first octet. Class A addresses always start with the first or high-order bit set to 0. Class B addresses always start with 10, Class C addresses always start with 110, and so on. The address range for the first octet for Class A networks is 1 to 126 (0 is invalid and 127 is reserved), 128 to 191 for Class B networks, and 192 to 223 for Class C networks.

Class A through Class C address blocks were intended for publicly connected devices, whereas the Class D block was originally reserved for future use and is currently used for multicasting on IP-based networks. Class E addresses are used for experimental purposes and are not valid host addresses on the Internet.

Recall from the discussion on telephony that a network address is composed of a minimum of two parts: a network part and a host part. The difference in the class addresses is how many bits are used for the **network ID** and how many bits are used for hosts. Class A address blocks, for example, identify the first 8 bits (first octet) as the network portion with 24 bits (the other three octets) used for hosts. The number of hosts that a single Class A address can support is determined by taking 2^n, where n is the number of bits used for addressing hosts. In this case it would be 2^{24}, or 16,777,216 possible hosts. Class B address blocks use the first 16 bits for the network ID and the last 16 bits as host bits, and can support 2^{16} (or 65,536) hosts. Class C addresses use the first 24 bits as the network ID and 8 bits for host addressing (2^8, or 256 hosts). Examples of each address are:

Class A = **15**.0.0.0–**15**.255.255.255

Class B = **160.10**.0.0–**160.10**.255.255

Class C = **198.10.1**.0–**198.10.1**.255

NOTE

The bolded values cannot be changed and are referred to as the network ID. Once you are assigned a network ID, the only portion that is modified can be the host (nonbolded) portion.

To help keep things straight, let's review:

- An IP address is 32 bits long.
- The address is evaluated in binary form by the computer system but entered and manipulated in decimal form by humans.
- The addresses are split into blocks or classes.
- The difference between the class addresses is the number of bits used for the network ID.
- The class of an address can be found by evaluating the decimal or binary value of the first octet.

Our next step in IP addressing is understanding the purpose of the subnet mask.

Subnet Mask

The **subnet mask** is used by an IP host to answer a critical question in the communications process: Is the destination host local on my network or not? The process that answers this question occurs on any device running IP that is capable of generating, receiving, or forwarding IP packets (routers, servers, workstations, etc.). Keeping this question in mind, we now cover a few examples and identify the logical process that is used to generate an answer. Figure 7.2 depicts two clients on different networks.

1. Client A wishes to communicate with Client B and uses a name resolution process to discover the IP address of Client B.

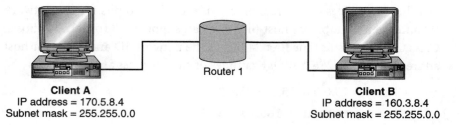

Figure 7.2
Clients on different networks

Client A
IP address = 170.5.8.4
Subnet mask = 255.255.0.0

Router 1

Client B
IP address = 160.3.8.4
Subnet mask = 255.255.0.0

2. Client A, using its local subnet mask, compares the first two octets in its address, to see if the values are the same as Client B. The first two octets are compared because the mask is set at 255.255.0.0 (a Class B address), indicating that the first 16 bits are the network ID.

3. Because the numbers in the first two octets are different (170.5.x.x vs. 160.3.x.x), Client A sends the frames to Router 1 for delivery to Client B.

The process of comparing the source address with the destination address is called **ANDing**. The IP host initiating the communications process (the source) ANDs its own address with its subnet mask and the result is the local network ID. The process is then repeated using the destination address. The *source* subnet mask is used in both calculations. The ANDing process for our example looks like this:

Source address   10101010.00000101.00001000.00000100 (170.5.8.4)

Source subnet mask   11111111.11111111.00000000.00000000
                     (255.255.0.0)

ANDed result   **10101010.00000101**.00000000.00000000 (local
                     network ID)

Destination address 10100000.00000011.00001000.00000100 (160.3.8.4)

Source subnet mask   11111111.11111111.00000000.00000000
                     (255.255.0.0)

ANDed result   **10100000.00000011**.00000000.00000000 (destina-
                     tion network ID)

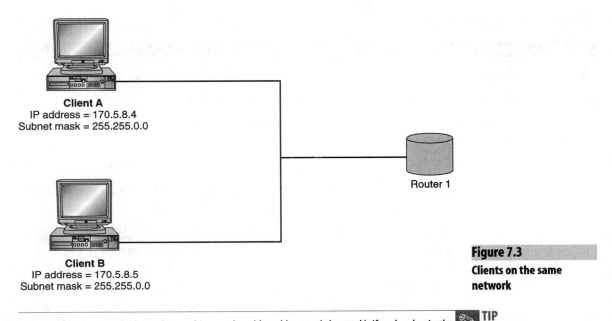

Client A
IP address = 170.5.8.4
Subnet mask = 255.255.0.0

Router 1

Client B
IP address = 170.5.8.5
Subnet mask = 255.255.0.0

Figure 7.3
Clients on the same network

TIP

ANDing is similar to multiplying the two binary values (the address and the mask). If each value in the address and subnet mask is 1, then the result is a 1; any other combination results in 0.

If the two ANDed results match, communication is local; if the results do not match, the clients are on different subnets. The two ANDed results in the preceding example do not match and therefore Client B is not on Client A's network. However, Figure 7.3 illustrates Client A and Client B on the same network with the ANDing results as follows:

Source address   10101010.00000101.00001000.00000100 (170.5.8.4)

Source subnet mask 11111111.11111111.00000000.00000000
(255.255.0.0)

ANDed result   **10101010.00000101**.00000000.00000000
(local network ID)

Source address   10101010.00000101.00001000.00000101 (170.5.8.5)

Source subnet mask 11111111.11111111.00000000.00000000
(255.255.0.0)

ANDed result   **10101010.00000101**.00000000.00000000
(destination network ID)

TABLE 7.8   Default Subnet Masks

Class	Default Mask (decimal)	Default Mask (binary)	Default Mask (bits)
A	255.0.0.0	11111111.00000000.00000000.00000000	8
B	255.255.0.0	11111111.11111111.00000000.00000000	16
C	255.255.255.0	11111111.11111111.11111111.00000000	24

In this case, the ANDed results are identical, and Client A can send its data packets directly to Client B without using the router.

In each of the examples, we used a subnet mask of 255.255.0.0, which makes it easy to determine when a host is or isn't on the same network. If the first two octets do not match, we know the host is on a different network segment and our packets go to the router. Stated another way, a subnet mask of 255.255.0.0 lets the host know that the first 16 bits of its address are the network ID. In our example, for a client to be on the same network, it must match the first 16 bits of its address with that of the destination host address.

Earlier in this section, we discussed classes of addresses and identified the numeric range of each block. The first three classes have default subnet masks assigned, as shown in Table 7.8.

Common practice annotates the subnet mask by using the number of bits rather than the decimal. So a Class B address of 160.10.0.0 /16 signifies the default mask of 16 bits, or 255.255.0.0.

Keep the following details in mind when using IP addresses:

- All clients using the same network ID must be in the same broadcast domain.
- Each client's IP address must be unique.
- A router (or a device that functions as a router) must be used when clients are addressed using different network IDs.
- Each client must have a subnet mask properly configured for consistent and correct communications to take place.

Up to this point, we have discussed the basics of IP addressing, the format of the address, and the function and format of the subnet mask. Recall that a Class A address can support 16,777,216 host IDs. An issue with Class A addresses is that no current Network layer protocol supports that many hosts in one broadcast domain. At some point on an Ethernet or Token Ring network, there would be so many hosts that broadcasts would completely saturate the available bandwidth. To better utilize Class A or Class B address spaces, we use a technique called subnetting.

7.3.4   Subnetting IPv4 Networks

Subnetting is the process of creating multiple, smaller address blocks from a single address block. Several reasons exist for subnetting, and some of the most common are:

- More efficient utilization of a large address space
- Creation of smaller networks for administrative efficiency (troubleshooting, management, documentation, etc.)
- Integration of geographically separated sites
- Reduction of broadcast domain size
- Creation of smaller network groups with similar traffic patterns

Each of these reasons by itself warrants creation of subnets. However, a combination of many of these reasons often drives network administrators to create smaller and more efficient networks out of one large block of IP addresses. As we begin our task of understanding subnetting, remember that the focus is on the subnet mask and its manipulation to create subnets.

We begin again by referencing the familiar and then transferring it to the unfamiliar. The next example uses an analogy between city streets and houses and an IP network. Subnetting is one of the more difficult networking concepts to understand, so take your time and read the information thoroughly. In our example, we assume that you live on a street named Maple, in the third house. We annotate your address as Maple.3 for the purposes of sending and receiving mail. (See Figure 7.4.)

You are responsible for mail delivery to everyone on your street. Therefore, you must determine whether each destination address is on your street. To qualify all outbound mail, you check the first five values of the destination address. If the five values equal Maple, the recipient lives on your street and you deliver the mail locally rather than forwarding it outside of your area. The common annotation for the street address is Maple /5.

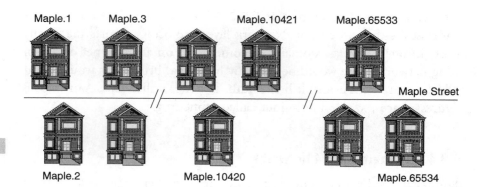

Maple.1 Maple.3 Maple.10421 Maple.65533

Maple Street

Maple.2 Maple.10420 Maple.65534

Figure 7.4

Houses and addresses on Maple

Currently, let's assume that over 65,000 people live on your street, and you are overwhelmed with unsolicited mail. In addition, workers providing essential city services such as fire control, ambulance, police, and garbage pickup have a difficult time finding specific houses and navigating their way through traffic. To solve the problem, the city decides to break up Maple into substreets by extending the street name. The city devises the following names:

Maple St   Maple Pl

Maple Wy Maple Av

Maple Ct   Maple Tr

Maple Cr   Maple Pk

Maple Bl   Maple Ln

Maple Rd   Maple Hy

After the substreets are created, your new address is Maple St.3, and you now have to check the first eight values of the street address to determine whether or not you deliver mail locally. Your street address is now annotated as Maple St /8, resulting in shorter streets, fewer houses per street, and smaller delivery areas for you and the city workers providing services. (See Figure 7.5.)

"Maple" is the equivalent of an IP network address. The process of creating the substreets is analogous to IP subnetting, which uses numeric addresses rather than street names. At this point, you should understand the need for subnets and have a general idea of the concept of subnetting. Next, let's venture into the actual mechanics of generating subnetted networks from one master network ID.

Creating subnets starts with the manipulation of the subnet mask. For our example, we will use the network address of 172.16.0.0. This is a Class B

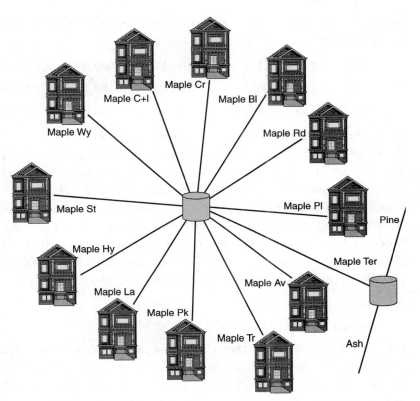

Figure 7.5
Substreets

address, capable of supporting 65,000+ hosts. Recall that the default subnet mask for a Class B address is 255.255.0.0, or 16 bits. Extending the subnet mask beyond 16 bits creates additional networks much like extending Maple from five to eight values created additional substreets. Let's look at two hosts using the default subnet mask configuration:

    Host A   172.16.1.1 /16
    Host B   172.16.129.1 /16

Because these two hosts are using the default mask, we only need to look at the first two octets to know that they share a common bit pattern for the left-most 16 bits as shown:

    Host A   172.16.1.1   **10101100.00010000.**00000001.00000001

    Host B   172.16.129.1   **10101100.00010000.**10000001.00000001

    Mask   255.255.0.0   11111111.11111111.00000000.00000000

Because the bolded bits are identical, these two hosts are on the same network and can communicate with each other locally, without the help of a router. Note how the pattern changes if we extend the network mask by a single bit, making it a 17-bit mask:

Host A   172.16.1.1   **10101100.00010000.0**0000001.00000001
Host B   172.16.129.1   **10101100.00010000.1**0000001.00000001
Mask   255.255.128.0   11111111.11111111.10000000.00000000

Notice that the third octet of the network mask now displays 128. This is the value of the bit that has been turned on in that octet. By extending the subnet mask by a single bit, we have successfully created two subnets from a single network address. Extending the mask (subnetting) borrows the bits from the host portion of the address and is also referred to as **stealing** bits. Remember the question that an IP host must answer: Is the destination host on my network or not? Using our new subnet mask, the first 17 bits of Host A no longer match the first 17 bits on Host B, and they are therefore on different networks. The address ranges for our two subnets are:

Subnet 1   172.16.1.0–172.16.127.255
Subnet 2   172.16.128.0–172.16.255.255

Each host on Subnet 1 has the same 17-bit pattern in the network portion of the address (left-most bits), and the same is true with each of the range of hosts in Subnet 2. Now that you have a little insight into the mechanics of how to extend the subnet mask, we can explore the question of how far to extend it.

Only two factors control how far to extend the subnet mask:

- The desired number of total available networks
- The desired number of total clients per network

Either of these factors can be used alone or together to set the constraints for the extension of the subnet mask. We illustrate each possibility in the next section.

Subnetting Using Desired Number of Networks

Assume that you are a network administrator for a large company and are currently configuring the IP addressing scheme. You have 16 campus locations and need to create 16 subnetted networks from the current network ID of 172.16.0.0 /16. The first step is to determine how far the subnet mask must be extended to create the proper number of subnets. Using our default mask of 16 bits, we get one network with a possible 65,000+ hosts. If we extend it by 1 bit to 17 bits, we have two possible subnet values in binary, 0 and 1.

172.16. |0|0 0 0 0 0 0 0. 0
172.16. |1|0 0 0 0 0 0 0. 0
255.255.   1 0 0 0 0 0 0 0. 0

In our example, we show the binary results for the third octet because the first and second octets remain constant. (Remember that the first two octets are Maple, and we are extending the name to make new streets.)

If we extend our mask by 2 bits to 18 bits, we have four possible subnet values: 00, 01, 10, and 11.

172.16. |0 0|0 0 0 0 0 0. 0
172.16. |0 1|0 0 0 0 0 0. 0
172.16 |1 0|0 0 0 0 0 0. 0
172.16 |1 1|0 0 0 0 0 0. 0
255.255.   1 1 0 0 0 0 0 0. 0

If we borrow 3 host bits to extend the mask by 3 bits, we have eight possible networks; 4 bits will give us 16 possible networks; and 5 bits will give us 32 possible networks. Hopefully you can see that the number of extra bits masked gives a resulting set of subnets that is a power of 2. The formula is 2^n, where n is the number of extended bits. Rather than trying to memorize powers of 2, use Table 7.9 as a shortcut.

! WARNING

An older formula for calculating the number of networks is $2^n - 2$. This formula was required for older equipment that treated the all 1s and all 0s network IDs as invalid. You should not use this formula unless legacy equipment is still in use.

TABLE 7.9   Calculating Networks

Bits masked	1	2	3	4	5	6	7	8
Networks created	2	4	8	16	32	64	128	256

Extending the subnet mask by 1 bit allows two networks to be created, and for each additional bit masked, you double the previous number of networks. Continuing the table, borrowing 9 host bits creates 512 networks, borrowing 10 host bits creates 1,024 networks, and so on. Using Table 7.8, you can rapidly discover how many additional bits need to be masked to generate the correct number of networks for a given configuration. In our example, we need to mask an additional 4 bits to produce 16 networks. Our network ID with its new subnet mask now looks like this:

172.16.0.0 /20 (the original 16-bit mask plus the 4 extended bits)

To calculate the decimal value for the mask, let's first look at the binary pattern:

11111111.11111111.11110000.00000000

You convert each of the octets by adding the values of each place as demonstrated earlier. An octet that is completely masked is equal to the sum of all of the place values, or 128 + 64 + 32 + 16 + 8 + 4 + 1 = 255. In our example, the third octet only has the first 4 bits turned on, so we must add the value of just those four places, 128 + 64 + 32 + 16 = 240. We now have a decimal equivalent of a 20-bit mask, or 255.255.240.0. By configuring a client with this mask, you are telling the internal network software to AND the first 20 bits of the configured IP address to find the local network ID. If the first 20 bits of the destination address match the local network ID, the host is on the local network and communications take place locally. If they do not match, the frames are sent to a router for proper delivery. Adding a row to our table allows us to determine the decimal mask for a given octet when extra bits are borrowed from the host and masked. (See Table 7.10.)

We can now use our table to determine how many extra bits to mask, how many networks can be created, and what the decimal value is for the partially masked octet.

The first step to subnetting is determining what subnet mask to use. We have determined that we need to mask an additional 4 bits to get 16 networks. The second step is determining our new network IDs so that we can

TABLE 7.10   Calculating Networks and Masks

Bits masked	1	2	3	4	5	6	7	8
Decimal mask	128	192	224	240	248	252	254	255
Networks created	2	4	8	16	32	64	128	256

properly configure IP subnetted addresses on network devices. We do this by evaluating the binary patterns produced with our new mask. Starting with our original network ID we have:

172.16. $\boxed{0\,0\,0\,0}$ 0 0 0 0. 0 0 0 0 0 0 0 0
255.255. $\boxed{1\,1\,1\,1}$ 0 0 0 0. 0 0 0 0 0 0 0 0

The bolded values represent the subnetted portion of our address. As long as the pattern in the boxed area remains constant, all clients are on the same subnet. The first address of each subnetwork is all 0s in binary, as we see in our current example. This address is often referred to as the **wire address**. It is an invalid host address and should never be configured on a network device as its local address. This address is often used by routers and other equipment when advertising network routes and availability. Addressing a host using the wire address would be the equivalent of saying that you live on Maple Street . . . the whole street.

WARNING

Many different software interfaces exist for entering network address information. Some interfaces allow you to enter the wire address without warning. You must pay close attention and remember not to use the wire address as a host address.

Our first wire address is 172.16.0.0 and our first valid host is 172.16.0.1, shown here in binary:

172.16. $\boxed{0\,0\,0}$ 0 0 0 0 0. 0 0 0 0 0 0 0 1
255.255. $\boxed{1\,1\,1}$ 1 0 0 0 0. 0 0 0 0 0 0 0 0

Remember that as long as the bolded values remain constant, all hosts are on the same network. This means that all possible 0 and 1 combinations would be on the first network, up to and including the following two:

172.16. $\boxed{0\,0\,0\,0}$ 1 1 1 1. 1 1 1 1 1 1 1 0 (last host)
172.16. $\boxed{0\,0\,0\,0}$ 1 1 1 1. 1 1 1 1 1 1 1 1 (broadcast address)
255.255. $\boxed{1\,1\,1\,1}$ 0 0 0 0. 0 0 0 0 0 0 0 0

Notice that the bolded pattern has not changed. The broadcast address, similar to the wire address, is an invalid host address. The broadcast address is defined by all host bits set to 1. In our last address example, the *right-most* 12 bits are all 1s in binary and therefore represent the broadcast address for the first subnet. This address is used by any host to reach all other hosts on a network (or subnetwork, in our case). Addressing a host with this address results in the host sending all packets with a broadcast source address. (If you haven't already guessed, that would be bad.) The address prior to the broadcast address is the last valid host address. We can now put the four elements of an address range together:

- **Wire address:** 172.16.0.0
- **First host address:** 172.16.0.1
- **Last host address:** 172.16.15.254
- **Broadcast address:** 172.16.15.255

Our second subnet looks like this:

172.16.	**0 0 0 1** 0 0 0 0. 0 0 0 0 0 0 0 0 (wire)	172.16.16.0
172.16.	**0 0 0 1** 0 0 0 0. 0 0 0 0 0 0 0 1 (first host)	172.16.16.1
172.16.	**0 0 0 1** 1 1 1 1. 1 1 1 1 1 1 1 0 (last host)	172.16.31.254
172.16.	**0 0 0 1** 1 1 1 1. 1 1 1 1 1 1 1 1 (broadcast address)	172.16.31.255
255.255.	1 1 1 1 0 0 0 0. 0 0 0 0 0 0 0 0	

The third subnet looks like this:

172.16.	**0 0 1 0** 0 0 0 0. 0 0 0 0 0 0 0 0 (wire)	172.16.32.0
172.16.	**0 0 1 0** 0 0 0 0. 0 0 0 0 0 0 0 1 (first host)	172.16.32.1
172.16.	**0 0 1 0** 1 1 1 1. 1 1 1 1 1 1 1 0 (last host)	172.16.47.254
172.16.	**0 0 1 0** 1 1 1 1. 1 1 1 1 1 1 1 1 (broadcast address)	172.16.47.255
255.255.	1 1 1 1 0 0 0 0. 0 0 0 0 0 0 0 0	

As a last example in binary, the fourth subnet looks like this:

172.16.	**0 0 1 1** 0 0 0 0. 0 0 0 0 0 0 0 0 (wire)	172.16.48.0
172.16.	**0 0 1 1** 0 0 0 0. 0 0 0 0 0 0 0 1 (first host)	172.16.48.1
172.16.	**0 0 1 1** 1 1 1 1. 1 1 1 1 1 1 1 0 (last host)	172.16.63.254
172.16.	**0 0 1 1** 1 1 1 1. 1 1 1 1 1 1 1 1 (broadcast address)	172.16.63.255
255.255.	1 1 1 1 0 0 0 0. 0 0 0 0 0 0 0 0	

If you look at each one of the wire addresses, you should see a pattern forming. The increment for the wire addresses is 16, allowing us to identify the rest of the subnets by adding 16 to the third octet. The final wire addresses are:

Subnet 5	172.16.64.0	Subnet 11	172.16.160.0
Subnet 6	172.16.80.0	Subnet 12	172.16.176.0
Subnet 7	172.16.96.0	Subnet 13	172.16.192.0
Subnet 8	172.16.112.0	Subnet 14	172.16.208.0
Subnet 9	172.16.128.0	Subnet 15	172.16.224.0
Subnet 10	172.16.144.0	Subnet 16	172.16.240.0

The first host, last host, and broadcast address can be found for any of the custom subnets using the pattern that we learned by looking at the binary. Assume we are going to deploy subnet 12 over the weekend and need to know what addresses are valid for that subnet. We know that the wire address for the twelfth subnet is 172.16.176.0 and the next subnet wire is 172.16.192.0. Using these two points, we can discover the first host, last host, and broadcast addresses for subnet 12, as follows:

172.16.176.0	Wire address
172.16.176.1	First host (found by adding 1 to the wire address)
172.16.191.254	Last host (found by subtracting 2 from the next subnet address)
172.16.191.255	Broadcast address (found by subtracting 1 from next subnet address)
172.16.192.0	Next subnet wire

This example illustrates how to create subnets based on a need for a certain number of networks. We accomplished this by doing the following:

- Identified the number of networks we needed (16).
- Used the formula 2^n, identified the number of bits required to create our subnets; 4 bits are required to create 16 different binary combinations.
- Extended our subnet mask by the correct number of bits ($16 + 4 = 20$).
- Showed how to convert a 20-bit mask into the decimal 255.255.240.0.

TABLE 7.11   Calculating Bits to Leave for Hosts

Bits left unmasked	1	2	3	4	5	6	7	8	9	10	11	12	13	14	15	16
Possible hosts ($2^n - 2$)	0	2	6	14	30	62	126	254	510	1,022	2,046	4,094	8,190	16,382	32,766	65,534

- Identified the new network addresses for all 16 networks.
- Illustrated the proper procedure for finding the wire, first host, last host, and broadcast address for any of the wires.

Subnetting by Desired Number of Hosts

Rather than subnetting based on networks needed, let's look at a an example based on the number of hosts per subnet. You are still the administrator for a large company that is changing its network address configuration. You are deploying advanced switching techniques, and will support up to 1,000 hosts per subnet. You would like to create a subnetted network that allows for up to 1,000 hosts per network. Your network ID is 172.16.0.0 /16.

The first step in this subnetting problem is determining how many host bits are required for at least 1,000 host IDs. We can use the same formula we used previously (2^n) with one exception; we need to subtract 2 from the final result because we cannot use the wire address or the broadcast address when assigning IP addresses to hosts. Table 7.11 shows how many bits are required to generate a given number of hosts.

Referring to Table 7.11, we see that 10 bits support 1,022 host IDs. This means we cannot mask the 10 right-most bits of the address. Using our network ID in binary, we can calculate how many bits are left available to extend our subnet mask and still support at least 1,000 hosts in each subnet:

```
172.16.   _ _ _ _ _ _ _ _ . _ _ _ _ _ _ _ _
255.255.  1 1 1 1 1 1 h h   h h h h h h h h
```

The *h*s in our illustration represent the bits that are left unmasked because they are needed for the host IDs. The remaining 6 bits can be masked to create new subnets. Using Table 7.12, we can determine the number of network subnets and the subnet mask.

Borrowing 6 bits gives us a new subnet mask of 22 (16 default bits for a Class B + 6 bits for our new networks = 22). The subnet mask for our

TABLE 7.12   Calculating Networks and Masks

Bits masked	1	2	3	4	5	6	7	8
Decimal mask	128	192	224	240	248	252	254	255
Networks created	2	4	8	16	32	64	128	256

clients is 255.255.252.0; 64 networks subnets can be created. However, we still need to determine the valid subnet ranges for our new networks. The first subnet looks like this in binary:

172.16.	0 0 0 0 0 0 0 0 . 0 0 0 0 0 0 0 0 (wire)	172.16.0.0
172.16.	0 0 0 0 0 0 0 0 . 0 0 0 0 0 0 0 1 (first host)	172.16.0.1
172.16.	0 0 0 0 0 0 1 1 . 1 1 1 1 1 1 1 0 (last host)	172.16.3.254
172.16.	0 0 0 0 0 0 1 1 . 1 1 1 1 1 1 1 1 (broadcast address)	172.16.3.255
255.255.	1 1 1 1 1 1 0 0 . 0 0 0 0 0 0 0 0	

The second subnet looks like this:

172.16.	0 0 0 0 0 1 0 0 . 0 0 0 0 0 0 0 0 (wire)	172.16.4.0
172.16.	0 0 0 0 0 1 0 0 . 0 0 0 0 0 0 0 1 (first host)	172.16.4.1
172.16.	0 0 0 0 0 1 1 1 . 1 1 1 1 1 1 1 0 (last host)	172.16.7.254
172.16.	0 0 0 0 0 1 1 1 . 1 1 1 1 1 1 1 1 (broadcast address)	172.16.7.255
255.255.	1 1 1 1 1 1 0 0 . 0 0 0 0 0 0 0 0	

The third subnet looks like this and we begin to see a pattern once again:

172.16.	0 0 0 1 0 0 0 0 . 0 0 0 0 0 0 0 0 (wire)	172.16.8.0
172.16.	0 0 0 1 0 0 0 0 . 0 0 0 0 0 0 0 1 (first host)	172.16.8.1
172.16.	0 0 0 1 0 0 1 1 . 1 1 1 1 1 1 1 0 (last host)	172.16.11.254
172.16.	0 0 0 1 0 0 1 1 . 1 1 1 1 1 1 1 1 (broadcast address)	172.16.11.255
255.255.	1 1 1 1 1 1 0 0 . 0 0 0 0 0 0 0 0	

As you can see, the wire addresses are incrementing by 4, which provides us a clue to our last shortcut in subnetting. The value of the last bit masked is the increment of the wire addresses. Figure 7.6 shows the third octet in our subnet mask and the place values.

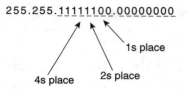

Figure 7.6

Lowest-bit masked pattern

The value of the lowest-bit masked sets the interval for the subnet wire addresses.

TABLE 7.13   The Subnet Calculator

Bits masked	1	2	3	4	5	6	7	8
Subnet interval	128	64	32	16	8	4	2	1
Decimal mask	128	192	224	240	248	252	254	255
Networks created	2	4	8	16	32	64	128	256

Understanding the impact of the lowest masked bit and its value allows us to complete what we call the subnet calculator. (See Table 7.13.)

We can now take any network address, plug it into the subnet calculator, and find information necessary to properly deploy subnets. Let's look at one final example by finding the answers using the subnet calculator.

You need to subnet 172.16.0.0 /16 into 28 smaller networks. Your team will deploy the first three subnets this weekend. You need to tell them what network mask to use and what the first three subnet address ranges are. You want to create only enough subnets to cover the current requirement (do not add for growth):

1. Using the last row of the calculator (labeled "Networks created"), move to the right until you reach a number that is 28 or greater. The number 28 is not in the table, so you stop in the column that contains the value of 32. This column will give us the remainder of the necessary information.

2. Determine the subnet mask. Creating 32 networks requires that you mask 5 extra bits in the third octet. Moving up the column (from 32), we discover that our decimal mask is now 255.255.248.0, or /21 (16 for a Class B, plus 5 extra bits for subnetting).

3. The column also provides us with a subnet interval of 8, allowing us to plot out the wire addresses for our new subnets as follows:

Subnet 1	172.16.0.0	Subnet 9	172.16.64.0
Subnet 2	172.16.8.0	Subnet 10	172.16.72.0
Subnet 3	172.16.16.0	Subnet 11	172.16.80.0
Subnet 4	172.16.24.0	Subnet 12	172.16.88.0
Subnet 5	172.16.32.0	Subnet 13	172.16.96.0
Subnet 6	172.16.40.0	Subnet 14	172.16.104.0
Subnet 7	172.16.48.0	Subnet 15	172.16.112.0
Subnet 8	172.16.56.0	Subnet 16	172.16.120.0

⋮

(interim subnets omitted for sake of brevity)

⋮

Subnet 31	172.16.240.0	Subnet 32	172.16.248.0

The correct IP address ranges for the first three subnets are as follows:

Subnet 1

172.16.0.0	Wire
172.16.0.1	First host
172.16.7.254	Last host (next wire address minus 2)
172.16.7.255	Broadcast (next wire address minus 1)

Subnet 2

172.16.8.0	Wire
172.16.8.1	First host
172.16.15.254	Last host (next wire address minus 2)
172.16.15.255	Broadcast (next wire address minus 1)

Subnet 3

172.16.16.0	Wire
172.16.16.1	First host
172.16.23.254	Last host (next wire address minus 2)
172.16.23.255	Broadcast (next wire address minus 1)

As you can see, the "subnet calculator" in Table 7.13 can come in handy when trying to determine the proper subnet mask for a given subnetting situation.

You can use software-based subnet calculators (a few are listed in Appendix A), but you may not always have access to them when you need them.

We have covered subnetting in considerable detail, so let's review the important points. Use the following list to help you review all of the concepts and procedures:

- IP addresses consist of two parts, network ID and host (node) ID.
- The subnet mask identifies the network portion of the address and the host portion of the address.
- An IP address and subnet mask are both 32 bits long.
- The three valid host address classes are A, B, and C.
- The value of the first octet identifies the class of the address.
- Each class has a default mask.
- When subnetting an IP address block, you must identify either the total number of networks needed, or the total number of hosts per network, or a combination of both.
- Use the formula 2^n when subnetting by the number of networks, where n is the number of bits used to extend the network mask.
- Use the formula $2^n - 2$ when subnetting by the number of hosts, where n represents the number of host bits that must remain unmasked.
- The all 0s and all 1s host (in binary) are invalid host addresses and represent the wire and the broadcast addresses, respectively.
- The value of the lowest bit used in the mask equals the interval between the wire addresses of the subnetted networks.
- To find the first valid host on a network, add 1 to the wire.
- To find the last valid host on a network, subtract 2 from the next wire.
- To find the broadcast address on a network, subtract 1 from the next wire.

The examples used and discussed in this section are often referred to as standard subnetting. After a network subnet mask is identified, it is used when configuring all network devices throughout the entire subnetted network. A newer method of subnetting, called variable-length subnet masking, is being rapidly deployed on networks of all sizes.

7.3.5   Variable-Length Subnet Masking (VLSM)

Variable-length subnet masking (VLSM) can best be described as subnetting a subnet. You use the same basic process described in the previous subnetting section and then continue to extend the network mask as needed to more precisely control the allocation of addresses. The name itself (variable-length subnet mask) implies much of its function. The subnet mask can vary in length throughout the network. Today's organizations and their complex networks require different numbers of hosts and different size subnets to maximize the use of valuable IP addresses. Creating variable-length subnet masks and deploying different size subnets for a given network ID is called variable-length subnetting. In this section, we cover VLSM in modest detail. The example we use is not meant to be extensive; rather, it introduces the methods and merits of using VLSM. For a thorough understanding of VLSM, consult one or more of the many books and Web sites devoted to this topic.

A few of the benefits of using VLSM include:

- Highly efficient use of address space
- Hierarchical addressing capability
- Reduction of the size of routing tables

Our example involves an enterprise network with five campuses, one of which has seven buildings. The network ID that we use is 10.0.0.0 /8 (Class A). We begin by subnetting our assigned network ID for at least five campuses. Recall that in order to obtain at least five networks, we have to mask an additional 3 bits ($2^3 = 8$). Our subnets increment by 32 and use a subnet mask of 255.224.0.0, or 11 bits. (Refer back to Table 7.13, as needed.) The subnet network addresses are:

Subnet 1	10.0.0.0 /11	Subnet 5	10.128.0.0
Subnet 2	10.32.0.0	Subnet 6	10.160.0.0
Subnet 3	10.64.0.0	Subnet 7	10.192.0.0
Subnet 4	10.96.0.0	Subnet 8	10.224.0.0

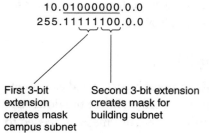

```
10.01000000.0.0
255.11111100.0.0
```

First 3-bit extension creates mask campus subnet

Second 3-bit extension creates mask for building subnet

Figure 7.7

Binary pattern of subnet mask

The next step in using VLSM is to subnet one of these address ranges again for use on our campus that has seven buildings. We'll use Subnet 3 (10.64.0.0 /11) to apply VLSM.

NOTE Your new network address starts with an 11-bit subnet mask and will be extended from that point. Be careful not to start over with an 8-bit mask.

We need seven additional subnet networks (one for each building). We already know that extending our mask by 3 bits provides eight networks, so we extend our mask an *additional* 3 bits. Our network ID is 10.64.0.0 and our mask is now 14 bits, or 255.252.0.0. See Figure 7.7 for the binary view of the address and mask.

To determine our subnet ranges, we look at the current total number of masked bits, which is six (three for the campus and three for the buildings). Six borrowed bits gives us a subnet interval of 4. We can now find our subnet IP addresses by starting at 10.64.0.0 and adding 4 to the second octet, as follows:

Subnet 1	10.64.0.0 /14	Subnet 5	10.80.0.0
Subnet 2	10.68.0.0	Subnet 6	10.84.0.0
Subnet 3	10.72.0.0	Subnet 7	10.88.0.0
Subnet 4	10.76.0.0	Subnet 8	10.92.0.0

If one of the buildings has 10 floors, we could use VLSM again and assign address blocks to each floor. See Figure 7.8 for an illustration of our example.

TIP One of the benefits of VLSM that impacts large network environments is the hierarchical addressing structure. The hierarchy reduces the size of routing tables for efficient and improved network traffic flow. For resources that provide additional information on VLSM, see Appendix A, "Online Networking Resources."

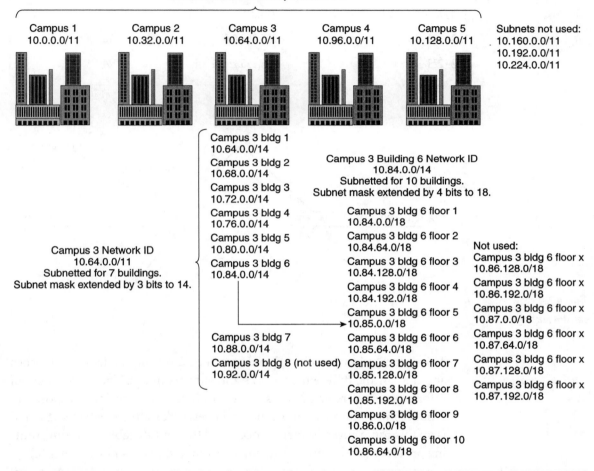

Figure 7.8
VLSM campus example

If you plan on using VLSM or subnetting, you will need to deploy **classless inter-domain routing (CIDR)** to make it work correctly.

7.3.6 Classless Inter-Domain Routing (CIDR) for IPv4

Routing is the process of forwarding frames from one interface to another based on a Layer 3 network address. To direct network packets efficiently, routers use protocols to exchange network information with other routers.

TABLE 7.14   Address Classes

Address Class	Numeric Range of First Octet	Default Mask (Decimal)	Default Mask (Bits)
A	1–127	255.0.0.0	8
B	128–191	255.255.0.0	16
C	192–223	255.255.255.0	24

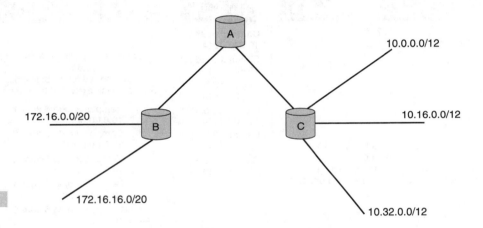

Figure 7.9

Classful routing

This information is collected and stored in a routing table. Routers learn about all of the different networks and subnets in use. These exchanges of information are referred to as *route advertisements* and are composed of sending information about subnets and network status. The focus of CIDR is on this route advertisement process and the routing table. (Routing, routing protocols, and routing functions are covered in detail in Chapter 8.)

One of the easiest ways to explain CIDR is to first look at what it is not. Think back to our discussion on IP address classes and recall that there are three classes used when assigning addresses to networked hosts. Each class is identified by looking at the numeric value of the first octet, and each has a default mask associated with it. Use Table 7.14 as a quick review.

If our routers and other key network devices are *classful*, they function by looking at the first octet and identifying the class of the address. After determining the class, the router or network device applies the default subnet mask. This process is called **classful routing**. Looking at Figure 7.9,

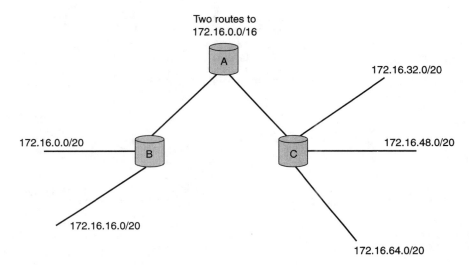

Two routes to
172.16.0.0/16

172.16.32.0/20

172.16.0.0/20

172.16.48.0/20

172.16.16.0/20

172.16.64.0/20

Figure 7.10
Classful routing failure

Router B would advertise its addresses to Router A as 172.16.0.0 /16 even though it is subnetted to a 20-bit mask.

Router C would advertise 10.0.0.0 /8 to Router A even though it is also subnetted. The advertisements and the routing procedure are referred to as classful because the mask is set to the default for the address class in use, not the configured subnet mask. Router A would route all destination traffic with a 172.160.x.x address to Router B and all traffic with a destination of 10.x.x.x to Router C. Using classful routing works well for smaller companies containing a few subnets. For larger companies with complex networks, another method must be used to avoid confusing the routers. (See Figure 7.10.)

In the situation depicted in Figure 7.10, if classful routing is used, both Router B and Router C would advertise their routes to 172.16.0.0 /16. Router A would believe that it has two routes to the same network and would load balance the traffic, sending half of the 172.16.x.x network traffic to Router B and half to Router C. Classful routing, in this situation, would result in some of the traffic bound for different subnetworks of 172.16.x.x being routed in the wrong direction. To solve this particular problem, you need to deploy CIDR at least on Router B and Router C. However, to avoid most problems, you should deploy CIDR on all routing equipment.

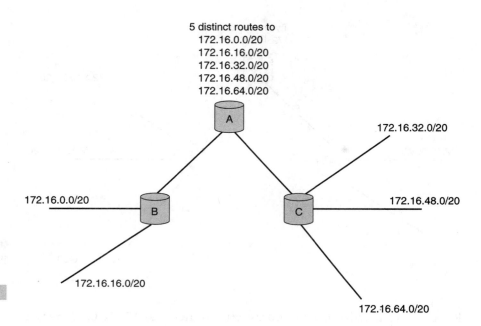

Figure 7.11
Classless routing

The word *classless* in CIDR refers to the fact that the routing equipment ignores the class of the network addresses and instead advertises the subnetted network ID in addition to the configured subnet mask, as shown in Figure 7.11.

The only requirement for using CIDR is to use equipment that can advertise and understand route advertisements that include both the network ID and the actual subnet mask in use. The important benefit of CIDR is that it allows the use of VLSM, which in turn allows us to more efficiently use our IP address blocks. Over the last 10 years, all available Class A, B, and C IP addresses have been taken (i.e., all class addresses have been assigned) and many companies are reconfiguring their networks to include CIDR and VLSM to extend the assigned address space. Another way to extend the address space is to use private addressing.

7.3.7   Private IP Networks

As the Internet has grown, available IP address blocks have diminished, making it more difficult to connect new systems to the World Wide Web. The Internet Engineering Task Force (IETF) realized that many companies might want to deploy TCP/IP without all their hosts (users) connected to the Internet. The IETF identified three address blocks that could be used privately, allowing any company the ability to create an autonomous, private IP network. These private addresses are not routed across the backbone of the Internet. The private IP address blocks are:

> 10.0.0.0–10.255.255.255 (or 10.0.0.0 /8)
>
> 172.16.0.0–172.31.255.255 (or 172.16.0.0 /20)
>
> 192.168.0.0–192.168.255.255 (or 192.168.0.0 /16)

Any company wishing to deploy TCP/IP clients is allowed to use the private address blocks. These addresses offer some additional security because they are not actively routed across the Internet—it's more difficult for hackers to gain access to a network using addresses from the private address blocks. Companies using **private IP addressing** must use an Internet gateway, such as a router or proxy server running network address translation (NAT), if they wish to have access to Internet resources. (NAT is covered in detail in Chapter 8.)

! WARNING

Because of the large private address space available, many network engineers and designers deploy private addressing using the *dartboard method* (that is, having no plan). The adage that poor planning leads to poor performance rings true in this case. We have consulted with clients that have run into numerous problems—large routing tables, routing table corruption, and troubleshooting problems—all because they handed out addresses without thought. Ensure that you have a plan any time you deploy TCP/IP addressing, whether private or public.

Earlier in the chapter we showed that IPv4 supports more than 4.2 billion hosts. Although that may appear adequate, we are close to depleting the current version of TCP/IP addresses completely. The newer routing protocols and addressing techniques such as CIDR and VLSM have bought us the time needed to create a replacement. That replacement is being deployed, as of the writing of this book, and it is IPv6.

7.3.8   IP Version 6 (IPv6)

IP version 6 (IPv6) or IPng (next generation) is designed to overcome some of the current limitations of IPv4 and also provide enhanced functionality for newer technologies. Some of these features include:

- Larger address space
- Header format simplification
- Improved support for options
- Native quality of services capabilities
- Built-in authentication and encryption capabilities

The address length of IPv6 is 128 bits, making the address space by today's standards almost infinite. Of course, that line of thinking got us into trouble with the address space of IPv4. But consider this: There are enough IPv6 addresses (2^{128}) to allow for 60,738,208,471,920,500,000,000 addresses per square foot on the Earth's surface. (The surface of the earth is roughly calculated at 5,602,443,264,000,000 square feet.) That's a lot of addresses!

As IPv6 becomes better understood and as more network device and software manufacturers support its use, you will see IPv6 coexist with IPv4, allowing for a smooth, gradual transition. During the transition period, IPv4 frames will be encapsulated inside IPv6 to maintain backward compatibility. Eventually, IPv6 will replace the older protocol. More detailed discussion of IPv6 would fill an entire book. It is mentioned here to encourage you to discover more about this emerging evolution of TCP/IP addressing.

7.4   Chapter Summary

- It is important to devise a standardized naming methodology for naming network devices. Device names should include location, function, and a unique ID.

- Security may be weakened by using a naming scheme, but is generally considered an acceptable trade-off for the benefits of standardized naming.

- IP addresses are 32 bits long and split into three main classes for host IP addressing: Class A, Class B, and Class C. The value of the first octet in an IP address identifies the class of the address. In addition, each class has a default mask.

- IP addresses consist of two parts, network ID and host (node) ID. The subnet mask identifies the network portion of the address and the host portion.

- The desired number of networks and/or the desired number of hosts affects how a network is subnetted. Extending the subnet mask (stealing or borrowing host bits) allows the creation of multiple subnetted networks from a single network address.

- Use the formula 2^n when subnetting by the number of networks, where n is the number of bits used to extend the network mask. Use the formula $2^n - 2$ when subnetting by the number of hosts, where n is the number of host bits that must remain unmasked.

- The all 0s and all 1s hosts (in binary) are invalid host addresses, and represent the wire and the broadcast address, respectively.

- The value of the lowest bit used in the mask equals the interval between the wire addresses of the subnetted networks.

- VLSM allows the use of different length subnet masks throughout a given network enterprise. CIDR is required for complex networks involving custom subnets separated by multiple routers or when using VLSM.

- IPv6 is the replacement for IPv4 and has an address that is 128 bits long.

7.5 Key Terms

ANDing: The process of adding the subnet mask to an IP address to determine the network ID.

borrowing: The process of extending the subnet mask into the host portion of a network address.

broadcast address: The last available address for a given network address range. This address can be identified when all host bits are set to 1.

classful routing: The process of routing using the default mask based on the class of the address rather than the actual network mask.

classless inter-domain routing (CIDR): A function of network devices where routing takes place using the full network ID and not the classful address boundary.

host: Any system configured with a TCP/IP address. This can include routers, switches, hubs, personal computers, mainframes, Unix systems, or any network-enabled device.

IP version 4 (IPv4): An abbreviation for Internet Protocol version 4. A widely deployed suite of protocols used in network communications. IPv4 is the most commonly deployed network communications protocol in the world today.

IP version 6 (IPv6): An abbreviation for Internet Protocol version 6. The newest version of the TCP/IP protocol that uses expanded features and addressing to overcome the limitations of version 4.

network ID: The number of bits (determined by the subnet mask) of an IP address that identify a client's network address.

private IP addresses: A set of three ranges of IP addresses defined by RFC 1918 that allows companies to use TCP/IP addressing and configuration without having valid public addresses. The ranges are defined as 10.0.0.0 /8, 172.16.0.0 /20, and 192.168.0.0 /16.

routing: The process of forwarding frames from one interface to another based on a Layer 3 network address.

stealing: The process of extending the subnet mask into the host portion of a network address.

subnet mask: A numeric value configured in networking software that gives an IP client the ability to determine the network ID.

subnetting: The process of extending the subnet mask to create multiple networks from one master network ID.

variable-length subnet masking (VLSM): The process of creating multiple subnetworks with using subnet masks that differ in length.

wire address: The first available address of a given network address range. The address is identified when all host bits are set to 0.

7.6   Challenge Questions

7.1   Which of the following characteristics should be included when assigning names to network devices? (Choose all that apply.)

a. Location

b. Serial number

c. Operating system

d. Function

e. Manufacturer ID

f. Unique ID

7.2   Which of the following is considered the biggest drawback to using a name code system?

a. Harder to understand the function and location of network devices

b. Easier to understand the function and location of network devices

c. May weaken security

d. Difficult for administrators to name network equipment

e. Easier for administrators to name network equipment

7.3   Which of the following is a valid Class C address?

a. 191.10.16.8

b. 224.15.6.5

c. 198.4.15.6

d. 160.10.8.1

7.4   What methods can be used to determine the class of an IP address? (Choose two.)

a. Evaluate the binary pattern of the first octet.

b. Evaluate the decimal value of the last octet.

c. Evaluate the hexadecimal value of the first octet.

d. Evaluate the hexadecimal value of the last octet.

e. Evaluate the binary pattern of the last octet.

f. Evaluate the decimal value of the first octet.

7.5   What is the purpose of the subnet mask?

a. Allows a host to send frames to the router

b. Used by routers to identify the network portion from the host portion of an IP address to enable proper routing of packets

c. Used by administrators to customize IP address blocks

d. Used exclusively by routers to determine whether a frame must be forwarded or blocked

7.6 Which of the following is not a Class B address?

    a. 191.18.4.10

    b. 170.6.33.4

    c. 120.16.8.5

    d. 144.15.8.254

    e. 128.109.113.220

7.7 If your host address is 160.10.22.1/20, which of the following is the wire address for your subnet?

    a. 160.10.0.0

    b. 160.10.4.0

    c. 160.10.8.0

    d. 160.10.16.0

    e. 160.10.24.0

7.8 Given the network ID and mask of 172.16.0.0 /21, which of the following is a valid range of subnet addresses?

    a. 172.16.0.0–172.16.15.255

    b. 172.16.0.0–172.16.16.255

    c. 172.16.4.0–172.16.7.255

    d. 172.16.32.0–172.16.64.255

    e. 172.16.24.0–172.16.31. 255

7.9 When reading an address annotated as 15.46.10.5 /21, what does the 21 represent?

    a. The number of subnetworks currently in use

    b. The number of bits used in the network ID

    c. The number of bits used in the host ID

    d. The number of hosts per network available

7.10 Which of the following two factors control how many bits are used when extending the subnet mask? (Choose two.)

    a. The number of network hosts needed per network

b. The number of technologies in use

c. The type of technologies in use

d. The number of networks needed

e. The total number of computer devices

7.11 Which of the following subnet masks would create at least 70 networks using the fewest number of masked bits with a network address of 190.15.0.0?

a. 255.255.224.0

b. 255.255.240.0

c. 255.255.248.0

d. 255.255.252.0

e. 255.255.254.0

7.12 What subnet interval is produced by a subnet mask of /19?

a. 4

b. 8

c. 16

d. 32

e. 64

7.13 Using a network ID of 160.10.0.0 /22, how many hosts are on each subnetted network?

a. 1,022

b. 510

c. 2,046

d. 1,024

e. 512

7.14 Using a network ID of 138.10.16.0 /22, what is the broadcast address for this subnet?

a. 138.10.23.255

b. 138.10.19.255

    c. 138.10.31.255

    d. 138.10.17.255

7.15 Which of the following are valid reasons to subnet? (Choose all that apply.)

    a. Easier software configuration

    b. Creation of smaller broadcast domains

    c. Better utilization of a large address space

    d. Creation of smaller networks for administrative efficiency (troubleshooting, management, documentation, etc.)

    e. Integration of geographically separated locations

7.16 What is the significance of the lowest bit masked?

    a. It creates the broadcast address.

    b. Its value is used to identify the subnet interval.

    c. Its value is used to identify the host range.

    d. Its value is used to identify the total number of hosts.

7.17 In large, complex networks using subnetted addresses, why is classless routing preferred over classful?

    a. Classless routing uses a default number of network bits, disregarding the class of the address in use.

    b. Classless routing uses a 24-bit network ID, disregarding the class of the address in use.

    c. Classless routing utilizes a default addressing hierarchy, disregarding the class of the address in use.

    d. Classless routing uses the first network ID along with the count of the total number of subnets, disregarding the class of the address in use.

7.18 You subnetted your large, complex network and are using 160.10.0.0 /22. To ensure that frames routers properly deliver, what type of routing should you use?

    a. VLSM

    b. CIDR

c. Classful

d. Source-based

7.19 Which addresses listed are part of the private IP addresses defined by RFC 1918? (Choose all that apply.)

a. 192.168.10.8

b. 10.25.8.4

c. 172.10.4.4

d. 223.14.200.6

7.20 What new features are incorporated into IPv6? (Choose two.)

a. Subnetting

b. Authentication

c. Encryption

d. Elimination of unicast packets

e. Elimination of multicast packets

7.21 How long in bits is an IPv6 address?

a. 32

b. 64

c. 128

d. 256

7.22 What statement best describes VLSM?

a. A routing technique that incorporates the network ID and mask with each route advertisement

b. The creation of a single subnet mask for the entire network

c. The creation of different subnet masks for subnetting different areas of the network

d. A subnetting technique that produces a different mask for each host on a network, useful in maximizing the entire address space

7.23 Given the address of 160.10.64.0 /20, what subnet mask creates an additional four subnets from this network ID?

a. 255.255.255.0

   b. 255.255.254.0

   c. 255.255.252.0

   d. 255.255.248.0

   e. 255.255.240.0

7.24 What is the decimal mask that matches a /26 bit annotation?

   a. 255.255.128.0

   b. 255.255.192.0

   c. 255.255.224.0

   d. 255.255.255.128

   e. 255.255.255.192

   f. 255.255.255.224

7.25 Given the IP address of 191.60.16.0 /24, what is the class of this address?

   a. A

   b. B

   c. C

   d. D

   e. E

7.7   Challenge Exercises

Challenge Exercise 7.1

In this exercise, you review the IP address configuration of your computer system. You need a computer running Windows 2000 Professional or Windows XP Professional with the TCP/IP protocol installed.

7.1 Log on to your computer.

7.2 On the desktop, right-click **My Network Places** and select **Properties**. The Network and Dial-Up Connections dialog box opens. (In Windows XP, the Network Connection dialog box opens.)

7.3 Right-click the **Local Area Connection** icon and select **Properties**. The Local Area Connection Properties dialog box opens.

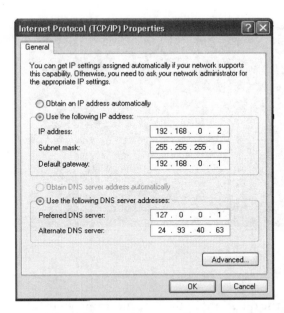

Figure 7.12

Internet Protocol (TCP/IP) Properties dialog box in Windows XP showing IP address, subnet mask, and default gateway settings

7.4 Select the **Internet Protocol (TCP/IP)** entry and click **Properties**. The Internet Protocol (TCP/IP) Properties dialog box opens, as shown in Figure 7.12.

  a. What is your current IP address?

  b. What is your current subnet mask?

  c. What is your default gateway?

  If your system is configured as a DHCP client, you won't see your IP address, subnet mask, or default gateway settings. To view your TCP/IP configuration settings, perform steps 7.5 through 7.7.

7.5 Click **Start** and then click **Run**.

7.6 Type **cmd** in the Open text box and click **OK**. A command prompt window opens.

7.7 On the command line, type **ipconfig /all** and press **Enter**. The resulting settings are displayed, as shown in Figure 7.13.

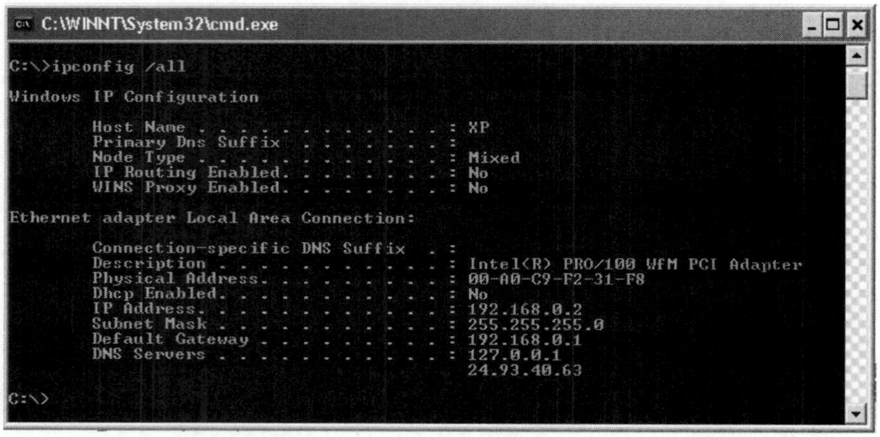

```
C:\WINNT\System32\cmd.exe                                              _□×

C:\>ipconfig /all

Windows IP Configuration

        Host Name . . . . . . . . . . . . : XP
        Primary Dns Suffix  . . . . . . . :
        Node Type . . . . . . . . . . . . : Mixed
        IP Routing Enabled. . . . . . . . : No
        WINS Proxy Enabled. . . . . . . . : No

Ethernet adapter Local Area Connection:

        Connection-specific DNS Suffix  . :
        Description . . . . . . . . . . . : Intel(R) PRO/100 VM PCI Adapter
        Physical Address. . . . . . . . . : 00-A0-C9-F2-31-F8
        Dhcp Enabled. . . . . . . . . . . : No
        IP Address. . . . . . . . . . . . : 192.168.0.2
        Subnet Mask . . . . . . . . . . . : 255.255.255.0
        Default Gateway . . . . . . . . . : 192.168.0.1
        DNS Servers . . . . . . . . . . . : 127.0.0.1
                                            24.93.40.63

C:\>
```

Figure 7.13

IPconfig settings displayed in Windows XP

You can now answer the questions in Step 4 concerning your TCP/IP address configuration.

Challenge Exercise 7.2

In this exercise, you research variable-length subnet masking (VLSM) on the Internet. You need a computer with a Web browser and Internet access.

7.1 In your Web browser, enter the following addresses:

http://cio.cisco.com/warp/public/701/3.html

http://swexpert.com/C4/SE.C4.NOV.98.pdf

7.2 Read the explanation of VLSM.

7.3 Repeat steps 1 and 2 for the following addresses:

http://www.tcpipguide.com/free/t_IPVariableLengthSubnetMask-ingVLSM.htm

http://www.wildpackets.com/compendium/IP/IP-VLSM.html

7.4 Write a two- to three-paragraph summary outlining the key benefits and methods used in VLSM.

Challenge Exercise 7.3

In this exercise, you research information on IPv6 on the Internet. You need a computer with a Web browser and Internet access.

7.1   In your Web browser, enter the following address:
http://playground.sun.com/pub/ipng/html/INET-IPng-Paper.html

7.2   Read the explanation of IPng, which is also called IPv6.

7.3   Repeat steps 1 and 2 for the following addresses:

http://www.microsoft.com/windowsserver2003/technologies/ipv6/default.mspx

http://www.6bone.net/

7.4   Write a two- to three-paragraph summary outlining the key benefits of IPv6 and additions made since IPv4.

7.8   Challenge Scenarios

Challenge Scenario 7.1

You are a network administrator for an international import/export company. You have offices worldwide and are reconfiguring your company's network. You have been asked to devise a naming scheme that incorporates location, function, and a unique ID for all of your computer network systems. Your locations are as follows:

Rio de Janeiro, Brazil	Paris, France
Sao Paulo, Brazil	Rome, Italy
Miami, United States	Berlin, Germany
Seattle, United States	Tokyo, Japan
Houston, United States	Moscow, Russia
Christchurch, New Zealand	Bangladesh, India
Perth, Australia	Pretoria, South Africa
London, England	Barcelona, Spain

Create a standard naming scheme and include the required elements.

Challenge Scenario 7.2

You are a network consultant/designer and are currently designing the subnet configuration for one of your clients. You need to subnet a network ID of 159.120.0.0 into 63 subnets. What subnet mask do you use? What is the wire, first host, last host, and broadcast addresses of the third, fourth, and fifth subnets?

Challenge Scenario 7.3

You are a network administrator who supports a large campus network environment. You have four buildings that host 7,000 clients, four buildings with 1,100 clients, and 14 smaller buildings containing 500 computers. How do you subnet your Class B network address of 150.18.0.0 while conserving the maximum number of host bits in the process?

CHAPTER 8

Routing

After reading this chapter you will be able to:

- Discuss routing tables
- Discuss the routing process
- Describe address resolution methods
- Describe routing protocols and their behavior
- Understand the administrative classification of routing protocols
- Understand and deploy hierarchical routing including summarization

The basic concept of routing and the reasons for implementing routing on your network have been previously discussed in this book. This chapter builds on these concepts and reasons in addition to taking a more in-depth look at the mechanics of routing, routing protocols, routing tables, and addressing. New subjects such as address resolution and route summarization are also discussed so that you may better understand routing and the routing process.

8.1   Routing Basics

When networking was first introduced only a small number of devices were interconnected, so behaviors such as broadcasts and collisions were of little concern to network designers and engineers. As networks grew, however, broadcasts and collisions caused significant problems. To overcome these problems, segmentation at OSI Layer 2 was introduced, reducing collisions and allowing greater access to network bandwidth. As networks continued to grow, broadcasts became the primary problem. The solution to greatly reducing broadcasts is to segment networks using Layer 3 devices, protocols, and addresses. Although broadcasts continue to be one of the main reasons to segment a network at Layer 3, others reasons include:

- Creation of small troubleshooting areas
- Creation of small administrator management areas
- Interconnection of remote offices using WAN technologies
- Grouping clients together with similar network resources

After your network is segmented, a router is required to properly forward data between all clients on different network segments. A router is a device that forwards data based on a logical Layer 3 address. (For more information on routers, see Chapter 2.) The type of address in use depends on the protocol used by the clients and servers. Many routers support the use of different protocols and addresses, such as Novell's IPX/SPX, AppleTalk, Pathworks, Banyan, and TCP/IP. Because of its popularity, our examples for this chapter will use TCP/IP.

The routing process usually occurs between physical network interfaces but can also happen between logical network interfaces. A router can be any network device with the proper software to make routing decisions and two or more network interfaces (logical or physical) used for forwarding packets between networks.

NOTE

When a single physical network interface has more than one address assigned, it said to have a logical rather than physical interface. The addresses can be from different subnets, allowing administrators to test configurations. This configuration is called *logical routing* or *logical subnetting*.

WARNING

It is possible to use a server or even a client workstation as a router. You may see this done in a test or lab environment. Using an actual device dedicated to routing in a production environment is strongly recommended, as dedicated devices are more stable and easier to troubleshoot when things go wrong. Unless otherwise noted, all discussions in this chapter deal with dedicated hardware routers.

8.1.1   The Routing Table

Now that the we have identified what routing is and the major types of routers (hardware and software), we need to examine the routing process and its requirements. Two key pieces of information required for any device to route packets are (1) a route to one or more networks and (2) a destination Layer 3 address. The routes to a given network are stored in the memory of the router and are referred to as a **routing table**. To better understand the function and structure of a routing table, see Figure 8.1.

In our example environment, we have a single router with four network interfaces interconnecting four networks. On Router A an entry for each network and its corresponding network interface is kept in memory; this is the routing table. The table allows the router to properly forward frames out of the correct interface once the frame is received and the destination address has been processed. A sample routing table for Router A would looks like this:

Network	Interface
192.168.1.0	N1
192.168.2.0	N2
192.168.3.0	N3
192.168.4.0	N4

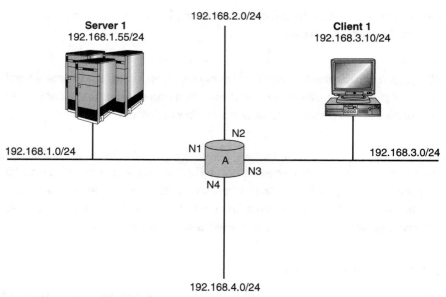

Figure 8.1

Basic routing environment   N = Network interface card (NIC)

In standard routing, the routing table is consulted every time a frame is received, so it plays a vital role in the proper delivery of data. If the routing tables are wrong, data may simply take a long time to get to its destination, but in the worse case data may never properly arrive at the destination host. An important concept to understand is that the routing table maintains only the *best* possible route to a given destination, not *all* possible routes. To illustrate this point, let's examine a more complex example, as shown in Figure 8.2.

Router A has two possible routes to network 192.168.10.0, through Router B (out the N4 interface) or through Router D (out the N3 interface). Which path will Router A use to send frames bound for the 192.168.10.0 network? The answer depends on several factors discussed later in the chapter, but there is only one route to network 192.168.10.0 in the routing table. In some cases, however, a router can have multiple interfaces associated with a single network route. For instance, Router B could send frames for the 192.168.10.0 network to Router A or Router C, or both, using load balancing. Router B would still have a single route entry in its routing table to network 192.168.10.0, but it could be associated with multiple interfaces, as shown here:

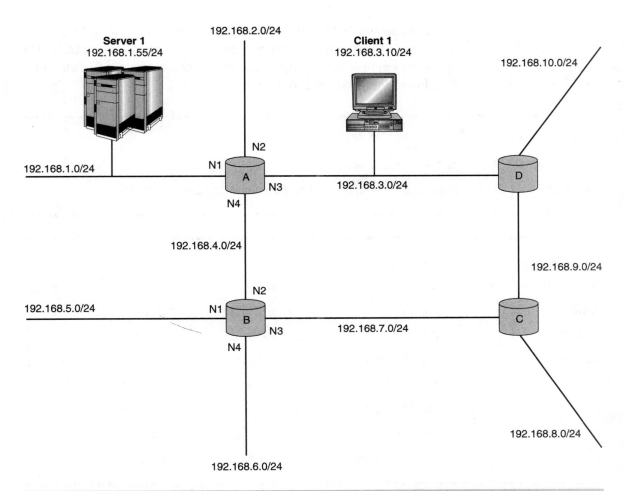

Figure 8.2

Routing with four routers

Network	Interface
192.168.10.0	N2
	N3

! **WARNING**

Do not confuse the concept of multiple *interfaces* associated with a network with multiple *route table* *entries* for a network. Having multiple entries for the same network is an illegal condition on a router and occurs only as a result of problems with the routing software or logic.

When managing TCP/IP as the Layer 3 protocol all IP enabled hosts, such as routers, servers and workstations, have some sort of routing table. The following example is the output of a route print command executed on a Windows XP Professional computer:

```
===========================================================================================

Interface List

0x1                     MS TCP Loopback interface

0x2 00 a0 c9 d3 a9 9b   Intel 82558-based Integrated Ethernet with Wake on LAN #2

===========================================================================================

===========================================================================================

Active Routes:
```

Network Destination	Netmask	Gateway	Interface	Metric
0.0.0.0	0.0.0.0	192.168.0.254	192.168.0.1	1
127.0.0.0	255.0.0.0	127.0.0.1	127.0.0.1	1
192.168.0.0	255.255.255.0	192.168.0.1	192.168.0.1	1
192.168.0.1	255.255.255.255	127.0.0.1	127.0.0.1	1
192.168.0.255	255.255.255.255	192.168.0.1	192.168.0.1	1
224.0.0.0	240.0.0.0	192.168.0.1	192.168.0.1	1
255.255.255.255	255.255.255.255	192.168.0.1	192.168.0.1	1

```
===========================================================================================

Persistent Routes:

  None
```

The first few lines show us that this system has two network interfaces, one virtual and one physical. The loopback interface is a software-based virtual interface commonly used for testing and troubleshooting. The physical interface is an Intel NIC, and it shows the MAC address for the NIC as well as the description. Below the interface list is the actual routing table that is split into several columns. The columns have the following functions:

- **Network Destination:** Lists the destination networks that this host knows how to reach.

- **Netmask:** Identifies the subnet mask (network bits) associated with the network listed in the first column.

- **Gateway:** Identifies the IP address that is the next hop for a packet going to the network destination listed in the first column.

- **Interface:** The local interface responsible for sending the frame to the listed gateway.

- **Metric:** A cost value associated with a particular route. Generally, the lowest metric route is placed in the routing table. (This topic is covered in detail in the "Routing Protocol" section.)

The first row (starting with 0.0.0.0) is called the **default route, default gateway,** or the gateway of last resort. If a frame is received and no network in the routing table matches the destination network of the frame, the frame is forwarded to the default gateway listed. The next line is a route to the local host. The 127.x.x.x address range is reserved for troubleshooting and testing the local IP configuration of the given host. The second route to 192.168.0.0 (third line) is a route entry for the local subnet. The fourth line is similar to the loopback route entry, but it specifies the IP address of the local host (192.168.0.1). The fifth line (192.168.0.255) is the subnet broadcast address used to reach all hosts on the 192.168.0.0 network. The sixth line (224.0.0.0) is a multicast address (class D), and it is used here to indicate that this host is multicast capable although it is not currently multicast enabled. The last line (255.255.255.255) is the all-networks broadcast address that addresses a frame so that any system receiving it will process it. Note that all of the routes deal with the local host, the local loopback address, or the default gateway because this routing table is from an IP host, not a router.

NOTE

We chose a host routine table to familiarize you with basic routing table concepts. Routing tables on routers can be far more complex and hard to interpret at first. If the system were set up as a router (as you will see later), the routing table has additional entries and is a little more interesting.

Our next routing table comes from a single Cisco router with two configured Ethernet interfaces (E0 and E1):

```
Router#show ip route
Codes: C - connected, S - static, I - IGRP, R - RIP, M - mobile, B - BGP
  D - EIGRP, EX - EIGRP external, O - OSPF, IA - OSPF inter area
  N1 - OSPF NSSA external type 1, N2 - OSPF NSSA external type 2
  E1 - OSPF external type 1, E2 - OSPF external type 2, E - EGP
  i - IS-IS, L1 - IS-IS level-1, L2 - IS-IS level-2, ia - IS-IS inter area
  * - candidate default, U - per-user static route, o - ODR
  P - periodic downloaded static route

Gateway of last resort is not set
C 192.168.1.0/24 is directly connected, Ethernet0
C 192.168.2.0/24 is directly connected, Ethernet1
Router#
```

This routing table is quite different from our Windows XP example. The
top section of the output is a legend used to read the codes for the lines of
the routing table listed beneath. The only two entries in the actual routing
table have been bolded and are described as follows:

- **C:** This value identifies the network as directly connected. (See
  entry in the legend.)

- **192.168.1.0/24:** This is the destination network and subnet mask
  as a single entry. The /24 indicates the number of bits in the subnet
  mask and is the same as 255.255.255.0.

- **Ethernet 0:** This column represents the interface responsible for
  maintaining connectivity to the listed network, in this case
  192.168.1.0

Again, our sample is simple to allow you to learn more quickly. Later examples show a considerably wider range of network configurations, and will
better represent a production network environment.

The routing tables in our examples have been built by the hosts through an
internal mechanism associated with the TCP/IP protocol. These routes represent directly connected interfaces and little else. In simple environments
such as a small business or home office, the routing tables are rarely more
complicated than what has been shown in our examples. On larger networks, however, routers need to have routes to all possible networks, even
those not directly connected. The task of populating the routing table is
done by using either dynamic routing or static routing.

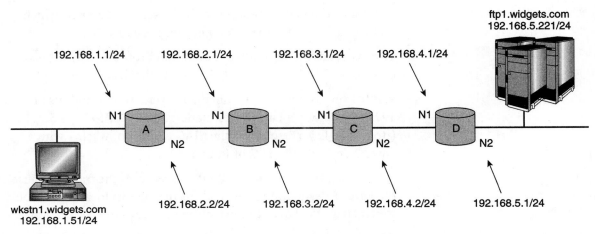

Figure 8.3

The routing process

Dynamic routing is accomplished by using routing protocols and allowing routers to build routing tables automatically. Static routing requires manual entry of routes and updates to different networks. Different situations will influence which type of routing to use, and many times you will find yourself using both. Before we discuss the details of static and dynamic routing, we need to take a closer look at the actual routing process.

8.1.2   The Routing Process

The routing process is more repetitions than it is complex. A majority of the work associated with routing a frame from source to destination is done before the frame is ever sent. Illustrating the process will help you better understand routing, routing protocols, and the function of routers. Looking at Figure 8.3, we see an internetwork composed of a workstation, a server, and four routers.

The following steps describe a simple routing process:

1.   A user at wkstn1.widgets.com wants to connect to the ftp1.widgets.com server to retrieve data. Name resolution (through DNS or a static mapping) returns an IP address of 192.168.5.221 for ftp1.

2.   Wkstn1 checks its local network ID to that of the destination and determines that ftp1 is not on its local network. Wkstn1 looks at

its local routing table and finds only the standard entries, which includes an entry for the default gateway of 192.168.1.1.

3. Wkstn1 sends out an Address Resolution Protocol (ARP) broadcast for the MAC address of 192.168.1.1 (the default gateway).

4. Wkstn1 builds frames that contain a Layer 3 source address of 192.168.1.51 and a Layer 3 destination address of 192.168.5.221 (ftp1). The Layer 2 source is the MAC address of wkstn1 with a Layer 2 destination MAC of Router A.

5. Wkstn1 sends its first frame. Router A retrieves the frame because the Layer 2 destination MAC address matches its local MAC. The router strips the Layer 2 information and reads the destination Layer 3 address of 192.168.5.221.

6. Router A consults its routing table (not shown) and determines that the route to 192.168.5.x (the destination network) goes through Router B at 192.168.2.1. Router A sends an ARP broadcast for the MAC address of Router B's N1 interface and rebuilds the Layer 2 encapsulation of the frame using the MAC address of the 192.168.2.2 interface (local N2) as the new source and the MAC address of Router B's N1 interface as the new destination.

7. Router A forwards the frame out of its local N2 interface. Router B retrieves the frame because the destination MAC address of the frame matches its N1 interface. Router B strips the Layer 2 encapsulation and reads the Layer 3 destination network address of 192.168.5.221.

8. Router B consults its routing table (not shown) and determines that the route to 192.168.5.x (the destination network) goes through Router C at 192.168.3.1. Router B sends an ARP broadcast for the MAC address of Router C's N1 interface and rebuilds the Layer 2 encapsulation of the frame using the MAC address of the 192.168.2.1 interface (local N2) as the new source and the MAC address of Router C's N1 interface as the new destination.

9. The process repeats until the frame arrives at Router D.

10. Router D consults its routing table and determines that it is directly connected to the 192.168.5.x network. Router D uses ARP to find the MAC address of the destination address 192.168.5.221 and then rebuilds the frame with the source MAC address of the

local N2 interface and the destination MAC of ftp1's network interface.

11. Router D transmits the frame onto the local 192.168.5.x network wire, and ftp1 retrieves the frame.

Our example shows the importance of both Layer 2 and Layer 3 addressing. Layer 3 addressing is critical for end-to-end reachability and does not change throughout the routing process. The Layer 2 address is used to speed the packet from one **hand-off point** (also called a "**hop**") to the next. This hopefully puts to rest the common misconception among network students that the router's IP address is the destination Layer 3 address of the frame. If this were true, the frame would lose the ability to get from wkstn1 to ftp1 (referred to as end-to-end reachability) because the Layer 3 address would be that of the router and the frame would stop there. Instead, the frame's destination is the router's Layer 2 address with the Layer 3 address remaining constant through each hop.

Although the process sounds time-consuming and even complicated, in the time that it took to read the 11 steps, you could have easily communicated with a server halfway across the world and received a response (probably from several servers). As mentioned previously, a majority of the routing process is done before the frame is even sent, including name resolution, routing table creation, and address resolution. Name resolution is covered in detail in Chapter 9, and routing table creation is covered later in this chapter, which brings us to a discussion of address resolution.

8.2   Address Resolution

Address resolution, as it pertains to our discussion, is the mapping of one address to another. It generally refers to mapping between a Layer 3 network address (logical) and a Layer 2 hardware address (physical), but the reverse process (mapping a Layer 2 to a Layer 3 address) is also address resolution.

TIP

WAN protocols also make use of address resolution, often mapping a Layer 3 network address to a Layer 2 WAN ID. An example is Frame Relay, in which a TCP/IP network address is mapped to a Data Link Connection Identifier (DLCI).

When network clients communicate, it is always with another device on the local network segment. Referring back to our routing process example

(Figure 8.3), wkstn1 did not directly communicate with ftp1 but instead with Router A configured on the same LAN. Because this process is used in every step of network communications (whether it is local or remote), understanding the address resolution process and characteristics helps you understand routing better and also illustrates the potential for making routing faster and more efficient. Address resolution is accomplished in one of the following ways:

- **Table lookup:** This procedure involves a static table that maps the Layer 3 and Layer 2 addresses together. The table is stored in memory (preferred), or on older systems may be stored in a text file and read when needed. This is a rarely used form of address resolution because it requires an enormous amount of time and maintenance even on modest-sized networks.

- **Closed-form computation:** This method of address resolution is used on networks with configurable Layer 2 and Layer 3 addresses. The MAC address is indexed to correspond to the Layer 3 host address. As an example, if your system were addressed on the fifth available address (192.168.2.5, for example), it would be the fifth MAC address in the table. This type of address resolution is only used in very specific networks and is also time-consuming to configure.

- **Dynamic message exchange:** This method of address resolution is the most common and involves an exchange of information between two hosts. Dynamic message exchange can be server-based or host-based. Server-based is centralized with the resolution table stored in a single location. Server-based dynamic message exchange is used in Asynchronous Transfer Mode (ATM) networks configured to use LAN emulation (LANE), and the table is stored on the LAN emulation server (LES). Host-based is the most common form of address resolution used in PC-based networks. In host-based dynamic message exchange, all systems participate and exchange Layer 2 data when requested.

Because dynamic message exchange is the most common, the rest of our discussion centers around TCP/IP-based networks and the use of the address resolution protocol.

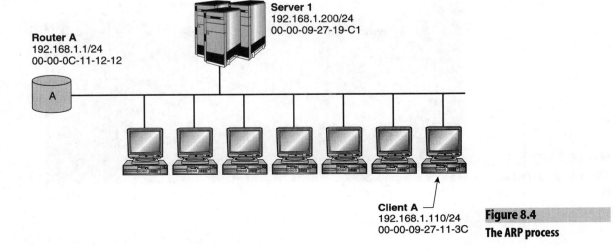

Figure 8.4
The ARP process

8.2.1   Address Resolution Protocol (ARP)

ARP is used when an IP host has a known destination IP address (Layer 3) and needs to retrieve the corresponding Layer 2 MAC address from the destination host. Use Figure 8.4 to help you follow the steps involved in an ARP exchange between Client A and Server 1.

The following steps illustrate an ARP frame exchange:

1.   Client A sends out an ARP broadcast with the following configuration:

      Source MAC address = 00-00-09-27-11-3C

      Source IP address = 192.168.1.110

      Destination MAC address = FF-FF-FF-FF-FF-FF

      Destination IP address = 192.168.1.200

2.   All clients receive and process the frame (because it is a broadcast) but only Server 1 responds because it is configured with the destination IP address of 192.168.1.200. Because Server 1 is now expecting to send and receive data with Client A, it enters the MAC and IP address of Client A into a temporary memory buffer called the **ARP cache** or **ARP table**.

Figure 8.5
ARP cache from Windows XP

3. Client A receives the response and places Server 1's MAC address in its ARP cache along with the corresponding IP address. Client A can now send frames to Server 1 with the proper destination MAC address, allowing all other hosts on the segment to disregard the frame because it is not a broadcast but a **unicast** conversation between Client A and Server 1.

The same sequence of events occurs between Client A and Router A during communications with a host on a different network segment. The difference (as shown in our routing process example) is that the Layer 3 address points to the ultimate destination while the Layer 2 address is that of Router A for the first hop.

Only one broadcast is required for this communication exchange, thus there is minimal impact on the other clients on the same network. The ARP cache is used to further reduce the need for broadcasts by storing the IP-to-MAC mapping in memory for a specified duration (usually measured in minutes). The ARP cache can include both static and dynamic entries and is shown in Figure 8.5. The ARP cache shown is from a Windows XP Professional system and is similar in layout to most IP hosts. The command used to retrieve the table is **arp a**.

Learning about ARP and its behavior helps identify performance enhancements that can reduce broadcast traffic on your network. If your goal is to eliminate as much broadcast traffic as you can, it is possible to statically enter numerous (or all) ARP cache entries on an IP host. These entries would include commonly used local resources and router interfaces. A significant drawback to a static ARP cache configuration is that MAC addresses and IP addresses change occasionally. Without a corresponding change in the static table, clients with static entries would attempt to communicate with systems using incorrect ARP table entries.

WARNING

When setting up static ARP table entries, do not enter the IP address and MAC address of remote hosts. When clients need to communicate with hosts on a different network, they use the router's MAC address, not that of the remote resource. All entries in a static ARP table should point to locally configured IP and MAC addresses.

Another network performance improvement can be achieved by extending the cache entry time. Most operating systems and IP devices such as routers have a configurable cache entry value. If your network and its components are stable, you can allow IP hosts to leave their cache entries in memory for extended periods (30+ minutes). Use caution when configuring ARP entries, particularly on a server or other device that is heavily used by numerous clients, as it takes more memory to store the entries for longer periods of time. Also be aware that if you replace a NIC or alter an IP address, clients will be unable to connect until the ARP cache entries are flushed from memory.

8.2.2   Reverse Address Resolution Protocol (RARP)

ARP locates the Layer 2 address when the Layer 3 address is known, while Reverse Address Resolution Protocol (RARP) finds the Layer 3 address when the Layer 2 address is known. A good example of RARP is found in TCP/IP address reservations and **Boot Protocol (BootP)**. Using BootP, IP hosts are assigned their IP addresses and other configuration information (DNS, default Gateway, NetBIOS name server, etc.) automatically through a BootP server. There are times when you want a network device to obtain the same address each time it is booted or when the configuration is renewed. This process is called a *reservation* and is commonly deployed for devices such as servers and network-connected printers. Using a BootP server, you create a reservation table with the MAC address of the specified client, and you associate an IP address and other configuration parameters with that MAC address. When the client with the configured MAC address boots, it uses RARP to retrieve its IP configuration from the BootP server.

8.3   Routing Protocols

In the previous section on routing tables, we pointed out that the tables are built dynamically with routing protocols or statically with manual entries. In this section, we explore dynamic and static routing in detail to provide you with information for making the correct decisions in given network environments. Realize that production environments often contain technological and political constraints that may make any given configuration or recommendation unsuitable. In these environments especially, the more information you have, the better and more complete the solution will be.

Our first topic is dynamic routing using routing protocols. There are several ways that routing protocols are classified, but keep in mind that they all have one purpose: to build a routing table with the best route to any given destination. Routing protocols are categorized into two types, loosely based on how the protocols communicate and their relative level of intelligence. The two classifications are:

- Distance vector
- Link state

8.3.1   Distance Vector

Distance vector routing protocols are simple—simple to set up and they use simple logic to determine the best path to a given destination. If you are considering a routing protocol, there are several questions to ask indicating which protocol to use. We will use the same questions for each routing protocol classification so that you can easily compare them.

- What metric does the protocol use to determine the best route among multiple routes to the same destination?
- What method does the protocol use to communicate, and how often does it communicate with other devices?
- How are routing loops prevented?
- How quickly do all devices learn of a change in the routing topology?

The term **metric** refers to the method or measurement used by the routing protocol logic to determine the best path to a given network. A distance vector routing protocol usually uses hop count as its metric. Looking at Figure 8.6, we see multiple paths to network 192.168.10.0. /24 from Router A.

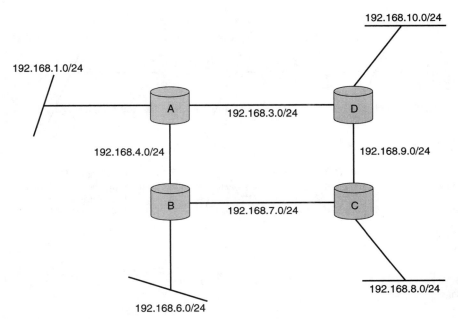

Figure 8.6
The best path

The two routes can be expressed as A-D and A-B-C-D. So which path is the *best* path? Based on the logic of distance vector protocols, it is the A-D path because it has the fewest number of hops to network 192.168.10.0. This might not always be the optimal path, as you will learn later in the "Link State" section.

A distance vector routing protocol is also characterized by how it communicates with other router devices and how often the communication takes place. Distance vector routing protocols use broadcasts to advertise their entire routing table to directly connected peer routers. This method is often very inefficient because the entire routing table is advertised at a periodic interval (usually 30 or 60 seconds) even when no changes have occurred, and also because it is broadcast-based, so all network devices on the LAN segment must process the frames. As the network grows, the entire process consumes large amounts of bandwidth, causing network congestion and communication problems especially if the protocol is configured over WAN connections.

Before we look at the next two questions concerning routing loops and topology changes, let's look at how a distance vector routing protocol builds a routing table. As you read through the steps, refer to Figure 8.7.

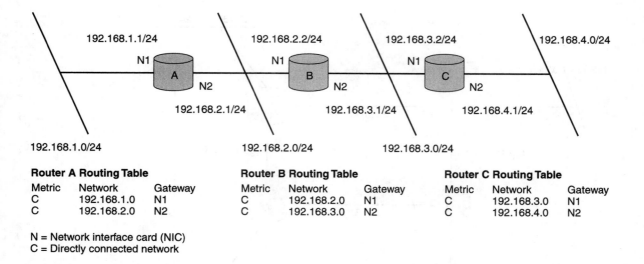

Figure 8.7

Distance vector communications

1. All of the routers know about their directly connected networks,
   so all three routers in Figure 8.7 start with two entries in their
   routing table marked as "C" for directly connected.

2. Assume Router A reaches its broadcast interval of 30 seconds first
   and advertises its entire route table to all of its directly connected
   neighbors, in our case Router B.

3. Router B receives the route table broadcast from Router A containing the following routes: 192.168.1.0 and 192.168.2.0.

4. Router B must now determine whether or not to enter any of
   these advertised routes into its routing table. Router B enters the
   route to 192.168.1.0 into its routing table because it has no current route to that network. Router B also associates the route with
   the next hop address of 192.168.2.1. In plain terms this means
   that if Router B has a frame with a destination network address of
   192.168.1.X /24, then Router B forwards the frame to Router A at
   192.168.2.1. Router A sent the advertisement for network
   192.168.1.0 and is 1 hop away. This value is entered in Router B's
   routing table as the metric for that route. Router B also receives a
   route to the 192.168.2.0 network from Router A. Router B adds 1

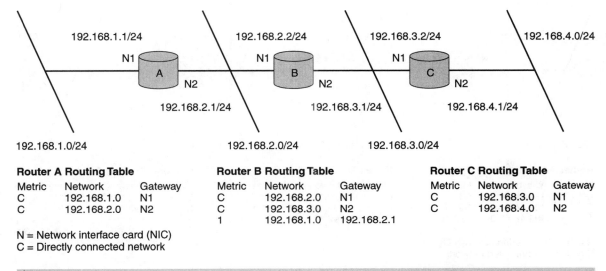

Figure 8.8

Processing route advertisements

for the metric and compares this route to the existing route already in its routing table. The route advertisement from Router A is dropped because Router B already has a route to the 192.168.2.0 network with a lower metric (directly connected). Router B's routing table is shown in Figure 8.8.

5. Router B now reaches its periodic advertising interval and advertises its entire routing table to all directly connected neighbors, Router A and Router C.

6a. Router A receives the broadcast with three routes: 192.168.1.0, 192.168.2.0, and 192.168.3.0. Router B is 1 hop away, so each route has a 1 added to its current metric value. Router A now compares each route to its routing table and selects the best route to each network. The routes to 192.168.1.0 and 192.168.2.0 are both dropped because Router A has a route with a better metric already in its table (both directly connected). The route to 192.168.3.0 is added with a metric of 1 and a next hop address of 192.168.2.2.

6b. Router C also receives the route broadcast from Router B that includes the same three routes. The metric for each route is incremented by 1 because Router B is 1 hop away. Router C adds the

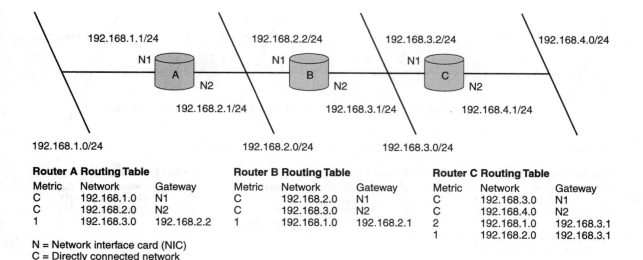

Router A Routing Table

Metric	Network	Gateway
C	192.168.1.0	N1
C	192.168.2.0	N2
1	192.168.3.0	192.168.2.2

Router B Routing Table

Metric	Network	Gateway
C	192.168.2.0	N1
C	192.168.3.0	N2
1	192.168.1.0	192.168.2.1

Router C Routing Table

Metric	Network	Gateway
C	192.168.3.0	N1
C	192.168.4.0	N2
2	192.168.1.0	192.168.3.1
1	192.168.2.0	192.168.3.1

N = Network interface card (NIC)
C = Directly connected network

Figure 8.9

Router B advertises

route to network 192.168.1.0 to its table with a metric of 2 (Router B advertised the route with a metric already at 1) and a next hop address of 192.168.3.1. The route to network 192.168.2.0 is also added to Router C's table with a metric of 1 and a next hop address of 192.168.3.1. The last route advertisement is dropped because Router C already has a route to the 192.168.3.0 network with a better metric (directly connected). The current status of the routing tables is shown in Figure 8.9.

7. Finally, Router C reaches its periodic advertising interval and advertises its entire route table to all directly connected peers (Router B).

8. Router B receives the broadcast and processes each of the entries received, adding 1 to the advertised metric value. The route to network 192.168.4.0 is added to Router B's route table with a metric of 1 and a next hop address of 192.168.3.2. All of the other routes advertised by Router C are dropped because Router B has better routes with lower metrics to each.

9. The process continues with each router advertising their routes every 30 seconds until each router learns a route to all of the avail-

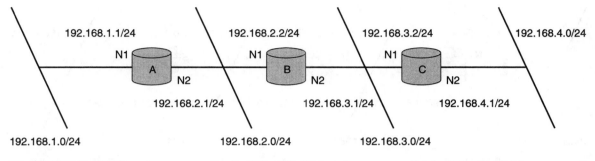

Router A Routing Table				Router B Routing Table				Router C Routing Table		
Metric	Network	Gateway		Metric	Network	Gateway		Metric	Network	Gateway
C	192.168.1.0	N1		C	192.168.2.0	N1		C	192.168.3.0	N1
C	192.168.2.0	N2		C	192.168.3.0	N2		C	192.168.4.0	N2
1	192.168.3.0	192.168.2.2		1	192.168.1.0	192.168.2.1		2	192.168.1.0	192.168.3.1
2	192.168.4.0	192.168.2.2		1	192.168.4.0	192.168.3.2		1	192.168.2.0	192.168.3.1

N = Network interface card (NIC)
C = Directly connected network

Figure 8.10

The converged tables

able networks. When the routers reach this stage they are referred to as **converged**. Figure 8.10 illustrates the complete routing tables for all three of the routers.

Convergence is the time it takes for a given set of routers to learn routes to all networks. After all routers learn of all networks and make appropriate entries in their respective routing tables, they have converged. Additionally, convergence describes the time it takes a set of routers to learn of a change on a network. Changes typically include a network being down (unavailable) or the addition of a new network. When comparing routing protocols, convergence is often used as part of the selection criteria. A faster convergence time is desired because the network is able to reflect changes and "route" around problems more quickly. Distance vector routing protocols generally take longer to converge than **link state** protocol because they use a periodic route advertisement schedule. This answers the third of our four questions posed at the beginning of the section. The last question is how are routing loops prevented. To answer this question, we need to know what a routing loop is.

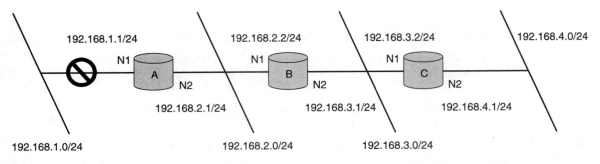

Router A Routing Table		
Metric	Network	Gateway
C	192.168.1.0	N1
C	192.168.2.0	N2
1	192.168.3.0	192.168.2.2
2	192.168.4.0	192.168.2.2

Router B Routing Table		
Metric	Network	Gateway
C	192.168.2.0	N1
C	192.168.3.0	N2
1	192.168.1.0	192.168.2.1
1	192.168.4.0	192.168.3.2

Router C Routing Table		
Metric	Network	Gateway
C	192.168.3.0	N1
C	192.168.4.0	N2
2	192.168.1.0	192.168.3.1
1	192.168.2.0	192.168.3.1

N = Network interface card (NIC)
C = Directly connected network

Figure 8.11

A routing loop

A **routing loop** occurs when routers get confused during update operations, causing frames to bounce back and forth between a set of interfaces. Refer to Figure 8.11 as we explore a routing loop.

The following steps illustrate a typical routing loop:

1. The routers are in a converged state when network 192.168.1.0 goes offline one second after Router A has sent out its periodic advertisement. Router A removes the route to 192.168.1.0 from its routing table and must now wait until its next periodic interval to notify its peers of the condition of network 192.168.1.x.

2. During Router A's wait time, Router B reaches its periodic interval and advertises its routing table to all of its peers including Router A. In the advertisement is a route to 192.168.1.0 with a metric of 1.

3. Router A goes through its normal route calculations looking for the best routes to all networks and consequently adds the route to network 192.168.1.0 (advertised by Router B) into its table because it has no route to that network. The metric is incremented to 2 and the next hop is set to 192.168.2.2.

This begins the routing loop, because Router A now has a route to network 192.168.1.0 that points to Router B. Router B has a route to network 192.168.1.0 that points to Router A. If Router C has a frame destined for network 192.168.1.0, the frame is delivered to Router B. Router B then forwards the frame to Router A, which then forwards it back to Router B and so on until the frame's time-to-live counter reached 0 and the frame is discarded.

There are two very easy ways to identify routing loops. The first is using the Tracert or Traceroute utility. If you trace an IP address using either utility and the frame hits a routing loop, you will see it bouncing back and forth between the routing devices, causing the loop. The second identification method involves viewing the routing table and the metric associated with the network in question. If you look back to our example in Figure 8.11 and extrapolate the behavior over several advertising intervals, you will note that the metric associated with the route to the 192.168.1.0 network keeps incrementing upward. On the first iteration of the routing loop, Router A incremented the metric by 1, making the metric 2. When Router A next advertises the route table to Router B, Router B will add 1 to the metric, making it 3. This process will continue infinitely unless some sort of protection or prevention logic is put into place.

Preventing routing loops involves the use of one or more of the following software-based methods added to the routing logic:

- **Split horizon:** This logic states that a router should not accept updates about a network from a peer to which the network was first advertised. In other words, Router A told Router B about network 192.168.1.0 first. Split horizon prevents Router A from accepting updates about that network from Router B.

- **Hold-down timers:** A hold-down timer prevents Router A from accepting updates about a particular route that has become unavailable for a predetermined amount of time. This prevents Router A from accepting route updates about the 192.168.1.0 network for the duration of the hold-down timer. This can cause problems if an alternate route (such as a dial-up) is made available, as Router A cannot accept any updates until the hold-down timer expires. This can add a considerable amount of time to convergence.

- **Triggered updates:** This solves the main problem that first caused our routing loop. Router A was forced to wait the periodic interval before notifying its peers of the down status of network 192.168.1.0. Triggered updates would allow Router A to immediately inform Router B of the network condition and likely prevent the loop from occurring. If triggered updates are used in conjunction with hold-down timers (as they often are), loop prevention is all but guaranteed.

- **Hop-count limits:** Limits are put on how high a hop count is allowed to increment before it is identified as a probable loop. One of the more common distance vector routing protocols sets a hop count limit of 15, meaning that if the hop count goes above this, a loop exists and the route should be taken out of the routing table. A significant issue concerning this loop prevention technique is that on large networks, 16 hops might be common. This means that distance vector routing protocols employing hop-count limits should not be used on such networks.

- **Poisoning:** This loop prevention technique relies on the previous concepts of hop-count limiting or metric limiting. When a route to a particular network goes offline, rather than deleting the route, the routers with direct knowledge of the failure set the route metric to one above the maximum allowed and continue to advertise the route with its new configuration. Because the metric advertised is set above the maximum allowed, the router receiving the new route advertisement will drop the network route as "unreachable."

Our next type of routing protocol is called link state and overcomes many of the limitations of distance vector routing protocols.

8.3.2   Link State

Link state routing protocols are far more intelligent than distance vector protocols. This extra intelligence increases the complexity of protocol configuration, maintenance, and troubleshooting. Most large, complex network environments demand the features, functions, and flexibility of link state routing protocols. The same questions posed for distance vector protocols are answered in this section to maintain comparisons between distance vector and link state protocols. Basically, our four questions deal with metrics, communications, routing loops, and convergence.

The metric used by most link state protocols is bandwidth, which allows more complex routing configurations to be properly deciphered. See the

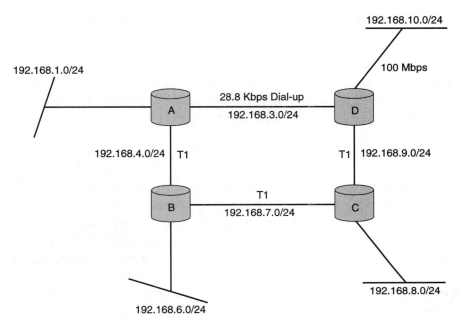

192.168.10.0/24

192.168.1.0/24

100 Mbps

28.8 Kbps Dial-up
192.168.3.0/24

A   D

192.168.4.0/24   T1   T1   192.168.9.0/24

T1
B   C
192.168.7.0/24

192.168.8.0/24

Figure 8.12
Link state intelligence

192.168.6.0/24

routing configuration in Figure 8.12, which shows a situation similar to our distance vector example.

The difference in this example is the addition of bandwidth on each of the links. A distance vector protocol still determines the route from A to D as the best route because it is calculating based on hop count. A link state protocol uses a mathematical formula involving bandwidth and determines that the path from A to B to C to D is the optimum path.

 NOTE

Routing protocols capable of making complex decisions use a mathematical formula for deriving the best path or route to a given network. The formula is referred to as an *algorithm* and is different for each routing protocol. Simple routing protocols (for example, distance vector) use a simple logic such as hop count to derive the best path.

In addition to bandwidth, some link state protocols are capable of determining the best route to a destination based on the following:

- **Delay:** The time it takes to deliver a frame to the destination
- **Load:** How busy a path or route is
- **Reliability:** How often the link goes down along a given route

- **Maximum transmission unit (MTU):** The maximum size of the frame that the network supports along the route to the destination

---

TIP Bandwidth is the most common metric used, but some link state protocols are more flexible than others and take into account more variables that affect network performance and frame delivery. Any or all of these metrics are used in link state protocols to generate a "best route" to a given destination. When more than one metric is used, it is referred to as a *composite metric*.

The communications process is another area of significant improvement of link state over distance vector. Link state protocols send updates only when changes occur but, more important, they send only the change and not the entire routing table. Additionally, link state protocols use multicast and unicast traffic instead of broadcast traffic to further reduce the impact of routing protocol traffic on a network. Link state routers also develop an overall picture of the available networks by establishing neighbor relationships. Routers communicate directly with all peer routers (neighbors). The neighbor relationships are created when the router initially boots and any time a new peer is discovered. After all routers are converged, change updates are all that are required to manage the routing tables.

The risk of developing routing loops is greatly reduced in routers using a link state protocol because of the initial "big picture" view of the network that is created by each router. Distance vector protocols are said to *route by rumor,* meaning you have to believe what your neighbor router heard from their neighbor and so on. Because link state routers build their own complete view of the network, they *route by reason.* Using triggered updates and only sending changes when they occur (instead of the entire table) are additional loop prevention mechanisms that are inherent in the link state protocol family.

Our last question to answer deals with convergence. Link state protocols excel in their ability to quickly and efficiently route around problems and add new routes to their routing tables. How quickly? When a change is detected on only one router, some link state protocols can converge in less than two seconds across 150+ routers. How do link state routers achieve such a quick response time? Let's look at another example of building routing tables and identifying network changes using link state. Figure 8.13 depicts a section of a network using eight routers.

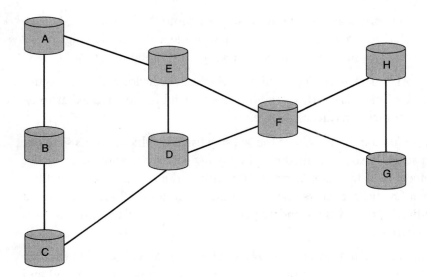

Figure 8.13
Link state initialization

The following steps illustrate router initialization for a router running the link state protocol Open Shortest Path First:

1. Router D is brought online and is not yet routing. It exchanges hello packets with its directly connected neighbors and establishes two-way communications.

2. Routers E, F, and C send back Router D hello packets identifying all known neighbors. These neighbor packets include Router D and complete the neighbor phase of the initialization process.

3. Router D now requests from its neighbors database packets concerning all known routes and neighbors. This allows Router D to build a local database and network view with itself at the center of the network view. The database is called the link state database, and all routers have a complete view of network routes and routers. (The link state database is different than the routing table.)

4. Router D uses the logic of the routing protocol (usually bandwidth) to determine the best path to any network and then populates its routing table with this information. When this process is complete, convergence communications continues until all routers have a complete view of all routers and routes on the network. When convergence takes place, Router D is initialized and begins communicating and routing frames. Updates about any

network changes are multicast throughout the network, and changes are made to the local view of the network allowing any and all routers to converge in a very short amount of time.

5.   All link state routers send out heartbeat, or hello, packets at regular intervals (5–10 seconds) to their neighbors to ensure that communications are still active.

The term *link state* comes from the last step listed in which routers send out hello packets. Using this method of two-way communication, each router is kept aware of the state or status of a link. If the link fails or a neighbor misses a few hello packets, the local router assumes the link is down and immediately transmits an update packet notifying all of the other routers of the change.

The only potential drawbacks to using link state protocols are that they are more resource intensive (require more CPU processing and memory) and are more complex to configure. The benefits often outweigh these issues. We have now explored two of the classifications of routing protocols, distance vector and link state. Use Table 8.2 to review the two before our next section on administrative classification.

8.4   Administrative Classification

Routing protocols are also separated by an administrative classification based on where they are used in the networking environment. The two classifications are:

- Interior routing protocols or interior gateway protocols
- Exterior routing protocols or exterior gateway protocols

Each classification contains several routing protocols. We discuss the most common protocols and their characteristics along with our examination of the two different administrative classifications in the following sections.

8.4.1   Interior Gateway Protocols (IGPs)

Interior gateway protocols (IGPs) can best be thought of as used within a company's network infrastructure to maintain routing tables and routing policy set forth exclusively by the company's network administrators. Contrast this with EGPs (discussed in the next section), which are configured to maintain routes on the Internet and across other public backbone net-

TABLE 8.2   Characteristics of Distance Vector and Link State

Protocol Type	Metric	Communication Process	Routing Loop Prevention	Convergence
Distance vector	Hop count	Broadcasts entire route table at periodic intervals	Split horizon, hold-down timers, triggered updates, metric limits, poisoning	Depends on size of network and routing update interval
Link state	Bandwidth (but can use other network parameters)	Only when changes occur, and only the change is transmitted as unicast or multicast	Triggered updates, common view of the network (link state database) transmitting only changes	Very fast regardless of network size

works. A collection of routers using IGPs, under common administrative control, are said to be in the same **autonomous system (AS)**. Routers using IGPs are administered and managed entirely by the company that owns the equipment and can use either distance vector or link state protocols. The two industry-standard IGPs are:

- Routing Information Protocol
- Open Shortest Path First

Routing Information Protocol (RIP)

Routing Information Protocol (RIP) was developed at the Palo Alto Research Center (PARC) in California. Many subsequent routing protocols rely on RIP as a model, including Novell's RIP for IPX and AppleTalk's routing protocol. RIP is a distance vector protocol that uses hop count for its metric when determining the best route to a given network. It advertises its entire routing table every 30 seconds.

WARNING Some implementations of RIP allow the broadcast interval to be modified to reduce the amount of traffic generated by RIP during normal operations. Ensure that all of your RIP routing devices support the modification before permitting this modification. If all devices don't support the modification, leave the route update interval at the default 30 seconds (the industry-standard time interval).

In most implementations, RIP uses split horizon, hop-count limit, and poisoning for routing loop prevention. These techniques are described in detail in the previous section on distance vector protocols. The hop-count limit of RIP is 15, forcing the protocol to discard any route with a metric above 15 as unreachable (preventing a routing loop). Given the limitations already discussed, RIP is useful on small- to medium-size networks with fairly straightforward connections and routes. An additional limiting factor of RIP is that it is a classful routing protocol. This means that the router transmits only the configured network and no network prefix or subnet mask. On networks with custom subnetting, this is a significant limitation that will likely push you to use RIP version 2 or a link state protocol.

TIP Many different server operating systems can use RIP. All that is required are two NICs installed in the server and an installation of the RIP software. Windows NT4/2000/2003, Unix, Linux, and NetWare servers all support RIP. However, keep in mind that the ability to route does not necessarily mean that a server is a good router. In most cases, if you need a router other than for lab purposes, you should buy a dedicated piece of hardware for the job.

RIP version 2 improves on its predecessor by allowing triggered updates in addition to the other routing loop prevention mechanisms. Using triggered updates significantly improves the convergence time of RIP, allowing its use on larger networks (but still within the limitations of 15 hops). RIP version 2 can be configured to be a classless routing protocol, allowing RIP to transmit not only the network but also the network prefix that is configured for a particular interface. Each of these improvements increases the usability of the protocol on networks, but eventually large networks become so complex that they outgrow RIP's ability to effectively route. Administrators then turn to Open Shortest Path First.

Open Shortest Path First (OSPF)

The shortest path as measured by **Open Shortest Path First (OSPF)** is actually the *fastest* path based on bandwidth. The term *shortest* in the name refers to the shortest time, not the shortest number of hops. OSPF can be a complex protocol allowing for routing hierarchies, **route summarization**, and areas not available in its simpler RIP counterpart. OSPF is used on large networks or networks that are composed of complex connections requiring more intelligence than simple distance vector routing protocols can provide.

OSPF conforms to features previously discussed in the link state section using bandwidth as its metric for determining its best route to a given network. It communicates using unicast and multicast packets that are more efficient in large routing environments and only transmits changes to the routing table when they occur. It uses hello packets to determine the current state of a link between itself and its neighbors, and utilizes a link state database to maintain a local view of the entire routing environment. Using Figure 8.14, let's review some of the advanced features of OSPF and the configurations that are possible using this link state protocol.

The following list describes the possible configurations using OSPF:

- **Areas:** Areas are used to separate or isolate smaller groups of routers. By using areas, routing updates and overall routing traffic

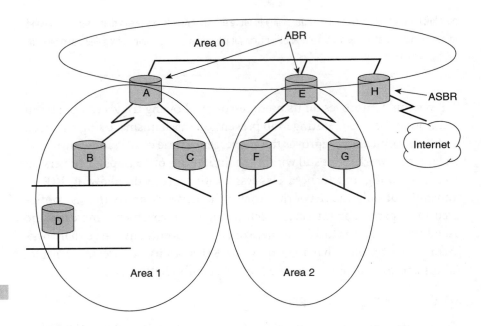

Figure 8.14
Routing with OSPF

are reduced. In Figure 8.14, Router A is an entry point into Area 1 and helps isolate other routers outside Area 1 from unnecessary route recalculations. If a route on Router B fails, routers E, F, G, and H should not spend time recalculating a path around the failure because one does not exist. Router A and the use of Area 1 helps, because the update packet that would normally be sent out to all OSPF routers is blocked at Router A and summarized to the other routers, preventing them from attempting to recalculate a best path to the network that has only one path through Router A. Areas can also be used to summarize routes (covered in a later section in this chapter), helping to reduce the total number of routes in the routing table. When using OSPF, the backbone is defined as Area 0, and all other areas must connect to Area 0 to have a valid OSPF hierarchy. If no other areas are needed, all routers are configured in Area 0.

- **Autonomous system (AS):** All routers connected to the same Area 0 are under common administrative control and are in the same AS. Administrative control does not mean that the routers have to be controlled by a single administrator or even the same team of administrators. AS indicates that a single business entity or company controls the routing policy and configuration. In our sample network, all of the routers shown are in the same AS.

- **Backbone router:** A **backbone router** has at least one interface in Area 0; routers A, E, and H are backbone routers.

- **Area border router (ABR):** An **area border router** has at least one interface in the backbone and one interface in another area. As mentioned in the definition of areas, ABRs serve the purpose of route summarization and traffic reduction to routers outside the area. Routers A and E are ABRs.

- **Autonomous system boundary router (ASBR):** An ASBR is used to connect an autonomous system to another. In many networks, as in our example, an ASBR connects the OSPF network to the Internet. (Router H in our example connects to the Internet.) This is not always the case. If you are connecting two companies, each running their own OSPF network with separate Area 0s, the connection between them would occur through an ASBR. The router with this configuration has special capabilities for summarizing routes and insulating internal routers from unnecessary outside traffic.

This is a brief overview of some of the components of an OSPF network. The subject of OSPF and its configuration easily fill numerous books dedicated solely to this one protocol. Hopefully, we have successfully illustrated the differences between distance vector and link state protocols by examining RIP and OSPF in more detail. We arrived at our current discussion by looking at the classification of these two protocols as interior gateway protocols. The other category of protocol in this classification is exterior.

8.4.2   Exterior Gateway Protocols (EGPs)

As illustrated in Chapter 7, a large company network can be compared to a city with houses, streets, and city services represented by hosts, network segments, and servers. Moving within your network is similar to driving in the city where you are subject to the traffic policies and routes dictated by the local transportation authority. What happens when you want to travel outside the city limits to another town, state, or country? Now you are subject to traffic policies and routing behaviors controlled by a collection of authorities. This realm outside your city is analogous to the area of the **exterior gateway protocols** (EPGs). Your city of routers is referred to as an AS and is assigned a number for the purposes of routing to and from your collection of routers. Users needing to get from one city to another have to use a highway controlled by an external authority. Although we teach this analogy often using the Internet as the backdrop, it can be applied to some of the enormous worldwide companies that maintain and manage hundreds if not thousands of routers.

The decision-making process of EGPs is far more complex than that of internal protocols. EGPs can alter their routing policy (the path a frame actually takes) based on current traffic load, traffic type, source address, destination address, or combinations of these parameters. Using our analogy again, it means that EGPs can dictate where and how trucks enter your city. If they are carrying important payloads, you can have them enter via a direct route on an eight-lane highway. If the trucks are carrying unimportant materials or equipment, you can send them down a slower path leaving the main roads open for the more important trucks. EGPs give you the freedom to route inbound and outbound traffic based on the needs of your company. Traffic to specified Web sites, e-mail, FTP, and Telnet can be routed and handled by the system differently, using EGPs and routing policies.

Proper use of the power and routing flexibility associated with EGPs requires an intimate knowledge and understanding of the complex nature of your network and its traffic. If you attempt to configure an EGP protocol and you do so incorrectly, or do not understand completely the consequences of what you are doing, the results can be catastrophic.

WARNING !

We are not attempting to sound melodramatic concerning the consequences of misconfiguration of an EGP protocol. A real-world example may help illustrate. One of our clients decided to take on the task of configuring their connections to the Internet using Border Gateway Protocol (discussed shortly). They maintained several sites worldwide, and each site had an independent connection to a local ISP. They misconfigured a routing policy at one of their sites and began routing all Internet traffic for the entire South Island of New Zealand back to the United States. The ISP promptly shut down their connection in New Zealand until the problem could be identified. In short, do not take the configuration or management of an EGP protocol lightly—a considerable amount of expertise is required to tap the power of these protocols.

After your network traffic leaves your control (after your truck leaves your city) you have *no* control over what happens to it. EGPs can let you influence and manage traffic only as it enters or leaves your AS, but when it's out on the "highway" you can only speculate what other policies are being applied as your traffic traverses other routing networks to its ultimate destination.

Given the cautions that we have stated, you are probably wondering when you should use an EGP. The most common situations are:

- You are an Internet service provider (ISP).

- Your company has multiple connections to the Internet connecting to different external ASs. A good example of this is if your company maintains offices in Europe, the United States and Asia, each with connections to the Internet and also connected to each other.

- Your company maintains multiple connections to the Internet through the same service provider but you need to control data traffic as it enters and/or exits your network.

- You need to control the data traffic flow among your own network routers, and you need the power and flexibility of an EGP. (You have an enormous network and are basically acting as an ISP for you internal network areas.)

Now that you know when you might want to use an EGP, let's look at some of the protocols that fall into this protocol classification.

Exterior Gateway Protocol (EGP)

No, this is not a printing mistake: The family of protocols is called exterior gateway protocols (EGPs), and one member of this family is called the **Exterior Gateway Protocol (EGP)**. This confusing bit aside, EGP was the first protocol developed that allowed isolation of ASs during the early development of the Internet. It is not used anymore, and was replaced by the Border Gateway Protocol.

Border Gateway Protocol (BGP)

Border Gateway Protocol (BGP) version 4 is the most widely used exterior protocol today. It is a well-established standard and commonly used by ISPs for very large companies. In the section on EGPs, we outlined when to use these particular types of protocols. It is also useful to know when not to use protocols such as BGP and instead use simpler alternatives. If your company or current situation falls into one of the following situations, do not use BGP:

- You have a single connection to the Internet.

- You do not need to control traffic into or out of your AS, or routing can be handled correctly with an IGP.

- You do not have the proper equipment to handle BGP. Exterior protocols require a significant amount of CPU processing and memory to perform their tasks properly.

- You have low-bandwidth links. BGP communicates frequently and requires lots of bandwidth.

- You have little or no understanding of exterior routing policies and protocols.

By following these guidelines and the guidelines provided in the "Exterior Gateway Protocols" section, you should be able to determine whether or not you need an exterior protocol. Alternatives include static routing, manually setting routes to different networks, and controlling your traffic flow as efficiently as needed without incurring the overhead and complexity of BGP. If you determine that you need BGP, the following paragraphs outline some of the capabilities and characteristics of this powerful protocol.

Figure 8.15 illustrates an important fact: There are actually two different classifications of BGP, internal and external. The annotations are used to help you identify the difference: iBGP is used for internal routing and eBGP is used for external routing. If two routers are running BGP and are in the same AS, they are running an iBGP connection as illustrated by the connections between A-C and A-B. If two routers are connected and each belongs to a different AS, they are using eBGP as shown between routers C-E and B-D. This is important because iBGP functions under different rules than eBGP.

To avoid getting lost in the details of this protocol, let's look back to the four questions we posed when comparing protocols: What metric is used? How does the protocol communicate? How are loops prevented? And, finally, how quickly can the protocol converge?

The metrics used by BGP are contingent on how you set up your routing policy. The policy can be built around different factors, as mentioned previously, including traffic type, outbound destination/source, inbound destination/source, administrative preference, and other proprietary factors based on which vendor's BGP implementation you are using.

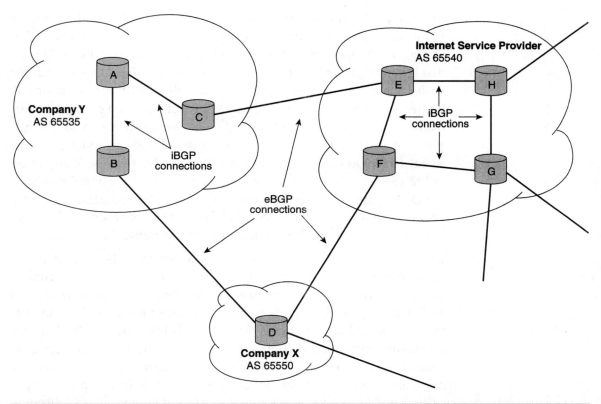

Figure 8.15
Routing with BGP

BGP communication starts by establishing peers. In Figure 8.15, Router C has two peers, A and E. However, peering (creating a connection between two routers) does not necessarily require a direct network connection. A TCP session is set up using command statements (usually a neighbor or peer statement of some kind) that form a continuous flow of BGP data between the two peers. This flow of data can actually occur over an IGP-routed network. After the peers have been established, BGP routing information is exchanged and updated as necessary. BGP is actually an advanced distance vector protocol that uses triggered updates for communicating changes in the routing environment.

Routing loops in BGP are avoided by using the AS-path attribute. When a BGP router advertises its locally connected networks, it appends its AS number to the route advertisement. If a route advertisement returns to the

AS from a different BGP peer with the local AS number in the path, the route advertisement is dropped. In Figure 8.15, assume that Router C is advertising the network 192.168.1.0 /24. It is telling each of its eBGP peers that it knows the path to that network. The route advertisement includes Router C's AS number of 65535. This advertisement is sent to Router E. Router E then adds the route and path to its BGP table and passes the information to all of its configured peers. Router F would eventually advertise its ability to get to 192.168.1.0, prepending its AS path information in the advertisement as 65540, 65535. Router D then advertises the ability to get to 192.168.1.0 to Router B, prepending its AS information as 65550, 65540, 65535. As soon as Router B receives this route advertisement, it drops it, because it's own AS is in the AS path of the route advertisement. This feature prevents any possible routing loops from forming.

The last of our four questions deals with convergence. Because BGP uses active TCP sessions that are set up and continuously maintained, convergence in the routing environment is very fast. You can use some features of BGP to help speed the convergence of the network routes under your control, but remember that in many cases there is little you can do about the routes and routing outside your administrative authority. It is important to emphasize again that our discussions here are introductory in nature. We have barely scratched the surface of BGP, but hopefully have provided you a better understanding of not only this protocol but also the classification and behaviors of both interior and exterior protocols as a whole. If you need more information, there are numerous books dedicated to routing and even specific routing protocols. Use Table 8.3 to help you review the key points and features of IGPs and EGPs.

8.5   Hierarchical Routing

The final subjects we tackle in this chapter are hierarchical routing and route summarization. Hierarchical routing techniques have taken hold over the last few years and are rapidly gaining wide acceptance. Hierarchical routing depends on hierarchical addressing and is a routing technique originally designed to help reduce the size of the routing tables on the Internet as well as speed up the overall routing process. The concept uses an address block (or blocks) to represent different sections of a network. Figure 8.16 illustrates hierarchical addressing well.

TABLE 8.3   Characteristics of Distance Vector and Link State

Protocol Type	Common Use	Routing Protocols in This Group	Key Characteristics
Interior gateway protocol	Internal networks	Routing Information Protocol, Open Shortest Path First	All routers are in the same AS. Easier to configure than EGPs. Routing logic is simpler than EGPs.
Exterior gateway protocol	Connecting networks to the Internet. Connecting huge private networks together.	Exterior Gateway Protocol, Border Gateway Protocol	Routers are not in the same AS. Can be very difficult to configure properly. Uses highly complex route selection logic.

Note that the campus is represented by one large address block. This was subnetted into smaller blocks, each assigned to a building. Each building was further subnetted by floor. After addressing is properly assigned, the hierarchy can be configured within your routing structure by using route summarization.

8.5.1   Route Summarization

Summarizing routes is best thought of as the opposite of subnetting and in fact is often referred to as supernetting networks. The process of summarization is built around the binary bit patterns just as it was in subnetting. The difference is that rather than extending the subnet mask, we remove bits. Look at the following addresses:

192.168.16.0	00010000 (binary of the third octet)
192.168.17.0	00010001
192.168.18.0	00010010
192.168.19.0	00010011

Looking at the binary of the third octet, note that the networks share the left six bits while bits 7 and 8 are responsible for creating distinct network IDs. This means that if we *unmask* two bits in the network prefix, all of the

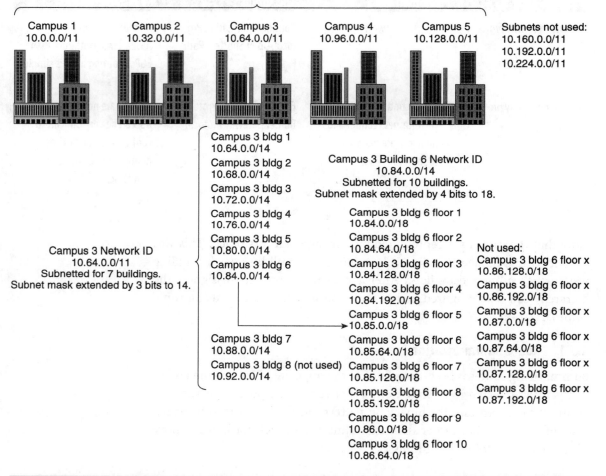

Figure 8.16

Addressing hierarchy

addresses would belong to the same network. This is the essence of summarization. The real benefit of this behavior is seen by examining a network involving summarization. Figure 8.17 shows us four routers (A, B, C, and D), each with several networks attached.

The routing tables on each router would contain 20 networks and would require a certain amount of time, memory, and CPU utilization to route

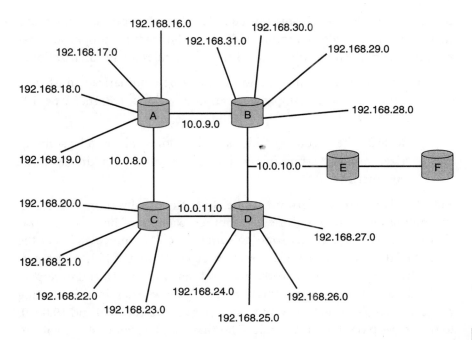

192.168.16.0   192.168.30.0

192.168.31.0

192.168.17.0   192.168.29.0

192.168.18.0

A   B   192.168.28.0

10.0.9.0

192.168.19.0   10.0.8.0

—10.0.10.0—   E   F

192.168.20.0   10.0.11.0

C   D

192.168.27.0

192.168.21.0

192.168.22.0   192.168.24.0

192.168.26.0

192.168.23.0

192.168.25.0

All networks are using 24-bit subnet masks.

Figure 8.17
Summarizing

frames and process routing updates. By using summarization we can reduce the routing tables on each router from 20 to 11. Here is how we do it:

- **Router A:** Advertises a single route of 192.168.16.0 /22. This informs all of the other routers that if the first 22 bits of the destination address match the first 22 bits of 192.168.16.0, then those frames should be routed to A.

- **Router B:** Advertises a single route of 192.168.20.0 /22.

- **Router C:** Advertises a single route of 192.168.24.0 /22.

- **Router D:** Advertises a single route of 192.168.28.0 /22.

By removing two bits from the classful 24-bit mask, we are obscuring or hiding the distinct network IDs from the other routers. This allows each of the other routers to simply match the first 22 bits of a destination address to locate the router to which the frame should be sent. When the frame arrives at the appropriate router, a longest match is performed against the destination address to determine the correct interface for the frame. A final route summarization and hierarchy can be seen from the perspective of routers E and F. The entire routing area (A, B, C, and D) produces 20 routes that appear on Router F. This can be reduced to two routes, producing a savings in terms of distinct routes of 90%! To illustrate the proper summarization technique on Router E, let's look at two rules for summarization:

- **Rule 1:** The number of addresses to be summarized must be a power of 2. For example, you can summarize 2, 4, 8, 16, 32, 64, 128 . . . networks.

- **Rule 2:** The beginning address of the address block to be summarized must be a multiple of the total number of addresses to be summarized.

Rule 1 is fairly straightforward, while Rule 2 is usually more confusing. Examining Figure 8.17, let's review another example of how summarization works. We have 20 networks to summarize. We immediately fail the first rule (20 is not a power of 2). Next, we separate out the 192.168.x.x networks from the 10.x.x.x networks and find that we have 16 and 4, respectively. By doing this we pass the first rule. Now we examine the starting range of each block that we want to summarize, 192.168.16.0 and 10.0.4.0, to see if we pass the second rule. The first block of addresses totals 16 (16–31 inclusively equals 16 networks) and the first address in the block is 192.168.**16**.0, which is a multiple of the total number of networks to be summarized. The second block of addresses totals 4 with the starting address 10.0.**8**.0 being a multiple of 4. We have passed both rules and therefore we can summarize these two address blocks.

To accomplish the summarization we need to determine how many bits to unmask (unsubnet) in order to make the networks appear as one big address block. We summarize the small address block using the long method and then show you a shortcut method to summarization using the larger address block. The following shows the binary values of the third octet in the four networks using the 10.x.x.x address range:

10.0.8.0   **000010**00

10.0.9.0   **000010**01

10.0.10.0   **000010**10

10.0.11.0   **000010**11

The left-most six bits in each address are identical, allowing us to peel back our network mask by two bits. Because we started with a 24-bit mask, eliminating two bits leaves a 22-bit mask. The summary address advertised by

TABLE 8.4   The Subnet Calculator

Bits Masked	1	2	3	4	5	6	7	8
Subnet interval	128	64	32	16	8	4	2	1
Decimal mask	128	192	224	240	248	252	254	255
Networks created	**2**	**4**	**8**	**16**	**32**	**64**	**128**	**256**

Router E to Router F is the beginning address of the block and the new network prefix, or 10.0.8.0 /22. The shortcut method of determining the summarization mask makes use of part of the subnet calculator that you learned in Chapter 7. The calculator is reprinted in Table 8.4.

The two lines that are important for this summarization shortcut are bolded to make them easier to follow. We need to summarize the block of 16 networks using the 192.168.16.0—192.168.31.0 address range. Using the shortcut method, slide from left to right on the calculator until you find the "networks created" value of 16, and then slide up the column to the bits masked. The value is 4. To get 16 networks, you mask 4 bits, so it stands to reason if you want to summarize 16 networks, you give 4 bits back (unmask them). Router E advertises a network of 192.168.16.0 /20 to Router F. This address lets Router F know that if the destination address of any frame matches the first 20 bits of 192.168.16.0, the frame should be forwarded to Router E.

TIP

Try using the shortcut on the 10.x.x.x address block. If you want to create four networks you mask two bits, so if you want to summarize four networks you unmask two bits. . . . It works, our answer matches the longhand method of summarization!

Because of summarization, Router F now only manages two routes to reach any network beyond Router E, 192.168.16.0 /20 and 10.0.8.0 /22. This reduces route processing time, memory and CPU use, route updates, and routing recalculations. One key point to be aware of when using summarization is that the routing protocol must transmit the network prefix along with the network address during route advertisements. This behavior is referred to as classless routing. RIP version 2 and OSPF both support classless routing and summarization. OSPF must be configured to use areas as summarization is accomplished on ABRs. BGP is also a classless routing protocol and generally only requires a single command to properly configure classless behavior.

8.6   Chapter Summary

- Routing is a process of forwarding frames based on a Layer 3 address. Routing is deployed to isolate broadcasts and create smaller, more manageable network segments.

- Routing requires two key pieces of information: a destination network address and at least one route (which can be just a default route).

- A routing table stores networks and associated interfaces for reaching those networks. Routing tables are built either dynamically or statically.

- The default gateway or default route is used when the destination address of a frame does not match any other entries in a routing table.

- The routing process involves stripping a frame of its Layer 2 header, performing a lookup in the route table using the Layer 3 destination address, ARPing for the next hop MAC address, and rebuilding the Layer 2 header with the next hop information.

- A Layer 3 address is used for end-to-end delivery of a frame, whereas Layer 2 addresses are used to forward a frame to the next hop.

- ARP is used extensively in TCP/IP networks and is a form of dynamic message exchange address resolution. ARP is used to map a known Layer 3 address to an unknown Layer 2 address, and RARP is used when the Layer 2 address is known and the Layer 3 address is needed. ARP data is cached in memory in an ARP table. The table entries can be dynamic or static.

- Routers use routing protocols to build routing tables and update other routers about the status of network routes.

- Routing protocols are classified as distance vector, link state, interior gateway, exterior gateway, classful, or classless.

- Distance vector protocols use broadcasts at specific intervals to send their entire routing tables to connected neighbors. The most common metric is hop count.

- Link state protocols use multicast frames only when changes occur to notify neighbors of a change in link status. Hello packets are used to verify communications capability, and the most common metric is bandwidth.

- Interior gateway protocols are used when all routers are under common administrative authority or in the same autonomous system.

- Exterior gateway protocols are used to connect different autonomous systems together, such as on the Internet.

- Border gateway protocol is the most common EGP and should be deployed only if needed and well understood.

- Routing hierarchies are built using addressing hierarchy and network summarization, which is the process of removing bits from the network prefix in order to make a collection of networks appear as one large network.

- The two rules of summarization require that (1) the number of networks to be summarized is a power of 2 and (2) the beginning network address must be a multiple of the total number of addresses.

8.7   Key Terms

area border router (ABR): An OSPF-configured router that borders more than one area.

ARP cache: A small portion of memory used on a client to store the ARP table.

ARP table: A table that maintains the association between an IP address and a corresponding MAC address.

autonomous system (AS): A collection of routers under common administrative authority or control.

autonomous system border router (ASBR): A router that borders an area not in the same autonomous system (usually the Internet).

backbone router: An OSPF router with at least one interface in the backbone (Area 0).

Boot Protocol (BootP): A protocol used to assign IP address and IP configuration information to IP hosts.

Border Gateway Protocol (BGP): An industry-standard EGP used to maintain routing tables for the Internet.

broadcast: A frame that has a Layer 2 MAC address of all Fs.

converged: The state at which all routers have a complete set of entries for the network.

convergence: The process of routing updates involved when a change occurs in the routing environment. Convergence can refer to the process or the time it takes to reach a converged state.

default gateway: An entry on a host or in a route table used when a destination address is unknown. Frames not matching any entries in the route table are forwarded to the default gateway.

default route: A routing table entry used when a destination address is unknown. Frames not matching any entries in the route table are forwarded to the next hop identified by the default route.

distance vector: A simple type of routing protocol whereby the basis for the best route decision is based on hop count.

Exterior Gateway Protocol (EGP): An early industry-standard exterior protocol replaced by BGP.

exterior gateway protocols (EGPs): A classification of protocols used to create and maintain routing tables and routing policy on the Internet.

hand-off point (hop): The next Layer 2 destination in an end-to-end Layer 3 communications path or route.

hold-down timer: A routing loop prevention mechanism that requires a router to disregard all route advertisements about an offline network until the hold-down timer expires.

hop: *See* hand-off point.

interior gateway protocols (IGPs): A family of protocols used to create and maintain routing tables and routing policy inside a company's network infrastructure.

link state: A complex type of routing protocol that uses advanced logic to determine the best path to a given network.

metric: The method or measurement used by a routing protocol to determine the best path to a given network.

Open Shortest Path First (OSPF): An industry-standard link state protocol.

poisoning: A routing loop prevention technique where the route metric is set above the allowed maximum in the route advertisement.

route summarization: The process of representing a block of networks using a single route advertisement.

Routing Information Protocol (RIP): An industry-standard distance vector routing protocol.

routing loop: A condition that occurs when routers get confused during update operations and cause frames to bounce back and forth between a set of interfaces.

routing table: A table stored in the memory of a router that associates a given destination network with an outbound interface.

split horizon: A routing loop prevention technique that requires a router to disregard route advertisements about locally propagated routes.

summarization: The process of removing network bits from the subnet mask until a collection of individual networks looks like one large network block (in binary format).

unicast: A frame addressed directly to a destination host.

8.8   Challenge Questions

8.1 How many route table entries to the network 192.168.1.0 /24 can a router hold?

a. 1

b. 2

c. 4

d. 8

e. It depends on the software and routing protocol in use on the router.

f. It depends on the amount of memory available on the router.

8.2 What is the purpose of the default gateway?

    a. All frames are forwarded to the default gateway.

    b. Frames are forwarded to the default gateway if the destination address does not match any other entries in the route table.

    c. Frames are forwarded to the default gateway after communications along the configured path fail.

    d. Frames are forwarded to the default gateway if the destination address does not match any other entries in the host table.

    e. Frames are forwarded to the default gateway if the source address does not match any other entries in the route table.

8.3 When resolving a Layer 3 TCP/IP address to a Layer 2 MAC, which of the following is used?

    a. RARP

    b. DNS

    c. ARP

    d. Default gateway

    e. Default route

8.4 Which of the following best describes convergence?

    a. The time it takes a router to develop its routing table

    b. The time it takes a router to develop a consistent routing table

    c. The time it takes a frame to get from source to destination

    d. The time it takes all routers to have a complete or common view of the network

    e. The time it takes a frame to get from source to destination and back

8.5 Which of the following are common characteristics of distance vector routing protocols? (Choose all that apply.)

    a. Uses hop count to determine best route

    b. Converges very fast on large networks

    c. Simple to configure

d. Uses periodic update intervals for route table advertisements

e. Only advertises changes to the network when they occur

8.6 Which of the following can be used to prevent routing loops? (Choose all that apply.)

a. Hold-down timers

b. Split horizon

c. Van Jacobsen algorithm

d. Triggered updates

e. Periodic updates

f. Poisoning

g. Route loop feedback detection

8.7 Which of the following best describes poisoning?

a. A router sets the metric of a route advertisement to below the minimum allowed setting.

b. A router sets a maximum metric limit for all downed routes.

c. A router disregards route advertisements from routers with known downed routes.

d. A router sets the metric of a route advertisement to above the maximum allowed setting.

e. A router sets a minimum metric limit for all downed routes.

8.8 What significant advantage does a link state protocol have over distance vector?

a. Simple, easy to configure

b. Uses more intelligent routing logic

c. Uses minimal CPU

d. Uses minimal memory

8.9 Which of the following best describes an IGP?

a. Used to maintain routes on the Internet

b. Capable of making complex decisions based on bandwidth

    c. Used to maintain routes on private networks

    d. Capable of making simple decisions based on hop count

8.10 By default, link state protocols base their routing decisions on what common metric?

    a. Bandwidth

    b. Hop count

    c. Total number of routers to destination

    d. Link delay

8.11 How often do link state routing protocols advertise their entire network tables?

    a. Every 30 seconds

    b. Every 60 seconds

    c. Only when changes occur

    d. Only when initializing a new neighbor router

8.12 When a change occurs on a network, how does a link state protocol notify its neighbors?

    a. Hello packet

    b. Triggered update

    c. Broadcast packet at the normal periodic route update interval

    d. Broadcast packet using a special triggered packet

8.13 Which of the following is an industry-standard distance vector IGP?

    a. BGP

    b. EGP

    c. OSPF

    d. RIP

8.14 Which of the following is most likely to be used by an ISP configuring network connections between autonomous systems?

    a. BGP

    b. EGP

c. OSPF

d. RIP

8.15 What is the purpose of an ABR?

a. It reduces the amount of network traffic.

b. It increases convergence time.

c. It reduces the amount of routing traffic.

d. It reduces the amount of broadcast traffic.

8.16 _____ is a classification for a complex family of routing protocols that allows routing policies to be set based on traffic type, link load, source address, destination address, or a combination.

a. EGP

b. IGP

c. Distance vector

d. Link state

e. Classless

f. Classful

8.17 What is the purpose of route summarization? (Choose all that apply.)

a. Reducing the speed of routing decisions

b. Reducing the size of routing tables

c. Reducing the time required to make routing decisions

d. Increasing the time required to make routing decisions

e. Increasing the memory required for routing decisions

8.18 What type of routing protocol must be used when using route summarization?

a. Hierarchical

b. Classful

c. Classless

    d. Link state

    e. Distance vector

    f. IGP

    g. EGP

8.19 Which of the following would *not* be a reason to use BGP?

    a. You have multiple connections to the Internet.

    b. You have a single connection to the Internet.

    c. You want to control traffic in and out of your AS.

    d. You control traffic to multiple AS networks across a shared backbone.

8.20 Which of the following best describes BGP?

    a. A distance vector IGP

    b. A link state IGP

    c. A distance vector EGP

    d. A link state EGP

    e. An advanced distance vector EGP

    f. An advanced link state EGP

8.21 What address and mask would you use to summarize only the following networks?

    192.168.4.0

    192.168.5.0

    192.168.6.0

    192.168.7.0

    a. 192.168.4.0 /20

    b. 192.168.4.0 /21

    c. 192.168.4.0 /22

    d. 192.168.4.0 /23

8.22 What address and mask would you use to best summarize the following networks?

172.16.8.0

172.16.9.0

172.16.12.0

172.16.14.0

172.16.15.0

a. 172.16.0.0 /16

b. 172.16.0.0 /20

c. 172.16.8.0 /20

d. 172.16.8.0 /21

e. 172.16.8.0 /22

f. 172.06.8.0 /23

8.23 What method does BGP use for routing loop prevention?

a. Poisoning

b. Split horizon

c. Hold-down timers

d. AS path

e. TCP sessions

f. Neighbor statements

8.24 What step is associated with route summarization?

a. Decreasing the length of the network mask

b. Increasing the length of the network mask

c. Summarizing only an even number of networks

d. Summarizing only an odd number of networks

8.25 If a routing protocol advertises routes without the network prefix, the protocol is _____?

a. Classless

b. Classful

c. Distance vector

    d. Link state

    e. IGP

    f. EGP

8.9   Challenge Exercises

Challenge Exercise 8.1

In this exercise, you review the routing table configuration of your computer system. You need a computer running Windows 2000 or Windows XP Professional, the TCP/IP protocol installed and properly configured, and access to the Internet.

8.1 Log on to your computer and connect to the Internet.

8.2 To open a command prompt window, click **Start**, click **Run**, type **cmd** in the Open text box, and press **Enter**.

8.3 At the command prompt, type **route print** and press **Enter**.

8.4 Analyze and identify as many components of your routing table as possible.

Challenge Exercise 8.2

Using the routing table in Figure 8.18, answer the following questions:

8.1 Which line represents the all-networks broadcast routing entry?

8.2 Which line identifies the route that is used if a destination address of a frame does not match other routes in the table?

8.3 Which line represents the all-subnet broadcast address for the 192.168.0.0 network?

8.4 What is the purpose of the 127.0.0.1 route table entry?

Challenge Exercise 8.3

Summarize the following three blocks of network addresses:

8.1 192.168.32.0–192.168.63.0

8.2 172.16.0.0–172.31.0.0

8.3 10.1.128.0–10.1.255.0

```
     Active Routes:
     Network Destination              Netmask            Gateway
     Interface
1)   0.0.0.0          0.0.0.0         27.234.145.247     27.234.145.247
2)   27.234.128.10    255.255.255.255 27.234.145.247     27.234.145.247
3)   27.234.145.247   255.255.255.255 127.0.0.1          127.0.0.1
4)   27.255.255.255   255.255.255.255 27.234.145.247     27.234.145.247
5)   127.0.0.0        255.0.0.0       127.0.0.1          127.0.0.1
6)   192.168.0.0      255.255.255.0   192.168.0.1        192.168.0.1
7)   192.168.0.1      255.255.255.255 127.0.0.1          127.0.0.1
8)   192.168.0.255    255.255.255.255 192.168.0.1        192.168.0.1
9)   224.0.0.0        240.0.0.0       192.168.0.1        192.168.0.1
10)  224.0.0.0        240.0.0.0       27.234.145.247     27.234.145.247
11)  255.255.255.255  255.255.255.255 192.168.0.1        192.168.0.1

12)  Default Gateway: 27.234.145.247

13)  Persistent Routes:
14)  None
```

Figure 8.18
Routing table

8.10 Challenge Scenarios

Challenge Scenario 8.1

You are the network administrator for a small firm with eight sites and 1,600 employees. You currently manage the network infrastructure and are migrating from static to dynamic routing. You have been asked to identify the routing protocol and configuration for the new network design. Each of the eight sites has 200 employees configured on a single LAN segment, and all sites are connected back to a central office at the corporate headquarters office in Seattle. Each site also maintains a single IP subnet with clients receiving their IP addresses through DHCP. Each office is a separate subsidiary and has its own server systems for Web services and its own connection to the Internet. In the past, issues have come up concerning network traffic taking suboptimal paths through the corporate network out onto the Internet. Management wants the new network configuration to be able to control traffic into and out of the corporate network as well as route around a link failure at any of the sites.

Using this scenario, answer the following questions:

8.1 What routing protocol would you recommend for the internal network?

8.2 What strategy would you recommend for routing to and from the Internet?

8.3 Given the constraints imposed by management, would static routing to the Internet be sufficient?

8.4 Does your new design require a reconfiguration of the current IP addressing configuration?

8.5 Could a routing hierarchy be developed and deployed?

Challenge Scenario 8.2

You have been hired to design and administer the network infrastructure for a new import/export company. Current plans include the development of over 150 sites worldwide with regional offices in North America, Europe, Asia, Australia, South America, and Africa. The total number of employees is currently 1,000. Because of security, all Internet traffic will enter or exit the company through a single T3 line in the headquarters office in Sydney, Australia. All of the smaller sites on each continent will connect with a variety of speeds to the regional offices, with the regional offices connecting back to the corporate office over a T1 link. Because WAN links in some areas of proposed development are unreliable, management wants to be capable of routing around problems and isolating issues from other sections of the network.

Using this scenario, answer the following questions:

8.1 What routing protocol would you recommend for the internal network?

8.2 How would you configure the network to help route around problems and isolate issues from the rest of the network?

8.3 What strategy would you recommend for routing to and from the Internet?

8.4 Could a routing hierarchy be developed and deployed?

CHAPTER 9

Network Services and Applications

After reading this chapter you will be able to:

- Use the various Application layer services and protocols
- Determine how domain names are resolved
- Identify the different e-mail formats
- Understand how Web browsers and Web pages work
- Understand the function of middleware

So far we have worked our way up the OSI model through the protocols and devices that operate at just about every layer. You have learned how IP addressing works and how packets get routed between networks. Now it's time to move to the Application, or top, layer services and protocols.

Almost all companies have Internet connectivity and a variety of devices connecting to their network, such as personal digital assistants (PDAs) and IP phones. Security and productivity are top issues, so many companies also use global positioning satellites (GPSs) to track their employees. They may also use digital surveillance. As a network administrator, you will need to know how to manage and support these devices. In this chapter, we will learn how TCP/IP networks provide these and other services, as well as what protocols each of these services relies upon.

9.1   Understanding Network Services

The Application, or top, layer of the OSI reference model allows access to network services such as file transfers, message handling, and database query processing. The Application layer enables commercial software to use these network services. Because the Application layer is the user interface, it is important to understand how these services work and how to troubleshoot problems. Today's multi-tier applications follow a more complex path across enterprise infrastructure than did early client/server applications.

9.1.1   Services Defined

Services help the operating system and applications communicate with each other. One of the most important services is the naming service, which associates names with values in a system. Later in the chapter we discuss Domain Name System (DNS). When using a naming service, clients can query a value using names. This name-to-value association is called a name binding. Name bindings are defined in relation to a *context*, which is a collection that contains a set of name bindings in which each name is unique. A name is always bound relative to a context. This concept is also used in directory services in NetWare and Microsoft operating systems. The directory service allows computers to find an object via a name and context. Directory services are discussed in Chapter 11.

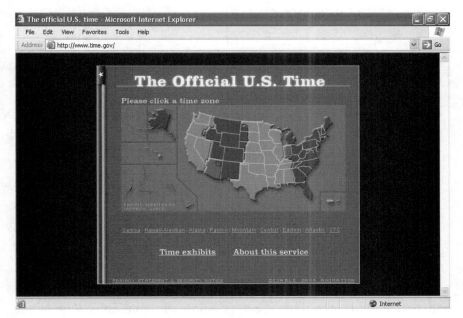

Figure 9.1
Time service Web site

A time service provides accurate, fault-tolerant clock synchronization for computers connected in local area networks and wide area networks. Synchronized time services are important in systems that require multiple hosts to maintain accurate global time. The Network Time Protocol is used to synchronize the computer clocks on the network. It is an Application layer protocol that communicates over User Datagram Protocol (UDP). It is critical that all clocks be in unison because many packets have predetermined periods of time in which to reach their destination before they expire. This allows events to be tracked and logged properly. Figure 9.1 shows an example of a time service Web site. Two other Web sites that offer time-related services are *http://tycho.usno.navy.mil/frtime.html* and *http://www.boulder.nist.gov/timefreq/service/its.htm*.

These are just two examples of the services that run on TCP/IP networks. In the next section we will go a bit further into services and protocols. Remember from Chapter 6 that connections are determined by the IP addresses and the socket numbers of computers trying to communicate. In

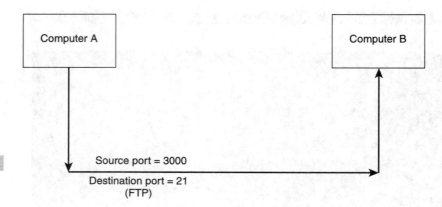

Figure 9.2

Establishing sessions with a destination port

order to establish a connection, a machine needs to know the IP address and port number on which the application communicates. One of the main functions of TCP and UDP is to be a port manager for the applications and services that are in the top layer. The destination port number is placed in the header and is used to pass traffic to the correct application.

There are 65,535 ports that can be accessed on a computer. The well-known ports are those from 0 through 1023. Internet Assigned Numbers Authority (IANA) assigns the numbers, which can be used only by system processes. Ports 1024 through 49151 are registered, and ports 49152 through 65535 are dynamic or private. Because the first 1,023 ports are reserved for system services, outgoing requests will usually come from port numbers higher than 1023. See Figure 9.2 for an example. Incoming connections communicate on the well-known ports that are listening for particular services controlled by system processes or service daemons.

These processes are handled either by the registry on Windows systems or the Internet Servers Database (inetd) daemon on Unix systems. Inetd is a control process that handles network services operating on a Unix system. The Windows registry is comparable to the inetd daemon, where all programs store their initialization and configuration settings. Unix systems use the inetd.conf file to configure service activation, including File Transfer Protocol (FTP), Telnet, and rlogin.

9.1.2   Services and Related Protocols

Due to the number of ports used for system services, quite a few services can run simultaneously. Some additional application services provided through TCP/IP are Telnet, FTP, Simple Mail Transfer Protocol (SMTP), and Simple Network Management Protocol (SNMP). Before we delve into these protocols, Table 9.1 shows the most common port numbers along with the services and protocols that operate on them. Many more ports and services exist but are not listed here.

9.2   File Transfer Protocol (FTP)

File Transfer Protocol (FTP) allows a person to transfer files between two computers, usually a client and a server site, while being connected to the Internet. The FTP server maintains the file security and transfer control. The client—which can be run from a command-line prompt, be built into the browser, or be a specialized program—receives the files and places them onto the local hard drive. Essentially, FTP makes it possible to move one or more files between computers with security and data integrity controls appropriate for the Internet.

FTP is a TCP-based service that utilizes two ports, a data port and a control port. Traditionally these are port 21 for the command port and port 20 for the data port. FTP has two modes, active and passive. In active mode, the FTP client connects from a random unprivileged port to the FTP server's command port (port 21). Then the client starts listening and sends the port command to the FTP server. The server then connects back to the client's specified data port from its data port (port 20). In active mode, the FTP client doesn't make the actual connection to the data port of the server; instead, it simply states what port it is listening on and the server connects to the specified port on the client. In passive mode, the client initiates all connections to the server. The client opens two random unprivileged ports locally. The first port contacts the server on port 21, but instead of issuing a port command and allowing the server to connect to its data port, the client will issue a pasv command. The server opens a random unprivileged port and sends the port p command to the client. The client then initiates the connection from the second port to port p on the server to transfer

TABLE 9.1   Common Port Numbers and Corresponding Services and Protocols

Port	Service or Protocol	Description
7	Echo	Allows return replies for network connectivity tests such as Ping
11	Systat	A Unix server function that allows remote access to the listing of running processes
15	Netstat	Allows the status display of active network connections
19	Chargen	Generates a stream of characters for testing
20, 21	FTP	Allows file transfers—port 20 is used for data; port 21 is used for control
23	Telnet	Provides access to and administration of a remote computer over the Internet or the network
25	SMTP	Allows mail transfers among servers
37	Time	Allows for time synchronization
42	NameServ	Supports Microsoft WINS directory replication
53	Domain	Used by the Domain Name System
67, 68	Bootps, Bootpc	Used to automatically configure system settings; this is an older version of DHCP—Bootps is the server protocol and Bootpc is the client protocol
69	TFTP (Trivial File Transfer Protocol)	Allows file transfers
79	Finger	Reveals detailed information about users
80	HTTP (Hypertext Transfer Protocol)	Permits active Web server communication
110	POP3	Allows mail transfers from servers to clients
111	Portmap	Allows Remote Procedure Call (RPC) client programs to make remote connections to RPC servers
119	NNTP (Network News Transfer Protocol)	Used for newsgroups
137, 138, 139	NetBIOS-ns, dgm, ssn	Allows the NetBIOS Name Service (used to resolve IP addresses to NetBIOS names), Datagram Service (used for local communication), and Session Service (used for file and print sharing) to communicate on Microsoft networks
160, 161, 162	SNMP (Simple Network Management Protocol)	Used for SNMP trapping

data. This is useful when trying to provide FTP connections through fire-walls. Most browsers only support passive mode.

To open an FTP connection, type FTP at a command prompt. When the ftp prompt appears, you can open a connection. The following are the most common commands for FTP:

- **ascii:** Used for transferring text files. Most FTP hosts store in binary as well as ASCII formats. ASCII mode is the default mode.

- **binary:** Switches to binary mode, which may be used for transferring binary files such as Zip files.

- **bye:** Closes the FTP connection.

- **cd:** Changes the working directory on the remote computer.

- **delete:** Deletes a file on the host computer.

- **dir:** Lists the files in the current directory on the remote computer.

- **get:** Copies a file from the remote computer to the local computer.

- **help:** Displays help on the use of commands within the FTP program.

- **ls:** Same as dir, but shows more limited information in the directory listings.

- **lcd:** Changes the directory on the local computer.

- **lpwd:** Shows the present working directory (pwd) on the local computer. This may not work on all computers. On a Unix machine, try !pwd.

- **mget:** Copies multiple files from the remote computer to the local computer.

- **mkdir:** Creates a new directory on the remote computer.

- **mput:** Copies multiple files from the local computer to the remote computer.

- **open:** Opens a connection with a remote computer.

- **put:** Copies a file from the remote computer to the local computer.

- **pwd:** Shows the present working directory (pwd) on the remote computer.

- **quit:** Ends the FTP session and closes the utility.

Figure 9.3
FTP connection

Usually, FTP lists the commands if you type "help" or "?". Your computer's help command may also have information about FTP. In Linux, type "man ftp" or "man ftpd". To connect to Microsoft's FTP server, for example, type "open ftp.microsoft.com" (see Figure 9.3).

When you have an open connection, you must supply a logon name and password. However, many sites offer files through anonymous FTP, which means that you can access a computer without needing to have an account on the remote computer. You simply type in the word "anonymous" as the logon prompt. These anonymous FTP servers are usually used for software updates, configuration files, pictures, music, and, of course, document files.

Although you can use FTP with your Web browser or through a command-line prompt, FTP client programs such as Fetch, Cute FTP, and WS_FTP also are available for transferring and managing files.

TRICKLE provides an alternative to FTP. It distributes files upon request or by subscription. You send commands in the text of an e-mail message, one command per line. If you subscribe to a directory, you will receive a list of files that have been added to it. If you subscribe to a file, TRICKLE will send you a new version of the file as soon as it is available on its FTP site.

9.3 Telnet

Telecommunications Network or **Telnet** is a protocol that provides a way for clients to connect to servers on the Internet. It was one of the Internet's first tools, created to work across a broad range of platforms and displays. It is the standard Internet application protocol for remote logon. The Telnet application is built over TCP/IP and provides a local computer with the means to emulate a terminal session compatible with a remote computer. It allows the user to create a connection and send commands and instruc-

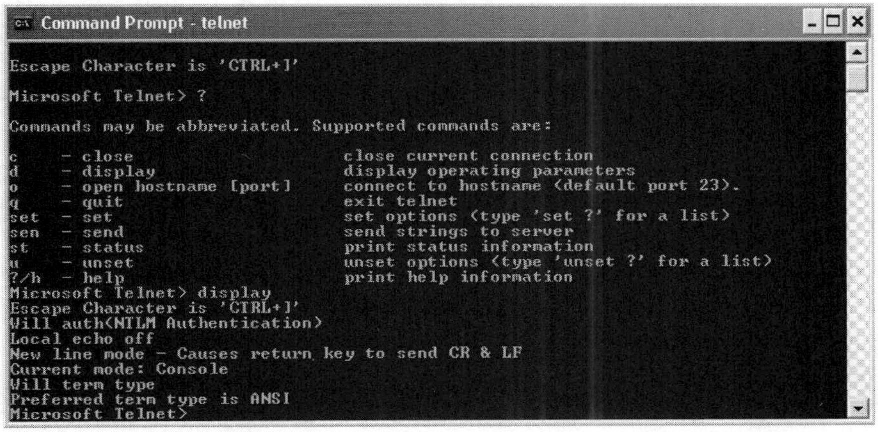

Figure 9.4
Telnet commands

tions interactively to the remote computer. The local system looks, to the user, just like the remote computer. The commands typed by the user are transmitted to the remote computer and the response is then displayed on the user's screen.

To start a Telnet session, you must log on to a server by entering a valid user name and password. The Telnet command is similar to the FTP command. The user name you use to access the system determines what actions you can perform. Telnet has no graphical user interface (GUI). It's all ASCII and command-line typing, so you'll need to learn the menu commands. Programs can be run on the remote system to let you access files, including e-mail programs such as Pine, Elm, and Mail or common editors such as Pico, VI, and EMACS. When accessing public Telnet sites, be sure to read and follow instructions because each Telnet site may have a different menu system or set of commands. Try typing "help" or "?" at the Telnet prompt to get a list of the commands available in the Telnet software. See Figure 9.4 for an example of a Telnet session.

When you have established a remote session, all commands you type will be sent to the remote host for execution. If you want a Telnet command issued in the remote environment to be executed locally, on most systems you precede the command with an escape sequence. The escape sequence for the version of Telnet running in Figure 9.4 is the Control key (CTRL) and right bracket (]) pressed simultaneously.

The Telnet TCP connection is established between a random unprivileged port on the client and port 23 on the server. Because a TCP connection is full-duplex and identified by the pair of ports, the server can engage in many simultaneous connections involving its port 23 and different random unprivileged ports on the client. Telnet's normal data stream, Network Virtual Terminal (NVT) mode, is 7-bit ASCII with escape sequences to embed control functions. Communication is based on a set of terminal characteristics and sequences that both sides agree to use to transmit data from terminals across the network, regardless of the terminal used. The Telnet client program maps incoming NVT codes to the actual codes needed to operate the display device and maps user-generated keyboard sequences into NVT sequences. NVT uses 7-bit codes for characters. The display device is required to display only the standard printing ASCII characters represented by 7-bit codes and to recognize and process certain control codes. The 7-bit characters are transmitted as 8-bit bytes, with the most significant bit set to 0. NVT is capable of generating 128 ASCII codes through keys, key combinations, and key sequences. A variety of options also can be negotiated between a Telnet client and server using commands at any stage during the connection. NVT ASCII also is used by many other Internet protocols such as FTP and TFTP.

9.4   Trivial File Transfer Protocol (TFTP)

Trivial File Transfer Protocol (TFTP) is a simple form of the File Transfer Protocol that uses the UDP. It is often used for booting or loading programs on diskless workstations. Because it uses UDP, it does not guarantee delivery and provides no security features. TFTP provides its own reliable delivery using a simple stop-and-wait acknowledgment system. When a client issues a read or write request to the remote host, the host responds with an acknowledgment before any data is transferred. Its services run at port 69.

TFTP does not require a user logon, but instead issues read and write requests to the remote computer. In order for files to be transferred, they must have full read and write privileges, so sensitive data should never be sent using TFTP. The TFTP file interface is very simple, providing no access control or security. TFTP commands do not provide the ability to list remote files or change directories at the remote host, and only limited file access privileges are given to the remote TFTP server. The following is a list of common TFTP commands:

- **?:** Displays help information. If a subcommand parameter is specified, only information about that subcommand is displayed.

- **ascii:** Switches to ASCII mode.

- **binary:** Switches to binary mode.

- **connect:** Connects to the remote host, and optionally the port, for file transfers.

- **get:** Copies a file or set of files from the remote host to the local machine.

- **mode:** Sets the type of transfer mode to either ASCII or binary. ASCII is the default.

- **put:** Puts a file or set of files from the local host onto the remote host.

- **quit:** Exits the TFTP session.

- **status:** Shows the current status of the TFTP program including the current transfer mode connection status and time-out value.

- **timeout value:** Sets the total transmission time to the number of seconds specified.

- **trace:** Turns packet tracing on or off.

- **verbose:** Sets verbose mode, which displays additional information during file transfer, on or off.

TFTP's most important application is bootstrapping a host over a local network. Because it is such a simple protocol, it can be implemented within the firmware on network devices that do not contain hard drives. It is often used in conjunction with BOOTP, which will be discussed in the "Dynamic Host Configuration Protocol (DHCP)" section later in this chapter.

9.5   Domain Name System (DNS)

If we had to remember the IP addresses of all of the Web sites we visit every day, what would we do? Human beings are much better at remembering words than remembering strings of numbers. The **Domain Name System**

(DNS) helps us by resolving the names we type into a Web browser to a proper network address. Originally, Internet host name translation was done by searching a table of host files on the local computer.

NOTE On Linux-based computers the host file is called HOSTS. On Windows computers, it is called LMHOSTS if resolving NetBIOS names to IP addresses; if it resolves DNS names to IP addresses, it is called HOSTS.

Paul Mockapetris designed DNS in 1984 to solve the escalating problems with the old mapping system. DNS is a distributed database, which means it lives on many different servers with no one server storing all the information. DNS is most commonly used by applications to translate domain names of hosts to IP addresses.

DNS consists of name servers and resolvers. Domain name servers store authoritative data about sections of a distributed database and respond to browser requests by supplying name-to-address conversions. A DNS client is called a resolver. Domain resolvers query domain name servers for name resolution on behalf of user processes. Resolvers are typically located in the Application layer of the networking software of each TCP/IP-enabled computer.

There are several implementations of DNS; one of the more popular is called Berkeley Internet Name Domain (BIND). BIND is an Internet name server for Unix operating systems whose development is funded by the Internet Software Consortium. It also consists of a server and a resolver library. BIND source code is freely available, and the resolver library in the distribution provides the standard application program interfaces (APIs) for translation between domain names and Internet addresses. BIND has been ported to Windows and VMS, but it is most often found on Unix machines. Because most of the development on the DNS protocols is based on this code, the BIND name server is the most widely used on the Internet.

NOTE DNS is sometimes referred to as Domain Name Service or Domain Name Server.

9.5.1   DNS Server Hierarchy

Having a basic understanding of how DNS works is important for administering an Internet-connected network successfully. We first look at the hierarchy of Internet host names. The last portion of a host name, such as .com, is the top-level domain to which the host belongs. There are seven original top-level domains assigned by the Internet Network Information Center (InterNIC), the coordinating body for Internet name services. InterNIC was formed in 1993 to handle domain name registrations. It makes the rules, administers the registration process, and maintains the official database of registered domain names. The original seven top-level domain names are as follows:

- **.com:** Introduced in 1995, it is unrestricted but intended for commercial registrants.
- **.edu:** Introduced in 1995 for use by United States educational institutions.
- **.gov:** Introduced in 1995 for use by the United States government.
- **.int:** Introduced in 1998 for use by organizations established by international treaties between governments.
- **.mil:** Introduced in 1995 for use by the United States military.
- **.net:** Introduced in 1995, it is unrestricted but intended for network providers.
- **.org:** Introduced in 1995, it is unrestricted but intended for organizations that do not fit elsewhere.

Top-level domains with two letters, such as .us, .uk, and .jp, have been established for over 240 countries and external territories. These are referred to as country-code top-level domains (ccTLDs). In 2001, the following additional top-level domains were introduced:

- **.aero:** For the air-transport industry
- **.biz:** For businesses
- **.coop:** For cooperatives
- **.info:** For all uses
- **.museum:** For museums
- **.name:** For individuals

The .pro extension was introduced in 2002 and is available exclusively for professionals, initially, doctors, lawyers, and CPAs. In order to be eligible

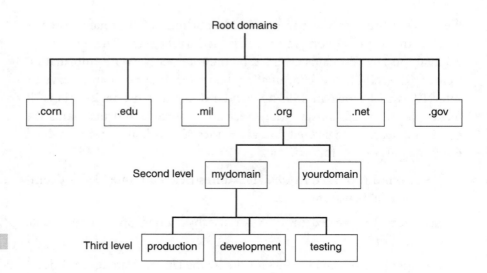

Figure 9.5
DNS hierarchy

for a .pro domain name, professionals must certify that they are professionals and that they meet the requirements in their jurisdiction. The information provided is verified against appropriate state, local, or professional licensing databases. These measures are designed to enforce the .pro domain name eligibility restrictions, something that no other top-level domain has done to date.

Within every top-level domain there is a second-level domain, such as *novell.com*. Every name in the .com top-level domain must be unique, but there can be duplication across domains. For example, *novell.com* and *novell.org* are completely different. *Development.novell.com* is a third-level domain. The leftmost word is the host name, which specifies the name of a specific machine in a domain. See Figure 9.5 for an example. The fully qualified domain name (FQDN) consists of the host name appended to the computer's domain. For example, a computer called mycomputer in the domain.com domain would have an FQDN of *mycomputer.domain.com*. A given domain can possibly contain millions of host names as long as they are all unique within that domain.

TIP Domain names can contain up to 127 levels, although more than four is not very common. The more levels, the harder it is for users to remember.

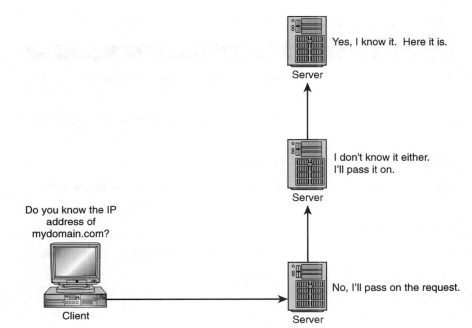

Server

Yes, I know it. Here it is.

Server

I don't know it either.
I'll pass it on.

Do you know the IP
address of
mydomain.com?

No, I'll pass on the request.

Client

Server

Figure 9.6
DNS name resolution

9.5.2   Structure of DNS Database Records

When you type in *www.yahoo.com*, the browser sends a request to the clos-est name server. If that server has ever had a request for *www.yahoo.com*, it will locate the information in its cache and reply. Name servers do not have complete information, so often it is necessary to obtain information from more than one server to resolve a query. If the name server is unfamiliar with the domain name, the resolver will ask a server further up the tree. If that doesn't work, the second server will ask yet another and another until it finds one that knows. After the information is located, it's passed back to your browser. See Figure 9.6 for an example.

At the top of the DNS database tree are root name servers, which contain pointer records to master name servers for each of the top-level domains. The master name servers contain a record and name server address for each domain name. So in trying to locate the IP address of *www.yahoo.com*, the DNS server asks the .com server for the name of the server that handles the yahoo.com domain. The DNS server then asks the yahoo.com server for the name of the server that handles the yahoo.com domain. The name server

TABLE 9.2   DNS Resource Records

Record Type	Description
SOA (Start of Authority)	The first record created in a zone database. It defines the name server that has authority for the zone.
A	Contains host address records that matched a host name to an IP address.
NS (Name Server)	Identifies other name servers.
CNAME (Canonical Name)	An alias for host names. CNAMEs allow the association of more than one host name with the same IP address.
MX (Mail Exchange)	Identifies mail routing servers.
PTR (Pointer)	Used for IP address to name resolution in reverse lookup zones.
WINS (Windows Internet Name Service)	Used to identify WINS servers.

supplies the DNS server with the IP address of the machine called *www.yahoo.com.*

Each name server manages a group of records called a zone. Zones are set up to help resolve names more easily and for replication purposes. DNS zones specify the domain name boundary in which a DNS server has authority to perform name translations. Each zone contains records that specify how to resolve the host names associated with the zone. Depending on the operating system used, the zone types can be primary and secondary or master and slave. Each of these types may then be either a forward zone, which maps names to addresses, or a reverse zone, which maps addresses to names. When a zone is set up you can enter records. Table 9.2 contains a list of the types of resource records contained in the DNS database.

The .arpa domain is used for reverse name resolution. Normally you type the Web site that you want to access into your Web browser. What happens when you know an IP address and want to find out what name goes with it? The .arpa domain maintains a reverse list of IP addresses to Internet addresses.

WARNING ▮

The IP addresses in the .arpa domain are listed in reverse order. Keep this in mind when configuring a DNS server. If your IP address is 202.216.185.95, it will be listed as 95.185.216.202.

You can either administer your own DNS servers or have an Internet service provider (ISP) do it for you. Both methods have advantages and disadvantages. If you choose to administer the primary name server yourself, you'll have to maintain the DNS records. Depending on the operating system used, you may be able to implement dynamic updates, which can certainly save on administrative work.

9.6   Dynamic Host Configuration Protocol (DHCP)

Dynamic Host Configuration Protocol (DHCP) was created by the Dynamic Host Configuration Working Group of the Internet Engineering Task Force (IETF), an organization that defines protocols for use on the Internet. DHCP provides a framework for passing configuration information to hosts or clients in a TCP/IP environment. It enables individual computers to automatically obtain their network configurations from a server rather than be manually configured. This reduces administrative overhead and configuration errors. DHCP is an extension of the Bootstrap Protocol (BOOTP), the previous IP allocation specification. There are two primary differences between DHCP and BOOTP. First, DHCP has capabilities for assigning clients a network address for a fixed period of time, allowing for reassignment of network addresses to different clients. Second, DHCP provides the means for a client to acquire all of the IP configuration parameters that it needs in order to operate. BOOTP allows only two types of messages, request and reply, whereas DHCP has seven possible message types that can be used during the address assignment sequence. Figures 9.7 and 9.8 show the differences between the two message formats. The numbers in parentheses indicate the number of bits allocated to each field.

The most important piece of data distributed by DHCP is the IP address. DHCP supports three methods of IP address allocation: manual, automatic, and dynamic. In manual allocation, DHCP relays a manually assigned address to the host. In automatic allocation, DHCP assigns a permanent IP address to a client. In dynamic allocation, DHCP assigns an IP address to a host for a limited period of time. Dynamic addressing simplifies network administration because the IP addresses are tracked by the software rather than an administrator. This means that a new computer can be added to a network with little administrative effort. It is the only one of the three methods that allows the server to automatically reuse an address that is no longer needed, and is especially useful for assigning an address to a client that will be connected to the network temporarily. This

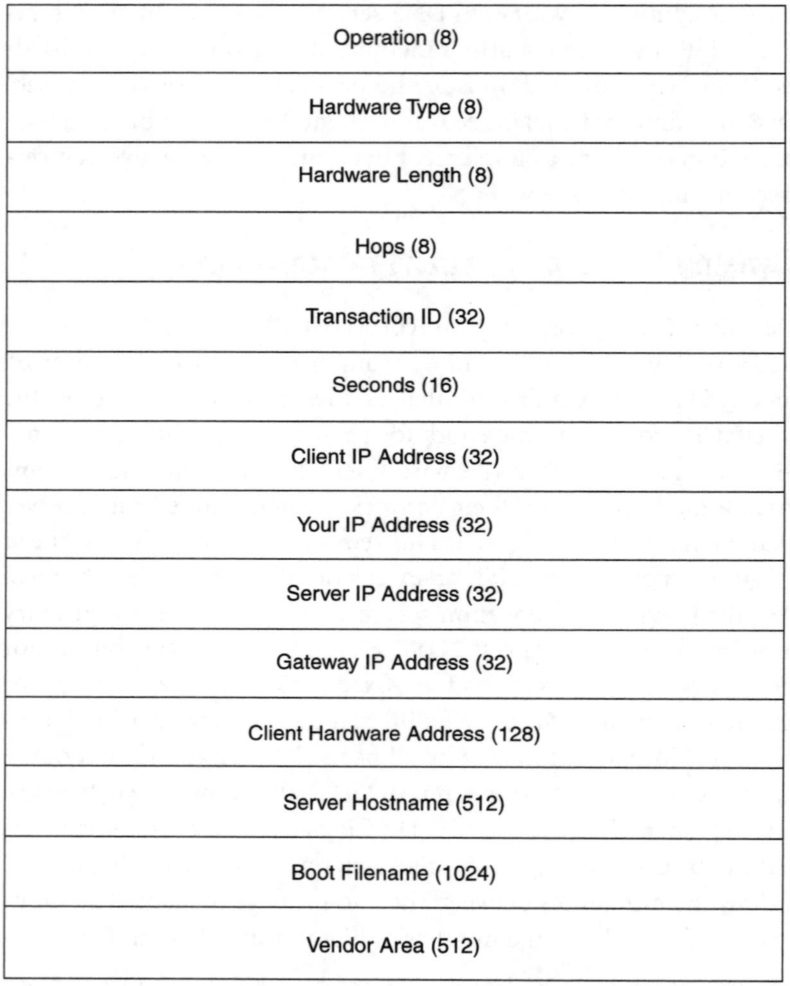

Operation (8)
Hardware Type (8)
Hardware Length (8)
Hops (8)
Transaction ID (32)
Seconds (16)
Client IP Address (32)
Your IP Address (32)
Server IP Address (32)
Gateway IP Address (32)
Client Hardware Address (128)
Server Hostname (512)
Boot Filename (1024)
Vendor Area (512)

Figure 9.7
BOOTP message fields

is a common situation for ISPs: All users are dynamically assigned an address when they connect for service. This type of addressing is also used for sharing a limited pool of IP addresses among a group of clients who do not need permanent IP addresses, such as contract employees, or for situations in which IP addresses are scarce and it is necessary to reuse them when they are no longer needed by a client. Server-based allocation eliminates the errors that may occur when manually configuring clients in environments in companies that have decided, for whatever reasons, to manage

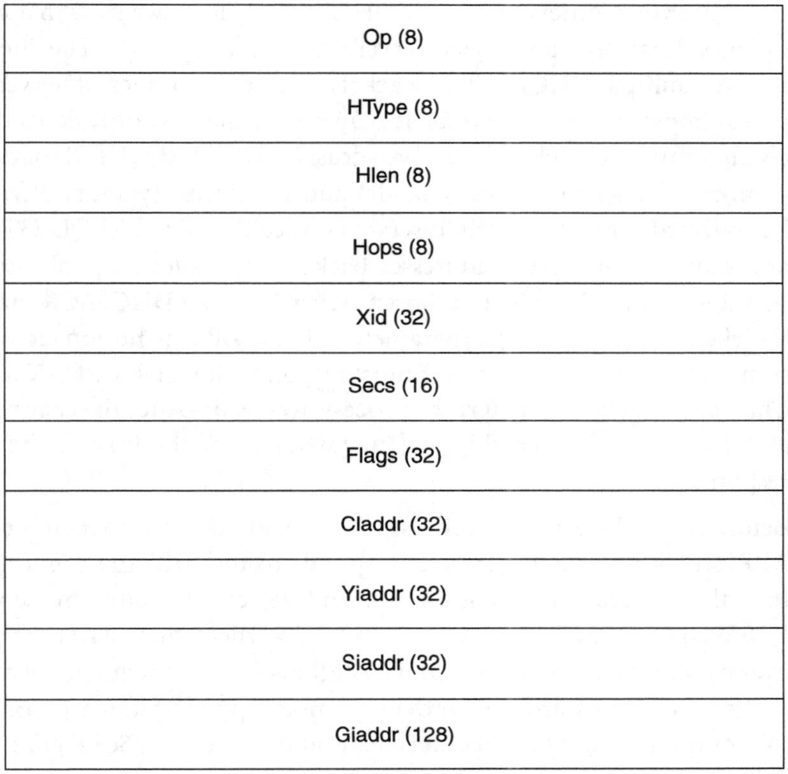

Op (8)
HType (8)
Hlen (8)
Hops (8)
Xid (32)
Secs (16)
Flags (32)
Claddr (32)
Yiaddr (32)
Siaddr (32)
Giaddr (128)

Figure 9.8
DHCP message fields

IP address assignment outside of DHCP. Networks can use one or more of these methods, depending on network administration policies.

> **WARNING**
>
> DHCP is not supported by all operating systems; it works only with TCP/IP. It does not work with AppleTalk or Internetwork Packet Exchange/Sequenced Packet Exchange (IPX/SPX) because it is tied to IP. These protocols have no need for DHCP because they have their own automated mechanisms for assigning network addresses.

When a DHCP device attaches itself to the network for the first time, it broadcasts a DHCPDISCOVER packet using UDP on port 67. All DHCP servers on the local segment see the broadcast and then broadcast a DHCPOFFER packet, on port 68, that contains proper configuration for the client based on parameters that are specified on the DHCP server. If your network does not have a DHCP server on every segment, you need to configure your routers to provide DHCP/BOOTP relay agents that forward the broadcasts to a predefined server on remote segments. The client may receive multiple DHCPOFFER packets from any number of servers, so it must choose between them, or it may accept the first one, depending on configuration. The client then broadcasts a DHCPREQUEST packet that identifies the server address (siaddr) and IP address (yiaddr) offer that it has selected. The other DHCP servers notice the DHCPREQUEST packet and return their offered addresses back to their address pool. Assuming that the offer is still valid, the chosen server returns a DHCPACK that sends the client all the requested parameters. If the offer is no longer valid for some reason, the selected server must respond with a DHCPNAK message. This causes the client to start the process over again. After the client receives a DHCPACK, all ownership and maintenance of the lease is the client's responsibility.

Before using the assigned address, clients should test it by conducting an ARP broadcast. If another node responds to the ARP, the client assumes that the offered address is in use and rejects the offer by sending a DHCPDECLINE message to the server. The client then starts the process over by sending a new DHCPDISCOVER packet. This sequence of events is pretty straightforward and provides ample opportunities to correct any miscommunication between the clients and the servers. See Figure 9.9 and Table 9.3 for a recap.

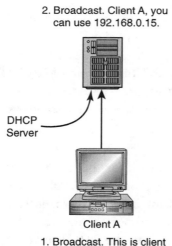

Figure 9.9
DHCP process

2. Broadcast. Client A, you can use 192.168.0.15.

4. Broadcast. Client A has IP address 192.168.0.15.

DHCP Server

DHCP Server

Client A

Client A

1. Broadcast. This is client A. I need an IP address.

3. Broadcast. This is client A. I'll take 192.168.0.15.

TABLE 9.3   DHCP Message

DHCP Message	Meaning
DHCPDISCOVER	Broadcast by the client to locate available servers.
DHCPOFFER	Servers respond to client with offer of configuration parameters.
DHCPREQUEST	Client broadcasts to servers requesting offered lease from one server, thereby implicitly declining offers from the others.
DHCPACK	Server gives client configuration parameters, including committed IP address.
DHCPNAK	Server refuses request for configuration parameters. The requested network address is already allocated.
DHCPDECLINE	Client indicates to server that the network address is invalid.
DHCPRELEASE	Client relinquishes network address to server and cancels remaining lease.
DHCPINFORM	Windows message used by clients to obtain local configuration options.

When the client has the lease, it must be renewed prior to expiration through another DHCPREQUEST message. Generally, a client attempts to renew its lease halfway through the lease process. If a client finishes using a lease prior to its expiration date, the client sends a DHCPRELEASE message to the server so that the lease can be added back to the address pool. If the server doesn't receive a lease renewal request from the client by the end of the lease period, it marks the lease as not renewed and makes it available for use by other clients.

 TIP

The amount of time assigned for a client to hold a lease depends on your goals, your patterns of use, and how you service the DHCP server.

9.7   Simple Network Management Protocol (SNMP)

Simple Network Management Protocol (SNMP) is part of the TCP/IP protocol suite and was developed in the 1980s as a solution to network management requirements arising from growing network infrastructures.

It is an Application layer protocol that is used to exchange management information between network devices. SNMP enables network administrators to manage network performance, find and solve network problems, and plan for network growth. SNMP management infrastructure consists of three main components:

- **SNMP managed node:** Any network-enabled device running an SNMP agent. Managed devices, sometimes called network elements, can be routers and access servers, switches, routers, hubs, computer hosts, or printers.

- **SNMP agent:** Stores and retrieves device-specific information from its management information base (MIB). The SNMP agent is a software module that resides in a managed device and interacts with the SNMP network management station to supply warning information and set thresholds received from the management station.

- **SNMP network management station (NMS):** An NMS executes applications that monitor and control managed devices. It displays a list of warnings and errors reported by the agents, allows configuration control, and provides statistical information on network operations.

Figure 9.10 shows the relationships among these components.

Three versions of SNMP exist. SNMP version 1 (SNMPv1) and SNMP version 2 (SNMPv2) have a number of features in common, but SNMPv2 offers enhancements, such as additional protocol operations. SNMPv3 is in progress but has not been standardized—it currently exists as a draft. SNMPv3 addresses major security and authentication concerns of SNMPv1 and SNMPv2.

Managed devices are monitored and controlled using four basic SNMP commands—read, write, trap, and traversal operations:

- **Read:** Used by an NMS to monitor managed devices.

- **Write:** Used by an NMS to control managed devices.

- **Trap:** Used by managed devices to report events to the NMS.

- **Traversal operations:** Used by the NMS to determine which variables a managed device supports and to gather information in variable tables.

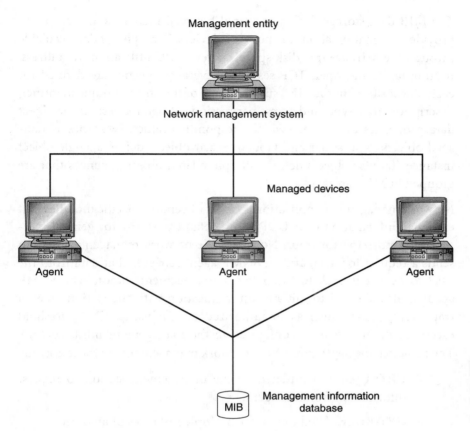

Figure 9.10
An SNMP-managed net-
work consists of managed
devices, agents, and NMSs

An MIB is a collection of information that is organized hierarchically. It contains managed objects and is identified by object identifiers. SNMP defines standards for device information organization and for communication between agents and management stations. SNMP contains two standards:

- **Structure of Management Information (SMI):** An OSI standard that governs how data structures should be organized. Management information within devices is organized into hierarchical structure of objects that have properties and values. SMI defines the structure and rules for objects, properties, and values.

- **Abstract Syntax Notation One (ASN.1):** The syntax standard for all SNMP messages between agents and network management stations. ASN.1 provides reliable interoperability among different vendors.

The MIB data storage facility is shared between managers and agents to provide information about the network devices. Examples of data available through the MIB are free disk space, current CPU utilization, IP address, routing table, and open TCP sessions. Several properties are defined for each object stored in the MIB, such as name of the object, unique identifier, description, data type, and access permissions. When requesting the object data, properties are returned with corresponding values. Two types of managed objects exist: scalar and tabular. Scalar objects define a single object instance. Tabular objects define multiple related object instances that are grouped in MIB tables.

Network management applications consist of vendor-specific modules that exchange information over UDP using default port 161 for general messages and port 162 for traps. Normally, the network management station sends a request for data, and an SNMP agent retrieves that data from the MIB to deliver it back to the network management station. The SNMP agent is also allowed to initiate communication with the station when a trap event occurs, such as unauthorized system usage, CPU threshold excess, or other events as configured in the management infrastructure. The principal messages involved in network management are the following:

- **GET:** Used and initiated by the management station to request information from the agent.

- **GET-BULK:** Used to retrieve multiple instances of an object.

- **GET-NEXT:** Used in the same way as GET, to request the next object in the MIB tree.

- **GET RESPONSE:** Used to return information from the agent to the process that issued the GET, GET-NEXT, or GET-BULK request.

- **INFORM:** Allows trap information to be exchanged between several management stations without having to requery agents.

- **SET:** Sent from the management station, and accepted and processed by the agent committing the changes to its MIB. Typically this is used to reduce network traffic or to do maintenance on hardware.

- **TRAP:** Also known as NOTIFY. Trap events trigger trap messages to be sent from the agent to the management station. Its purpose is to notify a device about pertinent network activity.

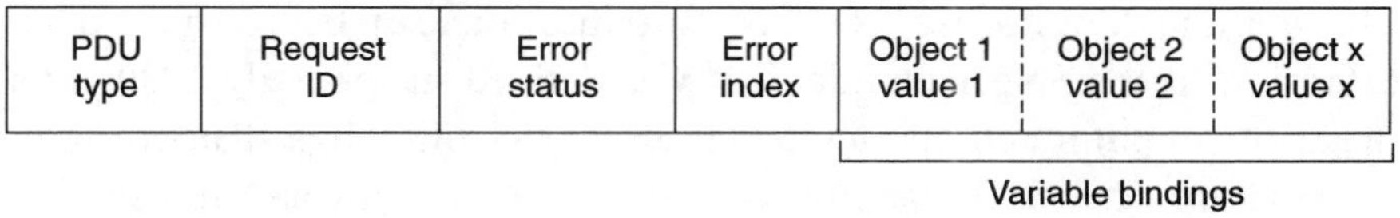

PDU type	Request ID	Error status	Error index	Object 1 value 1	Object 2 value 2	Object x value x

Variable bindings

Figure 9.11
SNMP protocol data unit (PDU)

Figure 9.11 shows the information that is contained in the SNMP protocol data unit (PDU).

Every agent has to be configured with at least one trap destination, which could be an IP address, an IPX address, or a hostname of a target management station, to be able to send traps. The trap destination must also point to a network device that is running SNMP management software.

! WARNING

A trap destination is a very important security configuration that, if not properly set, can reveal a wealth of information about the host and network infrastructure to unauthorized individuals.

All agents and management stations must belong to an SNMP community, the purpose of which is to provide a very basic form of authenticating SNMP messages. SNMP and management stations that belong to the same community can accept messages from each other and communicate as defined in the community properties. It is very important to define hard-to-guess community strings, because if the community string becomes known or is guessed by an attacker, he or she could gain a lot of information about the host being queried.

SNMPv1 is the initial and still most widely used implementation of the SNMP protocol and functions within the specifications of the SMI. SNMPv1 operates over protocols such as UDP, IP, OSI Connectionless Network Service (CLNS), AppleTalk Datagram-Delivery Protocol (DDP), and Novell Internetwork Packet Exchange (IPX). SNMPv1 is widely used and is the de facto network-management protocol in the Internet community. SNMPv2 is based on the first version of the protocol and was designed to extend the functionality of its predecessor. SNMPv3 primarily addresses security problems inherent in the first two versions. Like SNMPv1, SNMPv2 is based on SMI, but introduces new data types, the ability to group different information into modules, and capability and compliance statements.

The Remote Monitoring (RMON) specification can be considered an extension to the SNMP standard. It was defined in the early 1990s as a means to monitor remote devices. It also relies on MIB's structuring of information and SMI. Its purpose is to deliver network information grouped into nine major monitoring elements:

- **Alarm group:** Contains statistics data that is sampled at regular intervals and compared to the threshold information. If threshold levels are exceeded, an alarm is generated.

- **Event group:** Controls event generation and notification on a monitored device.

- **Filter group:** Contains streams of packets logged if matched against a specified filter.

- **History group:** Includes information, sampled at regular intervals over a period of time, that is stored for later analysis.

- **Host group:** Contains basic statistical information on the hosts discovered in the network.

- **HostTopN group:** Used to prepare reports that describe the hosts that top a list ordered by rate-based statistics. The management station can also select the number of hosts reported.

- **Matrix group:** Stores statistics on conversations between participating hosts.

- **Packet capture group:** Allows the logging and analyzing of actual packets.

- **Statistics group:** Contains statistical information collected by RMON probes from each of the configured interfaces on the device.

Cisco Systems includes SNMP and RMON functionality in its software. There are a number of software packages available as add-ons to HP Openview, IBM, SUN, and DEC, so network monitoring can be done without needing to implement an expensive management infrastructure.

9.8   Electronic Mail (E-mail)

Electronic mail (e-mail) was one of the first Internet applications. It can be traced back to the ARPANET. In 1972, Ray Tomlinson wrote a program to send and receive messages over the network. Today, e-mail applications enable users to send messages along with files, text, and embedded data as attachments.

E-mail uses a store-and-forward method of transmission. The messages are stored in an electronic mailbox and when a user logs on, the messages are downloaded onto the workstation. Likewise, outgoing e-mail is stored until it can be forwarded on the network. Windows, Linux, and NetWare all have their own versions of e-mail software, such as Eudora, Messenger, Outlook, and Sendmail. There are also Web-based e-mail systems such as HotMail and Yahoo!Mail. Besides message delivery, many e-mail products offer address books for storing contact information, filtering software for eliminating junk mail, and the ability to make distribution lists.

9.8.1   E-mail Message Formats

Multipurpose Internet Mail Extensions (MIME) is the standard that defines the format of text messages. The basic idea behind this standard is that the content of e-mail messages is logically divided into two pieces, the header and the body. Requests for comments (RFC) 822 addresses the contents of the header in great detail; however, the message body is limited to short lines of printable text. Several different formats can be chosen for the e-mail body besides basic text formatting, such as Hypertext Markup Language (HTML) and Rich Text. Each has its own characteristics, advantages, and disadvantages. Formats to ensure secure e-mail messages, such as Pretty Good Privacy (PGP) and Secure/MIME (S/MIME), exist as well.

The various formats are:

- **HTML:** Supports text formatting, color and background images, horizontal lines, alignments, HTML styles, and Web pages. If the recipient's e-mail program cannot read HTML, the message will be received in plain text format with an attachment that can be opened in a Web browser. Be careful where you send HTML mail. Many e-mail lists and newsgroups do not allow HTML because there is a security risk that it might contain destructive code.

- **MIME HTML (MHTML):** Enables full Web pages from the Internet to be sent inside e-mail messages.

- **Rich Text:** Supports text formatting, bullets, color, and alignment. Because this is a Microsoft-specific format, other mail programs may not be able to read it.

- **Plain Text:** Does not contain any formatting. This may be the best choice for most situations because all recipients will be able to read the message.

- **S/MIME:** Helps ensure the security of e-mail by enabling users to digitally encrypt and sign messages.
- **Pretty Good Privacy (PGP):** Like S/MIME, allows messages to be digitally signed and encrypted.

9.8.2   E-mail Transfer

E-mail client programs perform several different functions, including creating messages, sending mail to and receiving mail from the server, displaying messages, and storing inbound and outbound messages. Electronic mail generally consists of three basic pieces: (1) the link level transport, which is the transport medium such as TCP/IP, (2) the Mail Transport Agent (MTA), which is responsible for transporting mail from source to destination, and possibly transforming protocols and addresses and routing the mail, and (3) the User Agent (UA), which is the software that the user uses to read his mail.

In its simplest form, an e-mail server has a list of e-mail accounts, with one text file account for each person who can receive e-mail. So the server would have a file named myname.txt, another named yourname.txt, and so on. If you want to send me a message, you compose a message in an e-mail client and type my name in the "To" field. When you send the message, the e-mail client connects to its e-mail server and transfers the name of the recipient, the name of the sender, and the body of the message. The server formats the information and attaches it to the bottom of the myname.txt file. As other people send mail to me, the server simply appends those messages to the bottom of the file in the order that they arrived. The text file stores the messages. When I want to read my e-mail, my e-mail client connects to the server and requests a copy of the myname.txt file. Then it resets the file, as well as saves the myname.txt file on my local computer and parses the file into the separate messages. When I double-click a message, my e-mail client finds that message in the text file and shows me the body.

TIP
To receive e-mail, you must have an account on a mail server. To send e-mail, you need a connection to the Internet and access to the mail server that forwards your mail.

The standard protocols used for sending Internet e-mail are Simple Mail Transfer Protocol (SMTP) and Post Office Protocol (POP). When you send an e-mail message, your computer routes it to an SMTP server. The server looks at the e-mail address, and then forwards it to the recipient's mail server, where it is stored until the addressee retrieves it. Now that you have an understanding of how e-mail works, let's go on to look at the different types of protocols and how they are used.

9.8.3   Post Office Protocol 3 (POP3)

Post Office Protocol 3 (POP) is used to retrieve e-mail from a mail server. Most e-mail clients use the POP protocol, although the Internet Message Access Protocol (IMAP) can also be used. IMAP is discussed in the next section, "Internet Message Access Protocol 4 (IMAPv4)." Several versions of POP have been developed. The first, called POP2, became a standard in the mid-1980s and requires SMTP to send messages. The most current version is POP3. POP3 servers are required to listen on TCP port 110 while clients use any port number above 1024, just like any other TCP-based client application. The idea behind POP3 is that the UAs on client workstations can use the protocol to dynamically access a mail drop on a server. After the messages are delivered to the client, the client takes responsibility for management features such as creating folders. If a user wants to maintain message folders, they must copy the message to a folder on the local system. The POP3 protocol carries a couple of assumptions. One is that the user's mail is kept on a reliable system accessible over TCP/IP. The second is that the user should be able to connect to the mail server, provide a user name and password, and retrieve any mail that is waiting.

 TIP

In POP3, the client performs all mailbox and message management.

The core POP3 protocol has no provision for transferring mail—the outbound mail is forwarded to an SMTP relay as shown in Figure 9.12. POP3 only specifies a mechanism for downloading messages—it does not provide a method for sending mail back to a server. POP3 is designed for user-to-mailbox access via authentication and mailbox manipulation. Authentication takes the form of a password transmitted as clear text, so POP3 should be used carefully if security is of concern.

When you check your e-mail, your e-mail client connects to the POP3 server using port 110. The POP3 server requires an account name and a password for validation. After you have logged in, the server allows you to access your text file. Your e-mail client then issues a series of simple commands to transfer copies of your e-mail messages to your local computer.

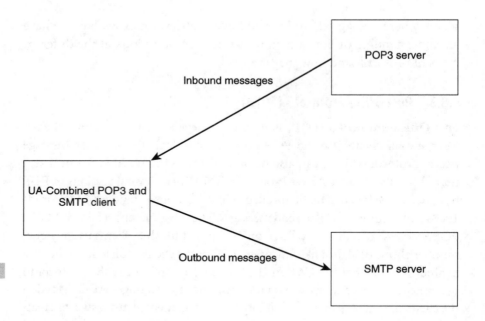

Figure 9.12
POP3 client
communications

Generally, it then deletes the messages from the server. The following are the most common commands:

- **USER:** Account user name for logging in to retrieve messages
- **PASS:** Account password for user name
- **QUIT:** Logs out and closes the connection
- **STAT/LIST:** Lists the number and size of messages waiting in mailbox
- **RETR:** Retrieves a specific message from the mailbox
- **DELE:** Deletes a specific message from the mailbox
- **TOP:** Shows the top lines of a message
- **RSET:** Undeletes a message
- **NOOP:** Specifies no action ("no operation" command)

POP3 uses a command/response syntax and relies on two simple status messages: "+" indicating that the command was accepted and executed properly, and "-" indicating that the command was not understood or was not executed. POP3 servers are allowed to put whatever text messages they want after the "+" or "-". The POP3 client must wait for a response before issuing any more commands. An example of the order of events follows:

1. User myself opens her POP3 mail client, which connects to the POP3 server running on TCP port 110.

2. POP3 server—"+" OK indicating that it is operational and ready.

3. POP3 client—USER myself.

4. POP3 server—"+"OK password required.

5. POP3 client—PASS password.

6. POP3 server—"+" OK.

7. POP3 client—"STAT" (for information about the mailbox and the messages that are waiting).

8. POP3 server—"+" myself has 15 messages containing 23,476 octets.

9. POP3client—"RETR" (to retrieve messages).

10. POP3 server—"+" marks end-of-messages with <crlf>.

11. POP3 client—"DELE" (deletes them from the server).

12. POP3 server—"+" OK.

13. POP3 client—"QUIT" (to close the session).

14. POP3 server—"+" OK, and then drops the connection.

A main advantage of POP3 mail services is that it is an "offline" protocol. Electronic mail messages are downloaded and read offline by the user with a local mail application. POP3 also allows you to make the most of services offered by e-mail clients such as Outlook, Messenger, and Eudora.

9.8.4   Internet Message Access Protocol 4 (IMAPv4)

Internet Message Access Protocol (IMAP) was originally developed in 1986 at Stanford University for communication over TCP/IP networks, but did not attract the attention of mainstream e-mail vendors until a decade later. The protocol includes operations for creating, deleting, and renaming mailboxes as well as checking for new messages, deleting messages, setting and clearing flags, and server-based parsing and searching. E-mail stored on an IMAP server can be accessed from a computer at home, at the office, and while traveling, without the need to transfer messages or files back and forth between computers. The most current version is IMAP4.

NOTE

IMAP4 is the fourth revision of the Internet Message Access Protocol, which was formerly known as the Interactive Mail Access Protocol. IMAP4 deals strictly with the client-side handling of e-mail.

IMAP4's ability to access messages from more than one computer has become extremely important as we rely more and more on e-mail, and as the use of multiple computers and devices increases. IMAP4 allows client computers to work with messages stored in mailboxes on remote mail servers. A client mail application connects to the mail server computer and provides an account name and password. The mail application then sends commands to the mail server that instruct the server as to which function the user wants to perform, such as list all messages in the mailbox, retrieve or delete messages, or move messages between mailboxes. IMAP4 uses the same command/response syntax that POP3 does. Table 9.4 shows the IMAP4 commands.

Before one can enter an IMAP4 command, an identifier must be placed in front of the command. For example, if you type "login," the server issues an error message; however, if you type "*username* login," you can log in. All output from the server starts with the same tag you placed on the beginning of your input. In addition, each response has the tag followed by one of the following keywords:

- **OK:** The command was completed successfully.
- **NO:** The command could not be completed.
- **BAD:** The command is unknown.

Any input that needs to be entered on separate lines requires a "+" before each line. All output lines end with a CR&LF, and an "*" precedes any multi-line outputs.

IMAP4 has several advantages over POP3. It offers more order and organization on the server end, including multiple mailboxes as well as nested folders. The startup time is shorter because it only has to download the headers; messages aren't downloaded until the user selects them. It also offers better offline mail handling than POP3 because it only marks a message for deletion; it doesn't delete it until it is clear that it is no longer

TABLE 9.4   IMAP4 Commands

Command	Description
CAPABILITY	Requests a list of supported capabilities
AUTHENTICATE	Indicates an authentication method to be used
LOGIN	Identifies the user and password
SELECT	Specifies the mailbox for access
EXAMINE	Specifies the mailbox for access in read-only mode
CREATE	Creates a mailbox
DELETE	Deletes a mailbox
RENAME	Changes the name of a mailbox
SUBSCRIBE	Adds a mailbox to the active list
UNSUBSCRIBE	Removes a mailbox from the server's active list of mailboxes
LIST	Lists mailboxes
LSUB	Lists subscribed or active mailboxes
STATUS	Lists the number and size of messages waiting in a mailbox
APPEND	Adds a message to the mailbox
SEARCH	Searches a mailbox for messages meeting specific criteria
FETCH	Fetches data contained in a specific message
COPY	Copies message to another mailbox
EXPUNGE	Removes messages from a mailbox
LOGOUT	Informs the server the client is ready to close the connection
CLOSE	Commits deletion of messages and closes mailbox
NOOP	No operation command, specifies no action
STORE	Alters data within a specific message

needed. It also offers automatic resynchronization with the server, if needed, and supports advanced authentication.

A companion protocol to IMAP4, which was developed at Carnegie Mellon University, is called the **Application Configuration Access Protocol**

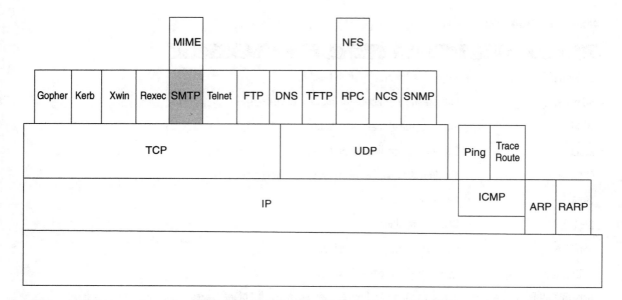

Figure 9.13
SMTP protocol stack

(ACAP). ACAP was originally derived from the Internet Message Support Protocol (IMSP). Although originally designed to support Internet mail clients in conjunction with IMAP4, ACAP can operate completely independently of IMAP4 and messaging.

ACAP is considered a solution to the problem of client configuration for mobile users on the Internet. Almost all Internet applications currently store user preferences, options, and other personal data in local disk files. ACAP provides a protocol to store and retrieve client-specific configuration from a server for arbitrary clients. RFC 2244 defines ACAP's specifications. ACAP falls somewhere between a directory service, a file system, and a specialized single-service protocol support. (Directory services will be discussed in Chapter 11.)

9.8.5   Simple Mail Transfer Protocol (SMTP)

Simple Mail Transfer Protocol (SMTP) is an asymmetric request-response protocol that was popular in the early 1980s. It is used as a transport protocol for sending e-mail server to server and does not deliver mail to a user's mailbox. It also does not allow remote users to retrieve mail from the server; POP3 and IMAP4 serve this function. SMTP works above the TCP/IP layer on port 25. Figure 9.13 shows the protocol stack. SMTP is

TABLE 9.5   SMTP Commands

Command	Description
HELO	Used to identify the sender to the receiver.
EHLO	In the extended protocol (ESTMP), the command EHLO is used instead of HELO.
MAIL FROM	Initiates a mail transaction including the "From" field or the sender of the mail.
RCPT TO	Identifies the recipient of the message, which dictates the destination mailbox for the message.
DATA	Announces the beginning of the actual mail data, which is the body of the message.
RSET	Aborts or resets the current transaction.
VRFY	Confirms a user name.
NOOP	This is the "no operation" command and specifies no action.
QUIT	Used to end the connection.
SEND	Lets the receiving host know that the message must be sent to another terminal.

considered an Application layer protocol that defines a set of rules for addressing, sending, and receiving mail between servers.

How does it work? A mail client will make a TCP connection to an SMTP server and upload a mail message and a destination to where the message should be delivered. If it knows the final recipient, the SMTP server delivers the message; if not, it passes the message along to another SMTP server. If the destination server is not available, the sending server will try again later. Eventually, the sender either makes it through or else gives up and returns the message to the originator as undeliverable.

A list of SMTP commands is provided in Table 9.5; the commands are fully documented in RFC 821. Additional extended commands have been added to the basic SMTP command list. Systems that recognize the extended commands are said to support Extended SMTP (ESMTP).

After each of these commands is sent, the SMTP server responds with a three-digit response code that indicates success or failure. The SMTP client is not allowed to issue any more commands until the last command has been confirmed with a response code. The following lists the category and description of the codes sent from the receiver Mail Transfer Agent (MTA):

- **2xx:** Command accepted and processed
  - **211:** System status
  - **214:** Help message
  - **220:** Server service ready
  - **221:** Service closing transmission channel
  - **250:** Requested action OK and completed
  - **251:** User not local; will forward on
- **3xx:** General flow control
  - **354:** Start message or mail input; end with <CRLF>.<CRLF>
- **4xx:** Critical system or transmission failure
  - **421:** Service not available, closing connection
  - **450:** Mailbox unavailable, requested mail action not taken
  - **451:** Requested action aborted; local processing error
  - **452:** Insufficient system storage, action not taken
- **5xx:** Errors with the SMTP command
  - **500:** Syntax error, command unrecognized
  - **501:** Syntax error in parameters or arguments
  - **502:** Command not completed
  - **503:** Bad sequence of commands
  - **504:** Command parameter not implemented
  - **550:** Mailbox unavailable
  - **551:** User not local
  - **552:** Exceeded storage allocation
  - **553:** Mailbox name not allowed

The actual conversation that an e-mail client has with an SMTP server is quite simple and human readable. A typical conversation, as shown in Figure 9.14, contains these steps:

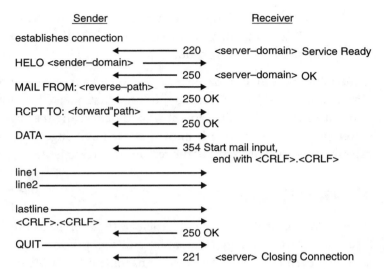

Figure 9.14
SMTP mail exchange

1. Your e-mail client connects to the SMTP server. It usually uses port 25.

2. The e-mail client prints a header to confirm it is an e-mail server running SMTP.

3. The e-mail client gets the attention of the SMTP server with a HELO or an EHLO command.

4. The SMTP server responds to let the client know it is running and waiting for commands.

5. The client sends the MAIL FROM command to identify who the e-mail is from.

6. The SMTP server responds with an OK to continue command.

7. The client sends the RCPT TO command to inform the SMTP server who the mail recipient is.

8. The SMTP server responds that this is OK.

9. The client sends the DATA command to tell the SMTP server it is sending the message. The text is sent line by line until the entire message has been transmitted, ending with a period on a line by itself.

10. The SMTP server replies that this is OK and the mail will be delivered.

11. The client can either start another message, quit by issuing the QUIT command, or receive messages from the other side by issuing the TURN command.

If the network uses a domain concept, SMTP cannot simply deliver mail sent by opening a TCP connection; it must first query the name server to find out to which domain name it should deliver the message. The name server stores resource records known as mail exchange (MX) records for message delivery. This is one of the reasons for creating MX records in DNS.

9.9   World Wide Web

In 1945, Vannevar Bush wrote an article in the *Atlantic Monthly* about the future uses of technology to organize and access information. He speculated that eventually we would have a machine called a Memex that would store all of a person's personal information on microfilm. In the 1960s, Ted Nelson described a similar system in which text on one page could be linked to text on other pages. He called this system hypertext. In 1987, Nelson published a book in which he outlined a global system for online hypertext publishing. Then, in 1990, Tim Berners-Lee developed the World Wide Web while he was working as a scientist for the world's largest particle physics laboratory, CERN. The Internet was already in existence, and at the time consisted of thousands of sets of individual files and text-based messages transmitted by the various transport protocols. They were accessible only to those who understood the command systems and the protocols necessary for their operation. What Tim Berners-Lee brought to the Internet was the ability to finally link all this data together. He did this by using three main elements: the HTTP protocol, the HTML language, and the URL addressing system. We will discuss all of these in further detail later in this section. These innovations allow us to send and receive pages that consist of many individual files. The images in a Web page are actually separate files within the text. Your browser assembles the document and formats the text and graphics according to the programming for that particular page.

TIP The Web consists of individual computers, Web browser software, connections to ISPs, servers that host data, and routers or switches that direct the flow of information.

The Web is based on a client/server architecture. Remember from previous chapters that in client/server architecture, the client requests a processing function or data from the server. The client sends the request and waits for a response. The server receives and processes the request and sends the data back to the client. The client then displays the data. Because the client is running on a completely separate computer from the server, it is able to focus on document display while the server handles only document retrieval. The World Wide Web is a distributed network. This allows for a many-to-many relationship between clients and servers. Any server on the Web can be accessed directly by any client. If a server on the World Wide Web fails, it doesn't affect the performance of other servers.

9.9.1   Hypertext Markup Language (HTML)

The language used to format pages on the Web is called the **Hypertext Markup Language (HTML)**. The current specification is HTML Version 4.01. Future versions and new features for HTML are under development. Information about these can be found through the World Wide Web Consortium (W3C). HTML is a document markup language that includes a set of tags for defining the format and style of documents. The codes describe the relationships among the document's text elements. In essence, HTML is a collection of platform-independent styles indicated by markup tags that define the various components of a Web document. HTML is based on Standard Generalized Markup Language (SGML). It is actually an instance of one SGML document type, Document Type Definition (DTD), that is easier to use and learn than SGML.

Information that you view on the Web consists of text and graphical images. This information is displayed one document, or page, at a time. Web pages are written in HTML so that Web browsers can understand them. These documents are simple text files that contain only numbers and the characters of the alphabet with formatting codes.

As stated earlier, HTML is simply a series of commands called flags or tags, written in plain text, that determine how a Web page displays in a browser. HTML tags are always written within angle brackets (<>) that let the browser know that these are commands. Almost all commands consist of a beginning tag and an ending tag. The text between the tags is the information that will be visible in your browser. The words/letters between these two angle brackets are called elements. Elements tell the browser how to display the Web page. You can view the HTML source code of a Web page by directing your browser to any Web site. With your mouse, right-click on any blank portion of the page and choose View Source. If you are using Internet Explorer, you can also use the View drop-down menu and choose Source. A new window appears, displaying words and characters. This is the HTML programming code. Each element within that code is known as an HTML tag. When you are done looking at the page's source code, simply close the source page to return to the original page.

TIP

HTML files can be created using any text editor. You can even use the text editor that's already on your system—SimpleText for Macs and Notepad for Windows.

It is possible to use word-processing software for HTML if you remember to save your document as text only with line breaks. HTML is not designed to be the language of a word processor, such as Word or WordPerfect, because the same HTML document may be viewed by different browsers of different abilities. Some WYSIWYG (what you see is what you get) editors are also available, including FrontPage, GoLive, and Dreamweaver. With these programs, instead of writing the markup tags in a plain-text file and then looking at the resulting page, you design your HTML document visually through a graphical user interface (GUI). You should wait to try one of them until after you learn the basics of HTML tagging, because you will want to know enough HTML to code a document in case you want to add HTML features that your editor doesn't support.

NOTE

HTML may not be viewed the same by all browser software. If you are creating a Web page, you should test the viewability of the page in several different browsers.

Any Web page you create contains the following tags at the start of the page:

- **<HTML>:** Tells the browser that this is the beginning of an HTML document.
- **<HEAD>:** Tells the browser that this is the header for the page.
- **<TITLE>:** Lets the browser know that this is the title of the page.

- **<BODY>:** Informs the browser that this is the beginning of the Web page content.

The end tag looks just like the start tag, except a slash (/) precedes the text within the brackets. The tags needed to end any Web page are </BODY> and </HTML>.

HTML is also not case sensitive. You may use either lowercase or uppercase. For consistency, use one or the other rather than a mix. You must have the <HTML>, <HEAD>, and <BODY> container tags in every HTML file.

9.9.2　Hypertext Transfer Protocol (HTTP)

Web clients and servers use **Hypertext Transfer Protocol (HTTP)** to communicate with each other. HTTP was developed in 1991. There are three versions of HTTP. The first one was HTTP 0.9, which was a bit primitive and was never specified in any standard. This was followed by HTTP 1.0, which was issued as a standard in RFC 1945. The current version, HTTP 1.1, extends and improves on HTTP 1.0 in a number of areas. The major improvements are some extensions for authoring documents online and a feature that allows clients to request that the connection be kept open after each application request, thereby saving wait time and server load if several requests have to be issued quickly.

HTTP is an application-level stateless protocol. When "http://" appears in a URL, it means that the user is connecting to a Web server to transfer files from the server to a browser in order to view a Web page. It only defines what the browser and Web server say to each other, not how they communicate—TCP/IP takes care of that. Each command is executed independent, without any knowledge of the commands that came before it, allowing systems to be built independent of the data being transferred. This is one of the reasons that it is difficult to implement Web sites that react intelligently to user input.

HTTP is a one-way system. Files are transported from the server to the client's browser. Only the contents of the Web page are transferred to the browser for viewing. The files are transferred but not downloaded, so they are not copied into the memory of the receiving device. The transfer process is quite simple; it consists of a connection, request, response, and close. Here are the basic HTTP commands:

- **GET:** Requests to read a page.

- **HEAD:** Requests to read a page. This request is similar to the GET command and is often used for testing hypertext links for validity, accessibility, and recent modifications.
- **PUT:** Requests to write to a page.
- **POST:** Appends to a named resource.
- **DELETE:** Removes the page.
- **LINK:** Connects two existing resources.
- **UNLINK:** Breaks an existing connection between two resources.

After the request, the server responds to the browser with a status line that has three parts: (1) the HTTP version, (2) a three-digit integer response status code, and (3) a reason phrase describing the status code. Typical status lines are:

- HTTP/1.0 200 OK
- HTTP/1.0 403 Forbidden

Following is a list of the status codes:

- **1xx:** Indicates an informational message only
- **2xx:** Indicates success of some kind
  - **200:** OK
  - **201:** Created
  - **202:** Accepted
  - **204:** No Content
- **3xx:** Redirects the client to another URL
  - **301:** Moved Permanently
  - **302:** Moved Temporarily
  - **304:** Not Modified
- **4xx:** Indicates an error on the client's part
  - **400:** Bad Request
  - **401:** Unauthorized
  - **403:** Forbidden
  - **404:** Not Found

- **5xx:** Indicates an error on the server's part
  - **500:** Internal Server Error
  - **501:** Not Implemented
  - **502:** Bad Gateway
  - **503:** Service Unavailable

Because HTTP allows an open-ended set of methods to be used to indicate the purpose of a request, it can also be used as a generic protocol for name servers, distributed object management systems, and proxies/gateways to other Internet protocols such as SMTP, Network News Transport Protocol (NNTP), and FTP. Messages are passed in a format similar to that used by Internet Mail and MIME.

9.9.3   Web Browsers

A **Web browser** is the client software that allows you to access and view any document on the Web. The number of available Web browsers is growing constantly. You access Web pages by typing a **Uniform Resource Locator (URL)** into the address text box of the browser. A URL represents a link to a Web page. Every Web site and every Web page has a unique URL, which is an electronic address that allows your browser to locate pages. URLs are broken down into three parts: The first part specifies the Internet protocol. The second part is the domain name of the computer hosting the HTML documents, the address of which may be modified by appending a port that is different from the default port after the domain name. The third part is the name of file directory and the file you are viewing. A URL is depicted in Figure 9.15.

Sometimes the URL contains an additional part known as the anchor name. This is a pointer to a specific part of an HTML document. It is preceded by the pound sign (#) and is especially useful for locating information in large documents.

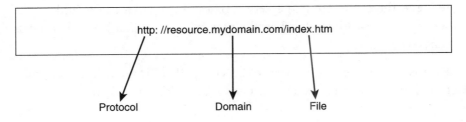

Figure 9.15

URL

When you type a URL into your browser or click a hypertext link, your browser sends a request to a Web server to download the requested file. The browser contacts a domain name server to translate the server name into an IP address that it can use to connect to the server. After the DNS server returns the site's IP address, the browser uses the IP address and the HTTP protocol to send a GET request to the server asking for the file index.htm. The request string is the only piece of information the server sees, so it doesn't care where the request came from. It could be from a browser or a search engine robot, or it could have been typed in manually. When the server receives the browser's request, it returns a signal to acknowledge that a connection has been formed.

TIP In a Web browser, when you request a Web page, the bar at the bottom of your browser window gives you information on the status of the request.

If you enter a URL incorrectly, your browser cannot locate the site or resource you want. When you receive an error message or access the wrong site, check the address you typed—the address field accepts only exact matches. The server then returns the HTML text for the Web page to the browser using TCP/IP. The server also tells the browser what kind of document it is so the browser can display the document with the appropriate program, if necessary.

As you learned in earlier chapters, the file that you request does not travel to your computer in one piece—it's broken up into separate data packets. As the packets arrive at your computer, they are stored in a cache. Your Web browser interprets the data and displays it on your computer screen. As the browser uses elements in the cache to reassemble the Web page on screen, it follows the HTML tags, which causes different parts of the page to appear on the screen before others. The browser displays HTML documents directly; if there are references to images, such as Java applets or sound or movie clips, and the browser has been set up to display these images, it requests these also from the server. These separate requests add to the server and network load. When the user follows another link, the process starts over again.

Because there are many Internet services, Web browsers support additional protocols, such as FTP and NNTP, in addition to Web clients. Different Web browsers have different features, and they all display Web pages with slight variations. Older Web browsers are still in widespread use and often have trouble displaying some of the newer HTML features. In fact, some sites list the browser versions they support, so that if you have difficulty viewing the page you know why.

9.9.4   Web-Based Services

Because most companies rely on the Internet for business activity, most IT professionals have to contend with Web-based services. A Web-based service is a distributed application that functions by using a set of markup language standards. This offers the opportunity for a better return on investment in Internet technology by allowing companies to implement business applications using components from various platforms. Some examples are automated banking capabilities, airline ticket purchases, and manufacturing part purchases. As with all emerging technologies, the Web services model presents its own set of challenges. How to cope with system outages, programming defects, or performance bottlenecks are important considerations when choosing a model for Web services standards.

Each day more acronyms related to Web services come into existence. The Web services architecture is modeled through several types of technologies. These technologies can generally be organized into layers that build upon one another. Each layer of the Web services stack addresses a separate business concern. These include messaging, security, transaction handling, proper routing, and workflow. The four basic layers are: (1) transport, (2) extensions/packaging, (3) description, and (4) discovery. The following lists each layer along with the technologies that fall under that category:

Transport
- DIME (Direct Internet Message Encapsulation)
- HTTPR (Reliable HTTP)

Packaging and Extensions
- SOAP (Simple Object Access Protocol)
- SOAP-DSIG (SOAP Security Extensions: Digital Signature)
- SWA (SOAP Messages with Attachments)

- WS-License (Web Services License Language)
- WS-Referral (Web Services Referral Protocol)
- WS-Routing (Web Services Routing Protocol)
- WS-Security (Web Services Security Language)

Description
- WSCL (Web Services Conversation Language)
- WSCM (Web Services Component Model)
- WSDL (Web Services Description Language)
- WSEL (Web Services Endpoint Language)
- WSFL (Web Services Flow Language)
- WSML (Web Services Meta Language)
- WSXL (Web Services Experience Language)
- WSUI (Web Services User Interface)
- XLANG (Web Services for Business Process Design)

Discovery
- UDDI (Universal Description, Discovery, and Integration)
- USML (UDDI Search Markup Language)
- WS-Inspection (Web Services Inspection Language)

Several companies, such as IBM and Microsoft, have come up with a set of specifications that are the foundation for their own versions of a Web services architecture.

9.9.5   Other Markup Languages

Other markup languages besides HTML exist. As you read earlier, HTML is based on **Standard Generalized Markup Language (SGML)**. In addition to HTML and SGML, **Extensible Markup Language (XML)**, a relatively newer language, exists.

SGML is a standard used to describe markup languages in general that originated from Generalized Markup Language (GML) in 1986. It is data encoding that allows the information in documents to be shared by other document-publishing systems and by applications for such functions as electronic delivery, database management, and inventory control. SGML contains an international standard that is independent of any software applications, devices, and operating systems. It was designed for massive document collections, such as repair manuals for fighter jets, and is used by the Department of Defense, Hewlett-Packard, and Kodak. Because it provides a vendor-neutral international standard for information exchange, SGML has been widely adopted for sharing document-based information in open systems environments.

SGML is costly and difficult to set up. The tools available are expensive compared to HTML tools, and it has a long learning curve. However, SGML has useful features that HTML lacks, such as supporting user-defined tags and architecture for rich documents. Plus, because it is nonproprietary, it will outlive most current applications.

To solve some of SGML's problems and capitalize on its advantages, markup language and software experts have developed XML, which contains the most useful features of HTML and SGML. XML is a markup language for documents containing structured information. It defines which data is displayed on a Web page, as opposed to how data is displayed. XML allows structured information to be displayed from any application in a standard, consistent way. HTML is more about the format of the page, whereas XML is about the amount of data displayed. Structured data contains both content and the role that content plays. XML satisfies two basic objectives of representing information hierarchically by providing a mechanism and a language for data structured in a streamed logical hierarchy. As with all hierarchies, there are family-tree–like relationships of parent, child, and sibling. In other words, XML marks data in much the same way that you would define a record structure in a database. It tells systems how information should be rendered and specifies the kind of information. XML simplifies the exchange of data between companies without using expensive software, and it provides data about information.

In addition to SGML, HTML, and XML, the following markup languages exist:

- **XHTML (Extensible Hypertext Markup Language):** The successor of HTML that contains a family of document types and modules that extend HTML, reformulated in XML.

- **DHTML (Dynamic Hypertext Markup Language):** HTML that can change even after a page has been loaded into a browser.

- **RDF (Resource Description Framework):** A framework for describing and interchanging metadata.

- **DAML (DARPA Agent Markup Language):** A language designed to have a greater capacity than XML for describing objects and the relationships between them, as well as creating a higher level of interoperability among Web sites.

9.10   Remote Procedure Call (RPC) and Middleware

Remote Procedure Call (RPC) is a protocol that a program can use to request a service from a program located on another computer in a network without understanding network details. It uses the client/server model: the requesting program is a client and the service program is the server. The remote procedure call is intended to act across the network transparently. RPC spans the Transport and Application layers, making it easier to develop an application that includes multiple programs distributed in a network. RPC allows the remote component to be accessed without knowledge of the network address or any lower-level information. Most RPCs use a synchronous, request-reply type protocol that involves blocking the client until the server fulfills the request.

By using RPC, programmers of distributed applications avoid the details of the interface with the network. The transport independence of RPC isolates the application from the physical and logical elements of the data communications mechanism and allows the application to use a variety of transports. RPC does not care how a message is passed from one process to another; it deals only with specification and interpretation of messages.

The process makes a remote procedure call by pushing its parameters along with a return address onto the stack, and then jumping to the start of the procedure. The procedure itself is responsible for accessing and using the network. When an RPC is made, the client makes a procedure call that sends a request to the server and waits. The thread is blocked from processing until either a reply is received or it times out. When the request arrives, the server calls a routine that performs the requested service, and then sends the reply to the client. After the remote execution, the procedure

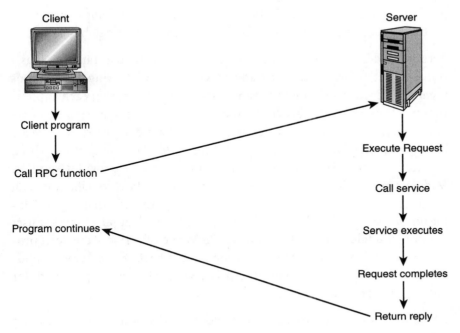

Figure 9.16
RPC process

jumps back to the return address and the client program continues. Figure 9.16 shows the process that takes place during an RPC.

When using RPC over a distributed network, the performance of the network should be considered. Even though the synchronous, blocking mechanism of RPC guards against overloading a network, when recovery mechanisms are built into a RPC application it may increase the network load, making the application inappropriate for an already congested network. There is no single standard for implementing an RPC, so different features may be offered by individual RPC implementations.

Middleware is software that connects applications, allowing them to exchange data. Essentially, it is a general term for any programming that provides messaging services so that two separate and often already existing applications can communicate. It is software that consists of a set of services that allow multiple processes running on one or more machines to interact across a network. This technology evolved during the 1990s to provide for interoperability in support of the move to client/server architectures and is essential for providing communication across heterogeneous platforms. A common application of middleware is to allow programs written for access to a particular database to access other databases.

Because middleware adds an independent third party to a transaction as a translator, it offers several key advantages over hardwiring applications together. The first is simplicity. Using middleware means that each application needs only an interface to the middleware instead of a separate interface to each application in which it needs to share data. Next, it provides persistence. Middleware can capture and hold data until it has been processed appropriately by all applications. Lastly, it provides services. Middleware can handle checking, printing, and data reconciliation with other applications as well as merging, splitting, or reformatting it. This means that services don't have to be rewritten for each application that uses them. As middleware products evolve, the range of services they can provide grows. It isn't uncommon for companies to have several types of middleware at work in a single enterprise, with different types used for different integration purposes.

Other middleware technologies that allow the distribution of processing across multiple platforms are:

- Object Request Brokers (ORB)
- Distributed Computing Environment (DCE)
- Message-Oriented Middleware (MOM)
- Component Object Model/Distributed COM (COM/DCOM)
- Transaction processing monitor technology
- Three-Tier software architectures

9.11   Chapter Summary

- Services help the operating system and applications communicate with each other. This is done through TCP and UDP acting as port managers for the applications and services that are in the top layer. There are 65,535 ports that can be accessed on a computer. The well-known ports are those from 0 through 1023, which can be used only by system processes.

- FTP makes it possible to move one or more files between computers with security and data integrity controls appropriate for the

Internet. The Telnet application allows a computer to create a connection and send commands and instructions interactively to a remote computer. TFTP is a simple form of the File Transfer Protocol that is often used for booting or loading programs on diskless workstations. Because it uses UDP, it does not guarantee delivery and provides no security features.

- The Domain Name System (DNS) takes the names we type in a Web browser and resolves them into a proper network address. DNS consists of name servers and resolvers. Domain name servers store authoritative data about sections of a distributed database and respond to browser requests by supplying name-to-address conversions.

- DHCP provides a framework for passing configuration information to hosts or clients in a TCP/IP environment. It enables individual computers to automatically obtain their network configurations from a server rather than be manually configured. The most important piece of data distributed by DHCP is the IP address. DHCP supports three methods of IP address allocation: manual, automatic, and dynamic.

- SNMP is used to exchange management information among network devices. SNMP enables network administrators to manage network performance, find and solve network problems, and plan for network growth. SNMP management infrastructure consists of three main components: managed nodes, agents, and network management stations.

- Electronic mail consists of three basic pieces: the transport medium, such as TCP/IP; the Mail Transport Agent (MTA), which is responsible for transporting mail from source to destination; and the User Agent (UA), which is the software that enables the user to read his or her mail. Post Office Protocol 3 (POP3) and Internet Message Access Protocol 4 (IMAP4) can be used to retrieve e-mail from a mail server. IMAP4 has several advantages over POP3, the main one being that mail can be accessed from anywhere instead of having to be downloaded to a computer. SMTP is used as a transport protocol for sending e-mail from server to server and does not deliver mail to a user's mailbox. It also does not allow remote users to retrieve mail from the server.

- The World Wide Web consists of three main elements: the Internet protocol that Web clients and servers use to communicate with each other, called Hypertext Transfer Protocol (HTTP); the Hypertext Markup Language (HTML), which is used to format pages on the Web; and the URL addressing system, which represents a link to a Web page.

- Remote Procedure Call (RPC) is a protocol that a program can use to request a service from a program located on another computer in a network without understanding network details.

- Middleware is software that connects applications, allowing them to exchange data. A common application of middleware is to allow programs written to access a particular database to access other databases.

9.12   Key Terms

Application Configuration Access Protocol (ACAP): A protocol to store and retrieve client-specific configuration from a server for mobile clients.

Domain Name System (DNS): Used to resolve the names typed into a Web browser and match them to a proper network address.

Dynamic Host Configuration Protocol (DHCP): Enables individual computers to automatically obtain their network configurations from a server rather than be manually configured.

Extensible Markup Language (XML): A markup language for documents containing structured information.

File Transfer Protocol (FTP): Allows a person to transfer files between two computers.

Hypertext Markup Language (HTML): The language used to format pages on the Web.

Hypertext Transfer Protocol (HTTP): A protocol that Web clients and servers use to communicate with each other.

Internet Message Access Protocol (IMAP): Allows the client e-mail program to access remote message stored as if they were local.

middleware: Software that connects applications, allowing them to exchange data.

Multipurpose Internet Mail Extensions (MIME): The standard that defines the format of text messages.

Post Office Protocol 3 (POP3): The current version of a protocol used to retrieve e-mail from a mail server.

Remote Procedure Call (RPC): A protocol that a program can use to request a service from a program located on another computer on a network without understanding network details.

Simple Mail Transfer Protocol (SMTP): A transport protocol for sending e-mail from server to server.

Simple Network Management Protocol (SNMP): An Application layer protocol that is used to exchange management information between network devices.

Standard Generalized Markup Language (SGML): An international markup standard that is independent of any software applications, devices, and operating systems.

Telecommunications Network (Telnet): A protocol that provides a way for clients to create a connection and to send commands and instructions interactively to the remote computer.

Trivial File Transfer Protocol (TFTP): A simple form of the File Transfer Protocol that is often used for booting or loading programs on diskless workstations.

Uniform Resource Locator (URL): An electronic address that allows a browser to locate pages.

Web browser: The client software that allows a user to access and view any document on the Web.

9.13 Challenge Questions

9.1 Which port number is associated with FTP?

    a. 21

    b. 25

c. 110

d. 443

9.2 Port 80 is associated with which service?

a. SMTP

b. SNMP

c. HTTP

d. IMAP

9.3 Which of the following rely on SMTP? (Choose all the apply.)

a. POP2

b. IMAP

c. HTTP

d. POP3

9.4 Which type of organization uses the .org top-level domain suffix address?

a. Noncommercial groups

b. Government

c. Education institutions

d. U.S. military organizations

9.5 SNMP is used for _____.

a. network file transfers

b. e-mail management

c. name resolution

d. network management

9.6 HTML is used for _____.

a. downloading e-mail

b. remote terminal management

c. formatting Web pages

d. transferring Web data

9.7 RPC is an acronym that stands for _____.

   a. Remote Protocol Class

   b. Remote Procedure Call

   c. Resource Procedure Call

   d. Resource Protocol Class

9.8 A hierarchical method of tracking domain names and their addresses, which was developed in the mid-1980s, is called the _____ .

9.9 To access the Web, a client requires the TCP/IP protocol, a unique IP address, a connection to the Internet, and a _____ .

9.10 Any clients on the Internet that need to look up domain name information are called _____ .

9.11 The _____ is a simple form of the File Transfer Protocol that is often used for booting or loading programs on diskless workstations.

9.12 A _____ is a distributed application that functions by using a set of markup language standards.

9.13 Name three reasons why a company would use DHCP.

9.14 What is middleware and how does it function?

9.15 What is the difference between POP3 and IMAP4?

9.14 Challenge Exercises

Challenge Exercise 9.1

In this exercise, you explore the purpose of Netstat. You learn how information can be obtained through the use of various commands. You need a computer with a Windows-based operating system and TCP/IP installed, network connectivity, and Internet access.

9.1 Log on to your computer.

9.2 Click **Start**, click **Run**, type **cmd** in the Open text box, and click **OK**. A command prompt window opens.

9.3 At the command prompt, type **netstat ?** and press **Enter**. All the switches that can be used with Netstat are displayed.

9.4 At the command prompt type, **netstat** and press **Enter**. The current TCP connections are displayed. See Figure 9.17 for an example.

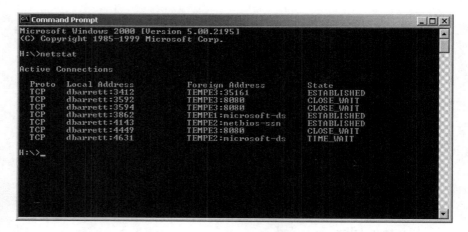

Figure 9.17

Netstat

9.5 Type **netstat -a** and press **Enter**. What happens? How many ports are listening on your computer?

9.6 Type **netstat -r** and press **Enter**. What does it show?

9.7 Type **netstat -s** and press **Enter**. What does it show? When would this information be useful?

9.8 Close the command prompt window.

Challenge Exercise 9.2

In this exercise, you explore the purpose of Nbtstat and learn how Nbtstat displays various parameters. You need a computer with a Windows-based operating system and TCP/IP installed, network connectivity, and Internet access.

9.1 Log on to your computer.

9.2 Click **Start**, click **Run**, type **cmd** in the Open text box, and click **OK**. A command prompt window opens.

9.3 At the command prompt, type **nbtstat ?** and press **Enter**. Review the list of commands you can use.

9.4 Type **nbtstat -c** and press **Enter**. The results should look similar to Figure 9.18.

9.5 Type **nbtstat -r** and press **Enter**. What does it show?

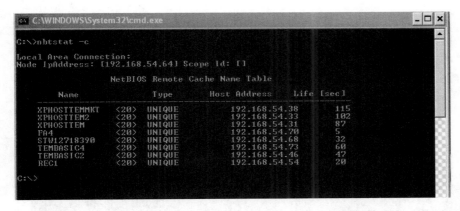

Figure 9.18

Nbtstat -c

9.6 Type **nbtstat -s** and press **Enter**. What does it show? When would this information be useful?

9.7 Close the command prompt window.

Challenge Exercise 9.3

In this exercise, you explore the purpose of Nslookup. This exercise will show you how information about an IP address and domain name can be obtained through the use of the Nslookup command. You need a computer with a Windows-based operating system and TCP/IP installed, network connectivity, and Internet access.

9.1 Log on to your computer.

9.2 Click **Start**, click **Run**, type **cmd** in the Open text box, and click **OK**. A command prompt window opens.

9.3 At the command prompt, type **ipconfig** and press **Enter**. The IP configuration of your computer displays.

9.4 At the command prompt, type **nslookup** and the connection-specific DNS suffix from the results of the ipconfig command. Press **Enter**. A list of current name servers is displayed. It should look similar to Figure 9.19. What information does this display? How would you use this information?

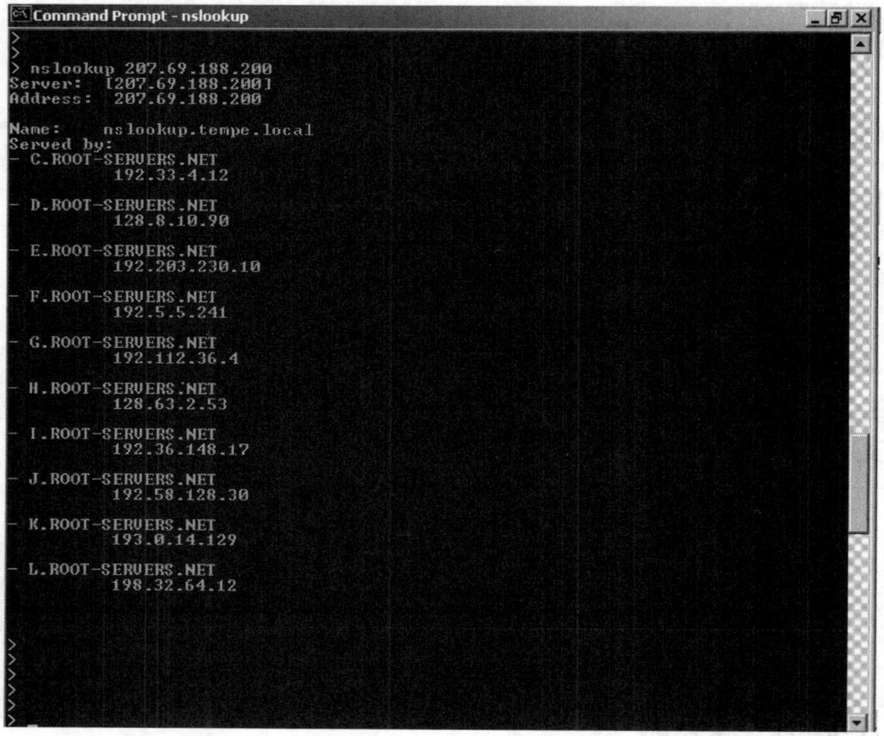

```
Command Prompt - nslookup                                     _ 8 X
>
>
>
> nslookup 207.69.188.200
Server:  [207.69.188.200]
Address:  207.69.188.200

Name:     nslookup.tempe.local
Served by:
- C.ROOT-SERVERS.NET
              192.33.4.12

- D.ROOT-SERVERS.NET
              128.8.10.90

- E.ROOT-SERVERS.NET
              192.203.230.10

- F.ROOT-SERVERS.NET
              192.5.5.241

- G.ROOT-SERVERS.NET
              192.112.36.4

- H.ROOT-SERVERS.NET
              128.63.2.53

- I.ROOT-SERVERS.NET
              192.36.148.17

- J.ROOT-SERVERS.NET
              192.58.128.30

- K.ROOT-SERVERS.NET
              193.0.14.129

- L.ROOT-SERVERS.NET
              198.32.64.12

>
>
>
>
>
```

Figure 9.19

Nslookup

9.5 Type **ext** and press **Enter** to exit Nslookup.

9.6 Close the command prompt window.

Challenge Exercise 9.4

In this exercise, you learn about FTP. This exercise will show how you can use the FTP command to display various parameters. You need a computer with a Windows-based operating system and TCP/IP installed, network connectivity, and Internet access.

9.1 Log on to your computer.

9.2 Click **Start**, click **Run**, type **cmd** in the Open text box, and click **OK**. A command prompt window opens.

9.3 At the command prompt, type **ftp** and press **Enter**. An ftp > prompt appears.

9.4 Type **?** and press **Enter**. Review the available FTP commands.

9.5 Type **open ftp.gnu.org** and press **Enter**. What happens?

9.6 Type **close** and press **Enter** to disconnect the connection.

9.7 Type **open ftp.Microsoft.com** and press **Enter**. When the logon prompt appears, type **anonymous** for the logon name and press **Enter** for the password. What happens?

9.8 Type **ls** and press **Enter**. What does it show?

9.9 When you are finished, type **close** and press **Enter** to close the connection.

9.10 Type **bye** and press **Enter** to exit FTP.

9.11 Close the command prompt window.

Challenge Exercise 9.5

In this exercise, you learn how to create a simple Web page using a text editor. You need a computer with a Windows-based operating system, a Web browser, network connectivity, and Internet access.

9.1 Log on to your computer.

9.2 Open Notepad. (In Windows 2000 Professional, click **Start**, point to **Programs**, point to **Accessories**, and click **Notepad**.)

9.3 When Notepad is open, type the following HTML text into the window:

```
<html>
<head>
<title>My First Web Page</title>
</head>
<body>
Hello everybody. This is my very first Web page!
```

```
</body>
</html>
```

9.4 Save it to the desktop as a file name **first.html**.

9.5 Open the page in your Web browser (e.g., Microsoft Internet Explorer or Netscape Navigator). All Web browsers can open a file stored on the local computer. In Internet Explorer or Netscape, point to **File** and click **Open** (or **Open File**) at the top of the window. Browse your computer to locate your desktop. Open the file **first.html**.

9.6 The URL displayed in the address window is C:\WINDOWS\ DESKTOP\first.html, showing that it is from the local hard disk, rather than the usual *http://<URL>*.

Challenge Exercise 9.6

In this exercise, you learn how to look up RFCs. You will learn how different protocols work. You need a computer with a Windows-based operating system and TCP/IP installed, network connectivity, a Web browser, and Internet access.

9.1 Log on to your computer.

9.2 In your Web browser, go to *http://www.faqs.org/rfcs/*. The Internet RFC/STD/FYI/BCP Archives Web page appears.

9.3 In the Display the Document by Number text box, type **821** and press **Enter**. The RFC 821-Simple Mail Transfer Protocol document appears.

9.4 Read the RFC and write down three items of interest regarding this RFC.

9.5 Click the **Back** button in your browser to return to the Internet RFC/STD/FYI/BCP Archives Web page.

9.6 Click the **Complete Index** link. Find the RFC for DNS.

Why are RFCs useful in network administration?

Challenge Exercise 9.7

In this exercise, you go to Whois.com and search for a domain to use for your network. You need a computer with a Windows-based operating system and TCP/IP installed, network connectivity, a Web browser, and Internet access.

9.1 Log on to your computer.

9.2 In your Web browser, go to **http://www.whois.com**.

9.3 In the Type the Domain Name You Want text box, type your first initial and last name and click **Go** (or press **Enter**).

9.4 Is the domain available? If not, search additional names until you find one that is available for all six top-level domain extensions.

9.15 Challenge Scenarios

Challenge Scenario 9.1

Bob Brown, your neighbor, has decided to start his own business selling insurance. He rented an office and purchased seven PCs and a server, and a laptop for himself. He knows you have good computer knowledge and asked you to help him set up Internet connectivity for the computers. He heard he must get a domain name and arrange for a company to host it. He is confused and would like you to explain to him what all of this means and what options he has. What will you tell him about getting a domain name? What suggestions would you offer him for DNS hosting?

Challenge Scenario 9.2

Bob thinks you did a great job helping him with his domain issues and now has some additional questions for you. The consultant who set up his network gave the workstations static IP addresses. One of Bob's friends told him that he can use *dynamic addresses* instead. His business is growing and he plans to add more staff. The consultant costs him a lot of money and takes a long time to complete a job. What will you tell him about dynamic addressing and how it works?

Challenge Scenario 9.3

Bob now decides he is ready to set up a Web site. His business is booming, and he wants to grow even bigger by having an Internet presence. One of his friends recommended a good designer, but the designer wants to know what language he wants the Web site programmed in and who is hosting the site. He comes to you again, asking you to explain Web site programming. What would you tell him?

Challenge Scenario 9.4

Bob approaches you about e-mail. His staff members are complaining that they have to use their personal e-mail addresses because the company has not provided them with business e-mail addresses. He realizes that he needs to do this, but one of his friends told him about how his network bogged down because of all the e-mail his employees were getting, so he switched to IMAP for mail. Bob has no idea what IMAP is or what it means. Because you are so good at explaining and clarifying technical issues, he once again asks you to tell him about e-mail and how it works. What will you tell him? Which e-mail protocol will you recommend?

CHAPTER 10

Network Security

After reading this chapter you will be able to:

- Identify threats
- Understand encryption types
- Understand the types of firewalls that are available
- Secure Web and e-mail servers
- Follow industry best practices to protect the network

The concept of security within the network environment includes all aspects of operating systems, software packages, hardware, and networking configurations, as well as any network sharing connectivity. This is not the only scope of security. As a professional, you will find that in today's world, physical security is also linked to IT security. Security cameras need IP addresses and space to store recordings, disaster recovery plans must now cover the entire business entity and not just the IT department, and physical access to unauthorized areas can be disastrous for a company. In this chapter, we cover the basics of properly securing your network, which includes learning about threats and vulnerabilities, encryption, firewalls, server security, and best practices.

10.1   Principles of Security

The modern computer world is a complex mix of different components with the purpose of making resources available to those who need it. Unfortunately, over the last decade, access to networks by unauthorized users has grown at a rate that far outpaces anything we could have imagined. We react by quickly developing and deploying hardware and software to meet the demands of business and home consumers, but fail to properly test and secure these technologies. This puts our networks at risk not only from the professional hacker but also from curious or disgruntled employees.

Security is not just a policy or a plan, it is a mindset. You must properly train and cultivate employees to be security aware. Remember that your network is only as strong as its weakest link, which is usually a human being, a concept that we will discuss further in the "Social Engineering" section later in this chapter. You will also have to stay current on threats and available patches to be sure that the servers and workstations are properly secured. Learning to implement encryption on sensitive data will be part of your job. Disaster recovery and incidence response plans need to be tested and updated on a regular basis. It all starts with proper planning.

10.2   Threats

An IT professional has the responsibility of ensuring that the network is secure and safe from attacks—quite an undertaking. A **threat** is anything that endangers the safety of the network. Threats come in all forms and sizes. The assessment of threats must begin when setting up the server. Most servers come with a wide range of services and protocols, many of which are turned on by default. This leaves them open to unauthorized access or threats, especially if you are unaware that these services are running. Another area of concern regarding threats is the use of a public Web server. Poorly written applications leave computers open to buffer overflows. (We will discuss buffer overflows later in this section.) **Malware**, or viruses, pose a threat to e-mail servers and can spread extremely fast. Humans pose probably the greatest threat to a network because their behavior cannot be easily controlled.

As you can see, threats are a part of the everyday life a network administrator. Because you can't make an environment completely threat-proof, you must be constantly attentive to be sure that your network is secure as possible. The first step to sound security is establishing a security policy.

10.2.1   Security Policy Issues

To ensure that threats are properly managed and maintained, it is important to establish clear and detailed security policies that are supported by an organization's management and practiced by its users. Policies that lack management support may prove to be unenforceable and those that users have no knowledge of are ineffective. Security policy planning details are quite extensive, and after the policy is in place it must be tested and updated on a regular basis.

Since September 11th, more companies are taking security seriously and have taken steps to implement an effective plan. Part of the problem with getting security funding and policies in place is that the return on investment can be difficult to calculate, and this type of expense shows no income. It is sometimes hard for a company to be proactive rather than reactive where security is concerned. Many companies take the approach that they will deal with the situation when it occurs.

Users must be made aware of security policies and expectations to minimize potential weaknesses in security. Without reminders, education, and testing, users may accidentally grant an attacker access to your network by such actions as not logging out when leaving for the day, sharing passwords with friends and coworkers, or by simply using easy-to-guess passwords.

> **TIP** Education about security should include management-level employees. Many times we assume that because they are management, this portion of the population is security aware. You will find this is not true in many cases.

10.2.2   Back Door

A **back door** is a program that allows access to a system without using security checks. In other words, it allows access to a computer without the user's knowledge or authorization. Programmers often put back doors in programs so they can debug and change code during test deployments of software. Because many of these are undocumented, they may be left in, causing security risks. Some viruses also install back doors for later access by a host to gather information such as passwords or account numbers. A type of back door can also be installed through applications that are hidden inside of games or software such as screen savers. When harmful code is hidden inside another application, it's called a Trojan horse. Trojan horses are discussed later in this chapter. Some applications that are meant for network administration can be installed by internal users to gain unauthorized access to servers or PCs from the Internet. Users should not be able to install this type of software, and if there is a good security policy in place, you may be able to keep this type of situation from happening.

Some of the better-known software programs used as back doors include:

- **Back Orifice:** This is a remote administration tool allowing system administrators to control a computer from a remote location. It is a dangerous back door designed by a group called the Cult of the Dead Cow Communications. Back Orifice consists of two main pieces: a client application and a server application. The client application, running on one machine, can monitor and control a second machine running the server application.

- **W32/Mofei-C:** This is a worm that spreads via network shares and a backdoor Trojan server, which allows remote access and control of the computer. It can be run on Microsoft Windows 95, 98, Me, NT, 2000, and XP. W32/Mofei-C provides backdoor access and control over a computer by creating a back door and then listening for instructions being sent from a remote client. The remote intruder can then carry out a variety of actions such as deleting files and folders, executing files, and downloading files from the Internet.

- **Sub7 (or SubSeven):** This is a Windows 9x Internet back door Trojan similar to Back Orifice and W32/Mofei-C. It can affect Windows 95, 98, NT, 2000, Me, and XP. When it is running, anyone running the appropriate client software has unlimited access to the system while it is connected to the Internet.

NOTE

Back Orifice, W32/Mofel-C, and Sub7 have two essential parts: a server and client. The server is the infected computer, and the client is used to remotely control the server. These programs are known as illicit servers.

Remote administration programs are available to network administrators. These non-Trojan, commercial products include pcAnywhere, Real Virtual Network Computing (VNC), and Microsoft Terminal Services. pcAnywhere is a remote control software with encryption and authentication produced by Symantec. It is used by many companies in their help desk departments for resolving user issues. Virtual Network Computing is remote control software created by AT&T Laboratories that allows you to view a desktop environment from anywhere on the Internet and from a wide variety of machine architectures. Microsoft operating systems use Terminal Services for remote control. Terminal Services delivers the Windows desktop and applications by means of terminal emulation. Even though these are tools used for administration, they can also be used with malicious intent.

Another type of back door comes in the form of a privileged user account. An existing user who already has privileges often creates the back door account. This account is set up to look like a normal user's account and is given high-level privilege. This allows the user or an attacker to come in under an alias. To prevent this situation, you need to set proper access so that users will not have the right or privilege to alter operating system files.

10.2.3 Brute Force

Brute force is a term used to describe a way of cracking a cryptographic key or password. It involves systematically trying every conceivable combination until a password is found or until all possible combinations have been exhausted. Brute force is a method of pure guessing. Password complexity plays an important role when dealing with brute force programs—the more complex the password, the longer it takes to crack. Many programs exist that try to decipher password files. L0phtCrack is one such program.

It's designed to crack passwords in network traffic streams or in captured password files. L0phtCrack works very quickly. As processor speeds increase, the time to recover passwords will shorten.

A dictionary attack is the first step of a brute force attack. This type of attack checks through known words in a data file, trying to match the password with a word in the dictionary. A birthday attack is a type of brute-force technique that uses hash functions. (We discuss hash functions in the "Encryption and Decryption" section later in this chapter.) The probability is greater than 50% that two or more people in a group of 23 will share the same birthday, hence the term birthday attack.

> **TIP** As users, we tend to choose passwords that have special meaning to us or relate to our everyday life. This makes the passwords easy to crack because they are usually found in the dictionary.

Some of the more popular password-guessing programs include:

- **Crack:** A password-cracking program designed to quickly locate insecurities in Unix (or other) password files by scanning the contents of a password file.

- **John the Ripper:** A password-cracking program that is available for Unix, DOS, and Windows NT/95. It has its own modules for different ciphertext formats and architectures.

- **L0phtCrack:** A Windows and Unix password auditing tool that produces user passwords from the cryptographic hashes that are stored by the operating system.

10.2.4   Buffer Overflow

The most popular attacks are **buffer overflow** attacks, which are constantly being launched. These attacks are called buffer overflows because more data is sent to a computer's memory buffer than it is able to handle, causing it to overflow. Usually the overflow crashes the system, leaving it in a state in which arbitrary code can be executed or an intruder can function as an administrator. Buffer overflows are currently the most common way to cause disruption of service and lost data. This condition occurs when the data presented to an application or service exceeds the storage space allocation that has been reserved in memory for that application or service. Poor application design might allow the input of 100 characters into a field linked to a variable only capable of holding 50 characters. As a result, the application doesn't know how to handle the extra data and becomes unstable. The overflow portion of the input data must be discarded or somehow handled by the application, otherwise it could create undesirable results. Because there is no check in place to screen out bad requests, the extra data overwrites some portions of memory used by other applications, causing failures and crashes. A buffer overflow can result in the following:

- Overwriting of data or memory storage
- A denial of service due to overloading the input buffer's ability to cope with the additional data
- The originator can execute arbitrary code, often at a privileged level

Buffer overflow attacks are often waged against applications such as e-mail clients and against Internet-accessible services of Web servers. The following are examples of buffer overflow issues:

- In the fall of 2002, the Linux Slapper worm infected about 7,000 servers. The worm exploited a flaw in Secure Sockets Layer (SSL) on Linux-based Web servers. The premise behind this vulnerability is that the handshake process during an SSL server connection can be made to cause a buffer overflow by a client using a malformed key.
- Buffer overflows in the Java Virtual Machine (JVM), which is the client-side environment supporting Java applets, cause execution stack overwriting. Improperly created applets can potentially generate a buffer overflow condition, crashing the client system.

Data input should always include a default value and character limitations to avoid buffer overflow exploitation.

10.2.5   Denial of Service (DoS) Attack

The purpose of a **denial of service (DoS) attack** is to disrupt the resources or services that a user would expect to be able to access. These types of attacks are executed by manipulating protocols and can happen without the need to be validated by the network. Many of the tools used to produce this type of attack are readily available on the Internet. In fact, administrators use them to test connectivity and troubleshoot problems on the network. Internet Control Message Protocol (ICMP) utilities such as PING are used in such attacks. Examples of DoS attacks include:

- **Smurf/Smurfing:** This attack is based on the ICMP echo reply function. The attack sends PING packets to the broadcast address of the network in which the attacker replaced the original source address in the PING packets with the source address of the victim. This causes a flood of traffic to be sent to the unsuspecting network device.

- **Fraggle:** This attack is similar to a Smurf attack. The difference is that it uses the User Datagram Protocol (UDP) instead of ICMP.

- **Ping flood:** This attack attempts to block service or reduce activity on a host by sending PING requests directly to the victim. A variation of this type of attack is the PING of death, in which the packet size is too large and the system doesn't know how to handle the packets.

- **SYN flood:** This attack takes advantage of the TCP three-way handshake. The source system sends a flood of Transmission Control Protocol/Internet Protocol (TCP/IP) synchronization (SYN) requests and never sends the final acknowledgment (ACK), creating half-open TCP sessions. Because the TCP stack waits before resetting the port, the attack overflows the destination computer's connection buffer, making it impossible to service connection requests from valid users.

- **Land:** This attack exploits a behavior in the operating systems of several versions of Windows, Unix, Mac OS, and Cisco IOS with respect to their TCP/IP stacks. The attacker spoofs a TCP/IP SYN packet to the victim system with the same source and destination IP address as well as the same source and destination ports. This confuses the system as it tries to respond to the packet.

- **Teardrop:** This form of attack targets the behavior of UDP in the TCP/IP stack of some operating systems. A teardrop attack sends fragmented UDP packets to the victim with odd offset values in subsequent packets. When the operating system attempts to rebuild the original packets from the fragments, the fragments overwrite each other, causing confusion. Because some operating systems cannot gracefully handle the error, the system will most likely crash or reboot.

Another form of attack is a simple expansion of a DoS attack referred to as a **distributed DoS (DDoS) attack**. Downloadable software on the Internet can be used to launch DDoS attacks from inside the network, allowing disgruntled or malicious users to disrupt services without any outside influence. The attacker distributes software that allows the attacker partial or full control of the infected computer system. When an attacker has enough systems compromised with the installed software, he can initiate an attack against a victim from a wide variety of hosts. The attacks come in the form of the standard DoS attacks, but the effects are multiplied by the total number of machines under the control of the attacker.

10.2.6   Man-in-the-Middle Attack

The **man-in-the-middle attack** takes place when an attacker intercepts traffic and then tricks the parties at both ends into believing that they are communicating with each other. The attacker can also choose to alter the data or merely eavesdrop and pass it along. A man-in-the-middle attack can be compared to inserting a receptive box between two people having a conversation. This attack is common in Telnet and wireless technologies. It is generally difficult to implement because of physical routing issues, TCP sequence numbers, and speed. If the attack is attempted on an internal network, physical access to the network is required. All TCP/IP connections negotiate a TCP session between the hosts. Each sent packet has a sequence number included in the packet header. If the sequence numbers are out of sequence, they will most likely be discarded. An attacker would have to use a tool that could predict TCP sequence numbers. Considering the speed at which data packets travel, it would be difficult to change packet data on the fly. Because the hacker has to be able to capture and analyze, or *sniff*, both sides of the connection simultaneously, programs such as Juggernaut, T-Sight, and Hunt have been developed to make this type of attack easier.

To avoid man-in-the-middle attacks, be sure that access to wiring closets and switches is restricted; if possible, the area should be locked. Next, you should look at the services that can be exploited. DNS can be compromised and used to redirect the initial request for service, providing an opportunity to execute a man-in-the-middle attack. Domain Name System (DNS) access to should be restricted to read-only for everyone except the administrator. The best way to prevent these types of attacks is to use encryption and secure protocols.

10.2.7   Session Hijacking

Session hijacking is a term given to an attack that takes control of a session between the server and a client. The authentication mechanism is one way, it making easy for a hijacker to wait until the authentication cycle is completed and then generate a signal to the client. This signal causes the client to think it has been disconnected from the access point. In the meantime, the hijacker begins to transact data traffic, posing as the original client. This starts as a man-in-the-middle attack and then adds a reset request to the client. The result is that the client is kicked off the session, while the rogue machine still communicates with the server. This commonly happens during Telnet and Web sessions in which security is lacking or when session timeouts aren't configured properly.

Forcing a user to reauthenticate before allowing transactions to occur could help prevent this type of attack. Other protection mechanisms include the use of unique initial sequence numbers (ISNs) and Web session cookies.

10.2.8 Spoofing

Spoofing is the act of making data appear to come from somewhere other than where it really originated. This is done by modifying the source address of traffic or source of information. Spoofing seeks to bypass IP address filters by setting up a connection from a client and sourcing the packets with an IP address that is allowed through the filter. The idea behind spoofing can be seen in the Land attack in which the attacker creates a packet with the source and destination IP addresses both set to the victim's address. A special program or utility is required for a computer to generate traffic in this fashion.

Services such as e-mail, Hypertext Transfer Protocol (HTTP), and File Transfer Protocol (FTP) can also be spoofed. A hacker can impersonate a valid service by sourcing traffic using the service's IP address or name. Instructions are readily available on the Internet on how to generate e-mails that appear to come from a different user. These forms of attacks are often used to get additional information from network users in order to complete a more aggressive attack.

10.2.9 Social Engineering

The next type of attack that needs to be addressed can be one of the easiest and most productive attacks of all. It is called **social engineering**. It plays on human behavior and how we interact with one another. The attack doesn't feel like an attack at all. In fact, we teach our employees to be customer service-oriented, so often they think they are being helpful and doing the right thing. It is imperative that you understand how prevalent social engineering has become.

Some scenarios of social engineering attacks are described in the following list:

- A vice president calls you and states that she's in real trouble. She's attempting to do a presentation for a very important client and has forgotten her password. She just changed it yesterday and can't remember what it is. She needs to have it right away because she has a room full of clients waiting and she's starting to look incompetent. This is an extremely important client and means a lot of money to the company.

- Someone you have never seen before approaches you as you are entering a secured building. She has her hands full carrying coffee and doughnuts. She smiles and says she just doesn't seem to have an extra hand to grab the door. She asks that you please hold it for her.

- You receive a call from the corporate office saying that they are deploying a new mail server and need to verify current user accounts and passwords. You are told that it is not secure to send this information via e-mail, so please print it and fax it directly to a number given to you that is direct line for the person deploying the new server.

In each of these situations, an attacker tries to manipulate corporate users to gain access or knowledge that allows him entry either into the building or network. Empathy and urgency are played upon in the first two scenarios. This makes users feel that it is okay to give out information or allow access to the building. In the third scenario, use of e-mail will be affected if you don't comply. Each attack plays on human behavior and our willingness to help and trust others.

10.2.10   System Bugs

To meet the demands of business and home consumers, we develop and deploy software so quickly that we do not take the time to properly test. This can lead to a vulnerability called bugs. Improperly programmed software can be exploited. Software exploitation is a method of searching for specific problems, weaknesses, or security holes in software code that takes advantage of a program's flawed code. One of the most used flaws is the buffer overflow, which we discussed earlier.

Many open source code operating systems, such as Linux and Unix and applications, are particularly vulnerable to system bugs, but once discovered can often be fixed within a relatively short period of time because the code is freely available. When closed-source operating systems or applications such as Windows, Mac OS, and Oracle contain system bugs, the users of these applications are dependent on the manufacturer to properly patch the problem once it has been identified. Some manufacturers are slow to admit a problem exists because it usually brings with it negative publicity. This can cause delays in correcting an identified weakness or security problem.

The most effective way to prevent an attacker from exploiting software bugs is to diligently apply the latest manufacturer's patches and service packs as well as monitor the Web for new vulnerabilities.

10.2.11   Malicious Software

In today's network environment, malicious code, or malware, has become a serious problem. The target is not only the information stored on local computers but other resources and computers as well. As a network professional, part of your responsibility is to recognize malicious code and know how to respond appropriately. In this section we will cover the various types of malicious code you might encounter: viruses, Trojan horses, and worms.

Viruses

A program or piece of code loaded onto your computer without your knowledge that is designed to attach itself to other code and replicate is called a **virus**. It replicates when an infected file is executed or launched. At this point it attaches to other files, adding its code to the application's code, and continues to spread. Even a simple virus is dangerous because it can use all available resources and bring the system to a halt. Many viruses can replicate themselves across networks, bypassing security systems. Several types of viruses exist:

- **Boot sector (also called master boot record or master boot sector):** Places a virus into the first sector of the hard drive so that when the computer boots up, the virus loads into memory
- **Polymorphic:** Developed to avoid detection by antivirus software, it has the ability to change form each time it is executed
- **Macro:** Is inserted into a Microsoft Office document and e-mailed to unsuspecting users

NOTE Viruses have to be executed by some type of action, such as running a program.

Since 2000, the majority of viruses released are actually worms. The following short list of viruses/worms, and their descriptions, have had a significant impact on computer users:

- **LoveBug:** This virus originated in an email with the subject line "I love you." Once the attachment was launched, the virus sent copies of the same email to all e-mail addresses listed in the user's address book. The virus came as a VBS attachment and deleted files, including MP3, MP2, and JPG and sent user names and passwords to the virus's author. LoveBug infected some 15 million computers and crashed servers located around the world.

- **Melissa:** This virus first appeared in March 1999. It is a macro virus, embedded in a Microsoft Word document. When the recipient receives the Word document as an attachment to an e-mail message and opens the document, the virus sends e-mail to the first 50 addresses in the victim's e-mail address book and attaches itself to each message.

- **Michelangelo:** This virus is a master boot record virus. It is based on an older virus called Stoned. The Michelangelo virus erases the contents of the infected drive on March 6 (the birth date of the virus' namesake) of the current year.

The number of new viruses and worms is growing at an alarming rate, and newer viruses cause more damage as virus writers become more sophisticated. Some Web sites offer low-cost subscriptions for access to the code for nearly every virus that exists. Some schools now teach virus writing. In any case, viruses cost you money due to the time it takes to clean the software and recover lost data.

A virus hoax uses system resources and consumes users' time. Many times, hoaxes come in the form of a chain letter bragging of free money. One of the more popular ones is about receiving millions of dollars for opening a bank to help a Nigerian investor. Some hoaxes tell users to delete files from their systems or inform them that a certain program will destroy their system on a certain date. If there is any doubt as to whether the virus threat is real, investigate it. Many good Web sites list these hoaxes. Visit the following antivirus Web sites for more virus information:

- Symantec: *http://www.symantec.com/avcenter/index.html*
- McAfee Security: *http://us.mcafee.com/virusinfo*

- Sophos: *http://www.sophos.com/*
- UrbanLegends.com: *http://www.urbanlegends.com*

Trojan Horses

Trojan horses are programs disguised as useful applications. Trojan horses do not replicate themselves like viruses but they can be just as destructive. Code hidden inside the application can attack your system directly or allow the system to be compromised by the code's originator. The Trojan horse typically is hidden, so its ability to spread is dependent on the popularity of the software and a user's willingness to download and install the software.

Examples of Trojan horses include:

- **Acid Rain:** This is an old DOS Trojan that, when run, deletes system files, renames folders, and creates many empty folders.
- **Trojan.W32.Nuker:** This is a Trojan designed to function as a DoS attack against a workstation connected to the Internet.
- **Simpsons:** The user is tricked into running a file that deletes files on selected drives via an extracted .bat file. This Trojan uses the program deltree.exe found on Windows 9x systems.

As with viruses, Trojan horses can do a significant amount of damage to a system or network of systems.

Worms

Worms are similar in function and behavior to a virus, Trojan horse, or logic bomb (described in the next section), with the exception that worms are self-replicating. A worm is built to take advantage of a security hole in an existing application or operating system, find other systems running the same software, and automatically replicate itself to the new host. This process repeats with no user intervention. After the worm is running on a system, it checks for Internet connectivity. If it exists, the worm then tries to replicate from one system to the next.

Some examples of worms include:

- **Morris:** This is probably the most famous worm of all. It took advantage of a Sendmail vulnerability and shut down the whole Internet in 1988.

- **Nimda:** This worm virus infects using several methods, including mass mailing, network share propagation, and several Microsoft vulnerabilities. Its name is admin spelled backward.

- **Code Red:** The exploit, a buffer overflow, is used to spread this worm. This threat only affects Microsoft Windows 2000 running Web servers.

There are many variants to each of these worms. Often they are quite difficult to remove, so antivirus companies have downloadable tools available to remove them.

 NOTE

A worm is a similar to a virus and Trojan horse, except that it replicates by itself without any user interaction.

Other Malware

Besides viruses, worms, and Trojan horses, other types of malware are available including logic bombs, spyware, sniffers, and keystroke loggers. A *logic bomb* is a virus or Trojan horse that is built to go off when a certain event occurs or a certain amount of time passes. For example, a programmer might create a logic bomb to delete all of his code from the server on a date after he has left the company. Several cases have been reported recently in which former employees have been prosecuted for their role in this type of destruction. During software development, it is a good idea to bring in a consultant to evaluate the code to keep logic bombs from being inserted. Although this is a preventative measure, it will not guarantee that a logic bomb won't be inserted after the programming has been completed.

Sometimes, undesirable code often arrives with commercial software distributions. The term *spyware* refers to software that communicates information from a user's system to the software developer. You might not be aware that many common personal productivity programs send information to the vendor at regular intervals. Be careful with freeware programs. Some of these contain spyware that scans systems for proprietary data and forwards it on to unauthorized remote hosts.

The degree to which utilities such as network sniffers and vulnerability scanners constitute malware is a matter of opinion. Many IT security departments use these tools to test networks for weaknesses and holes.

However, such tools are also used by employees to gain access to unauthorized resources. Keystroke loggers also border between security administration and security breach. As with scanners and sniffers, the intent can be good or bad. Some companies use commercial loggers to monitor employees, and law enforcement agencies may use keystroke loggers to gather evidence on suspected criminals. On the other hand, employees may download keystroke loggers from hacker sites to spy on their bosses and coworkers.

10.3 Encryption and Decryption

A cryptosystem or cipher system provides a way to protect information by disguising it into a format that can be read only by authorized systems or individuals. The use of these systems is called cryptography, and the disguising of the data is called **encryption**. Cryptography dates back to the ancient Assyrians and Egyptians. The first appearance of cryptography was when Julius Caesar sent messages. He didn't trust the messengers, so he replaced A with D, B with E, and so on, so only someone who knew his transposition could read the messages. Since the early manual systems of cryptography, we have evolved into using mechanical cryptography, which came into being with the use of computers. Modern cryptography has become increasingly important in securing data that is passed thorough networks or stored on hard drives.

Encryption is the transformation of data into a form that cannot be read without the appropriate key to decipher it. It is used to ensure that information is kept private. **Decryption** is the reverse of encryption. Decryption deciphers encrypted data into plain text that can easily be read. Encryption is amongst the most important concepts to understand. It is necessary to secure our environments due to the increasing sophistication of hackers and their tools. By studying and learning how encryption and decryption work, we can better understand how they interact with various applications, design concepts, and operating system security features.

A *cipher* is a combination of encoded or symbolic letters. There are two basic types of encryption ciphers: substitution and transposition. Both are covered in the following sections.

10.3.1 Substitution Ciphers

A substitution cipher replaces characters or bits with different characters or bits, keeping the order in which the symbols fall the same. The resulting

```
MVLP SWPPXQW LP PQFXSUKWN

KEY
F=R
K=L
L=I
M=T
N=D
P=S
Q=G
S=M
U=B
V=H
W=E
X=A


AFTER DECIPHERING, IT SAYS:
THIS MESSAGE IS SCRAMBLED
```

Figure 10.1
Substitution cipher

text is called ciphertext, which uses a key to decipher the code. (Both substitution and transposition ciphers result in ciphertext.) We use substitution ciphers, such as Morse code and shorthand, regularly. The only difference between these and ciphertext is that the preceeding examples are public; therefore, everyone knows how to decode them. Another example of a substitution cipher is a child's decoder ring. It has two concentric wheels of the letters of the alphabet. You rotate the outside ring and substitute the letters in your message found on the outside ring with the letters directly below on the inside ring. Julius Caesar used this same scheme. In the Caesar cipher, each letter is replaced with the letter three spaces away. This is also called a shift alphabet. It is possible to make your ciphertext a little tougher to decode by putting 26 pieces of paper into a hat, each with a letter of the alphabet written on it, drawing them out one at a time, and then placing them under the letters of a normal alphabet. Figure 10.1 shows a simple substitution cipher. Substitution is used in algorithms today but is much more complex than the example in Figure 10.1.

10.3.2 Transposition Ciphers

In a transposition cipher, the information is scrambled by keeping all of the original letters intact but mixing up their order. This is called permutation.

```
MEETME

AFTERW

ORKFOR

DRINKS
```

Figure 10.2

Transposition cipher

The key determines how to encode and decode the message. In the 5th century B.C., the Spartans used a transposition cipher called a scytale. The scytale uses a cylinder with a ribbon wrapped around it from one end to the other. The message was written across the ribbons, and then unwrapped from the cylinder. Only someone with an identical-diameter cylinder could rewrap and read the message. If the cylinder was captured by the enemy, the whole system was compromised. Because both the sender and receiver of a transposed ciphertext must remember the method for enciphering and deciphering, many times something simple is chosen. Geometrical figures are easy to remember and serve as the basis for a whole class of transposition ciphers. In the example shown in Figure 10.2, the message will be the shape of a rectangle. Because there are 24 characters, the message is written in a 6×4 box.

We can now transcribe the message by moving down the columns instead of across the rows. The characters are broken into groups of four to give no clues about word sizes. The result looks like this: MAOD EFRR ETKI TEFN MROK EWRS. This is a simple example and is only one of a variety of ways that a transposition cipher can be done. When it is used with complex mathematical functions, it can be difficult to break. The more complex the mathematical function, the more difficult it is to figure out.

Word lengths are telltale signs as to the nature of the code and are vulnerable to attacks that use frequency analysis. Frequency analysis relies on the fact that certain words are used more often, which can help attackers figure out a pattern and put together the key used to encode the message. The following are the most frequently used two-letter words: of, to, in, it, is, be, as, at, so, we, he, by, or, on, do, if, me, my, up, an, go, no, us, and am. To help conceal your message, don't use spaces and break up the message into equal-size pieces. Although we used four letters in the example, five are customary.

10.3.3   Data Encryption Standard (DES)

The original idea behind the Data Encryption Algorithm was developed by IBM in the 1960s to protect financial transactions. They called this technique Lucifer. Lucifer was submitted for use as a public standard, refined, and adopted as a standard called the Data Encryption Algorithm (DEA) in 1976. **Data Encryption Standard (DES)** was adopted for use by the National Institute of Standards and Technology in 1977. The Data Encryption Standard suggests the use of a certain mathematical algorithm in the encrypting and decrypting of binary information. The system consists of an algorithm and a key. It is a block cipher using a 56-bit key on each 64-bit chunk of data. In a block cipher, the message is divided into blocks of bits. These blocks are then put through mathematical, substitution, or transposition functions. The key has a length of 64 bits, of which 56 are used as the key and the remaining 8 bits are parity bits used in checking for errors. Even with just 56 bits, there are (2^{56}) or over 72,000,000,000,000,000 (72 quadrillion) possible encryption keys that can be used. For each given message, the key is chosen at random from among this enormous number of keys. Although it is considered a strong algorithm, it is limited in use because of its relatively short key length.

Here is how DES works: DES enciphers data in blocks of 64 bits of binary data. A 64-bit key must be selected and then the plaintext converted to binary form. The order of the blocks of 64 bits is important. The left-most bit is in the first position. The right-most bit is the 64th bit, or in last position. The first step is to change the order within each block. For example, the 48th bit in the original string becomes the first bit in this new block. Bit 40 becomes bit 2 and so forth (see Figure 10.3). This is called permutation. Remember from the section on transposition, in permutation only order is changed. The results of this are then broken down into two halves. The process then runs in several modes and involves 16 rounds of transformation. The key and the message become interwoven. This makes it difficult to break apart the cipher. Decoding is accomplished by running the process backward.

Modern day cryptosystems are classified as either public key or private key. Private-key encryption methods, such as DES, use the same key to both encrypt and decrypt the data. Therefore data can be recovered only by using the same key with which it was encoded. Private-key systems suffer from this key distribution problem. To be successful, both the sender and receiver must know the key and, for a secure communication to occur, first the key must be sent securely to the other party. Anyone who has the key and the algorithm can easily decipher the code and read the original message. In 1997, Rivest, Shamir, and Adleman, developers of the next type of

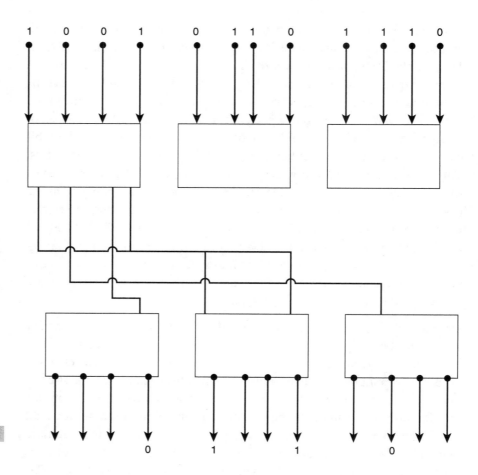

Figure 10.3

Block cipher algorithm

encryption we will discuss, offered a $10,000 reward for breaking the encryption on a DES message. A joint effort of over 14,000 computer users deciphered the message after running through only 18 quadrillion of the 72 quadrillion possible keys.

Although DES is considered strong encryption, many companies use Triple Data Encryption Standard (3DES), which applies three keys in succession. First, the data is passed through a 56-bit key to provide encryption. Next, the data is decrypted using a different 56-bit DES key. Finally, the data is passed through the original key again. It may seem odd to encrypt the data with one key and decrypt it with a different one. 3DES is designed so that when decryption is performed, it isn't with the original key, which changes the data seen by the third run of the algorithm with the original key. This is what 3DES uses for increased strength and protection against hacking because there are essentially two different keys applied, making the reconstruction of data very difficult.

10.3.4   Rivest-Shamir-Adleman (RSA)

Rivest-Shamir-Adleman (RSA) is an Internet encryption and a digital signature authentication system that uses an algorithm developed in 1977 by Ron Rivest, Adi Shamir, and Leonard Adleman. This encryption system is currently owned by RSA Security. (For additional information, visit the RSA Web site at *http://www.rsasecurity.com.*) The RSA algorithm is the most commonly used encryption and authentication algorithm. It is often included as part of Web browsers and various other products. The RSA key length may be of any length, and it works by multiplying two large prime numbers. (More math!) How many of us remember what a prime number is? A prime number is a number divisible only by itself and 1. After some additional functions, it derives a set of numbers—one for a public key and the other for a private key. This is known as a *public-key cryptosystem.* The public key is readily available. The private key is kept confidential. We will discuss this further in the "Public-Key Cryptography" section later in this chapter.

How does RSA work? As stated previously, the algorithm involves multiplying two large prime numbers and, through additional operations, derives a set of two numbers that make the public and private keys. The security of the RSA system is based on the assumption that factoring is difficult. The fastest known factoring algorithm would take an extremely long time for an attacker to break the code. Many times, attacks are aimed not at the cryptography itself but at a weakness in a specific implementation of it. For example, if you store your private key insecurely, it may be discovered by an attacker.

Both keys are needed for encryption and decryption, but only the owner of a private key needs to know it. The private key is used to decrypt text that has been encrypted with the public key. If you want to send me a message, you can find out my public key and encrypt a message using that key. When I receive the message, I decrypt it with my private key. Because messages are encrypted with a public key and decrypted with a private key, keys do not need to be distributed for a secure communication to occur. A user wishing to exchange encrypted messages using a public-key cryptosystem places their public encryption key in a public file. The user's corresponding decryption key is kept confidential. The following is a recap of how public encryption works:

1. User 1 wants to send a private message, M, to User 2.
2. User 1 gets User 2's public key from a public server.
3. User 1 encrypts message M using User 2's public key.
4. This results in an encrypted message, E.
5. User 1 sends Message E.
6. Upon receipt, User 2 decrypts message E using his or her private key.
7. This results in User 2 possessing the original message M.

The RSA public-key cryptosystem can also be used to authenticate or identify another person or entity by use of a digital signature. This works because everyone has a private key that no one else has access to, allowing for positive and unique identification. We discuss digital signatures in the "Digital Signatures" section later in the chapter.

10.3.5 Public-Key Cryptography

In 1973, a few years before RSA was invented, Cliff Cocks of Communications-Electronics Security Group (CESG) invented the first practical method for what we now call public-key cryptography (PKC). This was inspired by James Ellis's work on the possibility of nonsecret encryption in 1970. Then in 1976, Whitfield Diffie and Martin Hellman introduced the concept of public-key cryptography. This key exchange algorithm was previously developed in 1974 by Malcolm Williamson. As the PKC concept spread, other methods came into being. We will discuss the Diffie-Hellman and other algorithms shortly.

As you learned in the previous section, public-key cryptosystems use different keys to encrypt and decrypt data. The public key is readily available whereas the private key is kept confidential. We are now going to introduce two new terms into the mix: *symmetric* and *asymmetric*. There are two major types of algorithms used today: symmetric, which has one key that is private at all times; and asymmetric, which has two keys, a public one and a private one. In an asymmetric algorithm such as RSA, there is always a public key available for whoever is going to encrypt the data to send to the keeper of the private key. The private key is maintained on the host system. The public key can be made available through e-mail or a centralized server. The environments where public-key encryption is very useful include unsecured networks where data is vulnerable to interception and abuse, and the Internet because the public key is all that needs to be distributed. Symmetric encryption can work over the Internet as well, but providing the key securely to everyone who requires it can be challenging. Besides RSA, some of the more popular asymmetric encryption algorithms are:

- **Diffie-Hellman Key Exchange:** This is also called the exponential key agreement. It is a key exchange design whereby two parties dynamically exchange a secret key that is known only to them. The keys are passed in such a way that they are not compromised using encryption algorithms to verify that the data is arriving at its intended recipient. This algorithm is used only for key distribution. It is not used for encrypting or decrypting messages.

- **El Gamal Encryption Algorithm:** This was designed in 1985 by Dr. El Gamal. Rather than focusing just on the key design, El Gamal designed a complete public-key encryption algorithm that includes a means for signature verification. It consists of both encryption and signature variants based on the use of a finite field to calculate discrete logarithms. The encryption algorithm is similar to the Diffie-Hellman key agreement protocol.

- **Elliptic Curve Cryptography (ECC):** This was proposed separately by Victor Miller and Neal Koblitz in the mid-1980s. It is a method by which elliptic curves could be used to calculate simple but very difficult-to-break encryption keys to use in general-purpose encryption. ECC encryption algorithms have a compact design because of the advanced mathematics involved. ECC is more efficient than RSA and is often used in devices that have limited processing power such as wireless devices and cell phones.

The main advantage of public-key cryptography is increased security and convenience. Because there are two keys, the private keys never need to be transmitted or accessed by anyone other than the owner. Another advantage of public-key systems is that they can provide a method for digital signatures. In public-key authentication, each user is responsible for protecting his or her private key so the signature cannot be disputed. This is called nonrepudiation. We will cover nonrepudiation and digital signatures in the "Digital Signatures" section later in this chapter.

A disadvantage of using public-key cryptography is speed. It is much slower than private key encryption and often they are both used together to get the best of both worlds. Public-key cryptography is best suited for an open multiuser environment.

Public Key Infrastructure

The next level for Internet transactions will require a method for providing legally binding identities to individuals while they are online so that they can do online voting and mortgage document signing. The concept of the **Public Key Infrastructure (PKI)** allows you to bring strong authentication and privacy to the Internet. This infrastructure includes all of the technology, processes, and procedures involved in supporting a public key-based solution. By using the public-key cryptographic techniques and encryption algorithms we have previously discussed, you can provide authentication to users and ensure that only the intended recipients have access to data. PKI is comprised of several standards and protocols that are necessary for interoperability among different security products. With PKI, we can look at the elements of a security solution that provide integrity and privacy to information but are not tied to any vendor or application. The most interesting portions of a PKI solution tend to be the policies, procedures, and protocols (not the technological elements) required to have an effective solution.

To make a PKI work, we need to examine what PKI does and how it works. PKI provides for the secure exchange of data over a network by using an asymmetric key system. PKI provides the secure infrastructure for applications and networks, which includes access control to resources such as Web browsers and secure e-mail. The system consists of digital certificates and the **certification authorities (CAs)** that issue the certificates. **Certificates**

Figure 10.4
Certificate details

identify sources that have been verified as authentic and trustworthy. A registration authority (RA) provides authentication to the CA of the validity of a client's certificate request. One of the most commonly used certificate and registration authorities is VeriSign, a vendor that specializes in the issuance of certificates for secure Web site connections. (For more information on the service it provides, go to *http://www.verisign.com.*) This type of CA is often used to connect workstations to servers, especially with remote users connecting to the server from the Internet. In the end-of-chapter exercises, you will look at a digital certificate on a Web site to get a better idea of what they are. For now, see Figures 10.4 and 10.5 for examples. CAs are trusted entities.

The CA's job is to verify the holder of a digital certificate and ensure that the holder of the certificate is who they claim to be. A way to understand this is to compare a CA to a birth certificate-issuing authority. To obtain a birth certificate, a higher authority verifies your identity and then issues the certificate. Birth certificates are trusted, because the issuing authority is trusted. Any organization may choose to establish its own CA instead of using a third party such as VeriSign or Thawte, but typically these are used

Figure 10.5
Certificate general
information

only within the organization. See Figure 10.6 for an example of a CA. Each certificate holds all the necessary information for identification.

The following is an example of how communication exists within a PKI: I go to work for a company that has a PKI. I need to establish a key pair (public/private), so I request one from the CA. The CA requests identification information from me. After the CA receives and verifies the identification information, I am registered in the CA database. The CA issues me a certificate that has my identification and public key embedded. I want to exchange messages with you. I request your public key from the CA. I then use this key to encrypt a session key that is used to encrypt the messages we send each other. I send my certificate to you, which contains my public key. When you receive my certificate, your browser checks whether the CA is trusted and whether the certificate is valid. As long as everything is fine, you can decrypt the session key with your private key. See Figure 10.7 for an illustration of this process.

Multiple standards and protocols are associated with a PKI. Each one has a specific purpose and may or may not be needed in a PKI solution. The following are several different standards that can be used in PKI:

- Public Key Infrastructure for X.509 Certificates (PKIX) is a group of protocols and standards for X.509-based Public Key Infrastructures.

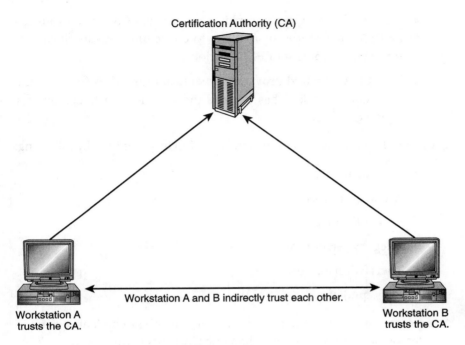

Figure 10.6
Certification Authority

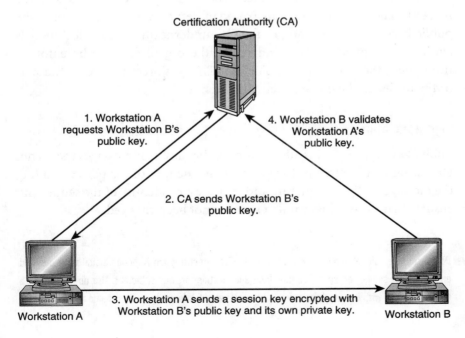

Figure 10.7
PKI process

- The Public-Key Cryptography Standards (PKCS) were produced by RSA Laboratories in an effort to create universal specifications for the development of PKI solutions.

- The X.509 standard provides authentication services for a system. The X.509 standard has become the Internet's PKI standard for digital certificates.

These standards are used to protect information by providing the following:

- Confidentiality
- Access authorization
- Authentication
- Integrity verification
- Transaction authorization
- Nonrepudiation

At times you may hear PKI referred to as a trust hierarchy. This occurs in PKI deployments in which more than one CA exists within a single organization. In a hierarchical structure, a root CA is placed at the top of the hierarchy and then other CAs are placed underneath. The root CA signs the public keys in the certificates of the CAs underneath. Hierarchical models allow for the policies and standards of the organization to be enforced throughout the infrastructure. The root CA takes precedence over the subordinate CAs in the hierarchical structure.

Digital Signatures

Public-key cryptosystems allow a user to digitally sign messages they send. Digital signatures attempt to guarantee the identity of the person sending the message. A digital signature authenticates the identity of the sender and ensures that the original content sent has not been changed.

WARNING ❗ Do not confuse a digital signature with a digital certificate or encryption. Although digital signatures and encryption use similar concepts, their intentions and functions are quite different. Also, do not confuse a digital signature with an e-mail signature that contains sender information such as name and address.

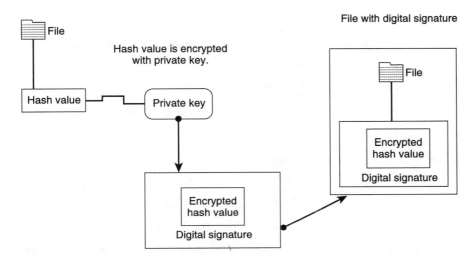

Figure 10.8
Digital signature process

A digital signature does not have to accompany an encrypted message. It can simply be used to guarantee the sender's identity and the message's integrity. The digital signature contains the digital signature of the CA that issued the certificate for verification. This is to prevent or alert the recipient to any data tampering. If a packet of data is digitally signed, it can only bear the mark of the sender. If the mark is different, the receiver would know, and the packet is either not unencrypted or is dropped. This works based on either asymmetric or hash algorithm principles.

We have talked about asymmetric algorithms, but what are hash algorithms? Let's start with hashing. **Hashing** is the transformation of a string of characters into a shorter fixed-length value or key representing the original string. Hashing is used in database indexing as well as encryption algorithms and digital signatures. The hashing algorithm is called the hash function. The digital signature is transformed with the hash function and then both the hashed value, which is also referred to as a message digest, and the signature are sent in separate transmissions. Using that same hash function, the receiver obtains a message digest from the signature and compares the two. If the message is genuine, they will be the same. The exchange would look similar to Figure 10.8.

For example, let's assume I need to digitally sign an e-mail and send it to you. I need to guarantee the integrity of the message and assure you that it is really from me. Here is the sequence of events:

1. I type the e-mail.

2. Using software built into the e-mail client on my machine, I obtain a hash of the message.

3. Next, I use my private key to encrypt the hash.

4. This encrypted hash is the digital signature for the message.

5. The message is then sent to you.

6. You receive the message, and using the software on your machine, you make a hash of the received message.

7. You use my public key to decrypt the message hash.

8. A match of the hashes proves that the message is valid.

Because digital signatures can prove who sent what messages when, the government put standards into place for use. The Digital Signature Standard (DSS) was developed for federal agencies. Government agencies are required to use the Digital Signature Algorithm (DSA) and the Secure Hash Algorithm (SHA). The DSA is used to digitally sign the message and the SHA is used to ensure the integrity of the message. Most vendors have designed their products to meet these standards.

TIP Besides the SHA algorithm, the asymmetric algorithms RSA, ECC, and El Gamal can be used for digital signatures.

Digital signatures are used to authenticate the identity of the sender, as well as ensure that the original content sent has not been changed. Authentication is a verification process that ensures the identity of a user or system. Digital signatures are often used to identify the author of an e-mail or to identify a Web transaction. Authentication and encryption each have their own function, but combining the two provides better security. Nonrepudiation is intended to provide a method in which there is no way to refute where data has come from. It guarantees that the sender cannot later deny having been the sender and that the recipient cannot deny having been the receiver. This of course does not take into account the possibility that the system used to create the private key and the encrypted digital signature may have been compromised. The key elements that nonrepudiation services provide on a typical client/server connection are proof of origin, proof of submission, proof of delivery, and proof of receipt. Although authentication and nonrepudiation may seem to be similar, the difference is that with nonrepudiation, proof can be demonstrated to a third party. A sender of a message signs a message using his or her private key. This provides unforgeable proof that the sender generated the message. Nonrepudiation is unique to asymmetric systems because private keys are not shared.

Let's review what choices we have with digital signatures. Different processes and algorithms provide different degrees of security:

- If a message is encrypted, it offers confidentiality.
- If a message is hashed, it offers integrity.
- If a message is digitally signed, it offers integrity and authentication.
- If a message is digitally signed and encrypted, it offers integrity, authentication, and confidentiality.

10.3.6 Virtual Private Networks (VPNs)

A **virtual private network (VPN)** is a network connection that allows you access via a secure tunnel built on top of a publicly accessible infrastructure, such as the Internet or the public telephone network. VPNs are called private because encryption and tunneling protocols (discussed in the next section, "Protocol Tunneling") are used to protect and maintain the data's confidentiality and integrity while it travels across the Internet. VPNs are very popular for the following reasons:

- Users in an organization can dial a local Internet access number and connect to the corporate network for the cost of a local phone call. This has the potential for enormous savings on the phone bill.
- Administrative overhead is reduced with a VPN because the Internet service provider (ISP) is responsible for maintaining the connectivity once the user is connected to the Internet.
- They use some combination of encryption, digital certificates, strong user authentication, and access control to provide security to the traffic they carry.
- They can provide connectivity to many machines behind a gateway or firewall.

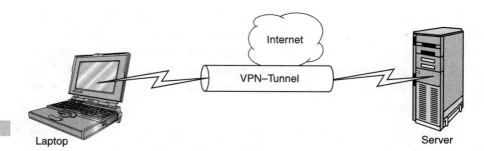

Figure 10.9
VPN

Here is how a VPN works, demonstrating a client accessing a corporate LAN through the Internet:

1. The remote user dials in to his or her local ISP and logs into the ISP's network.

2. The user initiates a tunnel request to the server on the corporate network. The server authenticates the user and creates the other end of the tunnel.

3. The user then sends data through the tunnel, which is encrypted by the VPN software before being sent over the ISP connection.

4. The server receives the encrypted data, decrypts it, and forwards the packets to the destination on the corporate network. Any information sent back to the remote user is encrypted before being sent over the Internet.

See Figure 10.9 for an illustration of what takes place when a VPN is used.

So how is this different from a client accessing an ordinary network? Virtual private networks allow any valid remote user to become part of a company's network, using the same network and addressing scheme as regular users. In addition, each company's network can be responsible for validating anyone coming into the network, despite the fact that they are actually dialing in to a public network. Besides being used by remote users to access the network, VPNs can be used to provide a connection between two routers. This is commonly called a gateway-to-gateway connection. In this scenario, each device has a dial-up connection, VPN software, and compatible protocols and encryption methods. They can also be implemented as an intranet, extranet, or a site-to-site VPN, or can occur between firewalls that have VPN functionality. (Firewalls are discussed in detail later in the chapter.)

In a VPN, encryption and decryption take quite a bit of CPU and memory usage, especially if implemented on a firewall that has VPN functionality. This is because there is extra work being done on the packets as they enter and leave the network, requiring more processing power. When implementing a VPN solution, be sure to consider that dedicated hardware or existing hardware upgrades may increase the cost of the proposed solution.

10.3.7   Protocol Tunneling

VPN technology is based on tunneling. **Tunneling** uses one network to send its data through the connection of another network. It works by encapsulating a network protocol within packets carried by a public network. In the case of a VPN connection over the Internet, packets of one protocol are encapsulated within the IP packets. In other words, tunneling is the process of placing an entire packet within another packet and sending it over a network. The protocol of the outside packet is understood by the network and both interfaces where the packet enters and exits the network. In this case, the outer protocol is IP. For a tunnel to be established, both the client and the server must be using the same tunneling protocol. Tunneling technology can be based on either a Layer 2 or Layer 3 tunneling protocol. Remember from Chapter 2 that Layer 2 protocols correspond to the Data Link layer and use frames to transmit data, whereas Layer 3 protocols correspond to the Network layer and use packets.

Tunneling actually requires a carrier, passenger, and encapsulating protocol. The protocol used by the network that the information is traveling over is called the carrier protocol. Remember that the end interfaces must also understand this protocol. The protocol that is wrapped around the original data is the encapsulating protocol, such as IP Security (IPSec), Point-to-Point Tunneling Protocol (PPTP), or Layer Two Tunneling Protocol (L2TP). The original data being carried is the passenger protocol. You can place a packet that uses a protocol not supported on the Internet, such as NetBios Enhanced User Interface (NetBEUI), inside an IP packet and send it over the Internet. You can also put a packet that uses a nonroutable IP address inside a packet that uses an external IP address to access a private network over the Internet.

Four different protocols can be used for creating VPNs over the Internet: Layer 2 Forwarding (L2F), IPSec, PPTP, and L2TP.

PPTP was created by the PPTP Forum, a consortium that includes US Robotics, Microsoft, 3Com, and Ascend. The Point-to-Point Protocol

(PPP) is the basis of both PPTP and L2TP. VPN tunneling is supported no matter which protocol is used on the LAN because all TCP/IP, Sequenced Packet Exchange (SPX), and NetBEUI communications are encapsulated into PPP. PPP is then encapsulated into either PPTP or L2TP.

PPTP allows tunneling that works at Layer 2 and enables a single point-to-point connection. There are two main connection types for which PPTP may be used: over the Internet or via a dial-up connection. Point-to-Point Tunneling Protocol (PPTP) technology embeds its own network protocol within the TCP/IP packets carried by the Internet. After the PPTP tunnel is created, user data is transmitted between the client and PPTP server in IP datagrams. The datagrams are created using a modified version of the Generic Routing Encapsulation (GRE) protocol. PPTP supports 40-bit and 128-bit encryption and can use any of the PPP authentication protocols, including Microsoft Challenge Handshake Authentication Protocol (MSCHAP) version 1 or version 2 and Shiva Password Authentication Protocol (SPAP).

L2TP is the product of a partnership between the members of the PPTP Forum, Cisco, and the Internet Engineering Task Force (IETF). L2TP is an extension of the PPP protocol, created by combining the best qualities of PPTP and L2F. L2TP is a data-link extension of PPP that sets up a single point-to-point connection between two computers. Because L2TP defines its own tunneling protocol, it requires support on the routers of the ISP, but it can encapsulate PPP packets for transmission over protocols such as X.25, Frame Relay, and ATM tunnels. L2TP encapsulates and transfers PPP frames and data over IP networks in the form of UDP packets using port 1701. The L2TP tunnel directs user requests via a L2TP Access Concentrator (LAC) to the central network server L2TP Network Server (LNS), which is either a router or a server and is the end point of all PPP sessions. It is specifically designed for client-to-gateway and gateway-to-gateway connections. It can handle any of the supported protocols implemented higher up the OSI model such as Password Authentication Protocol (PAP), Challenge Handshake Authentication Protocol (CHAP), MSCHAP version 1 or version 2, and SPAP or Extensible Authentication Protocol (EAP).

TIP Tunneling should not be used as a substitute for encryption. The strongest level of encryption possible needs to be used within the VPN.

Tunneling presents an issue for firewalls. For your firewall to allow the tunnel to be established, you need a set of rules configured to permit such activity. Unfortunately, once the VPN tunnel is created, it is considered a communication channel that already passed necessary security checks. Many times, VPN traffic is not filtered by the firewall. After establishing the communications channel, one could pass any traffic through, bypassing the rules instituted by the firewall. In addition, when encryption is used within a tunnel, filtering may not be possible because the firewall does not see the contents due to the end-to-end encryption between the peers. Of course, there are firewalls available that have VPN functionality. Here the packets arrive encrypted, and then they are decrypted to allow the firewall to inspect them.

Both PPTP and L2TP have advantages and disadvantages:

- PPTP can only run on top of IP networks, whereas L2TP can use other protocols such as Internetwork Packet Exchange (IPX) and Systems Network Architecture (SNA).

- PPTP does not support dial-in authentication protocols such as Remote Authentication Dial-In User Service (RADIUS) and Terminal Access Controller Access Control Systems (TACACS+), whereas L2TP does.

- PPTP is an encryption protocol, whereas L2TP is not, so it lacks security.

Combining more than one technology ensures the same level of security over public WANs as if the information were traveling over LAN wires. The most widely accepted mechanism to strengthen the security of encapsulated traffic is IPSec. L2TP/IPSec is considered the best standard for implementing VPN connections. We discuss IPSec after the next section on firewalls.

10.4   Firewalls

A **firewall** is a component placed between computers and networks to help eliminate undesired access by the outside world. It can be composed of hardware, software, or a combination of both. A firewall is the first line of defense for the network. How firewalls are configured is important, especially for large companies in which a compromised firewall may spell disaster in the form of bad publicity or a lawsuit, not only for the company, but also for the companies with which it does business. For smaller companies,

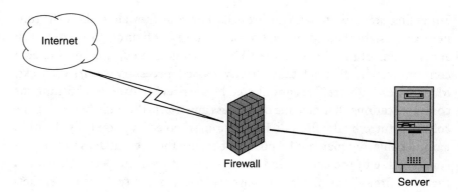

Figure 10.10
Firewall

a firewall is an excellent investment because most small companies don't have a full-time technology staff, and an intrusion could easily put them out of business. Everything considered, a firewall is an important part of your defense, but you should not rely on it exclusively for network protection. See Figure 10.10 for an example of a firewall.

Network firewalls operate at different levels of the OSI model and use different criteria to restrict traffic. There are four broad categories that firewalls fall into: packet filters, circuit-level gateways, application-level gateways, and stateful inspection. These four categories can be grouped into two general categories: network-level and application-level firewalls. Packet filters and stateful inspection firewalls are considered network-level, and circuit-level and application-level gateways are considered application-level firewalls. The lowest layer a firewall can operate at is the Network layer (Layer 3). Layer 3 firewalls are concerned with packets and their destinations. As the layers go higher the sophistication increases, but if a packet can be intercepted at the network level, the risk level decreases.

Very often these days you find that firewalls are used to implement a demilitarized zone (DMZ). This is a network segment located between two firewalls (see Figure 10.11). This is used as a buffer zone to keep the internal network safe from the outside world while offering services that are useful outside of the internal network without allowing the entire network to be available to Internet users. Many times the DMZ contains devices that need Internet access: Web, DNS, and e-mail servers. These servers all have to be hardened to keep them from being attacked by malicious users. Also, care should be taken when choosing what data and services are available on these machines.

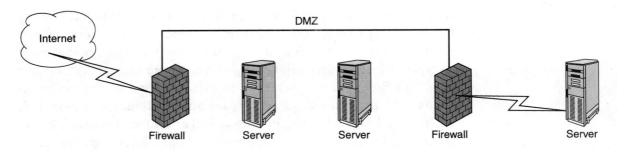

Figure 10.11
DMZ

Sensitive data should be located on the internal network, not the DMZ. If the DMZ is compromised, you want to be sure that the information that is stored there cannot cause harm to the company should the compromise become a matter of public knowledge. If fact, some states have passed legislation that says you must disclose compromises.

10.4.1   Packet Filtering

A packet-filtering firewall is typically a router. Packets can be filtered based on IP addresses, ports, or protocols. They operate at the Network layer (Layer 3) of the Open System Interconnection (OSI) model. Packet-filtering architecture involves checking the traffic for source and destination addresses and source and destination port numbers, as well as protocol types. Packet filtering is based on the information contained in the packet header. Each header is compared against a set of rules and then either forwarded or dropped. Typically, you can either allow or deny access. This set of rules is formulated in an access control list (ACL). This type of firewall can be set up to deny access to packets that have source addresses that are nonroutable internal addresses to prevent denial-of-services attacks.

Packet-filtering solutions are generally considered less secure firewalls because they still allow packets inside the network, regardless of communication pattern within the session. This leaves the system open to DoS attacks. Even though they are the simplest and least secure, they are a good first line of defense. They are low cost, but their main advantage is speed, which is why they are sometimes used before other types of firewalls to perform first-filtering pass.

A *stateful inspection firewall,* also referred to as a dynamic packet filtering firewall, takes packet filtering a step further and keeps track of all active and pending network connections through the firewall. It is a combination of all types of firewalls and relies on algorithms to process Application layer data. This firewall filters packets at the Network layer, determines legitimate session packets, and evaluates packet contents at the application level. Filtering decisions are based on rules as well as content. Because it knows the connection status, it can protect against IP spoofing. It has better security controls than packet filtering, but is more complicated to configure.

10.4.2 Application Gateway

To make up for some of the shortcomings associated with packet filtering, firewalls use software applications to forward and filter connections for services such as HTTP and SMTP. This application is referred to as a proxy service. An application-level gateway is known as a proxy, which is the host running the proxy service. It functions on the highest layer of the OSI model: the Application layer. Proxy service firewalls act as go-betweens for the network and the Internet. This type of firewall has a set of rules that the packets must pass to get in or out of the network. They hide the internal addresses from the outside world and don't allow the computers on the network to directly access the Internet. They do this by receiving all packets and replacing the IP address on the outgoing packets with their own address, and then change the address of the packets coming in to the destination address. Proxy service firewalls can also serve as caching servers by holding frequently visited Web pages in cache to reduce the time it takes to get a response from the Internet. The two basic types of proxies are circuit-level gateways and application-level gateways.

A circuit-level gateway operates at the OSI Session layer by monitoring the TCP packet flow to determine whether the session requested is legitimate and acting as a forwarding agent. Fundamentally, it relays TCP connections while applying filter rules based on port address. It is more secure than packet filtering, but not as secure as an application-level gateway. Because it can understand what a packet is, DoS attacks are detected and prevented in circuit-level architecture by discarding suspicious requests.

In an application-level gateway, all traffic is examined to check for OSI Application layer (Layer 7) protocols that are allowed. Examples of this type of traffic are File Transfer Protocol (FTP), Simple Mail Transfer Proto-

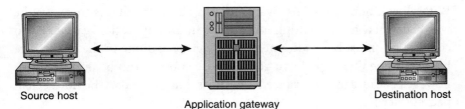

Source host

Application gateway

Destination host

Figure 10.12
Application gateway

col (SMTP), and Hypertext Transfer Protocol (HTTP). See Figure 10.12 for an example.

When a user wants to connect to an inside system from the outside, he or she first has to connect to the application gateway. Here's how it works using FTP as an example:

1. The user FTPs to the application gateway and enters the name of the FTP server.

2. The gateway checks the source address and either accepts or rejects the request, based on the filtering rules in place.

3. Depending on access, the user then may be required to authenticate with a login and password.

4. The proxy service creates an FTP connection between the FTP server and the gateway.

5. Communication is passed between the user and the server by the proxy service.

6. The application gateway logs the connection information.

Application gateways offer several advantages over packet-filtering methods. These include information hiding, strong authentication and logging, less complex filtering rules, and cost-effectiveness. We spoke earlier about how they hide the internal addresses from the outside world and don't allow the computers on the network to directly access the Internet. Because a packet travels all the way up the stack on an application gateway, developers may implement application-based security controls. This allows access to be controlled individually, by using group policies or filtering by content type. Because the filtering is application specific, it adds overhead to the transmissions but is more secure than packet filtering. Rules at the packet-filtering router now become less complex because they only need to allow application traffic intended for the gateway and reject the rest.

With all solutions come disadvantages as well as advantages that must be weighed when implementing a solution. In an application gateway, two connections must be made, one to the gateway and one to the server. The higher up the OSI model you go, the more controls can be implemented; however, because more advanced filtering is done, it tends to be slower than packet filtering.

10.5   IP Security (IPSec)

Short for **IP Security**, **IPSec** is a set of protocols developed by the IETF that operate at the Network layer (Layer 3) to support the secure exchange of packets. IPSec is used most commonly in firewalls, VPNs, and authentication products. Remember from our earlier discussion that in virtual private networks companies can exchange sensitive data over public networks with the assurance that data is going to the intended receivers, that it was kept confidential in transit, and that it did not change during transmission. The IPSec protocol suite adds an additional security layer in the TCP/IP stack that protects TCP/IP traffic by using a set of open standards and cryptographic security services. It provides security techniques and a mechanism that implements security services before it exchanges information between two entities. See Figure 10.13 for the reference between the various IPSec components. Because it is open standard, it does not rely on proprietary protocols or techniques while bringing a higher level of interoperability to the Internet. Business partners can communicate with each other without having to purchase proprietary equipment.

The IPSec suite attains a higher level of support for data transport by using a set of protocols and standards together. Each of these can be used independently to provide additional security, but when used together they ensure the highest data security during transport over public networks like the Internet. The most important of these are Authenticated Header (AH), Encapsulated Security Payload (ESP), and Internet Key Exchange (IKE). Depending on the encapsulation process used, the set of security services offered by AH and ESP can include:

- Integrity (both)
- Data origin authentication (both)
- Partial sequence integrity (AH for replay attacks)

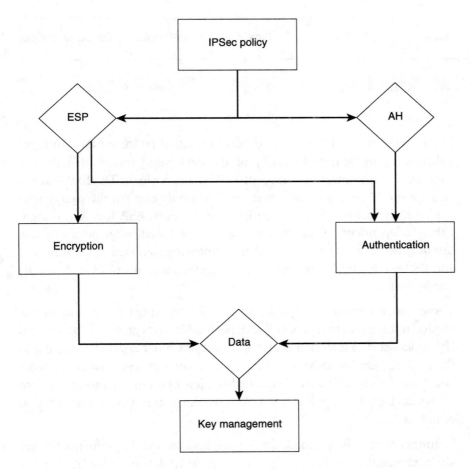

Figure 10.13
IPSec components

- Confidentiality (ESP)
- Limited traffic flow confidentiality (ESP)

AH provides integrity, authentication, and antireplay capabilities whereas ESP provides all that AH provides, plus data confidentiality. The specific information associated with each of these services is inserted into the packet in a header that follows the IP packet header. AH will ensure that the fields identifying the source and destination of the IP packet are valid and have not been modified during transmission. It ensures the integrity and authenticity of the entire packet with the exception of the destination address. This is accomplished by using digital signature techniques or one-way hash functions.

Original IP header	ESP header	TCP	Data	ESP trailer	ESP authentication

Figure 10.14

Transport mode ESP header

ESP is the portion of the IPSec protocol suite that addresses the confidentiality, integrity, and authenticity of the data being transmitted. It uses encryption techniques to encrypt the IP packet payload. The ESP will not encrypt the IP header or information; it will only encrypt the packet payload, which ensures the confidentiality of the data. ESP, like AH, is algorithm independent. IPSec does not define the specific algorithms to use, but only provides a framework for implementing standard algorithms. AH and ESP can be used independently or together, but most of the time only one is used.

There are two modes of operation for ESP: transport mode and tunnel mode. In transport mode, only the IP payload is encrypted and the original IP headers are left intact. In transport mode, the ESP header is inserted into the IP datagram immediately prior to the Transport layer protocol header (see Figure 10.14). This mode only adds a few bytes to each packet. It also allows devices on the public network to see the final source and destination of the packet.

In tunnel mode, the payload, the header, and the routing information are all encrypted in a new IP packet. The original IP datagram is placed in the encrypted portion of the ESP, and the whole frame is placed within a datagram having unencrypted IP headers. The information in the unencrypted headers is used to route the secure datagram. All traffic is passed to the IPSec device, and then it acts as a proxy element for this type of traffic. An unencrypted IP header might be included between the IP header and the ESP. See Figure 10.15 for an example.

Now that we have covered protocols and modes, it is time to address the cryptography part of IPSec. Users of IPSec implementations are issued

Figure 10.15

Tunnel mode ESP header

New IP header	ESP	Original IP header	TCP	Data	ESP trailer	ESP authentication

public keys and private keys. When a message is sent from one user to another, it is automatically signed with the user's private key. The receiver uses the sender's public key to decrypt the message. For key management, IPSec uses two methods of key management, manual keying for a small number of sites and IKE for automated key management for supporting many remote users. IKE is a hybrid protocol that implements the Oakley key exchange and Skeme key exchange inside the Internet Security Association and Key Management Protocol (ISAKMP) framework. Let's back up and define some of the terms we just mentioned:

- **Internet Key Exchange (IKE):** A protocol that provides authentication of the IPSec peers and negotiates IPSec keys and security associations.

- **Internet Security Association and Key Management Protocol (ISAKMP):** A general protocol framework that supports the mechanics of implementing a key exchange protocol, and the negotiation of a security association.

- **Oakley:** A key determination protocol that uses a public-key exchange algorithm and also supports a method to prevent key reuse called Perfect Forward Secrecy.

- **Skeme:** A key exchange protocol that defines how to derive authenticated keying material, with rapid key refreshment.

IKE automatically negotiates an authenticated and secure tunnel between the sender and the receiver, and then negotiates the security associations (SAs) for IPSec. An SA is a logical connection between two IPSec systems; that is, one security service carried by one protocol in one direction at one time. Because an SA is unidirectional, there are at least two security connections, one from A to B, and one from B to A. The security association is identified by a randomly chosen number called the security parameter index (SPI) and the destination IP address. After the connection is negotiated, authentication takes place. This can be through preshared keys in which the same key is preinstalled on each host, public key cryptography, or digital signature.

The IPSec Policy is similar to packet filter rules. It is stored in the Security Policy Database (SPD). Each packet entering the IP stack has to be compared with the Security Policy. Let's walk through how this all works together:

1.   A message is sent between company A and company B.

2. The IPSec driver of company A attempts to match the packet type against the IP Filter.

3. The IPSec driver asks ISAKMP to initiate security negotiations with company B.

4. Company B's ISKAMP receives the security negotiations request.

5. Both companies initiate a key exchange, establishing an SA and a shared secret key.

6. Both companies negotiate the security level, establishing IPSec SAs and keys.

7. Company A's IPSec driver transfers packets to the connection for transmission.

8. Company B receives the packets and transfers them to the IPSec driver.

9. Company B's IPSec uses the inbound SA and key to check the digital signature and then start decryption.

10. The provider's IPSec driver transfers decrypted packets for further processing.

10.6   Web Security

It is an IT professional's responsibility to be sure that the network is secure and safe from attacks. When you install a Web server, you open a window into your local network that the entire Internet can see through. Things get complicated in an intranet environment, where the Web server must typically be configured to recognize and authenticate various groups of users, each with distinct access privileges. There are many risks involved in conducting business online, so how do you make your Internet transactions safe?

There are various Web servers available, including Microsoft's Internet Information Services (IIS), Apache for Linux and Unix, Novell Netscape, Macintosh WebSTAR, and IBM WebSphere. Most servers come with a wide range of services and protocols, many of which are turned on by default. By identifying the role that each server plays, it can more easily be determined which services and protocols are required or needed. A Web server is used to host Web-based applications and internal or external Web sites. Because it can be either, you should also determine whether the server is to be accessed from the internal network, from the external world, or both. This helps identify the services and protocols you need on your server. The best way to ensure that only necessary services are running is to do a clean install. When a computer system is shipped to you, there is usually additional software, such as the manufacturer's tools, or additional configuration changes that have been made. Deploying a server out of the box may have services installed that actually pose security risks. Therefore, you need to determine which services can be uninstalled or disabled. It is not wise to run services that aren't going to be used. If they are left installed and improperly configured, someone else may use them to do harm to the network. This can happen from inside the network as well as from the outside. These days, more harm is done by disgruntled and curious employees than from outside hackers.

One primary concern of network security involves the use of a public Web server. When a Web server is visible to the outside world, security holes and vulnerabilities are sought by people looking to take valuable information from it, use it as a zombie server for DDoS attacks, or worse. Web servers contain large, complex programs that may have some security holes because many companies use custom Web applications to fit their business needs. Applications are often rushed to market without being programmed or tested properly. Besides misconfiguration and poor programming, client-side vulnerabilities and server-side vulnerabilities exist to add to the security concerns. Client- or browser-side vulnerabilities include ActiveX and JavaScript. Server-side vulnerabilities include Common Gateway Interface (CGI) script and protocol vulnerabilities.

Many Web sites use a scripting language known as JavaScript. JavaScript code is transferred to the client's browser where it is used to manipulate many browser settings. This mainly poses privacy-related vulnerability issues such as file access and manipulation. There is also a Java-based mini-program, called an applet. Improperly created applets can potentially generate a buffer overflow condition, crashing the client system. ActiveX is an application technology that can be embedded in a Web page much the same way as Java applets. ActiveX controls may be digitally signed and are restricted based on whether or not they are signed. If a user configures his or her browser to allow the execution of unsigned ActiveX controls, any action may be invoked by visiting a Web site that hosts an HTML page with a control embedded in it. This can crash the browser or damage the user's system.

A server-side interpretation option includes the use of CGI script, which is often written in the Perl language. These should be written with care because, in a way, they are miniature servers. CGI scripts are interpreted on the server system, generally by using user input values, so they are subject to exploitation in many ways. They may intentionally or unintentionally leak information about the host system that can help a hacker. Because most scripts process user input, it is possible for the user to trick them into executing commands. CGI scripts used to display such items as Web site guest books or display counters can make use of an account that has very little privileges; therefore, it is possible to cause a buffer overflow or run a script using an account that has very few privileges. To protect the server, you may want to disable scripting of objects marked as safe. Another option would be to implement a proxy server along with a content-filtering solution to protect the network.

Many protocols contain common vulnerabilities that may be manipulated to allow unauthorized access, including SSL connections. SSL was originally designed by Netscape to secure HTTP traffic passing through Web browsers. It is a Session layer protocol allowing communications to occur between the HTTP Application and TCP Transport layers of Internet communications. SSL establishes a stateful connection by negotiating a handshaking procedure between client and server. SSL connections are particularly vulnerable during the handshake process, when the client and server exchange information about the shared encryption keys to be used.

NOTE In the fall of 2002, 7,000 servers were affected by a worm that exploited a flaw in SSL on Linux-based Web servers. The premise behind this vulnerability is that the handshake process during an SSL server connection can be made to cause a buffer overflow by a client using a malformed key.

Basic Web connectivity using HTTP occurs over TCP port 80. An alternative to this involves the use of SSL transport protocols operating on port 443. When you access a site that uses HTTPS, the URL will show as *https://<website>*. Notice that there is an "s" after the http. HTTPS and SSL support the use of X.509 digital certificates from the server so that a user can authenticate the sender. HTTPS should not be confused with S-HTTP, which is a security-enhanced version of HTTP. HTTPS is the use of SSL as a layer under the HTTP application layer. S-HTTP allows the client to send a certificate to authenticate the user, whereas when using SSL, only the server can be authenticated.

A Web server should be patched after a new vulnerability is discovered and the patch should be tested to be sure there are no adverse effects. It is wise to subscribe to a security alert list or check various sites daily, as this is how quickly these occur. Whereas patching a Web server is a matter of due diligence, the actual challenge is to write better applications.

10.7   E-mail Security

E-mail has become an important part of our everyday life. It is fast, convenient, and now the preferred method of communication over using the telephone. It is used for company correspondence and for ordering products; it can even be used as evidence in court. However, its speed and accessibility also carry several security considerations. The public transfer of sensitive information exposes it to interception or being sent to undesired recipients. In addition, unsolicited e-mail may contain dangerous file attachments such as viruses, Trojan horses, or worms.

! WARNING

Viruses, Trojan horses, worms, and other forms of malicious programming often transmit themselves using electronic mail as their carrier.

10.7.1   Pretty Good Privacy (PGP)

When we wanted more out of our e-mail than just text, the Multipurpose Internet Mail Extension (MIME) protocol extended the ability of the original Simple Mail Transfer Protocol (SMTP) to allow embedded data within a message for the transmission and receipt of images, applications, and audio and video files. To provide a secure method of transmission, the Secure Multipurpose Internet Mail Extension (S/MIME) standard was developed. S/MIME originated around 1995 using the RSA algorithm, and is now in version 3. Because S/MIME was developed to provide an envelope around the mail, its content protection stops once the mail has been unpacked. An alternative to the use of S/MIME is the proposed PGP/MIME standard. S/MIME v3 and PGP are both protocols for adding authentication and privacy to messages.

Pretty Good Privacy (PGP) is derived from the application program developed by Phillip R. Zimmerman in 1991. Not only is PGP a specification, but it is also an application available from the PGP Corporation, which has integrated it into popular e-mail packages. PGP has become a powerful cryptographic product family that enables people to securely exchange messages and to secure files, disk volumes, and network connections with both privacy and strong authentication. It encrypts and decrypts e-mail messages based upon public-key encryption using either RSA or Diffie-Hellman. PGP can also be used for applying a digital signature without encrypting the message.

There are three different versions of PGP:

- **PGP 2.x:** All the 2.x versions are derived, more or less, from a common source base, PGP 2.3a, although all versions of PGP after 2.3 produce messages that cannot be read by 2.3 or earlier.

- **PGP 5.x and higher:** The PGP 5.x and higher series include OpenPGP compatibility. Most versions include both a command-line version and one with a graphical user interface.

- **GNU Privacy Guard:** GNU Privacy Guard is an OpenPGP program that is compatible with both the PGP 2.x and the PGP 5.x and higher versions, used mostly on Unix or Linux systems.

10.7.2   Privacy Enhanced E-Mail (PEM)

Privacy-Enhanced Mail (PEM) was one of the first standards for securing e-mail messages by encrypting 7-bit text messages. It specifies a PKI for key exchange over large networks like the Internet, providing for the secure exchange of electronic mail using cryptographic techniques, allowing for confidentiality, authentication, and message integrity. PEM can be employed with either symmetric or asymmetric cryptographic key mechanisms. It works at the Application layer, using a hierarchical authentication framework compatible with X.509 standards. The first entity in the hierarchy is a central authority called the Internet Policy Registration Authority (IPRA). This is the root of the hierarchy and validates all the certificates in the hierarchy. It is responsible for certifying and reviewing the policies of the entities in the next lower level called policy certification authorities (PCAs). PCAs in turn are responsible for certifying the next lower level consisting of certification authorities (CAs). The CAs are responsible for certifying subordinate CAs and individual users. Individual users are the lowest level of the hierarchy.

When MIME was introduced, PEM became less important because it only supported 7-bit text messages. PEM was then extended with MOSS (MIME Object Security Standard), which was PEM compatibility with support for MIME attachments. MOSS is difficult to implement and use, so it is not used often. At the same time, due to the proprietary nature of the encryption scheme that PEM uses, it too is little used. Despite this, there are at least two different implementations of PEM available. One is Riordan's Internet Privacy Enhanced Mail (RIPEM), written by Mark Riordan. This is a useful but partial implementation of PEM, allowing e-mail to have all the security features of PEM. The other was originally called TIS/PEM, written by Trusted Information Systems, Inc. However, it has since been succeeded by TIS/MOSS.

10.8   Best Internet Security Practices

As technology advances, our networks become more complex and grow more so every day, and hackers get more sophisticated. As the discussion continues about whether new vulnerabilities should be disclosed and whether it is good to teach courses such as virus writing and hacking, we must still protect our networks. Developing a sound security strategy involves balancing the changes in threats and technology with our corporate environment. Knowing how and what to protect, and what controls to put in place, is not always easy. It takes planning, procedures, and policy development. The planning and implementation for network security can be time-consuming and overwhelming. This is where best practices come in. Best practices are really a set of good controls. When putting your plan together, make sure that your practices include assessing risks, prevention, detection, response, and vigilance. Here are some best practices for being able to detect network attacks:

- Assume everyday that a new vulnerability has surfaced overnight.
- Make it part of your daily routine to check the log files from firewalls and servers.
- Have a list of all the security products that you use, and check vendor Web sites for updates.
- Know your infrastructure so that you can detect abnormal behavior.
- Ask questions and look for answers.

The following is an example of best practices for password policies:

- Make the password length at least eight characters, and require the use of uppercase and lowercase letters, numbers, and special characters.

- Lock user accounts out after three to five failed logon attempts. This stops programs from deciphering the passwords on locked accounts.

- Monitor the network for the use of questionable tools. If password files can be captured, they can be run though password-guessing programs on another machine.

Here is an example of protecting the network from malicious code:

- Install antivirus software and update the files on a regular basis. Antivirus software doesn't do a company any good if it is not updated often.

- Only open attachments sent to you by people you know. Many viruses infect user address books, so even if you know who the attachment is from, be sure to scan it before you open it.

- Do not use any type of removable media from another user without first scanning the disk.

- Perform backups on a daily basis.

- Install firewalls on client machines.

- Subscribe to security-related newsgroups and check security-related Web sites on a regular basis.

As you can see, putting best practices into place will make the computing environment a much safer and secure place. It takes planning, testing, and education. Although each company must have its own unique security plan, best practices can be shared among companies. Listed below are some Web sites that offer good information on best practices:

- *http://csrc.nist.gov/fasp/*

- *http://www.cert.org/security-improvement/*

- *http://www.sans.org/rr/*

- *http://www.securityfocus.com*

10.9   Chapter Summary

- Security is not just a policy or a plan—it is a mindset. It means properly training and cultivating employees to be security aware. Remember that your network is only as strong as its weakest link.

- Threats come in all forms and sizes. The assessment of threats must begin upon the setup of the server. Most servers come with a wide range of services and protocols, many of which are turned on by default, leaving them open to unauthorized access or threats. Another large area of threats involves the use of a public Web server. Web threats lie in script code running within the client's browser, server-side vulnerabilities, and the transfer of cookies or unsigned applets. Malware or viruses pose a threat to e-mail servers and can spread extremely fast. Humans probably pose the greatest threat to a network.

- A cryptosystem or cipher system provides a way to protect information by disguising it into a format that can be read only by authorized systems or individuals. Modern cryptography has become increasingly important in securing data that is passed through networks or stored on hard drives. Private-key encryption methods, such as the Data Encryption Standard (DES), use the same key to both encrypt and decrypt the data. In public-key encryption, two keys are used. The public key is readily available whereas the private key is kept confidential. Diffie-Hellman Key Exchange, RSA, El Gamal Encryption Algorithm, and Elliptic Curve Cryptography (ECC) all use this type of encryption.

- Public Key Infrastructure (PKI) allows you to bring strong authentication and privacy to the Internet. This infrastructure includes all of the technology, processes, and procedures involved in supporting a public key-based solution. By using the public-key cryptographic techniques and encryption algorithms, you can provide authentication to users and ensure that only the intended recipients have access to data.

- VPNs use encryption and tunneling protocols to protect and maintain the data's confidentiality and integrity while it travels across the Internet. VPN technology is based on tunneling. Tunneling uses one network to send its data through the connection of another network. It works by encapsulating a network protocol within packets carried by a public network. In the case of VPN connection over the Internet, packets of one protocol are encapsulated within the IP packets.

- The IPSec protocol suite adds an additional security layer in the TCP/IP stack to protect TCP/IP traffic by using a set of open standards and cryptographic security services. It provides security techniques and a mechanism that implements security services before it exchanges information between two entities. Because it is an open standard, it does not rely on proprietary protocols or techniques while bringing a higher level of interoperability to the Internet.

- Basic Web connectivity using HTTP occurs over TCP port 80. An alternative to this involves the use of SSL transport protocols operating on port 443. HTTPS and SSL support the use of X.509 digital certificates from the server so that a user can authenticate the sender. HTTPS is the use of Secure Sockets Layer (SSL) as a layer under the HTTP Application layer. S-HTTP allows the client to send a certificate to authenticate the user, whereas with SSL only the server can be authenticated.

- Pretty Good Privacy (PGP) is used to securely exchange messages, and to secure files, disk volumes, and network connections with both privacy and strong authentication. PGP can also be used for applying a digital signature without encrypting the message. Privacy-Enhanced Mail (PEM) was one of the first standards for securing e-mail messages by encrypting 7-bit text messages. PEM may be employed with either symmetric or asymmetric cryptographic key mechanisms.

10.10   Key Terms

back door: A program that allows access to a computer without the user's knowledge or authorization.

brute force: Term that describes a way of cracking a cryptographic key or password by trying every conceivable combination until a password is found, or until all possible combinations have been exhausted.

buffer overflow: Condition that occurs when the data presented to an application or service exceeds the storage space allocation that has been reserved in memory for that application or service.

certificate: A digital document that attests to the truth that you are who you say you are. Besides providing authentication, a certificate also secures the exchange of information

certification authority (CA): An organization or system that issues and manages security certificates.

cipher: The process of replacing letters or numbers with different characters. The letters can also be rearranged without changing their identities to form an enciphered message.

Data Encryption Standard (DES): A block cipher using a 56-bit key on each 64-bit chunk of data used to encrypt data.

decryption: The act of converting a message from code into plaintext.

denial of service (DoS) attack: A type of attack that disrupts the resources or services to which a user would expect to have access.

distributed denial of service (DDoS) attack: Attacks that come in the form of standard DoS attacks but the effects are multiplied by the total number of machines under the control of the attacker.

encryption: Transformation of data into a form that cannot be read without the appropriate key to decipher it.

firewall: A component placed between computers and networks to help eliminate undesired access by the outside world.

hashing: The process of transforming a string of characters into a shorter fixed-length value or key that represents the original string. Hashing is used in many encryption algorithms.

IP Security (IPSec): A set of protocols operating at the Transport layer to support the secure exchange of packets.

malware: Software designed with the intent to damage or disrupt a system. Malware is a shortened version of the words "malicious software."

man-in-the-middle attack: Attack that takes place when an attacker intercepts traffic and then tricks the parties at both ends into believing that they are communicating with each other.

Pretty Good Privacy (PGP): Encrypts and decrypts e-mail messages based on public-key encryption and provides for digital signatures.

Privacy-Enhanced Mail (PEM): One of the first standards for securing e-mail messages by encrypting 7-bit text messages, it specifies a PKI for key exchange over large networks.

public-key cryptography: Uses different keys to encrypt and decrypt data. The public key is readily available whereas the private key is kept confidential.

Public Key Infrastructure (PKI): A set of standards and protocols that allows data to be transported with strong authentication and privacy on the Internet.

Rivest-Shamir-Adleman (RSA): Developed in 1977 by Ron Rivest, Adi Shamir, and Leonard Adleman, this is an encryption and digital signature authentication system that uses an algorithm based on the multiplication of prime numbers.

session hijacking: Attack that takes control of a session between the server and a client.

spoofing: Method to make data appear to come from somewhere other than where it really originated.

social engineering: Method of attack that plays on human behavior to obtain private information.

threat: In terms of network security, anything that endangers the safety of the network.

Trojan horse: A program that disguises itself as a useful application.

tunneling: Uses one network to send its data through the connection of another network.

virtual private network (VPN): A network connection that allows access via a secure tunnel built on top of a publicly accessible infrastructure, such as the Internet or the public telephone network.

virus: A program or piece of code that is loaded onto your computer without your knowledge.

worm: Generic term for a self-replicating virus, Trojan horse, or logic bomb.

10.11   Challenge Questions

10.1   Which of the following accurately describes the difference between a Trojan horse and a virus?

a. A virus needs no user intervention to replicate.

b. A Trojan horse needs no user intervention to replicate.

c. A virus is open source code and attacks only open source software.

d. A Trojan horse buries itself in the operating system software and infects other systems only after a user executes the application in which it is buried.

10.2 You have created a utility for scanning hard drives. You have hidden code inside the utility that will install itself and cause the infected system to erase the hard drive's contents on April 1. Which of the following attacks has been used in your code?

a. Virus

b. Spoofing

c. Logic bomb

d. Trojan horse

10.3 Which of the following is *not* a potential exploit for CGI scripts?

a. Providing information on processes running on the server

b. Executing arbitrary commands on the client

c. Buffer overflows

d. Arbitrary commands executed on the server

10.4 You have implemented a proxy firewall technology that can distinguish between an FTP get command and an FTP put command. What type of firewall are you using?

a. Packet-filtering firewall

b. Circuit-level gateway

c. Application-level gateway

d. FTP proxy

10.5 The company wants to secure their Web services and provide a guarantee to online customers that personal information is securely transferred. Which technology would you suggest?

a. VPN

b. SSH

c. S/MIME

d. SSL/TLS

10.6 What type of algorithm breaks data into chunks and applies encryption to those chunks of data?

    a. Symmetric encryption algorithm

    b. Elliptic curve

    c. Block cipher

    d. None of the above

10.7 Which type of algorithm generates a key pair of a public key and a private key that is then used to encrypt and decrypt data and messages sent and received?

    a. Elliptic Curve

    b. Asymmetric encryption algorithm

    c. Symmetric encryption algorithm

    d. All of the above

10.8 When encrypting and decrypting data using an asymmetric encryption algorithm, you use the _____ key to decrypt data encrypted with the _____ key.

10.9 The _____ portion of the IPSec protocol suite provides authentication and integrity but not privacy for a packet.

10.10 _____ integrates with current messaging platforms as a protocol to provide secure messaging.

10.11 Who is responsible for security in an organization? Explain your answer.

10.12 List the reasons why it is unsafe to allow signed code to run on your systems.

10.13 What is IPSec?

10.14 What protocols can be used for creating VPNs over the Internet?

10.15 Describe what a stateful inspection firewall does.

10.12 Challenge Exercises

Challenge Exercise 10.1

In this exercise, you install Real Virtual Network Computing (VNC) and use it to remotely control the computer of another person in the room. You need a desktop or laptop computer running a Windows-based operating system, TCP/IP installed, network connectivity, and Internet access.

10.1 Log on to your computer and open an Internet connection.

10.2 Go to **http://www.realvnc.com/download.html**.

10.3 Enter your contact information, select **Windows 9x/2000/NT/XP**, and then click the **Proceed to download** button.

10.4 In the Download Area, click the executable link for **Full installation**. (If you have compression software, you can download the .zip file; otherwise, simply download the .exe file.)

10.5 In the download dialog box, click **Save** and save the file to your desktop.

10.6 After the download is complete, double-click the VNC setup file on your desktop. Install the software using the default settings.

10.7 After the setup is complete, run **VNC Server** and enter a password. An icon should appear in your system tray.

10.8 Open the program and run VNC Viewer to connect to a computer name or IP address.

Challenge Exercise 10.2

In this exercise, you look at the digital certificate on Amazon.com to determine whether it is valid and who issued it. You need a desktop or laptop computer running a Windows-based operating system, TCP/IP installed, network connectivity, and Internet access.

10.1 Log on to your computer and open an Internet connection.

10.2 Go to **http://www.amazon.com**.

10.3 Browse through the products, pick something you'd like to order, and add it to your shopping cart. Don't worry, we are not really going to order, but we need to get to the secure part of the site.

10.4 Go to the area where you check out (click the **Proceed to checkout** button or link). It will ask for an e-mail address and a password if you are a returning customer.

10.5 Leave the e-mail box blank, enter any password, and press **Enter**. You will get an error about failing to provide an e-mail address, but you will be redirected to the secure page.

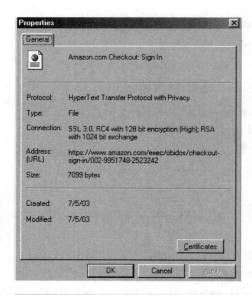

Figure 10.16

Properties dialogs box, General tab

10.6 Notice the "https" in the address bar.

10.7 Right-click anywhere on the page. On the resulting menu, click **Properties**. The General tab should look similar to Figure 10.16.

10.8 Click the **Certificates** button. The General tab should look similar to Figure 10.17.

10.9 Click the **Details** tab. What information does it give you?

10.10 Click the **Certification path** tab. What information does it give you?

10.11 From the information supplied, what can you determine about the certificate?

10.12 Close all windows or click the **Back** button on the toolbar to exit from the page.

Challenge Exercise 10.3

In this exercise, you install a password-revealing program and evaluate the information it gives you. You need a desktop or laptop computer running a

Figure 10.17

Certificate dialog box, General tab

Windows-based operating system, TCP/IP installed, network connectivity, and Internet access.

10.1 Log on to your computer and open an Internet connection.

10.2 Go to **http://www.openwall.com/**.

10.3 Scroll down the page and click the **password recovery resources** link.

10.4 In the left pane near the bottom of the page, click the **Win9x/ME (*.PWL)** link if you are using one of these operating systems, or click the **WinNT/2000/XP** link if you are using one of these operating systems.

10.5 If you are using Win9x/Me, you will download Write All Stored Passwords (WASP). If you are using WinNT/2000/XP, you can download John the Ripper or any other program that can be used for these operating systems. Save the setup file to your desktop.

10.6 Double-click the setup file on your desktop to install the program you downloaded. After installation, open the program.

10.7   This example is for John the Ripper. On the right side of the window, click **Analyze password file**.

10.8   What did you find out?

Challenge Exercise 10.4

In this exercise, you learn to fix a computer that is infected with a virus. You will research the virus and clean the computer. You need a desktop or laptop computer running a Windows-based operating system, TCP/IP installed, network connectivity, and Internet access.

10.1   Log on to your computer and open an Internet connection.

10.2   Go to **http://www.McAfee.com**.

10.3   Click **Home User**. Click the **McAfee FreeScan** link and then click the **Scan Now** link.

10.4   Scan your computer. Assume it found the Klez virus.

10.5   On the McAfee Home + Home Office Web page, click the **Downloads** link. On the Downloads page, click the **Virus Removal Tools** link.

10.6   Click the **back** button in your Web browser. Find Klez and click the **Removal Tool** link. Download the kremove.exe file to your desktop. Double-click **kremove.exe** to run the removal tool.

10.7   After running the program, reboot the computer and scan it again to be sure the virus is gone.

Challenge Exercise 10.5

In this exercise, you look at the IPSec policy on a computer to be sure you know where and how policies are set. You need a desktop or laptop computer running Windows 2000 or Windows XP, TCP/IP installed, and network connectivity.

10.1   Log on to your computer.

10.2   For Windows 2000, click **Start**, point to **Settings**, click **Control Panel**, double-click **Administrative Tools**, and double-click **Local Security Policy**. (In Windows XP, omit the step of pointing to **Settings** and click **Performance and Maintenance** in the Control Panel.)

Figure 10.18

IPSec Custom Security Method Settings dialog box

10.3   Click **IP Security Policies on Local Computer** in the left pane. Look at each of the selections in the right pane. You should have Client (Respond Only), Secure Server (Require Security), and Server (Request Security).

10.4   Double-click **Client (Respond Only)**. The Client (Respond Only) Properties dialog box opens.

10.5   On the Rules tab, click **Edit**. The Edit Rule Properties dialog box opens.

10.6   You should be on the Security Methods tab. What does the information tell you about AH and ESP?

10.7   Highlight the first line and click **Edit**. The Modify Security Method dialog box opens. You should be on the Security Method tab.

10.8   Select the **Custom** option, and then click the **Settings** button. The Custom Security Method Settings dialog box opens, as shown in Figure 10.18.

10.9   What choices do you have for each type of algorithm? Why are there session key settings?

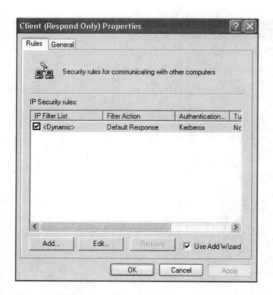

Figure 10.19

Client (Respond Only) Properties dialog box

10.10 Click **Cancel** three times. You should now be back in the Client (Respond Only) Properties dialog box, as shown in Figure 10.19. Click the **General** tab.

10.11 Click the **Advanced** button. The Key Exchange Settings dialog box opens.

10.12 Click the **Methods** button. The Key Exchange Security Methods dialog box opens.

10.13 Highlight the first selection and click **Edit**.

10.14 What choices do you have? Why?

10.15 Click **Cancel** four times. You should be back to the Local Security Settings screen.

10.16 Highlight **IPSec Security Policies on Local Computer** in the left pane. Click the **Action** menu, and then click **Manage IP filter lists and filter actions**.

10.17 Click each tab and look at all the options. How would you use these?

Challenge Exercise 10.6

In this exercise, you research best practices and make an outline for a Web server. You need a desktop or laptop computer running a Windows-based operating system, TCP/IP installed, network connectivity, and Internet access.

10.1   Log on to your computer and open an Internet connection.

10.2   Using your favorite search engine, such as Google.com, search for "best practices". You can go to *http://csrc.nist.gov/fasp/* as an example of what to look for.

10.3   Formulate a best practices plan for Web servers.

10.13   Challenge Scenarios

Challenge Scenario 10.1

Technaguardian is a large online educational company with several offices throughout the United States. It expanded rapidly, mostly by purchasing other smaller companies. The company does business with several different vendors and has hired many contract employees to teach online classes as well as write curriculum. Technaguardian has learned that its curriculum is somehow ending up the hands of its competitors. Because the expansion has been so quick, the company offices have many different protocols and services running.

Management is extremely concerned and wants to be sure that its proprietary information is protected from theft and alteration. They have contacted you about implementing encryption. You have a meeting set up with them. At this initial meeting, what questions should you ask about their network and business to help them determine an appropriate method of encryption?

Challenge Scenario 10.2

Technaguardian was pleased with the help you gave them on encryption and has asked you to set up another meeting to discuss further security issues. Remember from Scenario 10.1 that the company expanded rapidly, mostly by purchasing other smaller companies. To maintain the diversity in the networks it has acquired, the company has many different protocols and services.

Many of the smaller offices don't have virus protection or use blank passwords on the desktops. Because of the acquisitions, a lot of foot traffic moves in and out of the offices and many of the offices don't keep logs of visitors. Technaguardian wants to minimize the risks of vulnerabilities to its ever-growing environment. In your meeting, you are asked how you would test the network for vulnerabilities and what changes you would recommend to protect the network from vulnerabilities. How would you respond?

Challenge Scenario 10.3

Technaguardian wanted to secure communications between remote offices located in Dallas and Phoenix, and the headquarters office in Chicago. Their goal is that any type of communication between any of the offices must remain completely secure and be impossible to decrypt. In addition, receivers must be sure that the sender's identity is verifiable and trusted. They also want legacy plaintext authentication programs to be secured without the need to migrate to a superior technology and the processing power requirements for encryption and decryption of packets to be kept at a minimum.

To achieve this, their IT department implemented a VPN solution between satellite offices and the headquarters office. They used hardware to facilitate end point encryption. Will this solution do what the company expects? Why or why not?

Challenge Scenario 10.4

After several meetings with you, Technaguardian decided that it would be good to secure communications between users and has implemented encryption on their network as well as for e-mail. You have been retained as a consultant. As a consultant, you have been working on a best-practices document and have been requesting additional information about the network and the structure of the business. Much of this information is confidential and could pose great danger if it ends up in the wrong hands. After sending several encrypted e-mails, recipients are complaining that they have no way of knowing for sure that the e-mails are from you. What can you do to allay their concerns?

CHAPTER 11

Network Operations

After reading this chapter you will be able to:

- Understand different operating systems and their requirements
- Discuss what role software components play in networking
- Install a network operating system
- Configure the operating system after installation
- Understand basic network services
- Work with directory services

Now that we have learned about how data travels across the network, the protocols that are used, IP addressing, and security issues, the time has come to install an operating system and configure it, along with some services. As a network professional, you will be exposed to many network operating systems and possibly different versions of each. You must understand the inner workings of operating systems. You will encounter them not only on servers but on desktops and laptops as well. For the purpose of this chapter, we will focus on server operating systems. Let's begin by looking at the different types of operating systems and what their requirements are, and then move on to the different software components that make an operating system function. After that, we will install the operating system and configure it. Finally, we will work with network services, such as printing and directory services.

11.1   Network Operating Systems

Network operating systems (NOSs) have existed for more than 30 years. In the early 1980s, NOSs were mainly research projects. Many of the original ones were actually a type of software package added to stand-alone operating systems, rather than a true NOS. Windows 95 and Windows for Workgroups were Microsoft's first NOS products, and Novell NetWare became the first popular NOS for personal computers. By contrast, from the beginning Unix was designed to support networking.

The choice of operating system should be based on the demands of business and not personal preference. Numerous factors, such as the size and topology of the network, should be considered when choosing a NOS and determining hardware requirements. The next few sections will cover these concepts so that an intelligent assessment can be made as to which operating system to install.

11.1.1   Overview

The first networks allowed computers to exchange data by means of a basic network protocol. The application programs running on these computers controlled the exchange of data and used the network to share data for specific purposes. One of the first successful attempts at integrating networking extensions into an operating system resulted in Berkeley Unix, also known as BSD. Unix was an operating system created at Bell Labs and licensed freely to most universities and research facilities. The major innovation in Berkeley's version was support for TCP/IP networking. This integration of TCP/IP and Unix allowed all processes on a Unix computer to communicate with other processes on any computer connected to the network. As the number of networked computers increased, it became apparent that some type of uniform networking support within the operating system would be necessary to effectively use the underlying network. For example, a person could only use a computer on which he or she had an account, so users wanted accounts on all computers. As another example, two users worked together but on two different computers. To work collectively, they had to move files back and forth, requiring them to know each other's passwords as well as manually track the versions of the files.

The first popular commercial network operating system was SunOS from Sun Microsystems. SunOS, a derivative from BSD, had two major improvements: (1) a network file system allowing a file on one computer to be visible to other computers and (2) a directory service. This service allowed user accounts created in one central computer to be replicated to user computers. (Directory services are covered in the last section of this chapter.) Current operating systems provide many services so that application programs have a unified view of the network. The basic functions of an operating system include directing and controlling activities of a computer's hardware components, and coordinating the interaction between software applications and computer hardware.

Some of the commonly available network operating systems include Linux, Novell NetWare, SunOS/Solaris, FreeBSD, Unix, and Windows. Table 11.1 shows some of the NOSs and their attributes.

11.1.2   Requirements

A network operating system utilizes device drivers as well as protocol stacks for networking hardware. We will discuss drivers and stacks in the next section. The environment managed by a network operating system consists of a group of computers that interconnect by external interfaces running under the control of software. Typically, there is at least one shared server providing access to files and shared hardware resources. It coordinates the activities of multiple computers across a network. The network operating

TABLE 11.1   Comparison of Network Operating Systems

Network Operating System	Attributes
Banyan Vines	Hardware independent. Based on Unix. Supports a variety of LAN types. Supports IBM mainframe communications. Supports third-party development application programming interfaces (APIs). Supports both asynchronous and synchronous WANs.
Novell NetWare	Novell Directory Services allows replication and distribution, enhanced security, file compression, and data migration. Includes advanced media management for CD-ROMs and GUI-based network management tools. Has its own proprietary set of network protocols that can be added to enhance network services. Fast for transaction processing.
Microsoft Windows 2000	Easy to integrate with desktop PCs. Strong tools such as Visual Basic and Visual C++. Offers remote access for incoming ports. Runs on different RISC architectures. Open architecture for third-party client redirectors. Includes security and fault tolerance features, file sharing and printer sharing, a transaction tracking system, and directory services.
Unix	Supports multiple users, multiple tasks, open architecture, multiple platforms. Uses TCP/IP as its Internet suite of protocols. Good choice for LAN servers running large databases and other enterprise-scale jobs. Popular platform for PC connectivity.

system acts as a director to keep the network running smoothly, and is a complete operating system in addition to managing communication across the LAN. It turns all computers and peripherals on a network into a functioning whole by coordinating and controlling how they communicate across the network. It also supports security and privacy for the network and individual users by controlling access to resources on a user authentication basis.

The network operating system advertises and manages resources from a centralized directory, provides mechanisms to easily add and remove services, reconfigures the resources, and is able to support multiple services of the same kind. These qualities make network operating systems indispensable in large networked environments. Network operating systems provide three basic mechanisms that are used to support the services provided by the operating system and applications. The first of these mechanisms is Message Passing, which is the basis for distributed systems, which we discussed in Chapter 4. The second is Remote Procedure Calls (RPCs), which we covered in Chapter 9. The last of these is Distributed Shared Memory

(DSM). DSM provides a logical equivalent to shared memory; two or more processes on two or more computers can map a single shared memory segment to their address spaces. These mechanisms support a feature called Inter Process Communication, or IPC, which allows processes to share information. After you have completed Challenge Exercise 11.1 and the operating system is installed, look at the shares. You will find an IPC$ share listed. This is automatically created when the operating system is installed. The $ denotes that the share is hidden.

Besides the mechanisms for supporting services, the NOS also needs to draw as much power out of its hardware as possible. One way of doing this is through a process called multitasking. Multitasking refers to doing more than one thing at a time, which is what the NOS does because it needs the capability to support numerous processes at one time. True multitasking can support as many processes as CPUs, but because most computers only have one CPU, time slicing is used to simulate multitasking. Time slicing works by dividing the CPU's clock cycles between tasks, giving the perception that many applications are operating simultaneously. There are two types of multitasking:

- **Preemptive:** The processes are assigned CPU time slices by the operating system; after the item slice expires, the process is halted and the next process gets computing time.

- **Cooperative:** The operating system has no control over the processes. After a process has control of the CPU, it cannot be interrupted. It finishes its computing needs before another process can use the CPU.

When determining which operating system to use, preemptive multitasking should be a key factor. In addition to the method of multitasking, here are some other factors that should be taken into consideration:

- Multiprocessor support
- Hardware support and hardware independence
- Reliability
- Recoverable file system
- Storage volume management
- Multiple server support

- Security and access control
- File-level access permission
- Scalability
- Mass storage options

The preceding list doesn't cover all the factors that should be considered when purchasing a NOS, but it is a start. Now that we have had an overview of a NOS, let's look closer at the software components that make up a NOS.

11.2   Software Components of Networking

As stated previously, the environment managed by a NOS consists of a group of computers that interconnect by external interfaces running under the control of software. Because a NOS provides a large variety of services and functions, quite a few software components are part of a network operating system, including naming and directory services, client and server network software, and drivers and stacks. We will start with drivers and stacks, then look at server and client communications, and finish the section with request-reply architectures.

11.2.1   Drivers and Stacks

For the devices on the network to communicate, they use a special interface card. You will hear this referred to as a network card, network adapter, or the most common name, a network interface card (NIC). Before the card can be used, a software or device driver must be installed on the computer. In the early days of network computing, each vendor had its own proprietary driver, making it difficult to integrate different vendors into the same network and to keep up with hardware and software updates. The operating system vendors eventually developed a way to integrate device drivers into the operating system for easier communication between the operating system and the devices. A driver, acting as the intermediary, is a program that communicates between the operating system and the device. Figure 11.1 illustrates this.

A **driver** is a program that interacts with either a particular device or type of software. The driver contains specific information about a device or a software interface that programs using the driver do not. In personal computers, a driver is often packaged as a dynamic link library (DLL) file.

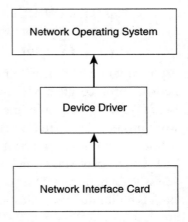

Figure 11.1
Purpose of a device driver

Packet drivers provide a software interface that is independent of the card you are using, but not independent of the network technology. Some of the driver technologies that you should be familiar with are:

- **Network Device Interface System (NDIS):** A communication interface between the MAC sublayer and the network interface driver, this allows Windows operating systems to communicate multiple protocols to the NIC. The specifics of a NIC's hardware implementation are wrapped by a MAC device driver so that all NICs for the same media can be accessed using a common programming interface. The wrapper serves to make development of both MAC and protocol drivers easier.

- **Open Data-Link Interface (ODI):** This is similar to NDIS except that it supports Novell and Apple operating systems. It allows these operating systems to communicate multiple protocols to the NIC. The ODI interface resides in the Data Link layer of the OSI protocol stack. ODI standardizes the development of NIC drivers so that vendors don't need to write separate drivers to work with each of the network protocols.

- **Win32 Driver model (WDM):** This architecture divides drivers into various classes by functions. It is a complete card interface that enables generic class drivers to handle bus and device functions. It works by channeling some of the work of the device driver into portions of the code that are integrated into the operating system.

This is not restricted to just NICs; it is also used for printers, scanners, and other network devices. All versions of Microsoft Windows after Windows 95 have implemented WDM.

A phrase you may hear is "binding a stack," which refers to linking a set of network protocols to a NIC. Every NIC must have at least one stack bound to it. (We will discuss binding later in the chapter.) A **stack** is a set of network protocol layers that work together. The set of TCP/IP protocols that define communication over the Internet is the most common stack. The TCP/IP protocol stack runs on top of the driver software and uses it to access your hardware. Due to the nature of DOS, in many cases a TCP/IP stack is built into the applications. This is true for many of the packet driver applications. In Windows, the Winsock DLL implements the TCP/IP stack. Windows Sockets is a socket interface, which was created as a Windows DLL. Each TCP/IP implementation requires its own version of Windows Sockets; WINSOCK.DLL provides 16-bit support and WSOCK32.DLL provides 32-bit support.

TCP/IP stacks have been written for NDIS, ODI, and WDM driver interfaces, so remember that when choosing a NIC, you must consider whether your chosen stack is compatible with the interface available for your card. If you are running a TCP/IP protocol stack that requires drivers that aren't available for your hardware, you're sure to end up with some complications. Some computers can load and run multiple protocol stacks, which correspond to layers of the OSI model. We will discuss how to decide which stack takes preference in the section on binding.

NOTE

The term *stack* also refers to the actual software that processes the protocols. Programmers sometimes talk about "loading a stack," which means to load the software required to use a specific set of protocols.

11.2.2   Servers and Clients

Client/server network operating systems allow the network to centralize services and applications in one or more dedicated servers. Figure 11.2 illustrates this concept. The servers become the core of the system, providing security and access to resources. Individual workstations are then given access to the resources on the servers. The network operating system provides the means to combine all the pieces of the network and allow multiple users to simultaneously share the same resources no matter where they

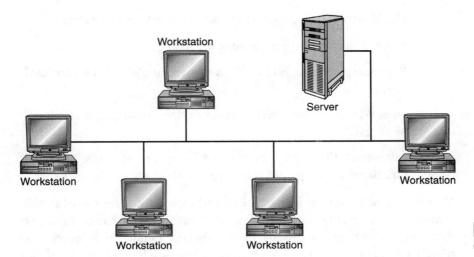

Figure 11.2
Client/server network

are located. Novell NetWare and Windows 2000 Server are examples of client/server network operating systems.

There is usually a clear distinction between client and server NOS software. Client software is fairly simple: Its purpose is to interface with the user's operating system, such as Windows XP, and provide easy access to network resources. Server software is more complex: Its implementation depends on the type of NOS. For example, in Novell NetWare the server NOS is essentially its own distinct network operating system. It is used only on network servers; there is no Novell client operating system. In contrast, Windows 2000 Server NOS is more like an extension of the basic client operating system with additional sharing and security features. Because the operating system has evolved with networking and TCP/IP in mind, NOS features are part of the client operating system in Unix.

Before we discuss how a client/server network operates, let's go over their advantages and disadvantages. The advantages of a client/server network include:

- **Centralization:** Resources and security are controlled through one central location.
- **Interoperability:** All components work together, including different types of hardware and operating systems.
- **Scalability:** The components can be expanded as needs increase.

- **Flexibility:** Newly developed technology can be integrated.

Disadvantages of a client/server network include:

- **Expense:** It requires an initial investment in dedicated server hardware and software.

- **Dependence:** If the server goes down, the network operations will be affected.

- **Administration:** Large networks will require administrative staff for efficient management and operation.

A client operating system is the type of software designed for workstation computers that enables the use of network resources. It has components that simplify network access by hiding specific details from users. The client NOS makes network resources look to the user like they are local. For example, you can print to a network printer on the second floor as easily as you can print to one that is directly attached to your own computer. It also lets you access files on the network as if they were on your own computer. Network files can be reached through networked drives or naming services.

The server NOS is much more sophisticated. It handles resources and services to be distributed to clients. It also provides the following functions:

- Manages a directory that contains user permissions to resources, their security permissions, and passwords.

- Supports file access compatible with various client operating systems; it tricks the client operating systems so that the directories and files look like they are local.

- Supports a relatively consistent user environment such that when a user logs on to the network, he is set up to access files, printers, and other resources.

- Helps maintain a productive computing environment by providing interfaces to Internet services.

- Manages shareable mass storage that can vary in size and span several physical disks.

Figure 11.3 shows the relationship between the server and the client. With some NOSs, the computer running the server software cannot be used as a workstation. This is called a dedicated server.

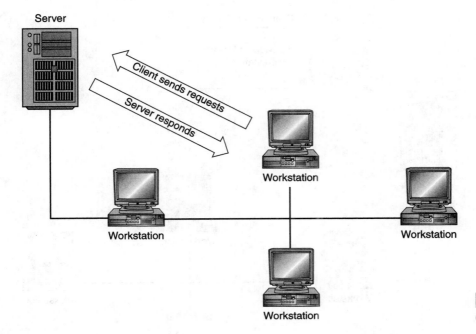

Server

Client sends requests

Server responds

Workstation

Workstation

Workstation

Workstation

Figure 11.3
Client/server relationship

As mentioned earlier, Novell NetWare uses this kind of setup almost exclusively. With some other NOSs, all workstations on the network can also be servers. These are called nondedicated servers and are usually found on a peer-to-peer network. Peer networks allow users to access resources on other computers and share the resources on their computers. Windows 2000 Professional and Windows XP are good examples of this type of operating system. Linux workstations and servers run the same version of the operating system, but servers have more network services installed than the workstations. Nondedicated servers allow for more flexibility, because users can make resources available on their computers as necessary. But this requires that users be willing to take some administrative responsibility, so they must be somewhat network-literate. Some of the advantages of a peer-to-peer network are:

- **Less initial expense:** A dedicated server does not have to be purchased.

- **Setup:** A current client operating system already in place may be used.

The disadvantages of a peer-to-peer network include:

- **Decentralization:** There is no central place to store files and applications.

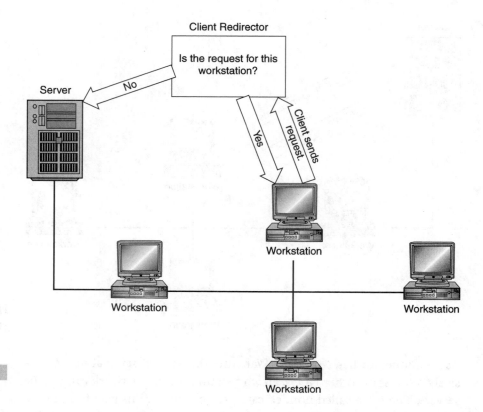

Figure 11.4

Redirector process

- **Security:** It does not provide the security available on a client/server network.

- **Performance:** It often suffers some performance degradation when being used simultaneously as a workstation and as a server.

The most important component of a NOS is redirection. Redirection in computing is exactly that—taking something headed in one direction and making it go in a different direction. Network operating systems depend heavily on redirection. In this case, data is being redirected from one computer to another over the network cable. With redirection, an operating program does not know or care where its output is going. The component that does this is called the **redirector**. It operates at the Presentation layer of the OSI model, and its function is to accept requests from applications and determine whether network access is needed. If it is, it sends the request over the network to the server. If the request is for local resources, the redirector passes the request to the CPU for processing. Figure 11.4 shows this process.

For example, if at a command prompt, you type **copy C: thisfile.doc J:**, thisfile.doc will be copied from your local drive C to the network drive J. The NOS makes it appear to the copy command that drive J is local, even though it really resides on another computer somewhere on the same network. The copy command doesn't know or care that drive J is across the network. The NOS reroutes the file across the network to drive J by means of the redirector. Redirection can be done with printers and other peripherals. In the instance of a printer, LPT1: or COM1 can be a network printer instead of a local printer and the NOS redirects files to these devices. In order for the output from the user's PC to be redirected successfully, the computer with drive J must expect data. It does this by making the drive available to network users as part of the NOS's function.

This process is called the *requestor* in NetWare operating systems and the *network shell* in Unix. Not all computers need to run the server software, because not all need to share their resources; but all network workstations must run redirector software, because every client has to be able to put data onto the network. Another process used by a NOS is a **designator**. This works in coordination with the redirector and is associated with drive mapping. It exchanges a locally mapped drive letter with the correct network address of a directory share. So, in other words, if the server has a shared folder on its D drive and you mapped it to the letter J, the designator takes you to the shared folder on the server's D drive even though you click drive J.

11.2.3 Request/Reply Architectures

Computing styles have evolved from highly centralized systems with mainframes to decentralized and distributed systems with workstations and PCs. The PC evolution has been so successful primarily because of the rapid development in both processing power and the bandwidth of connections between computers. In many organizations, the information technology infrastructure has become many different products provided by various vendors. This produces increased requirements for integration and flexibility.

Since the first program was divided into modules, software systems have had architectures, and programmers have been responsible for making the modules all work together. In the 1990s client/server computing became the dominant distributed systems architecture. In the previous section we learned that any component that submits a request becomes a client, and any component that replies becomes a server. The distinction between client and server is a really a conceptual one, because the same computer can be a client in one transaction and a server in another interaction.

Because of this structure, the client /server style is sometimes referred to as request/reply architecture. Remember from earlier in the chapter that this process includes message passing, workflow, and distribution of tasks among the programs in a business system. In distributed message-oriented request/reply architecture, a central exchange service exists, to which all participating processes connect. Services assign themselves a name and export the methods by which these services are remotely accessible. Client services, in turn, are then able to make calls against the exported methods. In this architecture, the processes are always connected through a central exchange process such as IPC to avoid the time of setting up and taking down individual socket connections for each request. So, in essence, the client has a generic connection, requests information, and then waits while it is searched for. This can occur either on the Internet or within a network.

The vast majority of business systems are based on this request/reply architecture in which a client seeking information must actively locate where the information is stored and then request it in such a manner as to get a reply. Each request for information is queued and then individually fulfilled by the provider. Networks based on this type of architecture can become clogged when a large number of clients are searching for and requesting data that must then be sent individually to them. This limitation of the request/reply architecture resulted in an effort to develop systems that can push or multicast information on the network as everyone wants it. As a result, many request/reply architectures are now being replaced by event-driven, publish/subscribe architectures in an effort to achieve real item data delivery. The premise behind publish/subscribe architecture is that data should come to us in a steady, unimpeded stream. The network should already know what data you need. In this way, data and software can be more useful in helping us make more intelligent decisions about our business needs.

Now that we understand the software components of a network and how they exchange information between the client and the server, let's move on to learning about how an operating system is installed.

11.3   Installing a Network Operating System

The installation of a NOS is a bit different than the installation of a desktop operating system because you will be configuring network services that determine the framework for the rest of the network and clients. In this section, we will discuss the steps required in preparing the computer for installation, making sure the installation cleans up after itself, and how to keep it updated.

11.3.1   Preparing for the Installation

Before the server operating system can be installed, some decisions need to be made about how the computer will interact on the network. These concepts apply whether you are installing a Microsoft, Novell, or Linux operating system. The first consideration is the size and layout, or topology, of the network. For example, if you have 10,000 users and intend to use one server to host applications, Web services, and e-mail, you just may overwork the computer and the response time will be extremely slow. Here are some additional configuration issues about the computer that we will explore:

- Function of the server
- File systems to be used
- Naming convention to be used
- Other operating systems and applications found on servers and clients
- How data will be stored and protected
- Hardware compatibility

We will start with the function of the server. By identifying the role that each server plays, it is easier to determine which services and protocols are required or needed. Most servers come with a wide range of services and protocols, many of which are turned on by default. To have a secure environment you need to determine the role of the server, along with the default configuration, the services, protocols, and applications required to meet business needs and any configuration changes that should be made to the default installation. For example, if we are using a server as a file server, it wouldn't necessarily have Web services installed on it. Here are come of the most common server uses and their functions:

- **Logon server:** These servers authenticate users when they log on to their workstations. They can function as other types of servers as well.

- **Network services server:** These servers host services that are required for the network to function as per the configuration. These include Dynamic Host Configuration Protocol (DHCP), Domain Name System (DNS), Windows Internet Name Service (WINS), and Simple Network Management Protocol (SNMP).

- **Application server:** Used for hosting applications such as custom accounting packages and office suites.

- **File server:** Used for access to common user files and home directories.

- **Print server:** Used for access to the network-shared printers.

- **Web server:** Used to host Web-based applications and internal or external Web sites.

- **FTP server:** Used to store files that are downloaded or uploaded. These can be internal as well as external.

- **E-mail server:** Used for e-mail but can also be used to host public folders and groupware applications.

- **News/Usenet (NNTP) server:** Used as a newsgroup server where users can post and retrieve messages in a common location.

You should also determine whether the server will be accessed from the internal network, from the external world, or both. This helps identify the services and protocols that will be necessary.

After you choose the server type, you must decide on a file system. The term **file system** describes the operating system's method of organizing, managing, and accessing of files through logical structuring on the hard disk. The disk is an array of fixed-size chunks, and the operating system's job is to implement a file system of these chunks. A disk partition contains numbered sectors. Operating systems add a directory structure to break up the partition into smaller files, assign names to each file, and manage the free space available to create new files. Different file systems reflect different operating system requirements, and some work better on small computers while others work better on large servers. The same hard disk can have partitions with file systems belonging to DOS, NT, or Linux. When more than one file system type is installed on a hard drive, this is called a multi-boot or dual-boot configuration. These are good for testing and learning purposes but normally are not used on a live network server.

File systems interact with the operating system to ensure that the operating system can find files requested on the hard disk. The file system keeps a table of contents of the files on the drive, so when a file is requested it is searched to locate and access the file. The most common file systems are FAT, HPFS, and NTFS.

FAT stands for File Allocation Table. In the 1970s, PC file systems were designed to support floppy disks. Hard disk support came later. The FAT file system is used by DOS and is supported by all other operating systems. It is simple, reliable, and uses little storage. The file allocation table is stored at the beginning of the partition to act as the table of contents we talked about earlier. To protect the partition, two copies of the FAT are kept in case one becomes damaged, and the FAT tables and the root directory are stored in a fixed location so that the system's boot files can be located properly. If the FAT table is not updated regularly, it can lead to data loss. Updating the FAT table is very time-consuming because the disk-read heads must be repositioned to the drive's logical track zero each time the FAT table is updated. The FAT directory structure doesn't have a lot of structure, so files are given the first open location on the drive. Here are some additional characteristics of FAT:

- It supports only read-only, hidden, system, and archive file attributes.

- FAT uses the traditional 8.3 file-naming convention. The name of a file or directory can be up to eight characters long, then a period (.) separator, and up to a three-character extension.

- The name must start with either a letter or number and can contain certain characters. Those considered special characters, such as " / \ [ ] : ; | = , cannot be used because unexpected results may occur.

- The name cannot contain any spaces.

- Because of FAT's low overhead, it can write data to a hard disk very quickly.

- FAT partitions are limited in size to a maximum of 4 gigabytes (GB) under Windows NT and 2 GB in MS-DOS.

- FAT uses 16-bit fields to store file size information.

Virtual FAT (VFAT) is an enhanced version of the FAT file system. This file system, also called FAT32, is available in Windows 95 and early versions of Windows NT. It allows files to have longer names than the 8.3 convention adopted by DOS. FAT32 also accommodates the use of smaller allocation units on a disk.

High-Performance File System (HPFS) was designed for the OS/2 operating system to allow for greater access to larger hard drives. HPFS maintains the directory organization of FAT, but adds automatic sorting of the directory based on filenames. Here are some of the qualities of HPFS:

- Filenames are extended to up to 256 characters.

- It allows for increased flexibility, as it supports other naming conventions, and security.

- The unit of allocation is changed from clusters to sectors (512 bytes), which reduces lost disk space.

- It offers greater efficiency and reliability than FAT.

- Directory entries hold more information than under FAT. This includes information about the modification, creation, and access date and times.

- It requires more memory than FAT and may not be a reasonable choice on systems with limited amounts of RAM.

HPFS organizes a drive into a series of 8 MB bands. Between each of these bands are 2 K allocation bitmaps, which keep track of which sectors within the band have been allocated. This increases performance because the drive head returns to the nearest band allocation bitmap, instead of returning to the top of the disk, when determining where a file is to be stored. HPFS also includes two unique special data objects called super block and spare block. The super block contains a pointer to the root directory, and the spare block is used for hot-fixing bad sectors.

> **WARNING** ❗ If the super block is lost or corrupted due to a bad sector, the contents of the partition are as well, even if the rest of the drive is fine.

New Technology File System (NTFS) was developed expressly for versions of Windows NT and Windows 2000. NTFS 4.0 supports Windows NT, and NTFS 5.0 supports Windows 2000 and higher. NTFS was developed as a platform for added functionality and for reliability, which is especially desirable for high-end systems and file servers. Here are some of the features of NTFS:

- Filenames can be a maximum of 256 characters.
- Stores file size information in 64-bit fields.
- Files or partitions can be as large as 16 exabytes.
- It incorporates sophisticated, customizable compression routines.
- It keeps a log of file system activity to facilitate recovery if a system crash occurs.

NTFS supports long filenames, large volumes, data security, and universal file sharing. Keep in mind that an NT file server will probably have all its partitions formatted for NTFS because the other operating systems cannot use it. Only Windows NT and higher can use data on an NTFS volume. NTFS is required to provide full security on a Windows file server and to support Macintosh datasets.

NTFS organizes files into directories, which are sorted much like HPFS. However, unlike FAT or HPFS, there is no dependence on the underlying hardware, such as 512-byte sectors or special locations on the disk, such as FAT tables or HPFS super blocks. NTFS keeps track of transactions against the file system, making it a recoverable file system. CHKDSK needs only to roll back transactions to the last commit point in order to recover consistency within the file system. To ensure reliability of NTFS recoverability, removal of fatal single-sector failures and hotfixing were built into the file system. Windows NT, 2000, and higher, are also designed to provide a platform that can be added to and built upon so that it is flexible enough for other file systems to be able to use. Windows servers also support fault-tolerance features, which we discuss later in this section.

A **naming convention** is a process by which names are created for the workstations and servers on the network. It is important to incorporate a scheme for user accounts, computers, directories, network shares, printers, and servers so that there is uniformity and logical structure.

A naming convention should make it simple to devise new names by modeling them on the composition of existing names. They should be descriptive enough to be able to locate devices quickly, yet not have silly names.

For example, if all the workstations are named by their asset number, and all the printers are named after cartoon characters, how will anyone find any device on the network? Here are some general guidelines for naming devices:

- Construct user names from the first and last name of the user, and by identifying their job title or department, such as JonesJmktg. This method uses last name first, first initial, and then department.

- Construct group names from resource types, or from the name of the department, location, project, or a combination of these, such as PhxHRprinters.

- Construct computer names for servers and clients from their location, department, or type, such as PhxHR01.

Although it may sound trivial, identifying the name of a server, workstation, or device on the network is an important part of the installation process. Think about the consequences of being new to the job and your first task is to set up a server. Without thinking, you name it GoodyearBlimp!

Check the operating system limitations for the length or number of characters allowed in naming conventions. For example, in a Novell NetWare environment the server names can be up to 47 characters. However, in a Windows networking environment, this may be limited to 15 characters, depending on the version of the NOS you are running.

Network naming conventions apply to all objects on the network. This includes computers, users, groups, and all shared network devices.

Microsoft Windows 2000 (and higher) and Novell NetWare utilize directory services, which have a distinct naming convention based on the DNS structure. We will discuss this structure in the "Directory Services" section later in this chapter.

Before an operating system is installed, check to see what other operating systems and applications are being used on the servers and clients. Be sure that all systems can be integrated easily, because you don't want to introduce a new operating system into the environment only to find out that it is incompatible with the current system. All computers on a network should communicate using the same protocol. Should you choose to use different protocols, be sure you have some type of bridge or gateway that can interpret the protocols so that all computers can communicate properly. Remember from Chapter 6 that each protocol has special designations for network addresses. Pay special attention to the setup of IP addresses, subnet masks, default gateways, and services such as DNS, WINS, and DHCP. When in doubt, put it in a test environment first to be sure that everything can be integrated properly.

TIP

You should also check compatibility with existing applications, especially when you upgrade an operating system. Imagine the surprise when an office's operating system is upgraded and now a vital application doesn't work.

Next, determine how data will be stored and protected. We talked earlier about file systems, and now it's time to look at what options are available to provide for data redundancy. It is shortsighted to set up an operating system without knowing how to salvage data should a component fail. The most common approach to this dilemma is called **Redundant Array of Inexpensive Disks (RAID)**. RAID organizes multiple disks into a large, high-performance logical disk. In other words, if you have three hard drives, you can configure them to look like one gigantic drive.

Disk arrays are created to stripe data across multiple disks and access them in parallel. This allows for:

- Higher data transfer rates on large data accesses,
- Higher I/O rates on small data accesses, and
- Uniform load balancing across all of the disks, eliminating hot spots that saturate one or two disks while the rest of the disks sit idle.

Large disk arrays are highly vulnerable to disk failures. To solve this problem, redundancy in the form of error-correcting codes can be used to tolerate disk failures. With this method, a redundant disk array can retain data much longer than an unprotected single disk can. With multiple disks and a RAID scheme, your system can stay up and running not only when a disk fails, but also while the replacement disk is being installed and its data restored.

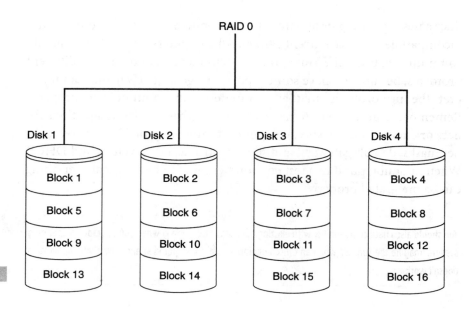

Figure 11.5
RAID level 0

There are two major goals in the implementation of disk arrays: data striping for better performance and redundancy for better reliability. Data striping distributes data over multiple disks to make them appear as a single large, fast disk. This improves I/O performance by allowing multiple I/Os to be serviced in parallel. Because there are more disks, the overall reliability of the array is lower, so it is important to have a way to tolerate disk failures and allow for the continuous operation of the system without any loss of data. This is why redundancy is incorporated in disk arrays.

Although there are many types of RAID, here is an explanation of some of the more common ones:

- **RAID Level 0:** Striped disk array without fault tolerance. RAID 0 implements a striped disk array, the data is broken into blocks, and each block is written to a separate disk drive. See Figure 11.5.

- **RAID Level 1:** Mirroring and duplexing. This solution requires a minimum of two disks and offers 100% redundancy because all data is written to both disks. See Figure 11.6. The difference between mirroring and duplexing is the number of controllers; mirroring uses one controller whereas duplexing uses a controller for each disk.

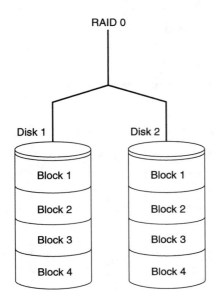

Figure 11.6
RAID level 1

- **RAID Level 2:** Hamming code ECC. In RAID 2, each bit of a data word is written to a disk. Four disks require three redundant disks, one less than mirroring. RAID 2 requires the use of extra disks to store an error-correcting code. With 32 data disks, a RAID 2 system would require seven additional disks for a Hamming code ECC. No commercial implementations exist today, and because modern disk drives contain their own internal ECC, RAID 2 is not practical because of the high initial cost. ECC is covered in Chapter 1.

- **RAID Level 3:** Parallel transfer with parity. In RAID 3, the data block is striped and written on the data disks. This requires a minimum of three drives to implement. In a parallel transfer with parity, data are interleaved bit-wise over the data disks, and a single parity disk is added to tolerate any single disk failure.

- **RAID Level 4:** Independent data disks with shared parity disk. Entire blocks are written onto a data disk. RAID 4 requires a minimum of three drives to implement. It is similar to RAID 3 except that data are interleaved across disks of arbitrary size rather than in bits.

- **RAID Level 5:** Independent data disks with distributed parity blocks. In RAID 5, each entire block of data and parity is striped. RAID 5 requires a minimum of three disks. See Figure 11.7.

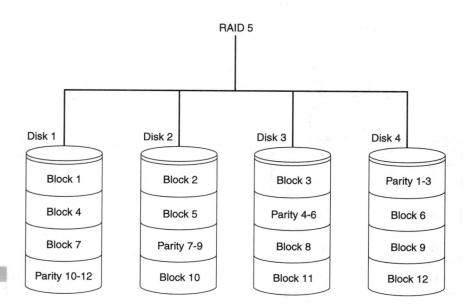

Figure 11.7
RAID level 5

Because it writes both the data and the parity over all the disks, RAID 5 has the best small-read, large-write performance of any redundancy disk array.

- **RAID Level 6:** Independent data disks with two independent parity schemes. This is an extension of RAID 5, which allows for additional fault tolerance by using two-dimensional parity. This method uses Reed-Solomon codes to protect against up to two disk failures using the bare minimum of two redundant disk arrays.

- **RAID Level 10:** High reliability combined with high performance. RAID 10 requires a minimum of four disks to implement. This solution is a striped array that has RAID 1 arrays. Disks are mirrored in pairs for redundancy and improved performance, and then data are striped across multiple disks for maximum performance.

There are three additional levels of RAID—7, 53, and 0+1. RAID 7 is a proprietary solution that is a registered trademark of Storage Computer Corporation. This RAID has a fully implemented, process-oriented, real-time operating system residing on an embedded-array controller microprocessor. RAID 53 is an implementation of a striped array that has RAID 3 segment arrays. This takes a minimum of five drives, three for RAID 3 and two for striping. RAID 0+1 is a mirrored array that has RAID 0 segments. RAID

0+1 requires a minimum of four drives, two for striping and two to mirror the first striped set.

When choosing a method of redundancy, choose a level of RAID that is supported by the operating system. Not all operating systems support all versions of RAID. For example, Microsoft Windows servers support RAID levels 0, 1, and 5. Also keep in mind that even though you set up the server for redundancy, you must still back up your data. RAID does not protect you from multiple disk failures. Regular tape backups allow you to recover from data loss, such as human, hardware, and software errors that are not related to a disk failure. We will discuss the different methods of backup in the next chapter.

We should mention hardware compatibility before we discuss how to install the operating system. After carefully installing the operating system, you don't want to discover that a vital piece of hardware isn't compatible with it. Hardware compatibility is just as important as the other items we have mentioned. Most NOS vendors publish and update a list of hardware that has been tested with their NOS for compatibility. Before installation, check the Web site of the operating system manufacturer for any known problems with hardware. Microsoft publishes a **Hardware Compatibility List (HCL)** which details compatible hardware for their operating systems.

⚠ WARNING

If you use incompatible hardware with your operating system, chances are the vendor will not provide technical support for any difficulties that may arise because it is an unsupported device.

Now that we have covered all the preparation steps, let's move on to the actual installation process.

11.3.2   Working through the Installation

Although all NOSs have different installation steps, the basic process is quite similar. In this section, we will first go over the installation of Windows 2000, and then look at Novell NetWare and Linux. All NOS installations start with a method of installation, choosing a partition size, and then formatting it with a file system. Today most NOSs are installed from a CD-ROM, but some can be installed over the network if you have a shared directory and a network boot disk. Another similarity is that all operating systems can be either an upgrade installation or a new install. Even though new installs are much cleaner and give us a chance to get rid of old files, sometimes it makes more business sense to upgrade.

There are three distinct sections to the Microsoft Windows 2000 Server installation: text-based, GUI, and networking. During the text-based portion of the installation, hard drives are partitioned and formatted with a file system. During the GUI phase, the license mode is chosen, the computer name is assigned, the administrator account is assigned a password, and the additional components to be installed are chosen. During the networking portion, the domain or workgroup is chosen and networking components are installed. We will do an actual install in the exercise at the end of the chapter.

Each operating system has minimum hardware requirements. Windows 2000 installation requires that the computer has the following processor, memory, and disk space capabilities:

- 133 MHz Pentium or higher CPU
- 64 MB of RAM, with 128 MB suggested
- The setup process requires 1 GB of free space; the recommended partition size is 2 GB.
- Additional space is needed for each component installed.
- If you choose to use FAT, an additional 100 to 200 MB of free space is required.
- Installation across the network takes an additional 100 to 200 MB of free space.
- In case of an upgrade, additional space is needed to import the existing user database.

Remember: These are only minimum requirements. It is not a good idea to try to run a database server on 128 MB of RAM—it will run too slow. Microsoft NOS and applications are RAM hungry, so when in doubt, the more the better. As you can see, many factors affect how much space you allocate for the operating system, so before you install, plan—plan carefully.

> **NOTE**
>
> When choosing the amount of space to allocate on the first partition, plan carefully, especially if you are installing applications that install to the root such as mail or database apps. The object is to make it big enough for needed files, but not too big as to encourage unnecessary files being placed in the root directory.

Installing Novell NetWare is similar to installing any other operating system. The current version at this writing is NetWare 6.5. This version brings accessibility, security, and high availability to the network. It also features extensive Internet and Web-based products such as iFolder, iPrint, and eDirectory. Novell provides additional information and online support from its Web site. Should you choose to investigate further, the Web site is *www.novell.com*.

Netware can be installed from a CD-ROM or over the network. The NetWare installation is text based. The installation will start the INSTALL.NLM utility and then go through the installation process: license agreement, server settings, device types, creating a partition, defining NetWare volumes, protocols, and services configuration. This is similar to the Windows 2000 server installation except that there is not a GUI portion of the setup.

When installing NetWare, take into consideration the number of NetWare-loadable modules (NLMs) used by each service. NLMs are routines that enable the server to run a range of programs and offer a variety of services. They consume resources just as installing additional applications do. Novell provides a worksheet so that you can calculate the amount of memory that the server requires. The minimum processor, memory, and disk space requirements are as follows:

- K7 processor (Pentium III 700 MHz recommended for multiple-processor computers)
- 256 MB RAM (512 MB recommended)
- DOS partition with 200 MB available space (1 GB recommended)
- 2 GB available space on volume SYS (4 GB recommended)

Again, remember that these are minimum requirements. One noticeable difference between Novell and Microsoft systems is that in Windows systems we often manage a server from the console. The Novell management console (NWAdmin) is very resource-intensive. It is better to run it remotely, such as from a Windows workstation, so as not to tax the server system resources. NetWare servers can have multiple NICs and use built-in bridging and routing software. Third-party NLMs for servers as well as client software are available.

Linux installations have become easier as the versions and products have evolved. Linux operating systems are a variety of Unix. The earlier versions were all text-based, and many times the hardware support had to be compiled into the kernel. (The Kernel is the core program component of the operating system.) Newer versions now all have GUI-based installs, making the process much less complicated. Various versions of Linux can be installed; some of the more popular ones are Mandrake, SuSE, Caldera, Slackware, and Red Hat. Red Hat is among the most popular and easiest to install. The installation process is similar to that of the other two operating systems we discussed. We will use Red Hat 9.0 as an example. The operating system can be installed from a CD-ROM. The setup takes you through creating a Linux partition and a swap partition.

NOTE ▣ In a Linux installation, you must configure two partitions—one native and one for swap space.

After the partitions are made, the installation walks you through selecting the devices on your computer, selecting whether the installation is a server or workstation install, and setting a root password. As with all NOSs, the computer has to be rebooted after the installation. You will find that Linux is popular due to cost and hardware requirements. The typical minimum processor, memory, and disk space requirements for a Linux server are:

- Intel-compatible CPU

- 32 MB of RAM

- Minimum of 500 MB free space

Linux is a bit different from Windows. Here are some tidbits about Linux that are worth knowing:

- Help is called the manpages.

- All devices have to be mounted before they can be used.

- Several different GUIs can be installed, such as Gnome and KDE.

- The X Window system is a client/server user interface that separates the client application processing from the server display functions and allows them to communicate over a network.

- Linux computers should be shut down properly. The files and system can be damaged if you just hit the power button, as we so often do in Windows.

After the operating system is installed, it needs to be configured. In the next section, we will look at the network configuration of the operating system.

11.3.3   Post-Installation Cleanup and Configuration

What happens when we start a NOS installation and for some reason it fails? Or, what happens when we install an application on the server and the installation fails? There are setup logs created when an operating system is installed that can tell us what happened to cause the install to fail. Instead of reading them, we usually just start over again and hope it works the second time around. A failed installation leaves behind a trail of files that need to be cleaned up. This is also often true when the operating system is upgraded instead of being a brand-new install or an application installation fails. You can clean up software products and service updates after an interrupted or failed installation. The cleanup procedure attempts to delete items that were partially installed or left in an incomplete state. Many operating systems have their own set of cleanup tools; some may have to be cleaned up manually. Here, because we will install a Microsoft NOS, we will mention the Windows Installer CleanUp Utility. This utility is designed to allow you to safely remove Windows Installer settings from your computer in the event of a problem. Windows Installer may become damaged if the computer's registry becomes corrupt or changes are made to registry settings used by the Windows Installer. You may also find that installations will fail if the CD-ROM is scratched or dirty, or if there isn't enough disk space allocated. The important point to remember is that many times when an installation fails, unnecessary files are left behind that should be cleaned up.

After the installation, the server needs to be configured. Earlier when we discussed the information needed before the install, we mentioned IP addresses, subnet masks, default gateways, and services such as DNS,

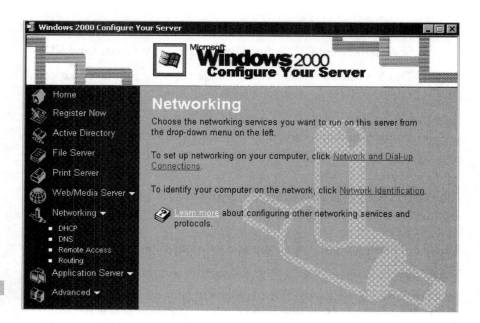

Figure 11.8
Configure your server

WINS, and DHCP. During the installation, some of these items may have been addressed, but not all of them. DHCP still needs scopes configured, WINS replication partners should be configured if necessary, and DNS zones will need to be configured as well. We'll only briefly review each of these and their configurations here because they are covered in Chapter 9:

- **DHCP scope:** This is the range of IP addresses that the DHCP server can assign. Each DHCP server must have at least one scope containing all the IP addresses to be made available for the subnet. DHCP scopes cannot overlap, otherwise IP addresses will be given out that have already been assigned.

- **WINS:** WINS resolves IP addresses to NetBIOS names. In a pure Windows 2000 environment, all connectivity is handled through DNS resolution. WINS is for backward compatibility on Microsoft systems. Novell and Linux know nothing of WINS.

- **DNS zones:** The DNS namespace is divided into zones, and each zone must have a server that is the authority for the name mapping for the zone. A Zone can be divided into multiple zones.

These are just a few of the items that can be configured. Figure 11.8 shows that many options are available in Windows 2000 Server.

11.3.4   Applying Checklists, Service Packs, Updates, and More

After the operating system is installed and configured it must be kept up to date. Updates can come in the form of service packs, or fixes. A **service pack** is an update to an existing release that includes solutions to known problems and other product enhancements. It may include bug fixes, system tools, and drivers. A service pack is not a replacement for an installation but an additional package of changes and enhancements for it. Between service packs, patches are issued to provide bug fixes for individual components. Depending on the operating system you are using, these can be applied different ways. Most operating system manufacturers recommend installing service packs as soon as they are released. It is always a better idea to test a service pack before installing it.

Because we install Windows 2000, we look at the methods of managing operating system updates and service packs. Before updating a Windows system, you'll need to know which service pack is currently installed. You can find this information in Windows in the following ways:

- In Windows 2000 and XP, the easiest way to determine which service pack is installed is to look on the System Properties General tab, which displays the build number as well as the service pack version.

- Type **winver** at a command prompt. This brings up the About Windows dialog box and displays the build number as well as the service pack version.

Many virus and vulnerability attacks happen because operating systems aren't updated or patched. Applying the latest manufacturer's operating system patches or fixes can also help prevent attacks. Subscribing to newsgroups and checking security Web sites daily will ensure that you are current as to the latest attacks and exploits. This requires constant vigilance. Keep in mind that, besides the servers, the workstations also need to have their operating systems updated and patched. When you have a large quantity of workstations on the network, managing and rolling out Windows updates can take a significant amount of your time. Windows 2000 includes features that can reduce your administrative tasks, including allowing for streamlined installations. Slipstreaming is a process whereby service packs are included with a distribution image. You can use slipstreaming to automatically roll service packs into Windows installations so that every new install is automatically updated to the latest version. This can save you a lot of time and hassle because you won't have to manually install the service packs after installing Windows.

11.4   Understanding Basic Network Services

The emergence of networking in the 1970s and its explosive growth since then have had a significant impact on the networking services provided by an operating system. As more network management features are added into the operating systems, more services are offered. In Figure 11.8 we saw that a variety of server components can be configured. Among these components are a myriad of system services. Services are provided by the operating system and form a foundation that is used by applications and accessed by the clients. When a service request comes in, the server process reacts to the request, performs the task requested, and then returns a response to the requestor. NOS services tend to be much more complex than those provided by regular operating systems. In addition, the implementation of these services often requires the use of multiple devices, message passing, and server processes. Some typical services provided by a network operating system include directory or naming, file, communication, mail, and printing.

Of these, the two most-used shared resources are directory and printing services. We will discuss each of these in detail a little later. But first we will do an overview of network services; next, look at installing, managing, and removing services; and then discuss network bindings. From there, we will move on to printing and directory services.

11.4.1   Overview

Every operating system requires different services for it to operate properly. The services installed will be different, depending on the role of the server. Ideally, the process of configuration should start with installing only the services that are absolutely necessary for the server to function. The manufacturer should have these services listed in the documentation. Using documentation to standardize the methods used to set up servers will make new deployments easier and more secure.

The best way to ensure that only necessary services are running is to do a clean install. New computer systems, especially servers, come from the manufacturer loaded with services, software, and protocols that will never

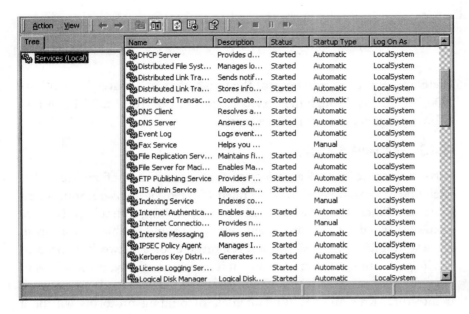

Figure 11.9
Managing services

be used. Additional software, such as the manufacturer's tools, or additional configuration changes also have been made. The only way to be sure the computer meets the specifications of the plan is to perform a clean installation using predetermined checklists or policies. This task is very time-consuming but, in the end, it's worth it. An additional benefit is that it ensures that you have all of the software and skills required to rebuild the server should that ever need to be done. Taking the time to do it right the first time will certainly save many headaches down the road.

11.4.2   Installing, Removing, and Managing Services

As mentioned above, only the services that are absolutely necessary for the server to function should be installed. As the network configuration changes, the role of the server may also change. You will end up having to either install or configure at least one of the services we have discussed at some point. Most NOSs have some type of administrative tool for removing or adding services. Figure 11.9 shows the services window on a computer running Windows 2000 as an example. These tools make it easier to stop and start all the basic services once they are in place.

There are several ways to control the parameters of services in Windows 2000. The first is through the Services applet in Control Panel. The second is through a management console snap-in.

11.4.3 Network Bindings

Networks can consist of a variety of topologies and configurations. We often find Microsoft Windows integrated with Novell NetWare. Some companies use Ethernet protocols, others use Token Ring technology. Because we have such a diverse environment, our NIC should be able to work in all of these conditions. When you are responsible for a network or need to maximize a computer's performance, it is imperative that you know how to properly link network components from the various levels of network architecture. Knowing the fundamentals of binding protocols will be a great advantage in making all this happen. Let's start with defining binding. **Binding** is the process of linking network components on different levels to enable communication between the components. Bindings are links that enable communication between network adapter card drivers, protocols, and services. You bind a protocol suite to a network interface whether it be a card, VPN, or dial-up modem. Bindings establish a logical link between the upper protocols and lower protocols on the NIC to provide interoperability. This allows one system to support and run any number of network protocols.

The number of protocols run and the order of the bindings on the client side can affect network performance. There are administrators who install unnecessary protocols because they either misunderstand the protocol's function or may need them at some future time. Protocols, like services, should not be installed unless required. The more protocols installed, the more network traffic. The most frequently used protocol, service, or adapter should be bound first. Figure 11.10 shows where the bindings are configured in Windows 2000.

11.4.4 Network Printing

Configuring and managing network printing services is a bit different than working with a printer connected to your workstation. With network printing, there are different operating systems, printer languages, and vari-

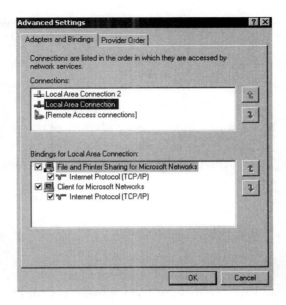

Figure 11.10
Network bindings

ous user or department requirements to meet. As with other network devices, network printers deliver different levels of performance depending on the quality of the printer and driver. There are three ways a printer can be networked:

1. Connect via serial/parallel to a server

2. Connect either serial or parallel to a remote print server

3. Connect via an internal NIC such as HP JetDirect's Ethernet interface

You will install a printer in Challenge Exercise 11.6 at the end of the chapter, so we will not go over the steps in detail at this point. Instead, let's look at some factors you should consider when choosing a strategy for network printing:

- Determine what speed the connection should be, such as 10 or 100 MB Ethernet.

- Check the amount of RAM in the printer. Users often send large print jobs. If the printer doesn't have sufficient memory, printing will be slow.

- A poorly written driver can significantly degrade print performance. Vendors update their print drivers periodically and make them available on their Web sites. Make sure new versions of the drivers are downloaded when they become available.

- It might be better to deploy several smaller printers rather than one large printer. If your only printer breaks, the users will have to wait for it to be repaired.

- Make sure that the printer, print server, and users are close to each other, if possible.

Managing print services involves more than hooking them up, creating the printer objects, and sharing them. Access needs to be established, print jobs may need to be redirected, or priority may need to be established on a print queue.

11.4.5   Directory Services

A network of computers managed by a network operating system can get rather large, making it difficult to maintain information about the location and availability of services. How would the client know whether the particular service is available, and if so, on what server?

Directory services, sometimes called name services, address such problems. The directory server is responsible for knowing the current locations and availability of all services so that the client can quickly locate the unique network address of the service. The **directory service** is a database of service names and service addresses. Different operating systems have different techniques for doing this, but they all supply a client with enough information about contacting the directory service because all servers register themselves with the directory service upon startup. To ensure the directory service is not dependent on one computer, the directory service is often replicated or mirrored. As long as one directory service is reachable, the client gets the information it seeks. As this concept develops, the directory service has been expanded to handle service addresses as well as users, groups, printers, folders, and Web information. Here is a summary of the features of a directory service:

- It is a network service that identifies all resources on a network and makes them accessible to users and applications.

- It stores information about objects that are name-related.

- It makes it easier to locate and manage network resources.

Directory services differ from a directory in that it is both the source of the information and the services making the information available to the users.

Two standards for using directory services over large networks such as the Internet have been developed:

- **X.500 directory service:** In the X.500 directory architecture, the client queries and receives responses from one or more servers in the server's Directory Service, with the Directory Access Protocol (DAP) controlling the communication between the client and the server. X.500 has been criticized as being too complex and difficult to implement.

- **Lightweight Directory Access Protocol (LDAP):** LDAP offers much of the same basic functionality as DAP and can be used to query data from proprietary directories as well as from an open X.500 service. It is fast becoming a de facto directory protocol for the Internet. Although LDAP started as a simplified component of the X.500 directory, it has evolved into a complete directory service.

Microsoft Windows 2000 offers directory services support in the form of Active Directory. Active Directory is an essential component of the Windows 2000 architecture that acts as the central authority for network security and allows organizations to centrally manage and share information on network resources and users. Figure 11.11 illustrates this concept.

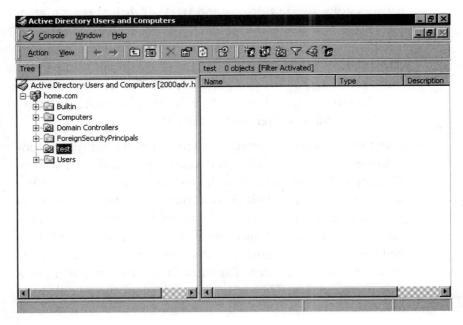

Figure 11.11

Active Directory

Linux Directory Services integrates LDAP and SSL to provide a secure network directory services architecture replacing Network Information Service (NIS). LDAP is now incorporated into most vendor releases of Linux. Novell NetWare Directory Services (NDS) is an object-oriented implementation of directory services that allows sophisticated naming schemes and databases across network-wide resources. The NDS architecture provides access to all network resources regardless of where the resources are physically located.

11.5   Chapter Summary

- Current operating systems provide many services to give application programs a unified view of the network. The basic functions of an operating system include directing and controlling activities of a computer's hardware components, and coordinating the interaction between software applications and computer hardware. Some of the commonly available network operating systems include Linux, Novell NetWare, SunOS/Solaris, FreeBSD, Unix, and Windows.

- A NOS provides a large variety of services and functions. Quite a few software components help make up a network operating system, including naming and directory services, client and server network software, and drivers and stacks. A driver is a program that interacts with either a particular device or type of software. The driver contains specific information about a device or a software interface that programs using the driver do not. Some of the driver technologies that you should be familiar with are the Network Device Interface System (NDIS), Open Data-Link Interface (ODI), and Win32 Driver model (WDM).

- Client/server network operating systems allow the network to centralize services and applications in one or more dedicated servers. The servers become the core of the system, providing security and access to resources. Individual workstations are then given access to the resources on the servers. The network operating system provides the means to combine all the pieces of the network and allow multiple users to simultaneously share the same resources no matter where they are located. The most important component of a NOS is redirection. The component that does this is called the redirector.

- After the server type is chosen, a file system must be decided upon. The term file system is used to describe the operating system's method of organizing, managing, and accessing of files through logical structuring on the hard disk. File systems interact with the operating system to be sure that the operating system can find requested files on the hard disk. The file system keeps a table of contents of the files on the drive; when a file is requested, the table of contents is searched to locate and access the file. The most common file systems are FAT, HPFS, and NTFS.

- An important aspect of protecting a NOS is providing for redundancy of data. It would be irresponsible to set up an operating system without considering how to salvage the data should a component fail. The most common approach to this is called RAID (Redundant Array of Inexpensive Disks). It organizes multiple disks into a large, high-performance logical disk. There are various levels, each providing a different method of redundancy.

- After the operating system is installed and configured, it must be kept up to date. Updates can come in the form of service packs or fixes. A service pack is an update to an existing release that includes solutions to known problems and other product enhancements. It may include bug fixes, system tools, and drivers. A service pack is not a replacement for an installation but an additional package of changes and enhancements to it.

- Binding is the process of linking network components on different levels to enable communication between the components. Bindings are links that enable communication between NIC drivers, protocols, and services. You bind a protocol suite to a network interface whether it be a card, VPN, or dial-up modem. Bindings establish a logical link between the upper protocols and lower protocols on the NIC to provide interoperability. This allows one system to support and run any number of network protocols.

- A network of computers managed by a network operating system can get rather large, making it difficult to maintain information about the location and availability of services. Directory services, sometimes called name services, address such problems. The directory service is a database of service names and service addresses that is responsible for knowing the current locations and availability of all services so that the client can quickly locate the unique network address of the service.

11.6   Key Terms

binding: The process of linking network components on different levels to enable communication between the components.

cooperative multitasking: A form of multitasking in which the operating system has no control over the processes. The operating system transfers control to an application. Once an application has control of the CPU, the operating system cannot interrupt it.

designator: Exchanges a locally mapped drive letter with the correct network address of a directory share.

directory service: A database of service names and addresses that exist on a network.

driver: A program that interacts with either a particular device or type of software. It contains specific information about a device or a software interface that programs using the driver do not.

File Allocation Table (FAT): A file system used by DOS that is supported by all the other operating systems. It is simple, reliable, and uses little storage.

File System: Describes the operating system's method of organizing, managing, and accessing of files through logical structuring on the hard disk.

Hardware Compatibility List (HCL): A manufacturer list that details compatible hardware for operating systems.

High-Performance File System (HPFS): Designed for the OS/2 operating system to allow for greater access to larger hard drives.

naming convention: The process by which names are created for the workstations and servers on the network.

Network Device Interface System (NDIS): A communication interface between the MAC sublayer and the network interface driver that allows Windows operating systems to communicate multiple protocols to the NIC.

network operating system (NOS): Acts as a director to keep the network running smoothly, and is a complete operating system in addition to managing communication across the LAN.

New Technology File System (NTFS): Developed expressly for versions of Windows NT and Windows 2000 as a platform for added functionality, reliability, and security features.

Open Data-Link Interface (ODI): Similar to NDIS except that it supports Novell and Apple systems. It allows these operating systems to communicate multiple protocols to the NIC.

preemptive multitasking: Processes are assigned CPU time slices by the operating system, and after the item slice expires, the process is halted and the next process gets computing time.

redirector: Operating at the Presentation layer of the OSI model, its function is to accept requests from applications and determine whether network access is needed.

Redundant Array of Inexpensive Disks (RAID): Organizes multiple disks into a large, high-performance logical disk.

service pack: An update to an existing release that includes solutions to known problems and other product enhancements.

stack: A set of network protocol layers that work together. The set of TCP/IP protocols that define communication over the Internet is the most common stack.

virtual FAT (VFAT): An enhanced version of the FAT file system, this file system is also called FAT32.

Win32 Driver model (WDM): Architecture that divides drivers into various classes by functions. It is a complete card interface that enables generic class drivers to handle bus and device functions.

11.7 Challenge Questions

11.1 Which of the following is not a common server use?

   a. Logon server

   b. Application server

   c. Music server

   d. Print server

11.2 When managing print services, which of the following should be taken into consideration? (Choose all that apply.)

a. Determine what speed the connection should be, such as 10 or 100 MB Ethernet.

b. A poorly written driver can significantly degrade print performance. Vendors update their print drivers periodically and make them available on their Web sites.

c. Make sure that the printer, print server, and users are close to each other if possible.

d. It might be better to deploy several smaller printers rather than one large printer.

11.3 Which of the following levels of RAID does Windows 2000 support? (Choose all that apply.)

a. RAID Level 0: Striped disk array without fault tolerance

b. RAID Level 1: Mirroring and duplexing

c. RAID Level 4: Independent data disks with shared parity disk

d. RAID Level 5: Independent data disks with distributed parity blocks

11.4 In which of the following NOS installations must you configure two partitions—one native and one for swap space?

a. Linux

b. Windows 2000

c. Novell

d. Windows 3.11

11.5 What term is used to describe the process of linking network components to enable communication?

a. Redirection

b. Designator

c. Binding

d. Requester

11.6 Which of the following NOSs does not have a GUI-based setup process?

a. Linux

b. Windows 2000

c. Novell

d. Windows NT

11.7 A naming convention should apply to which of the following objects on the network? (Choose all that apply.)

a. Passwords

b. Users

c. Printers

d. Servers

11.8 Which of the following issues should be addressed before starting the setup of a server?

a. Role of the server

b. Number of partitions

c. Naming conventions

d. The name of the HR director

11.9 The _____ is a database of service names and service addresses that is responsible for knowing the current locations and availability of all services so that the client can quickly locate the unique network address of a service.

11.10 The most common method for providing redundancy for data accumulated on hard disks is called _____.

11.11 To verify hardware compatibility before you install a NOS, you should check the _____.

11.12 Name and give a brief description of the most commonly used network operating systems.

11.13 Describe multitasking and the different methods that exist.

11.14 Why must you plan your organization's naming structure carefully?

11.15 List four factors you should consider before purchasing a network operating system.

11.8   Challenge Exercises

Challenge Exercise 11.1

Planning is an important part of setting up a network server. In this exercise, you plan the setup of your server. Use Table 11.2 as a checklist and fill in all the information. You need the computer on which you intend to install the operating system and a pen.

Challenge Exercise 11.2

In this exercise, you install the Windows 2000 Server or Windows 2000 Advanced Server operating system. You need a computer with the following components:

- 133 MH2 Pentium processor or higher

- 128 MB of RAM

- 2 GB free space

- An installed NIC

- Windows 2000 Server or Advanced Server CD-ROM

11.1   To start the installation, place the CD-ROM in the drive and reboot the computer. Make sure your BIOS is set to boot from the CD-ROM. Setup will begin with the text mode portion of the setup. If you have third-party controllers such as SCSI or RAID, press **F6** to install them.

11.2   The Welcome to setup screen appears. You can choose from the following three options:

- Run Windows 2000 setup. Press Enter for this option.

- Repair an existing Windows 2000 installation. Press R for this option.

- Exit setup without installing Windows 2000. Press F3 for this option.

Press **Enter** to run the Windows 2000 setup program.

TABLE 11.2   Server Setup Checklist

Item	Information
Date	
Setup person	
Computer manufacturer	
Model	
Serial number	
Number of hard drives and size	
RAM	
Processor(s)	
NIC(s)	
Disk controller type	
Number of partitions	
Partition size(s) and type(s)	
File system type	
Server purpose	
Server type	
Registration key	
Server name	
Domain	
Licensing mode	
Components to be installed	
Network protocols to be installed	
Location of log files	
IP address	

11.3 If the hard drive has an incompatible operating system already installed, you will get a message stating that you could lose data if you continue with setup. You have two choices:

- Continue setup. Press C.
- Quit setup. Press F3.

Press **C** to continue.

11.4 Read the license agreement. If you do not agree with the license agreement, setup cannot continue. Use PageDown to scroll through the agreement. When finished, press **F8** to accept the agreement.

11.5 The next step allows you to choose which partition the operating system is installed on. This is the point when you partition the drive. You have three options:

- To setup Windows on the selected partition, press Enter.
- To create a new partition in the unpartitioned space, press C.
- To delete the selected partition, press D. Any files stored here will be lost.

Press **C** to create a new partition. When you choose this option, you can decide how large to make the partition or return to the previous screen without making a new partition. You may either choose to accept the default size or select a different size. Select a size of 2 GB.

11.6 After the partition is created, you must format the partition. The choices are NTFS or FAT. NTFS is the default. If the partition size is larger then 2 GB, it will default to FAT32. Choose the file system you want to use and press **Enter**. A bar appears across the screen showing the progress of the formatting. When the formatting is complete, setup copies the startup files to the hard drive and initializes the Windows 2000 GUI portion of the setup.

11.7 A message appears telling you to remove any floppy disks from the drive and to press Enter to restart the computer. Press **Enter**.

11.8 Upon reboot, the Starting Windows bar appears at the bottom of the screen. When the computer is finished booting, you will be at the GUI portion and the setup wizard appears.

11.9 Click **Next** to continue. The setup wizard detects the devices on the computer.

11.10 The Regional Settings screen appears. Select **Regional settings**. When finished, or if you choose to accept the default, click **Next**.

11.11 The Personalize Your Software screen appears. Enter your name and organization information. When finished, click **Next**.

11.12 The Your Product Key screen appears. Enter your product key. This is found on the case of the CD-ROM. If you do not have a case, your instructor will provide a key for you. Click **Next**.

11.13 The Licensing Modes screen appears, which allows you to choose the license mode. You can choose either per server or per seat. After you choose the mode, click **Next**.

11.14 The Computer Name and Administrator Password screen appears. In the Computer Name text box, enter a name for your computer. In the Administrator Password text box, enter the password for the Administrator account. The computer name must be unique; the password is to be entered twice. The second time is to confirm it. Click **Next**.

11.15 The Windows 2000 Components screen appears. This screen allows you to decide which additional components you want to install; however, do not choose any at this time. Click **Next**.

11.16 The Date and Time Settings screen appears. Set the date, time, and time zone. Click **Next**.

11.17 Setup now moves to the networking portion. The Networking Settings screen appears and allows you to choose typical settings or customize them. Click **Typical settings**, and then click **Next**. This option installs TCP/IP, Client for Microsoft Networks, and File and Print Sharing for Microsoft Networks.

11.18 The Workgroup or Computer Domain screen appears. You now can join either a workgroup or a domain. Because we will install Active Directory later in the exercises, you must temporarily join a workgroup at this point in the installation. Select **No, this computer is not on a network, or is on a network without a domain**, type **WORKGROUP** in the Workgroup or Computer Domain text box, and then click **Next**.

11.19 The Installing Components screen appears. Setup installs the network components, copies files, and removes temporary files.

11.20 The Completing the Windows 2000 Setup Wizard screen appears. Remove the CD-ROM from your drive and click **Finish**.

11.21 Windows 2000 is now installed on your computer.

Challenge Exercise 11.3

Directory Services identifies all resources on a network and makes them accessible to users and applications. In this exercise, you install Microsoft Active Directory. This will be a new domain controller as the root of a forest. You need a computer with a NIC and with a Windows 2000 Server or Advanced Server installed. Be sure the network card is plugged into the network; many times Directory Services fails to install because the card is not plugged in.

11.1 To start Active Directory installation, click **Start**, click **Run**, and type **cmd** in the Open text box, and press **Enter**. At the command prompt, type **DCPROMO** and click **OK**.

11.2 The Active Directory Installation Wizard starts. Click **Next**.

11.3 The Domain Controller Type screen appears, which allows you to choose the domain controller type. Because you are working with a single server, select **Domain Controller for a New Domain**. Click **Next**.

11.4 In the Create Tree or Child Domain screen, you can choose whether to create a domain or create a new child domain in an existing tree. Because we want to create a new domain, select **Create a New Domain Tree**. Click **Next**.

11.5 In the Create or Join Forest screen, select **Create a New Forest of Domain Trees**. Click **Next**.

11.6 In the New Domain Name screen, type the name of the domain that you wrote on the installation checklist in Challenge Exercise 11.1. Keep in mind that you must use a DNS domain name. For example, if the domain we picked was TEST and we were installing in a local domain, the domain name would be TEST.LOCAL. After you enter a domain name, click **Next**.

11.7 In the NetBIOS Domain Name screen, enter the NetBIOS domain name. This is used for backward compatibility. Enter **TEST**. Click **Next**.

11.8 In the Database and Log Locations screen, specify where the Active Directory database and the log files should be stored. For better performance and fault tolerance, it is recommended that these not be on the same drive as the operating system. Click **Next**.

11.9 In the Shared System Volume screens, specify where you want the SYSVOL folder to be installed. Click **Next**.

11.10 A warning dialog box opens, stating the installation wizard cannot contact the DNS server. This is normal. You have created the root of a new forest, and DNS has not been set up yet. Click **OK**.

11.11 In the Configure DNS screen, select the **Yes, Install and Configure DNS on this Computer** option. This automatically installs and configures DNS. Click **Next**.

11.12 In the Permissions screen, you are given the choice to select whether you will be working strictly with Windows 2000 computers or need backward compatibility. Select **Permissions Compatible Only with Windows 2000 Servers**. Click **Next**.

11.13 The Directory Services Restore Mode Administrator Password screen appears.

! WARNING

For security purposes, the Directory Services restore password and the administrator password should not be the same, because if the system is compromised, Directory Services will not be compromised as well.

Enter a password, enter it again to confirm it, and click **Next**.

11.14 The Summary screen appears. Read through this carefully because it recaps all the information you have entered. If anything needs to be corrected, click **Back** to correct the information. If all of the information is correct, click **Next**.

11.15 Active Directory now installs. If the installation fails, verify that the NIC is plugged in. After Active Directory finishes installing, click **Finish**. You now must reboot the computer for the changes to take effect.

Challenge Exercise 11.4

In this exercise, you complete an installation checklist for installing a Linux operating system. This is a three-step exercise: In Step 1, you research the different types of Linux operating systems that are available and choose one. In Step 2, you write down the system components that are in the system you are currently using and check that they are compatible with the operating system you chose. In Step 3, you create a Linux installation checklist. For this exercise, you need a computer with Internet access, and a pencil and paper.

11.1 Access the Internet and research the different Linux operating systems that are available. Choose one. Which one did you choose? Why? Write your answers on a separate sheet of paper.

11.2 In Table 11.3, fill in the information as it pertains to the computer that you are using. Check the compatibility list for the operating system to be sure that the operating system can be installed on the computer.

TABLE 11.3   Computer Compatibility Information

Item	Manufacturer	Model
CPU		
Hard disk		
Controller		
CD-ROM		
NIC		
Sound card		
Monitor		
Keyboard		
Mouse		
Tape drive		

11.3 In Table 11.4, list the items you want in your Linux installation. Refer to Table 11.2 in Challenge Exercise 11.2 as a guide.

TABLE 11.4   Linux Installation Checklist

Item	Information

Challenge Exercise 11.5

Network operating systems allow the user to access shared resources. In this exercise, you create a new folder, share the folder, set permissions on the share, and then place the share in Active Directory. You need a computer with Windows 2000 Server installed.

11.1 Log on to your computer.

11.2 Double-click **My Computer**.

11.3 Click the **C** drive. On the menu bar, click **File**, point to **New**, and then click **Folder**.

11.4 For the filename, replace New Folder with **Shared**.

11.5 Right-click the folder, click **Properties**, and then select the **Sharing** tab, as shown in Figure 11.12. Click the **Share this folder** option and type **Shared** in the Share name text box. Enter a description in the Comment text box.

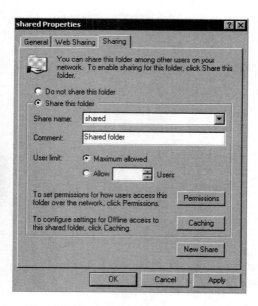

Figure 11.12

Properties page of the Shared folder

11.6   Click the **Permissions** button. Verify that the Everyone group has been given Full Control. Click **OK**.

11.7   Click the **Security** tab in the Properties dialog box. Assign permissions to the Everyone group. This allows users to list what is in the folder, read the contents of any file, and use applications but not make any changes to the folder.

11.8   Click **Add**. We will add permissions for the Administrators group. Select the **Administrators** group from the list in the top pane of the window. Click **Add**. The Administrators group should now appear in the bottom pane of the window. Click **OK**.

11.9   Give Full Control permission to the Administrators group. Click **OK**. Close any open windows.

11.10   Click **Start**, click **Programs**, point to **Administrative Tools**, and then click **Active Directory Users and Computers**.

11.11   Click the directory root (**C**). From the top menu, select **Action**, point to **New**, and then click **Shared folder**.

11.12   In the New Object-Shared Folder dialog box, type **Shared** in the Name text box, and then type the path to the share in the Network path text box, as shown in Figure 11.13. Click **OK**.

11.13   Verify that the shared folder is available in the Active Directory Users and Computers window.

11.14   Right-click the new share to open the properties dialog box. Type a description for the share in the Description text box. Click **OK**. Close Active Directory Users and Computers.

Challenge Exercise 11.6

In this exercise, you install and share a local printer connected via a TCP/IP port. You need a computer with Windows 2000 Server installed, but do not need a local printer attached.

11.1   Log on to your computer.

11.2   Click **Start**, click **Settings**, click **Printers**, and then double-click the **Add printer** icon.

11.3   The Add Printer Wizard starts. Click **Next**.

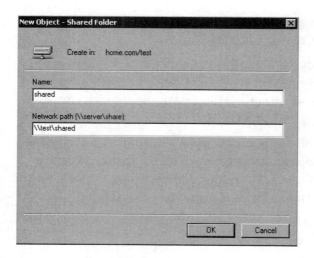

Figure 11.13
New Object-Shared Folder dialog box

11.4 Click the **Local Printer** radio button and deselect the **Automatically detect and install my Plug and Play printer** option. Click **Next**.

11.5 Click the **Create a new port** radio button and then select **Standard TCP/IP Port** from the type menu. Click **Next**.

11.6 The Add Standard TCP/IP Port Wizard starts. It will guide you through setting up the port. Click **Next**.

11.7 In the Printer Name or IP Address text box, type **192.168.0.25** or the IP address given to you by your instructor. The port name automatically fills in, as shown in Figure 11.14. Click **Next**.

11.8 You will get an error that the wizard cannot identify the printer. This is acceptable for exercise purposes. In a real network environment, you would investigate why this is happening. Click **Next**.

11.9 The summary screen appears. Click **Finish**.

11.10 The Add Printer Wizard screen appears again. In the Manufacturers list, select **HP**. In the Printers list, select **HP Laserjet 5si**. Click **Next**.

11.11 In the Printer name field, type the room number you are in. For example, Room 235. Click **Next**.

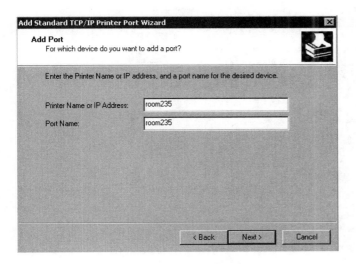

Figure 11.14

Add Standard TCP/IP Printer Port Wizard port name field

11.12 Click the **Share as** option and specify the share name of the printer as **Room XXX**, where *XXX* is the actual room number. Click **Next**.

11.13 In the Location text box, type a description of the location such as the one shown in Figure 11.15. Click **Next**.

11.14 Click the **No** option in the Print Test Page screen. Click **Next**.

11.15 Review the information shown on the summary page. Click **Finish**.

11.16 After a few moments, you should see a printer icon in the Printers window. Close the Printers window.

Challenge Exercise 11.7

In this exercise, you go to the Microsoft Web site and search for the latest service pack for Windows 2000 Server. For this exercise you need a computer with Internet access.

11.1 Log on to your computer and connect to the Internet.

11.2 In the Address text box, type **www.microsoft.com**.

11.3 In the Resources section in the left pane, click **Downloads**.

11.4 In the Download Categories section in the left pane, choose **Windows (Security & Updates)**.

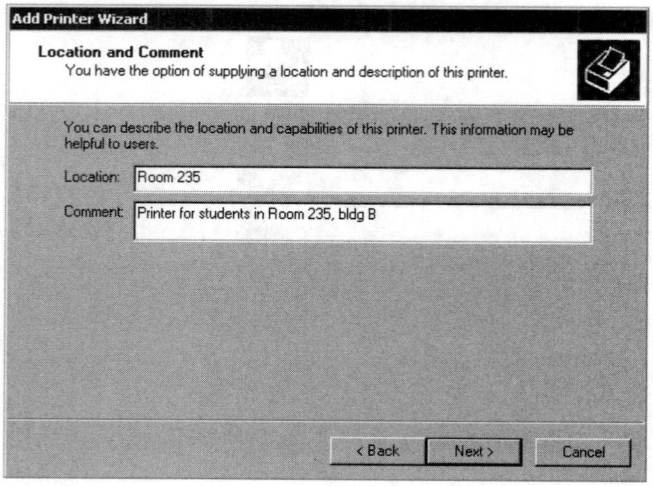

Figure 11.15

Location and Comment screen in the Add Printer Wizard

11.5 In the results pane, click the + box to show all results.

11.6 Search through the results until you find the latest service pack for the Windows 2000 Server. In the Related Resources section on the right side of the page, click the **Readme for Windows 2000 Service Pack X**, where X is the number of the latest service pack. What types of things does the service pack add or correct?

11.7 Answer the following general questions about service pack installation:

a. Why would a network manager want to install a service pack?

b. When would be the best time to install it?

c. What possible pitfalls might one encounter as a result of installing a service pack?

11.9   Challenge Scenarios

Challenge Scenario 11.1

A new client calls and wants to install a network. The client is unsure of the different operating systems available and would like some help. From your experience, describe the different operating systems and explain why they would choose one over the other.

Challenge Scenario 11.2

A potential client calls and explains the following situation: They are planning a network installation for their medium-size company. Sixty-five computers, four servers, and 15 printers will be installed. All computers will be installed in four divisions of the company: Administration (#1220), Finance (#1222), Development (#1200), and QA (#1256). They are installing Windows 2000 Server servers and Windows XP workstations. They want the naming convention to provide a unique name for each user and device on the network, and the naming convention should be easy to understand and administer.

They have come up with this naming scheme: User names will consist of the first four letters of first name of the user, followed by their department number (DAVI1222). Computer names will follow the same naming convention: first four letters of the user's first name followed by their department number. Server names will be SERVER1, SERVER2, SERVER3, and SERVER4. Printer names consist of the type of printer (HPLJ4), the department number (1200), and the printer number (1, 2, etc.). They ask for your opinion. What do you tell them?

Challenge Scenario 11.3

Your client has eight workstations and soon will add more. You suggest that they implement a client/server network. Even though your main contact thinks it's a great idea, the owner is opposed to it. He is afraid that if something happens to the server, all the data will be lost and no one will be able to work. He also believes a network of that type is expensive to install considering the cost of the server and software.

The network is growing. The owner needs to consider a client/server network to avoid problems in the future. What will you say to convince him that your solution has the company's best interests in mind?

Challenge Scenario 11.4

Technoguardian has asked you to help plan a Windows 2000 network. They have been using Windows NT until now and have decided to upgrade the NOS because they would like to use Active Directory and don't want to switch to Novell NetWare. Your job is to check to be sure that the servers and workstations have the processing power, memory, and disk space to provide for this upgrade, and that the current hardware is compatible. Create a checklist for the servers and workstations, and a checklist for hardware compatibility.

CHAPTER 12

Network Administration and Support

After reading this chapter you will be able to:

- Manage user and group access
- Understand what Group Policy objects are and how to work with them
- Effectively manage network performance
- Implement and maintain security
- Protect the physical, data, and system environments in a network
- Establish proper planning for business continuity

One of the most challenging parts of network administration is managing user access. Often a fine line exists between enough access and too much access. In this chapter, we look at how to manage user access by using groups and group policies. Then we discuss methods for keeping the network running smoothly and efficiently. Knowing what to look for and how to fix it is an acquired skill. From the examples in this chapter you will gain some insight into issues that cause performance problems on your network. From there, we progress to ensuring that you have a sound security policy in place and knowing how to maintain it. You will find that security today involves physical, data, and system security as well as general network security, and all of these must be addressed in your security policy. We finish the chapter with a detailed analysis of business practices and support requirements that may be needed to ensure that your company can continue to function in the event of failure.

12.1   Network Management Tasks and Activities

A large part of network management involves configuring a mix of different components that makes resources available to those who need them while prohibiting access to those who don't. Determining what is enough access and what is too much can be tricky. You will find that creating groups and assigning users to these groups will make the administration process much easier. Although managing users is part of network management, it is not all of it by any means. You must also do network monitoring, which involves checking parameters, avoiding bottlenecks, and optimizing network performance. Once you have the monitoring process down, it's time to figure out how you are going to protect the infrastructure. This starts with the physical aspects and includes protecting sensitive information, such as payroll records, as well as network servers and workstations. A security plan must be put into place, and users need to be trained. It's an endless job, but somebody has to do it! This is where you come in. To get started, we'll discuss how to manage user accounts and access.

12.2   Managing Access and Accounts

Setting up user accounts is usually much less complicated than allowing access. Every operating system has a method for setting up user and group accounts, most of which include some type of user interface. Even though each system has its own method for setting up these accounts, the basic principles of user management can be applied no matter which operating system you are using. When allowing user access, remember that you are dealing with human beings. Your access plan is always better received when rights or privileges are added rather than taken away. For example: When I set up your user account, I give you full access to a database that you really don't need to access. As a new user, and naturally a curious person, you are looking around and accidentally delete the entire database, not even realizing you did. The next day you are poking around and notice the database is missing. Upon asking why, you are told that *you* deleted this very important database and that your rights have been taken away. How does that make you feel? The phrase "we took away your rights" has a very strong impact on users. This is why you should be extremely careful with access. Remember the phrase "less is more" whenever determining proper levels of access. This is the security practice known as least privilege, that is, an account is granted no more access rights than the minimum needed to perform assigned tasks. We will go into more detail on access rights and levels later in the chapter, but for now we will look at user and group accounts.

12.2.1 User and Group Accounts

As mentioned earlier, every operating system has a method for setting up user and group accounts. A **user account** holds information about the specific user. It can contain basic information such as name, password, and the level of user permission. It can also contain much more specific information, such as the user's department, a home phone number, and the days and hours the user is allowed to log on to specific workstations. Groups are created to make resource sharing more manageable. A **group** contains users who share a common need for access to a particular resource. For example, the sales support staff requires access to a folder that contains the contact information for all new leads the sales people generate. Instead of giving each individual access to the folder, a group called "sales support" can be created, granting access to the leads folder to all users in that group. Depending on your operating system, you may find that permissions will be used in granting access to perform actions, and rights will be used to describe access to perform a task. For example, in Microsoft operating systems, rights and permissions denote two different things; Novell rights; Unix permissions; and some versions of Linux uses privileges. Even though

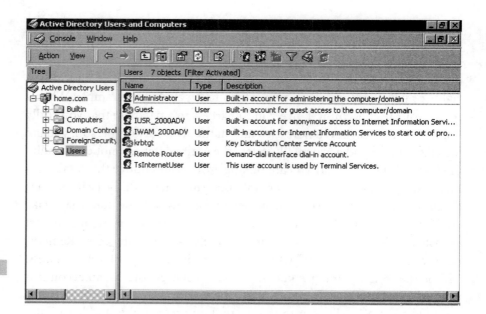

Figure 12.1

Windows 2000 Server default accounts

the connotations may differ with each operating system, all of these terms still refer to the access granted to a user or group account.

All operating systems have an administrative account. Again, because operating systems differ, this account is not named the same in all operating systems. (For example, in Linux or Unix it is called root, in Windows it is called Administrator, and in Novell it is called Supervisor.) Even though the names are different, the purpose of the account is the same: It is used to manage the system.

WARNING ! The administrative account should be used *only* for the purpose of administering the server. Granting users this type of access can lead to disastrous results. An individual using the administrative account can put a company's entire business in jeopardy.

Most operating systems set up the administrative account during installation and then set up additional user accounts after the installation is complete. Windows, however, has several accounts set up by default. In this chapter, we look at Windows 2000 Server. Figure 12.1 shows the default accounts created when the operating system is installed. No matter which

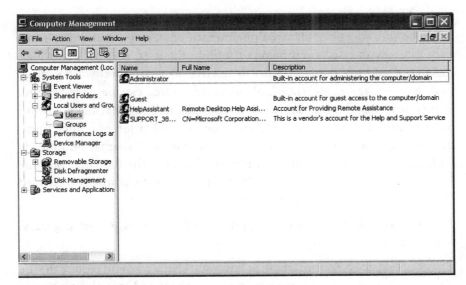

Figure 12.2
Windows XP Professional user accounts

system is used, it is important to know what accounts are installed by default and what access each account has. As a comparison, Figure 12.2 shows the screen of a computer running Windows XP Professional.

As you see, the built-in user accounts for each operating system may be different. One built-in account common to all Microsoft operating systems since Windows NT is the Guest account. The purpose of the Guest account is to allow temporary access for a user who doesn't have an account set up. The Guest account has limited access, but many times it is disabled to keep intruders from accessing the machine.

TIP

By knowing which accounts are installed by default, you can determine which are really needed and which can be disabled, thereby making the system more secure.

When setting up user accounts, proper planning and policies should be determined. The first item we will look at is passwords, simply because a password is one of the first pieces of information entered by a user.

Allowing users to create their own passwords produces an insecure environment because users typically choose passwords that contain easy-to-remember words. On the other end of the spectrum, if the passwords are too difficult to remember, users will write them down and post them on monitors, keyboards, and any number of obvious places. A weak password might be very short or only use alphanumeric characters, containing information easily guessed by someone profiling the user, such as a birthday, nickname, address, name of a pet or relative, or a common word such as *God*, *love*, *money*, or *password*. Stronger passwords can be derived from events or things the user knows. For example, let's say that the password must be nine characters long and must be a combination of letters, numbers, and special characters. The user is going to the Bahamas on June 10, with his spouse named Jean. The phrase "Going to the Bahamas on June 10 with Jean" can become gtBH610@J. Now we have a complex password that is easy for the user to remember.

The following items should be given consideration when setting password policies:

- Make the password length at least eight characters, and require the use of uppercase and lowercase letters, numbers, and special characters.

- Lock user accounts out after three to five failed logon attempts. This stops programs from deciphering the passwords on locked accounts.

- Require users to change passwords every 60 to 90 days, depending on how secure the environment needs to be. Remember that the more frequently users are required to change passwords, the greater the chance that they will write them down.

- Set the server to not allow users to use the same password over and over again. Certain operating systems have settings that do not allow users to reuse a password for a certain length of time or within a certain number of password changes.

- Never store passwords in an insecure location. Sometimes a company may want a list of server administrative passwords. This list may end up in the wrong hands if not properly secured.

- Upon logon, display a statement to the effect that network access is granted under certain conditions and that all activities may be monitored. This way you can be sure that any legal ramifications are covered.

Password policies help protect the network from hackers and define the responsibilities of users who have been given access to company resources. You should have all users read and sign security policies as part of their employment process.

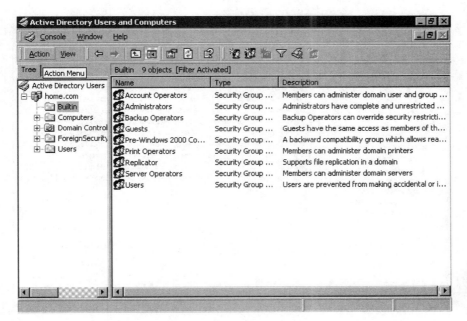

Figure 12.3
Windows 2000 Server default groups

Besides password restrictions, logon hours can also be restricted in many operating systems. Many times it is necessary to restrict logon hours for maintenance purposes. For example, at 11 P.M. each evening the backup is run, so you may want to be sure that everyone is out of the system. Or, if databases get re-indexed on a nightly basis, you may have to be sure that no one is in them. This is also a good way to ensure that a hacker isn't logging on with stolen passwords. Logon hours can be restricted by days of the week, hours of the day, or both. Each operating system is different, so the effect of the restrictions will differ if the user is currently logged on when the restriction time begins. In a Microsoft environment, the connection is immediately broken. In a Novell environment, the user is allowed to stay logged on, but once logged off, a user cannot log back in. **Auditing** is the process of keeping track of who is logging in and accessing what files. We will go over auditing in detail in the section on implementing policy.

Finally, the network administrator has to assign user rights and set user permissions. Besides having built-in user accounts, most operating systems come with built-in groups. Figures 12.3 and 12.4 show the built-in groups that come with Windows 2000 Server and Windows XP. Although each system has nine groups, some of the groups are not the same.

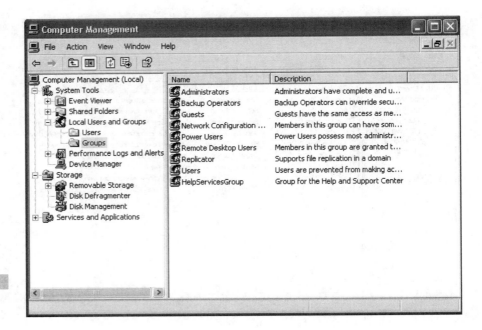

Figure 12.4
Windows XP default groups

As a network administrator, you have the option to assign rights and permissions to individual user accounts. This usually is not a good idea. For example, the owner of the company requests that you make a folder called private for her and her executive assistant to exchange confidential documents. They are the only two people who should have access to the folder. This assistant has been with the company for a long time. Suddenly she is taken ill and can no longer work. A replacement has been hired, but the owner wants her to have access to only certain information, and very little information in the private folder. In normal circumstances, you would just rename the account of the former executive assistant to the name of the new one. In this case, that cannot happen. Furthermore, operating systems do not have an easy way for you to tell what rights and permissions an individual has. Once you start assigning rights and permissions to individuals, you could create a tangled mess. That is why groups were created. Groups ease administrative overhead by combining accounts that require similar access to resources in a single object that is assigned rights and permissions.

When working with groups you should remember a few key items. First, no matter what operating system you are working with, if you are giving a user full access in one group and no access in another group, the result will be no access. However, rights are cumulative, so if a user belongs to two groups and one has more liberal access, the user will have the more liberal access, except where the no access right is involved.

! WARNING

When assigning user rights, if the groups to which the user is assigned have liberal rights but one group has no access, the result is no access. There are no exceptions. If a user has difficulty accessing information after he or she has been added to a new group, the first item you may want to check is conflicting rights.

Next, in enterprise networks, groups may be nested. Let's take Microsoft Windows 2000 as an example. Users can be placed in universal, global, or local groups. Before we describe the difference between them, we'll discuss group types. In Windows 2000, Active Directory Services provides flexibility by allowing two types of groups: security groups and distribution groups. Security groups are used to assign rights and permissions to groups for resource access. Distribution groups are assigned to a user list for applications or nonsecurity-related functions. For example, a distribution group can be used by Microsoft Exchange to distribute mail.

Both types of groups have what is called a scope, which determines where the group can be used in the network and who can be a member. The three group scopes available are domain local, global, and universal. Universal groups can contain user accounts, global groups, or other universal groups. Because universal groups did not exist in Windows NT, the network must contain all Windows 2000 servers. This is also described as operating in native mode. Global groups can contain user accounts and other global groups from within their own domain. Domain local groups can contain user accounts, global groups, and universal groups. If you have both Windows NT servers and Windows 2000 servers, otherwise known as operating in mixed mode, this type of group can contain user accounts and global groups. In Linux, groups can be nested with a bit more flexibility, unless add-on directory services are installed.

TIP

The acronym GULP will help you remember how groups are placed into other groups. Global groups go into Universal groups, either can go into Local groups, and then you set Permissions.

12.2.2   Access Management Regimes

The access level that users are given directly affects your level of network protection. Although it may sound strange that the network should be protected from its own users, the internal user has the greatest access to data and the opportunity to either deliberately sabotage it or accidentally delete it. For example, at one company, upon a user's insistence, management directed the network administrator to give this user administrative privileges. One day while this employee was formatting floppy disks, he received a phone call from the help desk. He helped the user resolve the issue at hand, took another phone call, and was ready to get back to formatting. He typed in "format *.*". He continued until he realized that he never switched back to the A drive, and instead of formatting a floppy disk he was formatting the whole production directory. Users started calling saying that they were having problems accessing files, so he tried to fix it himself but made matters worse. Only after being confronted by the network administrator did he confess what he had done. This kind of situation happens more often than you would think, and only through proper access policies can it be avoided.

The days of storing centralized data on mainframes, all controlled by a trusted few well-trained employees, are gone. In today's world, users, often with little or no training, have access to huge volumes of critical business data. The method of implementing privileges can be based on user, group, or role, and should be decided early in the policy-planning stage.

Within a user-based model, permissions are uniquely assigned to each account. One example of this would be a peer-to-peer network or a workgroup where access is granted based on individual needs. This access type is also found in government and military situations, or in private companies where patented processes and trademark products need to be protected. User-based privilege management usually is used for very specific parts of the network or specific resources. This type of policy is time-consuming and difficult for administrators to handle, plus it does not work well in large environments. For example, with a small network of 300 users using 2,000 files and folders, it would be unreasonable to expect that the entire environment could be based on individual user-based privileges. Even if each user needed access to only 25% of the data, it would result in 150,000 individual privileges! Note that this only includes files and folders; printers and other devices are not figured into the equation.

Access control over large numbers of user accounts can be accomplished more easily by managing the access permissions on each group, which are then inherited by the group's members. This is called **group-based access control**. In this type of access, permissions are assigned to groups, and user accounts become members of the groups. Each user account has access based on the combined permissions inherited from its group memberships. These groups often reflect divisions or departments of the company such as human resources, sales, development, and management. By using groups, access control can be accomplished more efficiently and effectively by fewer administrators with less overhead. Take the same example of 300 users with 2,000 files and folders. If they could all be grouped into five groups, permissions could be assigned to these five groups instead of each individual. If user access remained constant at 25%, the number of permissions needing to be set would drop from 150,000 to 2,500, which is a much more reasonable number to manage and control.

The next method of control we will look at is **role-based access control**, which is a variation of the group-based access control method. A role is generally associated with a particular job assigned to a person. It is based on an organization's structure and the role a user plays in the organization. In this type of access control, it is determined by what job functions each employee performs, and then access is assigned based on those functions. Each role is given the proper permissions necessary for the defined role, and then the roles are assigned to the appropriate user accounts. Because users are assigned roles and then permissions are assigned to the roles, this sounds a lot like group membership, right? Not necessarily. Both roles and groups are ways of controlling user access, but in a group environment users can belong to other groups. In a role-based model users can be assigned only one role. Another difference is that sometimes in a group environment users are assigned separate or individual permissions. A role-based model does not support this. So if you are assigned the role of "developer," you have access to the resources that are allowed for that role—nothing more, nothing less.

Many times this type of access control model will be used in companies that have many independent contractors or high employee turnover. This saves on administrative overhead because the administrator can more easily remove and add users to a role. For example, let's look at the difference between a user in a group scenario and a user in a role scenario. Let's say you had a developer who belonged to the following groups: development, testing, and production. He also had administrative permissions on two of the servers in the development office. He has left the company, and you have hired a new developer to replace him. You don't want the new developer to have the excessive permissions the original developer had, so you cannot just rename the old account. This creates a lot of work for the administrator and, if turnover is high, before you know it either there will be very little control or the administrator will be spending all of his or her time setting permissions. In a role-based scenario the permissions are much cleaner because the developer could be assigned only one role. So when a new developer is hired, he either has the same role as the previous developer or is assigned a different one, but he can have only one role, making administration much easier.

The last type of access control we will look at is rule-based access control, which is based on access control lists (ACLs). The most common use of this type of control is on routers and firewalls. Access is determined by looking at a request to see whether it matches a predefined set of conditions. An example would be if you configured your router to deny any IP addresses from the 10.10.0.0 subnet and allow addresses from the 192.168.10.0 network. When a machine with an address of 192.168.10.15 requests access, the router looks at the rules and will accept the request. In rule-based access control, the administrator sets the rules, so the users cannot change them. In other words, if the administrator set the above router conditions, you, as a user, could not have the router accept requests from a 10.10.0.25 address.

In a rule-based access control solution, accounts may be granted different levels of access, such as Read, Write, or Edit. These rights may vary by account, by group membership, by time of day, or by many other forms of conditional testing. An example of this is configuring filtering of IP packets on a proxy server or firewall. Say that you don't want the production staff to download JPG files, but you do want the development staff to do so. Before any file is downloaded, the file type, as well as the group membership conditions, are checked. The most common form of rule-based access control involves testing against an ACL that details systems and accounts with access rights and the limits of their access for the resource. ACLs are used within operating systems such as Novell NetWare, Microsoft Windows, DEC OpenVMS, and most Unix and Linux packages.

Now that we have discussed the possible types of access management, it should be noted that most companies and even operating systems use some combination of these regimes. It is common to find a simple network that uses more than one of these methods; in large networks, you will find group management for file and print access, role assignments for tasks such as installing software and backing up information, and special access assigned to individual users such as the CEO. So how do you implement all this?

12.2.3   Implementing Policy

Implementation of access management is based on one of two models: centralized or decentralized. Both the group-based and role-based methods of access control have either a centralized database of accounts and roles or groups to which the accounts are assigned. This database is usually maintained on a central server that is contacted by the server providing the resource when a user's access control list must be verified for access. Centralized privilege management is more secure than decentralized because all privilege assignments and changes made to existing accounts are done through one department or group. The drawback to the centralized model is the ability to scale. As the company and network grow, it becomes more and more difficult to keep up with the tasks of assigning and managing network resource access and privileges.

Decentralized security management is less secure but more scalable. Responsibilities are delegated, and employees at different locations are made responsible for managing privileges within their administrative areas. Decentralized management is less secure because more people are involved in the process, resulting in a greater possibility for errors.

Most companies use a hybrid approach to making the network work. Management may decide to centralize the creation of user accounts while decentralizing resource access and privilege assignment to the owners of the servers and data.

After you have established the proper access control scheme, it is important to monitor changes to access rights. Auditing of access use and rights changes should be implemented to prevent unauthorized or unintentional access for a Guest or restricted user account to sensitive or protected

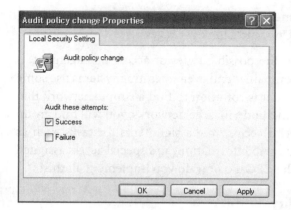

Figure 12.5
Windows XP audit policy

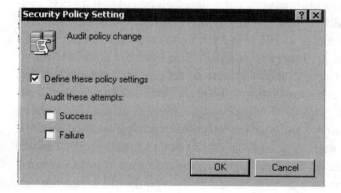

Figure 12.6
Windows 2000 Server
audit policy

resources. Figure 12.5 provides an example of a Windows XP auditing policy configured to log audit policy changes on the local computer. Figure 12.6 shows the audit policies in Windows 2000 Server. Notice that in Windows 2000, policies must be defined first.

Some of the user activities that can be audited include:

- Reading, modifying, or deleting files
- Logging on or off the network
- Using services such as remote access or terminal services
- Using devices such as printers

How much you should audit depends on how much information you want to store. Keep in mind that auditing should be a clear-cut plan built around goals and policies. Without proper planning and policies, you probably will quickly fill your log files and hard drives with useless or unused information. Here are some items to consider when you are ready to implement an audit policy:

- Identify potential resources at risk within your networking environment. These resources typically might include sensitive files, financial applications, and personnel files.

- After the resources are identified, set up the audit policy through the operating system tools. Each operating system will have its own method for tracking and logging access. Auditing can easily add an additional 25% load on a server. If the policy incorporates auditing large amounts of data, be sure that the hardware has the additional space needed as well as processing power and memory.

- After you have auditing turned on, log files will be generated. Take time to view the logs. If an intrusion is recorded in your logs, and you haven't read them for the last three months, the log files will not help protect the system against compromise. Visually sorting through log files should be a last resort. Many operating systems produce log files in text file format. It is much easier to view the data graphically, so if possible, import them into some type of database.

- When configuring an audit policy, it can be useful to monitor successful as well as failed access attempts. Failure events allow you to identify unauthorized access attempts; successful events can reveal an accidental or intentional escalation of access rights.

NOTE

You can audit as much or as little as you want, but if you don't read the logs, they are not serving the purpose for which they were intended. When deciding what to audit, remember that auditing takes up system resources and space.

Auditing can be as simple or complex as you want to make it. Be consistent, whatever your plan. As you learn the patterns of your users and the network, it will be easier than you think to identify odd or suspicious behaviors.

12.2.4   Working with Group Policy Objects

After you create groups, Group Policy can be used for ease of administration in managing the environment of users. This can include installing

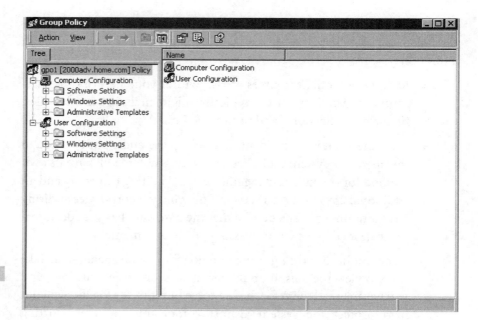

Figure 12.7
Windows 2000 Server GPO choices

software and updates or controlling what appears on the desktop based on the user's job function and level of experience. The **Group Policy object (GPO)** is used to apply Group Policy to users and computers. A GPO is a virtual storage location for Group Policy settings, which are stored in the Group Policy container or template. Figure 12.7 shows a GPO for Windows 2000 Server.

Although we won't discuss the mechanics of Group Policy (because you will be working with it in the exercises), we will discuss briefly how you determine what policies to put in place and why. How companies use Group Policy depends on what level of client management is required. Too many group policies can create longer logon times, and if conflicting policies are implemented, you may have a difficult time tracking down why one of them isn't working like it should. To properly implement Group Policy, first you should determine which areas require what levels of management. In a highly managed environment where users cannot configure their own computers or install software, there will be considerable control over users and computers with Group Policy. In a minimally managed environment where the users have more control over the environment, Group Policy will

Figure 12.8

Windows 2000 Server GPO link

be used minimally. Group Policy is versatile and can be used with Active Directory to define standards for the whole organization or for the members of a single workgroup, location, or job function.

Group Policy allows you to set consistent common security standards for a certain group of computers, enforce common computer and user configurations, simplify computer configuration by distributing applications, and restrict the distribution of applications that may have limited licenses. To allow this wide range of administration, GPOs can be associated with or linked to sites, domains, or organizational units. Figure 12.8 shows the GPO links for an organizational unit. Because Group Policy is so powerful, various levels of administrative roles can be appointed. These include creating, modifying, and linking policies.

Group policies are applied in a specific order, or hierarchy. By default, Group Policy is inherited and cumulative. GPOs are processed in the following order:

1.   The local GPO

2.   GPOs linked to sites

3. GPOs linked to domains

4. GPOs linked to organizational units

TIP

To remember the order in which a group policy is applied, use the acronym LSDOU, which stands for local, site, domain, organizational unit.

The order of GPO processing is important because a policy applied later overwrites a policy applied earlier. Group policies get applied from the bottom up, so if there is a conflict, the policy higher up in the list will prevail. Now let's talk about the exceptions. The default order of processing has the following exceptions:

- If the computer is a workgroup member instead of a domain member, only the local policy will be applied.

- Any policy except for the local one can be set to No Override, meaning that none of its policy settings can be overridden.

- Block inheritance can be set at the site, domain, or organizational unit level to not inherit any policies; however, if the policy is marked No Override, it cannot be blocked.

- Loopback setting is an advanced setting that provides alternatives to the default method of obtaining the ordered list of GPOs.

As you can see, the GPO can be tricky to configure after you put numerous policies in place. Group Policy can be audited to track any changes. Figure 12.9 shows the audit screen; again, there any many choices that can be made.

Now that you have user access, and auditing and Group Policy are in place, something odd has happened to your network. It has become very slow, and the users are complaining. How are you going to fix it? The next section will guide you through managing and improving network performance.

12.3   Managing Network Performance

As your network changes, its performance must be monitored and improved. Ideally, this would be taken into consideration before changes are implemented, but this is seldom the case. Opinions often differ as to how a network should perform and what is acceptable. Sometimes the

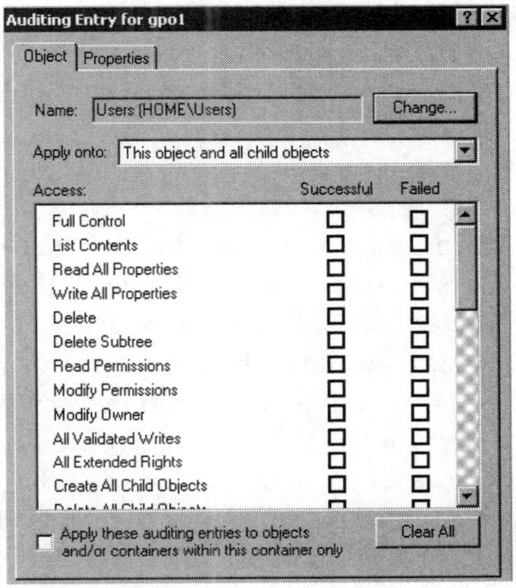

Figure 12.9
Windows 2000 Server Auditing Entry screen

slightest change can affect the performance. For example, a small company suddenly started experiencing poor performance on the network. Management brought in several consultants and numerous changes were made to server configurations, all to no avail. Finally, at her wit's end, the system administrator installed monitoring software to track the traffic on the network. She found that excessive traffic was coming from an area in the corner of the room. Apparently the new help desk technician had decided to set up his own little network. In the process, he used several network cards that were old and noisy, causing excessive traffic on the network. After the technician's own network was disabled, performance returned to normal for the company. Something as simple as some network cards caused poor performance and consultant fees. Notice that the normal performance level was restored for the company. It's a good thing the system administrator knew what was normal. So how do you know what is normal for your network? We'll start with something called baselining.

12.3.1 Understanding Performance Basics

It is essential to identify what typical behavior is in order to identify what abnormal behavior is. This measure of normal activity is known as a **baseline**. Baselines must be updated regularly, and certainly when the network has changed or new technology has been deployed.

> **WARNING** ⚠ Baselining should be done for both network and application processes so that you can tell whether you have a hardware or software issue. Sometimes applications have memory leaks, or a new version may cause performance issues. Without having a baseline on applications, you may spend a long time trying to figure out the problem.

When doing a baseline, be sure that it's done during normal business hours under normal conditions. Taking a baseline on a day when there is little activity will later cause alarm for probably no reason; conversely, taking a baseline when there is a denial of service attack taking place causes you not to pay attention when you should. Speaking of denial-of-services attacks, security monitoring during baselining is important because an ongoing attack during the baselining process could be registered as the normal level of activity. To be sure the network is secure when establishing baselines, it is important to harden all technologies against as many avenues of attack as possible. The major areas of concern should be the network itself, the machine operating system, applications, and services.

Once the baselining is done, several tools can be used to monitor performance. The first two we will look at are Performance Monitor and Event Viewer, both of which are covered in the next section.

12.3.2   Monitoring Performance

With your baselines established, you need to monitor the network to be sure that it is performing properly. Often it is necessary to make adjustments and possibly change the topology or structure of the network. Many tools can help you monitor the performance of the network. Event Viewer, Performance console, Network Monitor, and Task Manager are tools designed for Windows operating systems. Other operating systems have comparable programs, and there are certainly many third-party tools available that will also do the job. Because we installed a Windows operating system in Chapter 11, we will look at those tools. First, we explore Event Viewer.

Event Viewer

Event Viewer allows you to audit certain events. Event Viewer maintains three log files, as shown in Figure 12.10: one for system processes, one for

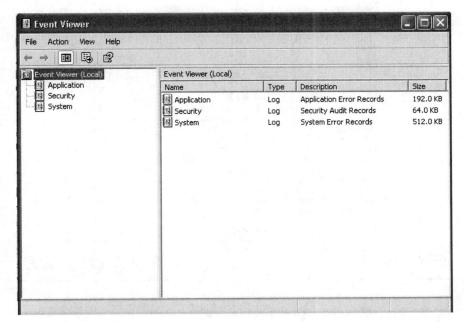

Figure 12.10
Event Viewer

security information, and one for applications. This figure came from a Windows XP machine. In Windows 2000 Server, you also find Directory Services, DNS server, and file replication logs.

The security log records security events and is available for view only to administrators. To monitor security events auditing must be enabled. The application and system logs are available to all users to view. The application log can be used to tell how well an application is running. The system log shows events that happen on the individual system. Inside each of the three log files are three types of events: information, warning, and error. Figure 12.11 displays the application log with each of the three types of events showing.

If you select one of the events, the screen shows additional detailed information. Settings such as the size of the file and the filtering of events can also be configured; for example, you can set the filter to show only errors. Figure 12.12 shows only the errors on a specific machine.

After looking at only the errors in this log file, it becomes apparent that there has been a problem with the hard disk controller for the past four months. This is why it is important to make reading the files part of your

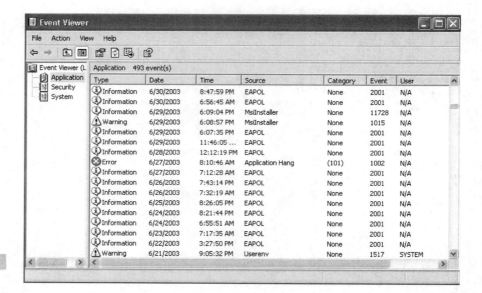

Figure 12.11
Application log

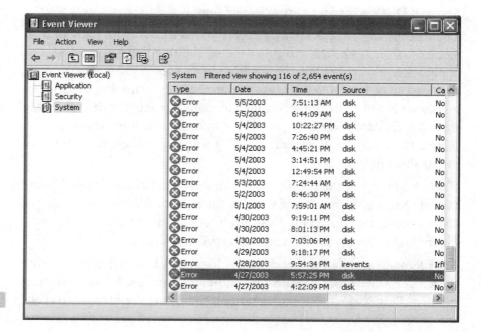

Figure 12.12
Errors filter screen

everyday routine. At some point the disk controller will fail, but this problem could be avoided if it is addressed when it starts to show up in the log files. Another case in point: A network administrator came in one morning to find that no one was working because the main server had failed. After the situation was resolved, the network administrator looked at the log files and discovered that a fan in the server had failed one week earlier. No one was reading the log files. As a result, the company lost revenue and paid the employees to sit around for several hours until the matter could be resolved. Had the log files been read, the fan could have been replaced without any down time or guessing as to why the server wasn't working.

Task Manager

The next tool we look at is Task Manager. **Task Manager** can end processes or applications that get hung up or cause the operating system to become unstable, without having to reboot the computer. It also gives you an instant view of CPU and memory usage. It should be one of the first places to check when something seems awry. Figure 12.13 shows the Processes tab of the Task Manager screen. In the exercises at the end of the chapter, you will explore all the screens in Task Manager.

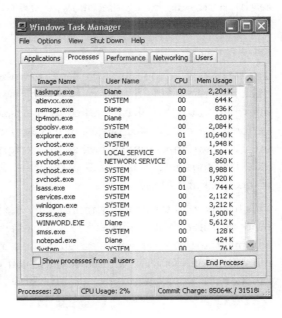

Figure 12.13
Task Manager

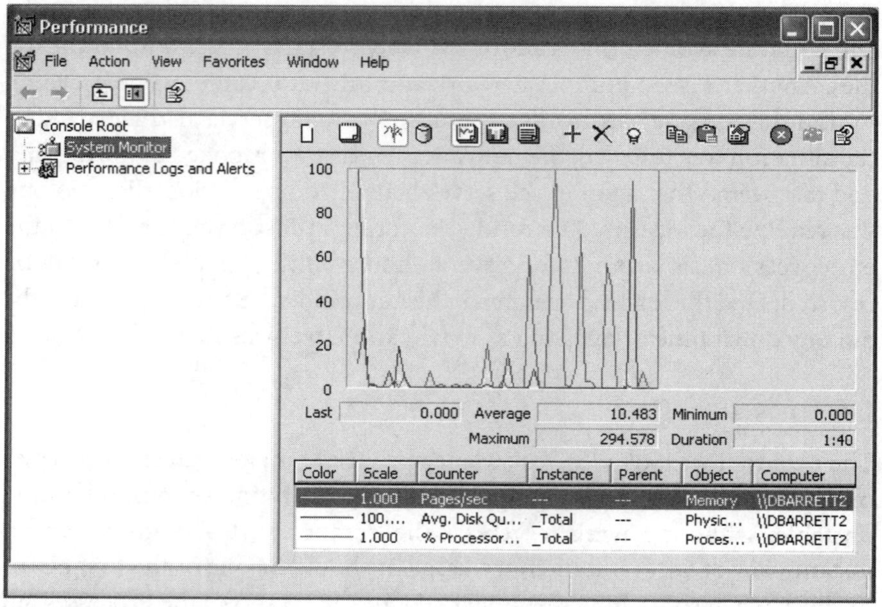

Figure 12.14
Figure 12.14
Performance console

TIP

The Users tab of Task Manager is a quick way to disconnect or log off users should the need arise. For example, let's say that in the middle of the workday an application locks up and needs to be re-indexed. While the re-indexing is being done, all users must be out of the application. They can be disconnected and, if necessary, logged out from the Users tab, rather than waiting for them to do it themselves.

Performance Console

The next tool we look at is the **Performance console**, which is used for tracking and viewing the use of operating system resources. You can view information that you have tracked in charts, alerts, logs, and reports. The Performance console keeps track of set counters for system objects. See Figure 12.14 for an example of what the Performance console screen looks like. The console consists of two snap-ins, System Monitor and Performance Logs and Alerts.

This tool is used for properly monitoring the physical disks, memory, and processor, along with other services. It can also send alerts to an assigned administrator or user when thresholds hit a certain level, and monitor more than one server at a time. Because you will configure some of these functions in the exercises, let's go over how and what to monitor. Figure

Figure 12.15
Performance Console
System Overview
Properties tab

12.15 shows the screen that reflects what counters are set. It is from this screen that any additional counters will be set.

Remember that if you log everything, you end up with too much data consuming system resources. Here are some of the parameters that should be monitored:

- **Random Access Memory (RAM):** Microsoft operating systems are memory intensive; therefore, it is important to monitor the memory. Also, sometimes applications have memory leaks that affect performance.

- **Logical and physical disks:** Monitor them for excessive disk usage. Keep in mind that if memory is insufficient, excessive disk usage will occur as the system swaps memory into and out of disk.

- **CPU:** Track the utilization rate to help determine which programs or processes have excessive time usage.

- **Protocols:** Some protocols have a tendency to grab more processor power, causing other protocols to drop packets.

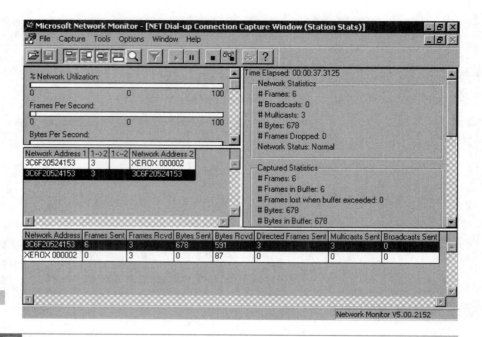

Figure 12.16

Network Monitor

NOTE Running the user interface portion of the Performance console takes up system resources and can significantly affect the performance of the computer. It is better to run this tool on a nonserver computer, such as one running Windows 2000 Professional. Although you are not running the user interface on the server, you will still have performance consequences, just in a different area: network traffic. Overall, however, this is a much better choice.

Network Monitor

The last tool we look at is **Network Monitor**, which is a protocol analyzer. It can be used to capture network traffic and generate statistics for creating reports. Novell's comparable network monitoring tool is called LANalyzer. In the Unix environment, many administrators use the tools that come with the core operating system, such as ps and vmstat. Sun Solaris has a popular utility called iostat that provides good information about I/O performance. Other third-party programs also can be used for network monitoring.

Network Monitor is not installed by default in Windows 2000; it must be added as an optional Windows component. However, once it is installed, it becomes a valuable part of the administrative toolkit. Figure 12.16 shows the Network Monitor screen.

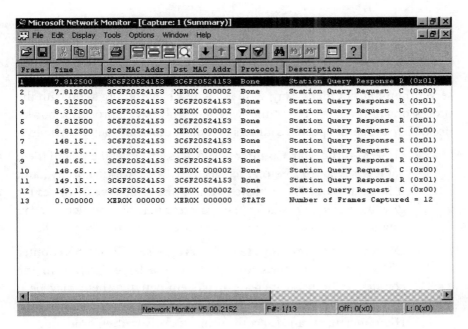

Figure 12.17
Network Monitor output

After packets have been captured, the information can be viewed as shown in Figure 12.17. It records the source address, destination address, headers, and data. Network Monitor detects other installer instances of Network Monitor and identifies the computer name and user running them. Often Network Monitor is used in conjunction with Microsoft's System Management Server (SMS) so that it routes and resolves IP addresses from names. You can also access to Performance Monitor from within Network Monitor.

Now that we have looked at the tools that we can use to monitor our performance, it's time to learn what to look at when performance becomes an issue.

12.3.3 Detecting Bottlenecks

A **bottleneck** occurs when we try to push too much data into a narrow opening. As a result, it jams up and has to wait. Internet and network traffic commonly bottleneck due to not having enough bandwidth. What happens when the network bandwidth is fine? Where do you look? It is important to look at what is happening on the servers.

The first item we will look at is the processor. Many times you will notice that if someone's system is slow, the user will tell you the processor must not be working properly. For example, not long ago a user reported that something was wrong with the server processor because it took a long time to open a particular application. What the user did not realize is that the application he was trying to open was accessing a database on a corporate server thousands of miles away, so the slowness had nothing to do with the processor. However, there are times when we truly have a processor bottleneck. Here are some specific counters to look at in Performance console:

- **Object—Processor, Counter—%Processor Time:** If either of these values rises above 75% on average, the CPU is working pretty hard; if it remains at 80% or higher without the same type of values for disk and network counters, the processor may be a bottleneck. You might want to keep an eye on the interrupts/sec counter as well.

- **Object—Processor, Counter—Interrupts/sec:** Check this counter when system activity is low. If there is a large increase in the counter without an increase in system activity, there may be a hardware problem, such as the board sending out false interrupts. High interrupts can also come from a poorly written program.

- **Object—System, Counter—Processor Queue Length:** A constant value of 3 or higher usually indicates a processor bottleneck.

- **Object—Process (_Total), Counter—%Processor Time:** If too many processes are contending for most of the process time, you should consider adding processors or upgrading to a faster processor.

When looking at the values associated with the preceding counters, keep in mind that when an application or program starts, it will automatically cause the CPU to spike to 100%. This is normal; in fact, when you are monitoring the processor, you should see the utilization spike up and down. However, if the usage goes to 100% and stays there, there is a concern. Even though you can view these counters in a real-time chart window, it might give you a more complete picture if you create a log file and let it run during a typical 24-hour period.

If your statistics indicate that your system has a processor bottleneck, you can either add more processors or upgrade the current processors to faster ones. Another option is to move some of the load to a different machine. For example, say that currently the mail and database server programs are running on one machine. You have a domain controller that at some point will be used for a Web server, but right now is only being used for user validation. You may want to consider moving the mail server program to the other server. Of course, if money is not a factor, you should look into clustering or load balancing options.

One of the most common bottlenecks that Windows 2000 systems face is memory. Windows servers are designed to page data out of memory into a paging file when not in use or if the memory is needed for other data. So by design, the more memory, the better. Counters are available that can show how well the system is using the RAM and that can help you determine whether you need more. There are two general areas to monitor to determine whether your system needs more RAM: the paging file and the various memory pools. As mentioned earlier, the paging file is an actual file on your hard drive. When the operating system runs out of physical RAM, it will temporarily move data out of RAM to this file, so if this file shows heavy usage, you know that the system is probably low on RAM. The following are some counters to check:

- Object: Memory, Counter: Pages/sec
- Object: Logical Disk Counter: Avg. Disk sec/Transfer

The Logical Disk in the preceding list is the disk on which the pagefile resides. You can determine the percentage of disk access time being used by paging if you multiply these two counters. If this percentage is greater than 10% for a prolonged period, or if the Pages/sec value is consistently greater than 5%, you should add more RAM.

The Logical Disk counter is not turned on by default. To use it you must turn it on by typing diskperf -yv at a command prompt, and then restarting the computer. To monitor whether a server requires additional RAM, enable the following counters in Performance Monitor:

- Object: Server
  - Counter: Pool Nonpaged Failures
  - Counter: Pool Paged Failures
  - Counter: Pool Nonpaged Peak

Failures in the Pool Nonpaged counter indicate that the computer's physical memory is too small. Pool Paged Failures indicates that either physical memory or a paging file is near capacity, and the Pool Nonpaged Peak shows the maximum number of bytes of nonpaged pool the server has had in use at any one point, indicating how much physical memory the computer should have.

Next we look at the physical disk drives to determine whether they are affecting the performance of the rest of the system. Remember that if there is a bottleneck with physical RAM, there will be excessive disk usage as the system swaps memory into and out of disk. Here are some counters to look at:

- Object: Physical Disk
  - Counter: %Disk Time
  - Counter: Average Disk sec/Transfer
  - Counter: Current Disk Queue Length
  - Counter: Disk Bytes/sec

The %Disk Time is the amount of elapsed time that the selected disk drive is busy servicing read or write requests. This value should be evaluated with the disk queue length to determine whether your disk is a bottleneck. The next counter is the time in seconds of the average disk transfer. If this value is greater than 0.3, it is an indication that the disk controller is having to retry over and over because of disk failures. The Current Disk Queue Length is the number of requests outstanding on the disk at the time the performance data is collected. Requests are experiencing delays in proportion to the length of the queue minus the number of spindles on the disks. This difference should be less than 2 for good performance. Microsoft has provided a formula for determining what it calls the Average Queue Time:

$$\text{Avg. Queue Time} = \text{Disk Queue Length} \times \text{Avg. Disk sec/Transfer.}$$

The last counter is the rate at which bytes are transferred to or from the disk during write or read operations. This rate should be checked during read or write operations. If the count is lower than 20,000, there may be a bottleneck.

Several options are available if your disks present a bottleneck to your system. The first option is to purchase faster disks or disk controllers. Another option is to add more drives and use RAID configurations. A third option is to move some data or applications off the disk volumes that are causing the bottleneck to other drives or different systems. Last, storage area networks (SANs) can be investigated.

Now that we have looked at how to detect bottlenecks, realize that bottlenecks never go away—they usually just move to a different area of the network. It's time to look at how to improve performance before a bottleneck occurs.

12.3.4 Correcting or Improving Performance

When we look at correcting or improving our network performance, one of the first factors to consider is the servers. Servers have a way of growing after they are in production. We are constantly adding users, applications, and data. Can your servers handle these new loads? To help you decide whether your server can meet your current and your future needs, we will first cover benchmarks. **Benchmarking** is determining how much of a load the server can handle by comparing two or more systems or components of a system. The most common use of a benchmark is to measure performance. However, a benchmark also can be used to burn in a new piece of hardware or a new application. When a server is set up, you should allow a burn-in period. During burn-in, the server is placed under a heavy stress level for long periods of time to determine whether any part of the system fails. In performing a burn-in, you often will catch problems that would arise only after extended use or that would not turn up unless the system is under a heavy load.

Living or real-world benchmarks attempt to measure the performance of the system under a load that would exist in a production environment. These are often application-based and may be customized based on your specific application and user environment. In smaller organizations, instead of using software products, the IT department may have a gaming weekend and play games such as Quake. Because games are very graphic and are hard on system resources, they help determine how well the server performs. Once you know your servers' capabilities, only then can you figure out how to improve their performance. Remember from the last section that changing the memory, hard disk performance, or processor utilization on the server can affect the performance. Of course, performance isn't just about the servers, but they are a big factor.

Performance can also be improved through application tuning, which is more of an art than an exact science. Preventing the application from going to disk to retrieve information will maintain performance, so in a database application, memory is very important. Database settings affect performance, and because each database has its own set of parameters, one wrong setting will have an impact. Some applications are so poorly written that it is almost impossible to tune them so they perform efficiently. Processor quality may be a factor in applications that calculate complex mathematical functions. Some of the old Cirrus processors did not handle complex mathematical functions well, and some of the Intel processors had similar problems. When purchasing or installing new applications, especially Web-based applications, implement them in a test environment to see how they react.

Network segments or the lack of them may affect performance. For example, say that it has been determined that there is too much traffic on the network, and a portion of it will be segmented. All the machines have 100 MB cards, and a 10 MB hub is in place. Did you just make the situation better or worse? It is worse, for two reasons:

1. If you want to segment the network, a switch should be used instead of a hub.

2. If the machine cards are 100 MB, then the switch should also be capable of handling the same bandwidth.

Many times performance will be an issue, and the cause will be something like several 10 MB hubs that have been daisy-chained together instead of using a large port switch. In this same area, network cards should be similar, should be the highest speed available on the network, and, if possible, should be from the same manufacturer. This just makes it easier to troubleshoot.

To improve our performance, the main areas to be addressed are network segmentation, application tuning, and server performance. Now that we know how to manage our network performance, it's time to look at managing our network security.

12.4   Managing Network Security

Recall from Chapter 10 that the concept of security within the network environment includes all aspects of operating systems, software packages, hardware, and networking configurations, as well as any network-sharing connectivity. It is the responsibility of the IT department to keep the whole environment safe and secure. Whether that information is stored on a local computer or transmitted across the Internet, you need to make sure your data is secure, unaltered, and delivered to the intended recipient on demand. Although network administrators used to spend much of their time protecting their networks from the Internet, now you must remember to protect the network from the inside as well. In order to accomplish such a task, you must have security policies in place.

12.4.1   Establishing Network Security Policies

A **security policy** is a set of security controls that dictate the company rules for providing a safe and secure working environment. It is important to establish clear and detailed security policies that are supported by the organization's management. The management has an ethical and legal responsibility to provide security for all assets of the organization. Investors, board members, officers, and employees can all be held liable in a lawsuit involving a breach in security. Insurance companies now place a great deal of weight on the security policy and perform audits. It is also important that the users are aware of and follow these policies. Most companies today have some type of policy in place that is included in the employee handbook or as a separate policy that must be shared by the employees.

The most crucial part of a security policy is the planning. The quality of the policy indicates how sophisticated an organization is as well as how well it can cope with security threats. The first step in establishing a network security policy is to appoint a planning committee. This should be a joint administrative–IT committee. This committee should designate the information security analyst or officer, a security administrator, and a security team. When the management hierarchy is established, planning can begin.

One way to begin is by examining the network for security risks or what is called **risk assessment**. Risk is the potential of a threat to exploit a vulnerability found in an asset. Risk assessment refers to how likely it is that the scenarios listed might actually occur. The security policy team must perform a detailed risk assessment to determine what assets must be protected by the policies, and then identify the users and vendors who must abide by the policies. By identifying assets, threats, and vulnerabilities, and comparing them with the probabilities and costs, you can calculate risk assessment. Be as prepared as possible and comfortable with the levels of risk in your environment.

It is important to specify what use is acceptable to an organization and then to inform users of these expectations. **Acceptable use** details specifically what users may do with their network access. This would include e-mail and instant messaging use for personal purposes, as well as what can be stored in the network space available to each user. An acceptable use policy defines proper use of an information system and the data it contains. One way to do this is through an access agreement with log-on banner reminders.

Every organization has the responsibility to conduct its business in a manner that complies with all applicable laws and regulations. Furthermore, it has the responsibility to ensure that its employees comply with these laws and regulations. This is what we call compliance. Failure to ensure compliance can result in legal liabilities. The security policy must strictly state the consequences of noncompliance, which can include measures ranging from loss of network privileges to legal action, depending on the severity of the breach.

An organization may be negligent in its duties if it fails to take common and necessary precautions to avoid a security threat. It also may be negligent if its actions contribute to an environment that allows a security threat to happen. For example, if an employee hacks into a vendor's network, the company can be held liable for lack of due care. **Due care** is the knowledge and actions that a reasonable and prudent person would possess or act upon. Because of this, it is important to establish clear lines of responsibility and expectations for users and administrators.

Your security policy must specify how your organization operates within applicable laws and regulations to ensure data privacy. This is especially important in industries that now have to comply with legislation such as the Health Insurance Portability and Accountability Act (HIPAA) and the Gramm-Leach-Bliley Act. Users and administrators must be made aware of privacy issues and the consequences of unintentional disclosure of private data that may arise over file, e-mail, and instant-messaging traffic within the organization's network.

NOTE
> Too much power can lead to corruption, whether it be in politics or network administration. Most governments and other organizations implement some type of a balance of power through a separation of duties.

It is important to include a **separation of duties** when planning for security policy compliance. Without this separation, all areas of control and compliance may be left in the hands of a single individual. The idea of separation of duties hinges on the concept that multiple people conspiring to corrupt a system is less likely to occur than a single person corrupting it. Often you will find this in financial institutions, where in order to violate the security controls, all of the participants in the process would have to agree to compromise the system. For security purposes, you should avoid giving one individual complete control of a transaction or process from beginning to end. Also, you should implement policies such as job rotation, mandatory vacations, and cross-training.

Users should have access to only the resources and information necessary to perform their roles. This is called "need to know." This part of the policy outlines the manner in which a user is associated with necessary information and system resources. There must be justification for any request to access information. Each person must have a unique ID and password to access a secure system. It is key to give users only the minimum possible level of access necessary to perform normal duties.

In Chapter 10 we discussed some best practices for passwords. Remember that weak passwords are security risks that may be exploited by an attacker. Besides password duration and complexity requirements, the password policy should recognize that:

- A password based on personal information can be guessed easily.

- Short words or common acronyms are easy to crack and provide very little security.

- Hard-to-remember passwords tempt users to write down the password.

The password policy needs to spell out that passwords such as *god, password, sex,* names of children, pet names, birthdays, and the like should not be used. It is important that users are made aware of these requirements and that existing passwords are tested using auditing tools to ensure that users are in compliance with these policies.

Proper disposal of data and equipment should be part of the security policy. Outdated hardware and discarded paper often may be used by attackers to obtain access to a network. "Dumpster diving" and other forms of access to discarded materials are common jackpots for hackers. How many times have you seen TV news stations doing articles on what was found in dumpsters? They have found items such as tax returns and medical records. How much information do you think is obtained from used equipment sold on eBay? Not long ago, a large quantity of hard drives were sold that contained medical records of veterans. Because of this, it is prudent to have a policy in place that requires shredding of all documents and security erasure of all types of storage media before they may be discarded.

Security planning must include procedures for the human resources department. It should detail the who, what, and when in regard to the authorization and creation of accounts for newly hired personnel, as well as removal of privileges following employment termination. The hiring process should also include training to make new employees aware of all security policies, along with a formal code of ethics that all employees should be made to sign after reading and reviewing all policies.

Your incident response policy must begin with what defines an incident and how to identify when one occurs. Each security policy is different, and each organization has different criteria for defining incidents. Incident response planning policies should be documented, including handling procedures, proper reporting, and recovery procedures for each defined type of incident.

This section by no means lists everything that is included in a security policy. It is merely a starting point. Each company is unique, has its own needs, and operates differently. Most important is that each company have a security policy in place, not only to keep the network and users safe, but also to protect the board of directors and stockholders in the event of a lawsuit.

12.4.2   Understanding Security Models

When dealing with security issues, two basic models can be used: one that addresses the risks associated with hardware and designs, which are physical, and one that deals with protocols and software, which are data. We will cover the basics here; both will be covered in detail later in the chapter.

Eavesdropping on transmissions usually requires a device such as a sniffer, so the intruder must have physical access. If the workstations, cables, and servers are not physically secure, it would be quite easy for someone to come in and steal data from the company. Another consideration is the type of equipment that is purchased. If wireless devices running on the network are not secured, someone sitting outside the building could easily gain access to the network without even entering the building. This has become a common practice, and there are now Web sites devoted to showing where unsecured wireless networks are located. What if the company has modems or modem pools in use? Many modems are configured to accept incoming calls. If they are not properly protected, dialing programs can easily detect them, leaving them vulnerable to abuse. These are just a few considerations. The point is to be sure that the equipment is properly secure and protected.

Similar to hardware, software is only as secure as the configuration. In most cases, security is compromised by poor configuration or not properly understanding how file access and rights work.

NOTE

Most operating systems contain security flaws that are open to exploitation if they are not patched properly. Many times network administrators leave default accounts in place, such as the Administrator account. Should this happen, a hacker is already halfway in, because you have just provided a logon name.

12.4.3   Implementing Security

We have already discussed some of the considerations that a security policy should address. We have talked about the different security models and access types. Now that you have a plan and a policy, how do you implement it? The first step is to set up the systems according to a plan that will make them as secure as possible. The next step is to train the users on how to use the systems properly, teach them why they must follow policy, and be sure that they realize the consequences for not complying with these policies. Setting up the systems according to plan will require manpower and change coordination. For example, let's say that the current password policy is that passwords never expire. What happens when Monday comes and all users have to change their passwords because a new policy is put in place? How many calls will the help desk get asking what is going on? Users need to know ahead of time when changes are coming.

Besides being notified of upcoming changes, users must be trained to properly use the system. Do not assume that users should know better than to reply to a chain letter, or to try and send a 15 MB file of marketing material to a potential client. Users must be explicitly told what they can and cannot do with the system they are given. They must also be trained to avoid falling victim to social engineering attacks. Planning, training, regular reminders, and firm and clear security policies are important when attempting to minimize vulnerabilities.

12.4.4   Security Maintenance

Maintaining security is an ongoing process. You cannot implement a plan and just forget about it. As the business needs and the network requirements change, so must your security plan. A security plan is a living document, just like a disaster recovery or incident response plan. When the plan is in place, you may find that certain parts do not work the way they should and thus need modification. There should be a policy describing the method for change control so that when it has been decided that the policy should be changed, these changes are documented and communicated to the employees affected.

12.5   Protecting Data and Systems

In business, there is a wide range of data to be protected. In human resources, personnel data, including home phone numbers, social security numbers, salary information, and employee review information, have to be kept confidential. Management has to protect business plans such as merger information, reorganization, and division sell-offs. The development team wants to protect proprietary information concerning business products, including chemical formulas, designs, and research data. Part of a network administrator's job is to protect this data, as well as the systems, people, and buildings that store and use the data in daily operations. In order to do this properly you must understand the different security components and how they affect each other.

12.5.1   Understanding Security Components

Because today's networks have become so intricate and far-reaching, they have many points of entry. These various points are all vulnerabilities that an intruder can explore. With so many ways of getting into the network, the components must be divided into separate elements so that the security process becomes easier to manage. The security components of a network can therefore be broken down into the following three elements: (1) physical, (2) data, and (3) system security. Each plays an important part in the overall security of a company, and a complete plan must include all three.

Physical Security

When planning security for networks, physical security can often be overlooked because we may assume that someone else is taking care of it, or that it has never been an issue before. September 11, 2001, changed all that. Securing physical access and making sure that access requires proper authentication is necessary to avoid exposure of sensitive data to attackers. Implementing physical security involves understanding a different set of vulnerabilities and threats. Physical security identifies physical dangers to the hardware and buildings that store the equipment on which the data resides. A company must identify the probability that an event will happen, estimate its impact, and then implement measures that help reduce the effects should the disaster actually occur. The following list describes some of the threats to consider when planning physical security:

- Someone breaking into a building and stealing network hardware
- An employee gaining unauthorized physical access to a server system
- Natural disasters, such as tornadoes, hurricanes, earthquakes, and floods
- Manmade disasters such as fires and chemical spills

Physical access to a system creates many avenues for breach of security, because many tools are available to extract password and account information that may then be used to access secure network resources. This applies not only to outside sources, but also to internal ones. Given the capability to reboot a system and load software from a floppy disk, attackers may be able to access or destroy data. Here are some ways to control physical access to systems that host data:

- Physically secure a system within a locked room or cabinet.
- Attach the system to fixed, nonmovable furniture using locking cables.
- Lock the system case itself to prevent the removal of components.
- Use locking screws for publicly accessible terminals.
- Use frosted or painted glass to eliminate direct visual observation in areas where secure systems are stored.

- Implement security guards, surveillance cameras, motion detectors, or token-based and biometric access requirements for restricted areas.

The security team should coordinate the security setup of the facility and surrounding areas, identify which groups are allowed to enter different areas, and determine the method of authentication to be used. As you deploy the new security systems, you should include training on how to use the systems. The timing of training should be coordinated so that training and physical deployment finish at about the same time.

As with all facets of security, physical security must be maintained. If maintenance is overlooked, the system will begin to fall apart. Broken locks, loose doorknobs, and cracked windows will let a potential intruder know that you are not maintaining your security systems. In addition, if security mechanisms are left in poor or nonfunctional condition, employees will bypass the security to get their jobs done. This will compromise the entire system and make the original investment of time and money worthless.

Data Security

To show the importance of how physical security affects data security, let's look at a scenario: In an amicable separation, an executive leaves a company. The company believes that, because the separation is amicable, there is no need to change locks, delete the executive's network access, or be concerned about any negative animosity. The next night, the main data center is broken into. Bleach is poured onto all the servers, switches, and phone equipment. The wiring is pulled out of all the patch panels, the hot-swappable hard drives are missing from the servers, and all the backup tapes have been removed from the servers and shelves, smashed with a hammer, and then doused with bleach. The former executive is found to be responsible for the damage. How quickly can this company recover without disrupting business?

In this situation, a large quantity of data was lost. The company did not plan for this event and, unfortunately, the only backup they had was in the room that was vandalized. First, no matter which way you choose to back up your data, back it up! You should ensure that you also have offsite copies of your backups to help you recover in case the entire facility is destroyed. In this case, only one day's worth of data would have been lost if the backups were stored off site.

The most popular backup strategies are:

- **Full backup:** Copies all selected files and resets the archive bit. This method allows you to restore using just one tape.

- **Incremental backup:** Contains all the information that was modified since the last incremental backup and resets the archive bit. If there is a need to restore, the number of tapes will include the last full backup and all incremental tapes. For example, if the server dies on Thursday, four tapes will be needed: the full tape from Friday and the incremental tapes from Monday, Tuesday, and Wednesday.

- **Differential backup:** Copies all information changed since the last full backup, regardless of if or when the last differential backup was made because it doesn't reset the archive bit. If there is a need to restore, the number of tapes will include the last full backup and one differential tape. For example, if the server dies on Thursday, two tapes will be needed—the full tape from Friday and the differential tape from Wednesday.

- **Copy backup:** Very similar to full backup in that it copies all selected files, but it doesn't reset the archive bit.

Normal backups should include only data. It is unnecessary to back up application files and operating system files with daily backups because they can easily be reinstalled if necessary. Backing up and restoring data is a security issue as well. If someone has the right to back up your data, that person could potentially take the tapes off site and recover the data, removing file permissions as they did so.

The second half of the backup process is your ability to restore the data. Backup tapes should be tested regularly. Many companies think they are backing up their data but then discover that the tapes are blank because the tape heads became worn or dirty, and now they can't restore their data. Numerous companies provide offsite data backup and recovery should you choose not to do it in-house. If you decide to trust someone else with your data, be sure the company is reputable and the employees are bonded.

System Security

Workstation security is often overlooked, yet this is one of the most attractive areas to intruders because it is the path of least resistance. These attacks generally happen because users are unaware of the dangers in which they put themselves and the company by doing some of the following:

- Installing unauthorized software
- Downloading infected music and movie files
- Opening e-mail that has a virus
- Forwarding e-mail hoaxes
- Not logging off the network when leaving the building

This by no means covers all the possible situations users face. There is also theft and lost equipment, failed components, and physical access by visitors to consider.

Servers are more sensitive to attacks than workstations, and these attacks can be more costly. Therefore, all network servers should be isolated in a server room and locked to prevent any kind of unauthorized physical access. Visitors to these premises must be justified and supervised. Besides having physical controls, availability must also be ensured. This can be done via Redundant Array of Inexpensive Disks (RAID, discussed in Chapter 11), uninterruptible power supply (UPS) equipment, and clustering.

Software that can help protect the data includes antivirus and intrusion detection software. Antivirus software can be used to scan for e-mail and downloadable malicious code. When using this type of software, be sure that the definitions are updated on a regular basis. Intrusion detection systems (IDS) are designed to analyze data, identify attacks, and respond to the intrusion. IDS systems are also designed to catch attacks in progress within the network, not just on the boundary between private and public networks.

12.5.2 Planning for Business Continuity

A **business continuity plan (BCP)** is similar to a **disaster recovery plan (DRP)** except that it is a long-term look at recovery in the case of a complete loss of facilities. Disaster recovery seeks to fix systems, utilities, facilities, and business function in the short-term; business continuity plans extend this to cover a longer time frame. In order to formulate this plan, the main areas of the DRP should be reevaluated for long-term issues and problems. A set time period should be determined for the transition from disaster recovery to business continuity. A business continuity plan must also include a detailed analysis of business practices and support requirements that are needed to ensure that business continuity can be maintained in the event of failure. Business continuity planning should include tactics and cost estimates for required services, such as network access and utility agreements and automatic failover of critical services, to redundant offsite systems. Some other considerations that may be included in continuity planning are:

- **Network connectivity:** An organization's continuity plan should include options for alternate network access if the ISP can no longer function.

- **Facilities:** The plan should include considerations for recovery in the event that existing hardware and facilities are rendered inaccessible or unrecoverable.

- **Fault tolerance:** Common fault-tolerant solutions such as RAID, hot-swapping of failed drives, and alternate sites should be included.

- **Clustering:** High-availability clustering can be used to ensure that automatic failover will occur in the event that hardware failure prevents primary equipment from providing normal service.

Even though the plans are similar, a separate business continuity plan should be created and updated whenever the DRP changes.

12.6 Chapter Summary

- Every operating system has a method for setting up user and group accounts. A user account holds information about the specific user. It can contain basic information such as name, password, and the user's level of permission. Groups ease administrative overhead by combining accounts that require similar access to resources in a single object that can be assigned rights and permissions.

- The Group Policy object (GPO) is used to apply Group Policy to users and computers. A GPO is a virtual storage location for group policy settings, which are stored in the Group Policy container or template. It is used to set consistent common security standards for a certain group of computers, enforce common computer and user configurations, simplify computer configuration by distributing applications, and restrict the distribution of applications that may have limited licenses.

- It is essential to identify what constitutes typical behavior in order to identify abnormal behavior. This measure of normal activity is known as a baseline. After you have established your baselines, the network will need to be monitored to be sure that it is performing properly. Many tools can be used to help monitor performance on the network: Event Viewer, Performance console, Network Monitor, and Task Manager are tools designed for Windows operating systems. Other operating systems have comparable programs that can be used, and there are many third-party tools that can be purchased that will do the job as well.

- It is important to establish clear and detailed security policies that are supported by the organization's management. Management has an ethical and legal responsibility to provide security for all assets of the organization. The most crucial part of a security policy is the planning. The quality of the policy indicates how sophisticated an organization is as well as how well it can cope with security threats.

- When dealing with security issues, two basic models can be used: one that addresses the risks associated with hardware and designs, which are physical, and one that deals with protocols and software, which are data. If the workstations, cables, and servers are not physically secure, it would be quite easy for someone to come in and steal data from the company. Likewise, software is only as secure as its configuration allows it to be. In most cases, security is compromised by poor configuration or not understanding how file access and rights work.

- Maintaining security is an ongoing process. You cannot implement a plan and just forget about it. As the business needs and the network requirements change, so must your security plan. A security plan is a living document just like a disaster recovery or incident response plan.

- With so many ways of getting into the network, the components must be divided into separate elements so that the security process becomes easier to manage. The security components of a network can therefore be broken down into the following three elements: (1) physical, (2) data, and (3) system security.

- A business continuity plan is similar to a disaster recovery plan except that it is a long-term look at recovery in the case of a complete loss of facilities. Disaster recovery seeks to fix systems, utilities, facilities, and business function in the short-term, whereas business continuity plans extend this to cover a longer time frame.

12.7   Key Terms

acceptable use: Defines the proper use of an information system and the data it contains.

auditing: The process of keeping track of who is logging in and accessing what files.

baseline: A measure of normal network activity.

benchmarking: The process of determining how much load the server can handle by comparing two or more systems or components of a system.

bottleneck: Occurs when too much data is pushed into a narrow opening, causing it to jam.

business continuity plan (BCP): A plan that takes a long-term look at recovery in the case of a complete loss of facilities.

disaster recovery plan (DRP): A plan that aims to restore essential computer and network functions shortly after a disaster strikes.

due care: The knowledge and actions that a reasonable and prudent person would possess or act upon.

Event Viewer: A Windows-based tool that maintains log files and allows you to audit certain events.

group: Contains users who share a common need for access to a particular resource.

group-based access control: A type of access control in which permissions are assigned to groups, and user accounts become members of the groups. Each user account has access based on the combined permissions inherited from its group memberships.

Group Policy object (GPO): A virtual storage location for Group Policy settings used to apply Group Policy to users and computers.

Network Monitor: A protocol-analyzing tool that can be used to capture network traffic and generate statistics for creating reports.

Performance console: A Windows-based tool used for properly monitoring the physical disks, memory, and processor along with other services.

risk assessment: Determines how likely it is that certain scenarios might actually occur.

role-based access control: A type of access control that determines what job functions each employee performs and then assigns access based on those functions.

security policy: A set of security controls that dictate the company rules for providing a safe and secure working environment.

separation of duties: The concept that the completion of a task should require more than one person.

Task Manager: A Windows-based tool that can be used to end processes or applications that get hung up or cause the operating system to become unstable.

user account: Holds information about the specific user. It can contain basic information such as name, password, and the user's level of permission.

12.8   Challenge Questions

12.1   You have been assigned the task of configuring auditing on the network. What is the first action you should take?

   a. Determine where the log files will be stored.

   b. Start auditing resources immediately.

   c. Use a vulnerability scanner to determine which resources are poorly protected.

   d. Plan.

12.2   The main fan in your server failed on Wednesday morning. It will be at least two days before it can be replaced. You decide to use another server instead, but need to restore data from the original server. You have been doing incremental backups, and the last full backup was performed on Friday evening. The backup doesn't run on weekends. How many backup tapes will you need to restore the data?

   a. 2

   b. 4

   c. 1

   d. 3

12.3   Which of the following security policies would stipulate that a user may be fined for using the Web server to run a personal business?

   a. Acceptable use

   b. Privacy

c. Due care

d. Separation of duties

12.4 Which of the following statements best describes a business continuity plan?

a. It reduces the impact of a hurricane on a facility.

b. It is an action plan used to bring a business back online immediately after a disaster has struck.

c. It is a long-term look at recovery in the case of a complete loss of facilities.

d. It attempts to manage risks associated with theft of equipment.

12.5 Which of the following is true when discussing physical security? (Choose all that apply.)

a. Physical security attempts to control unwanted access to specified areas of a building.

b. Physical security attempts to control access to data from Internet users.

c. Physical security attempts to control the impact of natural disasters on facilities and equipment.

d. Physical security attempts to control internal employee access to secure areas.

12.6 Which of the following is a good password policy?

a. Make the password length at least four characters and require the use of uppercase and lowercase letters.

b. Lock out user accounts after one failed logon attempt.

c. Upon logon, show a statement to the effect that network access is granted under certain conditions and that all activities may be monitored.

d. Allow passwords to be stored in non-password-protected Excel files on users' machines.

12.7 Which of the following is a way in which users jeopardize system security? (Choose all that apply.)

a. Installing unauthorized software

    b. Logging off the network when leaving the building

    c. Forwarding e-mail hoaxes

    d. Deleting e-mail from unknown users

12.8 _____ is used to set consistent common security standards for a certain group of computers, enforce common computer and user configurations, or simplify computer configuration.

12.9 It is essential to identify what typical behavior is in order to identify what abnormal behavior is. This measure of normal activity is known as a _____ .

12.10 There are many tools that can be used to help you monitor performance on the network. _____, _____, _____ and _____ are tools designed for Windows operating systems.

12.11 Why is the order of GPO processing important?

12.12 What are some of the activities that can be audited?

12.13 Security planning must include procedures for the human resources department. Why?

12.14 What are some of the considerations that should be included in a business continuity plan?

12.15 What is the most crucial part of security policy?

12.9 Challenge Exercises

Challenge Exercise 12.1

In this exercise, you use the Active Directory Users and Computers console to create, delete, and rename domain user accounts on the domain controller. You need a computer with Windows 2000 Server or Windows 2000 Advanced Server installed, a domain set up, and Administrator privileges.

12.1 Log on to your computer as Administrator.

12.2 Click **Start**, point to **Programs**, point to **Administrative Tools**, and then click **Active Directory Users and Computers**.

12.3 Select the domain, right-click the **User** container, point to **New**, and click **User**.

12.4 In the New Object-User dialog box, set the domain user name options, as follows:

- **First Name:** The user's first name
- **Initials:** The user's initials
- **Last Name:** The user's last name
- **Full Name:** The user's complete name
- **User Logon:** Uniquely identifies the user throughout the entire network
- **User Logon Name (Pre-Windows 2000):** User's unique logon name that is used to log on from earlier versions of Windows; entry is required and must be unique within the domain

12.5 Click **Next**. Enter the password information, as follows:

- **Password:** Used to authenticate the user
- **Confirm Password:** Confirmation that the password was typed correctly
- **User Must Change Password at Next Logon:** Requires user to change password when logging on the first time; leave blank
- **User Cannot Change Password:** Only administrators are allowed to control passwords; leave blank
- **Password Never Expires:** Password will never change; leave blank
- **Account Is Disabled:** Prevents use of the user's account; leave blank

12.6 Click **Finish**. Notice that this screen gives you an option to go back before the actual creation of the account. It also gives you a synopsis of what is being created.

12.7 After the account is created, right-click the newly created account and select **properties**.

12.8 Your screen should look similar to Figure 12.18.

12.9 Examine each of the tabs and the information contained within. When finished, click the **Account** tab.

12.10 To set the logon hours for this account, click **Logon Hours**.

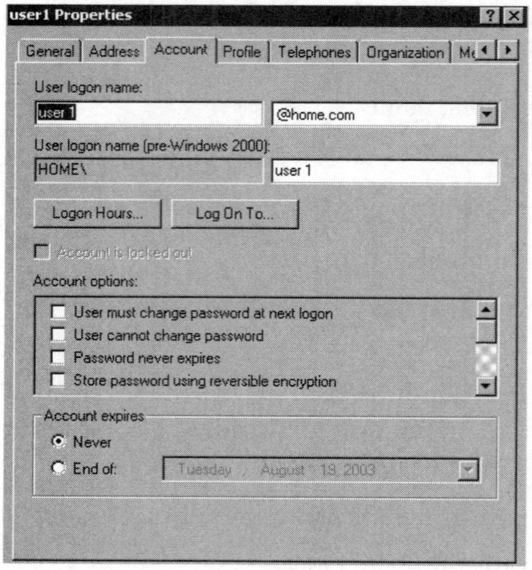

Figure 12.18
User Properties screen

12.11 Select the rectangles of the days and hours for which access is to be allowed. Click the start time, drag to the end time, and then click **Logon Permitted**.

12.12 Select the rectangles of the days and hours for which access is to be denied. Click the start time, drag to the end time, and then click **Logon Denied**.

12.13 Click **OK**.

12.14 When you finish setting up this account, repeat steps 3 through 13 to create a total of 12 accounts.

12.15 Select the last account you created. You will now reset the password, rename the account, and then delete it.

12.16 In the Active Directory Users and Computers console, expand the console tree until the appropriate user account is visible, and then select the user account.

12.17 On the Action menu, click **Reset Password**.

12.18 Enter a new password for the user, confirm the password, and then click **OK**.

12.19 In the Active Directory Users and Computers console, select the user account.

12.20 On the Action menu, click **Rename**.

12.21 Enter a new name for the user. When the Rename User dialog box opens, verify that all information is correct, and click **OK**.

12.22 In the Active Directory Users and Computers console, select the user account.

12.23 On the Action menu, click **Delete**.

12.24 Click **Yes** in the Active Directory message box.

12.25 Close the window.

Challenge Exercise 12.2

In this exercise, you use the Active Directory Users and Computers console to create, delete, and manage group accounts on the domain controller. You need a computer with Windows 2000 Server or Windows 2000 Advanced Server installed, a domain set up, and Administrator privileges.

12.1 Log on to your computer as Administrator.

12.2 Click **Start**, point to **Programs**, point to **Administrative Tools**, and then click **Active Directory Users and Computers**.

12.3 Click the domain, right-click the **User** container, point to **New**, and click **Group**.

12.4 Complete the information fields in the New Object-Group dialog box and click **OK**.

12.5 Repeat the process, creating five more groups.

12.6 Now you will delete a group and then add users to groups. Select the last group you created, right-click the group, and then click **Delete**.

12.7 Click **Yes** on the Active Directory message box.

12.8 Start the **Active Directory Users and Computers** console and expand the **User** container.

12.9 You will add four users to each of the groups that you have created. Right-click the appropriate group, and then click **Properties**.

12.10 The Select Users, Contacts, Computers, or Groups dialog box opens. In the Look In list, select a domain from which to display user accounts and groups, or select **Entire Directory** to view user accounts and groups from anywhere in Active Directory.

12.11 In the Name column, select an object to add, and click **Add**.

12.12 Review the accounts to be certain they are the ones to be added, and then click **OK** to add the members.

12.13 In the Properties dialog box, click **OK**.

12.14 Repeat this process until there are four users in each group. There should be 11 users, so one of them will have to be added to two different groups.

12.15 Close the window.

Challenge Exercise 12.3

In this exercise, you create a GPO snap-in, delegate administrative control of the GPO, specify settings, and test the GPO. You need a computer with Windows 2000 Server or Windows 2000 Advanced Server installed, a domain set up, and Administrator privileges.

To create a GPO snap-in console:

12.1 Log on to your computer as Administrator.

12.2 Click **Start**, point to **Programs**, point to **Administrative Tools**, and then click **Active Directory Users and Computers**.

12.3 Right-click the **Domain Controller OU** container, click **Properties**, and click the **Group Policy** tab.

12.4 Click **New** and then type **NewGPO**.

12.5 Click **Close**.

12.6 Click **Start** and then click **Run**.

12.7 In the Run dialog box, type **mmc** in the Open box and click **OK**.

12.8 In the new MMC console, from the Console menu, select **Add/Remove Snap-In**.

12.9 In the Add/Remove Snap-In dialog box, click **Add**.

12.10 In the Add Standalone Snap-In dialog box, select **Group Policy**, and then click **Add**.

12.11 In the Select Group Policy Object page, click **Browse** to find NewGPO.

12.12 In the Browse For a Group Policy Object dialog box, click the **All** tab, click **NewGPO**, and then click **OK**.

12.13 In the Select Group Policy Object page, click **Finish**, and then click **Close** in the Add Standalone Snap-In dialog box.

12.14 Click **OK** in the Add/Remove Snap-In dialog box.

12.15 On the Console menu, click **Save As**. In the Save As dialog box, type **NewGPO** in the File Name box and click **Save**. The GPO is now available on the Administrative Tools menu.

To delegate administrative control of the GPO to the Domain Administrators group:

12.1 Access the Group Policy snap-in for **NewGPO**.

12.2 Right-click the root of the console and click **Properties**.

12.3 Click the **Security** tab and then click the Administrators group using the **Add** button.

12.4 To provide administrative control of the GPO, set both the Read and Write permissions to Allow. A user or administrator who has Read access but not Write access to a GPO cannot use the Group Policy snap-in to see the settings that it contains. See Figure 12.19.

12.5 Click **OK**.

12.6 In the **NewGPO** console, expand the root of the console.

12.7 Expand **User Configuration**, and then expand **Administrative Templates**.

12.8 In the console tree, click **Start Menu & Task Bar**.

12.9 In the details pane, double-click **Remove Documents Menu from Start Menu**.

12.10 Click **Enabled**, and then click **OK**.

12.11 Repeat Steps 9 and 10 for Remove Network & Dial-in Connections and Favorites.

To test the GPO:

12.1 Log off as Administrator.

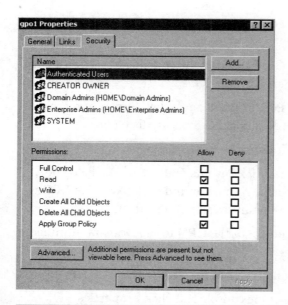

Figure 12.19
GPO Properties

    12.2 Make sure that you have the rights to log on locally.

    12.3 Log on as User1.

    12.4 Click **Start**. Is the Documents menu there? What about Favorites?

    12.5 Log off as User1.

Challenge Exercise 12.4

In this exercise, you learn to use Event Viewer, enable the security log, filter events, set log file sizes, and export the file. You need a computer with Windows 2000 Server or Windows 2000 Advanced Server installed and Administrator privileges.

To explore Event Viewer set log file sizes, and filter events:

    12.1 Log on to your machine as Administrator.

    12.2 Click **Start**, point to **Programs**, point to **Administrative Tools**, and then click **Event Viewer**. Your screen should look like Figure 12.20.

    12.3 Select the **Application** log.

    12.4 Look through the events to familiarize yourself with the screen.

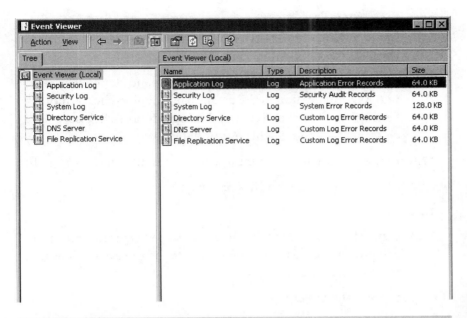

Figure 12.20
Event Viewer

12.5 Look through the rest of the logs. Are there any events in the Security log? Why or why not?

12.6 Highlight the **Application** log. Click **Action** and select **Properties**.

12.7 Change the maximum log size to 2048 KB.

12.8 In the When Maximum Log Size Is Reached area, change to Overwrite Events As Needed.

12.9 Click the **Filter** tab.

12.10 Deselect **Information and Warning under Event Types**.

12.11 Click **Apply**, and then click **OK**.

To enable the Security log:

12.1 Click **Start**, click **Run**, type **mmc /a** in the Open text box, and then click **OK**.

12.2 On the Console menu, click **Add/Remove Snap-in**, and then click **Add**.

12.3 Under Snap-in, click **Group Policy**, and then click **Add**.

12.4 In the Select Group Policy Object dialog box, type **Local Computer** in the Group Policy Object text box (if necessary), click **Finish**, click **Close**, and then click **OK**.

12.5 Click **Local Computer Policy** in the Tree pane, double-click **Computer Configuration** in the details pane, double-click **Windows Settings**, double-click **Security Settings**, double-click **Local Policies**, and then double-click **Audit Policy**.

12.6 In the details pane, click the attribute or event you want to audit.

12.7 Click **Action**, and then click **Security**.

12.8 Click **OK**.

12.9 Repeat Steps 6, 7, and 8 for other events you want to audit. You will probably have to wait a few minutes before events show up in the Security log.

To export the System log file:

12.1 Go back to Event Viewer, select the **System** log, click **Action**, and then select **Export list**.

12.2 In the file name box, type **systemlog**. Save the file as a .txt file.

12.3 Open the file and look at the contents.

12.4 Save the same log as a .csv file. Open the file and look at it. Which format do you think would be more useful? Why?

12.5 Close Event Viewer.

Challenge Exercise 12.5

In this exercise, you learn to use Performance Monitor, set counters for the processor and memory, and then play pinball or any action-intensive game to see the effect graphic programs have on the system. You will need a computer with Windows 2000 Server or Windows 2000 Advanced Server installed and Administrator privileges.

12.1 Log on to your computer as Administrator.

12.2 Click **Start**, point to **Settings**, click **Control Panel**, double-click **Administrative Tools**, and then double-click **Performance**.

12.3 Right-click the **System Monitor** details pane and click **Add Counters**.

12.4 To monitor any computer on which the monitoring console is run, click **Use Local Computer Counters**. To monitor a specific computer regardless of where the monitoring console is run, click **Select Counters from Computer** and select your computer name from the list.

12.5 In the Performance Object list, select the **Processor performance** object.

12.6 Select the **Counter: %Processor Time** and **Counter: Interrupts/sec** counters to monitor.

12.7 Select the System Object, **Counter: Processor Queue Length**.

12.8 Select the Memory Object, **Counter: Pages /sec**.

12.9 Select the Physical Disk Object, **Counter: Current Disk Queue Length**.

12.10 Shrink the window. Click **Start**, point to **Programs**, point to **Games**, and then click **Pinball** (or any action-intensive game). Play a game and watch the counters. What happens? Why?

12.11 Close Performance Monitor.

Challenge Exercise 12.6

In this exercise, you learn to install and use Network Monitor to capture frames traveling to and from the server's network interface card (NIC). You will analyze this information to determine the protocol that the frames are carrying. You need a computer with Windows 2000 Server or Windows 2000 Advanced Server installed and Administrator privileges.

To install Network Monitor Tools:

12.1 Log on to your machine as Administrator.

12.2 Click **Start**, point to **Settings**, click **Control Panel**, and then double-click **Add/Remove Programs**.

12.3 Click **Add/Remove Windows Components**.

12.4 When the Windows Components Wizard starts, choose **Management and Monitoring Tools**.

12.5 Click **Details**, and then choose **Network Monitor Tools**.

12.6 Click **OK**. The tools are installed.

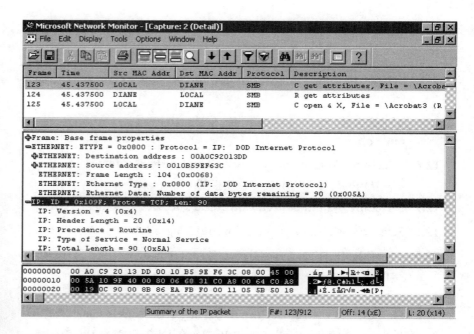

Figure 12.21

Capture screen of Network Monitor

To use Network Monitor:

12.1 Click **Start**, point to **Settings**, click **Control Panel**, double-click **Administrative Tools**, and double-click **Network Monitor**.

12.2 Click **Capture** on the menu bar, and then click **Start** to begin capturing packets.

12.3 You should now start to see traffic being generated on the screen.

12.4 Wait a few minutes, and then in the Network Monitor menu bar, click **Capture**, and then click **Stop**.

12.5 In the Network Monitor menu bar, click **Capture**, and then click **Display Captured Data**.

12.6 The screen should look like Figure 12.21.

12.7 Network Monitor displays three panes: the captured frames, the header and delivery details, and the hexadecimal representation of the frame.

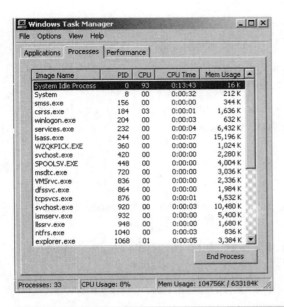

Figure 12.22

Task Manager Processes tab

12.8 In the top frame, choose a frame to view. Browse through the fields, and find the frame's protocol type and source address. Why is this information important?

12.9 Close Network Monitor.

Challenge Exercise 12.7

In this exercise, you learn to use Task Manager to get an instant view of what is happening on your system. You will analyze this information to determine what processes are running and which ones, if any, have high CPU usage. You will need a computer with Windows 2000 Server or Windows 2000 Advanced Server installed and Administrator privileges.

12.1 Log on to your computer as Administrator.

12.2 Press **CTRL+ALT+DELETE**. When the Windows Security screen appears, click **Task Manager**.

12.3 Click the **Processes** tab and look at System Idle Process. It should look similar to Figure 12.22. In the CPU column, how much usage is shown (what's the number displayed in the column)? What does this mean?

12.4 Click the **Performance** tab. What is the percentage of CPU usage? When is this screen helpful?

12.5 Go through the rest of the tabs, carefully examining each one. Discuss the usefulness of each screen.

12.6 Close Task Manager.

Challenge Exercise 12.8

In this exercise, you examine the building you are in for places where security can be improved. You will need a pencil and paper.

12.1 Walk around the outside of the building. How many outside entrances are there? Can people simply walk in?

12.2 Observe the reception area. Do guests have to sign in? What about students?

12.3 Walk around the inside of the building. Is the server area secure? What about the equipment in the library?

12.4 After you have made your observations, discuss in class the difference between the physical security requirements for a business and those for a school environment.

12.10   Challenge Scenarios

Challenge Scenario 12.1

Jim Jones has decided to start his own travel agency. He has rented an office, hired 35 employees, and purchased 35 PCs, along with a server and a laptop for himself. He knows you have good computer knowledge and has asked you to help him. He wants to get the server set up and will have the following departments: Sales and Marketing, Management, Sales Support, Human Resources, Administrative, and Help Desk. He wants to be able to tell who is logged in to the network at all times and wants the departments to have access to only the information that they need. He wants access to the server to be as secure as possible. He will have employees only—no contractors. Put together a plan for Jim detailing what type of naming convention(s) you would suggest, how to be sure the server access is secure, and what groups should be created on the server.

Challenge Scenario 12.2

Jim Jones was happy with the plan you gave him for naming conventions and groups. He followed through by having one of his sales people set up the accounts and groups. But he is finding that not everything is working out the way he expected. Many employees belong to more than one group, and others have access to files they should not. This time, he has contracted you to come in and fix the problem. He has a very specific list of who gets access to what. He also informs you that he has hired three outside sales people who dial in for access and need to be set up as well. He doesn't want these employees to be able to browse the network or the server; they should have access to only the Sales and Marketing material. Put together a plan with the steps you will take to rectify this situation.

Challenge Scenario 12.3

Jim Jones was very pleased with the work you did with the user accounts. Recently he has added 10 new employees and installed several new applications, one of which is Web-based. The users are complaining that the network is slow, but not all the time. This not only affects his business, but also he often hears the employees grumbling about the network and thinks it is affecting their morale. He is having a hard time figuring out why sometimes the network works fine and other times it is extremely slow. He once again has contracted you, but this time your job is to find out what is going on with the network. Where will you begin, and how will you figure out what is causing the network to be slow at times?

Challenge Scenario 12.4

Mr. Jones has expanded his travel agency business tremendously in a short amount of time. He has doubled the number of employees to keep up with the demand. The outside sales force has tripled, and these sales people come in for meetings once a week. People are constantly coming and going. Some days when Mr. Jones comes in there are many faces that he does not recognize. He has become concerned about the physical security of the building but does not want to hire a security guard. The server room is not secured very well, and he also has concerns about a competitor stealing his customer database. He has contracted you to evaluate the physical security of the facility and suggest some recommendations for improvement. List the items you would evaluate, why, and the recommendations you would suggest.

Challenge Scenario 12.5

All your hard work has finally paid off. Mr. Jones has become quite successful and now is ready to hire a full-time network administrator. He has offered you the job. You have accepted. You are very eager to start. Mr. Jones has expressed concern that because he now has over 100 employees, his payroll cost is too high. He knows that the employees are not monitored closely because he often sees them surfing the Internet, downloading music files, and sending personal e-mail. He has done nothing about this because there are no policies in place to prevent this type of behavior. Your first order of business is to put together a security policy and make sure all employees are aware of it. What will you include in the policy, and how will you implement it?

CHAPTER 13

Network Troubleshooting

After reading this chapter you will be able to:

- Avoid potential problems through proper preventative techniques
- Measure, monitor, and audit network resources
- Understand the principles of good troubleshooting
- Identify key information resources
- Know how to handle some common sources of network problems

We would like to believe that if we plan properly the network will run trouble free. However, things will go wrong: Systems will crash and applications will hang—part of everyday life for a network administrator. To have as little down time as possible, you must be proactive in managing the environment and know how to effectively troubleshoot any issues.

This chapter will guide you through preventing problems by being proactive, show you a methodical process for troubleshooting, and expose you to related tools and resources that are available to help make the process easier.

13.1   Avoiding Potential Problems

There are two approaches to troubleshooting: preventing potential problems through proper planning and quickly fixing what fails. The former is often referred to as trouble avoidance or preemptive troubleshooting, and the latter is referred to as troubleshooting or damage control. To be effective, both of these should be used in combination. Let's look at a few real-world scenarios:

- A company hires a consultant to resolve why customers are having trouble accessing the company Web site. After initial tests are performed, the consultant determines that the problem lies with the Web server. The consultant requires physical access to the server, but no one in the company knows where it is located. The company paid someone to set up the server about a year ago, but the person who arranged everything is no longer with the company and no records were kept. After two days of searching, the consultant finds the Web server in a closet that the company has been using for storage. At this point, the consultant learns that no one in the company knows the root password.

- A company is having problems with its e-mail server; sometimes it works fine, other times it doesn't. There is no documentation on the server. What is known is that a friend of the owner put the computer together for a good price, and some consultants came in and set up everything. It is discovered that the e-mail program is an obscure software package, and the friend of the owner doesn't remember what kind of components he used in the server. How long do you think it will take to resolve this issue?

These scenarios happen in real life; in fact, both are true stories. Documentation is important. It's a tedious job, and we all would rather be working with new technology, but documentation is imperative. Both of the preceding scenarios could have been avoided if this information was available. We will begin this section by discussing the first method of troubleshooting: preventing problems. This will include making sure we have ongoing access, proper security, good hardware and software standards, and monitoring and auditing.

13.1.1 Ensuring Ongoing Access

In a networked environment, you must ensure that users have ongoing access by making sure that if a problem arises, you have a backup plan so that the normal course of business operations is not interrupted. In the last chapter, we discussed the different methods available for backing up data. Here are the points to remember in regard to data backup:

- Identify the data that should be backed up.
- Determine the backup type and schedule.
- Designate someone to be responsible for performing the backup and changing the tapes.
- Be sure the tapes are properly labeled.
- Keep a log verifying that these procedures are being followed.

TIP

Normal backups should include only data. It is unnecessary to back up application files and operating system files with daily backups because they can easily be reinstalled from the original CDs, if necessary.

Keeping a log may seem like a trivial detail, but the following scenario is a good example of why it needs to be done. Say you have a large database to back up and have chosen the incremental method of backup. The person who is supposed to be changing the tapes forgets to do so two days in a row. A system component fails midday today. How much data have you lost? You have lost the equivalent of 2.5 days of data.

Make sure that you have a plan in place for storing the backup data. If the building burns down, will you be able to restore your data? You should be able to answer yes to that question.

An important part of the backup process is your ability to restore the data. Many companies think they are backing up their data, and later find out that the tapes are blank, or the tape heads have become worn or dirty. When the need arises, they can't restore their data. Therefore, backup tapes should be tested regularly.

13.1.2   Establishing Proper Security

Think about the many ways that the security of your company could be compromised. We discussed vulnerabilities and best practices in Chapter 10. Remember that a security policy should encompass hardware and software, along with some of these areas:

- There should be clear paths of responsibility and user expectations, including identification of what may be done with generally accessible data available to users and administrators.

- Users should be aware of privacy issues that may arise, including adequate notice of access rights claimed by the company over file, e-mail, and instant messaging traffic within the organization's network.

- A separation of duties policy should exist so that total control is not left in the hands of a single individual for whom the check-and-balance process is not applied. This policy might include details such as identifying which group is responsible for updating security hotfixes or updating data records in the company database.

- Users should be aware of password length, duration, history, and complexity requirements, along with the reasons they exist.

- There should be a clear policy for the destruction of data. Outdated or bad hardware and discarded documents may often be exploited by attackers to obtain access to a network.

- Procedures should be established for creating and authorizing accounts for newly hired personnel, as well as removal of privileges following employment termination.

- Incident response and disaster recovery planning policies should be included.

As you can see, proper security entails formulating a set of instructions on how to conduct business and interact with information systems while maintaining an acceptable level of security. Once this is done, users must be made aware of these security policies because your network is only as strong as its weakest link.

13.1.3   Creating Hardware and Software Standards

The goal of security is expressed in terms of confidentiality, integrity, and availability. Confidentiality ensures that information is not intentionally or unintentionally disclosed, integrity protects from unauthorized modifications to data, and availability makes sure any needed data is available when it is requested. These goals can be achieved through creating hardware and software standards.

When establishing standards for hardware and software, desktop systems should be included. Workstation consistency is often overlooked, yet this is one of the areas that can attract the most problems. Users are often unaware of the consequences to themselves and the company when performing the following:

- Installing unauthorized software
- Downloading infected music and movie files
- Opening an e-mail message that contains a virus
- Using weak passwords
- Not logging off the network when leaving the building

Should a component in a workstation fail, such as a hard drive, running nightly backups will be instrumental in making sure the data can be recovered. You may also want to consider removing floppy drives or disabling devices that aren't absolutely necessary. This prevents users from bringing in infected files and intruders from gaining access.

When trying to keep hardware components standardized, network administrators often tend to favor one particular manufacturer and order several desktops or components at a time, not only for convenience but also because it makes good sense. The components or parts can be interchanged should a vital system go down. This principle can be applied to various devices. For example, if a company uses the same type of external backup drive for all servers, if one tape drive fails, one from another computer can be used until the faulty tape drive is fixed. In addition, the tapes from each drive are interchangeable, so if data must be restored on a different computer, all that is needed is the tape. However you choose to order your equipment, be sure it is from a vendor with a solid reputation. From an administrative and support standpoint, standardization is imperative.

Besides consistency in desktop hardware standards, you should also have some system of identifying and tracking the hardware on your network.

This is needed not only for inventory and insurance purposes but also for troubleshooting purposes. We will cover documentation in more detail later in this chapter. Keep in mind that documentation for workstations should also include security.

Standards for laptops, personal digital assistants (PDAs), Palm Pilots, and Pocket PCs may be more difficult to define because each user has his or her own preference. However, if these devices are company issued or company supported, they must be standardized as well. These devices are susceptible to theft because they are small and valuable, and many times they contain important information about a company. You need to be sure that encryption is enabled to keep the data safe if the device is lost or stolen. If possible, you should protect these devices with passwords so there is at least an initial deterrent.

You must also define and document standards for new server installations along with guidelines for current server configurations. Most servers come with a wide range of services and protocols, many of which are turned on by default. Every operating system requires different services for it to operate properly. Ideally, the configuration process should start with installing only the services necessary for the server to function. Besides having only the necessary services and protocols installed, you should limit physical access to the server. In addition, you must ensure availability. You can accomplish this by using Redundant Array of Inexpensive Disks (RAID), uninterruptible power supply (UPS) equipment, and clustering.

The computer industry changes constantly—what works today might not work tomorrow. To keep pace, be sure to evaluate standards often. Ideally this would be once per quarter. If this seems too time-consuming, remember that a solid set of standards helps keep the network safe and running.

13.1.4   Managing Change

Change is part of life, especially for a network administrator. Vendors constantly update their operating systems, drivers, and equipment. Because the network will continually change, it is critical to plan for changes. Policies should include provisions for change authorization, documentation, and notification, along with procedures to be used when hardware, software, or storage media is replaced or discarded.

Changes can have serious consequences on the productivity of the users and the network. If not done properly, the system can be exposed to corruption or data deletion during changes. Planning and testing eliminates the majority of these types of problems, and sufficient time must be spent to ensure that the transition and implementation go as smoothly as possible. As a guideline, the following steps should be considered when creating a change management policy:

1. Establish a schedule for changes.
2. Make sure users are notified of the changes.
3. Conduct proper testing.

By following these three steps, you should be able to better control the changes made to your network and the equipment used on it.

When setting up a schedule for changes, be sure they are not implemented during key business times. Scheduling changes also ensures that multiple changes that could conflict or cause problems are not implemented on the same day or at the same time of day. Changes should be scheduled during off hours, if possible, or only after extensive testing. This doesn't always happen. For example, a relatively inexperienced network administrator applies a new service pack to a server during business hours to fix a security hole. However, the service pack was not tested first, and now the users are having problems because the service pack adversely affected the operating system.

! WARNING

If it takes months to schedule a change, get it approved, and implement it properly, you'll find that administrators might bypass that process to get their jobs done. Long, bureaucratic processes have a tendency to worsen the situation, not help it.

A change request should be submitted to the IT management team along with a staging plan outlining the proposed method for the deployment. This procedure will help eliminate problems quickly. For example, a network administrator wants to upgrade a software package and install new memory on a server. The change request and staging plan call for the software upgrade to be performed first, then a testing period, and finally the memory installation. If the server stops functioning, the problem can easily be attributed to either the software upgrade or memory installation because they are not scheduled to take place at the same time.

Documentation is critical. Documentation eliminates misunderstandings and provides vital information should there be problems with a change. Change documentation should include:

- A schedule of the proposed and approved changes
- Specific change details regarding what is changing, such as files being replaced, configuration updates, or software upgrades
- Specific change problems and issues that occurred during the testing phase of the change process
- Recommendations and notes on this particular change event
- Who approved and who performed the change tests

After the change has been requested, documented, and approved, you should then send notification. Change notification can be done either by distributing a physical copy of the change request to those affected by the change or via e-mail. This can be also be used for feedback in the event some detail was overlooked in the original request. Before actually deploying the change, testing should be conducted. This should be performed first on equipment in a test lab. Deploying to test lab equipment first can uncover immediate problems and give you time to deal with issues before deployment in the production environment begins. Testing should be well documented and should involve simulated end-user activity on the system. In many instances, testing eliminates problems when the change is finally deployed in the production environment. However, problems can still occur when you upgrade your production systems. In these cases, a rollback strategy is necessary.

A rollback strategy should be part of every change plan. Although this seems redundant, you are changing network components, software, or configurations that might impact the ability of the company to conduct business. Something as simple as upgrading a network interface card (NIC) driver can be disastrous if you can't find a copy of the old driver when the new one doesn't work. We will discuss this concept further in the "Reversing Recent Changes" section later in the chapter.

13.1.5 Maintaining Documentation

Although it can be a tedious aspect of network management, thorough documentation is a necessary part of an administrator's job. Document everything you do, and be as detailed as you can. It is a hard habit to develop, and many administrators think that if they document everything, they can then be easily replaced. This is far from true—documentation is more valuable to you as an administrator than you may realize. When it is time to upgrade the network, purchase additional equipment, or troubleshoot a problem, a complete set of network documents is priceless. Documenting is particularly important because of the impact it can have on business and the impact if legal action is involved. Most, if not all, of the documentation should be generated throughout each and every process. From planning to deployment to ongoing management, documentation is the key to long-term success.

All documents should be kept in both hard- and soft-copy form, and it is imperative that both copies of this information be updated regularly. Part of the frustration in putting together documentation is that the information is constantly changing. As our systems, employees, vendors, and business partners change, so do our business needs. Many hours are spent looking for information that is not documented. Although it is commonly overlooked, documentation is critical to the ongoing functionality of your network.

Documentation will also give users, managers, and executives a clear understanding of the systems and software they are using. Your network documentation should include these components:

- **Policies and procedures:** Documents all roles and tasks performed by the network staff, which may include, but are not limited to, setting up and deleting user and group accounts, naming conventions, backup procedures, and incident response policies.

- **Network history:** Documents the changes that have occurred in the network since its inception. It should list all protocols and standards in use and include the who, what, when, where, why, and how of all changes that occur.

- **Network map:** Includes a map of all network equipment such as servers, switches, hubs, and the location of electrical equipment such as fuse boxes, along with all telephone equipment, including PBXs and T-1(s). Network and electrical capacity information should also be included in this component.

- **Cable diagrams and layouts:** Includes details about the wall plate information so that you will know which cable goes into which port on the switch. This is very valuable especially when troubleshooting connectivity issues.

- **Contact list:** Includes contact information for all pertinent personnel. It should start with company contacts for emergencies including vendors, business partners and information on leased lines, telephone numbers, and who to contact.

- **Equipment list:** Similar to an inventory list, includes the date of purchase, manufacturer, warranty information, and serial numbers. More than one list can be kept, especially if there is a large quantity of computers on the network.

- **Computer and network device configuration:** Includes configuration details on the configuration files for all desktops, servers, routers, and other devices in this document.

- **Software and its configuration:** Defines the configuration for each type of software installed on the network. It should also state whether it is client/server or the configuration for both and any exceptions to the standard configuration.

- **Network address list:** Tracks all static IP addresses issued and MAC addresses for servers, routers, printers, and switches. It should also include IP scope ranges for DHCP servers and their purpose. Ideally this list will also include the MAC address of the individual computer's NIC and where the machine is located.

- **Software licensing information:** Lists all software in use and the number of licenses issued for each software package. In the past, when you purchased licensing for Microsoft products, the licenses came with the equipment. Now most commercial licensing is done through Worldwide Fulfillment, and you must be sure to have the information sent to you to be able to track the number of licenses you have.

WARNING **!** If you have outdated documentation, it provides no useful purpose for network troubleshooting. It also provides neither liability protection nor due diligence obligations that businesses might have to meet under current insurance requirements or laws.

13.1.6   Preempting Problems

Preemptive troubleshooting, also called trouble avoidance, may seem time-consuming, but it will save time and may help save data when problems arise. In the last chapter, we showed an example of a computer with a disk controller error. In a preemptive environment, this issue would be addressed before the controller fails. Preemptive troubleshooting can also prevent additional expense and downtime while trying to figure out what happened after a failure. Preemptive troubleshooting can also protect data integrity. For example, if a SQL server fails in the middle of posting transactions, the database will likely become corrupt. If so, not only do you have a computer to fix, you also have to recover the database. Preemptive troubleshooting would have avoided the failure entirely.

The International Organization for Standardization (ISO) defines five preemptive troubleshooting network management categories, as follows:

- **Accounting management:** Accounting management collects statistics on resource consumption for the purposes of capacity and trend analysis, cost allocation, auditing, and billing. The goal of accounting management is to provide a set of tools that can be used to meet the requirements of each application, because they do not have uniform security and reliability requirements.

- **Configuration management:** Configuration management is the process of managing products, facilities, and processes by managing the information about them, including changes, and ensuring they are what they are supposed to be in every case. It is typically a formally defined process to be used by an organization's systems engineers.

- **Fault management:** The task of fault management is to find, identify, and fix malfunctions in the network and its control subsystem. It also includes implementing fault-tolerant hardware systems and fault-tolerant procedures. This process may require equipment replacement, change of system configuration, or software removal of bugs.

- **Performance management:** Performance management actually refers to how well the network serves its users. Performance management includes the processes of reporting, measuring, and controlling the availability and utilization for different network components. However, what truly matters is the performance of the network as a whole.

- **Security management:** Good security management is the key to success. Your everyday security management tasks should include best practices and guidelines for monitoring and controlling access to network resources and the environment.

Be sure that your preemptive troubleshooting techniques cover all these areas. This gives you a better chance to prevent problems before they occur and a better handle on them if they do happen.

13.1.7   Measuring, Monitoring, and Auditing

In Chapter 12 we covered some of the tools that can be used to manage and monitor network performance. Many of these tools also help identify conditions that may lead to problems and often can ultimately help in the prevention of network failures. They are long-term troubleshooting tools because you often have to collect data for a while before any of it can be useful in troubleshooting. Let's review some of these tools and what they are used for, starting with baselining.

It is essential to identify what typical behavior is in order to identify what abnormal behavior is. This measure of normal activity, known as a baseline, gives you a point of reference when something on the network goes awry. Without a baseline, it is harder to see what is wrong because you don't know what is normal. Baselines must be updated regularly and certainly when the network has changed or new technology deployed. Baselining should be done for both network and application processes so that you can tell whether you have a hardware or software issue.

Event Viewer allows you to audit certain events. Event Viewer maintains several log files, as shown in Figure 13.1, that are used to monitor system processes, security information, and applications.

Task Manager can be used to end processes or applications that get hung up or cause the operating system to become unstable without having to reboot the machine. It also gives you an instant view of CPU and memory usage. It is should be one of the first places to check when something seems awry. Figure 13.2 shows the Processes tab of Task Manager.

The Performance console is used for tracking and viewing operating system resources. You can view information that you have tracked in charts, alerts, logs, and reports. The Performance console keeps track of set counters for system objects. You can use it to monitor the physical disks, mem-

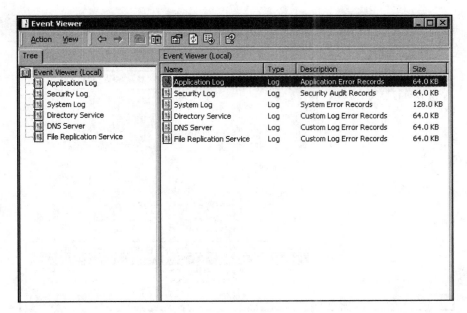

Figure 13.1
Event Viewer

Figure 13.2
Task Manager

ory, and processor, along with other services. It can also send alerts to an assigned administrator. Figure 13.3 is a reminder of what the Performance console screen looks like.

A network monitor can be used to capture network traffic and generate statistics for creating reports. After the packets have been captured, the information can be viewed. It records the source address, destination address,

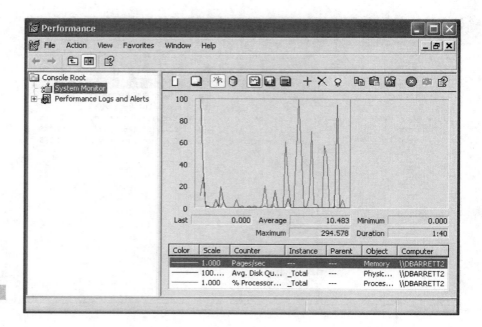

Figure 13.3

Performance console

packet headers, and data. Almost all operating systems come with a network-monitoring tool. Figure 13.4 shows the network monitor screen for Microsoft Network Monitor.

Auditing is the process of tracking users and their actions on the network. Some activities that can be audited include reading, modifying, or deleting files; logging on or off the network; using services such as remote access or Terminal Services; and using devices such as printers. How much you should audit depends on how much information you want to store. You can audit as much or as little as you want, but if you don't read the logs, they are not serving the purpose for which they were intended. When deciding what to audit, remember that auditing takes up system resources and space. Auditing can be as simple or complex as you want to make it. As you learn the patterns of your users and the network, it will become easy to identify odd or suspicious behaviors.

Simple Network Management Protocol (SNMP), as discussed in Chapter 9, is an Application layer protocol that is used to exchange management information between network devices. SNMP enables network administrators to manage network performance, find and solve network problems,

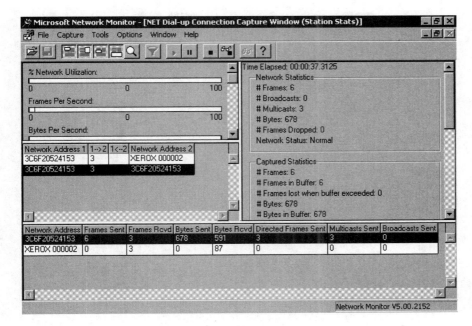

Figure 13.4
Network Monitor

and plan for network growth. SNMP management infrastructure consists of three main components: (1) SNMP-managed nodes or devices, (2) SNMP agents that store and retrieve information from its management information base (MIB), (3) and SNMP network management stations that execute applications that monitor and control the managed devices. It displays a list of warnings and errors reported by the agent, allows configuration control, and provides statistical information on network operations. SNMP can manage network devices such as servers, bridges, and routers. Figure 13.5 shows a SNMP-managed network.

All of these tools can be used to gather information that can help us identify devices that create bottlenecks, monitor trends in network traffic, and identify events that arise from software or hardware changes.

13.2   Principles of Troubleshooting

Although we put much effort into preemptive troubleshooting, proper planning, and vigilant monitoring and auditing, problems do occur. Many are obvious, such as the fans in a server going out or a circuit breaker that

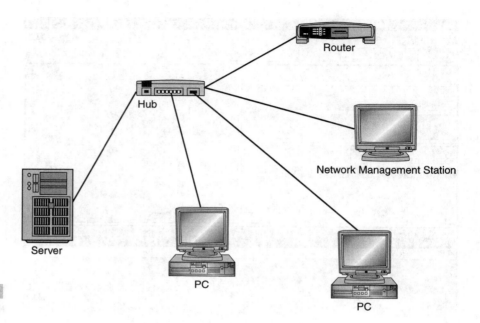

Figure 13.5
SNMP-managed network

trips. Some are not so obvious, and these are the ones that are harder to troubleshoot. So how do you figure out what is wrong?

This is what troubleshooting is all about. Troubleshooting skills are exactly that—skills. They are acquired through experimentation and experience. You cannot learn the resolution to every problem that exists. You can, however, learn a methodology to find and diagnose nearly every problem in a systematic and logical manner. Each one of us eventually develops "a method to our madness," but remember that your mental state greatly influences your ability to troubleshoot effectively. Stay calm and try to keep composed when working on a problem. If you feel yourself getting frustrated, or if you get stuck, these are probably signs that you've been working on the problem too long. Take a break, walk away, and do something else for a while. High levels of frustration can occur when you haphazardly troubleshoot without any logical steps.

The following are the most common network problems:

- **User error:** Eliminating user error is a good place to start. You will often find that users try to do things the network doesn't support, or they make mistakes. Many times you will find that they have changed settings or deleted files, causing the problem.

TABLE 13.1   Various Structured Troubleshooting Approaches

Approach 1: Microsoft Recommended	Approach 2: Fluke Networks Recommended	Approach 3: Troubleshooting Model (Ethernet networks as defined by Charles Spurgeon, University of Texas)
Set the problem's priority.	Collect information.	Discover problem.
Collect information about the problem.	Localize the problem.	Gather facts.
Develop a list of possible causes.	Isolate the problem.	Create hypothesis.
Test each hypothesis to isolate the actual cause.	Correct the problem.	Develop an action plan.
For each potential cause, attempt at least one solution.	Verify problem resolution.	Implement action plan.
N/A	N/A	Test and observe results.

- **Physical connections:** Verify that all cables are plugged in and that you have lights on the NIC and hubs. Watch out for loose cables or cables that are not properly secured.

- **System needs a reboot:** Often, system processes or software applications hang up, and the only way to get them to unlock is to reboot the computer. You will find this true especially with Microsoft operating systems. When all else fails, reboot.

If these steps don't help, then it's time to move on and try other troubleshooting options. Although troubleshooting is different for a programmer than for a network administrator, there are some common skills and training that apply to both. Research on problem solving and reasoning is fundamental to understanding troubleshooting skills, which is why troubleshooting methodologies have been developed. You can choose from several different methodologies of troubleshooting. These give us guidelines for logically solving problems using a step-by-step process. Table 13.1 lists several different approaches.

As you can see, although each method may be a little different, the basic premise is the same and the procedure should be followed step by step. We will look at the first approach so that you get an idea of how this all works.

The first step is to determine the scope of the problem by identifying the symptoms. Ask questions such as "Is anyone else in the area having the same problem?" or "Can you print from other applications?" When you first encounter a problem, it is very important to determine its scope. Does this problem lie with a specific computer, or does it exist across the network? If more than one computer is having the same problem at the same time, it is obvious that you are having a network problem and not a computer-specific problem. This phase often requires you to check the status of other computers on the network to determine whether they are having the same problem. Quickly determining the scope of the problem is the first step in gathering information about the nature of the problem. After the scope is determined, the priority can be set. In other words, if none of the users in the building can access the Internet, this should be a much higher priority than if one user can't print an e-mail message. If more than one problem has surfaced, deal with them according to priority.

The next step is to collect specific information about the problem at hand. You will find that most of the time when users have a problem, they make general or vague statements such as "The printer isn't working" or "I can't access the network." You must ask specific questions about the situation to be able to fix it. Here are some questions to ask:

- What exactly is happening? Does it happen all the time or just sometimes?

- What has changed? Have you installed any new applications or programs?

- When was the last time it worked properly? Have you tried to fix it yourself?

To illustrate this process, let's look at the "printer isn't working" issue. You ask the questions above and are told:

- The printer isn't printing. It is happening all the time.

- Nothing has changed.

- It worked fine until about 10 minutes ago. No one had tried to fix it.

Once you have the pertinent information, then the scope is determined: No one in the department can print from any application.

Sounds pretty serious, huh? Well, in the next step we establish possible causes. From experience, you would start by creating a list of probable causes. First, look to the obvious and never assume anything, especially when working with users. What would cause the printer to suddenly stop printing? Here is a list of the most likely causes:

- It is out of paper.
- The paper is jammed.
- The printer is offline.
- Someone sent a large print job and the printer queue is full.
- The printer is unplugged.
- The printer is turned off.

Now that you have a list of probable causes, begin to isolate the problem by testing each of the causes, starting with the most obvious first. In our scenario, for simplicity sake, let's say there is no paper in the top printer tray and the printer won't print unless there is paper in both trays. The printer being out of paper is the most common cause for a printer not to print.

This is the stage where you may attempt to re-create the problem. During this phase, while you are trying to isolate the problem, it is important to understand the problem and make only one change at a time. If you change too many things at one time and the problem is suddenly solved, you will have no idea what fixed it. On the other end, if the problem gets worse, you will have no idea what happened that created the additional concerns or worsened the condition.

TIP

Don't be afraid to ask for help. It can be an excellent way to learn and can save precious time in urgent matters. There are many knowledgeable people who are willing to share their solutions—all you have to do is ask.

If you encounter an issue that is the result of having installed a new application or device, read the documentation that came with the hardware or software. Speaking from experience, some students once had a problem with a video card installation and after two frustrating days came to ask for help. We found the answer only three lines into the readme.txt file. They spent two days trying to troubleshoot a problem that was solved in 20 seconds!

When a problem is isolated, test each change. In the preceding printer scenario, after paper is added to the printer, it starts to print again. A short time later, it stops printing again. You must begin the troubleshooting process all over again. This means starting back at step one and continuing from there. As for our hypothetical printer issue: While the printer was out of paper, a sales assistant sent an extremely large print job that contained graphics that the printer couldn't understand and that jammed the queue. When the printer didn't print the first time, the sales assistant resent the job several more times, adding to the problem. In this instance, we ended up with two problems instead of one.

> **WARNING !**
> To have an organized method of troubleshooting, don't forget about the obvious. Do not assume anything or think a question is too basic, because often these basic questions help solve the problem.

Connectivity problems can occur when a workstation cannot communicate with its own devices or other devices on a LAN or WAN. More than 70% of all computer problems are related to cabling and connections. Ensure that all cables are connected firmly. IDE, floppy ribbon cables, network cables, and power cables can often become loose. Ensure that the microprocessor, memory modules, and cards such as video and sound are inserted correctly and didn't unseat during a recent move. If a computer doesn't start after being moved, this is usually an indication that something became unseated. One company found that, for some reason, certain processors in one manufacturer's case always came loose when moved, so the computers never booted until the processor was reseated. Connectivity problems can include total loss of connectivity, intermittent connectivity, and timeout problems.

If response times are slow, the network is not as reliable as usual, or users are reporting that it takes them longer to do their work, you may have performance issues. Performance problems such as instances of duplicate addresses can be intermittent, while consistently high utilization rates for memory, processors, and disks can indicate a growing strain on your network. If you regularly examine your network for performance problems by using the methods outlined in Chapter 12, you can extend the usefulness of your existing network configuration rather than waiting for a performance problem to adversely affect productivity. We will discuss fixing performance problems later in the chapter.

By using a defined strategy for network troubleshooting, you can approach a problem methodically and resolve it with minimal disruption to network users. It is also important to have an accurate and detailed map of your current network environment handy to easily identify the location of connectivity problems. Beyond that, a good approach to problem resolution is to be able to recognize symptoms and understand the problem. Sometimes having a good approach isn't enough to get the job done. You may need the help of some tools. Let's now look at the different tools you may use.

13.2.1   Creating a Hardware Toolkit

More complex network environments mean that the potential for connectivity and performance problems in networks is high, and the source of problems is often hard to pin down. By understanding how network troubleshooting fits into the framework of the OSI model, you can identify at what layer problems are located and which type of troubleshooting tools to use. For example, a problem with the transmission media or with a router configuration can cause unreliable packet delivery. Many networking problems occur at the lower layers of the OSI model where it is better to use diagnostic tools for troubleshooting. In this section, we will look at some of the most common physical tools, such as crossover cables, volt-ohm meters or digital voltmeters, cable testers, time-domain reflectometers, and oscilloscopes, along with their use on the network.

A **crossover cable** looks just another twisted-pair cable, but two wires are crossed, which makes the cable not suitable for regular connectivity on a computer or a hub. Remember from the exercises in Chapter 2 that you actually made a crossover cable. A crossover cable is used to connect two computers to each other directly, without the use of a hub. It is useful in troubleshooting because it allows you to easily verify that the NIC is functioning properly. For example, if a user is having trouble connecting to the network, by using a crossover cable you can try to access the user's workstation from another computer. If it works, you know that the NIC is fine, and it is probably the network cable that is bad.

A hardware **loopback adapter** is a way to test the ports on a system without having to connect to an external device. For example, you can use a serial

Figure 13.6
Tone generator and tone locator

loopback adapter to make sure that a transmitted signal is leaving your serial port and returning through the loopback adapter, thereby verifying that your serial port is working correctly. You can test the loopback on a NIC by typing ping 127.0.0.0 at a command prompt. This is called a loopback address, and if it replies you know the NIC is working.

Often, our telecommunications closets become unorganized, and it's difficult to determine where a pair of wires begin and end. You can use a **tone generator** to perform tests on phone and network lines to help identify wires during the wire-tracing process. The tone generator issues a signal on the wire pair while the tone locator emits a tone when it detects activity in the wire pair. See Figure 13.6 for an example. To locate the proper end wire, you have to use the process of elimination, which is referred to as "fox and hound." You begin by attaching the fox (tone generator) to the cable, jack, or panel that you would like to trace, and you continue with the hound (tone locator) on the other end of the cable to find the fox's tone. When you find the tone, you will know that you have correctly traced the cable.

This is very helpful for determining which cable in a group of many cables, such as in a wiring closet, has gone bad and needs to be replaced. This type of device cannot be used for anything other than locating the end of a wire pair. They are not used much on today's networks because of their limited functionality, but they are still widely used by telephone technicians.

Do not use a tone generator on a wire that is connected to a network adapter or a computer port. The tone generator transmits electricity that can possibly damage the port or adapter.

Cable checkers and testers enable you to check physical connectivity. **Cable testers** operate at higher layers of the OSI model and provide more detailed information than a cable checker.

Testing of cables is important especially if you make your own. Use a cable tester to be sure that the end connections are solid and wire order is correct before you use the cable.

A **cable checker** determines whether your cabling can provide connectivity, whereas a cable tester performs the same continuity and fault tests but also provides these functions:

- It ensures that the cable is not too long.
- It measures the distance to a cable fault.
- It tests and reports on cable conditions, including near-end crosstalk, attenuation, and noise.
- It performs traffic monitoring and wire map functions.
- It issues pass or fail ratings for Cat3, Cat5, Cat6, or even Cat7 standards.
- It displays MAC sub-layer information about LAN traffic, stores and prints cable testing results, and performs limited protocol testing.

Cable testers are available for shielded twisted-pair (STP), unshielded twisted-pair (UTP), 10BaseT, and coaxial cables. Similar testing equipment is available for fiber-optic cable.

Because of the relatively high cost of fiber cable and its installation, fiber-optic cable should be tested both before installation, which is called on-the-reel testing, and after installation.

Analog **volt-ohm** meters or digital **voltmeters** (DVMs) are at the lower end of the spectrum of cable-testing tools. These devices measure alternating

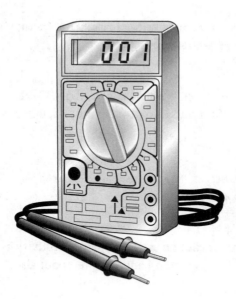

Figure 13.7
Digital voltmeter

current (AC) and direct current (DC) voltage, current, resistance, capacity, and cable continuity. The analog volt-ohm meter, sometimes referred to as a VOM, was the most common type available until the late 1980s. It has a left-to-right needle that moves across a physical meter called a movement, some sort of rotary switch, and a set of wire probes. The switch setting allows you to select which mode that it operates in. Because of the impedance of the physical meter, the accuracy for measuring certain types of signals or levels can be a problem. A VOM has two wires, called probes, attached to it. Typically, one is red and the other is black. Always plug the red lead into the plug marked + and the black lead into the plug marked − or Ground.

A DVM provides the same functionality as any other VOM and is also referred to as a VOM. The digital type is far more common than the analog today, and the cost for a DVM is quite reasonable. It has a digital display, wire probes, and possibly a rotary switch to select operational mode. See Figure 13.7. The input stage normally has very high impedance.

WARNING ❗ Always disconnect the cable completely before testing with the ohm setting on your VOM. Having the cable connected to something will invalidate your readings or could damage your VOM if power is hooked up to it.

These types of devices are used to check physical connectivity or to determine whether the cable is intact. The most common failure is called an open circuit, which is a total disconnection from one cable connector to another. The next most common is a dead short, which is caused by something heavy falling or rolling over the cable such as a chair, or the cable, being mishandled by being twisted, knotted, or severely bent. Less frequently, but still common, is a high-resistance failure, which is often caused by stretching the cable, thereby breaking the wire inside.

The way to test for these problems is to test the resistance of the wire. Resistance is measured in ohms. The ohm setting on the meter can be used to test the conductivity of a wire, a switch, or almost anything that is supposed to carry electricity from one point to another. If the DVM finds no resistance or resistance within the cable's limitations, the cable is fine. However, if the DVM shows infinite resistance, a cable break exists that's preventing electronic flow.

At the top end of the cable-testing spectrum are time domain reflectors (TDRs) and optical time domain reflectors (OTDRs), which are devices that assist in the location of cable breaks, impedance mismatches, and other physical cable problems. A **time domain reflectometer (TDR)** works by bouncing a signal off the end of the cable. It sends a signal down the cable and then, at some point, it is reflected back. The TDR calculates the distance down the cable that the signal traveled before being reflected by measuring the amount of time it took for the signal to be returned. This is similar to how sonar works. If this distance is less than your overall cable length, a cable problem exists that distance from your location. TDRs can also be used to measure the length of a cable. Some TDRs can also calculate the propagation rate based on a configured cable length.

Fiber-optic measurement is performed by an **optical time domain reflectometer (OTDR)**. OTDR is an advanced diagnostic tool for optical fibers that allows you to take a snapshot of a fiber link. It can accurately measure the length of the fiber, locate cable breaks, measure the fiber attenuation, and measure splice or connector losses as well as locate a break within a few feet of actual fault. Like optical radar, the OTDR sends short pulses of light down one end of a fiber at a specified rate. Light is then reflected back to where the tool records the optical power and arrival time. OTDRs are well equipped for troubleshooting problems because they allow you to find connections, fiber breaks, splices, and tight bends by studying the graphical trace. Just like a TDR, an OTDR can be used to take the characteristics of a particular installation. This baseline measurement can then be compared with future readings when a problem in the system is suspected. Here are some uses for a TDR:

- Locates crushed, pinched, or kinked cables
- Locates opens and shorts in the cable
- Locates bad splices
- Locates water or moisture in the cable
- Locates unknown splices
- Documents the integrity of your cabling
- Documents or maps cable networks
- Locates problems caused by construction companies
- Documents cable installations prior to construction work

An **oscilloscope** can determine when there are shorts, crimps, or attenuation in the cable. The oscilloscope displays its output in a graphical format. In other words, it draws a graph of an electrical signal. The graph shows how signals change over time: The vertical (Y) axis represents voltage and the horizontal (X) axis represents time. The device itself looks a lot like a small television set, except that it has a few more controls and a grid on its screen. The front panel of an oscilloscope normally has control sections divided into three sections: vertical, horizontal, and trigger. There are also display controls and input connectors. See Figure 13.8 for an illustration.

Oscilloscopes, like VOMs, also come in analog and digital types. An analog oscilloscope works by directly applying a voltage being measured to an electron beam moving across the oscilloscope screen. When you connect an oscilloscope probe to a circuit, the voltage signal travels through the probe to the vertical system of the oscilloscope. Next, the signal travels directly to the vertical deflection plates of the cathode ray tube (CRT) and on to the trigger system to start or trigger a horizontal sweep. Together, the horizontal sweeping action and the vertical deflection action trace a graph of the signal on the screen. In other words, the voltage deflects the beam up and down proportionally, tracing the waveform on the screen. This gives an immediate picture of the waveform. In Chapter 1, we discussed analog and digital signals, and that analog equipment works with continuously vari-

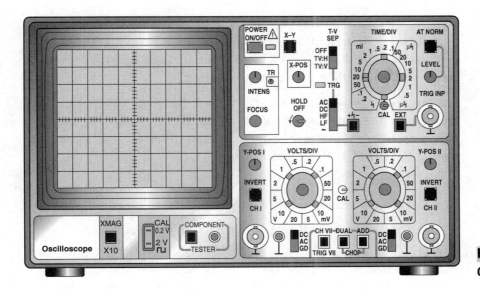

Figure 13.8
Oscilloscope

able voltages, while digital equipment works with binary numbers that may represent voltage samples. In keeping with this principle, a digital oscilloscope samples the waveform and uses an analog-to-digital converter to convert the voltage being measured into digital information. When you attach a digital oscilloscope probe to a circuit, the vertical system adjusts the amplitude of the signal, just as in the analog oscilloscope. Next, the analog-to-digital converter in the system samples the signal at discrete points in time and converts the signal's voltage at these points to digital values called sample points. It then uses this digital information to reconstruct the waveform on the screen. Oscilloscopes are useful for:

- Determining the time and voltage values of a signal
- Calculating the frequency of a signal
- Calculating how much of a signal is either DC or AC
- Tracking how much of the signal is noise and whether the noise is changing with time
- Seeing the actual moving parts of a circuit represented by the signal
- Determining whether a malfunctioning component is distorting the signal

Oscilloscopes are used by everyone from television repair technicians to physicists. In the networking environment, oscilloscopes are commonly used to test cables that have been recently run through walls to ensure there are no problems with the cable prior to using it.

Fox boxes, breakout boxes, and bit or block error-rate testers are digital interface testing tools used to measure the digital signals at peripheral interfaces such as printers, modems, or a channel service unit/digital service unit (CSU/DSU). These devices can:

- Monitor data line conditions
- Trap and analyze data
- Diagnose problems common to data communication systems

13.2.2   Creating a Software Toolkit

Besides hardware tools, your toolkit should also contain tools such as network monitors, protocol analyzers, and connectivity utilities so you can monitor traffic on the network and display the packets that have been transmitted across the network, if necessary.

Connectivity utilities such as PING, Netstat, Nbtstat, and Traceroute (Tracert) are very useful in figuring out where the issue lies when there are connectivity concerns. In Chapter 6 we discussed Ping and Traceroute, and in Chapter 9 we discussed Netstat and Nbtstat. Let's start with PING, because you will use it frequently. Remember that PING is a standard troubleshooting tool available on most network operating systems. The PING utility sends specially marked ICMP packets from the local computer to a remote device. Besides determining whether the remote computer is currently available, PING also provides information pertaining to the general speed or reliability of the network connection. With connectivity issues, first try to ping another computer on the same network. If you receive a response from this computer, try pinging the gateway. After you receive a proper response, try pinging a host on a remote network. If the network information has changes for some reason and you are using DHCP, it may be easier to release the IP address and then reboot the computer. This will allow it to pick up the proper configuration settings. When using host names with the ping command instead of IP addresses, a network name service such as DNS is needed to translate that name into the address that ping eventually uses. However, name services can take time to receive the latest addressing updates.

TIP

Devices that use frequently changing dynamic addresses, such as mobile computers, can be difficult to track via PING.

Traceroute (also Tracert) is used to track the path a packet takes to get to its destination. In other words, it measures how long it takes to travel through each hop to get to its target. It is useful in finding out why a packet isn't reaching its destination. For example, let's say a company uses one ISP for both the mail and the Web server. A user calls and says customers are complaining that they can't access the Web server. Depending on the network setup, the first question you might ask is: "Can you access the e-mail server?" This may sound like an odd question but:

- Because more than one customer has called, it is not a configuration issue on the client side.

- If the user can't get e-mail, and both e-mail and Web servers are going through the same ISP, you know that it could be an ISP problem.

In this case, let's say the user can't access e-mail. By using Traceroute, you will be able to tell exactly where the issue lies. Here, what is happening is that the ISP has a machine that is looping the IP address, so when you trace the route, you see an IP address going back and forth between two addresses. In this case, you would call the ISP, give them the information, and hopefully they would fix the problem immediately. As you can see, Traceroute is a valuable tool for quickly resolving connectivity issues. Be sure to use it.

Netstat is used to display active TCP connections; ports on which the computer is listening; Ethernet statistics; the IP routing table; and IP statistics for the IP, ICMP, TCP, and UDP protocols. Nbtstat displays NetBIOS over TCP/IP protocol statistics, NetBIOS name tables for both the local computer and remote computers, and the NetBIOS name cache. As their names imply, they are used to display statistics about the connections and ports on the computer, which can help you tell what is going on if the issue is isolated to the individual machine.

Network monitors provide an accurate picture of network activity over a period of time by continuously tracking packets crossing a network. They do not decode the contents of frames because usually they can only interpret information up to Layer 3 of the OSI model, but they are very useful for collecting information. Monitors collect information such as packet sizes; the number of packets; error packets; the number of hosts, their MAC addresses, and overall usage of a connection; along with details about communications between hosts and other devices. This data can be used for baselining, distributing traffic more efficiently, and planning for network expansion, as well as to assist in locating traffic overloads and detecting intruders.

Earlier in this chapter we mentioned Microsoft Network Monitor. Network Monitor, also known as NetMon, is a software-based tool that you can use to capture and observe network traffic patterns and problems. It can continually monitor traffic on the network from a server or workstation attached to the network. Often, Network Monitor is used in conjunction with Microsoft Systems Management Server (SMS) so that it can be used across routers and resolve IP addresses from names. The two primary components of Network Monitor are the Network Monitor Agent and the user interface. The Network Monitor Agent binds to the user interface and passes traffic up to the program. The Network Monitor Agent can run on any compatible computer while the program is running on a separate computer. Some of the functions that NetMon provides are:

- Capturing frames sent from or to a specific computer
- Capturing network data on one or more network segments
- Detecting other copies of NetMon on the network
- Recording statistics about network activity

To use Network Monitor, your computer must have a network card that supports promiscuous mode. If you are using Network Monitor Agent on a remote computer, the local workstation does not need a network adapter card that supports promiscuous mode, but the remote computer does. Promiscuous mode is a state in which a network adapter card captures all frames on a network, not just frames that are addressed to the card itself. This mode enables Network Monitor to capture and display all network traffic. **LANalyzer** is a complete monitoring and analysis tool for troubleshooting Novell networks. It monitors the network for anomalous events and can decode NetWare, SNA, TCP/IP, and AppleTalk traffic along with supporting Ethernet and Token Ring.

Figure 13.9
Protocol analyzer

 NOTE

Some products, such as Microsoft Network Monitor and Novell LANalyzer, are a combination of network monitors and network analyzers. They provide some of the same functions as protocol analyzers, but also are monitoring tools included with the operating system.

For information on the wide range of network monitoring products that have been developed, access one of these Web sites:

- *http://www.slac.stanford.edu/xorg/nmtf/nmtf-tools.html#nmp*

- *http://www.monitoring-software.net/network-monitoring-software.htm*

A **network analyzer**, also called a protocol analyzer, is a hardware-based tool that a network administrator connects to the network expressly to determine the nature of more complex network problems. This is usually a combination of hardware and software, which can test network cable for compliance to specified standards, troubleshooting cable problems, analyzing problems, and monitoring network health by capturing network traffic and creating reports and graphs from the data collected. These hardware and software combinations provide the most advanced network troubleshooting and are also the most expensive equipment available. See Figure 13.9 for an example.

A network or protocol analyzer decodes the various protocol layers in a frame. Then it presents them in a readable format, detailing which layer is involved—such as physical or data link—and what function each byte of data serves. Network analyzers such as sniffers decode problems at all seven OSI layers and can be identified automatically in real time, providing a clear view of network activity. Most network analyzers can perform many of the following functions:

- Filter traffic based on certain criteria—for example, all traffic to and from a particular device
- Present protocol layers in an easy-to-read format
- Generate frames and transmit them onto the network
- Timestamp captured data

Listed below are some of the most commonly known protocol analyzers:

- **Network General Corporation Sniffer:** Provides continuous monitoring to give you real-time network status updates.
- **WildPackets EtherPeek:** A software based protocol analyzer that offers both diagnostics and frame decoding in real time during capture.
- **Ethereal:** A free network protocol analyzer for Unix and Windows.

After you determine exactly the cause of your network problem, you have to determine how to fix the problem. In many cases, the solution may be obvious, such as replacing a bad cable or NIC. But in other cases additional solutions may be required. Remember that no one knows everything, but knowing where to look definitely helps. The next section will provide you with some resources that are readily available to help you search for the solution to your problems.

13.3   Accessing Key Information Resources

Where do you go when you don't know how to solve a problem? Earlier we mentioned that it is okay to ask other people for help. Even though many times our egos get in the way, there are knowledgeable people out there with more experience who can help us. They can be found in user groups and newsgroups. Besides other human beings, there are a myriad of resources you can use while troubleshooting network issues. They include online services, Web sites, subscription services, books, and magazines. We discuss the most commonly used methods in the following sections.

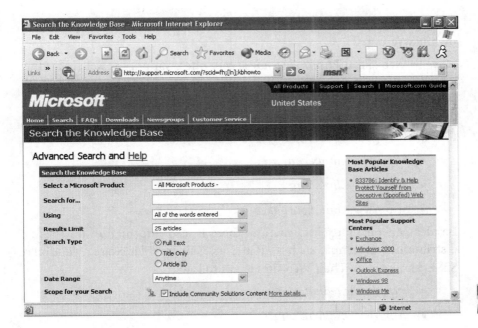

Figure 13.10
Microsoft Knowledge Base

13.3.1   Identifying Key Web Sites

One of the best places for troubleshooting a problem is the manufacturer's Web site. Because Microsoft has a large share of the market, we will first look at the information that is available at *http://www.microsoft.com*.

> **NOTE**
>
> Microsoft continually changes and updates its Web sites. At this time, you can access the Knowledge Base by going to *http://www.microsoft.com*, pointing to Support in the left pane, and selecting the Knowledge Base menu item. This may change in the future.

The Microsoft Knowledge Base, as shown in Figure 13.10, is a search engine that offers support for Microsoft products. From here, you can choose several options. To look up a topic, use the options in the Search the Knowledge Base area.

If your developers need help making their applications work with Microsoft products, they can access the Microsoft Developer's Network. This is not only a good place for developers, but as a network administrator you may find some very useful information when integrating applications or operating systems. Besides these resources, Microsoft also operates its own newsgroups.

Novell's Web site at *http://www.novell.com* offers support as well, including a knowledge base, newsgroups, support, and documentation. Just as with Microsoft and Novell, Linux has good Web site resources. Because there are so many different versions of Linux, we will start with some generic pages that can be a good source of information:

- *http://www.linux.com*
- *http://www.linux.org*
- *http://www.linuxjournal.com*

Besides general Linux information, there is also information on specific distributions of Linux, such as Red Hat, Caldera, Slackware, Mandrake, SuSE, and Debian. Their Web sites are as follows:

- *http://www.redhat.com*
- *http://www.caldera.com*
- *http://www.slackware.com*
- *http://www.mandrakelinux.com/en/*
- *http://www.suse.com/us/index.html*
- *http://www.debian.org*

Thus far, we have only discussed operating system manufacturers, but the same holds true for just about any computer, device, or application. For example, if you are having a problem with a video card that doesn't work properly in a specific type of computer, a good place to start is the Web site of the video card manufacturer or the computer manufacturer. Most sites provide troubleshooting information, suggest steps to resolve common problems, offer the latest updated drivers, and list phone numbers for technical support.

13.3.2   Identifying Support Services

In addition to Web sites, you can use subscription services to obtain a wealth of information. TechNet is one such service that is used for supporting all aspects of networking, with an emphasis on Microsoft products. It is updated via monthly CD-ROMs and can be accessed online. TechNet includes a searchable database of Microsoft articles and documentation on

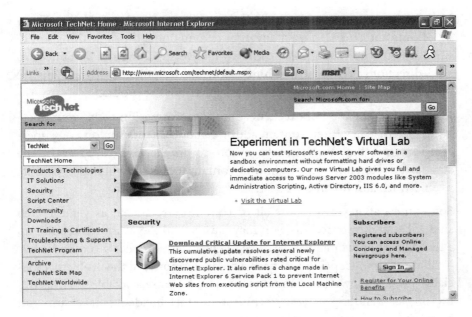

Figure 13.11
TechNet main screen

nearly all of the products, updated drivers, the most recent service packs, and beta copies of new releases and tutorials. Figure 13.11 shows the main TechNet screen at *http://www.microsoft.com/ technet/default.mspx.*

TIP

There is a very good chance that someone else has already had the same problem that you are having, and TechNet is likely to contain some documentation about how that person solved the problem.

The TechNet CDs contains a plethora of information for planning, maintaining, and troubleshooting Windows-based networks. You may find yourself using TechNet almost daily as a first line of defense for solving problems.

Vendor-provided CDs should also be one of the first places you look for information. They may contain a technical information base, with a number of known issues and their resolutions or workarounds. Many technicians overlook these CDs and spend countless hours troubleshooting on their own. You should at least look at the readme.txt file even before the product is installed, because usually the CD provides preinstallation tips and warnings that are critical for a smooth installation. Remember the students who spent two days trying to make a video card work with Linux?

Had they read the known issues before installation, they could have saved a lot of time and effort. Sadly, many of us end up doing the same thing sometime. It's our nature to think we know what we are doing and don't need to read directions. Vendor CDs should not be overlooked, whether you are planning to implement, support, or troubleshoot the product.

Resource kits are another excellent source of information about your operating system. They often contain additional documentation on your operating system that may have been too comprehensive to cover in the standard documentation. Often they contain tools that will make your life as a network administrator easier.

Sometimes, after you exhaust all of your resources such as vendor Web sites, CDs, and resource kits, you may have to call the vendor and open up a technical support incident to solve the problem. There is a good possibility that the support personnel have already encountered the problem, especially if it is a known issue and documented fixes are available. To improve the proper handling of your technical support incident, make sure you have the following information ready to assist the support department:

- The operating system you are running
- Service packs installed
- Version numbers of hardware and software
- Serial numbers
- Detailed account of the problem
- Troubleshooting steps attempted so far, and the results

WARNING Be careful opening a computer case and replacing the components on your own—this could void the warranty. Before opening up a computer, check the warranty information carefully.

13.3.3 Identifying Information Resources

Other excellent sources of information are periodicals and white papers. These documents provide valuable information on current as well as and new practices, products, and trends. These resources often can help guide you through procedures such as setting up VPNs or writing automated scripts. Many new magazines and periodicals are introduced each year, some of them dealing with specific computing environments such as Windows 2000 and Windows Server 2003 networks or Linux systems, while others may concentrate on hardware or networking. Often you will find that as a networking professional, you will be offered free subscriptions to some of these magazines.

Besides white papers and periodicals, don't forget to keep a couple of good reference books handy, especially when you first begin. Remember that no one knows all the answers, but it certainly helps to know where to look for them. In the next section we will discuss some of the more common network problems you will encounter and offer some suggested solutions.

13.4   Handling Common Sources of Trouble

Unfortunately, all problems won't be easy to fix, and for many you will have to do additional research and testing. But if you start with the basics, you are on your way to solving any network problem that occurs. Because networks are designed to move data from a transmitting device to a receiving device, if a device cannot communicate, you must determine why the data is not traveling as expected and then find a solution. The two most common causes for data not moving reliably are (1) physical connection breaks, such as the cable being unplugged or broken, or (2) a network device isn't working properly. Of course, always eliminate any potential user errors first. With that said, let's look at the one of the most common sources of problems, cabling and connections.

13.4.1   Physical Layer: Cables and Connections

The majority of networking problems occur at the Physical layer of the OSI model and include problems with cables, connectors, and NICs. Experienced network administrators know that cabling and connections are probably the most common source of network failures. For this reason, you should check cabling and connections first during your network troubleshooting process. Are all cables firmly connected, including the power cord and the network patch cable? Remember that IDE, floppy ribbon cables, network cables, and power cables can often become loose, especially when equipment is moved around. Ensure that the microprocessor, memory modules, and video and sound cards are inserted correctly and didn't unseat during transportation. If the equipment was not moved, reach around and unhook the network cable, and reconnect it into the ports on both ends. This may seem trivial, but it is important. Speaking from experience, users do some strange things with their network cables:

- There is the case of the vice president who was having difficulty connecting to the network. He blamed the technician because the operating system had recently been upgraded. Come to find out, the vice president had plugged in his network cable upside down!

- A user moved his PC so he could have a better view. This presented a problem with the cable because it had to run across the floor. The user kept running over the cable with his chair, so he decided to run the cable underneath the chair mat, which had large spikes in it to grip it to the carpet. What do you think happened?

Most often, cable that is damaged is cable that runs from the workstation to the wall jack. This cable receives the most mistreatment. Sometimes you can fix the problem by simply plugging the cable back in, or plugging it back in properly. If you have determined that a cable may be the cause of a network-related problem, the next logical step is to test this theory by replacing the cable with a known good cable. You will have one of two results: (1) If the machine can access the network again, then the old cable was bad. (2) Or, if you still cannot communicate, you need to continue troubleshooting or find another cable to test. Devices are available to determine whether cables have gone bad, such as those we discussed earlier in the chapter. But these devices can be expensive, so you can simply swap out the cables to determine whether a cable is bad.

After you have a known good cable in place, if the machine still doesn't work, you may want to swap network jacks: If the machine is close enough or can be moved easily to another active network jack, try plugging the malfunctioning machine into the second network jack. If the machine works in the second jack, then there is a network problem with the first jack. If the machine doesn't work with a different network jack, it's time to look at the link lights. Link lights are a good indicator in determining whether a network connection is present. A link light is a green or amber LED on the networking device that lights up if it detects a network connection. Most network devices, such as routers, hubs, and network cards, are equipped with link lights. Most network cards have two lights: a link light used to indicate the connection, and a light that displays the current activity of the network card, which goes off and on as data is transferred to and from the computer or device. If the link light on the device determines that a network connection is present, then it's time to move on and look at TCP/IP configurations by using PING.

13.4.2 Power Problems

Power problems will arise in various ways. One of the most obvious is when power strips are daisy-chained together. Many times the devices will not get enough power. The other end of the spectrum is that this will occasionally trip the circuit breakers or start a fire. Be aware that power problems can burn out equipment. For example, in several cubicles the flow of power was not regulated by a line conditioner or surge protector. One day, a cloud of smoke emerged from the center of the room and the motherboards in eight computers and eight modems were burned out. If power is not properly conditioned, it can have devastating effects on equipment. Let's look at some of the power variations that can occur, and then discuss how we can protect our network in the event that these conditions occur:

- **Noise:** Also referred to as electromagnetic interference (EMI) and radio frequency interference (RFI), **noise** can be caused by lightning, load switching, generators, radio transmitters, and industrial equipment. It can cause glitches and errors in executable programs and data files.

- **Spikes:** These are instantaneous, dramatic increases in voltage that result from lightning strikes or when electrical loads are switched on or off. **Spikes** can destroy electronic circuitry and corrupt stored data.

- **Surges and overvoltages:** These are short-term increases in voltage that are commonly caused by large electrical load changes and from utility power line switching. A **surge** can seriously damage electrical equipment.

- **Sags and brownouts:** These are short-term decreases in voltage levels that commonly occur when motors are started up or by faults on the utility power system. You may experience a **sag**, or brownout, if your facility is located near another one that requires large sources of power, such as a professional ballpark. They can cause malfunctions or sudden shutdowns in computer or process control equipment.

- **Blackouts:** These are caused by faults on the utility power system and refer to a complete loss of utility power. If you live in California, you may have experienced **rolling blackouts**. Rolling blackouts occur when the utility company turns off the power in a specific area. Power is turned back on in about an hour and then the power is shut off in another area. This process continues until the amount of surplus electricity begins to exceed the demand.

How then do you protect your environment from such damaging fluctuations in power? Always connect your sensitive electronic equipment to power conditioners, surge protectors, or, for the best protection, an **uninterruptible power supply (UPS)**. This is a power supply that sits between the wall power and the computer. In the event of power failure at the wall, the UPS takes over and powers the computer so that you can take action, such as saving your work or shut down your servers without data loss.

Three different types of devices are classified as UPSs:

- **Standby power supply (SPS):** This is also referred to as an "offline" UPS. In this type of supply, power is usually derived directly from the power line, until power fails. After a power failure, a battery-powered inverter turns on to continue supplying power. Batteries are charged, as necessary, when line power is available.

- **Hybrid or ferroresonant UPS systems:** This device conditions power using a ferroresonant transformer. This transformer maintains a constant output voltage even with a varying input voltage and provides good protection against line noise. The transformer also maintains output on its secondary power source (battery) briefly when a total outage occurs.

- **Continuous UPS:** This is also called an "online" UPS. In this type of system the computer is always running off of battery power and the battery is continuously being recharged. There is no switchover time, and these supplies generally provide the best protection from power line problems.

! WARNING

Never plug a printer into a UPS. Printers use large amounts of power and will drain the battery quickly. The purpose of having a UPS is to have enough time to properly shut down equipment before damage is caused.

Even if you always connect your sensitive electronic equipment to power conditioners, surge protectors, or a UPS, power problems cannot be eliminated, but the damage they cause can be minimized or possibly prevented.

13.4.3   Reversing Recent Changes

If you are running a Microsoft operating system, you may have connected to the Internet only to be taken to Microsoft's site to update your software. Technology is constantly changing and so is software. This means you will have to upgrade both of these on a regular basis. So you upgrade your system or apply a service pack, and now you find that one of the custom applications you use doesn't work properly. Now what?

If a software upgrade causes a problem on the system even though you tested the upgrade before deploying it on your production network, you should be prepared to roll back or reverse the process. This process is also referred to as **backleveling**. Most often the best source of help when a problem occurs is the manufacturer's documentation. Quite often, patches, client software, and applications will have an uninstall utility that will put the system back to where it was, but not always. For example, Windows XP has a system restore feature that can be used to revert your system to its state prior to the problem, whereas MSN cannot be rolled back, as you must uninstall the current version and then reinstall the old version. As for server operating systems, before you upgrade, make a complete backup and then restore the entire system from backup if necessary.

As with software, you will also have to provide for a backup plan in the event that a hardware upgrade doesn't go as planned. It is important not to discard the old device in case the upgrade causes problems. This applies to the drivers that may be necessary as well. It is much easier to swap the hardware back out and then do some additional research into why the device is not working properly. The Windows XP operating system provides for driver rollbacks, but not all operating systems do. So, as always, it is important to have a backup plan in case things don't go the way they should.

13.4.4   Fixing Performance Problems

With the rapid growth and implementation of technology, performance management becomes increasingly challenging. Due to the ever-growing demand for powerful applications and expanding data-processing networks, the complexity of network topology and communication equipment becomes more and more sophisticated. Performance management, as well as response time management, becomes more difficult. If you have been properly monitoring your network and keeping up with growth, you should be able to manage performance in a timely manner, but sometimes you will find that for an unknown reason the network performance begins to suffer. Here are some avenues to consider when there are problems with performance:

- Change is the biggest factor that can cause poor network performance. So the first question to ask is "what has changed?"

- Another big factor that affects network performance is playing games or downloading music and movie files. Check whether any of the users are involved in these types of activities.

- Sometimes applications have memory leaks, or a new version may be bloated or have an improperly programmed query function that may cause performance problems.

- Adding new electrical equipment may have a negative effect on the network, especially if the electrical equipment is close to network equipment, because it can generate interference.

- Adding new hardware, such as additional servers or workstations, may cause performance to decrease.

- Other changes in workload or workplace behavior, including adding more users, could affect performance.

Because we often stretch our networks to their limits, you may want to consider expanding your network by implementing devices such as additional switches and routers or upgrading the backbone to increase the capacity the network can handle before it becomes a bigger issue. Remember that serious networking problems can sometimes begin as performance problems. Addressing performance problems as they occur will help prevent larger network issues down in road.

13.5 Chapter Summary

- The goal of security is expressed in terms of confidentiality, integrity, and availability. These goals can be achieved through creating hardware and software standards. When establishing standards for hardware and software, desktop systems should be included. You must also define and document standards for new server installations along with guidelines for current server configurations.

- Changes can have serious consequences on the productivity of the users and the network. If not done properly, the system can be exposed to corruption or data deletion during changes. Planning and testing eliminates the vast majority of these types of problems, and sufficient time must be spent to ensure that the transition and implementation go as smoothly as possible. Changes should be scheduled during off hours, if possible, or only after extensive testing.

- You cannot instantly resolve every problem that exists. You can, however, learn a methodology to find and diagnose nearly every problem in a systematic and logical manner. The first step is to determine the scope of the problem by identifying the symptoms. After the scope is determined, the priority can be set. The next step is to collect specific information about the problem at hand. Finally, begin to isolate the problem by testing each of the causes, starting with the most obvious first.

- Connectivity problems can occur when a workstation cannot communicate with its own devices or other devices. On LANs or WANs, connectivity problems can include loss of connectivity, intermittent connectivity, and timeout problems.

- Many networking problems occur at the lower layers of the OSI model where it is better to use diagnostic tools for troubleshooting. Some of the most common tools are crossover cables, volt-ohm meters or digital voltmeters, cable testers, time domain reflectometers, and oscilloscopes.

- Besides hardware tools, your toolkit should also contain tools such as network monitors, protocol analyzers, and connectivity utilities so you can monitor traffic on the network and display the packets that have been transmitted across the network, if necessary. Connectivity utilities such as PING, Netstat, Nbtstat, and Traceroute

(Tracert) are very useful in figuring out where a connectivity problem lies.

- Help can be found by contacting others in user groups and newsgroups. A large variety of resources are available for use while troubleshooting network issues, including online services, Web sites, subscription services, books, and magazines.

- If power is not properly conditioned, it can have devastating effects on equipment. Always connect your sensitive equipment to power conditioners, surge protectors, or a UPS. Although this will not eliminate power problems, it can minimize or possibly prevent damage to components and equipment.

13.6   Key Terms

auditing: The process of tracking users and their actions, and other events, on a network.

backleveling: The process used to roll back or reverse an upgrade or change.

blackouts: Caused by faults on the utility power system, they are a complete loss of utility power.

cable checker: Device that determines whether your cabling can provide physical connectivity.

cable tester: Device that determines whether your cabling can provide physical connectivity. Operates at higher layers of the OSI model and provides more detailed information than a cable checker.

crossover cable: Cable that looks just like a twisted-pair cable, but with two wires crossed, making the cable able to directly connect two machines without using additional equipment.

LANalyzer: A complete monitoring and analysis tool for troubleshooting Novell networks. It monitors the network for anomalous events and can decode and support various protocols.

loopback adapter: A way to test the ports on a system without having to connect to an external device.

network analyzer: Also called a protocol analyzer, a hardware-based tool that a network administrator connects to the network expressly to determine the nature of more complex network problems.

noise: Also referred to as EMI and RFI, it can be caused by lightning, load switching, generators, radio transmitters, and industrial equipment.

optical time domain reflectometer (OTDR): An advanced diagnostic tool for optical fibers that allows you to take a snapshot of a fiber link and can accurately measure various statistics.

oscilloscope: An instrument that can determine when there are shorts, crimps, or attenuation in the cable. It displays its output in a graphical format.

sags: Short-term decreases in voltage levels that commonly occur when motors are started up or by faults on the utility power system.

spikes: Instantaneous, dramatic increases in voltage that result from lightning strikes or when electrical loads are switched on or off.

surges: Short-term increases in voltage that are commonly caused by large electrical load changes and from utility power line switching.

time domain reflectometer (TDR): A device that bounces a signal off the end of the cable. It sends a signal down the cable, which at some point it is reflected back.

tone generator: A device used to perform tests on phone and network lines to help aid in the identification of wires during the wire-tracing process.

uninterruptible power supply (UPS): A device that sits between the wall power and the computer that, in the event of power failure, takes over and powers the computer.

volt-ohm meter or **voltmeter:** A device used to check physical connectivity or to determine whether the cable is intact by measuring AC and DC voltage, current, resistance, capacity, and cable continuity.

13.7   Challenge Questions

13.1 What type of UPS continually uses its battery to supply a connected device with power?

   a. Continuous

   b. Standby

   c. Hybrid

   d. Dual purpose

13.2 Which of the following is the best way to reverse a server operating system upgrade?

a. Delete any new folders created by the upgrade.

b. Restore from backup.

c. Reinstall the operating system.

d. Use the rollback feature.

13.3 Which of the following will have the least effect on network availability?

a. Adding a switch

b. Adding a user account to the server

c. Adding a router

d. Adding AC ductwork and power to the server room

13.4 Which of the following best describes baselining?

a. Network monitoring

b. The process of burning in a server

c. Measuring normal network behavior

d. Reversing a server operating system upgrade

13.5 Which of the following are power problems that can affect the network? (Choose all that apply.)

a. Spikes

b. Turning on the radio

c. Blackouts

d. Turning off a computer

13.6 When upgrading a NIC in the server, what should you have on hand? (Choose all that apply.)

a. The old NIC

b. A list of all employee contact information

c. The server documentation

d. The driver for the old NIC

13.7 Which of the following is not a tool for testing lower-layer connectivity?

  a. A cable tester

  b. A volt-ohm meter

  c. Traceroute

  d. An oscilloscope

13.8 _____ is an Application layer protocol that is used to exchange management information between network devices.

13.9 Reversing a software upgrade is also known as

  _____.

13.10 A(n) _____ is an advanced diagnostic tool that allows you to take a snapshot of an optical fiber link and can accurately measure various statistics.

13.11 The majority of networking problems occur at the _____ layer of the OSI model and include problems with cables, connectors, and NICs.

13.12 Why is documentation important?

13.13 Why is a rollback strategy needed when you upgrade components or applications?

13.14 Name three factors that should be taken into consideration when developing a change management policy.

13.15 To improve the handling of your technical support incident, list the information you should have ready to assist the support department.

13.8   Challenge Exercises

Challenge Exercise 13.1

In this exercise, you download and install Microsoft Baseline Security Analyzer (MBSA). You need a computer with Internet access to download the analyzer and a computer running Windows 2000 Server to run the analyzer.

  13.1 Log on to your computer.

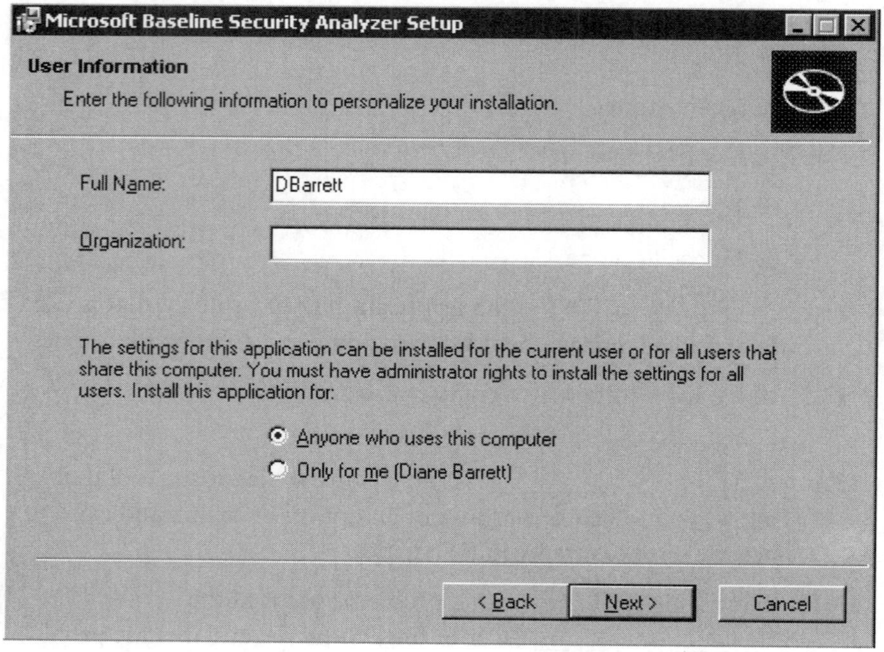

Figure 13.12

MBSA user information

13.2 Open an Internet connection.

13.3 Go to *http://www.microsoft.com/technet/treeview/default.asp?url=/ technet/security/tools/mbsahome.asp* and download the analyzer.

13.4 Run the setup program, accept the license agreement, and then click **Next**.

13.5 Enter the appropriate user, company information, and which users you want to be able to run the program, as shown in Figure 13.12. Click **Next**.

13.6 Choose the destination folder for the installation, and then click **Next**.

13.7 Choose the install options. (They should all be checked by default.) This will place a shortcut on the desktop, and open the readme.txt file and the application when the installation is complete.

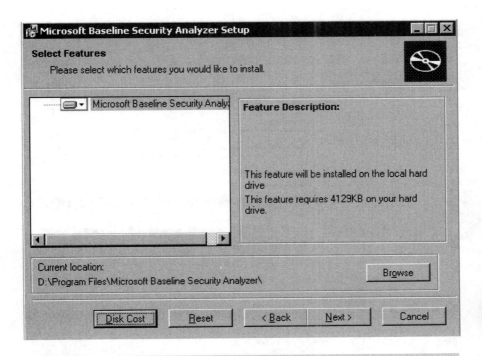

Figure 13.13
MBSA feature selection

13.8   Select the features as shown in Figure 13.13. Click **Next** twice and then click **Finish**.

13.9   The readme file should now be displayed on the screen. Read it so you understand what the analyzer does.

13.10   Start the application by clicking the desktop icon.

13.11   Choose **Scan a computer**. Your computer name should automatically appear in the top drop-down box on the right side of the screen. If not, enter it or the IP address in the next line.

13.12   Move down to the bottom of the screen and choose **Start scan**.

13.13   After the scan runs, you will have a screen that looks similar to Figure 13.14.

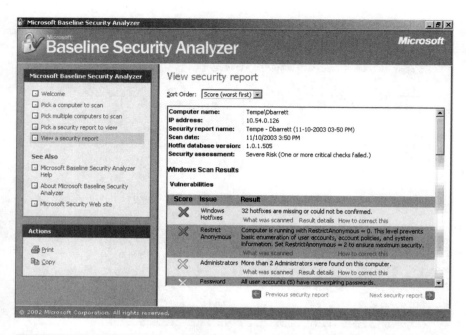

Figure 13.14

View security report

13.14 As you can see from the results, the computer that was scanned is a severe security risk. How well did your machine do?

Challenge Exercise 13.2

In this exercise, you learn to troubleshoot using the traceroute and ping commands. You need a computer running a Windows-based operating system, TCP/IP installed, a gateway, and Internet access.

13.1 Log on to your computer.

13.2 To open a command line window, click **Start**, click **Run**, type **cmd** in the Open text box, and click **OK**. At the command prompt, type **ipconfig /all**, and press **Enter**. Record your IP address, subnet mask, and default gateway or the DNS server address.

13.3 At the command prompt, type **ping 127.0.0.1**, and press **Enter**. Do you get a response? Unplug your network cable, retype **ping 127.0.0.1**, and press **Enter**. What happens? Why?

13.4 Plug your network cable back in. At the command prompt, ping the address of another computer in the room. What happens? Unplug your network cable and ping the same address. What happens? Why?

13.5 Plug the network cable back in. At the command prompt, ping the address of the gateway or DNS server. What happens?

13.6 At the command prompt, type **ping www.microsoft.com**. What happens? Write down the IP address displayed on the screen.

13.7 At the command prompt, type **tracert www.microsoft.com**. How many hops did it take to reach the destination?

13.8 Look at the last address where the tracert stops. Why might this address be different than the one you wrote down from the ping to the same address?

Challenge Exercise 13.3

In this exercise, you document the current network configuration. You need drawing software, such as Visio, or a pencil and paper. Your instructor should also have arranged for you to tour the network room.

13.1 Draw the configuration of the classroom.

13.2 After you are finished, tour the network room.

13.3 Take your pencil and paper and make notes about the configuration. Ask the administrator about policies for the users such as passwords, security, and so forth, and about topology.

13.4 When you get back to the classroom, make a rough draft of the network layout and include standards and policies.

13.5 Make a list of the documentation that a network administrator should have handy.

Challenge Exercise 13.4

In this exercise, you use a digital volt-ohm meter to test the voltage on a battery. You need a volt-ohm meter and a AA, C, or D battery.

13.1 Insert the black test lead in the hole marked Ground on the meter. Depending on the meter, it might be marked Common Com, Gnd, or "-".

13.2 Insert the red test lead in the hole marked Pos. Depending on the meter, it might be marked Volts, V, or "+". (Some meters have multiple holes for the red lead, so be sure you use the one for volts.)

13.3 Turn the dial to the DC Volts section. There are multiple voltage ranges available in this section. The battery will have a voltage of 1.25 volts. Find the closest voltage greater than 1.25 volts.

13.4 Hold the black lead to the negative terminal of the battery and the red lead to the positive terminal. You should be able to get a reading close to 1.25 volts off the meter. (It is important that you hook the leads up properly. The black lead goes to negative and the red lead goes to positive.)

Challenge Exercise 13.5

In this exercise, you install SNMP to help monitor the network. You need a computer running Windows 2000 Server.

13.1 Log on to your computer.

13.2 Click **Start**, point to **Settings**, and then click **Control Panel**.

13.3 Double-click the **Add/Remove Programs**.

13.4 Click the **Add/Remove Windows Components** option.

13.5 Highlight **Management and Monitoring Tools**, click the **Details** button, and then select **Simple Network Management Protocol** as shown in Figure 13.15.

13.6 Click **OK**, click **Next**, click **Finish**, and then click **Close**. Close any open windows. Now that the SNMP service is installed, we will configure it.

13.7 Click **Start**, point to **Programs**, point to **Administrative Tools**, and then click **Computer Management**.

13.8 In the details pane, expand **Services and Applications**. Scroll down to and click **SNMP Service**.

13.9 On the Action menu, click **Properties**.

13.10 On the Agent tab in Contact, type the name of the user or administrator for the computer.

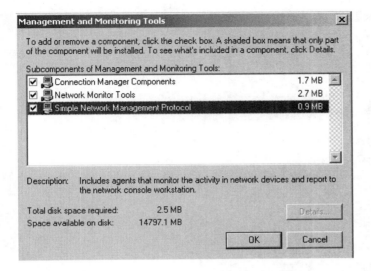

Figure 13.15

Subcomponents of Management and Monitoring Tools

13.11 In Location, type the physical location of the computer, as shown in Figure 13.16.

13.12 Under Service, select the appropriate check boxes for this computer, and then click **OK**.

13.13 Click the **Traps** tab. The screen shown in Figure 13.17 appears. This tab contains the names of SNMP communities and where to report events.

13.14 Browse the rest of the tabs to become familiar with the interface.

Challenge Exercise 13.6

In this exercise, you start to develop your own method of troubleshooting based on what you learned in this chapter. You will create a situation and then troubleshoot it with a partner.

13.1 Ask your partner to leave the room.

13.2 Unplug the cable from the network card on the back of the computer. Put it back in the jack, but not completely. It should have the appearance of being connected properly even though it isn't.

13.3 Reboot the computer.

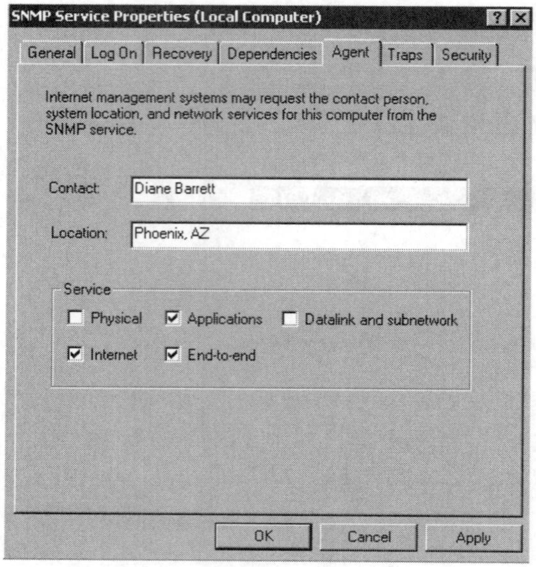

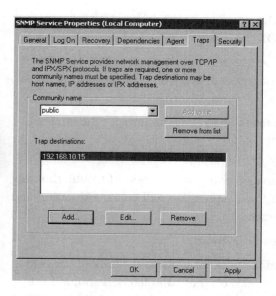

Figure 13.16
SNMP Service Properties Agent tab

Figure 13.17
SNMP Service Properties Traps tab

13.4   Allow your partner to reenter the room. Explain that you are having problems connecting to the network and ask him or her to help you figure out what is wrong. By following a logical process, the problem should be solved relatively quickly.

13.9   Challenge Scenarios

Challenge Scenario 13.1

You have a client who has added eight new workstations. When the workstations were set up, you were part of the process and verified that they all were set up correctly for network and Internet connectivity. Several weeks have passed since the workstations were added, and the owner calls to inform you that the network has become very slow. It is taking a long time to open some applications, and network access to the Internet has become extremely slow. You make an appointment to look at the problem the next day. Besides the information from the owner, you know that the company uses several Web-based applications. When you get to the work site, what steps should you take to troubleshoot the issue?

Challenge Scenario 13.2

Just as you are about finished resolving the issue from the last scenario, one of the users reports that he can't print. You know that several users have their own printers, there are two network printers, and some of the HR and administrative staff have two printers—one laser and one color printer. What questions should you ask the user before you go to the printer?

Challenge Scenario 13.3

You recently were hired as a network administrator for a small manufacturing company. Originally you were unable to get into the servers because the last network administrator left without giving notice and no one had the password to the server. You also do not know what applications are running on the network or how many licenses are available for each application because there is no documentation. You have decided that your first priority is to have proper documentation. You will formulate a plan to ensure that anyone hired after you will not be left in the same situation that you were. What would you say to management to convince them this is a necessary process? What would be included in your documentation plan?

Challenge Scenario 13.4

Now that you have proper documentation for the network, you decide that it is time to standardize the desktops. You have been discussing this with some of the users. However, they don't like the idea one bit. You know that not having workstation consistency is one of the areas that can attract the most problems for a network administrator. Present a good case for and cite reasons why the workstations should be standardized.

APPENDIX A

Online Networking Resources

This appendix offers an array of networking-related resources available on the Web as of this writing. Should you encounter a problem with a URL (such as the dreaded 404: Not Found error message), open your favorite search engine and search for the appropriate terms. You might find an even better source of information!

A.1 General Networking Information and Support

- Microsoft Knowledge Base: *http://www.Microsoft.com/*. Point to Support in the left pane and then select Knowledge Base. You can search for support information on nearly every Microsoft product offered.

- Microsoft TechNet: *http://www.microsoft.com/technet/default.mspx*. An online version of the popular CD/DVD subscription, TechNet offers general support information for Microsoft products, security updates, patches, hotfixes, white papers, and much more.

- Novell: *http://www.novell.com*. Click the Support link to access Novell's knowledge base, patches and fixes, support forums, documentation, and downloads.

- Linux.com: *http://www.linux.com*; LinuxOnline: *http://www.linux.org*; Linux Journal: *http://www.linuxjournal.com*. These preceding

Linux URLs offer general information and support for Linux distributions, such as Red Hat, Caldera, Slackware, Mandrake, Debian, and SuSE.

- Cisco: *http://www.cisco.com*. Click the Technical Support link and choose from several networking-related categories of support that include hardware, software, technology, tools and utilities, and the software center.

A.2   General Protocol Information

- Protocol Directory: *http://www.protocols.com/pbook/toc.htm*. Protocols.com offers information on many types of networking protocols, and pin assignments for physical interfaces. Be sure to check out the TCP/IP Suite link for a list of protocols for each layer of the OSI model, and a protocol route map.

- ASL Protocol Decodes: *http://www.decodes.co.uk/content/chart.htm*. Here you'll find a protocol decode chart that lists the layers of the OSI model with the associated protocols that exist at each layer, along with the layer boundaries. You can view the chart online or download the file (in Microsoft Publisher format).

- Computer Networking and Internet Protocols: A Comprehensive Introduction: *http://www.cis.ohio-state.edu/cs/Services/index.html*. Visit this site for information on GNU, Internet RFCs, and Internet Engineering Notes (EINs).

A.3   Security

A.3.1   Best Practices

Each of the following sites provides information on best practices.

- *http://csrc.nist.gov/fasp/*
- *http://www.cert.org/security-improvement/*

- *http://www.sans.org/rr/*
- *http://www.securityfocus.com*

A.3.2   IP Security

- Computer Security FAQs: *www.faqs.org/faqs/computer-security/*. This is one of the best resources for IP security-related FAQs.

- SysAdmin, Audit, Network, Security (SANS) Institute: *www.sans. org.* SANS provides, by far, some of the best security training and information. It offers a weekly vulnerability digest and weekly news digest, access to the Internet's early warning system (Internet Storm Center), flash security alerts, and research papers.

A.3.3   Certificates and Encryption

- RSA Security: *http://www.rsasecurity.com.* RSA Security owns a digital signature authentication system that uses the Rivest-Shamir-Adleman algorithm. It is often included as part of Web browsers and various other software products.

- VeriSign: *http://www.verisign.com.* This is a popular certificate and registration authority. You can use VeriSign to issue certificates for secure Web site connections.

A.3.4   Password-Revealing Programs

- Openwall Project: *http://www.openwall.com/.* Openwall offers several password-revealing programs, such as WASP and John the Ripper.

A.3.5   Wireless LANS

- Wireless LANS: *http://www.wlana.org/security.htm.* This site offers links to several white papers that focus on WLAN security.

A.4 Requests for Comments (RFCs)

- Internet FAQs Archive: *http://www.faqs.org/rfcs/.* This site offers a search engine for Internet RFCs. We've found it to be an up-to-date depository.

- Internet Engineering Task Force: *http://www.ietf.org.* A must-visit site for all things networking. Be sure to check out the RFC Pages link in addition to the Overview of the IETF link.

A.5 IP Addressing, Subnetting, and Supernetting

- Understanding IP Addressing: Everything You Ever Wanted To Know: *http://www.3com.com/other/pdfs/infra/corpinfo/en_US/ 501302.pdf.* Chuck Semeria's paper offers comprehensive information on every part of IP addressing.

- IPv6: *http://www.ipv6.com;* IPv6 Forum: *www.ipv6forum.com/.* Both IPv6 sites offer the latest information on the development and pending deployment of IPv6.

A.6 Binary Arithmetic Overviews

- Binary Arithmetic: *http://www.freesoft.org/CIE/Topics/19.htm.* This article, from the "Connected: An Internet Encyclopedia" site, offers easy-to-understand illustrations that help the reader grasp binary arithmetic.

A.7 DHCP and DNS

- DHCP Resources: *http://www.dhcp.org/.* Ralph Droms offers outstanding DHCP resources and links to additional sources of information.

- DNS Resources Directory: *http://www.dns.net/dnsrd.* Need to brush up on DNS, or just get a handle on what it's really about? András Salamon shares information on nearly every DNS-related topic imagineable.

A.8　Routing and Switching

- Circuit Switching: *http://jhunix.hcf.jhu.edu/~tnaugler/770.512/Common_files/CircuitSwitching/CircuitSwitching.htm.* Thomas Naugler offers a fully illustrated primer on circuit switching, with additional Web references.

- Packet Switching Demo: *http://www.pbs.org/opb/nerds2.0.1/geek_glossary/packet_switching_flash.html.* This PBS Flash tutorial walks you through the basics of packet switching.

A.9　SNMP

- SNMPWorld.com: *www.snmpworld.com/.* You can find links, tools, RFCs, MIBs, and more at this SNMP-focused site.

APPENDIX B

Networking Standards

For networks to function properly, an amazing array of devices and technologies must all work well together. From the networking cables or media, to the hardware necessary to connect computers and other devices to such media, to the protocols and communication formats that give networks shared capabilities to get things done, ingenuity and technology are essential to coordinate all the required components.

A vast collection of networking standards and specifications explains how all of these pieces and parts can be successfully—and easily—assembled into working networks. The key to this is interoperability: the ability of devices of the same kind and capability to work with one another, even if made by different manufacturers in different parts of the world. At each layer of the OSI network reference model, which is covered in Chapter 2, network standards exist to ensure interoperability. From specifying common cable types and connectors (so that plugs fit network interfaces) to establishing common network protocols, such as HTTP for Web access and SMTP for e-mail access, various networking standards make it possible to plug different parts together and get them to work.

Standards help establish common sets of implementation guidelines, connectivity and behavioral specifications, message formats, error-handling requirements, and so forth, that create comprehensive sets of rules that make interoperability possible. Some standards even supply batteries of tests that implementers or manufacturers must use to demonstrate compliance with standards. Likewise, as new technologies are developed, participants hold regular "bake-offs" to provide ample opportunities to make sure that different implementations can and do indeed work together as required and desired. In the following sections, you'll find information about key networking standards that apply at various levels of the OSI network reference model and links where you can find more information.

B.1   Making Standards Happen

Before we present and examine various key networking standards, it's important to understand the processes whereby standards are made. Virtually all standards emerge from various committees of multiple individuals, such as working groups, special interest groups, and task forces from business, industry, academia, government, and other groups with particular agendas and investments to protect. Creating standards involves considering various points of view and looking for workable compromises and sometimes even alternative implementations that satisfy all parties involved equally.

In general, the process of creating a standard works like this:

- Standards are built by standards organizations, industry or trade associations, consortia, or other groups, which recruit assistance from volunteers and staff to document and maintain individual standards documents. Many such organizations have only a small number of paid staff who oversee ongoing efforts, but rely on support from interested parties to provide the manpower necessary to research, craft, and maintain standards and specifications.

- Oversight committees and/or members of the parent organization generate ideas for potential standards. Often, individuals who represent third parties that share common interests or avocations form groups to deal with specific networking-related technologies or issues to drive activity in specific areas.

- Within communities focused on special interests, working groups form to deal with specific topics, issues, or technologies. Such groups are usually run by a chairperson and staffed by volunteer members who share the workload involved in defining problems and crafting standards to address them.

- Starting with whatever ideas, prototypes, and existing allegiances members may bring to the working group, such groups work to build consensus around the problems a standard seeks to address and how it attempts to resolve them. Given sufficient time (often months to years), numerous proposals are drafted. The proposals are debated and amended until consensus is reached or efforts are abandoned, as sometimes happens when consensus fails to emerge. Internet standards, for example, aim at something called "rough consensus," which means that the majority of the working group backs a proposal and that dissenters are willing to play along.

- Once the working group agrees that its draft standard proposal is ready for outside review, the group turns the proposal over to the parent organization. There it's subjected to wider review and comment within a special interest group or technical team. It is then returned to the working group for further work, as needed. A draft proposal typically goes through several iterations in this phase, which normally takes between three and 12 months to complete.

- Finally, the special interest group turns the draft standard over to a higher-level parent group, often a standards committee, which provides an additional level of review and feedback. Then it is brought to the organization's membership for comment and discussion. If accepted, this final stage results in creation of an official standard. However, the draft may be rejected outright. This step can take from three to six months to complete.

- Once accepted and finalized, official standards are published in printed and/or electronic format. As such, they will often be subjected to formal editing procedures, in much the same way that manuscripts are readied for publication. Depending on length and complexity, this process takes between one and six months to complete.

- After publication, official standards must be reviewed regularly and updated or amended to keep up with changing times and technologie. An official author or technical editor is generally appointed to take stewardship of a standard; this person oversees the post-publication maintenance work. Reviews typically occur once or twice a year, unless the parent organization or its membership calls for an interim review earlier. Given their frequency, this process seldom takes more than a month or two to complete.

- Standards that are not superceded outright by updated versions are often declared obsolete. The newer version may be a revision of the original standard or an entirely new (but similar) standard taking into account new technology, protocols, or services. In any event, once a standard is made obsolete, another standard is invariably used in its place.

Creating standards, and especially achieving consensus, takes time and involves a lot of effort, discussion, and compromise. This explains why proprietary protocols and technologies so often come and go while related standards may still be under development. This creates an important dynamic between open, standard implementations and specifications and closed, proprietary ones: In many important ways, each of them helps to keep the other honest. Proprietary technologies and protocols help keep pressure on standards groups to finish up before their standards become passé; standards groups help make sure that proprietary solutions meet general market needs by specifying minimal accepted features and functions (which proprietary implementations usually seek to exceed rather than simply to meet).

Within the networking world, thousands of trade groups, professional societies and associations, standards bodies, and industry consortia exert considerable influence. In the following section, we provide a short but select list of those groups and bodies most deeply involved in and responsible for the state of networking as it exists today.

B.2 Key Standards Organizations

Networking standards come in many forms and from many kinds of organizations. Some are specifically international or global in scope (the International Organization for Standardization, or ISO, is a good example). Others focus only on particular countries or regions of the world, such as Underwriters Laboratories, which warrants electrical and electronic equipment for North American markets.

Standards organizations also tend to have specific areas of interest or focus: some concentrate on networking media, others on networking devices and technologies, and still others on networking protocols, services, and communications. IT professionals or those simply interested in networking should be familiar with the major networking standards organizations. The Computer and Communication Web site at *http://www.cmpcmm.com/cc/ standards.html* has one of the best overall lists of general networking-related standards that we've found. Be sure to visit it for a broader view of such organizations than we can cover in this appendix.

Here are our picks for key standards organizations related to networking:

- American National Standards Institute (ANSI)
- Electronic Industries Alliance (EIA)
- International Electrotechnical Commission (IEC)
- International Telecommunication Union-Telecommunication Standardization Sector (ITU-T)
- Internet Society (ISOC)
- Institute of Electrical and Electronics Engineers (IEEE)
- International Organization for Standardization (ISO)
- Telecommunications Industry Association (TIA)
- World Wide Web Consortium (W3C)

We'll review the areas of focus and coverage for each of these organizations, followed by information about resources for other networking technology and standards.

B.2.1 American National Standards Institute (ANSI)

Simply put, ANSI is involved in the development of technology standards in the United States. Although ANSI is an American organization, it exerts influence worldwide: the United States has been a technology leader in so many areas that its standards lead the rest of the world. In fact, this organization has created more than 10,000 standards. Also, although its primary areas of focus are networking technologies, programming languages, and communications techniques and methods, ANSI also acts as the American representative to the ISO, the ITU-T, and the IEC, all of which are discussed elsewhere in this appendix.

Well-known ANSI programming languages include C, COBOL, FORTRAN, and ANSI Standard SQL (Structured Query Language), a standard variant of the well-known database query language SQL. ANSI standards for networking technologies include joint efforts with the IEEE on various aspects of the 802 networking standards for Token Ring (802.5) and Ethernet (802.3 and others), as well as on FDDI and SONET. Communication standards include standards for voice and data transmission, encryption and privacy, and numerous types of signaling controls and technologies. To learn more about ANSI, visit the organization's Web site at *http://www.ansi.org*.

B.2.2 Electronic Industries Alliance (EIA)

Based in Arlington, Virginia, the EIA is a national trade organization that represents more than 2,500 members, mostly manufacturers who work in the electronics industry in the United States. The EIA represents its members on issues that are relevant to implementing successful technologies; its current focuses include broadband and Internet security. The EIA also works with other industry groups, including the TIA, to develop various recommended standards for electronics equipment and communications. EIA standard designations take two forms:

- RS-nnn, where RS stands for "recommended standard" and nnn is a three-digit sequence number

- EIA-nnn, where the same number is used but the standard designation is assumed

A well-known EIA standard is the RS-232C standard, which was originally approved in 1987. Although it's still most commonly known as RS-232, this standard was advanced to EIA/TIA-232-E in 1991, and remains the most common standard for serial communications. (The TIA was a joint sponsor for this standard; see the discussion of the TIA elsewhere in this appendix.) The EIA has defined newer standards for serial communications known as RS-422, RS-423, and RS-449 that offer faster data transfer and superior immunity to electrical interference. To learn more about the EIA and related standards, visit *http://www.eia.org*.

B.2.3 International Electrotechnical Commission (IEC)

The IEC is a Swiss-based, global organization that creates and publishes international standards for electronic, electrical, and related technologies. The organization's charter addresses all forms of electronics, including electronic circuitry and devices, magnetics and electromagnetics, electro-acoustics, multimedia, telecommunication, and energy production and distribution. The IEC also addresses related terminology and symbols, compatibility issues, measurement and performance, dependability, design and development topics, as well as safety and the environment.

IEC standards also represent the World Trade Organization's Agreement on Technical Barriers to Trade (WTO TBT), created to help central governments establish and recognize international standards as a way to improve global industrial efficiency and develop world trade. Hundreds of standardization bodies have accepted the IEC's Code of Good Practice for the Preparation, Adoption, and Application of Standards. This body also promotes conformity assessment and product certification schemes that ensure interoperability among components and devices manufactured worldwide. Key networking-related IEC standards govern standard cabling, broadband networking and ISDN, transformers, electrical motors, and other standard electrical components and devices. For information on this organization, visit *http://www.iec*.

B.2.4   International Telecommunication Union-Telecommunication (ITU-T)

The ITU-T was formerly known as the Comite Consultatif Internationale de Telegraphie et Telephonique (CCITT); it is probably still better recognized under its old name than its new one. This group operates as a permanent part of the ITU and under the authority of the United Nations (UN). The ITU itself includes members from more than 160 countries, representing the vast majority of UN member states. Often, delegates to the ITU-T work for national postal, telephone, and telegraph services, commonly known as PTTs.

The ITU-T manages standards that relate to various networking topics and technologies including communications, telecommunications, and outright networking services. The ITU-T works with ISO, which explains why many standards carry both ISO and ITU-T designations. The ITU-T is divided into 15 named topic and study groups, plus two sets of standards designated V (for modems) and X (for various forms of networking protocols and communications), as follows:

- *A, B:* working terms, definitions, procedures, and standards guidelines
- *D, E:* tariffs and fee exchanges

- *F:* telegraph, telemetric, and mobile services
- *G, H:* transmissions
- *I:* ISDN
- *J:* television transmission
- *K, L:* facilities protection
- *M, N:* maintenance
- *P:* telephone transmissions
- *R-U:* terminal and telegraph services
- *V:* telephone-based data communications
- *X:* data communication networks

This nomenclature explains the various V.nn standards (such as V.90 for 56 Kbps modem communications). When a standard is named V.nn *bis* or V.nn *ter*, the italicized terms refer to the second and third standards that share the common two-digit (nn) value. For more information about the ITU-T, visit the parent organization's Web site at *http://www.itu.org*.

B.2.5   Internet Society (ISOC)

The ISOC is a large, member-oriented organization that is deeply involved with all things related to the Internet. Numerous suborganizations within the ISOC are of greatest interest from a standards perspective:

- The Internet Engineering Steering Group (IESG), an oversight group that provides input and guidance over IETF working groups, allocates resources and set priorities. For more information, visit *http://www.iesg.org/iesg.html*.

- The Internet Research Task Force (IRTF) is a forward-looking group that researches Internet protocols, applications, architecture, and technologies that have potential social or technical significance. Some of this research is sent on to the IETF and results in the creation of actual Internet standards. For more information, visit *http://www.irtf.org*.

- The Internet Architecture Board (IAB) governs Internet architecture, services, protocols, and related technologies, and is the parent to many suborganizations responsible for researching, creating, and maintaining Internet standards. This group's Web site is *http://www.iab.org.*

- The Internet Corporation for Assigned Names and Numbers (ICANN) oversees names and addresses for the Internet, including IP address space allocation, protocol parameter assignments, domain name system management, and root server system management functions for the entire Internet. Although the Internet Network Information Center (InterNIC, *http://www.internic.net*) maintains information about domain name registries—third-party companies and organizations that manage various portions of the overall Internet domain name space—ICANN oversees all other aspects of Internet naming and addressing. Visit *http://www.icann.org* for more information about this organization.

- The Internet Engineering Task Force (IETF) is one body under the IAB that is responsible for proposing, developing, and maintaining Internet standards documents. Such documents, known as Requests for Comment (RFCs), come in numerous forms (draft, experimental, historical, best practices, official, and obsoleted) that reflect their relevance, currency, and importance. Individual standards are the focus of specific working groups, of which more than 100 may be active at any one time. The IETF's Web site is *http://www.ietf.org.*

As of this writing, there are nearly 4,000 RFC documents in the index of RFCs maintained by the IETF—a collection of documents far too large to document in this appendix. RFCs numbers are allocated in strict numerical order and always contains the most recent version of the "Internet Official Protocol Standards" (RFC 3700, at the time of this writing). Thus, the RFC ending in 00 is numerically closest to the highest-numbered current document. Keep this in mind to determine which official standard RFCs are currently in effect, what best current practice (BCP) documents are active, and so forth. You can locate the current document at *http://www.faqs.org/rfcs/ rfc3700.html*, or by searching for "RFC 3700" using your favorite search engine. Starting from this document, you can usually find the most important RFCs, except perhaps for those introduced since the last Internet Official Protocol Standards Document was published. Because this document is updated regularly, you'd seldom have to search through more than 18 months of new RFCs.

B.2.6   Institute of Electrical and Electronics Engineers (IEEE)

The IEEE (pronounced "eye-triple-e") is a nonprofit, technical professional association with members from more than 150 countries around the world. Although it's based in the United States, the organization acts as a technical authority on a broad range of topics and technologies than range from computer engineering and telecommunications to biomedical technology. As part of its focus, the IEEE produces and maintains a large body of networking-related specifications and standards. Work that originates in the IEEE is often shared with ANSI, and in turn may be shared with ISO. This explains why many important IEEE networking standards are also ANSI and ISO standards.

The most important IEEE networking project is its collection of standards known as the 802 project. This number indicates that it was the second project begun in 1980, although many additions have been made, and continue to be made, since then. At its inception, 12 working groups were designated for the 802 project, numbered 802.1 through 802.20. Today, there are 9 active working groups (A), eight hibernating groups (H: no longer active, published a standard), and two disbanded working groups (D: no longer active, did not publish a standard) in the 802 family, as shown in Table B.1.

For more information about the IEEE, visit *http://www.ieee.org*. For an excellent overview of the IEEE 802 standards, visit *http://www.ieee802.org*.

B.2.7   International Organization for Standardization (ISO)

The Paris-based ISO is sometimes incorrectly called the International Standards Organization, but "ISO" is not really an acronym. ISO's focus is on defining, maintaining, and promoting global standards for the worldwide community. Member countries may be represented by government officials or by national standards organizations, such as the ANSI in the United States. ISO representatives also include participants from business, research and development, or educational organizations and from other international standards bodies such as the IEC and the ITU-T. Overall, ISO's mission is to create and promote international standards for all manufactured products or goods, and for services as well.

ISO's focus in the networking arena is to establish global standards for information exchange, e-commerce, data communications, and network-

TABLE B.1   Working Groups in the IEEE 802 Project

Number	Status	Title
802.1	A	High Level Interface (HILI) Working Group
802.2	H	Logical Link Control (LLC) Working Group
802.3	A	CSMA/CD Working Group
802.4	H	Token Bus Working Group
802.5	H	Token Ring Working Group
802.6	H	Metropolitan Area Network (MAN) Working Group
802.7	H	BroadBand Technical Advisory Group (BBTAG)
802.8	D	Fiber Optics Technical Advisory Group (FOTAG)
802.9	H	Integrated Services LAN (ISLAN) Working Group
802.10	H	Standard for Interoperable LAN Security (SILS) Working Group
802.11	A	Wireless LAN (WLAN) Working Group
802.12	H	Demand Priority Working Group
802.14	D	Cable-TV Based Broadband Communication Network Working Group
802.15	A	Wireless Personal Area Network (WPAN) Working Group
802.16	A	Broadband Wireless Access (BBWA) Working Group
802.17	A	Resilient Packet Ring (RPR) Working Group
802.18	A	Radio Regulatory Technical Advisory Group
802.19	A	Coexistence Technical Advisory Group
802.20	A	Mobile Wireless Access Working Group

ing protocols. These standards are intended to permit interoperability among products and services on a global level, so that components and systems from around the world can be easily integrated. ISO's major efforts in this area are known collectively as the Open Systems Interconnection (OSI, or ISO/OSI). Although most such standards now serve primarily as teaching models, some components continue to exert real market influence today. For more information about ISO, visit *http://www.iso.ch.*

B.2.8 Telecommunications Industry Association (TIA)

The TIA is a leading, U.S.-based nonprofit trade association that serves communications and information technology industries. Its missions include market development, sponsoring of trade shows, and industry awareness promotion and advocacy, as well as standards development. Although based in the United States, the organization takes a global focus, primarily because its member companies serve the global community.

Although it can trace its roots back to trade show planning for independent telephone vendors in 1924, the TIA did not form under its present name until 1988 after a merger of the United States Telecommunications Suppliers Association (USTSA) and the Information and Telecommunications Technologies group of the EIA (covered elsewhere in this appendix). Between 1924 and 1988 the organization focused almost exclusively on telephony topics, as a committee of the United States Independent Telephone Association and, after 1979, as the USTSA.

With a dual focus on communications and information technology, the TIA has been involved in formulating standards across a number of broad technology areas, including fiber optics, user premises equipment (primarily telephone switches and systems), network equipment, wireless communications, and satellite communications. As such, it affects networking technology in all of these groups, especially in light of continuing convergence of voice and data networks and technologies. From wireless networking of many kinds to the cables that make wired networking possible, the TIA is likely to be involved in related standards. For more information, visit the organization's Web site at *http://www.tiaonline.org*.

B.2.9 World Wide Web Consortium (W3C)

A relatively new standards body, the W3C (pronounced "double-you-three-see"), formed in 1994 when the underlying technologies that support the Web were first introduced. The initial effort originated at the research labs at CERN (Conseil Européen pour la Recherche Nucléaire; European Laboratory for Particle Physics) in Geneva, Switzerland. This group decided to release its work on the Web markup language HyperText Markup Language (HTML) and the protocol and service environment known as HyperText Transfer Protocol (HTTP) to the world community, which led directly to the formation of W3C. In the United States, W3C makes its home on the campus of the Massachusetts Institute of Technology (MIT). W3C is also involved with INRIA (Institut National de Recherche en Informatique et en Atomatique, the French National Institute for Research in Computer Science and Control). Both organizations help to staff and house W3C as well.

Although the relationship between the Web and networking may not be immediately obvious, so much Internet access focuses on the Web and related services and capabilities that we'd be remiss in omitting it from this collection. IT professionals in general, including those who specialize in networking, regularly turn to the Web for news, information, updates, patches, fixes, and more. With a Web presence at nearly every organization, many network professionals are also responsible for or involved in Web sites.

Important W3C standards include:

- **Cascading Style Sheets (CSS):** A document markup language used to manage how pages are displayed within Web browsers (or other viewing software)

- **HyperText Markup Language (HTML):** The basic markup language for representing simple content and information in Web pages

- **HyperText Transfer Protocol (HTTP):** The collection of message formats used to request Web pages to be downloaded from a Web server and delivered to a client for access (and, usually, viewed within a Web browser)

- **eXtensible Markup Language (XML):** A sophisticated markup language designed to replace HTML with more abstract and powerful content representation, management, and presentation controls

- **XML vocabularies:** Any of a number of standard or named collections of markup built using XML; hundreds of standard XML vocabularies have been defined for content ranging from anatomy to zoology

The W3C operates an extensive Web site with complete documentation for its hundreds of standards at *http://www.w3c.org*. Robin Cover's "Cover Pages" at *http://xml.coverpages.org* is another great, comprehensive source of information about XML and XML vocabularies that includes news, information and overviews, as well as W3C pointers and third-party documents about XML and XML vocabularies.

B.3   Other Valuable Networking Technology and Standard Resources

In addition to the organizations mentioned in the preceding sections, a plethora of sites and information about networking topics and technologies is available online. When researching a specific standard, visit your favorite search engine and look for tutorial or overview documents on the subject by concatenating the subject name with the terms "standard tutorial" or "standard overview" in your search string. Also see Appendix A for more general pointers on sources of networking information online.

APPENDIX C

Binary Arithmetic and IP Address Calculation

Understanding TCP/IP means understanding IP addresses, those strange dotted-quad numbers such as 172.16.1.24 or 192.25.1.1. You'll sometimes see the numbers when surfing the Web, and you'll deal with them any time you must install or configure networking software or devices. Understanding IP addresses and learning how to subdivide or combine IP address ranges—sometimes called subnetting and supernetting, respectively—makes more sense if you understand the binary or Base 2 notation that computers use and see when they work with addresses.

Having some basic knowledge of binary numbers is extremely helpful; knowing how to convert from decimal to binary and binary to decimal is also quite helpful. (We "slow" humans understand numbers much better in decimal form, whereas our fast computers understand numbers much better in binary form.) This is not a terribly complex job, and can be accomplished by mastering several simple tasks:

- Learning how to convert binary numbers into decimal equivalents, and vice versa

- Understanding the concept of a mask, and how mask bits translate into specific decimal and binary numbers

- Learning to recognize specific bit patterns in 8-bit numbers and how they convert to decimal

- Understanding how to concatenate multiple 8-bit numbers and convert them into decimal

You should understand one more subtlety about numbers before we tackle the subjects outlined above—namely, the distinction between distance and the number of positions on a number line. This can be best summed up by asking the question: "How many numbers fall in the range from 1 to 6?" Subtracting 1 from 6, you get 5, but this is the distance (or difference, in arithmetic terms) between 1 and 6. If you count the number of values in this sequence—1, 2, 3, 4, 5, 6—you'll quickly see that there are 6 numbers in this range. The general formula that answers the question "How many numbers fall in the range from a to b?" is best expressed as $a - b + 1$ (to add back the starting value that the difference ignores). Please keep this notion in mind when dealing with address ranges, subnetting, and supernetting, because the maximum number of addresses needed is important when making such calculations.

C.1   Converting Between Binary and Decimal

C.1.1   About Binary Numbers

Binary numbers (Base 2) are either 0 or 1 for any possible power of 2, where all binary numbers may be expressed using exponential notation as follows:

$$c_1*2^n+c_2*2^{n-1}+c_3*2^{n-2}+\ldots+c_k*2^3+c_{k+1}*2^2+c_{k+2}*2^1+c_{k+3}*2^0$$

The c^i values are constants and, because of the way binary arithmetic works, must be either zeros (0s) or ones (1s). The 2^n values represent some power of 2, or the number of 2 raised to a specific exponent value. (Note that $2^1 = 2$ and $2^0 = 1$ by mathematical convention; this trick of notation is what makes it possible to represent any number in binary form.) Binary numbers aren't compact or easy for humans to read once those numbers get large, but they can represent any integer or whole number imaginable.

C.1.2   Converting Binary to Decimal

If you count the number of values in a binary number starting from right to left, each position you count specifies the exponent for the power of 2 associated with the specific value you're counting in the number at any given moment, as long as you start counting with 0 (zero).

Let's use the number 10010011 as an example. If you count the number of positions in this number you get 8, which means the highest power of 2 in this string of binary digits is 7 (counting from 0 to 7 gives you a total of 8

TABLE C.1 Decimal Values for Powers of 2

Power	Exp Value	Decimal
0	2^0	1
1	2^1	2
2	2^2	4
3	2^3	8
4	2^4	16
5	2^5	32
6	2^6	64
7	2^7	128
8	2^8	256

numbers, as explained earlier in this appendix). Thus, this number may be expressed in exponential notation, as follows:

$1*2^7 + 0*2^6 + 0*2^5 + 1*2^4 + 0*2^3 + 0*2^2 + 1*2^1 + 1*2^0$

As a quick check on your work, list only the constants that precede the values of 2 in this sum, and you get 10010011, which matches the original number exactly—as it must, to be correct.

Now, calculating the decimal value of the number means that you need only to add the decimal values for the powers of 2 that have a coefficient of 1 so that this number could be more compactly expressed by omitting all zero coefficient values, as follows:

$1*2^7 + 1*2^4 + 1*2^1 + 1*2^0$

Note that this transformation breaks the symmetry with the original binary number, but it also provides only those numbers you care about. By using a calculator or the values in Table C.1, you can determine that $2^7 = 128$, $2^4 = 16$, $2^1 = 2$, and $2^0 = 1$, so the decimal value of the binary number 10010011 is 128 + 16 + 2 + 1, or 147. This same approach works for all binary numbers, but gets tedious as numbers get large. (Hint: The Microsoft Calculator has a special button that converts from binary to decimal, and another that converts from decimal to binary!)

C.1.3 Converting Decimal to Binary

There are two traditional approaches to converting decimal numbers to binary—a brute force technique that is extremely easy to calculate but may be difficult to understand, and a value-fitting technique that depends on knowing the powers of 2 to fit decimal numbers to them. Each method depends on dividing or subtracting specific numbers and working on what's left over (the remainder, in mathematical terms).

The brute force technique takes the initial decimal number and keeps dividing it by 2 until the result is 0, while recording the results of those operations in a special way. The recipe is to divide the number by 2, and to write a 1 if the first number is odd or write a 0 if the first number is even. Repeat the technique on the result of the division until that result is a 0. The following is an example, using the number 147 for which we already know the binary value:

> 147 divided by 2 is 73 with a remainder of 1
>
> 73 divided by 2 is 36 with a remainder of 1
>
> 36 divided by 2 is 18 with a remainder of 0
>
> 18 divided by 2 is 9 with a remainder of 0
>
> 9 divided by 1 is 4 with a remainder of 1
>
> 4 divided by 2 is 2 with a remainder of 0
>
> 2 divided by 2 is 1 with a remainder of 0
>
> 1 divided by 2 is 0 with a remainder of 1

If you write the digits that result from this recipe, starting from the bottom of the list, you get the binary number 10010011 (which we already know is correct). This formula works for any binary number.

The other approach relies on knowledge of the powers of 2. Small decimal numbers—such as those that appear in IP addresses—can be readily obtained from Table C.1. In each case, we look for the power of 2 that is closest to and less than the value we're working on:

> 147 is between 256 and 128, 128 is less; record 2^7 for 128, then subtract 128 from 147 to get 19
>
> 19 is between 32 and 16, 16 is less; record 2^4 for 16, then subtract 16 from 19 to get 3

3 is between 4 and 2, 2 is less, record 2^1 for 2, then subtract 2 from 3 to get 1

1 is precisely 2^0, so record 2^0

Note that this formula indicates that $147 = 2^7 + 2^4 + 2^1 + 2^0$, which precisely matches our earlier calculation after dropping the numbers with zero coefficients.

C.2   Understanding Bit Masks

In computer terms, a bit mask is a pattern of zeros and ones in which the ones in the pattern "block off" bit positions in related binary numbers in a special way. The position of the ones in the mask is called high-order if it runs from left to right, and low-order if it runs from right to left. For example, a 3-bit high-order mask for an 8-bit number is expressed in binary terms as 11100000 (the three leftmost bits are set to 1); a 3-bit low-order mask for an 8-bit number is expressed as 00000111 (the three rightmost bits are set to 1). Converting the first number to decimal, we get $2^7 + 2^6 + 2^5 = 128 + 64 + 32 = 224$; converting the second number to decimal we get $2^2 + 2^1 + 2^0 = 4 + 2 + 1 = 7$. Tables C.2 and C.3 list the values of high- and low-order bit masks for 8-bit binary numbers, respectively. Each table explains a way to calculate the value of such a mask based on its size or value.

TABLE C.2   High-order Bit Masks and Decimal Values

Binary	Decimal	Calculation
10000000	128	2^7
11000000	192	$2^7 + 2^6$
11100000	224	$2^7 + 2^6 + 2^5$
11110000	240	$2^7 + 2^6 + 2^5 + 2^4$
11111000	248	$2^7 + 2^6 + 2^5 + 2^4 + 2^3$
11111100	252	$2^7 + 2^6 + 2^5 + 2^4 + 2^3 + 2^2$
11111110	254	$2^7 + 2^6 + 2^5 + 2^4 + 2^3 + 2^2 + 2^1$
11111111	255	$2^7 + 2^6 + 2^5 + 2^4 + 2^3 + 2^2 + 2^1 + 2^0$

TABLE C.3　Low-order Bit Masks and Decimal Values

Binary	Decimal	Calculation
00000001	1	$2^1 - 1$
00000011	3	$2^2 - 1$
00000111	7	$2^3 - 1$
00001111	15	$2^4 - 1$
00011111	31	$2^5 - 1$
00111111	63	$2^6 - 1$
01111111	127	$2^7 - 1$
11111111	255	$2^8 - 1$

A general formula for low-order bit masks is $2^n - 1$, where *n* is the number of bits set in the mask.

By becoming familiar with the values in Tables C.2 and C.3, you'll be well-equipped to handle most ordinary IP address calculations, including various forms of address masks often called subnets and supernets. These are discussed in the following two sections.

C.3　Working with Subnet Masks

As discussed in Chapter 7, a subnet permits you to divide an IP address range into a collection of distinct networks, all of which function together as a single routing domain. You use a higher-order bit mask called a subnet mask to steal bits from the host portion of an IP address, which you can then use to create subnetworks within an existing network address.

Here's what's involved in creating a subnet mask, in recipe form:

1. Calculate how many subnets are needed and add 2 to that number: one for the underlying network address, the other for a broadcast address.

2. Jump to the next highest power of 2. For example, if you need four subnet masks, adding 2 creates a value of 6. The nearest next highest power of 2 is 8, or 2^3, where the 3 tells you how many bits you need for your subnet mask.

3.   Use a high-order bit mask to block off space for these subnetworks. The mask that meets a need for four subnetworks is therefore 11100000, or 224.

4.   Check your work. Analyze the number of bits in the host portion of the address to make sure enough host addresses remain usable (if h is the number of bits in the host portion, $2^h - 2$ defines the number of usable host addresses). For a 3-bit subnet mask, the number of hosts on each subnet is $2^5 - 2 = 30$.

5.   If n is the number of bits in the subnet mask, remember that $2^n - 2$ represents the number of usable subnets that result from this mask (here again, the all-zeros version of this address is needed to address all subnets as a whole, and the all-ones version to broadcast to them as a group). For a 3-bit subnet mask, that number is $2^3 - 2 = 6$.

Here is another example that will help you understand this process:

1.   MegaInc needs nine subnets for a Class C address of 196.24.24.0, and each subnet must be able to accommodate 12 host addresses.

2.   Add 2 to the number of subnets (9) to get 11. The nearest power of 2 is 16 or 2^4, which dictates a 4-bit mask. Four bits are left over for the host portion, which equates to 14 hosts per subnet. That number meets MegaInc's host addressing requirements.

3.   Adding to the default Class C mask address of 255.255.255.0, we use the 4-bit high-order decimal value to extend that mask. Because a 4-bit mask produces a value of 240, this makes the complete subnet mask 255.255.255.240.

A more complex example that partitions a bigger address helps to show the power of subnet masking. Let's apply this example to Picture This!, a company with multiple locations around the world that uses a Class B address:

1.   Picture This! wants 240 subnets for its Class B address of 168.32.10.0. No subnet needs more than 200 host addresses.

2.   Add 2 to the host and subnet portions of the address to get 242 subnets and 202 hosts. The nearest higher power of 2 for 242 is 256, or 8 bits. This leaves 8 bits for the host portion, which meets the company's host addressing requirements.

3. Reserving 8 bits in the final 16 bits of the IP address creates a subnet mask of 11111111 00000000. In decimal terms, this is 255.0, so the default Class B subnet mask of 255.255.0.0 turns into 255.255.255.0 to meet requirements as stated. In fact, this basically breaks a single Class B address into 253 Class C addresses.

To learn more about this fascinating subject, visit your favorite search engine and searching for "IP subnetting tutorial". A recent visit to Google turned up more than 150 hits on this query.

C.4   Working with Supernet Masks

Subnets steal bits from the host portion of an IP address to subdivide that address space into logical subnetworks. Supernets go the other way. By concatenating multiple IP network addresses (which must be in sequence and fit the dictates of the bit patterns they'll attempt to use), they permit host address space to be extended so that bits "stolen" from the network portion of the address are "given" to the host portion of the address. This has the nice side effect of modestly increasing the total number of hosts that may be addressed, because the number of all-zeros network addresses and all-ones broadcast addresses that must be preserved is reduced as host address size increases. (It works out to about 1% of overall address space.)

When combining addresses to create supernets, the number of addresses required corresponds to the low-order bit mask patterns shown in Table C.3. The caveat is that the number of addresses required is the value of 2^n, where n is the number of bits to be used. (Two bits' worth of supernet mask requires $2^2 = 4$ sequential addresses.) Calculating supernets is similar to calculating subnets, except that bits come from the low end of the mask rather than the high end. Here's what this means:

- To use 3 bits of network address for host addressing, you need to reserve the 3 low-order bits in an address range. Because $2^3 = 8$, you need eight contiguous addresses to do this.

- If you're extending a Class C address, the resulting host address now covers 11 bits rather than 8. The resulting subnet mask (it's still called that, even though you're supernetting) is 255.255.248.0 instead of 255.255.255.0 because you've reduced the number of bits in the network portion of the third octet by 3 bits.

- You can calculate supernet masks in one of two ways:

  - You can work from the bit pattern. For the preceding example this produces 11111000, which translates to 248.

  - You can recognize that $2^3 - 1 = 7$ and subtract that value from 255 to get 248. (This only works because it's a low-order bit mask that borrows from the bottom up, as it were.)

Note that each of the eight Class C addresses that you're combining can address 254 hosts ($2^8 - 2$), for a total of 2,032 hosts. By combining them into a single address range, it can address $2^{11} - 2 = 2,046$ hosts. This produces a modest increase of 16 hosts overall.

C.5 Modern IP Addressing

Although it's still helpful to describe IP addresses as Class A, B, or C, modern Internet addressing uses a different type of notation called CIDR addressing. In CIDR addressing, an IP address is followed by notation that looks like /n, where n is typically a number between 4 and 20. This notation simply identifies the number of bits in the network (leftmost) portion of the address, so that you can calculate the number of bits in the host portion by subtracting that value from 32 (or 5, for the /27 example just stated).

Everything explained about subnetting and supernetting works for CIDR addresses, except that network and host portions seldom fall on octet boundaries. This requires a bit more mathematical sophistication and practice to master, but works according to all the rules explained herein.

APPENDIX D

IP Tools and Software

This appendix includes several IP-related tools, utilities, and software. They should become an essential part of your networking toolkit.

D.1   Command Prompt IP Utilities

D.1.1   Ipconfig

Ipconfig displays the MAC address of your computer (the physical address of your NIC), and displays your IP address, subnet mask, and default gateway or the DNS server address.

Syntax

ipconfig /? | /all | /release [*adapter*] | /renew [*adapter*] | /flushdns | /regis-terdns | /showclassid *adapter*

| /setclassid *adapter* [classidtoset]

For more information about Ipconfig and an explanation of the parameters, type **ipconfig /help** at a command prompt.

D.1.2   Tracert

Tracert (aka Traceroute) tracks the path a packet takes to get to its destination, measuring how long it takes to travel through each hop to get to its target. Tracert uses an ICMP echo request packet to find the path.

Syntax

tracert [-d] [-h *maximum_hops*] [-j *host_list*] [-w *timeout*] *target_name*

For more information about Tracert and an explanation of the parameters, type **tracert** at a command prompt.

D.1.3   Ping

Ping uses the ICMP echo function. A small packet containing an ICMP echo message is sent through the network to a particular IP address. The computer that sent the packet then waits for a return packet. If the connections are good and the target computer is up, the echo message return packet will be received. It is one of the most useful network tools available because it tests the most basic function of an IP network. It also shows the TTL value and the amount of time it takes for a packet to make the complete trip, also known as round trip time (RTT).

Syntax

ping [-t] [-a] [-n *count*] [-l *size*] [-f] [-i *TTL*] [-v *TOS*] [-r *count*] [-s *count*] {[-j *host-list*] | [-k *host-list*]}

[-w *timeout*] *destination-list*

For more information about Ping and an explanation of the parameters, type **ping** at a command prompt.

D.2   Networking Tools and Utilities

- Advanced Checksum Verifier: *http://www.irnis.net/soft/acsv*
- Download a free error-checking utility that verifies the integrity of your files via the CRC32 or MD5 algorithms.
- Whois: *http://www.whois.com*

Search for a domain name before you register.

D.2.1   Antivirus Software

- Symantec: *http://www.symantec.com/avcenter/index.html*
- McAfee Security: *http://us.mcafee.com/*

- Sophos: *http://www.sophos.com/*
- F-Prot: *http://www.f-prot.com*

The preceding list offers both shareware and retail versions of popular, downloadable antivirus software packages.

- McAfee FreeScan: *http://www.McAfee.com*

Click the Scan Now link to run a thorough check of your computer for viruses.

D.2.2   Synchronized Time Services

- U.S. Naval Observatory Time Service Department: *http://tycho. usno.navy.mil/frtime.html*
- NIST Internet Time Service: *http://www.boulder.nist.gov/timefreq/ service/its.htm*

Both of these URLs offer synchronized time services to help you maintain accurate global time across your network.

D.2.3   Hardware Addresses

- IEEE OUI and Company ID assignments: *http://standards.ieee.org/ regauth/oui/index.shtml*. IEEE offers a downloadable list of organizationally unique identifiers (OUIs) and an OUI search engine.
- Vendor/Ethernet MAC Address Lookup and Search: *http://www. coffer.com/mac_find/*. Jason Coffer provides a search engine for looking up vendors of Ethernet hardware.

D.3   Analyzers

D.3.1   Computer and Network Analyzers

- Microsoft Baseline Security Analyzer (MBSA): *http://www.microsoft. com/technet/security/tools/mb5ahome.mspx*. This Microsoft tool scans your computer for missing security updates and service packs.
- Microsoft Network Monitor: *http://www.microsoft.com/win-dows2000/en/server/help/default.asp?url=/windows2000/en/server/ help/sag_NETMNintro.htm*

- Novell LANalyzer: *http://www.novell.com*

Microsoft Network Monitor and Novell LANalyzer are a combination of network monitors and network analyzers. The URLs listed provide information about their features and functions.

- SLAC Network Monitoring Tools: *http://www.slac.stanford.edu/xorg/nmtf/nmtf-tools.html#nmp*

- Monitoring Software: *http://www.monitoring-software.net/network-monitoring-software.htm*

Both SLAC and Monitoring Software provide links to shareware and commercial versions of tools for network monitoring, Internet monitoring, intrusion detection, and more.

D.3.2   Protocol Analyzers

- Wildpackets EtherPeek: *http://www.wildpackets.com*

- Ethereal: *http://www.ethereal.com/*

Both WildPackets and Ethereal offer free, downloadable protocol analyzers.

Glossary

4B/5B encoding: A scheme that takes data in 4-bit codes and maps it to corresponding 5-bit codes.

4D-PAM5 encoding: Stands for 4-dimensional, 5-level pulse amplitude modulation. This is a way of encoding bits on copper wires to get a 1 GB per second transfer rate by employing a five-level signal called pulse amplitude modulation 5.

802.1x: A standard that governs internet working and link security. It governs authentication mechanisms for both wired and wireless technologies.

8B/6T encoding: An encoding scheme in which the value of the data byte is compared to the values in the 8B/6T table. The remapping table has nine symbols used for starting and ending delimiters and control characters.

8B/10B encoding: An encoding scheme in which 8-bit binary data values are represented by 10-bit symbols. The data octet is split up into the three most-significant bits and the five least-significant bits.

A

acceptable use: Defines the proper use of an information system and the data it contains.

ad hoc: A wireless network setup between clients without using a WAP.

addressing: A method of identifying network-connected equipment with a unique value.

Address Resolution Protocol (ARP): A protocol used by IP Network layer protocols to map IP network addresses to the hardware addresses used by a Data Link protocol.

all routes explorer (ARE): A frame used to discover the best path to a client in source route bridging networks.

ALOHA: One of the earliest multiple access schemes. It allows network stations to access the channel whenever they have data to transmit, but each station must add a checksum at the end of its transmission to allow the receiver to recognize whether the frame was properly received.

amplitude modulation (AM): The encoding of a carrier wave by the changes of its amplitude along with the changes in input signal.

analog signal: Adds information or encodes information to an AC base signal by modifying the frequency or signal strength.

ANDing: The process of adding the subnet mask to an IP address to determine the network ID.

AppleTalk: The protocol suite used to interconnect Macintosh computers. It is designed to be a flexible, simple, and inexpensive network means for connecting computers, peripherals, and servers.

Application Configuration Access Protocol (ACAP): A protocol to store and retrieve client-specific configurations from a server for mobile clients.

Application layer: Layer 7 of the OSI reference model. This layer provides services to application processes to ensure that effective communication with other application programs is possible.

application-specific integrated circuit (ASIC): A hardware circuit with embedded code used in switching.

arbitrated loop (AL): A Fibre Channel configuration that creates a multi-point configuration between a maximum of 127 nodes.

area border router (ABR): An OSPF-configured router that borders more than one area.

ARP cache: A small portion of memory used on a client to store the ARP table.

ARP table: A table that maintains the association between an IP address and a corresponding MAC address.

asynchronous communication: Communication that is not synchronized or kept in check with a clocking mechanism between communication devices.

Asynchronous Transfer Mode (ATM): A communications services technology that provides a common format for services with high bandwidth requirements, such as video conferencing and video on demand. ATM supports transmission rates up to 9953 Mbps.

attachment unit interface (AUI): A transceiver cable between the medium access unit (MAU) and the data terminal equipment.

auditing: The process of tracking users and then actions, and other events, on a network.

autonomous system (AS): A collection of routers under common administrative authority or control.

autonomous system border router (ASBR): A router that borders an area not in the same autonomous system (usually the Internet).

B

backbone: A single cable segment used in a bus topology to connect computers in a straight line.

backbone router: An OSPF router with at least one interface in the backbone (Area 0).

back door: A program that allows access to a computer without the user's knowledge or authorization.

backleveling: The process used to roll back or reverse an upgrade or change.

bandwidth: A measurement of how much information can be transmitted over a medium over a prescribed period of time.

base station (BS): A special fixed node on a network. It is located in a central location for use on a wireless or cellular network.

baseline: A measure of normal network activity.

benchmarking: The process of determining how much load the server can handle by comparing two or more systems or components of a system.

binding: The process of linking network components on different levels to enable communication between the components.

blackouts: Caused by faults on the utility power system, they are a complete loss of utility power.

blocking: A state on a bridge or a switch where traffic is not passed to or from the port.

Bluetooth: An open standard of wireless communications that allows communications between devices from different vendors.

Boot Protocol (BootP): A protocol used to assign IP address and IP configuration information to IP hosts.

Border Gateway Protocol (BGP): An industry-standard EGP used to maintain routing tables for the Internet.

borrowing: The process of extending the subnet mask into the host portion of a network address.

bottleneck: Occurs when too much data is pushed into a narrow opening, causing it to jam.

bridge: A device that connects two or more segments of a network to make them one.

bridge ID: A two-part ID consisting of bridge priority and MAC address.

bridge priority: A 2-byte user-configurable field that provides administrators control over which bridge becomes the root.

broadcast: A frame that has a Layer 2 MAC address of all Fs.

broadcast address: The last available address for a given network address range. This address can be identified when all host bits set to 1.

broadcast domain: A group of network devices that are capable of receiving each other's broadcast packets.

brute force: Term used that describes a way of cracking a cryptographic key or password by trying every conceivable combination until a password is found, or until all possible combinations have been exhausted.

buffering: The act of temporarily storing data in memory while waiting for access to the media for further processing.

buffer overflow: Condition that occurs when the data presented to an application or service exceeds the storage space allocation that has been reserved in memory for that application or service.

bus: A major network topology in which the computers connect to a backbone cable segment to form a straight line.

business continuity plan (BCP): A plan that takes a long-term look at recovery in the case of a complete loss of facilities.

busy-tone multiple access (BTMA): An access method designed for station-based networks, it divides a channel into a message channel and a busy-tone channel.

C

cable checker: Device that determines whether your cabling can provide physical connectivity.

cable tester: A device that determines whether your cabling can provide physical connectivity. It operates at higher layers of the OSI model and provides more detailed information than a cable checker.

capture-division packetized access (CDPA): An alternative to systems based on bandwidth subdivision methods such as TDMA, FDMA, and CDMA. In CDPA there is no subdivision of bandwidth.

carrier sense multiple access (CSMA): A fundamental advance in network access, it checks whether the medium is active before sending a packet; that is, it listens before it transmits.

carrier sense multiple access with collision avoidance (CSMA/CA): Designed to prevent collisions at the moment they are most likely to occur. All nodes are forced to wait for a random number of timeslots and then check the medium again before starting a transmission.

Carrier sense multiple access with collision detection (CSMA/CD): A method used in Ethernet that allows clients to access to the medium. Clients must listen for a carrier signal before transmitting and must then listen for collisions.

certificate: A digital document that attests to the truth that you are who you say you are. Besides providing authentication, a certificate also secures the exchange of information.

certification authority (CA): An organization or service that issues and manages security certificates.

checksum: A simple error-detection scheme whereby each message is accompanied by a value based on the number of bits in the message.

cipher: The process of replacing letters or numbers with different characters. The letters can also be rearranged without changing their identities to form an enciphered message.

classful routing: The process of routing using the default mask based on the class of the address rather than the actual network mask.

classless inter-domain routing (CIDR): A function of network devices where routing takes place using the full network ID and not the classful address boundary.

client: A computer on a network that requests resources or services from some other computer.

code division multiple access (CDMA): An access method that combines spread-spectrum technology with analog-to-digital conversion. After the data is digitized, it is spread out over the entire bandwidth available.

collision: Refers to when two network stations attempt to communicate at the same time and the signals crossover each other on the wire.

collision domain: All networking clients with the potential to send signals and have them collide are said to be in the same collision domain.

converged: The state at which all routers have a complete set of entries for the network.

convergence: The process of routing updates involved when a change occurs in the routing environment. Convergence can refer to the process or the time it takes to reach a converged state.

cooperative multitasking: A form of multitasking in which the operating system has no control over the processes. The operating system transfers control to the application. Once an application process has control of the CPU, it cannot be interrupted.

crossbar switch: A device that directly switches data between any input and any output port, without sharing a bus with other data.

crossover cable: Cable that looks like an ordinary twisted-pair cable, but with two wires crossed, making the cable able to directly connect two computers without using additional equipment.

cut-through switching: A type of switching method where the switch forwards packets as soon as the 6-byte destination MAC address is received.

cyclic redundancy checking (CRC): A sophisticated method of error-checking that is based on algebra. It is substantially reliable in detecting transmission errors and is commonly used in modems.

D

Data Encryption Standard (DES): A block cipher using a 56-bit key on each 64-bit chunk of data used to encrypt data.

datagram: A packet that consists of a header, data, and a trailer.

Datagram Delivery Protocol (DDP): An AppleTalk Network layer protocol used to connect more than one network.

Data Link Connection Identifier (DLCI): A method of identifying multiple virtual circuits in a Frame Relay network.

Data Link layer: Layer 2 of the OSI reference model. This layer packages raw bits from the Physical layer into logical, structured data packets.

DECnet: A proprietary network protocol designed by Digital Equipment Corporation.

decryption: The act of converting a message from code into plaintext.

default gateway: An entry on a host or in a route table used when a destination address is unknown. Frames not matching any entries in the route table are forwarded to the default gateway.

default route: A routing table entry used when a destination address is unknown. Frames not matching any entries in the route table are forwarded to the next hop identified by the default route.

delay: *See* latency.

denial of service (DoS) attack: A type of attack that disrupts the resources or services to which a user expects to have access.

designated port: In a looped bridge or switch environment, this is the port that is designated to forward traffic for a given segment. All other switches on that segment will filter all client traffic.

designator: Exchanges a locally mapped drive letter with the correct network address of a directory share.

Digital Network Architecture (DNA): A layered network architecture that supports standard and proprietary protocols.

digital signal: Uses steps to represent information in binary format as zeros (0s) or ones (1s).

directory service: A database of service names and addresses that exists on a network.

disaster recovery plan (DRP): A plan that aims to restore essential computer and network functions shortly after a disaster strikes.

distance vector: A simple routing protocol where the best route decision is based on hop count.

distributed denial of service (DDoS) attack: Attacks that come in the form of the standard DoS attack but the effects of which are multiplied by the total number of computers under the control of the attacker.

Domain Name System (DNS): Used to resolve the names typed into a Web browser and match them to a proper network address.

driver: A program that interacts with either a particular device or type of software. It contains specific information about a device or a software interface that programs using the driver do not.

Dual-Attached Concentrator (DAC): A network node in FDDI that is attached to both rings and can wrap the ring in case of a primary ring failure. It is also responsible for connecting end-nodes to the FDDI ring.

Dual-Attached Station (DAS): A network node in FDDI that is attached to both rings and can wrap the ring in case of a primary ring failure.

dual-homed: A network node in an FDDI network that is attached to two DACs.

due care: The knowledge and actions that a reasonable and prudent person would possess or act upon.

duplexing: Refers to the transmission of packets. Half-duplexing transmits packets in one direction only. Full duplexing transmits packets in two directions simultaneously.

Dynamic Host Configuration Protocol (DHCP): Enables individual computers to automatically obtain their network configurations from a server rather than be manually configured.

E

egress port: The designated outbound port for a given frame.

encapsulation: The process of packaging upper-layer protocol information and data into a frame.

encoding: The process of putting electronic data into a standard format.

encryption: Transformation of data into a form that cannot be read without the appropriate key to decipher it.

error checking and correcting (ECC): A more sophisticated form of checking where errors are corrected when they are detected. Also known as error-correction code.

Ethernet: A Layer 2 networking protocol used for delivering frames between two network interface cards. Network access is achieved through CSMA/CD.

Ethernet II: A modification of the original Ethernet standard. Ethernet II uses a Type field instead of an LLC field.

Ethernet raw: A Novell proprietary implementation of the original Ethernet I standard. It does not use an LLC field.

Ethernet SNAP: An extension of the Ethernet I specification that allows for more service access points.

Event Viewer: A Windows-based tool that maintains log files and allows you to audit certain events.

Extensible Markup Language (XML): A markup language for documents containing structured information.

Exterior Gateway Protocol (EGP): An early industry-standard exterior protocol replaced by BGP.

exterior gateway protocols (EGPs): A classification of protocols used to create and maintain routing tables and routing policy on the Internet.

F

fabric: A Fibre Channel configuration that creates a multipoint configuration between an infinite number of nodes. It requires a special switch.

Fiber Distributed Data Interface (FDDI): A Layer 2 protocol similar to Token Ring. It uses token passing for media access and a dual-ring topology for redundancy.

Fibre Channel: A Layer 2 networking protocol used to create a channel between communicating nodes.

File Allocation Table (FAT): A file system used by DOS and supported by all other DOS- and Windows-based operating systems. It is simple, reliable, and uses little storage.

file system: Describes the operating system's method of organizing, managing, and accessing of files through logical structuring of the hard disk.

File Transfer Protocol (FTP): Allows a person to transfer files between two computers.

filtering: The process of reading information in a packet, such as the destination address, and either forwarding or dropping the packet based on that information.

firewall: A component placed between computers and networks to help eliminate undesired access by the outside world.

flooding: When a bridge receives a broadcast, multicast, or a packet with an unknown destination and copies the packet to all ports except the port of entry.

flow control: A method by which the data flow between devices is managed so that the data can be handled at an efficient pace.

forwarding: The process that a bridge uses when copying a frame from one port to another using a known destination MAC address.

fragment-free switching: A form of switching used instead of cut-through to eliminate forwarding collision fragments. The packet is forwarded after the 64th byte of data is received.

Frame Relay: A packet-switched WAN technology whereby bandwidth is shared among subscribers.

frequency division duplex (FDD): Uses different frequency bands for uplink and downlink.

frequency division multiple access (FDMA): Provides multiple and simultaneous transmissions to a single transponder.

frequency division multiplexing (FDM): A method of transmission in which numerous signals are combined on a single communications line or channel.

frequency modulation (FM): The method of encoding data onto an AC wave by changing the instantaneous frequency of the wave.

full-duplex: A transmission method whereby data can be transmitted in both directions on a signal carrier at the same time. Full-duplex transmission implies a bidirectional communications (one that can move data in both directions).

G

giant: A frame that is larger than the defined current protocol and media.

group: Contains users who share a common need for access to a particular resource.

group-based access control: A type of access control in which permissions are assigned to groups, and user accounts become members of the groups. Each user account has access based on the combined permissions inherited from its group memberships.

Group Policy object (GPO): A virtual storage location for Group Policy settings used to apply Group Policy to users and computers.

H

half-duplex: A transmission method whereby data can be transmitted in both directions on a cable, but not at the same time.

hand-off point (hop): The next Layer 2 destination in an end-to-end Layer 3 communications path or route.

Hardware Compatibility List (HCL): A manufacturer list that details compatible hardware for operating systems.

hashing: The process of transforming a string of characters into a shorter fixed-length value or key that represents the original string. Hashing is used in many encryption algorithms.

hello packet: Also known as a heartbeat, a special message (packet) that a router sends out periodically to determine network adjacency relationships.

High-level Data Link Control (HDLC): A Layer 2 WAN protocol used on point-to-point serial links.

High-Performance File System (HPFS): Designed for the OS/2 operating system to allow for greater access to larger hard drives.

hold-down timer: A routing loop prevention mechanism that requires a router to disregard all route advertisements about an offline network until the hold-down timer expires.

home RF: A wireless technology being developed for use with home appliances.

hop: *See* hand-off point.

host: Any system configured with a TCP/IP address, which can include routers, switches, hubs, personal computers, mainframes, Unix systems, or any network-enabled device.

hub: A multiport repeater that retransmits a signal on all ports.

Hypertext Markup Language (HTML): The language used to format pages on the Web.

Hypertext Transfer Protocol (HTTP): A protocol that Web clients and servers use to communicate with each other.

I

Institute of Electrical and Electronic's Engineers (IEEE): A professional engineering organization that defines standards for networking devices, which include network interfaces, cabling, and connectors.

Integrated Services Digital Network (ISDN): A packet-switched digital connection method similar to phone service.

inter-frame gap: The 9.6-microsecond required wait time between the receipt of the last signal and the start of a new signal on an Ethernet network.

interior gateway protocols (IGPs): A family of protocols used to create and maintain routing tables and routing policy inside a company's network infrastructure.

International Organization for Standardization (ISO): An international standards organization responsible for developing a wide range of standards, including many that are relevant to networking, such as the OSI reference model and the OSI protocol suite.

International Telecommunication Union-Telecommunication Standardization Sector (ITU-T): An international organization that develops communication standards. The ITU-T developed X.25 and other communications standards.

Internet Control Message Protocol (ICMP): A part of the Internet layer that uses IP datagram delivery to send messages notifying the sender if something has gone wrong in the transmission process.

Internet Message Access Protocol (IMAP): Allows the client e-mail program to access remote message stored as if they were local.

Internet Protocol (IP): The Network layer protocol that's part of the TCP/IP suite.

Internet service provider (ISP): An organization that provides Internet access to customers, primarily as a paid service.

Internetwork Packet Exchange (IPX): A connectionless datagram-based Layer 3 (Network) protocol of the IPX/SPX suite that is used to route packets through networks.

interworking function (IWF): Provides the necessary protocol conversions so that wireless data users can continue to access existing network-wired applications without requiring modifications to the applications.

IP Security (IPSec): A set of protocols operating at the Transport layer that support the secure exchange of packets.

IP version 4 (IPv4): An abbreviation for Internet Protocol version 4. A widely deployed suite of protocols used in network communications. IPv4 is the most commonly deployed network communications protocol in the world today.

IP version 6 (IPv6): An abbreviation for Internet Protocol version 6. The newest version of the IP protocol that uses expanded features and addressing to overcome the limitations of version 4.

J

jitter control: A process that ensures that traffic travels through a network smoothly.

K

kernel: The core program component of an operating system.

L

LANalyzer: A complete monitoring and analysis tool for troubleshooting Novell networks. It monitors the network for anomalous events and can decode and support various protocols.

late collision: A collision that occurs after the first 64 bytes of data have been transmitted.

latency: Delay associated with the transmission, retransmission, or processing of network frames.

learning: When a bridge or switch adds an address to its forwarding table.

link state: Complex type of routing protocol that uses advanced logic to determine the best path to a given network.

listening: A phase used on a bridge or switch port that allows it to send BPDU traffic.

load shedding: Process of systematically reducing the system demand by temporarily decreasing the load in response to transmission or capacity shortages.

Local Access and Transport Area (LATA): A geographic zone supported by a single telephone service provider.

local area network (LAN): A group of devices under common administrative control, connected at high speed, and located close together.

Logical Link Control (LLC): A Layer 2 protocol defined by IEEE 802.2 and used in other protocols such as Ethernet and Token Ring.

Logical Link Control (LLC) layer: Sublayer of the Data Link layer that manages communications between devices over a single link. This layer includes error checking and flow control.

loopback adapter: A way to test the ports on a system without having to connect to an external device.

M

MAC address: The unique hardware or physical address of a hardware device. Manufacturers assign MAC addresses to hardware devices.

malware: A shortened version of the words "malicious software." It is software designed with the intent to damage or disrupt a system.

Manchester encoding: A synchronous clock encoding technique used to encode the clock and data of a synchronous bit stream. It uses the rising or falling edge in the middle of each bit time to indicate a zero (0) or one (1).

man-in-the-middle attack: An attack that takes place when an attacker intercepts traffic and then tricks the parties at both ends into believing that they are communicating with each other.

maximum transmission unit (MTU): The maximum frame size allowed to travel through a network, using a given protocol and media type.

Media Access Control (MAC) address: A unique physical address, also called a hardware address, that all NICs have.

Media Access Control (MAC) layer: A sublayer of the Data Link layer that manages protocol access to the physical network medium.

mesh: A hybrid network topology used for fault tolerance in which all computers connect to each other.

metric: The method or measurement used by a routing protocol that determines the best path to a given network.

metropolitan area network (MAN): A group of LANs connected using WAN and LAN technologies but limited in distance to a metropolitan area or LATA.

middleware: Software that connects applications, allowing them to exchange data.

Multi-Level Transition-3 encoding (MLT-3): A three-level form of data encoding used to concentrate the signal power below 30 MHz.

multiple access: Allows more than one device to communicate.

multiple access collision avoidance (MACA): A multiple access method that attempts to detect collisions at the receiver by establishing a request-response channel of communication between the sender and receiver.

multiplexing: Refers to sharing a communications line. It combines several connections into one larger channel.

multipoint: A network configuration that involves multiple network nodes or end points.

Multipurpose Internet Mail Extensions (MIME): The standard that defines the format of text messages.

Multistation Access Unit (MAU): A device used to attach clients to a Token Ring network.

N

naming convention: The process by which names are created for the workstations and servers on a network.

NetBIOS Extended User Interface (NetBEUI): Specifies the way that upper-level software sends and receives messages over the NetBIOS Frames Protocol (NBF). It has become an industry standard.

NetWare Core Protocol (NCP): One of the core protocols of the IPX/SPX suite. NCP handles requests for services, such as printing and file access, between clients and servers.

network: A group of computers that can communicate with each other to share information and resources.

network address translation (NAT): The process of replacing the source or destination network address in a frame with a valid address.

network analyzer: Also called a protocol analyzer, a hardware-based tool that a network administrator connects to the network expressly to determine the nature of more complex network problems.

Network Basic Input/Output System (NetBIOS): Developed in 1983 for International Business Machines Corporation (IBM) to allow applications on different computers to communicate within a local area network.

Network Device Interface System (NDIS): A communication interface between the MAC sublayer and the network interface driver that allows Windows operating systems to communicate multiple protocols to the NIC.

network ID: The number of bits (determined by the subnet mask) of an IP address that identify a client's network address.

Network layer: Layer 3 of the OSI reference model. This layer provides connectivity and path selection between two systems. This is the layer at which routing occurs.

network medium: Refers to the cable (metallic or fiber-optic) that links computers on a network. Because wireless networking is possible, it can also describe the type of wireless communications used to permit computers to exchange data via some wireless transmission frequency.

Network Monitor: A protocol-analysis tool that captures network traffic and generates statistics for creating reports.

network operating system (NOS): Acts as a director to keep a network running smoothly, and is a complete operating system in addition to managing communication across a LAN.

Network Services Protocol (NSP): A connection-oriented protocol developed by Digital to manage flow control, segmentation, and reassembly functions.

New Technology File System (NTFS): Developed expressly for versions of Windows NT and Windows 2000 as a platform for added functionality, reliability, and security features.

noise: Also referred to as EMI and RFI, it can be caused by lightning, load switching, generators, radio transmitters, and industrial equipment.

Non-Return to Zero (NRZ) encoding: Uses two levels of signaling or is bipolar. The two levels or states can be expressed as either on or off, or high or low.

O

Open Data-Link Interface (ODI): Similar to NDIS except that it supports Novell and Apple operating systems. It allows these operating systems to communicate multiple protocols to the NIC.

Open Shortest Path First (OSPF): An industry-standard link state protocol.

Open Systems Interconnection (OSI) reference model: A hierarchical, seven-layer abstract structure of communications between application processes running in computer systems.

optical time domain reflectometer (OTDR): An advanced diagnostic tool for optical fibers that allows you to take a snapshot of a fiber link and accurately measure various statistics.

oscilloscope: An instrument that can detect shorts, crimps, or attenuation in a cable. It displays its output in a graphical format.

over-subscription: A condition that exists when a network device is too slow or has too little memory for the current traffic load. The result is dropped packets.

P

packet: A small segment of a data stream message transmitted over a packet-switched network. A packet contains the destination address in addition to the data.

parity check: Ensures that when data is transmitted from one device to another or stored locally, there is a means to recover lost transactions.

path cost: The cost of a link between two bridges or switches. It is determined by dividing 1,000 Mbps by the speed of the link.

peer-to-peer: A type of networking in which each computer can be a client to other computers and act as a server as well.

Performance console: A Windows-based tool used for properly monitoring the physical disks, memory, and processor along with other services.

permanent virtual circuit (PVC): A circuit path defined in software for the delivery of packets between two end points. The circuit is up even when no data is being sent.

phase-shift modulation (PSM): Conveys digital signals by shifting phases.

Physical layer: Layer 1 of the OSI reference model. It defines mechanical, functional, procedural, and electrical aspects of networking. It includes connectors, circuits, voltage levels, and grounding.

PING: An ICMP echo function used to test network connectivity.

plain old telephone system (POTS): The public telephone system, also known as public switched telephone network (PSTN).

point-to-point: A network configuration involving only two nodes.

Point-to-Point Protocol (PPP): A newer protocol that does essentially the same thing as SLIP but has extra features, such as error detection and IP address negotiation.

poisoning: A routing loop prevention technique where the route metric is set above the allowed maximum in the route advertisement.

polling: A process in which the master broadcasts a query to every node on the network, asking each node in turn whether it has anything to communicate.

port address translation (PAT): The process of replacing the source or destination network and port address in a frame with a valid address and port number.

Post Office Protocol 3 (POP3): The current version of a protocol used to retrieve e-mail from a mail server.

preemptive multitasking: The process whereby the operating system assigns CPU time slices to processes. After each time slice expires, the process is halted and the next process gets computing time.

Presentation layer: Layer 6 of the OSI reference model. It translates data from the Application layer into an intermediary format, provides services such as data encryption, and data compression.

Pretty Good Privacy (PGP): Encrypts and decrypts e-mail messages based on public-key encryption and provides for digital signatures.

Privacy-Enhanced Mail (PEM): One of the first standards for securing e-mail messages by encrypting 7-bit text messages, it specifies a PKI for key exchange over large networks.

private IP addresses: A set of three ranges of IP addresses defined by RFC 1918 that allows companies to use TCP/IP addressing and configuration without having valid public addresses. The ranges are defined as 10.0.0.0 /8, 172.16.0.0 /20, and 192.168.0.0 /16.

propagation delay: The delay an electronic signal experiences when transmitted between two end points.

protocol data unit (PDU): A defined amount of data that can be transmitted using the current protocol and media.

protocol: A set of rules and conventions that specifically governs how computers exchange information over a network medium. A protocol implements the functions of one or more of the OSI layers.

proxy aware: Software applications that can be configured to use a proxy server.

public-key cryptography: Uses different keys to encrypt and decrypt data. The public key is readily available whereas the private key is kept confidential.

Public Key Infrastructure (PKI): A set of standards and protocols that allows data to be transported with strong authentication and privacy on the Internet.

public switched telephone network (PSTN): *See* plain old telephone system (POTS).

pulse code modulation (PCM): Transmits analog data using a digital scheme.

pure ALOHA: A multiple-access scheme that allows stations access to a communications channel whenever the stations have data to transmit, but each station must add a checksum to the end of its transmission to allow the receiver to determine whether the frame was properly received.

Q

quality of service (QoS): A standard that specifies the time frame in which data will be delivered after transmission. QoS helps control jitter, latency, and loss for long-distance, high-bandwidth applications.

quantization: Stage that allocates a level to a sample signal. The sampled analog signal can take any value, but the quantized signal can have a value only from a set of half voltages.

R

redirector: Operating at the Presentation layer of the OSI model, its function is to accept requests from applications and determine whether network access is needed.

Redundant Array of Inexpensive Disks (RAID): Organizes multiple disks into a large, high-performance logical disk.

Remote Procedure Call (RPC): A protocol that a program can use to request a service from a program located on another computer on a network without understanding network details.

repeater: A device that regenerates electronic signals so that they can travel a greater distance or accommodate additional computers on a network segment.

reservation ALOHA: A combination of a slot reservation design with slotted ALOHA. This channel allocation scheme divides the channel bandwidth into slot sizes equal to the transmission time of a single packet, assuming that the packet sizes are of constant length.

resources: The files, applications, and hardware that are shared by a server for clients to access.

Reverse Address Resolution Protocol (RARP): A network protocol belonging to the OSI Data Link layer used to resolve a Data Link layer address to the corresponding Network layer address.

ring: Topology consisting of computers connected in a circle, forming a closed ring.

risk assessment: Determines how likely it is that certain scenarios might actually occur.

Rivest-Shamir-Adleman (RSA): Developed in 1977 by Ron Rivest, Adi Shamir, and Leonard Adleman, this is an encryption and digital signature authentication system that uses an algorithm based on the multiplication of prime numbers.

role-based access control: A type of access control that determines what job functions each employee performs and then assigns access to a system or network based on those functions.

root bridge: The bridge with the lowest bridge ID in the Spanning Tree Algorithm. All traffic forwards along the best path toward the root bridge.

root port: The port with the lowest cost path to the root bridge.

router: A device that passes data among networks.

route summarization: The process of representing a block of networks using a single route advertisement.

routing: The process of forwarding frames from one interface to another based on a Layer 3 network address.

routing information field (RIF): A field used in source route bridging that maintains the correct path that a frame used to traverse a series of Token Ring networks. Token Ring bridges or switches populate this field.

routing information indicator (RII): A field used in source route bridging that identifies the packet as a local frame if set to 0, or a source route frame if set to 1.

Routing Information Protocol (RIP): An industry-standard distance vector routing protocol.

routing loop: A condition that occurs when routers get confused during update operations and cause frames to bounce back and forth between a set of interfaces.

routing table: A table stored in the memory of a router that associates a given destination network with an outbound interface.

runt: A frame that is smaller than the defined minimum size for the protocol and media.

S

sags: Short-term decreases in voltage levels that commonly occur when motors are started up or by faults on the utility power system.

security policy: A set of security controls that dictate the company rules for providing a safe and secure working environment.

self-interference: A process by which a large fraction of the signal energy leaks into the receive path when a node is transmitting data.

separation of duties: The concept that the completion of a task should require more than one person.

Sequenced Packet Exchange (SPX): Resides on top of IPX and is a reliable, connection-oriented protocol that supplements the datagram service provided by IPX. SPX works with IPX to ensure that data is received whole, in sequence, and error-free.

Serial Line Interface Protocol (SLIP): An extremely simple framing scheme for putting IP packets on a serial line.

server: A computer whose job is to respond to requests for services or resources from clients elsewhere on a network.

Service Advertising Protocol (SAP): A protocol in the IPX/SPX suite through which network resources, such as file servers and print servers, advertise their addresses and the services they provide.

service pack: An update to an existing release of an operating system that includes solutions to known problems and other product enhancements.

session hijacking: An attack that takes control of a session between a server and a client.

Session layer: Layer 5 of the OSI reference model. It allows two applications on different computers to establish dialog control, regulates which side transmits, and determines the time and length of the transmission

signaling: Communication of information between network nodes by initiation, transmission, control, and termination of telecommunications signals.

Simple Mail Transfer Protocol (SMTP): A transport protocol for sending e-mail from server to server.

Simple Network Management Protocol (SNMP): An Application layer protocol used to exchange management information between network devices.

Single-Attached Station (SAS): A network node in FDDI attached only to the primary ring.

sliding window: A method of flow control for data transfers. The window is the maximum amount of data that can be sent without having to wait for acknowledgments.

slotted ALOHA: Doubles the efficiency of the ALOHA protocol by completely overlapping packets when they collide so that each packet is retransmitted in a future slot until the transmission is successful.

social engineering: Method of attack that plays on human behavior to obtain private information.

Source Route Bridging (SRB): A type of bridging used on Token Ring networks where the client sends out a special frame used to determine the best path to a given destination.

space-division switching: Single transmission-path routing accomplished using a switch to physically separate a set of matrix contacts or cross-points. Space-division is closely related to the concept of the crossbar switch.

Spanning Tree Algorithm (STA): An algorithm that prevents bridging and switching loops.

spikes: Instantaneous, dramatic increases in voltage that result from lightning strikes or when electrical loads are switched on or off.

split horizon: A routing loop prevention technique that requires a router to disregard route advertisements about routes locally propagated routes.

spoofing: Method of making data appear to come from somewhere other than where it really originated.

stack: A set of network protocol layers that work together. The set of TCP/IP protocols that define communication over the Internet is the most commonly used stack.

Standard Generalized Markup Language (SGML): An international markup standard independent of any software applications, devices, and operating systems.

star: A network topology in which computers connect via a central connecting point, usually a hub.

star bus: A network topology that combines the star and bus topologies.

star ring: A network topology wired like a star that handles traffic like a ring.

stealing: The process of extending the subnet mask into the host portion of a network address.

store-and-forward switching: A standard type of bridging and switching process where the entire frame is received before a forwarding decision is made.

subnet mask: A numeric value that is configured in networking software that gives an IP client the ability to determine the network ID.

subnetting: The process of extending the subnet mask to create multiple networks from one master network ID.

summarization: The process of removing network bits from the subnet mask until a collection of individual networks looks like one large network block (in binary format).

surges: Short-term increases in voltage that are commonly caused by large electrical load changes and from utility power line switching.

switch: A special networking device that manages networked connections between any pair of star-wired devices on a network.

Switched Multimegabit Data Service (SMDS): A subscriber WAN service for connecting networks together over high-speed links.

switched virtual circuit (SVC): A circuit path defined in software for the delivery of packets between two end points. The circuit is up only when there is data ready to be sent.

switching fabric: The combination of hardware and software that transfers data coming into a network node to the appropriate output port on the next node on the network. Switching fabric includes the switches in a node, the hardware that they contain, and the software programs that control switching paths.

synchronous communication: Communication whereby a clocking mechanism keeps events in sync to manage flow of information.

Synchronous Optical Network (SONET): A subscriber WAN service that aggregates multiple signaling types into a single large pipe.

T

Task Manager: A Windows-based tool that can be used to end processes or applications that get hung up or cause the operating system to become unstable.

Telecommunications Network (Telnet): A protocol that provides a way for a client to create a connection and to send commands and instructions interactively to the remote computer.

terminator: A device used to absorb signals as they reach the end of a bus, thus freeing the network for new communications.

threat: In terms of network security, anything that endangers the safety of the network.

time-division duplex (TDD): Multiplexing of the transmission in different time periods but in the same frequency band.

time-division multiple access (TDMA): A digital transmission technology that allows users to access a single radio-frequency (RF) channel without interference by dividing the channel into time slots for each user.

time-division multiplexing (TDM): The process by which multiple data streams are combined in a single signal and transmitted over the same link by allocating a different time slot for the transmission of each channel.

time domain reflectometer (TDR): A device that bounces a signal off the end of a cable and measures the signal's travel time to detect faults in the cable.

time-division switching: Switching of TDM channels by shifting bits between time slots in a TDM frame.

time-slot interchange (TSI): In time-division switching, the process of coordinating time slots between the transmitting station and the receiving station.

time-space switching: A combination of space-division and time-division switching. Time-space switching precedes each input trunk in a crossbar with a TSI, and delays samples so that they arrive at the right time for the space-division switch's schedule.

time-to-live (TTL): A number, assigned to a frame, that is decremented to prevent the frame from circulating through the network infinitely.

token: A packet used in some ring topology networks to ensure fair communications between all computers.

Token Bus: An early definition of a token-passing environment in which systems were wired in a physical bus.

token passing: A method of passing data around a ring network.

Token Ring: A Layer 2 networking protocol used for delivering frames between two network interfaces. Network access is achieved by possessing an electronic token.

tone generator: A device used to perform tests on phone and network lines to help aid in the identification of wires during the wire-tracing process.

topology: The basic physical layout of a network.

Traceroute: An ICMP function used to track the path a packet takes to arrive at its destination. Traceroute was originally developed for the Unix platform.

Tracert: The Windows version of Traceroute.

traffic shaping: Regulates the flow of data across a network by changing bursts of traffic to uniform, regular traffic.

translational bridging: A form of bridging that allows bridging between Ethernet and Token Ring networks.

Transmission Control Protocol (TCP): The Transport layer protocol that's part of the TCP/IP suite.

Transmission Control Protocol/Internet Protocol (TCP/IP): The language of the Internet. This is a suite of protocols that enable packets to be routed across many networks to arrive at their destination.

Transport layer: Layer 4 of the OSI reference model. It helps provide a virtual error-free, point-to-point connection between two hosts so that communication between the hosts arrives uncorrupted and in the correct order.

Trivial File Transfer Protocol (TFTP): A simple form of the File Transfer Protocol, often used for booting or loading programs on diskless workstations.

Trojan horse: A program that disguises itself as a useful application but performs malicious actions, such as deleting data files, when launched.

Truncated Binary Exponential Backoff Algorithm: A mathematical formula used by Ethernet clients after a collision has occurred. It insures that clients do not attempt to communicate at the same time again.

tunneling: Uses one network to send its data through the connection of another network.

U

unicast: A frame addressed directly to a destination host.

Uniform Resource Locator (URL): An electronic address that allows a browser to locate pages.

uninterruptible power supply (UPS): A battery-operated power source that sits between the wall electrical outlet and the computer. In the event of a power failure, it takes over and provides power to the computer.

user account: Holds information about a specific user. It can contain basic information such as name, password, and the user's level of permission.

User Datagram Protocol (UDP): A connectionless datagram service in the TCP/IP suite that does not guarantee delivery and does not maintain an end-to-end connection. It merely pushes the datagrams out and accepts incoming datagrams.

V

variable-length subnet masking (VLSM): The process of creating multiple subnetted networks by using subnet masks that vary in length.

virtual FAT (VFAT): An enhanced version of the FAT file system, this file system is also called FAT32.

virtual local area network (VLAN): A configuration on a switch that groups ports into a single broadcast domain.

virtual private network (VPN): A network connection that allows access via a secure tunnel built on top of a publicly accessible infrastructure, such as the Internet or the public telephone network.

virus: A program or piece of code that is loaded onto your computer without your knowledge.

volt-ohm meter or **voltmeter:** A device used to check physical connectivity or to determine whether a cable is intact by measuring AC and DC voltage, current, resistance, capacity, and cable continuity.

W

wave-division multiplexing (WDM): A form of frequency-division multiplexing specifically for combining many optical carrier signals into a single optical fiber.

Web browser: The client software that allows a user to access and view any document on the Web.

wide area network (WAN): A group of LANs connected over a wide geographic area, at slower speeds than a LAN, and under shared administrative control.

Win32 Driver model (WDM): Architecture that divides drivers into various classes by function. It is a complete card interface that enables generic class drivers to handle bus and device functions.

wire address: The first available address of a given network address range. The address is identified when all host bits are set to 0.

wireless: The ability to transmit data without using wires.

wireless access point (WAP): A device used to connect wireless cards into a managed network.

wireless network: A type of LAN that uses high-frequency radio waves rather than physical connections, such as cables or wires, to communicate between devices.

worm: Generic term for a self-replicating virus, Trojan horse, or logic bomb.

X

Xerox Network Systems (XNS): A suite of protocols created by Xerox in the late 1970s and early 1980s to be used with Ethernet networks.

Index